World Chronology of Music History

of

Music History

VOLUME **V**

1736 - 1786

Compiled and Edited by

Paul E. Eisler

Foreword by Fritz Kramer

1978 OCEANA PUBLICATIONS, INC./Dobbs Ferry, New York

Library of Congress Cataloging in Publication Data (revised):

Eisler, Paul E.   1919-
    World chronology of music history.

    CONTENTS: v. 1. 30,000 D.C. - 1594 A.D. v. 2. 1594-
1684.   v. 3. 1685-1735   v. 4. Index   v. 5. 1736-1786
    1. Music — Chronology.   I. Title.
ML161.E4   780'.9   72-4354
ISBN 0-379-16080-3
    0-379-16085-4 (v. 5)

Manufactured in the United States of America

To my beloved wife, Edith
and
to my earlier chronology
Judith
Paul III
Karen
and
Peter
with deepest affection

Table of Illustrations

FOREWORD

The average music student, leaving school to enter life and embark on a career of his own, supposedly has a solid foundation of knowledge of the history of Eastern and Western music, both ancient and modern, and of the various musical styles and the ways to perform them. There is little doubt, however, that the sheer quantity of the material absorbed during the years of study is so overwhelming that for the young practicing musician it will take years for him to achieve true order and logic in his vision of historic perspective. There are also many professional musicians who pick up at random whatever they know about the different periods and styles of music, and the state of even their accumulated knowledge is deplorable.

The *World Chronology of Music History* is a concise survey of the art of music, especially its forms, its styles, the development of different theories, the ups and downs of music throughout the centuries and, of course, individual composers. Included, of necessity, are important highlights of what happened in other arts, what locations acquired transitory importance at any given time, and which crowned heads, emperors and kings and princes, and which theoreticians made their names known as relevant to music.

The importance of this particular *Chronology* lies in its comprehensiveness. Not only does it list the aforementioned items; it also gives literally thousands of examples of performances, premieres and — last but not least — performers. It is a gigantic undertaking. When it is complete, roughly 32,000 years of human evolution and culture will have been covered, starting with the Paleolithic Age and ending with electronic music.

Upon completion of the entire set (anticipated extent: 8-10 volumes) there will, of necessity, be added a separate index volume containing an alphabetical listing of the persons, works and events discussed in the *Chronology*.

The use of the book ought to be described. If a reader wants information about a specific time period, he will find this time period covered in chronological sequence. Should a reader wish to obtain information about a personage whom he cannot locate as to the exact time in which he lived, he may find his name listed in the Index, together with the pertinent page in the volume. The first volume, covering the ages up to the latter part of the 16th Century, will, for instance, have more to say about the Renaissance period than, let's say, about the 9th Century, the century whose only towering personage was Charlemagne, the initiator of certain chant codifications and founder of the first music schools to teach strictly Western music.

From about the middle of the 16th Century on, the material is so abundant as to require a year-by-year coverage. Let us, for example, take the year 1590. What knowledge opens up on the first Madrigal opera, on Mr. Byrd, on the "Liber Secundum Sacrarum Cantionum," on the Council of Brunswick, the popularity of lute music, the painter Zuccari, *young* Monteverdi's doings, and the violin makers in Brescia! And after having read up on the multiple facts of the year 1590, we may proceed to pages and pages of happenings in 1591, and so on. In quoting examples, the standard practice has been followed of referring to major collections of published music.

Reading about music or listening to lectures about music without listening to the music itself is definitely a profitless undertaking. It is the music itself that matters above anything else. Our author, therefore, has taken special pains to emphasize the importance of certain works by various composers which are not to be overlooked. Parallel with the emphasis on masterworks run entries of the pertinent periods in general, such as Classical Antiquity, the Middle Ages (including the Gothic centuries), the Renaissance (as far as Vol. I covers) composers up to the heavenly heights of Byrd, Orlando di Lasso, Palestrina and Victoria.

Now, *to understand music it is also necessary to have some knowledge of the forces which have conditioned the various epochs during their growth.* Music can be grasped in its very depth only if coordinated with the sum total of the art of its time of origin, with literature, painting, sculpture and architecture. The *Chronology* offers assistance even above and beyond these features by also keeping close watch over the war-and-peace-makers of different time periods, their most cunning counsellors, their most eminent philosophers.

Fritz Kramer

Introduction

This volume which deals with the late Baroque and Pre-Classical contributions to music history also initiates the Classical period and thus provides insight into this fascinating overlap. The contrast in the works of the various Bach songs points this out most vividly and the researcher using this volume cannot help but notice this.

Specific problems unique to this time-span arose in the preparation of this volume. In the case of Haydn the several catalogings of his works are not always in agreement as to the dates of various works and especially not in the numberings within distinct categories such as symphonies, string quartets, and the like. It should also be noted that collections of these categories on occasions omit some of the compositions only to include them in later issues of the same collections. The greatest care has been taken in the assembling of these important data, in order to provide the best possible guides for the user of the volume.

Kochel numbers for Mozart's works have been provided wherever possible as well as other pertinent information to serve as assistance in identifying interesting and important facets of his early career. This careful tracing of the young Mozart's accomplishments strongly underlined the genius that has been ascribed to him far more clearly than in the generalities so often applied in casual discussions of his accomplishments.

Considerable information has been collected in this volume concerning Beethoven's forebears, and it came as a revelation to find as much music as there was in his strange background. His violent personality became far more understandable in the light of the facts assembled here.

The assistance of many people in various stages of this volume must be mentioned here. Because of the complexity of the material at hand and the need for the utmost care in the search for accuracy a special note of gratitude is in order to Teresa Eichler, Joseph Pecorella, and Daniel A. Ricigliano. Their faith and encouragement helped beyond words throughout this arduous task. New researchers have been added to the staff in the persons of Laurie Hays and Julie Ziavras. Some valuable assistance by Roger Hussey in the proofreading area was welcomed. Most of all Edith Eisler, my wife, contributed the patience and understanding that this task requires from a generous helper. The tedious work she performed in adding various graphic touches, picking out pictures, and making corrections were tangible features. The emotional support was intangible but invaluable during this period.

Finally, a word of tribute to Neal Hatch for the typing of this manuscript which became more and more difficult as the volume progressed. His enormous help and his continuing good nature and wit during the difficult times revealed his deep friendship as well as his earnest desire for the excellency of the finished book.

Paul E. Eisler

(January 5, January 12, January 17, February 19) Handel's "Alexander's Feast" with text by Dryden with additions by Newburgh Hamilton was completed, one section on each of these dates.

(January 12) Arne's incidental music for "Zara" was produced in London's Drury on this date.

(January 12) S. M. Cibber made her début as a tragic actress in Aaron Hill's "Zara" on this date.

(January 15) The merchant guild of St. Maurus employed Claude Rameau (Jean-Philippe's brother) as its parish organist to play on Saint's Day.

(January 17) Cornelius van Beethoven became a citizen of Bonn.

(January 21) On this date Charles Theodore Pachelbel gave his first concert in New York.

(January 24) Porpora's "Mitridate", an opera and not a pasticcio as presumed by some, was performed at London's Haymarket Theatre on this date. It is not to be confused with the Roman "Mitridate" in 1730.

(January 31) Juvarra died before his designs for the Royal Palace were finished. He died on this date and the building was completed by his student Giovanni Battista Sacchetti.

(February 3) Johann Georg Albrechtsberger, Austrian organist, composer and teacher was born at Klosterneuburg near

(cont.) Vienna (died 1809, March 7 at Vienna). He was a great contrapuntalist.

(February 9) Araia's "La forza dell'amore e dell'odio" appeared at the Russian court.

(February 9) Carey wrote the music for a production of "Hamlet" on this date at Goodman's Fields.

(February 13) Caldara's opera "Achille in Sciro" was performed in Vienna in celebration of the wedding of Maria Theresa to Stephen Francis, the Duke of Lorraine.

(February 19) Handel's "Alexander's Feast" was produced in London on this date at Covent Garden.

(February 28) Arne's "The Fall of Phaeton" (with "Harlequin Restor'd, or Taste à la Mode") was performed at London's Drury Lane on this date.

(March 10) Rameau and Fuzelier added a fourth entrée, "Les Sauvages" to Les Indes Galantes, first produced on this date at Paris.

(March 13) John Walsh I, English or Irish music publisher and instrument maker, died on this date (birthdate unknown). He lowered the prices on reprinted Dutch editions.

(March 16) Giovanni Battista Pergolesi, Italian composer, died (born 1710, January 4 near Ancona). He was a pupil of Durante and Feo.

(March 17) Pergolesi was buried on this date in the common burial pit of the poor at

Pozzuoli.

(March 23) Bourgeois' "Le Paradis terrestre" composed to Milton's text appeared on this date.

(April 25) Ludwig and Maria van Beethoven Srs' second child, Marcus Josephus, was baptized on this date. He died as an infant.

(April 29) Cecilla Young sang at a benefit for her uncle, Anthony Young.

(May 4) Porpora's serenata "Festa d'Imeneo" was performed on this date for the marriage of Frederick, Prince of Wales. The production was at the Haymarket Theatre in London.

(May 5) Gioacchino Conti sang, in London, in the opera "Ariodante".

(May 7) John Weldon, English organist and composer, died at London (born 1676, January 19 at Chichester).

(May 12) Gioacchino Conti sang, in London, in the opera "Atalanta".

(May 12) Handel's "Atalanta", libretto by Belisario Valeriani, was first produced on this date at Covent Garden. Frederick, Prince of Wales, the principal patron of the "Opera of the Novility", was impressed with this work. Porpora left England as a result of the success.

(June 3) Ignaz Fränzl, German violinist and composer, was born at Mannheim (died 1811 at Mannheim). He was a prominent

(cont.) composer of the "Mannheim School".

(June 4) Daniel Henstridge died at Canterbury. He was an English organist and composer, possibly the son of a musician with the same name who had been an organist at Gloucester Cathedral (birthdate unknown but probably at Gloucester).

(June 7) Karl Friebert, Austrian tenor, was born at Wullersdorf, Lower Austria (died 1816, August 6).

(June 21) Jonathan Martin was appointed organist of the Chapel Royal. He promised "to compose anthems or services for the use of his Majesty's Chapel, when- ever required by the Subdean for the time being".

(July 12) Charles Avison was appointed organist of the Church of St. John on this date.

(August 15) Johann Christoph Kellner, German organist and composer was born at Gräfenroda, Thuringia (died 1803 at Cassel). He composed an operetta and a cantata as well as concertos, sonatas, and organ works. In addition he wrote a book on thorough bass.

(September 8) Bernardino Ottani, Italian composer, was born at Bologna (died 1827, October 26 at Turin).

(September 20) Tommaso Carapella, Italian composer, died at Naples (born 1653 at Cerreto).

(October 18) Mlle. Duval a French singer and composer's only known work was a four-act opera-ballet "Les Génie's," produced at the

1736(cont.)
Académie Royale de Musique of
Paris on this date.

(October 31 and November 18)
J. S. Bach wrote to Johann
Friedrich Klemm on these dates.
The latter was an official of
the town of Sängerhausen. Bach
requested his help for Johann
Gottfried Bernhard in obtaining
the vacant organist's position
at the Jacobi-Kirche in Sängerhausen.

(November 18) The London Daily
Post on this date announced that
Signoras Merighi,Chimenti, and
Francesina had the honour to
sing before the Queen on the
previous Monday night last and
received a "most gracious
reception".

(November 18) There was an
article about the singer
Elisabeth Duparc in the London
Daily Post on this date.

(November 18) Karl Friedrich
Fasch, German harpsichordist and
composer, was born in Zerbst.
(died, 1800, August 3) He gave
rebirth to the Concerts Spirituel at Berlin by forming the
Singakademie which revived
choral singing in Germany.

(November 19) J. S. Bach was
awarded the title of Royal
Polish and Electoral Saxon Court
composer* by Augustus III on
this date. (*Königlicher Hof-
Componist)

(November 22) Arne's incidental
music for "The Rival Queens, or
the Death of Alexander the Great"
was produced at Drury Lane
Theatre in London.

(November 23) Elisabeth Duparc
appeared in Hasse's "Siroe" at

(cont.) London. It was her
first appearance there.

(December 1) J. S. Bach performed
again on the Silbermann organ
in the Sophien-Kirche.

(December 2) Melchiorra Brigida
Scarlatti (second generation of
the Scarlatti family) died
(born, 1663, October 5).

(December 8) Annibali made his
London début on this date in
the title-role of "Poro"
(created at its first production
in 1731 by Farinelli).

(December 28) Antonio Caldara,
Italian composer, died at
Vienna (born, 1670 in Venice).
He had been Vice-Kapellmeister
at Vienna and a pupil of
Legrenzi.

(January) Vivaldi's opera
"Ginevera, principessa di
Scozia" (libretto by Salvi)
was produced in Florence at
the Teatro della Pergola.

(February) Pergolesi went to
the Capucian monastery in
Pozzuoli which had been founded
by his patron, the Duke of
Maddaloni's ancestors.

(March) None of Araia's works
seem to have ever been printed
except one single aria inserted
in the pasticcio "Orfeo",
performed in London at this time.

(June) A drinking song by
Villesavoye was published in
the "Mercure de France" this
month.

(September) J. S. Bach renewed
his application to Augustus III
this month.

(October) Charles Avison was

1736(cont.)
appointed organist of St. Nicholas at this time. It is now the Cathedral in Newcastle-on-Tyne.

(November) Riccardo Broschi was court composer at Stuttgart for a brief period.

(November) W. H. Grattan Flood gave this date as that when Pescetti went to England.

(Summer) Gottfried Theodor Krause of Herzberg was J. S. Bach's deputy at the Thomas-schule during this period.

Johann Georg Albrechtsberger, composer and musician, was born at Klosterneuburg (died, 1809, at Vienna). He was one of Beethoven's teachers.

Johann Christoph Bach, 7th generation, was born (died, 1808). He was the son of Johann Friedrich Bach.

Johann Heinrich Cario, German trumpeter was born at Eckern-förde, Holstein (death date unknown).

Margrave Christian Frederick was born (died, 1806).

Horace Coignet, French amateur composer, was born at Lyons (died, 1821, August 29 at Lyons).

Benjamin Goodison, English musician, was born at London (death date unknown).

Louis de Lully, French composer, died (born, 1664, August 4).

Johann Wilhelm Mangold, son of Johann H. Mangold, a German musician, was born at Umstadt (died 1806 at Darnstadt).

Karl Michael, Ritter von Esser, German violinist and composer, was born probably at Aachen or Zweibrücken (died c.1795).

Angélique Richer, wife of Philidor, was born (death date unknown).

Alessandro Scarlatti, son of Domenico, was born. Some sources give his birthdate as 1737. He was a member of the fourth generation of the Scarlatti family.

Antoine Trial, a renouned tenor, was born at Avignon (died, 1795, February 5 at Paris)

Karl Westenholz, German musician, was born at Lauenberg (died 1789, January 24).

Christian Ferdinand Abel retired from the court chapel at Cöthen where he had been a viola da gamba player and cellist. He was the son of Clamor Heinrich Abel.

J. Adlung's house was destroyed in the great fire at Erfunt.

Domenico Annibali, Italian soprano at the court of Saxony, was engaged by Handel for his opera company at London. He made his debut in "Arminio" at Covent Garden.

Johann Christoph Bach, son of Johann Christoph and grandson of Christoph, was an organist at Keula and dealer at Blank-enhain (born 1689, September 12).

J. S. Bach maintained control over the choir prefects at the Thomasschule. The head prefect, as his deputy, was in a close relationship with him.

J. S. Bach was awarded the title of Court Composer to the King-Elector of Poland-Saxony, Frederick Augustus.

J. S. Bach was musical editor of the "Musicalisches Gesang-Buch".

J. S. Bach's tunes he wrote for Schemelli's hymn-book were in print.

Barrière went to Italy for further studies.

John Beard appeared as a tenor at Covent Garden. He sang in "Alexander's Feast", "Acis and Galatea" and "Atalanta".

Pierre-Joseph Bernard supplied Rameau with the libretto for "Castor et Pollux".

Francesca Bertolli sang in "Onorio" this year.

Louis-Thomas Bourgeois was at Poitiers.

Josse Boutmy entered the service of the Prince of Thurn and Taxis. He taught harpsichord to the Princess d'Arenberg and to the young ladies and gentlemen at the court.

Boyce was appointed composer to the Chapel Royal. He also became organist at St. Michael's Cornhill.

S. M. Cibber tried unsuccessfully to take the part of Polly in "The Beggar's Opera" from Kitty Clive.

Clari was "maestro di cappella" at Pisa at this time.

Cobb sold his business to his

(cont.) brother-in-law William Dicey of Northampton. The latter had been associated with him and bought it for himself and his son Cluer Dicey, who managed it until 1764.

Composer Francisco Corselli, who came to Madrid from Parma, was appointed supernumerary maestro d'capella this year. He was promoted to first master two years later.

DeLange studied music this year at one of the Liège churches and was awarded a cash prize.

Farinelli went to Spain by way of France this year. Once in Spain he succeeded by means of his voice to bring Philip V back to participation in the affairs of government.

Ignazio Fiorillo this year made his debut as an opera composer with a production of his Mandane at Venice.

B. Fortier, English music engraver, produced Porpora's "Sinfonie da camera a tre istromenti . . . Opra II".

Benjamin Franklin advertised "Corelli's sonatas, Geminiani's Concertos, and ditto's Solos" this year.

Fux recommended G. C. Wagenseil for a court scholarship.

Georg Sigismund Gebel this year was appointed sub-organist at the church of St. Elisabeth at Breslau.

Gluck left for Vienna this year to become chamber musician to Prince Ferdinand Phillip Lobkowitz. He became acquainted

with Italian Opera while in
Vienna. He had come from Prague
and was only twenty-two years
old.

Johann Gottlieb Görner was
director of music at St. Paul's
church in Leipzig at this time.

The Bay Psalm Book, formerly
"John Edwards His Book 1736",
was at this time in the possession of his descendant Dr.
Samuel Abbot Green.

Handel's oratorio "Alexander's
Feast" was produced with John
Beard, tenor. The latter was
one of his greatest protegés.

Hoffmann this year was elected
Bürgomeister of his native
town (Rastenberg, Thuringia).
He later died there.

Johann Janitsch joined the
private orchestra of the Crown
Prince at Rheinsberg this year.
His compositions, in the style
of J. G. Graun, consisted of
trios, concertos, sonatas, a
"Te Deum", several cantatas and
other works.

Joseph Kelway was appointed
organist of St. Martin's-in-
the-Fields this year.

Johann Friedrich Lampe became
the brother-in-law of T. A.
Arne this year when Arne married
Lampe's sister Cecilia.

Jean Marie Leclair "l'aîné"
ceased to appear in the programs
at the Concert Spirituel.

The "Lettres Muscovites"
appeared in Paris this year.
Locatelli vented his wrath over
his ill-treatment and arrest

(cont.) in Kazan in the letters.

Lotti actually took over Biffi's
functions as maestro di cappella
at St. Mark's, Venice this year.

Giovanni Battista, the composer,
came to Madrid at this time.

James Oswald, dancing master,
moved to Edinburgh.

Charles Theodore Pachelbel,
the German organist, gave
concerts in New York and
Charleston this year. They
were for his own benefit.

The earliest record of John
Parry was a visit he made to
play in Dublin this year.

G. Porta operated Handel's
"Royal Academy of Music" until
this year.

Anton Raaff made his début
this year when he sang at
Florence at the betrothal of
Maria Theresa. He later sang
at many Italian opera houses
and theatres.

Rameau this year was also
organist at the church of the
Jesuit Novitiate.

The baptismal certificate of
Alexandro Scarlatti appeared
this year.

Tommaso Scarlatti sang in
various operas during this
season.

Johann Scheibe this year
settled in Hamburg as a teacher.

Gottfried Silbermann this year
gave two pianos he had made to
J. S. Bach.

1736(cont.)

Antonio Stradivarius made the "Habeneck" violin this year.

Antonio Stradivarius made the "Muntz" violin this year.

By this date Villesavoye was "maître de musique" at Strasbourg Cathedral.

Voltaire sent his completed text for "Samson" to Rameau. However the latter had lost interest by this time.

The building of the great organ at Versailles was not completed until this year.

The Amsterdam edition of the cello sonatas by Antoniotto of Milan appeared at this time.

"Le Berger Fidèle" and "Aquilon et Orithie" were published complete by this time.

Thomas Augustine Arne this year published "The Fall of Phaeton" at London.

Arne composed some music for Aaron Hill's tragedy of "Zara" this year. His sister made "her first attempt as an actress" in the production.

Charles Avison's "Six celebrated Sonatas in Three Parts" were published this year by Cooke.

J. S. Bach wrote Cantata #6 "Bleib bei uns, denn es will Abend werden" this year for Easter Monday.

J. S. Bach wrote the Cantata "Kommt, eilet und laufet: this year for Easter Day (Picander?). It is part of the Easter Oratorio.

Spitta attributed J. S. Bach's C minor Concerto for Two Claviers to this date.

J. S. Bach composed his Easter Oratorio this year.

Boismortier's opera-ballet "Les Voyages de l'amour" appeared this year.

"Les Voyages de l'Amour" libretto by Le Clerc de la Bruère) and music by Bodin de Boismortier was produced this year. The librettist also served for Rameau's "Dardanus".

Boyce's oratorio "David's Lamentation" appeared this year.

G. G. Brunetti's opera "Il corrivo" was produced at Naples.

Caldara's opera "Achille in Sciro" was produced at Vienna.

Metastasio's libretto "Achille in Sciro" was set this year by Caldara and later Chiarino Corselli, Gassmann, Hasse, Jommelli (2 settings), Leo, Naumann, Paisiello, Pugnani and Sarro.

Mestastasio's libretto "Ciro riconosciuto" was set this year by Caldara and later by Cocchi (G.), Duni (E. G.), Galuppi, Hasse, Jommelli, Leo, Piccinni, and Rinaldo di Capua.

Metastasio's libretto "Temistocle" was set this year by Caldara, and later by J. C. Bach, Durau, Jommelli and Leo.

Castel's "Remarques sur la lettre de M. Rameau" ("Mémoires de Trévoux") appeared this year.

E. R. Duni's opera "Alessandro nell'Indie" (Metastasio) may have appeared this year.

E. R. Duni's opera "La tirannide debellata" (Zenò and Pariati) was produced at Milan's Teatro Regio Ducal at this year's carnival.

Durante's oratorio "Abigaile" appeared at Rome this year. Only the libretto has survived.

"Les Génies, an opera by Mlle. Duval was written this year.

Johann Ernst Galliard wrote the music to "The Royal Chase", or "Merlin's Cave" this year.

Baldassare Galuppi this year wrote his opera "Elisa, regina di Tiro" in Venice (libretto: Zeno and Pariati).

Baldassare Galuppi this year wrote his opera "Ergilda" in Venice (libretto: Vitturi).

Lodovico Giustini's twelve clavier sonatas were published at this time.

Barnabas Gunn published his "Two Cantatas and Six Songs" this year.

A group of Günther's friends published his collection "Singende Muse an der Pleisse" at this time.

Handel's opera "Atalanta" was completed this year (see also 1736, May 12).

Handel's composition this year included:
    Concerto Grosso in C major
    (performed at the opening of

(cont.) Act II of "Alexander's Feast"). Another concerto, opus 4, #6, was used in Act I.

Wedding Anthem for the Prince of Wales ("Sing unto God")

"Not cloe that I better am" (vocal work)

Hasse was credited with composing "La Sorella Amante" at Malta this year. It was probably "Dalisa" with a new title.

Abraham Langford's ballad opera "The Lover his own Rival" appeared this year.

Leo wrote both "Onore vince amore" and "Farnace" this year.

Maichelbeck's Opus I, "Die auf dem Clavier spielende und das Geliör . . . ." was published this year at Augsburg.

Johann Mattheson this year published his "Kernmelodische Wissenschaft". He recommended the French style to young composers in this wrok.

Monteclair this year wrote "Principles de musique" in 4 parts. Fétis mistakenly thought it a 2nd edition of the "Methode".

Pergolesi's "Salve Regina" in C minor, for soprano and strings appeared this year.

Pergolesi's "Stabat Mater" appeared this year. It was his most celebrated work.

Rameau's rondo "Tourbillons" was included in his "Pièces de Clavecin" published this year at Paris.

1736(cont.)

J. S. Bach wrote the music for Schemelli's Hymn-book published this year by Breitkopf.

Sperontes' "Die singende Muse an der Pleisse", a collection of lieder, was published this year at Leipzig.

William Tansur's "A Compleat Melody, or, The Harmony of Zion" was published this year at London by Alice Pearson.

Domenico Terradellas' oratorio "Giuseppe riconosciuto" appeared at this time. He was a Spanish composer.

Hasse's pasticcio "Orfeo" was produced in London this year.

Charles Helmont's "italiaens opera", a setting of a Flemish version of Zeno's "Griselda", was performed this year at Brussels.

Giovanni Batista Lampugnani wrote two operas, "Egio" and "Antigone" for the Teatro Ducale in Milan this season.

Jean Marie Leclair ("le cadet") had his "Divertissement champêtre" performed at the Lyons Academy this year.

G. B. Mele's opera "Por amor y por lealtad" (Metastasio) was performed at Madrid this year.

Vivaldi's opera "Ginevra, principessa di Scozia" was produced in Florence at this time.

The Weissenfels court theater of the Dukes of Saxe-Weissenfels refused to allow interpolation of foreign words in their pro-(cont.) ductions at this time.

Cartaud de la Villatte wrote "Essai historique et philosophique sur le Goût" this year.

Juvara, prominent Italian Baroque architect, died (born 1678).

Jean Baptiste Pater, French painter, died (born 1695).

Pöppelmann, German Baroque architect, died (born 1662).

At Versailles this year Francois Lemoyne completed the ceiling of the Hercules Salon. It was the last great decorative project in the palace and showed 140 mythological figures amidst the clouds.

Tiepolo painted "Danaë" at Stockholm this year.

Johann Joachim Winckelmann, a German archaeologist, was active at this time.

(to 1737) A. T. Nawrat was praepositus of the Capella Rorantistarum during this period.

(to 1737) Chrystian Ruciński was a member of the Jesuit Chapel in Cracow for these years.

(to 1739) George Bickham, Jr. was most famous for his two illustrated folio volumes, "The Musical Entertainer". It was issued in parts during this period.

(to 1742) The singer Vittoria Tesi wrote a series of love letters to a priest, Enea Silvio Piccolomini during these years.

1736(cont.)

(to 1744) J. S. Bach composed fifty-three cantatas during these years, probably with several more that have been lost.

(to 1745) Micola Fago ("Il Tarantino") was maestro di cappella at the church of San Giacomo dei Spagnvoli during this period.

(to 1745) Polonaise tunes were included in Sperontes' collection "Die singende Muse an der Pleisse" during these years.

(to 1754) G. C. M. Clari was chapel master at Pisa Cathedral for this nineteen year period.

(to 1754) Lorenz Christoph Mizler's journal, "New-eröff- neter Musikalischer Bibliothek" appeared at intervals in these years.

(to 1770) Charles Avison conducted subscription concerts at Newcastle during this long period.

(to 1775) At least 46 concerts were advertised in New York newspapers during this thirty- nine year span.

c.1736

Pieter Joseph van den Bosch, Dutch organist and composer, was born at Hoboken (died 1803, February 19 at Antwerp).

Giuseppe Guadagnini, Italian violin maker, was born (died: c.1805).

Kohault, Bohemian composer, was born in Bohemia (death date unknown)

Jakob Kress, German violinist

(cont.) and composer, died at Darmstadt. His works included a Symphony, overtures, violin and flute concertos, quartets, trios and sonatas for various instruments (birthdate unknown).

Giusto Ferdinando Tenducci, Italian male soprano and composer, was born at Siena (death date unknown).

Jean-Baptiste Anet this year left Paris and retired to the court of ex-king Stanislas Leczinski of Poland at Lunéville.

N. Porpora was paid off for his disappointment in losing the appointment as maestro di cappella at St. Mark's in Venice by an invitation to London as principal composer to the "Opera of the Nobility".

J. S. Bach wrote Cantata #13, "Meine Seufzer, meiner tränen" for the second Sunday after Epiphany.

J. S. Bach wrote Cantata #28, "Gottlob! Nun geht das Jahr zu Ende" for the Sunday after Christmas.

J. S. Bach wrote Cantata #41, "Jesu nun sei gepreiset" for New Year's Day.

Handel at this time wrote the following cantatas for voices and instruments:
"Cecilia, volgi un sguardo" (soprano, tenor, strings and continuo)

"Carco sempre di gloria" (contralto, violins and continuo)

c. 1736(cont.)

Handel composed "Pieces for the Harpsichord" (Aylesford mss) this year and also earlier.

Handel composed two suites at this time, one in d minor and one in g minor.

Hasse's opera "Cleofide" (Metastasio) a new version was heard at Dresden at this time.

Richard Jones'book of "Chamber Airs" was published at this time at London.

Rameau published his third and last collection "Nouvelle Suites de pieces de clavecin" at this time at Paris.

Chardin painted "The Monkey Antiquarian" at this time at Chartres. (16¼" x 12¼")

1737

(January 12) Francesca Bertolli and Farinelli both sang in Handel's "Arminio" at Covent Garden on this date. The libretto was by Salvi and this was the première.

(January 13) James Kent on this day succeeded John Bishop as organist of both the Cathedral and College at Winchester.

(January 13, 14) Johann Göttfried Bernhard Bach passed his test for the vacant organ seat at the Jacobi-Kirche at Sängerhausen on the thirteenth and on the following day his appointment was approved, subject to testimonials of good character from Mühlhausen, his prior position.

(January 29) Arne's incidental music for "The King and the Miller of Mansfield" was heard (cont.) at Drury Lane Theatre in London.

(February 6) G. Bononcini's opera "Alessandro in Sidone" was heard on this date at Vienna.

(February 16) Francesca Bertolli sang in Handel's "Giustino" at its première on this date at Covent Garden in London. The libretto was by Niccolò Beregani but somewhat altered.

(February 18) The British ambassador reported on this date "The queen (of Spain) is endeavoring to look out for diversion for the King, who has a natural aversion for music".

(February 27) Hasse's Opera "Senocrito" (libretto by B. Pallavicino) was heard in Dresden on this date.

(February 28) Hercule Bréhy (also known as Pierre), a Netherlands organist and composer, died on this date at Brussels (born 1673 and baptized September 13).

(March 4) Antonio Stradivarius' second wife, Antonia Maria Zambelli, was interred in the Villani burial vault on this day.

(March 9) Joseph Mysliweczek, Bohemian composer, was born on this date at Prague (died 1781, February 4 at Rome).

(March 11, 12) Johann Gottfried Bernhard Bach succeeded in obtaining two testimonials as to his courteous and respectable conduct at Mühlhausen.

1737(cont.)

(March 15) At Lincoln's Inn
Chapel, Thomas Arne married
Cecilia Young, daughter of
Charles Young the organist, at
All Hallows, Banking.

(March 17-24) Benjamin Franklin
during this period advertised a
reprint of Watt's "Divine Songs
attempted in Easy Language for
the Use of Children" in the
Pennsylvania Gazette.

(March 25) Andrzej Todensz
Nawrat, Polish ecclesiastic
singer and conductor, died on
this date at Cracow (birthdate
unknown).

(March 26) Vivaldi's opera
"Catone in Utica" was produced
on this date at Vienna.

(March 28) N. Porpora's oratorio "Gedeone" was performed
on this date at the Imperial
Chapel in Vienna.

(April 4) The Leipzig consistory confirmed Johann Gottfried
Bernhard Bach's appointment as
organist at the Jacobi-Kirche.

(April 4) Jonathan Martin,
English organist and composer,
died at London on this day
(born 1715 at London).

(April 4) G. Bononcini's
oratorio "Ezechia" had its
first performance on this date
at Vienna.

(April 13) Handel's pasticcio
"Didone" with music by L.
Vinci and recitative by Handel
(libretto based on Metastasio)
was heard at Covent Garden in
London.

(April 19) Hasse's oratorio
"La virtu appie della croce"

(cont.) (libretto by
Pallavicino) was produced on
this date at Dresden.

(May 3) Friedrich Schwindel,
Dutch violinist, flautist,
harpsichordist and composer,
was born in Amsterdam (died
1786, August 7)

(May 9) François Lupin Grenet's
"Le Triomphe de l'harmonie"
was produced on this date at
the Paris Opèra.

(May 10) John Travers was sworn
in on this date as organist of
the Chapel Royal .

(May 12-19) Benjamin Franklin
during this week published
the words of a "New Year's
Ode by Colley Cibber, Esq.,
Poet Laureate and set to Music
by Dr. Green".

(May 16) Johann Friedrich
Lampe's "The Dragon of Wantley"
was produced at the Haymarket
Theatre in London on this date.

(May 18) Francesca Bertolli
sang in a revival of "Partenope"
this evening.

(May 18) Annibali appeared in
Handel's opera "Berenice" on
this date. The libretto was
by Salvi and the performance
was at Covent Garden in London.

(May 24) E. R. Duri's opera
"Demifoonte" was produced on
this date at the King's Theatre
in London. Three performances
were given during May and June.

(May 30) Jean Claude Gillier,
French composer, died in Paris
(born 1667).

(June 7) Jean-Baptiste von
Maldere, violinist, brother of

Pierre, and later a violinist at the Royal Chapel of Brussels, was born there on this date (death date unknown).

(June 8) Vivaldi's secular cantata "Ilmopso" for five violins and instruments was performed on this day at the Pieta.

(June 11) Farinelli set out on a trip to Madrid. Upon his arrival Italian opera received great imputus.

(July 6) Pietro Torri, organist and composer, died on this date at Munich (born c. 1655 at Peschiera, Verona).

(July 10) Handel's oratorio, "Il trionfo del Tempo e della verita" with words by Humphreys, based on Racine's "Panfili", was heard at the Oxford Theatre at London on this date.

(July 26) Hasse's opera "Atalanta" (libretto by Pallaviciero) was premiered on this date at Dresden.

(August 3) Hasse's opera "Asteria" (libretto by Pallaviciero) received its first performance on this date at Dresden.

(August 4) Corrette's "La Fete infernale" was performed on this date.

(August 7) A quotation from Farinelli's biographer Giovanni Sacchi said, "Farinelli arrived on August 7, 1737 (Madrid). Queen Elizabeth arranged a concert in a hall close to the King's own apartment. She asked Farinelli to recite a few

(cont.) of his most engaging songs. King Philip at first seemed surprised, then deeply moved. After the second aria, he summoned the singer to his chambers, overwhelmed him with compliments and asked for a third piece, in which Farinelli surpassed himself. Carried away, the King asked him what reward he wanted. Nothing would be denied him. Farinelli asked that the King allow himself to be shaved and dressed, that he rise from his depression and again appear in the Council of the State." "This was done and his affliction improved."

(August 22) Privileges were granted on this date to Charles Nicholas Le Clerc for "Les Pieces de Clavecin de M. Scarlati".

(August 30) John Beard on this date appeared at Drury Lane Theatre as Sir John Loverule in Coffey's ballad opera "The Devil to Pay".

(September 14) (Johann) Michael Haydn, Austrian organist, composer and brother of Franz Joseph Haydn, was born on this date at Rohrau, Austria (died 1806, August 10 at Salzburg).

(September 21) Francis Hopkinson, musical amateur, was born on this date. Although a lawyer by profession, he considered himself to be the first native composer. He was also a signer of the Declaration of Independence.

(September 27) Michel (Pinolet) de Monteclair, French composer, died near St. Denis (born 1667, baptized December 4 at Andelot, Haute Marne).

1737(cont.)

(September 28) J. S. Bach's "Angenehmes Wiederau", a secular cantata, was performed on the occasion of Johann Christian Hennicke taking possession of the estate of Wiederau.

(October 22) Vincenzo Manfredini, Italian composer, was born at Pistra (died 1799, August 16 at St. Petersburg.

(October 24) Rameau's opera "Castor et Pollux, tragédie en musique" (text by Bernard) was produced on this date at Paris.

(October 26) Louis Charles Joseph Rey, French cellist and composer, was born at Lauzerte. He was the brother of Jean-Baptiste Rey and first studied in Toulouse. Rey wrote several trios for two violins and cello and some violin and cello duets (died 1811, May 12 at Paris).

(October 28) Johanna Caroline Bach, daughter of J. S. Bach and Anna Magdalena, was born (died 1781, August 18). She never married.

(October 30) J. S. Bach's daughter Johanna Caroline was baptized on this day.

(November 4) Domenico Sarro's opera "Achille in Sciro" was given on this date at the Teatro San Carlo in Naples (libretto by Metastasio).

(November 16) Vivaldi on this day wrote to Marchese Guido Bentivoglio d'Aragono, describing his heart ailment.

(November 16) Vivaldi learned that he was forbidden to be artistically active in Ferrara at this time.

(November 20) Handel composed an anthem for the funeral of Queen Caroline, which took place on this date.

(November 24) Polish composer Jacek Szczurowski took Holy Orders at this time.

(December 17) A funeral service for Queen Caroline took place in London on this day.

(December 18) Antonio Stradivarius, the renowned violin maker, died on this date at Cremona (born 1644 or 1645).

(December 19) John Bishop, English organist and composer, died on this date at Winchester (born 1665)

(February) Lulli's "Persée" was given this month.

(March) J. Gottfried Bernhard Bach left Mühlhausen for his new position at Sängerhausen.

(March) Desmarets composed a motet and a "Te Deum" for the marriage of Princess Elisabeth Thérèse to the King of Sardinia.

(March) The oratorio "Teodora" (libretto by Papebrochio Fungoni) was sung at the monastery of Santa Chiara.

(May) Vivaldi's opera "Catone in Utica" (libretto by Metastasio) was produced on this date at Teatro Filarmonico in Vienna.

(June) Jean-Jacques Rousseau contributed an air to the "Mercure de France" this month.

(Fall) V. L. Ciampi's opera "Da un disordine nasce un ordine" was produced at this time at the Teatro dei Fiorentini.

(Fall) N. Porpora's opera "Rosbale" was performed at this time at the Teatro St. Giovanni Crisostomo in Venice. In the libretto Porpora is referred to as Maestro of the Ospedale degli Incurabile.

(October) Francesco Feo this month wrote a serenata "Polinice" for the celebration of the marriage of Charles of Bourbon, King of the two Sicilies, to Princess Maria Amalia of Poland.

(November) Pescetti probably went to England at this time. According to Flood it was 1736.

(December) Bellinzani was maestro di cappella at Recanati from this time to his death.

(December) Pere Louis-Bertrand Castel wrote "Extrait de la génération harmonique de M. Rameau" in the Journal de Trévoux this month.

Alday, a member of a family of French musicians, was born at Perpignan (date of death unknown). He was a mandolin player.

Pietro Maria Crispi, an Italian composer, was born at Rome this year (died 1797, June 16 at Rome).

Johann Georg Linigke, German violinist and composer, died sometime after this year (birthdate unknown).

Antoine Mahaut (b?d?), an 18th-century flutist, composer and editor, at this time lived in Amsterdam until he fled from creditors and entered a monastery. He was known for his work as an editor of "Monthly Musical Pastime".

Giovanni Mariani, Italian composer who taught Francesco Gnecco who later taught Niccolo Paganini, was born (died 1795).

William Paxton, English cellist and composer, and brother of Stephen, was born at London (died 1781 at London).

Frederick Charles Reinhold, English organist and bass singer, was born this year at London (died 1815, September 29 at London).

Christian Weiss, whose son was sponsor to Bach's daughter, Johanna Caroline, died this year (birthdate unknown).

Dorothea Wendling, opera singer, was born this year at Stuttgart (died 1811, August 20).

Bernardo Aliprandi this year was appointed chamber composer to the Munich court orchestra.

Aliprandi's serenata "Apollo tra le Muse in Parnaso" was performed this season at Nymphenburg.

Domenico Alberti was a member of the Venetian embassy in Rome this year.

Alcock became organist of St. Andrew's Church, Plymouth at this time.

Domenico Annibali sang the part of Giustino in Handel's opera of that name, and also the part of Demetrio in his "Berenice".

Johann Ernst Bach briefly attended the Thomasschule this year.

Johann Gottfried Bernhard Bach was organist at Sängershausen by now.

K. P. E. Bach this season performed his compositions before the Margrave Friedrich Wilhelm and Friedrich Wilhelm I of Prussia, the father of his future patron.

Baron this year made a tour to Merseburg, Cöthen, and Berlin, and was engaged by Frederick William I as theorist.

Benoît Blaise at this time joined the orchestra of the Comedie Italienne in Paris as a bassoonist.

Giovanni Bononcini apparently returned to Vienna this year.

Boyce conducted for the meeting of the three choirs of Gloucester, Worcester and Hereford this season.

Riccardo Broschi revived his "Adriano in Siria" this year at Stuttgart.

Cartel at this time reviewed Rameau's "Génération harmonique" unfavorably.

William Coxe this year said the following about Carlo Broschi: "In 1737 he went to Versailles, and was drawn to Madrid by Elizabeth Farnese, who was desirous to try the power of music in soothing the melancholy of her husband."

Carey wrote the libretto for "The Dragon of Wantley" this year.

Cervetto played cello in the performance of Arne's "Comus" during this season.

Chinzer was one of the composers from whose works Vivaldi selected part of the score for the centenary celebration of the Amsterdam Schouwburg.

Clegg had a benefit at Crow Street Theatre in Dublin this year.

Gioacchino Conti this season sang in the productions of "Arminio", "Berenice", "Giustino", and "Partenope" at London.

Cotumacci entered the Congregazione dei Musici di Napoli this year.

Jean-Baptiste Cupis was given a privilege to publish violin sonatas and othere instrumental pieces for the next nine years.

Elisabeth Duparc's portrait was engraved by J. Faber this year in mezzotint from a painting done by George Knapton.

Thérèse Deshayes this year gave an analysis of Rameau's "Generation harmonique" in "Le Pour et Contre".

Giovanni Ferrandini this year was appointed director of the electoral chamber music and a councillor at the court in Munich.

Michael Festing was appointed director of the Italian opera this season.

1737(cont.)

Castrucci was succeeded this year at the Italian Opera by Michael Festing.

Gabler provided a 12-rank mixture and many others for the organ at Weingarten Abbey.

Martin Gerbert von Hornau, German musical historian, entered the Benedictine monastery of St. Blasien this year.

Gluck this year discovered a book of Metastasio's that he would later (1752) use for his opera "La Clemenza de Tito".

Daniel Gough, proprietor of Marylebone Gardens, started charging one shilling per person. This entitled the buyer to refreshments up to that amount.

Handel closed his Covent Garden Theatre this season since it was on the verge of Bankruptcy.

Handel at this time refused to meet King Frederick, the Great at Aix-la-Chapelle.

Handel this year revised an oratorio by Cardinal Panfili titled "Il Trionfo del Tempo e del Desinganno".

Handel suffered a paralytic stroke and nervous collapse this year amounting to a physical breakdown.

Handel this year provided the music for Queen Caroline's funeral.

Harris' double organ at this (cont.) time was moved from Magdalen College, Oxford to Tewkesbury Abbey.

F. J. Haydn was sent away from home for an education. He went to Hainburg this year for that purpose.

Heidegger signed the dedication of Handel's "Arminio" issued this year.

John Keeble this year was appointed successor to Thomas Roseingrave in London as organist of St. George's, Hanover Square. Roseingrave was awarded half of his salary until his death.

Krebs at this time was appointed organist at Zwickau.

Johann Friedrich Lampe collaborated with Henry Carey on the opera (burlesque) "The Dragon of Wantley".

Johann Friedrich Lampe's theoretical work "A Plain and Compendious Method of Teaching Thorough Bass" was published this year.

Nicolas Matteis settled at Shrewsbury at this time as a teacher of languages and violin. Burney studied French and violin with him there.

The opera company run by Pietro and Angelo Mingotti toured Austria, Moravia and Bohemia and often visited Copenhagen and Germany from this year forward.

Prince Francesco Saverio Melzi, postmaster-general of Lombardy, induced Gluck to go with him to Italy this year.

1737(cont.)

Joseph Mondonville played at the Concert Spirituel in Paris this year and was well received by French audiences.

Michel Montéclair retired from the Opera orchestra this year with a pension.

Pepusch was appointed organist of Charter House at this time.

Porpora's Opera of the Nobility was practically bankrupt at this juncture.

From this year until his death, G. Porta was court "Kapell-meister" at Munich.

Rameau opened "a school of composition" at his house this year.

Rameau and Roy had a violent quarrel this year. Rameau gave up wearing a sword as a result of the fight.

Henry Roberts operated a music and a printshop in Holborn at this time. His name appeared on several pieces of decorative engraving on music as the engraver.

William Savage sang in a production of Handel's opera "Faramondo" this season.

Stratfield, the English music historian, tells of this event this year: "Hearing a stranger playing a Fugue in one of the Flemish churches, the organist embraced him, saying, 'You can be no other but the Great Handel'".

Johann Scheibe began the publi-cation of his weekly periodical

(cont.) "Der critische Musikus" this year. In the magazine he criticized Bach's compositions but also made clear the dif-ference between cantatas and oratorios, essentially stressing the difference in the location where they were presented.

Telemann this year visited Paris for a fairly good length of time.

Sophie Kauper Verocai was engaged this year as prima donna at Braunschweig. She continued to sing both there and at Wolfenbuttel until her death in 1747 on May 12.

Vivaldi this year in a letter to Marchese Bertwoglio said "for over fourteen years we have travelled together in many European cities". Records of his travels are vague.

Vivaldi left Venice this year because of a scandal concerning his not saying Mass. Rumors spread that he had been suspended from his priestly functions for leaving the altar during a Mass to make note of a musical idea.

John Wesley's book of hymns was notably received this year.

W. Wiklinski played horn, oboe and trumpet in the Jesuit band up to this time.

James Worgan this year became organist at Vauxhall Gardens.

A copy of the score of "La Semiramide Riconosciuta" written this year at St. Petersburg, was formerly in the possession of Queen Charlotte but is now in the Queens Library

in England. This was first
opera written by Araia for the
Russian court.

John Arthur's "The Lucky
Discovery" or "The Tanner of
York", a ballad opera, appeared
this year.

Auletta"s comic opera "Orazio"
was written this year.

Andrea Basili's oratorio "Il
martirio di Santa Sinforosa
e dei sette santi suoi
figliuoli" was performed this
year at Tivoli.

Andrea Bernasconi's opera
"Flavio Anicio Olibrio"
appeared at this time.

Bickham's engraving "Songs in
the Opera Flora" was done this
year at London.

Blanchard's motet "Laudate
Dominum quoniam bonus est
psalmus" was performed this
season before the King.

During the time he was in
Bohemia this year, Breunich
wrote the music for a serenata,
"Timandra". This was performed
by four Saxon princes and
princesses at a meeting of the
electoral family with the
Dowager Empress Amalia at
Neuhas (Jindřichův-Hradec).

Chinzer's "Arie diverse" was
published some time after this
date.

Chinzer's opera "Temistocle"
was performed this year at Pisa.

Feo and Sarri's oratoria "Gesu
adorato dei re mage", was
published this year at Genoa.

B. Fortier, music engraver,
this year printed E. Duni's
"Arie composte per il Regio
Teatro, cantate dal Signor
Carlo Broschi Farinelli".

Baldassare Galuppi composed
his opera "L'Avilda" (libretto:
Zeno) this year at Venice.

Baldassare Galuppi composed
his opera "Ciro riconosciuto"
(libretta: Metastasio) this
year at Venice.

Carmine Giordani composed his
famous pastoral motet this year.

Maurice Greene wrote his
oratorio "Jephtha" at this time.

Maurice Greene composed a
service in C major this year.

The pasticcio, "Hermann von
Balcke" was written this year
for the jubilee at Elbing.
The music was taken mainly
from operas by Handel. The
story was on a local subject
and the libretto by George
Daniel. Included were several
arias and recitatives by J. J.
DuGrain. The work was multi-
lingual and various sources
give the languages as German,
Italian, Latin and Polish.
Apparently the work was never
produced.

Handel's "I like the am'rous
youth that's free" was sung
by Mrs. Clive this year in
The Universal Passion".

Handel's funeral anthem for
Queen Caroline "The Ways of
Zion do mourn" was composed
at this time.

Handel's "Trionfo del Tempo"
was changed for performance at

1737(cont.)

London. In 1757 considerable was added to the work.

Hasse's pasticcios this year received the following performances: "Sabrina" at London, "Die Farbe macht die Königin" at Hamburg, "Die Hochzeit der Statira" at Hamburg.

Max Hellmann this year composed the allegorical serenata "21 premio dell'onore".

Jacques Hotteterre's "Méthode pour la musette" appeared this year at Paris.

Cooke published John Humphries' "XII Concertos", Opus 2 and Opus 3 in 1741.

Samuel Johnson's "An Opera in a Comedy" was performed this year at Lincoln's Inn Fields in London.

Niccolo Jommelli's first opera, "L'Errore Amoroso" appeared this year and was produced at Naples.

Lampe's opera "The Dragon of Wantley" was produced this year at London.

Giovanni Battista Lampugnani's opera "Antigone" was produced this year at Milan.

Gaetano Latilla's "La finta giardiniera" was produced this year at Naples.

Jean Marie Leclair "l'aine" wrote "Première Récréation de musique . . . pour deux flûtes ou deux violons et B. C.", "Six concertos", and "Deuxieme Récréation de musique . . . pour deux flûtes ou deux violons

(cont.) et B. C.", all three appearing at this time.

Leo's operas "L'amico traditore", "La simpatia del sangue" and "L'Olimpiade" all appeared this year. "L'Olimpiade" was produced at Naples.

A "moratorium" for five instruments was written by Linigke at this time. He must have died shortly after this.

P. Locatelli's "Sonates en trio", opus 5 was published this year.

P. Locatelli's "Sonatas for solo violin", opus 6 was published this year.

Maichelbeck's opus 2, entitled "Die auf dem Clavier lehrende Cäcilia . . ." was published this year at Augsburg.

Mattheson's, the "Kern melodischer Wissenschaft", a theatrical work was published at this time.

A Mesopatamian, Ahmad al-Muslim al-Mausili, this year wrote "Book of the Exquisite Pearl on the Theory of Music".

G. B. Mele's opera, "Amor, constanzia y mujer" (translated from Metastasio), was performed this season at Madrid.

Reverand James Miller's ballad opera, "The Coffee House", appeared at this time.

Pescetti's opera "Demetrio" (libretto: Metastasio) was produced this year in England.

Pescetti's opera "Sabrina" (a pasticcio) was produced this

season at London.

Porpora's opera "Lucio Papirio" was performed at the Teatro St. Cassiano this year at Venice during the carnival.

Cooke published J. F. Ranish's "Eight Solos for a German Flute with a Thorough Bass" this year.

Rameau published his "Géneration harmonique" at this time.

Book III of Rameau's "Traité de l'Harmonie" was translated into English this year and published by J. French.

Rousseau's "Air pour le Mercure de France" was published this year.

Nicola Sala's opera "Vologeso" was produced this year at Rome.

A Saxon clergyman this year published a universal song book. This volume included songs for christenings, marriages, and other holy events. Other music was for lawsuits, deafness, blindness and other handicaps.

Scheibe this year printed an anonymous attack on Bach in "Der Kritische Musikus".

F. M. Veracini's opera "La Clemenza di Tito" appeared this year.

Johann Caspar Vogler composed several choral preludes for a two-manualed organ with pedals and they were published this year.

The first of Weslye's trans-

(cont.) lations, as well as many by Isaac Watts', were published this year at Charleston, South Carolina. There was no music included.

W. Wiklinsky this year composed "Lauda Jerusalem ex C" as a psalm.

The first organ for Cape Town, South Africa, was completed at this time.

John Singleton Copley, the noted American painter, was born (died 1815).

Galilei, the Italian Baroque architect, died (born 1691).

Chardin this year painted "Boy preparing to Draw". The picture is at the Louvre in Paris.

Chardin this year painted "The Copper Cistern" (9" x 8½"). It is at the Louvre in Paris.

An oil painting of Jean-Baptiste Forqueray by Fredou was completed at this time.

The Marquis Scotti and the Queen attempted to interest the King of Spain in music. The Teatro de los Canos del Peral was restored in fine style. Carasano was the architect and plans were by Medrano. The work only took nine months.

Samuel Johnson went to London this year to start his literary career.

The Peace of Passarowitz took place at this time.

(to 1738) Arrigoni returned

from London and went to Italy
by way of Vienna at this time.
There he produced several
cantatas and an oratorio,
"Ester". The manuscripts are
preserved in Vienna.

(to 1738) The first issue of
Bickham's "The Musical
Entertainer" appeared during
this period.

(to 1738) Campra's two books
of Psalms were published this
season.

(to 1738) Elisabeth Duparc
sang in Pescetti's "Arsace"
at this time.

(to 1738) Leo composed six
concerti for the Duke of
Maddaloni during this period.

(to 1738) Thomas Roseingrave
was forced to give up his
position as organist of St.
Georges, Hanover Square at
this time. He then lived for
some time at Hampstead.

(to 1739) Leopold Mozart
studied at the University of
Salzburg during this period.

(to 1740) Of J. S. Bach's
four masses composed during
this period, one was in F major,
on in A major and one in g
minor.

(to 1740) Two volumes of
Carey's songs were issued
during this period.

(to 1740) An edition of J. A.
Scheibe's "Kritischer Musikus"
was published in Hamburg during
these years.

(to 1741) Gluck studied with

(cont.) Giovanni Battista
Sammartini in Milan during
these four years.

(to 1742) Brivio wrote a
number of operas for Turin
during this period.

(to 1743) "Sammlung verschied-
ener und auserlesener Oden"
edited by Johann Friedrich
Gräfe appeared at this time.
Seventy-two odes by Hurlebusch
were included.

(to 1744) Lorenzo Fago was
second master at the conservatorio della Pietà dei
Turchini during these years.

(to 1754) George Bickham, the
elder and the younger both
engraved music during this
period.

(to 1760) Rameau during this
period set to music at least
twenty-four plays and made the
majority of them into grand
operas.

(to 1765) Henry Roberts engraved music during this period.

c.1737
Jean Bapstiste Davaux, French
composer, was born at La Côte
Saint-Andre, Isère (died 1822,
February 22 at Paris).

Ignazio Raimondi, an Italian
violinst and composer, was born
at Naples this year (died 1813,
January 14 at London). He
wrote many operas and several
symphonies.

J. S. Bach this year wrote
Cantata #17, "Wer Dank opfert
der preiset mich" for the
fourteenth Sunday after
Trinity.

J. S. Bach this year wrote Cantata #118 "O Jesu Christ, Mein's Lebens Licht" for a funeral. It had parts for two-litui.

J. S. Bach wrote Cantata #197, "Gott ist uns're Zuversicht" for a wedding. It contained older material from 1728.

Some French song-writers this year started a club which they named "Le Caveau" after the place of meeting.

"The Exquisite Pearl in the Art of Music" by 'Abd al-Mu'min al-Bo appeared at this time.

B. Fortier, English music engraver, printed a song by Farinelli, "Ossequioso rin-graziamento" at this time.

Because of his occasional insanity, Roseingrave was superseded at St. George's Church this year by Keeble.

1738
(January 3) Handel's opera "Faramondo" (libretto by Zeno) was premiered at the King's Theatre in London on this evening.

(January 3) Elisabeth Duparc sang in Handel's "Faramondo" at its first production.

(January 3) Antonio Lottini sang bass in Handel's "Faramondo" on this date.

(January 6) Franz Xavier Murschhauser, German theorist and composer died on this day at München (born 1663, at Zabern and baptized on July 1 of that year.)

(January 7) Vivaldi conducted a festival program in Amsterdam on this day. His opera "Het Eeuweetiude van den Amstel-damschen Schouwburg" was produced for the first time on this occasion.

(January 17) Jean François Dandrieu, French organist, harpsichordist and composer, died at Paris (born 1682 at Paris).

(January 20) Francesco Feo's "Oreste" was performed in Madrid on the King's birthday.

(January 26) Carey and Henry Burgess, Jr. wrote music for James Miller's "The Coffee-House", produced on this date at the Drury Lane Theatre in London.

(February 8) Hasse's opera "Irene" (Pallavicino) was produced on this date at Dresden.

(February 25) Handel's pasticcio "Alessandro Severo", taken chiefly from Handel's earlier works but with a new overture, was produced on this date at the King's Theatre in London. The libretto was probably by Zeno.

(March 4) Arne's "Comus" was performed this date at Drury Lane Theatre in London.

(March 8) King João V decreed Scarlatti eligible for knight-hood in the Portuguese order of Santiago.

(March 22) By decree of King João V, by virtue of a Papal Bull, the customary restrictions on clothing and its richness

1738(cont.)
were eased and D. Scarlatti was
excused from the usual year in
the novitiate.

(March 25) Turlough Carolan,
Irish harper and composer,
died near Kilronan (born 1679
near Nobber, County Meath).

(April 15) Handel's opera
"Serse" ("Xerxes") (libretto
by Niccolo Minato) was
produced on this date at the
King's Theatre in London.
Antonia Merighi sang the role
of Amastre, her last appearnace
in England. His best known
aria "Ombra mai fu" ("Largo")
was in this opera.

(April 19) On this date Cata-
lina Scarlatti authorized
Domenico Scarlatti's entry into
the Order of Santiago.

(April 21) Domenico Scarlatti
was knighted in Madrid in the
Order of Santiago. The reception was described by Matheo
Albo Rivero, a notary.
Chaplain Nicolas Filiberti
certified the event. Scarlatti's
sponsor Joachim Fernandez
Solana de Maldonado also
certified the event which took
place between four and five in
the afternoon at the high altar
of the Capuchin Convent of
San Antonio de El Prado at
Madrid.

(April 28) Augustus visited
Leipzig on this date.

(April 28) J. S. Bach's
Cantata "Willkommen ihr
herrschenden Götter der Erden"
was performed on this date at
an "Abendmusik" in honor of
the marriage of Princess
Amalia and Charles IV (Charles

(cont.) III of Spain) of the
Two Sicilys. The music has
been lost.

(May 11) Hasse's opera "Alfonso"
(Pallavicino) was produced on
this date at Dresden.

(May 15) On this date João
Pereyra da Gama, chaplain of
the convent of Palmella of the
Order of Santiago, certified
the entry of Scarlatti's Knight-
hood in the archives of the
Order.

(May 24) J. S. Bach on this
date wrote a pathetic letter
to Klemm asking that J. G. B.
Bach's position at the Jacobi-
Kirche be held open until the
whereabouts of his son was
discovered. J. S. Bach had
assumed his debts.

(July 1) Johann Gottfried
Bernhard Bach had left Leipzig
clandestinely to avoid his
creditors and on this date the
town council implied to the
consistory that he had proved
to be unsatisfactory in other
ways.

(July 4) Corselli succeeded
Jose Torres as "maestro
compositor de cámara" to
King Charles III of Spain.

(July 16) Antonio (Maria)
Pacchioni, Italian composer,
died at Modena (born 1654,
July 5 at Modena).

(August 3-10 and 24-31) The
Pennsylvania Gazette on this
date stated that the dancing-
master at Philadelphia (a Mr.
Bolton) had a dangerous com-
petitor in Theobald Hackett,
who taught 'all sorts of
Fashionable English and French

Dances'".

(August 22) Geminiano Giacomelli became Tommaso Redi's successor at the Santa Casa in Loreto on this date.

(August 23) Andreas Düben, the younger, composer, died at Stockholm (born 1763, August 28 at Stockholm).

(August 26) Dall'Abaco on this date was appointed director of the chamber music as well as aulic councillor at a salary of 1000 florins annually.

(September 23) Carlo Agostino Badia, Italian composer, died at Vienna (born 1672 at Venice).

(October 8) Louis Joseph Francoeur, French violinist, conductor and composer, was born on this date at Paris (died 1804, March 10).

(October 22) E. R. Duni's name appeared on this date in the University registers at Leyden.

(October 29) Giuseppe Aprile, male contralto, was born at Bisceglia (died 1813, January 11 at Martinafranca).

(November 5) Pasquale Maiorano ("Coffarelli"), brother of Gaetano and Francesco, entered the Neapolitan Conservatorio dei poveri on this date.

(November 9) Maria Scarlatti, daughter of Domenico, (fourth generation of the Scarlatti family), was born (died between 1757, October 30 and 1760, June 10).

(November 13) Maria Scarlatti's

(cont.) baptismal was performed on this date.

(November 15) Friedrich Wilhelm Herschel (Sir William), German astronomer and musician who later became English and was knighted, was born on this day in Hanover (died 1822, August 25 at Slough, Buckinghamshire).

(November 25) Arne's incidental music for "The Tender Husband" was performed on this date at the Drury Lane in London.

(November 27) Rights were granted on this date to Charles Nicholas Le Clerc for "Les premiers, 2e et 3e Livres de Scarlati (sic) pour le Clavecin".

(December 9) Johann Friedrich Lampe's "Margery, or A Worse Plague than the Dragon" was produced at Covent Garden in London on this day.

(December 14) Jan Antonén Koželuh (Kozeluch), Bohemian composer, uncle of Leopold Kozeluch was born at Velvary (died 1814, February 3 at Prague).

(December 22) Jean Joseph Mouret, French composer, died at Charenton (born 1682, April 16 at Avignon).

(December 22) James Worgan was elected organist at St. Botolph Aldgate, and at St. Dunstan's, both on this date.

(January) Birnbaum at this time published an academic and anonymous reply to Scheibe's "Der Kritische Musikus".

(January) Montagnana this month

1738(cont.)
returned to his allegiance to
Handel by singing "Faramondo",
at this time first produced
as "Serse".

(January) Antonia Merighi
appeared in the new opera,
"Faramondo", finished by Handel
just after his return from
Aachen.

(February) Gaetano Latilla's
"Madama Ciana" was given this
month at the Teatro della
Pallacorda in Rome.

(Spring) Porpora's opera
"Carlo il Calvo" was performed
at Rome's Teatro delle Dame
this season.

(April) Philip Hayes, English
organist and composer and son
of William Hayes, was born at
Oxford (died 1797, March 19
at London).

(May) J. G. B. Bach was at
Jena this month.

(May) J. S. Bach performed again
on the Silbermann organ in the
Sophien-Kirche during this
month.

(June) The meeting at St. Paul's
of the Charity Children was
held this month at Christ
Church on Newgate Street.

(August) "Two Grand or Double
Bassoons, made by Mr. Stanesby,
jun." were introduced into
Marylebone Gardens this month.

(August) An anonymous writer in
the "mercure de France" this
month said: "Anet already had
a prodigious technique when he
arrived at Rome; Corelly (sic)
himself was surprised at this,

(cont.) and was delighted to
show him how to perform the
sonatas in his way".

Ernst Carl Gottfried Bach,
cantor, seventh generation,
was born (died 1801). He was
the son of Johann Christoph
Bach.

Johann Christoph Bach, (sixth
generation) son of Johann
Nikolaus, died (born 1717).
Spitta referred to him as
Johann Christian as did
Geiringer. He was a theologian.

Jonathan Battishill, a fine
anthem composer, was born
(died 1814).

Mary Blow, daughter of John
Blow, died (birthdate unknown).

Antonio Boroni, Italian, composer, was born at Rome
(died 1792, December 21 at Rome.

Chevalier de Boufflus, governor
of Senegal and a writer of
light verse was born (died
1813).

Johann Joseph Dussek, Bohemian
musician, was born (died 1818).

Thomas Ebdon, English organist,
conductor and composer, was
born at Durham (died 1811,
September 23 at Durham).

Johann Caspar Ferdinand Fischer,
German Kapellmeister to Mark-
graf Ludwig of Baden at Schloss
Schlackenwerth (Bohemia) died
(born c.1660 or c.1665).
Forkel is the source for these
disputed dates.

Karl Franz, German horn and
baritone player, was born at
Langenbielar, Silesia (died
1802).

1738(cont.)

Filippo Gherardeschi, Italian composer, was born at Pistoia (died 1808).

George III, King of England (House of Hanover) was born (died 1820). His reign spanned the years 1760-1820.

Joseph Melchior von Birkenstock, servant of Maria Theresia and Kaiser Joseph, was born (died 1809, October 30).

Johann Heinrich Müller (also known as Schröter), an actor and dramatist from Halberstadt, was born (died 1815).

Georg Reutter (sr.) died (born 1656).

Johann Samuel Petri, a pupil of Wilhelm Friedemann Bach was born (died 1808).

William Selby, English organist from London, was born (died 1798).

Johann Friedrich Agricola entered the University of Leipzig this year. Gottsched was professor of rhetoric at the time.

John Alcock became organist of St. Andrew's Church, Plymouth on this date.

Johann Elias Bach (sixth generation) came to Leipzig to study theology this year.

Johann Gottfried Bernhard Bach this year was a law student at Jena.

K. P. E. Bach left Frankfurt for Berlin at this time. He became accompanist for Frederick (cont.) the Great of Prussia.

Cornelius van Beethoven was the only Beethoven on the list of Bonn citizens this year.

Bini taught for some time probably after this at Naples. Olivieri died at the time.

Blanchard this year was appointed one of the four "sous-maîtres de musique" at the Royal Chapel.

The colonial settler's love for dancing, brought Mr. Bolton to Philadelphia this year as a master of the art.

Riccardo Broschi returned to Naples this year.

Caffarelli spent six months in England at this time appearing at the King's Theatre in Handel's "Faramondo" and "Serse", the pasticcio "Alessandro Severo", Pescetti's "La Conquista del Vello d'oro", and Veracini's "Partenio".

An action was brought by S. M. Cibber's husband this year against a man named Sloper, and it may have been the gossip which caused her to leave the London stage for a while.

Corrette this year was organist at the Jesuit College in Paris.

Francesco Corselli was chapel-master in Spain from this date forward.

Jean-Baptiste Cupis appeared at the Concert Spirituel this season.

William Felton was awarded a Bachelor of Arts degree by

St. John's College, Cambridge this year.

The Dutch writer Fischer at this time stated that for carillon playing, "a musician required nothing more than a thorough knowledge of music, good hands and feet, and no gout!"

Giovanni Antonio Giai this year became court composer to King Charles Emanuel III of Sardinia at Turin.

Gough started an orchestra this year and engaged players "from the opera and both theatres". They performed from 6 to 10 and played 18 pieces at Marylebone Gardens.

Louis Guillemain, violinist and composer, was a member of the Royal chapel at this time.

J. N. Hamal succeded Dillox-haille as choirmaster at the Cathedral in Liege this year.

Handel's oratorio period was not fully established prior to this time.

Haudek went to study with Schienderlarz, this year and studied with him for six years.

The Catholic Church this year arranged a "jubileum universale" for the victory over the Turks. Prayers were offered to accompaniment of considerable music in which Haydn took part.

Haydn received his first musical training from an uncle with whom he lived at this time.

Mathias Haydn attended a

guild meeting at Hainburg on Corpus Christi day of this year.

M. Heighington this year was admitted to the Gentlemen's Society at Spalding. It was a literary and antiquarian body corresponding to the Society of Antiquaries.

At Hickford's "Great Room in Panton Street" there were no concerts this year recorded in connection with Hickford. His name did not appear at all, nor was the entertainment typical of what he produced.

John James at this time resigned his position as organist of the London Church of St. Olave to go to St. George-in-the-East in the same position.

Joseph changed his style of composition and started to write motets this year.

Johan Kleinknecht was chamber musician at Eisenach and Bayreuth at this time.

Santo Lapis was in Prague this year and started to compose trio sonatas.

Gaetano Latilla was appointed second maestro di cappella under Pompeo Cannicciari this year at Rome.

Antonia Merighi sang in Pescetti's opera "La conquista de villo d'oro" this season.

L. Mizler von Koloj founded the "Association for Musical Science" at Leipzig this year. He also wrote an article on J. S. Bach.

J. G. Müthel was appointed

chamber musician and court organist at Schwerin at this time.

C. Nichelmann this year went to Berlin to study counterpoint with Quantz.

Rameau had left his job as organist at the church of the Jesuit Novitiate in Paris by this year but kept his position at Ste. Croix de la Bretonnerie. The date of his retirement from it is not known.

Though she was not a professional, Rameau's wife sang in the court performance of "Castor et Pollux" this year.

Reutter (jr.) became conductor at St. Stephen's this year and also headed the choir school.

By this time if not even earlier, Scarlatti was living in the Calle ancha de San Bernardo at the parish of San Martin.

John Stanley, English composer and organist, married a Miss Arnold this year.

Soprano Anna Strada del Pò had a quarrel with Heidegger this year. This ended her association with London and she left England.

Joseph Torres was first organist at the Royal Chapel until his death this year.

Tommaso Traetta, the composer, became a pupil of Durante at the Conservatorio di Santa Maria di Loreto at Naples this year.

Verocai stayed in Russia until this time.

Ferdinand Weber, a German organ-maker from Meissen, set up business in Ireland this year and worked there for forty-five years.

Aliprandi's opera "Mitridate" was performed this year at München.

Almeida's "Le virtù trionfanti", a serenata, appeared this season.

Another version of "Comis" was given to the public this season. T. A. Arne first showed his full talents in the production for which he composed the music. The presentation was at the Drury Lane Theatre in London.

Auletta's comic operas "Il Marchese Sgrana" and "La locandiera" both appeared at this time.

Johann Sebastian Bach this year wrote Cantata #30, "Freue dich, erlöste Schaar", for the Feast of Saint John the Baptist (Mid-Summer Day).

J. S. Bach wrote the Fantasia and Fugue in C minor for clavier this year. Forkel described it as "unfinished".

J. S. Bach's B minor Mass from the Credo on was composed this year.

J. S. Bach wrote a treatise, "Rules and Instructions for playing Thorough-bass or Accompaniment in Four Parts" at this time.

Josse Boutmy's first book was

published this year. It contained a "Fanfarinette". It
was issued at Paris and was
titled "Premièr Livre de
pièces de clavecin".

Riccardo Broschi added some
arias to Leo's "Demetrio" at
a revival this season.

Carey this year wrote the
libretto for "Margery".

Chiarini's opera "Argenide"
appeared at this time.

Corselli's "Alessandro nell'
Indie" was completed at this
time.

Raphael Courteville this year
published his "Memoirs of the
Life and Administration of
William Cecil, Baron Burleigh".

Jean-Baptiste Cupis published
a book of instrumental pieces
this year. He dedicated it to
the Duc d'Antin.

E. R. Duni published a volume
of "Minuetti et Contridanze"
at this time.

François Francoeur wrote his
opera "Ballet de la paix"
this year.

The opera "La rosa" (libretto
by Papebrochio Fungoni) was
produced at the Teatro Nuovo
in Naples this season.

Baldassare Galuppi this year
wrote his opera "Alessandro
nell'Indie" at Mantua
(libretto by Metastasio).

Baldassare Galuppi wrote his
opera "Issipile" this year at
Turin (libretto by Metastasio).

Baldassare Galuppi wrote his
opera "Li amori sfortunati di
Ormindo" in Burano this year.
The libretto was by Vitturi.

James Green's "Book of Psalmody"
was printed and published
this year by Alice Pearson.

Handel's choral drama "Saul"
was composed this year.

Samuel Howard this year wrote
songs for the pantomime "Robin
Goodfellow, or The Rival
Sistors".

Jommelli's secular drama
"Odoardo" was heard this year
at Naples.

König's "Harmonischer Lieder-
Schatz oder Allgemeines evan-
gelisches Choral-buch" was
published this year at Frankfurt. It contained 1940 tunes
and was his best known work and
was a major chorale book of
the Baroque period.

B. Cole this year engraved
"Songs and Duetto's in . . .
The Dragon of Wantley . . . by
J. F. Lampe".

J. F. Lampe this year composed
a sequel opera in burlesque
style, "Margery, or A Worse
Plague than the Dragon".

Lampugnani produced "Amelica"
this season at Milan.

Giovanni Battista Lampugnani's
opera "Demofoonte" was produced
at Milan this year.

G. B. Lampugnani's opera
"Angelica" was produced at
Piacenza this season.

G. B. Lampugnani's "Il passaggio

. . . di Maria Amalia", a serenata, was produced this year at Ferrara.

Gaetano Latilla's operas were first produced this year at Rome and later were heard throughout Europe.

Latilla's opera "Orazio" was produced this year at Rome.

Jean Marie Leclair "l'aîné" this year wrote his fourth book of "Sonatas".

Leo this year wrote "Demetrio", "Il conte", "Le nozze di Amore di Psiche", the chorus for "Sofronia" in Marchesi's "Tragedie cristiane" and "Sesostri".

Leo's oratorio "S. Francesco di Paola nel deserto" was written at this time.

Nicola Logroscino's "Inganno per inganno" was produced this year.

N. Logroscino's opera "Quinto Fabio" was produced this season.

Roland Marais published a book of "Pièces de violes" this year.

B. Marcello's "Il teatro alla moda" was reprinted this year at Venice.

On Sunday of carnival week this year, the Teatro de los Canos del Peral was opened with a performance of Metastasio's "Demetrio". The recitatives were by Hasse and arias by various composers.

Metastasio's libretto "Pace fra la virtu e la bellezza, La"

(cont.) was first set by Predieri and later Adofali and Bioni.

Metastasio's libretto "Parnaso accusato e difeso, Il" was first set by Reutter this year and later by Breunich.

Milton's "Comus" was presented this season in London at the Drury Lane Theatre.

Mizler's "Musikalische Biblio-thek" was published this year at Leipzig.

D. Paradisi wrote his opera "Alessandro in Persia" this year for Lucca.

Four chamber cantatas by Pergolesi were published this year.

Pergolesi's "La serva Padrona" was produced this year at Graz and also near Bologna. De Brosses was pleased with it.

The earliest recorded revival of Pergolesi's opera buffa "La serva Padrona" was at Parma this season.

Pescetti's opera "La conquista del vello d'oro" was heard this season at London.

P. Prelleur's "A Brief History of Music", a supplement to his "Modern Musick Master", was published this year.

Cooke published Ranish's "Twenty-four Country Dances for the year 1738" at this time.

B. Fortier, English music engraver, printed Giuseppe Sammartini's "VI Concerti grossi

. . . Opra II' this year.

A set of sonatas by Giuseppe
Sammartini was published at
this time.

"Essercizi per Gravicembalo/di/
Don Domenico Scarlatti/Cavaliero
di S. Giacomo e Maestro/dè/
Serenissimi Prencipe e Prenci-
pessa/delle Asturie & c."
appeared at this time.

The English edition of Scarlatti's harpsichord lessons
was published this year by
B. Cooke.

Amiconi designed the frontispiece for Scarlatti's
"Essercizi" this year.

Shortly after his knighthood
this year, Scarlatti dedicated
his first published collection
of harpsichord pieces to
João V ("Studies for the
Harpsichord by Don Domenico
Scarlatti Knight of St. James
and Master of the most serene
Prince and Princess of the
Asturias & c."). The work was
hailed as a miracle of sound
effects.

John C. Smith composed his
oratorio "David's Lamentation
over Saul and Jonathan" at
this time.

William Tansur's "Heaven on
Earth, or the Beauty of
Holiness . . ." was printed
and published by Alice Pearson
this year at London.

Adam Thompson's "The Disappointed Gallant", a ballad
opera appeared this year.

F. M. Verracini's opera

(cont.) "Partenio" was completed at this time.

Vivaldi's opera "L'Oracolo
di Messenia" was produced this
year at the Teatro Sant'
Angelo in Venice. The libretto
was by Zeno.

Vivaldi's opera "Rosmira"
(libretto by Silvio Stampiglia)
was produced at the Teatro
Sant'Angelo in Venice this
season.

This year the "Mercure de
France" felt the need to ad-
monish noblemen who made
public display of their talent
as violinists and dined with
professionals.

The Royal Society of Musicians
was founded at London this year.

Farinelli probably initiated
the remodeling of the Royal
Theatre in Spain this summer.

At this time it was the custon
to conduct opera performances
while sitting at the harpsichord.

Italian opera was introduced at
the Hamburg German Opera
this season.

The Hamburg Opera closed this
year due to lack of support
by the public.

Johnson's poem "London" was
published this year in England.

Claude Michel Clodion, French
sculptor was born (died 1814).

Benjamin West, American painter,
was born (died 1820).

Roubillac's statue was unveiled

1738(cont.)
in Vauxhall Gardens this year.

(and 1739) Bonporti was still
seeking a canonry at Trento
during these years.

(and 1739) Blamint's "Les
Caracteres de l'amour" ("ballet
heroique") and an additional
act, "Les Amours de printemps"
(1739) appeared during these
years.

(and 1739 and 1774) Giuseppe
Bonno studied composition at
Naples at the Emperor's expense
and this year was taken into
the imperial court chapel as
"Hofscholar". He later rose
to be court composer in 1739
and on Gassmann's death,
court chapel master in 1774.

(to 1740) The Elector Friedrich
Christian of Saxony visited
Venice during these years.

(to 1740) A series of letters
written by Johann Elias Bach
during these years while he was
a member of Bach's family,
showed the atmosphere of a
happy and pleasant household.

(to 1740) During this period
Johann Adolf Scheibe published
his "Critische Musicus" in
Germany.

(to 1740) Four collections of
songs by Couvard were issued
during these years.

(to 1741) Johann Friedrich
Agricola studied with J. S.
Bach during this period.

(to 1741) Handel's operas
were last produced in London
during these years.

(and 1738, 1741, 1747, 1750,

(cont.) 1762, 1770) William
Knapp published "A new Sett
of Psalms & Anthems in four
parts" this year. Subsequent
editions appeared at the years
indicated. All but the last
were from engraved plates, the
last from type.

(and 1742) Only about forty
of Scarlatti's Sonatas, including some of those written
in Venice in 1742, appeared
to antedate the "Essercizi"
published in 1738.

(to 1744) Johann Elias Bach
lived with his cousin Johann
Sebastian during this period.

(to 1748) Per Brandt was
conductor of the Royal
Orchestra at Stockholm during
this decade.

(and 1755) Seven operas by
Casali were produced during
these years.

(to 1760) Benjamin Cole's
engraving business was at the
corner of King's Head Court
near Fetter Lane, Holborn,
London for these twenty-two
years.

(to 1770) Joseph Mondonville's
religious motets appeared in
the programs at the Concert
Spirituel during these years.

(to 1778) T. A. Arne produced
numerous operas and operettas
at the Drury Lane Theatre for
these forty years.

c.1738
Carlo Besozzi, oboist, was
born at Naples this year
(death date unknown).

Ercole Ciprandi, Italian tenor,

c.1738(cont.)
was born this year (died after 1790)

Lady Hamilton, née Barlow, Welsh or English amateur keyboard player, was born at Colby, Pembrokeshire (died 1782, August 27 at Portici).

Prince Philipp Heinrich Lobkowitz died (birthdate unknown).

Joseph Vernon, English tenor and composer, was born at Coventry (died 1782, March 19 at London).

Burkat Shudi (the younger), English harpsichord maker, was born at London (died 1803).

Joseph Mondonville's "Les Sons harmoniques", sonatas for violin solo with continuo, was composed at this time.

Cooke this year published Ranish's "Caledonian Country Dances".

Cook published Ranish's "The Complete Country Dancing ,aster" this year in three volumes.

Verocai's twelve violin sonatas were published at St. Petersburg this year.

1739
(January 1) A copy of Praetorius's Syntagma which belonged to J. B. Bach and later to J. E. Bach has been preserved; "Alumnus Scholae Thom. 1739 d. (den, not "died") 1 Jan." is on the title page.

(January 2) Vivaldi on this

(cont.) date made reference to his "94 Opere", which indicates that many of his stage works have not yet been discovered.

(January 16) Handel's oratorio "Saul" with words by Chas Jennens had its first performance at King's Theatre in London on this date.

(January 20) Porpora's opera, "Semiramide riconosciuta" was revived at the Teatro San Carlo in Naples on this evening.

(February 3) D. Scarlatti's "Esercizi per gravicembalo" was advertised by Adamo Scola in "The Country Journal" on this date in London.

(February 9) A concert was advertised for the benefit of Valentine Snow on this date. Hickford's new Great Room in Brewer St. near Golden Square was the scene of the concert.

(February 16) Sampson Estwick, English priest and composer, died at London (born 1657 at London).

(March 19) Giuseppe Scarlatti's componimento sacro "La SSma Vergine Annunziata" was produced on this date at Rome. It was performed by the Congregation of the Oratorians.

(March 24) Christian Friedrich Daniel Schubart, German author, organist and composer, was born in Obersontheim in Swabia on this date (died 1791, October 10).

(April 4) Handel's oratorio "Israel in Egypt" was premiered on this date at the King's Theatre in London. The words were compiled from the

1739(cont.)
Bible and Prayer Book version
of the Psalms.

(April 10) Michael van Beethoven
on this date was made a citizen
of Cleves.

(April 13) Daquin became organist of the Royal Chapel
on Dandrieu's death this year.

(May 1) Handel's opera "Jupiter
in Argos" (libretto from
Antonio Lucchini's "Giove in
Argo" with modifications)
was produced on this date at
the King's Theatre in London.

(May 2) The solemn entry of the
imperial commissary Cetto a
Cronstorff into Hainburg took
place on this day.

(May 4) William Forster, maker
of spinning-wheels and violins,
was born at Brampton, Cumberland on this date (died 1808,
December 14).

(May 6) D. Scarlatti's first
wife, Maria Caterina Gentile,
died on this date at Aranjvez
(birthdate unknown).

(May 6) The joint will made by
Domenico and Catarina Scarlatti
is referred to in the notice of
her death on this day.

(May 8) Jacob Kirkman rented a
house in Great Pulteney St.
East at this time and carried
on his harpsichord business
there.

(May 12) Johann Wanhal, Austrian
composer, was born at Nechanice
near Hradec Kralove (died 1813,
August 26 at Vienna).

(May 13) Giuseppe Maria Buini,

(cont.) Italian composer,
died at Alessandria on this
date (born c.1695 at Bologna).

(May 21) Rameau's second opera-
ballet, "Les Fêtes d'Hébé du
Les Talents lyriques", was
produced at Paris on this date.
The libretto was by Montdorge.

(May 27) Johann Gottfried
Bernhard Bach, the third surviving son of Johann Sebastian
and Maria Barbara Bach, died
at Jena (born 1715, May 11 at
Weimar).

(June 10) A copy of the Royal
Decree concerning D. Scarlatti's
Portuguese revenues came on
this date from Lisbon.

(June 11) Francesco Mancini,
Italian composer, died at
Naples (born 1679 at Naples).

(June 14-21 and October 11-18)
The American Weekly Mercury on
this date stated that "Magnus
Falconar, of Bomess in Scotland,
Mariner", taught navigation in
Philadelphia.

(June 30) "Le Postillion
français" on this date named
Antoine Gautier de Montdorge
as the anonymous author of
Rameau's libretto "Les Fêtes
d"Hébé".

(July 6) Friedrich Wilhelm
Rust, composer and pupil of
Wilhelm Friedemann Bach, was
born at Wörlitz, Dessau,
Germany (died 1796, February
28 at Dessau).

(July 24) Benedetto Marcello,
Italian composer and brother
of Alessandro, died at Brescia
(born 1686, August 1 at Venice).

1739(cont.)

(July 28) Johann Adolf Scheibe made a statement this year in his "Critischer Musicus" rectifying his error concerning his "fight" with Bach.

(July 29) Francesco Geminiani on this date received a license from King George II to publish his works.

(August 6) The "London Daily Post" on this date announced the presence of "2 Grand or Double Bassoons" at the concert at Marylebone Gardens. They were "made by Mr. Stanesby junior the greatness of whose sound surpasses that of any other Basse instrument whatsoever".

(August 28) Agostine Accorimboni, Italian composer, was born this year at Rome (died 1818, August 13 at Rome).

(August 29) Charles de Brosses wrote to a friend on this date and told him about Vivaldi's great compositional abilities.

(August 29) Charles de Brosses wrote to M. de Blancey on this date and gave a description of the orchestral concerts.

(September 12) Reinhard Keiser, German opera composer, died at Hamburg (born 1674, January 9 at Teichern near Weissenfels).

(September 28) A letter of Johann Elias Bach's on this date clearly implied that J. S. Bach was associated with the Collegium Musicum.

(October 24) Anna Amalia, Duchess of Saxony and German amateur composer, was born at Wolfenbüttel (died 1807, April 10

(cont.) 10 at Weimar).

(November 2) Karl Ditters von Dittersdorf, Austrian violinist and composer, was born at Vienna on this date (died 1799, October 24 at Neuhof, Pilgran, Bohemia).

(November 15) Arne's "An Hospital for Fools" was performed at Drury Lane on this date.

(November 19) Rameau's "Dardanus" on this date opened its run of twenty-six performances at Paris. It was described as a "tragédie en musique" and the libretto was by LeClerc de la Bruére.

(November 22) Handel gave the first performance of his "Ode for St. Cecilia's Day" at Lincoln's Inn Fields Theatre on this date at London. The words were by Dryden.

(November 23) A document from Lisbon on this date gave a Royal Decree assigning to Scarlatti "47,119 Reis Annually".

(November 29) Hugh Montgomerie (later 12th Earl of Eglinton), Scottish amateur composer, was born (died 1819, December 14 or 15).

(December 6-13) The American Weekly Mercury during this week published (at Philadelphia) ("For the benefit of the poor in Georgia") "A Hundred and fifty-odd Hymns, composed by John and Charles Westly".

(December 19) Gottfried Grünewald, German composer, died at Darmstadt (born 1673).

1739(cont.)

(January) E. R. Duni's opera "Didone abbandonata" was produced at Milan at the Teatro Regio Ducal during this month.

(January) E. R. Duni was back in Italy this month.

(March) Pescetti's pastoral "Angelica and Medoro" was produced this month in England.

(Spring) Porpora's opera "Il Barone di Zampano" was performed at this time at Naples in the Teatro Nuovo.

(Easter) Pergolesi's "La Serva Padrona" was given at Graz at this time.

(June) N. Porpora was 1st maestro of the Conservatorio di Santa Maria di Loreto at this time.

(Summer) Caffarelli obtained leave to go to Madrid.

(September) Handel's "Ode on St. Cecelia's Day" was published at this time. He used some of Muffat's "Componimente musicales" in the work.

(Autumn) Porpora's opera "L'amico fedele" was performed at this time at Naples in the Teatro dei Fiorentini.

(Autumn) Vivaldi's opera "Feraspe" (libretto by Silvani and Vittieri) was produced at this time in Venice at the Teatro Sant'Angelo.

(October) DuGrain left Elbing this month.

(December) Pescetti's "Diana and Endymion" was produced in (cont.) England this month.

Johann Ernst Bach, Arnstadt organist, son of J. Christoph, grandson of Christoph, member of the 5th generation of the Bach family, died (born 1683).

Louis van Beethoven's son Johann was born. Some sources gave the date as 1740.

Jean Francois Boëly, "ordinaire de la musique du Roi" and harp master to the Countess of Artois, was born (died 1814).

John Bowman, English actor, singer and composer, died (born 1651).

Joseph Anton Ernst Gilowsky, older cousin of Maria Anna K. Gilowsky was born (died 1787).

Giuseppe Millico, Italian male soprano and composer, was born at Terlizzi, Modena (died 1802 at Naples).

Pierre-Louis Molire, French librettist, was born (death date unknown).

Luigi Antonio Sabbatini, Italian composer, was born at Laziale near Rome. He was educated at Bologna in the Franciscan monestary. He there studied music under G. B. Martini and stayed for 8 years (died 1809, January 29 at Padua).

Johann George Christoffer Schetky, German cellist and composer, was born at Darmstadt on this date (died 1824, November 29 at Edinboro).

Joshua Shudi, English harpsichord maker, was born in Schwanden (died 1774).

Gotthard Wagner, German composer, died at Tegernsee (born 1679).

Barrière settled in Paris this year.

John Beard this year married Lady Henrietta, Lord Edward Herbert's widow and the daughter of the Earl of Waldegrave.

Rumors of bankruptcy had begun this year concerning Beethoven's great-grandfather Machael van Beethoven.

Berteau made his début at the Concert Spirituel in Paris with great success.

Antonio Besozzi entered the Dresden court orchestra as first oboist this year.

Bioni's setting of Metastasio's serenata"La pace fra la virtù e la bellezza", was dedicated to the emperor this year. It has been preserved at the Austrian National Library.

Thomas Brome was appointed professor of music at Gresham College in London this year.

In a fragment of a letter from Charles de Brosses written at the end of this year, he spoke of how they enjoyed listening to the concerto of Corelli called "La Notte di Natale".(sic)

Bernard de Bury entered the Royal service this year as chamber accompanist.

Caffarelli at this time was involved in a brawl with another singer during a performance in a Neapolitan church. He was reprimanded and confined to his home.

Cernohorsky was conductor of the church choir at St. James's church from this year on.

Burney this year wrote that Cervetto, among others, "brought the violoncello into favour".

Captain Coram founded the Foundling Hospital this year. It was a charitable institution with which Handel was associated.

Cousser's spirited musicianship aroused the enthusiasm of his peers and this year Mattheson referred to him as the model of the "Vollkommene Kapell-meister".

Dauvergne was admitted to the Musique de la Chambre this year and went to Paris.

Doles this year went to Leipzig for a course in theology at the University.

Elisabeth Dupard sang in "Acis and Galatea", Israel in Egypt", and "Saul" this year at London.

Marie Fel, French soprano, was given her first leading role at the Paris Opéra this year.

Christoph Förster was appointed conductor at Sondershausen at this time.

Fux this year recommended G. C. Wagenseil as court composer in Austria.

Charles Gardner was appointed professor of music this year at Gresham College in London.

Johann Georg Gebel failed to get the position of principal organist at St. Elisabeth this season.

François Lupin Grenet at this time went to Lyons to teach, direct the Academie des Beaux-Arts and conduct the theatre orchestra.

C. A. Grenser went to Dresden this year from Wiehe, Thuringia.

The glorification of liberty, so frequently appearing in oratorios, appealed to the optimistic spirit of the new English nationalism and after this year the annual performance of an oratorio by Handel was recognized as a truly national tradition.

Salvatore Lanzetti went to London this year and brought favor to the cello while there.

Johann Mattheson, the Hamburg critic, insisted that "an oratorio is merely a sacred opera".

Mattheson, in his "Vollkommene Capellmeister" referred to "non nobis domine", a canon by Byrd.

Wincenty Maxylewicz succeeded Fatlor Andrzy Bargiel this year as conductor of the Capella Calthedrales, a position he held for life. He also wrote 5 four-part composition to be performed a-capella.

J. Pekalski this year became praepositus of the Capella Rorantistarum at Cracow.

Pescetti was appointed director of Covent Garden Theatre at this time.

N. Porpora was back at Naples by this time.

La Poupliniere at this time bought a mansion in the Rue de Richelieu. Rameau and his family lived there for a while in an apartment of their own.

Johann Adolph Scheibe replied to Bach's answer at this time. Scheibe answered with slurs on Bach's general education and culture.

Schroter at this time invented the earliest example of the tangent action for the piano.

Schroter was asked this year by a patron to make a piano with an optical display as suggested by F, Castel's Eye Organ.

"Senesino" sang in Florence this year.

Burkat Shudi moved to "Meards Street" in London this year.

The last double bassoon made by Thomas Stanesby junior was this year. It was over 8 feet in height and was preserved at the National Museum in Dublin.

Prior to this year Stanesby senior's instruments were no longer used.

Late this year Vittoria Tesi, the singer, was in Madrid.

Ferdinand of Bavaria heard Vivaldi's cantata "Mopso" this season at Venice.

Vivaldi became close friends with Charles de Brosses this year.

Karl Weideman helped found the Royal Society of Musicians at this time.

Esther Young sang at Covent
Garden this season.

Bernardo Aliprandi's opera
"Iphigenie" appeared this year.

Almeida's opera "La spinalba,
ovvero Il vecchio matto" was
produced this year at London.

Two more of Arrigoni's operas
"Scipinoe nelle Spagne" and
"Sirbace" were produced during
the Carnival season this year
at the Teatro di Via del
Cocomero in Florence.

Auletta's comic operas "Amor
cosstante" and "Don Chichibio"
appeared at this time.

J. S. Bach's four Duetti,
Catechism Chorale Preludes and
Organ Prelude and the Fugue in
Eb were published this year
in Part III of the "Clavier-
übung". The full title of the
work was "Excercises for the
Clavier consisting of Various
Organ Preludes to the Catechism
and other Hymns, composed for
the diversion of amateurs and
particularly of competent
judges of such works, Published
by the Composer". The renowned
St. Anne's Fugue was included.

The first publication of J. S.
Bach's organ works occured this
year.

Johann Caspar Bachofen's
"Vermehrter Zusatz von Morgen,
Abend . . . Gesängen" appeared
at this time.

Barrière this year published
his "Sonates de par-dessus de
la viole, livre 5".

Johann Philipp Bendeler's

(cont.) "Organopoeia" was reprinted at this time.

Benoît Blaise's cantata, "Le
Feu de la ville" was published
this year.

Blankenburg's "Elementa musica,
of nieuw licht tot het welver-
staan van de musiec en de bas-
continuo" was published at
The Hague this year by Laurens
Berkoske.

Giuseppe Brivio produced his
two operas "Didone Abbandonata"
and "Incostanza delusa" this
year at Milan.

G. G. Brunetti's opera "Orten-
sio" appeared at this time.

Camerloher's opera "Melissa"
was composed this year.

Rinaldo di Capua's opera
"Volugeso, rè dei Parti" was
produced this year at Rome.

Carey's interlude (or opera)
"Nancy, or The Parting Lovers"
was produced this year at the
Drury Lane Theatre in London.

Prospero Castrucci published
6 violin sonatas this year.

Chiarini's opera "Achille
in Sciro" appeared at this time.

Dauvergne's "Divertimenti a
tre", a book of violin sonatas
with a bass was composed this
year.

Francesco Feo's oratorio "La
distruzione dell'esercito de
Cananei" was published this
year at Prague.

Foppens' "Bibliotheca belgica"
was completed at this time.

Francesco Geminiani's "Rules for Playing in True Taste" was published this year at London.

Six Sonatas for violin by Geminiani were published this year at London. Also twelve violin sonatas were published and apparently this was a different collection.

Handel's oratorio "Alexander's Feast" was performed at the Three Choirs Festival this year.

Handel composed six concertos for woodwinds and strings, usually called the "oboe concertos", and twelve grand concertos opus 6 for two solo violins, string orchestra, and continuo this year. They were listed as follows:

Six Concertos (Set II)
   1. F ma.
   2. A ma.
   3. D mi.
   4. G ma.
   5. D ma.
   6. G mi.
Twelve Concerti Grossi, Op. 6
   1. G ma.
   2. F ma.
   3. E mi.
   4. A ma.
   5. D ma.
   6. G mi.
   7. Bb ma.
   8. C mi.
   9. F ma.
   10. D mi.
   11. A ma.
   12. B mi.

Handel this published Seven Sonatas or Trios, opus 5 for two violins or German flutes and continuo.

Hasse's intermezzo, "Rimario e Grilantea" (librettist and date of performance unknown)(revived at Dresden, 1883, December 29).

Hasse's opera, "Viriate" "Metastasio's "Siface", altered by Domenico Lalli) was produced this year at the Carnival in Venice.

Musgrave Heighington produced an ode at the Gentlemen's Society's anniversary this year. It was composed by him for the occasion.

B. Cole engraved "British Melody; or the Musical Magazine" by J. F. Lampe, etc. this year.

J. F. Lampe at this time wrote the songs for the collections "Wit Musically Embellish'd," and "British Melody".

Giovanni Battista Lampugnani's opera"Didone abbandonata" was produced this season at Padua.

Leo's opera "Amor vuol sofferenza" was produced this year at Naples.

Leo this year wrote "Achille in Sciro", "Amor vuol Sofferenze", "Ezio", "Festa teatrale for the Spanish Court", Intermezzo" and "Temistocle".

Leo's "Miserere", S.A.T.B. and S.A.T.B. and organ in C minor, was published at this time.

N. Logroscino's "L'inganno felice" was produced this season.

Mattheson's theoretical work "Ephorus Göttingensis" was published this year.

Mattheson's "Der Vollkommene
Capellmeister" appeared this
year at Hamburg.

Metastasio's libretto to
"Astrea Placata" was first set
this year by Prediere. Later
it was set by Breunich.

Metastasio's "Clemenza di Tito"
and "Siroe" both with music by
Hasse were produced this
season.

Mica composed his oratorio
"The Sung Meditations" at
this time.

A set of harpsichord sonatas
by Pescetti was published this
year at London. They were
contained in Farrenc's "Tresir
des pianistes" as well as
other collections.

Edward Phillips' ballad opera
"Britons, strike Home" appeared
at this time.

Porpora's "Intermezzo" for
the wedding of the Infante
Filippo was performed this
season at Madrid.

Porpora wrote two opera buffas
this year for the Teatro Nuovo
and Teatro dei Fiorentini at
Naples.

The founder of the English
Scarlatti cult was Roseingrave,
a close friend of D. Scarlattis
for many years. He published
an augmented reprint of the
"Essercizi" this year and a
supplement later.

Roseingrave's "XLII Suites de
Pieces" was issued at this time.

Nicola Sala's opera "Vologeso"

(cont.) was performed this
season at Lisbon.

Christopher Saur of Germantown
(a suburb of Philadelphia)
published the "Zionitischer
Weyrauch Huegel" and "Ein
abgenöthigter Bericht"
(Warrington) at this time.

Giuseppe Scarlatti's earliest
known compositions date from
this year.

B. Fortier, English music
engraver, printed D. Scarlatti's
"Essercizi per gravicembalo"
at this time.

Five of D. Scarlatti's sonatas
and the fugue in Parma (III,
30) were printed this year by
Roseingrave.

Jean Baptiste Stuck's opera
"Polydore" was revived this
season.

Domenico Terradellas's oratorio
"Ermengildo martire" was produced at the monastery of
Santa Chiara at Naples this
year during the Carnival
season.

"Fêtes d'Hebe" by Traetta was
seen this season.

Johann Triemer this year
published a work on the rudiments of music. He was a
German cellist and composer.

Euler's clavichord was tuned
to A=392 cps and S=1'0 at
this time.

Th. Muffat's "Componimenti"
showed staccato as reducing
the length of note by one hald.
It also included mordents,
trills and compound ornaments.

1739(cont.)

The Hamburg Opera was closed this season.

Two "good" clarinettists advertised their availability this year at Frankfurt am Main.

Cesare Ponsicchi wrote a pamphlet "Il primo pianoforte verticale" in 1898 describing an upright pianoforte by Don Domenico del Mela of Gagliano made this year.

Thomas Gray and Horace Walpole left this year on a joint tour or Europe.

Charles Simon Favart's play "Moulinet Premier" was published this year. It was his first work to be printed.

P. Fuhrmann's book "Alt und Neues Wien" of this time was based on the writings of a Silesian law student, Johann Konst.

Maurice Greene's collection of 25 sonnets was published this year.

"Julius Caesar" by John Sheffield, was produced this season at the King's Theatre in London.

William Tansur published his "Sacred Mirth, or The Pious Soul's Daily Delight" this year.

Chalgrin, a French architect, was born at this time (died 1811).

Jean Baptiste Chardin this year painted "Back from Market", oil on canvas.

Chardin this year painted "Housewife". It is at the Louvre in Paris.

Chardin painted "La Pourvoyeuse" at this time (Young woman carrying provisions). It is at the Louvre in Paris.

(end-1740 beginning) The official report in Bonn in 1784 mentioned Johann van Beethoven (son of Ludwig, Sr. and Maria) and places his birth at this time.

(to 1740) Handel produced his last operas this season with an inferior company put together in a rush.

(and 1740) Lorenz Mizler's "Musikalischer Staarstecher" was published during this period at Leipzig.

(to 1740) Rameau sold his house in Dijon to Bazier during this time span.

(to 1741) Johann Philipp Kirnberger studied under J. S. Bach during these years.

(to 1742) Jiří Antonín (Georg) Benda attended the Jesuit college of Jicin for these three years.

(to 1743) Francesco Feo was maestro di cappella at the Conservatorio dei Poveri di Gesù Cristo at this time. He had succeeded Durante.

(to 1744) Leo was Primo maestro at the Conservatorio di Sant' Anofrio for these five years.

(and 1744, 1746) In addition to pieces already in circulation included in other collections

and a few early movements used
by Avison for his transcriptions in 1744 or printed by
Roseingrave or Boivin (before
1746), most early keyboard
works by Scarlatti were
apparently lost or destroyed.

(to 1747) At this time at the
court of Braunschweig-Wölfen-
buttel, 14 operas by Verocai
were produced.

J. P. Kellner's "Certamen
musicum bestehend aus
Präludien, Fugen, Allemanden",
etc. in 6 suites appeared
during these years.

(to 1752) Dauvergne's compositions at this time were only
instrumental.

(to 1754) Mizler edited a
periodical, the "Neueröffnete
Musik-Bibliothek" this year
and also wrote a treatise on
thorough-bass, "Die Anfangs-
gründe des Generalbasses".
In the latter he seemed to have
pushed the connection between
music and mathematics too far.

(to 1770) Giovanni Battista
Gabbrielli, Italian violin
maker, worked during this
period.

c.1739

Georg Böhm, German organist,
died at this time (born 1661).

Eligio Celestino, Italian
violinist and composer, was
born this year at Rome (died
1812, January 14 at Rome.)

J. F. Lampe this year married
Isabella Young, daughter of
Charles Young.

J. S. Bach this year wrote

(cont.) Masses in A major and
G major.

Johann Sebastian Bach at this
time wrote his four miscalled
"short" Masses, in F, A, G
minor, and G major. They
belonged to the Leipzig period.

Handel's vocal work "Dank sei
dir, Herr" an arioso from a
cantata was written at this
time. (According to the A.M.Z.
of 10/2/42 it is a forgery
by Siegfried Ochs.)

Gottlieb Muffat published his
"Componimenti musicali" for
harpsichord this year. It
contained caprices, overtures,
sarabands, etc. and a preface
ending with "Parlicolar segni
delle maniere . . . dedicated
to Charles VI.

Chardin this year painted
"The Young Schoolmistress".
It is at the National Gallery
in Washington.

1740

(January 5) Antonio Lotti,
Italian singer, organist and
composer, died (born 1667).

(January 13) William Turner,
English composer, died at London
(born 1651 at Oxford).

(January 16) The 4th Earl of
Abingdon (Willoughby Bertic),
English music patron and com-
poser, was born at Gainsborough
(died 1799, September 26 at
Rycote).

(January 19) Michele Caballone,
counterpoint teacher, died
(born 1692).

(January 20) Porpora's opera
"Il trionfo di Camilla" was
performed on this date at Naples.

1740(cont.)

(January 23) Giuseppe Scarlatti's opera "Merope" was produced at the Teatro Capranica, in Rome (libretto by Zeno).

(January 24) Geminiano Giacomelli, Italian composer, died at Parma (born c.1692).

(February 3, 7) At Dublin, Faukner's Journal on these dates announced a benefit for a "Signior Scarlatti" which may well have been Francesco Scarlatti.

(February 4) Carl (Mikael) Bellman, Swedish poet who set many of his own lyrics to music, was born on this date at Stockholm (died 1795, February 11 at Stockholm).

(February 9) Ernst Eichner, German bassoonist and composer of the Mannheim School was born at Mannheim (died 1777 at Mannheim).

(February 9) Vincenz Lübeck, German organist and composer, died (born 1654, September).

(February 12) Johann Friedrich Lampe's "Orpheus and Eurydice" was produced at Covent Garden in London on this date.

(February 13) Sophie (Madeleine Arnould), French actress and singer, was born on this day at Paris (died 1802, October 22 at Paris).

(February 16) Willem de Fesch's oratorio "Judith" was heard on this date at Hickford's Room (libretto by William Higgins).

(February 27) Girolamo Amati, renowned violin maker, died on

(cont.) this date at Cremona (born 1649, February 26 at Cremona).

(February 27) Handel's secular oratorio in 3 parts had its first performance on this date at Lincoln's Inn Fields in London. "L'Allegro, il Penseroso ed il Moderato" was the title and a revised version was peformed in 1741. The texts for the first two parts were adapted from Milton by Charles Jennens, the third was set to a poem of its own in the same style but far inferior in quality.

(February 27) Catherine Plunkett made her debut as a "prodigy" violinist at Crow Street Music Hall in Dublin on this evening.

(March 10-1777, August 18) Andrea Basili was "maestro di cappella" of the Santa Casa at Loreto for these thirty-three years.

(March 19) Joseph Franz Weigl, cellist and composer, was born in Bavaria (died 1820, January 25).

(March 21) d'Alessandro's serenata, "Il coro delle Muse", libretto by Goldoni, was performed on this date in honor of the Electoral Prince of Saxony, Frederick Christian, at the Ospedale della Pieta.

(March 21) The Elector Friedrich Christian of Saxony visited the Ospedâle della Pietà in Venice on this day.

(March 31) On this date at Hickford's Room a concert in-

cluded Galliard's choruses for
"Julius Caesar" by John
Sheffield, Duke of Buckingham.
Handel's Holy Week anthems
"O Sing unto the Lord" and
"My Song Shall be always" were
performed for the first time.
The singers included Mrs.
Thomas Arne and John Beard.
The concert was a benefit.

(April 27) Vivaldi on this
date sold three concertis and
one sinfonia for 15 ducats
and 13 lire.

(May 8) Giovanni Paisiell,
Neapolitan composer noted for
opera buffa, was born at
Taranto (died 1816, June 5).

(May 12) Vivaldi on this date
sold twenty concerti for 70
ducats and 23 lire.

(May 21) Gasparo Pacchierotti,
Italian male soprano, was
baptised at Fabriano near
Ancona (died 1826, October 28
at Padua).

(May 27) Philipp Joseph Frich
(Frike), German organist and
armonica player, was born at
Würzburg (died 1798, June 15).

(June 8) Gabriele Piozzi,
Italian musician, was born on
this date at Brescia (died 1809,
March 26 at Dymerchion,
Denbighshire).

(July 1) Edward Purcell (II),
organist and composer, died on
this date at London (born
1689, August or September at
London).

(July 17-24) The American
Weekly Mercury at this time
published at Philadelphia

(cont.) ("For the benefit of
the poor in Georgia"), "A
Hundred and fifty-odd Hymns,
Composed by John and Charles
Westly".

(July 26) G. C. Wagenseil's
"I lamenti d'Orfeo" was performed on this date at Vienna.

(August 1) For the celebration
of the anniversary of the
accession of the House of
Hanover to the throne, Thomson
and Mallet's masque "Alfred",
with music by Arne, was performed for the first time in a
temporary theatre in the garden
of Cliveden, Bucks, at that
time the residence of Frederick,
Prince of Wales. The famous
hymn "Rule Brittania" was
included in the work.

(August 1) Arne's "The Judgment
of Paris" was performed this
day at Cliveden, Bucks.

(August 10) Samuel Arnold,
English organist, composer,
conductor and editor, was born
at London (died 1802, October
22 at London).

(August 29) Vivaldi on this
date sold many of his concertos
for one ducat per concerto.

(September 11) Thomas Lowe
sang in "The Devil to pay" in
London on this evening.

(September 14) Christian
Friedrich Georg Berwald,
violinist, was born at Hohenaspe,
Slesvig on this date (died 1825,
February 23 at Stockholm).

(October 7) Luigi Maria
Baldassare Gatti, Italian composer, was born on this date at
Lazise, Lago di Garda (died
1817, February 28).

(October 17) Thomas Lowe sang in "The Beggar's Opera" at London on this evening.

(November 4) Anselm Bayly matriculated at Exeter College, Oxford on this date.

(November 4) Davide Perez's first opera that was preserved "Siroe", written for the Teatro San Carlo at Naples, was produced at this time.

(November 22) Elisabeth Duparc sang in Handel's "Imenio" this evening.

(November 22) Handel produced the first performance of his "Imeneo" at Lincoln's Inn Fields this evening at London.

(December 2) John Broderip on this date became a vicar-choral of Canterbury Cathedral.

(December 19) Porpora's opera "Tiridate" was performed on this date at the Teatro San Carlo on Naples.

(December 20) Arne's incidental music for "As you Like It" was performed on this date at the Drury Lane in London. The text was as might be expected, Shakespeare.

(December 25) Joseph Corfe, English organist, was born on this date at Salisbury (died 1820, July 29 at Salisbury).

(December 26) Francesco Feo's opera "Arsace" was performed on this date at the Teatro Regio in Turin.

(December 28) Johann Gottfried Schwanenberg, German composer, (cont.) was born on this date at Wolfenbüttel (died 1804, April 5).

(July) A second edition of Bickham's "The Musical Entertainer" appeared this month.

Evaristo Felice Dall'Abaco, died on this date according to a major source (born 1675, July 12). See also 1742, July 12.

Domenico Alberti, Italian singer, harpsichordist, and composer, died at Formio, Rome (born c.1710 at Venice).

Gennaro d'Alessandro, Italian composer, died, probably at Venice (born 1717 at Naples).

John Antes, American-English missionary and amateur composer of German descent, was born at Frederick near Bethlehem, Pennsylvania (died 1811 or 1808 at Bristol).

Attillo Ariosti, Italian composer, died (born 1666).

Jane Ashley, English bassoonist, was born on this date at London (died 1809, April 5 at London.)

Michael Arne, English composer, was born at London on this date (died 1786, January 14 at London). Some sources give his birthdate as 1741.

Johann Christoph Bach, Erfurt musician, son of J. Egidius, grandson of Johann and member of the 5th generation of the Bach family, died (born 1685).

Rosa Borosini, singer (wife of

Francesco Borosini) died on
this date at Vienna (born c.
1693 at Modena).

Charles Clagget, Irish violinist
and inventor, was born on this
year at Waterford (died c.1795).

Richard Eastcott, English
clergyman musical historian
and composer, was born this
year at Exeter(died 1828 at
Livery Dale, Devon).

Samuel Green, English organ
builder, was born this year at
London (died 1796, September 14).

Matthys Hoffmans, Netherlands
violin maker, died this year
(born 1689).

Franciszek Ksawery Kratzer,
Polish musician, was born in
Austria this year (died 1818
at Cracow).

Johann Gotthelf Krieger,
German musician and son of
Johann Krieger (1) died at
Querfurt (born 1687, September
13 at Weisenfels).

Francesco di Majo, opera composer, was born at this time
(died 1771).

Bungo Miyakoji, founder of the
Bungo-bushi school of music,
died (birthdate unknown).

Cardinal Ottoboni died.

Johann Georg Christoff Schetky,
German cellist and composer,
was born at Darmstadt (died
1824, November 29).

Waclaw Sierakowski, Polish
musical organizer, was born
in Boguslawice (died 1806).

Samuel Webbe, composer, was
born (died 1816).

Zadarski, Polish composer,
died (birthdate unknown).

Francesco Zanetti, Italian
singer and composer, was born
this year at Volterra (death
date unknown).

Dall'Abaco was in London this
year where he was heard by
Burney. The latter mentioned
him in laudatory terms.

Avoglio was in London by this
date.

K. P. Emanuel Bach, son of
J. S. Bach, was appointed
court accompanist to Friedrich
"the Great" of Prussia at
this time.

Ludwig van Beethoven Sr. and
his wife Maria had another
child this year. Johann was
born but there are no records
of his baptism.

Jan Jiří Benda at this time
became chamber musician at
Berlin.

Bonporti retired this year and
went to live at Padua. He
died there nine years later.

An organ was erected at
Marylebone Gardens this year
by Bridge.

Charles de Brosses estimated
there were two hundred instru-
mentalists assembled in the
papal chamber at Monte Cavallo
at this time for the sacred
concert to be held on Christmas Eve.

De Brosses at this time stated

"the art of nuances and of
clair-obscur as practiced by
the Italians in 1740 either in
rapid succession or by imper-
ceptible degrees. These are
reflections, demi-tints, which
produce an incredible charm in
the coloring of the sounds".

Until this year Brusa held the
post of "organista del pal-
chetto" at St. Mark's in Venice.
Angelo Cortona succeeded him
at this time.

Wards "Lives of the Gresham
Professors" this year contained
a printed list of John Bull's
composition for virginal.

Caffarelli was back in Naples
this year.

F. A. Calegari was still in
Venice this season.

Caporale this year joined
Handel's opera orchestra.

John Clothier was "court
drummer" during this decade.

Mattheson this year mentioned
Conradi as conductor at
Oettingen. This started confusion in many subsequent
reference books.

W. Corbett returned to
England this year.

Marianna Cornelys made her
singing debut at Venice this
season.

A. Duni must have stayed in
Madrid at least until this year.

Nicola Fago ("Il Tarantino")
was succeeded this year in his
position as teacher at the

(cont.)Conservatorio della
Pièta dei Turchini.

Fritsch, the composer, studied
under Bach at the Thomasschule
this year.

Francesco Geminiani moved from
Dublin to London at this time.

Geminiani was teaching the
7th position on all strings of
the violin by this year.

de Giovannini (1st name unknown),
a composer, was living in
Berlin at this time.

James Grassineau this year
translated Brossard's
"Dictionnaire" as "A Musical
Dictionary--Carefully Abstracted
from the Best Authors".

Grassinian said at this time
that there were several instruments such as bellows-blown
organs, depressed and elevated
by the action of a water-wheel
in Italian grottoes and vine-
yards.

Johann Gottlieb Graun this year
became conductor of the royal
orchestra in Berlin.

Hakermann at this time, after
his patron's death returned
to Prague and worked as choirmaster in several churches there.

Handel used the contra this
year in "L'Allegro".

Handel's "Concerti Grossi"
of this year testified to the
knowledge he derived from
Corelli's works. Several
passages from his vocal compositions such as the chorus from
"Esther" also showed this
influence.

1740(cont.)

F. Hanot became attached to the maîtrise of Tournai Cathedral and taught violin and dancing in the town for several years from this date forward.

The firm of Harvis and Byfield built an organ this year for Doncaster. The cost was £525.

Franz Joseph Haydn went to Vienna this year and became a choirboy at St. Stephen's Cathedral. He spent all of his study years there.

John Johnson was established in London by this time or earlier at Cheapside "facing Bow Church", at the sign of the Harp and Crown.

Jommelli was summoned to Rome this year. He then was under the protection of the Cardinal Duke of York. His opera "Ricimero" was produced.

Leopold Mozart this year was awarded an appointment as musician and chamberlain to the Count Thurn and Taxis, Canon of Salzburg.

James Oswald this year announced he was leaving for Italy, but it is dubious whether or not he did so.

A one-manual choir organ with a number of stops was mentioned in the inventory of Cardinal Ottoboni's instruments prepared after his death this year.

Pescetti this year was appointed director of the King's Theatre at London.

Catherine Plunkett this year was sent as an "apprentice" to

(cont.) Dubourgh, who was master of the State Music in Ireland.

A. Pollarolo became maestro at St. Mark's Cathedral in Venice this season.

Rameau this year took out an annuity of 160 livres for himself, his wife and daughter.

Reutter Jr. was knighted this year by Emperor Charles VI.

J. H. Rolle entered the court chapel of Frederick the Great this year as a chamber musician (violist).

Tommaso Scarlatti sang in various operas this season.

Johann Scheibe became Kapellmeister to the Margrave of Brandenburg-Culmbach at this time.

Burkat Shudi made a harpsichord this year for Frederick, Prince of Wales, son of George II. (#94;2-manual) It still survives today.

Burkat Shudi this year made a 2-manual harpsichord (#103).

John Simpson took over the work from Henry Roberts at this time. They were both engravers of music.

Martin Smith became organist at Gloucester Cathedral this year replacing Barnabas Gunn.

John Snetzler settled in England this year. He came there from Germany.

In a eulogy to Somis, Hubert Le Blanc wrote this year, "He

cleared the post where people come to grief, in short he succeeded in the great feat on the violin of holding a whole-note".

Mattheson, in his "Grundlage einer Ehren Pforte" of this year stated that Sweelinck studied with Zarlino in Venice. This was apparently an error.

Daniel Gottlieb Treu entered the service of Count Schaff-gotsch at Hirschberg this year both as a violinist and com-poser.

Vivaldi this year left his position at the Ospedale della Pietà in Venice.

Many of A. Vivaldi's colleagues were present in Vienna with him after the Venetian scandal that had just ensued.

The business of Walker & Sons, organ builders, was originated this year by George England.

The nail violin was invented this year by a German violinist, Johann Wilde.

M. Zurowski was rector of the Jesuit Musical Bursary at this time at Cracow.

This year marked the publica-tion of a textbook on vocal pieces performed on various occasions during the reign of Clemens August, Componimento per Musica (music by Giuseppe dall'Abaco, Director of the Chamber Music).

The few works by which Gennaro d'Alessandro was known were all performed at Venice this season.

Gennaro d'Alessandro collabo-rated with Goldon this year in three cantatas: "Gli amanti felici", "La ninfa saggia", and "Le quattro stagioni".

Gennaro d'Alessandro's opera "Ottone" appeared at this time.

Aliprandi's opera "Semiramide Riconosciuta" was performed this year at München.

Arne published the masque "Comus" in folio this year. He identified it as his "Opera prima".

Arne reset Congreve's masque "The Judgment of Paris" this year and it was performed at Drury Lane in London.

Arne's song "When daises pied . . ." from "Love's Labour's Lost" was not sung in any production of that play, but was interpolated into "As You Like It" in this year's production.

Auletta's comic opera "L'impos-tore" appeared at this time.

Cooke published Charles Avison's "Six Concertos" this year.

J. S. Bach's Cantata #3, "Ach Gott, wie manches Herzeleid", was written this year for the second Sunday after Epiphany. It was from the Kirchencantaten in the Bach Gesellschaft edition.

Johann Caspar Bachofen's "Irdisches Vergnügen in Gott" (Brockes) was set to music this year.

Blavet published his third book

of flute sonatas at this time.

Four of Boyce's early works written shortly before this year included "Academy of Music held in the Apollo", the oratorio "David's Lamentation over Saul and Jonathan", two odes for St. Cecilia's Day and Lord Lansdowne's masque "Peleus and Thetis".

A list of manuscripts containing compositions by Bull was included this year in Ward's "Lives of the Gresham Professors".

Campra's "Les Nopces de Vénus" was probably performed this season. It certainly was published.

Casali's opera "Candaspe" was produced this year at Venice.

Castel's best-known work "Le Clavecin oculaire des couleurs" appeared at this time.

V. L. Ciampi's "Beatrice" was produced this year at the Teatro Nuovo during Carnival.

The Cracow Gradual appeared at this time.

E. R. Duni's opera "Catone in Utica" was produced this year in Florence at the Teatro della Pergola during the Carnival.

Christoph Förster this year wrote two scenic serenatas" "Der auserlesene Beytrag zum vergnügten Alter" and "Das Verlangen als die Quelle aller menschlichen Affecten".

François Francoeur's opera

(cont.) "Pirame et Thisbe" was revived at Paris this season.

Baldassare Galuppi this year completed his opera "Adriano in Siria" in Turin (libretto by Metastasio).

Baldassare Galuppi this year wrote his opera "Gustavo primo, ré di Svezia" in Venice (libretto by Goldoni).

Baldassare Galuppi at this time completed "Orono, ré de' Sciti" at Venice (libretto by Goldoni).

Geminiani's "The Art of Playing on the Violin" was published this year at London. A famous quote from the work was "One of the principal Beauties of the violin is the Swelling or encreasing and softening the sound".

Richard Cooper this year engraved Gibbon's "Six Sonatas".

James Grassineau's "A Musical Dictionary . . . of Terms and Characters . . . ." was published this year at London. In the book he credited J. de Muris with the invention of musical notes, the long, the breve, etc.

Maurice Greene wrote his pastoral "The Judgement of Hercules" at this time.

François Lupin Grenet's "Le Triomphe de l'amitié" was performed this season at Lyons.

C. P. Grua's oratorio "La conversione di Sant'Ignazio" was performed this season at Mantua.

William Hammond's ballad opera "The Preceptor" appeared at this time.

Johann Mattheson's "Grundlage einer Ehrenpfore", published this year at Hamburg concerned Handel.

In "Select Harmony", published this year, two of Handel's Concertos in Bbmajor for oboe, strings and continuo were included as well as a Concerto Grosso in C major.

Handel's "A second Set of Six Concertos for the harpsichord or organ" without instrumental parts was published this year.

Handel's "Hornpipe" in D major was published this year.

Handel's miscellaneous vocal works published this year included "The death of a stag" ("When Phoebus the tops of the hills does adorn") for 2 voices, "The Forsaken Nymph" ("Guardian Angels") and "Love's but the frailty of the mind". The latter was sung by Mrs. Clive in Congreve's "The Way of the World".

The pieces of the "Water Music" were collected for publication this year by Walsh in London. This was the earliest printing of the work.

Hasse's opera "Artasere" (libretto by Metastasio) was produced this season in a new version at Venice.

This year provided the first setting of Metastasio's "Attilio Regolo" by Hasse.

Hasse's opera "Demetrio"

(cont.) (later "Cleonice"), libretto by Metastasio, was produced this year in a new version at Venice.

Hasse's pasticcio "Olimpia in Ebuda" was performed this year at London.

A work dubiously attributed to Hasse was produced this year at Ljubljana during the Carnival. The work, "Rosmira", was in all likelihood a pasticcio identical with an anonymous opera of the same name produced by the same company, Mingotti's, the previous year at Graz.

Sir John Hawkins' "Memoirs of Steffani" was published this year.

Jommelli's opera "Ricimero, rè dei Goti" was produced this season at Rome.

Johann Friedrich Lampe's theoretical work "The Art of Musick" was published at this time.

Giovanni Battista Lampugnani's opera "Adriano in Siria" was produced this season at Vincenza.

Hubert Le Blanc's "Défense de la basse de viole" appeared at this time.

Leo wrote during this year "Alidoro", "Carlo in Alemagnia", "Scipione nelle Spagne" and "Viriati".

Leo's libretto for the opera "I viaggiatori" was published this year at Paris.

Leo produced his "Scipinoe nelle Spagne" this season at Naples.

J. Mattheson's "Grundlage einer
Ehrenpforte", a collection of
biographies of contemporary
musicians, was published this
year.

Metastasio's libretto to the
oratorio, "Isacco", had its
first setting this year by
Prediere (see also Dittersdorf
and Martines).

Metastasio's libretto for the
oratorio, "La Morte d'Abel",
had its first settings this
year by Reutter (see also
Arne).

Metastasio's libretto for "Il
Natale di Giove" had its
first setting this year by
Bonno (see also Hasse).

Metastasio's libretto for
Zenobia had its first setting
this year by Predieri (see also
Albinioni, Cocchi (G), Dieren
(extract) Hasse, Piccini,
Porpora). Other users of his
texts have included Angioline
(friend), Apell (canzonets),
Beethoven (5 songs and canon),
Davies (ode for sisters),
Glover (2 operas), Gluck (arias
in "Innocenza giustificate",
"Poro" (see "Alessandro"),
Gounod (song), libretto Luens
("Regicide, an opera), Maria
Antonia Walpurgis (altered
libretto), Mele (2 Spanish
operas), Mozart (17 concert
arias, 4 vocal trios), Rossini
(2 songs), Schubert (10 songs),
Wellesz (cantata for voice and
orchestra).

J. M. Molter composed for the
clarinet for the next decade.

Johann Molter's musical drama
"Die . . . drei Hauptstande"

(cont.) was performed at
Eisenach this season.

Georg Monn wrote his Symphony
in D major this year. It had
four movements, one of which
was a minuet.

D. Paradisi wrote the serenata
"Il decreto del fato" this
year for Venice.

Davide Perez's "Li travesti-
menti amorosi" was produced
this season at Palermo.

A book of "Concertini" was
published by Carlo Bacciccia
Ricciotti at the Hague this
year. It foreshadowed sonata
form and was perhaps written
by Pergolesi.

Pergolesi's opera buffa "La
Serva Padrona" was produced
this year at Dresden, Lucca,
München and Venice.

Pescetti's opera "Busiri" was
produced this season at London.

Rameau's wife sang in this
year's court performance of
his "Les Fêtes d'Hébé (Les
Talents lyriques)". She was
actually not a professional
singer.

Cooke at this time published
A. Scarlatti's "VI Concertos
in Seven Parts'.

Cooke this year published D.
Scarlatti's "XLII Suites"
in 2 volumes.

Scheibe's "Der critische
Musikus" was published this
year at Hamburg.

Hickford's Second Room was open
this year with larger concerts

than before. J. D. Smith's "Rosalinda" and his oratorio "The Lament of David over Saul and Jonathan" were both performed for the first time during this season.

Lorenzo Somis' book of 8 sonatas for violin and continuo was published this year at Paris.

Vitturi wrote a libretto this year for Albinoni. Gluck later used it for his "Artamene".

Le Clerc of Paris this year issued six sonatas for cello and continuo by Vivaldi.

G. Wagenseil this year published his "Suavis artificiose elaboratus" in six parts at Bamberg.

Ward's "Lives of the Gresham Professors" was published this year.

Zellbell published his treatise "Temperatur tonorum" this year.

Geminiani in his "Art of Violin" this year called virginalists double strokes "beats" in the text and mordents in illustrations. He also discussed "staccato" and recommended the use of "vibrato" as often as possible. He described the "close shake" and called for the "swelling of the note" (sforzando) or leaning on the appoggiatura.

Grassineau's "Dictionary" of this year showed ornament signs; used the work "curtal" which became obsolete after this; he showed virginalists double strokes as mordents.

An example of a canon "four in two" appeared in Travers' Service of this year.

The English guitar appeared as early as this date.

The French horn with crooks was introduced into England shortly prior to this time.

A master for musical theory was appointed at the Thomasschule in Leipzig this year.

By this date the operatic crescendo was practiced in all varieties of Italian music.

The magnificent imperial operatic establishments suddenly collapsed at this time.

The symphony replaced the concerto this year as the leading form of concerted instrumental music.

No public concerts existed at this time in Vienna.

The court theatre at Turin was called Regio from this date forward.

This year brought the beginning of the long reign of two rulers whose ascent to the thrones of their respective empires happened under circumstances that forecast disruptions.

The death of Charles VI and the accession of Maria Theresa at Vienna was a major event of this year. Frederick the Great of Prussia also became chief of state when King Frederick William I died.

King Frederick William I died (birthdate unknown).

1740(cont.)

Czar Ivan VI of Russia was born (died 1764). His reign spanned the years 1740-1741.

Johann Georg Jacobi, a poet, was born (died 1814).

James Boswell, biographer and friend of Dr. Samuel Johnson, was born. He was a descendant of a Scottish family and a very likable man. He studied law in Holland and became a close friend of the philosopher David Hume. He wrote about the lives and conversations of great men and often broached a subject in order to arouse commentary which he recorded (died 1795).

Antonio de Zamora, playwright who wrote Don Juan, died (Birthdate unknown).

Voltaire was looking for a composer for his "Pandore" at this time.

Samuel Richardson's novel "Pamela" was published this year.

Wesley, a Methodist preacher, tried to bring his new system of worship into vogue. His enthusiasm was great and came out of the growing rationalistic British Christianity of this century.

Tiepolo painted ceiling perspectives at the Palazzo Clerici in Milan this year.

(to 1741) Elisabeth Duparc was the "prima donna" during Handel's last opera season this year at Lincoln's Inn Fields. She sang Rosmene in "Imeneo".

(to 1742) Domenico Scarlatti married Anastasia Maxarti Ximenes sometime during this period. She was his second wife.

(to 1742) F. Meyer von Schauensee studied the violin with Galimberti at Milan during these years.

(to 1744) J. S. Bach wrote the second volume of the "Well-Tempered Clavier" during this period.

(to 1744) Emanuele Barbella studied under Leo for these four years.

(to 1745) Guillaume Coustou sculpts "One of the Horses of Marly" during these years.

(to 1745) During these years William Smith of London published T. A. Arne's "As You Like It', "Comus", "Lyric Harmony", "Rosamund", "Twelfth Night" and other works.

(to 1745) J. Wynne published his "Twelve English Songs" during this period.

(to 1746) The second edition of "Calliope" was published by John Simpson during these six years.

(to 1747) A selection of Clari's vocal duets and trios with continuo was published at London during this period.

(to 1748) Handel's Overture in D major for 2 clarinets and corno di caccia was published at this time.

(to 1749) Count Francesco Algarotti during these years

served as chamberlain at Berlin.

(to 1749) Giovanni Guadagnini's violin making business was in Piacenza for these nine years.

(to 1751) Handel's Six Concertos for organ and strings were completed during this period. The keys were as follows: 1. Bb major, 2. A major, 3. Bb major, 4. d minor, 5. g minor, 6. b^{b}minor.

(to 1757) N. Pasquali lived in Edinburgh all this time.

(to 1758) The papal reign of Pope Benedict XIV spanned these years. He was born at Bologna.

(to 1763) Johann Nikolaus Hemmerlein, teacher and composer, taught music at the Bamberg College at this time. He was chamber musician to the Prince-Bishop of Lwów.

(to 1765) John and Sarah Phillips operated a music shop at the Harp in St. Martin's Court at this time and worked for composers who published their own compositions.

(to 1767) During this period K. P. E. Bach was court cembalist for Frederick II of Prussia.

(and 1771) Franz Benda embarked on systematic musical study with Graun, and after Frederick's accession to the throne this year he followed him to Berlin and stayed in the Royal orchestra throughout his life. He became conductor in 1771.

(to 1773) Christoph Schetky

(cont.) wrote his undated quartets, opus 6, sometime during this period.

(to 1775) John and Sarah Phillips engraved music throughout this period.

(to 1776) Baldassare Galuppi during these years wrote about 30 Latin and Italian oratorios, most of them were performed at Venice.

(to 1786) Frederick the Great during this period had his own court orchestra of fifteen musicians with Carl Heinrich Graun as conductor.

(to 1786) Frederick II (Frederick the Great) reigned over Prussia for these thirty-six years.

(to 1788) George England, organ builder, flourished during this period.

(to 1799) Jean Oliver y Astorga during this period lived in London and lodged "at the Trunk Maker's in Cockspur St." under the protection of the 4th Earl of Abingdon.

c.1740

John Alcock (ii), English organist and composer, was born at Plymouth (died 1791, March 30 at Walsall Staffs).

Anna Lucia de Amicis, Italian soprano, was born at Naples (died 1816 at Naples).

John Ashley, who was later responsible for the premieres of Haydn's "Creation" and Mozart's "Requiem" in England, was born (died 1805).

Karl Friedrich Baumgarten, German organist, violinist and composer, was born at Lübeck (died 1824 at London).

Marcello Bernardini, Italian composer, was born at this time in Capua (died early 19th century).

Antonia Bernasconi, Italian singer, was born this year at Stuttgart (died after 1783 at Vienna).

Quirinus Gerbrandt Blankenburg, Dutch organist, theorist and composer, died this year at The Hague (born 1654 at Gouda).

Gaetano Brunetti, Italian violinist and composer, was born this year at Pisa (died 1808 at Madrid).

Nicolas Capron, French violinist and composer, was born this year (died 1784, September 14 at Paris).

Giovanni Battista Cirri, Italian composer, was born at this time in Forli (deathdate unknown).

Charles Dieupart, French violinist, harpsichordist and composer, died possibly at London (birthdate unknown).

Giovanni Mane Giornovichi, Italian violinist and composer, was born this year at Palermo (died 1804, November 21).

Cecilia Grassi, Italian soprano, was born this year at Naples (deathdate unknown).

Giuseppe Guarneri, Italian violin maker, died this year

(cont.) at Cremona (born 1666, November 25).

Carl Ludwig Junker, clergyman, musician and author, was born at this time (died 1797).

Charles John Frederick Lampe, English organist and composer, was born this year at London (deathdate unknown).

Andreas Lidl, Austrian baritone player, was born this year at Vienna (died at London).

William Napier, Scottish musician and music publisher who participated in the first musician's strike was born (died London 1812).

Antonio Rosales, Spanish composer, was born this year at Madrid (died before 1801, November 22 at Madrid).

João de Sousa, Portuguese composer, was born at this time (died 1802).

Charles de Brosses provided a description of Italian opera of this time. As an example of dramatic criticism it would fit into Wagner's Opera and Drama.

G. G. Brunetti left Naples this year.

Prior to this date Charke succeeded Richard Jones as first violin at the Drury Lane Theatre in London.

Demachi was violinist at the court chapel in Turin at this time.

H. F. Johnsen this year joined

c.1740(cont.)
the orchestra of Frederic
Adolphus, Duke of Holstein,
at Eutin.

Jean-François Rameau came to
Paris this year. He was well-
received by his uncle Jean-
Philippe, who helped him to
get some pupils.

William Smith's signboard on
a shop on the Strand that read
"Corelli's Head" was taken down
this year. It had been erected
in 1731. Smith then moved to
a new location in London for
the second time which was to
be the last such move.

A little before this year
Tartini travelled to Rome at
the request of Cardinal
Olivieri. At the latter's
palace he met all the nobility
of the city and Pope Clement
in person. Tartini was a
reputable violinist, teacher
and composer by this time.

Of J. S. Bach's Cantatas that
fell after the Ziegler year
(1735), the majority can only
be dated about this time.

The following cantatas by J.
S. Bach were composed at this
time.
Cantata #2, "Ach Gott, vom
Himmel sieh darein", written
for the second Sunday after
Trinity.

Cantata #135, "Ach Herr,
mich armen Sünder", written
for the third Sunday after
Trinity.

Cantata #114, "Ach lieben
Christen, seid getrost",
written for the seventeenth
Sunday after Trinity.

Cantata #26, "Ach wie flüch-
ting, ach wie nichtig",
written for the twenty-fourth
Sunday after Trinity.

Cantata #33, "Allein zu dir,
Herr Jesu Christ", written
for the thirteenth Sunday
after Trinity.

Cantata #38, "Aus tiefer Not
Schrei ich zu dir", written
for the twenty-first Sunday
after Trinity.

Cantata #121, "Christum
wir sollen loben schon",
written for the Feast of
Saint Stephen.

Cantata #7, "Christ unser
Herr zum Jordan kam", written
for Feast of Saint John Baptist (Midsummer Day).

Cantata #126, "Erhalt' uns,
Herr, bei deinem Wort",
written for Sexagesima.

Cantata #45, "Es ist dir
gesagt, Mensch, was gut ist",
written for the eighth
Sunday after Trinity.

Cantata #90, "Es reifet euch
ein schrecklich Ende", written for the twenty-fifth
Sunday after Trinity.

Cantata #91, "Gelobet seist
du, Jesus Christ", written
for Christmas Day.

Cantata #96, "Herr Christ,
der ein'ge Gottes-Sohn",
written for the eighteenth
Sunday after Trinity.

"Herr Gott, Beherrschen aller
Dinge".

Cantata # 130, "Herr Gott,

c.1740(cont.)
dich loben alle wir",
written for Feast of Saint
Michael the Archangel.

Cantata #113, "Herr Jesu
Christ, du höchstes Gut",
written for the eleventh
Sunday after Trinity.

Cantata #127, "Herr Jesu
Christ, wahr'r Mensch un
Gott", written for
Quinquagesima ("Estomihi").

Cantata #48, "Ich elender
Mensch, wer wird mich er-
lösen", written for the
nineteenth Sunday after
Trinity.

Cantata #92, "Ich hab'in
Gottes Herz und Sinn",
written for Septuagesima.

Cantata #193, "Ihr Pforten
zu Zion", written for
Inauguration of the Town
Council (c.August 24)
Incomplete.

Cantata #78, "Jesu, der du
meine Seele", written for
the fourteenth Sunday after
Trinity (this particular
cantata was an example of
Bach's most mature style).

Cantata #123, "Liebster
Immanuel, Herzog der
Frommen", written for the
Feast of the Epiphany.

Cantata #32, "Liebster Jesu,
mein Verlangen", written for
the first Sinday after the
Epiphany

Cantata #115, "Mache dich,
mein Geist, bereit", written
for the twenty-second Sunday
after Trinity.

Cantata #124, "Meinen Jesum
lass' ich nicht", written
for the first Sunday after
Epiphany.

Cantata #10, "Meine Seel'
erhebt den Herrn", written
for the Feast of the
Visitation.

Cantata #125, "Mit Fried'
und Freud' ich fahr'dahin",
written for the Feast of the
Purification.

Cantata #101, "Nimm von uns,
Herr, du treuer Gott",
written for the tenth Sunday
after Trinity.

Cantata #50, "Nun ist das
Heil und die Kraft", written
for Feast of Saint Michael
the Archangel (C.1749
according to Grove).

Cantata #62, "Nun komm, der
Heiden Heiland", written
for first Sunday in Advent.

Cantata #34, "O ewiges
Feuer", written for Whit
Sunday ("am Pfingstfeste")
The possibility of this can-
tata being composed a year
later exists.

Cantata #180, "Schmücke dich,
o liebe Seele", written for
the twentieth Sunday after
Trinity.

Cantata #57, "Selig ist der
Mann", written for the Feast
of Saint Stephen.

Cantata #151, "Süsser Trost,
mein Jesus kommt", written
for the Feast of Saint John
the Evangelist.

Cantata # 138, "Warum

c.1740(cont.)
betrübst du dich, mein Herz",
written for the fifteenth
Sunday after Trinity.

Cantata #111, "Was mein Gott
will, das g'scheh' allzeit",
written for the third Sunday
after the Epiphany.

Cantata #1, "Wie schön
leuchtet der Morgenstern",
written for the Feast of
the Annunciation.

Cantata #146, "Wir müssen
durch viel Trübsal", written
for the third Sunday after
Easter ("Jubilate" used
older instrumental material).

Cantat #178, "Wo Gott der
Herr nicht bei uns hält",
written for the eighth
Sunday after Trinity.

Cantata #139, "Wohl dem,
der sich auf seinen Gott",
written for the twenty-third
Sunday after Trinity.

J. S. Bach wrote an incomplete
cantata for a wedding this year.

J. S. Bach this year completed
three partitas for the lute.

Barsanti's "Dodeci Sonate a
tre, cioe due Flauti o Violini
e Basso (per Giuseppe San
Martini) . . . date in Luce da
F. Barsanti . . ." appeared
this year at London.

The flautist Blavet published
two books of Brunettes at this
time.

A solo for two cellos by
Giovanni Bononcini was included
in a collection published this
year at London.

M. F. Cannabich was probably
the composer of the last three
"Solos for a German Flute . . ."
published by J. Tyther this
year at London.

Georg Gebel composed his opera
"Serpillo und Melisse" at this
time.

Handel's "Gloria in excelsis"
was purportedly written at
this time but was not for
certain by him.

Handel composed his "Clock
Music" this year or perhaps
even earlier.

Handel's Concerto in F major
for 2 oboes, strings and
continuo (opus 6) was composed
at this time.

Handel's "Yes I'm in love"
(for voice) was composed this
year.

"The Pleasant Musical Companion"
was published by John Johnson
of Cheapside this year.

Rousseau composed his opera
"Iphis et Anayarette" this year
at Chambéry (fragments have
survived).

William Savage's song "My fair
is beautiful as love" was
written this year.

The vogue of the French cantatas lasted until this time.

From this date forward Turkish
or Janissary music began to be
used in European military music
(bass drum, cymbals, side-drum
and triangle).

A new mature form of "nagauta"
(love songs) was created at

c.1740(cont.)

this time. It had all the lyricism of the shorter forms in addition to the sustaining power of more narrative music.

Plans by Baron von Knobelsdorf, Frederick's minister for public works, were already in existence this year in Berlin. The clearing away of the old fortifications and leveling of sandy mounds was put in progress.

Boffrand's painting "Salon de la Princesse" (c.33"x26") was completed this year for the Hotel de Soubise in Paris.

Giambattista Piazzetta painted a "genre scene", "The Fortune Teller" at this time.

(to 1750) Handel's concerto (double concerto) in Bb major for oboes, bassoons, strings and continuo was composed during this period.

(to 1750) Handel's concerto (double concerto) for horns, oboes, bassoons, strings and continuo was composed during these years.

(to 1750) Handel's concerto (double concerto) in F major for horns, oboes, bassoons, strings and continuo was composed during this period.

(to 1750) Handel's concerto for organ and orchestra in F major with oboes, bassoons, horns and strings was completed during these years.

(to 1760) Miller, whom Burney described as "the best bassoon I can remember" was playing

(cont.) concertos throughout these years.

(to 1785) Nicola Gagliano, Italian violin maker, worked during these years at Naples.

1741

(January 1 to 1744, October) Leonardo Leo was primo maestro during this period at the Turchini.

(January 6) John Church, English composer, died this year at London (born c.1675 at Windsor).

(January 9) Richard Goodson (II), English organist, died at Oxford (birthdate unknown).

(January 10) Elisabeth Duparc sang the title role on this date in Handel's last opera "Deidamia".

(January 10) Handel produced the first performance of his last opera, "Deidamia" at Lincoln's Inn Fields Theatre at London on this date. The libretto was by Rolli.

(January 15) Arne's incidental music for "Twelfth Night" was produced at this time at Drury Lane Theatre in London.

(January 22) Anselm Bayly was appointed lay-vicar of Westminster Abbey on this date at London.

(January 29) Anselm Bayly on this date was admitted a Gentleman of the Chapel Royal.

(February 9) Heinrich Joseph Riegel, conductor and composer, was born on this date at

1741(cont.)

Wertheim Franconia (died 1799, May at Paris). He studied with F. X. Richter at Mannheim and Jommelli at Stuttgart. He composed operas, oratorios, symphonies (for strings, two horns and piano), as well as some chamber music.

(February 11) Andre Ernest Modeste Gretry, French (Belgian) composer, was born on this date at Liege (died 1813, September 24 near Montmorency).

(February 13) A concert for the benefit of Francesco Scarlatti was given this evening at Dublin, Ireland.

(February 14) Arne's incidental music for "The Merchant of Venice" was performed on this date at Drury Lane Theatre in London.

(February 14) Johann Joseph Fux, Austrian organist and composer, died at this time in Vienna (born 1660). He was Kapellmeister at Vienna. As a composer he was most active in the fields of opera and church music.

(February 15) Giovanni Bononcini's last dated composition, a "Te Deum Laudamus" was preserved at Vienna and was probably performed there at this time.

(February 16) Alessandro Maria Antonio Fridzeri (Frizeri), Italian violinist and composer, was born on this date at Verona (died 1825, October 16).

(February 20) The first performance of Charles Simon Favart's "La Chercheuse

(cont.) d'Esprit" was given on this date at the Opera-Comique de la Foire Saint-Germain. The opera ran for 200 nights.

(March 8) Joah Bates, English conductor, was baptised on this day at Halifax (died 1799, June 8 at London).

(March 12) Michael van Beethoven was so much in debt that he was forced to leave Malines on this date permanently. He left his remaining property and possessions to a relative who was also a creditor, Henry Willems, and left with his wife for Bonn where they joined their sons.

(March 28) Johann André, conductor, composer and publisher, was born on this day at Offenbach am Main (died 1799, June 18 at Offenbach). He composed primarily for the lyric stage.

(March 31) Hassé's oratorio "Giuseppi riconosciuto" (libretto by Metastasio) was performed at Dresden on this day.

(April 1) John Broderip on this date was appointed organist at Canterbury Cathedral.

(April 13) Arne's "The Blind Beggar of Bethnal Green" was produced on this date at Drury Lane Theatre in London.

(April 17) Johann Gottlieb Naumann, opera composer, church music composer and later conductor at the Court Chapel in Dresden, was born on this date at Blasewitz (died 1801, October 23 at Dresden).

(April 18) Johann Friedrich Lampe's "The Sham Conjurer" was performed on this date at Covent Garden in London.

(April 22) "The London Daily Post" on this date announced that James Oswald had arrived in the city to publish a 2nd collection of Scottish tunes.

(May 2) An "Abendmusik" for the King-elector was composed at this time by Görner to a text by Gottsched.

(May 28) Andrea Lucchesi, Italian musician, composer, and later Kapellmeister at Bonn, was born on this date at Motta in Venetian territory (deathdate unknown).

(June 22) Joseph-Hector Fiocco, composer and violin maker, died at this time at Brussels (born 1703).

(June 22) Luigi Tomasini, violinist and composer, was born on this date at Pesaro (died 1808, April 25 at Esterház).

(June 24) G. Scarlatti's opera "Arminio in Germania" was produced on this date at the Teatro della Pergola in Florence.

(July 8) Elizabeth Hare (the elder), wife of John Hare, was buried on this date at London (Islington).

(July 27) Grancois Hippolyte Bartshélemon, French violinist and composer, was born on this date at Bordeaux (died 1808, July 23 at London).

(July 28) Antonio Vivaldi was buried on this date in St. Stephen's cemetery in Vienna (born 1678, March 4 at Venice). He was a pupil of Legrenzi and was considered by many to be the greatest Italian master of the concerto.

(August 20) Benjamin Franklin on this date reprinted the 15th edition of Watts' "Hymns and Spiritual Songs" (Warrington), as well as the 13th edition of the "Psalms of David" by the same author.

(August 22) Handel began composing his oratorio "Messiah" on this date.

(August 28) Handel by this time had completed the first part of his "Messiah".

(September 1) Johann Paul Aesidius Schwartzendorf Martini, (Martini il Tedesco) was born on this date at Freistadt, Upper Palatinate (died 1816, February 16 at Paris). He was a highly successful German organist, conductor and composer.

(September 6) Handel had completed the second part of his "Messiah" by this time.

(September 7) Henri Desmarets, French composer, died on this date at Lunéville (born c.1662 at Paris).

(September 12) Handel finished the third part of his "Messiah" at this time.

(September 14) Handel had finished the instrumentation on his "Messiah" by this date. The entire work took him 23 days from start to finish.

1741(cont.)

(September 25) Wenzel Pichl (Pichel), Austrian composer and violinist, was born at Bechyně near Tábor (died 1804, June 4 at Vienna).

(September 29) Handel on this date completed the first part of the oratorio "Samson".

(October 2) The "Charitable and Musical Society" on this date opened a new hall designed by Richard Castell. It was called "New Musick Hall in Fishamble Street".

(October 2) Hasse's opera "Numa" (libretto by Pallavicino) was produced on this evening at Hubertusburg Palace near Dresden.

(October 7) Hasse's intermezzo "Pimpinella e Moorcantonio" was produced on this date at Huburtusburg Palace near Dresden.

(October 11) Handel completed the second part of the oratorio "Samson" on this date.

(October 31) Galuppi's opera "Alessandro in Persia" was produced on this date at the Haymarket Theatre in London. The work is also referred to as a pasticcio on occasion.

(November 1 to 1742, July 1) Eight men put up more than £1000 to guarantee opera performances during this period at the King's Theatre in London.

(November 20) Christoph Daniel Ebeling, German musical historian, was born on this date at Garmissen, Hildesheim (died 1817, June 30 at Hamburg).

(November 26) From the "Registers" of Gray's Inn on this date, William Sheffield was appointed chapel clerk. His varied duties included "setting the psalms".

(November 27) Jean Pierre Duport, French violoncellist, was born on this date at Paris (died 1818, December 31 at Berlin).

(December 13) Carl Heinrich Graun's opera "Bodelinda" was produced on this date at the Royal Palace in Berlin. It was the first Italian opera performed there.

(December 18) Maximilien Léopold Philippe Joseph Gardel, French dancer, was born on this date at Mannheim (died 1787, March 11).

(December 23) Handel gave the first of his series of "6 musical Entertainments' on this evening at the "New Musick Hall in Fishamble Street".

(December 26) Gluck's Italina opera "Artaserse" was produced on this date at Milan, at the Teatro Regio Ducal (libretto by Metastasio). This performance reopened the theatre.

(December 29) George F. Handel on this wrote a letter to Charles Jennens Jr., thanking him for some lines for the "Messiah", and expressing pleasure at his own reception in Ireland. In the same letter he remarked "Signora Avolio, which I brought with me from London pleases extraordinary".

(January) William Hayes succeeded Richard Goodsen this year as Professor of Music at the University.

(March) Jean-Baptiste Forqueray,
a viol composer and player and
Rameau's friend, was married
this month. "La Forqueray" by
Rameau was written for Forqueray.

(July) A "Magnificat" by
Blanchard was first performed
this month.

(July to September) The "Kongl-
Svenska Vetenskaps Acad.
Handlingar" at this time con-
tained the description of Dr.
Brelin's "Upright double
Clavecin".

(August) J. S. Bach visited
Berlin at this time.

(Autumn) Angelo Monticelli
this season made his London
début in the pasticcio
"Alessandro in Persia".

(October) Adam Craig, Scottish
violinist, died this month at
Edinboro (birthdate unknown
but he was born at Edinboro).

(October) James Oswald's
departure from Scotland became
the subject of a poetic "Epistle"
in "The Scots Magazine". It
gave many interesting details of
his compositions, arrangements
as well as his playing. Oswald
left for Edinboro.

(November) J. S. Bach performed
again this month on the
Silbermann organ in the Sophien-
Kirche.

(November) Rameau wrote a letter
this month to Christin, secretary of the Academy of Lyons,
in order to correct certain
misstatements made by Bollioud-

(cont.) Mermet in a "Memoire"
published by the Academy.

Johann Ludwig Bach, court
cantor and director of the
"Kapelle" at Meiningen during
J. S. Bach's residence at
Weimar, died this year (born
1677). According to Forkel
an eight-part Mass in G by
Johann Sebastian has been
attributed to him.

Johann Christian Frischmuth,
German composer, was born
this year at Schwabhausen,
near Gotha (died 1790, July 31).

William Hayes, English chorister,
clergyman and writer (3rd son
of William Hayes, Sr.) was born
at this time at Oxford (died
1790, October 22).

Giuseppe Jannaconi, Italian
composer, was born at this
time at Rome (died 1816, March
16 at Rome).

Honoré Francois Marie Langle,
French composer, was born
this year at Monaco (died 1807,
September 20 at Paris).

Theobald Marchand, theatrical
manager at Frankfort, Mannheim
and Munich, was born this year
at München (died 1800).

Thomas Norris, English singer,
organist and composer, was
born this year at Mere, Salisbury (died 1790, September 3
at Himley Hall, Dudley,
Worcestershire).

Giovanni Paisiello according
to a major source was born this
year (died 1816).

Giacomo Rust, Italian composer,
was born this year at Rome

1741(cont.)

(died 1786 at Barcelona). He studied in Naples and later with di Capua in Rome.

Franz Adam Veichtner, German violinist and composer, was born at this time at Ratisbon (died 1822 at St. Petersburg). He studied violin with Benda and composition with Riepel.

Jacob Adlung this year became professor at the "Rathsgymnasium" of Erfurt.

Johann Friedrich Agricola went to Berlin this year and continued his studies under Quantz. He also received advice on the dramatic style from Graun and Hasse.

Jean Le Rond d'Alembert was admitted to the Academy of Sciences at this time.

Angelo Amorevoli this year sang for the Earl of Middlesex in the opera at London.

Andrioni was an Italian singer engaged for this season at London.

Andrioni and the cellist Caporale appeared several times this season at the Friday subscription concerts held at Hickford's Second Room.

Avoglio was among several who went to Ireland with Handel this year.

Johann Elias Bach refused a position offered to him at this time for the sake of his family.

Johann Ernst Bach (6th generation) at his father's (J. Bernhard) request, left the University in

(cont.) Leipzig this year and returned to Eisenach.

During the performance of Latilla's "Olimpia nell' i sola d'Ebada" this season, Caffarelli behaved so badly toward the other singers and for the audience that he was arrested at the end of the evening and sent to prison.

Caffarelli sang regularly at the San Carlo theatre in Naples from this date forward.

After this year Caroli acted as deputy for Perti who had become senile.

Caroli was "principe" of the Accademia Filarmonica at this time.

Chiarini was a friend of Goldoni who this year wrote the libretto of "Statira" for him.

François Cupis was a violinist at the Paris Opéra this season.

Carl Gustaf Düben was conductor of the court orchestra until his death.

Pierre Gaviniès this year made his first successful appearance as a violinist at the Concert Spirituel in Paris.

Matthias van den Gheyn this year was appointed organist of St. Peter's Church in Louvain.

Thomas Griffin arranged for the organ at St. Helen's Church in Bishopsgate to be installed at this time.

Jean-Pierre Guignon this year was awarded the title of Roi des Violons et ménétriers.

1741(cont.)

According to a Mr. Streatfield, quoted by Forkel, Frederick the Great was not at Aix until this year, when Handel was composing the "Messiah" in London.

"Serse" and "Deidaria", Handel's last operatic works, reverted to the earlier 17th-century type in which humorous and serious scenes were mixed.

Handel produced the last of his 40 London operas this season and turned to oratorio.

John Hebden's portrait was painted by Mercier and engraved by Faber this year.

Ignaz Holzbauer was back in Vienna at this time after a short engagement as musical director to Count Rottack at Holešov in Moravio.

John Immyns founded the Madrigal Society this year at London.

Jommelli went to Bologna this year where he enjoyed the friendship of Martini.

Johann Friedrich Lampe at this time embarked on a provincial tour with his wife (a singer), who performed his burlesque operas.

Teresa Lanti, when a child, had the famous Salimbeni (castrato) as her protector. He later became her lover. This year he placed her, dressed as a boy, with a woman in Bologna and promised to send for her in 4 years. She scored her first success as a youth, Bellino (a castrato) rather than as a prima donna. Casanova "liberated her and

(cont.) made her again a woman".

Gaetano Latilla this year resigned from his position as second maestro di capella because of illness.

Jean Marie Leclair's (l'aîné") portrait was done by Alexis Loir this year. It was engraved by François at Lyons.

It was said this year of Locatelli, that he "plays with so much fire that he must use up a few dozen violins a year".

M. Palotta was dismissed at this time as a court composer at Vienna.

Raick assumed a position this year at the Cathedral of Saint-Bavon in Ghent as organist, choirmaster and chaplain.

Rameau this year dedicated one of his most beautiful "Pièce en concert" to the Comte de Livre.

Jean-Jacques Rousseau arrived in Paris at this time.

Royer continued at the Concert Spirituel in Paris this season.

Rémond de St. Mard said this year that the sarabande "toujours melancolique respire une tendresse serieuse et delicate".

William Savage was organist at Finchley Church in Middlesex at this time.

William Savage sang in a production of Handel's opera "Deidamia" this season.

Joseph Seegr was appointed organist at the Church of Tÿn this year.

John Snetzler built the organ for Chesterfield Church at this time.

John Snetzler built an organ for Handel this year. It was used in Dublin for the first performance of "Messiah".

Johann Stamitz, Bohemian composer, violinist and conductor, played the violin at the coronation festivities in Prague this year. He received attention from visiting princes and was engaged by the court at Mannheim at once.

Franz Tuma, violist and composer became Kapellmeister to the Dowager Empress Elisabeth at this time.

Viotti introduced Cherubini into the "Société Academique des Enfans d'Apollon", an association for concerts founded during this season.

G. C. Wagenseil was organist to the Dowager Empress Elizabeth Christine.

Johann Wenzel's performance this year in Prague at the coronation festivities was heard by Carl Theodor. The latter brought him to Mannheim to be the founder and leader of the Mannheim School of violinists and conductors.

John Arnold this year published "The Compleat Psalmodist" which contained many psalm tunes, chants and hymns.

Charles Baton wrote a "Disser-

(cont.) tation historique sur la vielle" under a privilege of 1741.

Blanchard's "Benedica anima mea" appeared at this time.

Boyce's "Cathedral Music" was written after this year.

Cailey's "Three Burlesque Cantatas" by "Signor Carini" was produced this season.

Chiarini's opera "Statira" appeared this year.

Michel Corette's "Theoretical and practical method for learning perfect playing of the cello in a short time" was published at this time.

P. Walmsley this year published Willem de Fesch's "Eight Concertos" and was responsible for its sale.

Baldassare Galuppi wrote his opera "Berenice" (libretto by Vittori) in Venice at this time.

Baldassare Galuppi's opera "Didone abbandonata" (libretto by Metastasio) was produced this season at Modena.

Baldassare Galuppi's opera "Penelope" (libretto by Rolli) was produced this year at London.

A set of concertos by Francesco Geminiani (opus 6) was published this year.

"6 violin concertos" by Francesco Geminiani were published at this time in London.

C. P. Grua's oratorio "Bersabea" was given this season at Mantua.

C. P. Grua's oratorio "Jaele" was sung this year at Mantua.

Handel's "22 Italian Duets with Continuo" (15."Quel fior ch'all' abba ride", 16."No di voi non vuò fidarmi") appeared this year.

Hasse's pasticcio "Alessandro in Persia" was heard this season in London.

"Der musikalische Patriot" edited by Henke was published this year at Braunschweig.

Holzbauer's first opera, a German version of Metastasio's "Ipermestra" was heard this season at the Stadttheater.

Jommelli's opera "Astianatte" was produced this season at Rome. It was later retitled "Andromaca".

Jommelli's opera "Ezio" was produced this year at Bologna.

Jommelli's opera "merope" was produced this season at Venice.

An aria by Giovanni Battista Lampugnani's was interpolated into the pasticcio "Alessandro in Persia" at its London production this season.

Giovanni Battista Lampugnani's opera "Arsace" was produced this year at Crema.

Giovanni Battista Lampugnani's opera "Semiramide riconosciuta" was produced this season at Rome.

Leo this year wrote both L'Alessandro" and "Il verbo eterno e la religione".

Leo this year published his

(cont.) motet "Dixit Dominus" for S.S.A.T.B. and S.S.A.T.B. and orchestra in D at Naples.

P. Locatelli's "Concerti a quattro" opus 7 was published at this time.

P. Locatelli's Trios for 2 violins and bass, opus 8, were published this year.

N. Logroscino's "Violante" was produced this season.

Abbé Gabriel Bonnot de Mably's "Lettres a Mme. la Marquise de P. . . sur l'opèra", appeared at this time.

B. Marcello's "Il teatro alla moda" was reprinted this year at Florence.

G. Martini's "XII Sonate d'intavolature" opus 2, was published this year at Amsterdam by Le Cène.

Davide Perez's "L'erosimo di Scipione" appeared at this time.

Rameau's "Pieces de clavecin en concerts" was published this year. It has a collection of instrumental ensemble music, a series of trio sonatas.

Metastasio's libretto to "L'Amor prigioniero" was first set this year by Reutter.

Rousseau this year composed the music for the 1st act of the tragedy "La découverte de Nouveau Monde" produced at Lyons but the work has been lost.

G. Scarlatti's opera "Dario" was produced this year at the Teatro Argentina in Rome

1741(cont.)
(libretto by Baldanza).

Zeno's "Lucio Vero" was produced this season at Alassio
during the Carnival. Antonio
Tonelli composed some inter-
ludes for the performance.

J. G. Walther at this time
composed a clavier concerto
without accompaniment.

J. G. Walther published a
Prelude and Fugue this year.

At the Dresden court chapel,
Buffardin's original salary
was doubled to 1000 thaler per
annum.

Austria already possessed
Turkish instruments by this
time and Ritter von der Trenck
marched into Vienna preceded
by a band with them included
in its instrumentation.

The rapid arpeggios and closing
broken chords were part of the
new concerto style and appeared
in "La Rameau" and "La Cupis"
of this year.

According to Schneider the
instrumentation of the Berlin
Opera orchestra this year was
as follows: 12 violins, 4
violas, 4 cellos, 3 double
basses, 4 flutes, 4 oboes,
0 clarinets, 2 bassoons, 2
horns, 0 trumpets, 0 trombones,
0 timpani, 2 harpsichords, 1
harp and 1 theorbo. Trumpets
and drums were however available.

The court orchestra at Eisenach
was disbanded at this time.

"Zwei paar Klarinettin" were
listed in the inventory of

(cont.) instruments owned by
the court of Sayn-Wittgenstein
this year.

Trinity Church, New York, has
an unbroken record of organs
from this year forward.

A Pennsylvania settlement of
great importance in American
musical history was founded in
Bethlehem this year by religious
refugees from Bohemia and
Moravia. Their leaders were
Bishop David Nitschman and
Count Zinzendorf, the founder
of the Herrnhut sect, who had
come to America to supervise
the establishment of the
colony. The new settlement had
a highly developed musical life
that surpassed any other music
centers in the area at the time.
They gave their first concert
this year.

Aberdeen poet and jeweler,
John Ewen, was born this year
(died 1821).

Favart's play "La Chercheuse
d'esprit" was produced this
season.

Samuel Johnson's "A Fool Made
Wise" was performed this year
at the Haymarket Theatre in
London.

Montdorge's "Reflexion d'un
peintre sur l'opéra" was
published this year in France.
He was a librettist to Rameau.

Charles W. Peale, American
painter, was born this year
(died 1847).

Hans Heinrich Füseli, known also
as Henry Fuseli, was born this
year at Zurich (died 1825).
He worked in England and

1741(cont.)
foreshadowed surrealism.

Jean Antoine Houdon, French
sculptor, was born at this time
(died 1828).

The town of Eisenach became
part of the principality of
Weimar this year.

(to 1742) Araia returned to
Italy from Russia at this time.

(to 1742) S. M. Cibber was in
Dublin during this year.

(to 1744) John Clemm, Jr. was
organist of Trinity Church,
New York during these three
years.

(to 1745) Gluck wrote nine
Italian operas during this
period.

(to 1746) Johann Heinrich Rolle
was violist at the court of
Friedrich "the Great" for this
period.

(to 1755) Joseph Barnabé Saint
Sevin L'Abbé, violinist during
this period played at the Concert Spirituel. He contributed
to the development of violin
execution in France and subse-
quently elsewhere.

(to 1757) Casanova maintained
that the singer Teresa Lanti
played an important part in
theatrical life of Naples for
these sixteen years.

(to 1759) Benedict Geisler, a
German composer, published
considerable music at Augsburg
and Bamberg throughout this
period.

(to 1762) Mathias Haydn held
the position of Marktrichter

(cont.) at this time.

c.1741
Walter Clagget, Irish composer,
was born this year at Waterford
(died 1798).

Jean-Baptiste Cupis, French
cellist and composer of Flemish
descent, was born this year at
Paris (deathdate unknown).

Francesco Scarlatti, violinist
and composer, died this year
(born 1666, December 5).

R. Pockrich made a speciality
of playing on musical glasses
at this time.

Lewis Granom's "Twelve Sonatas
or Solos for a German Flute,
with a thourough-bass for the
Harpsichord, or Violoncello ,
opera prima" was published
at this time.

Richard Jones' "6 Suites of
Lessons for a Violin . . . ."
was published this season at
London.

1742
(January 17) Alessandro Toeschi,
violinist and composer, provided the ballet music for
C. P. Grua's opera "Maride"
which opened the Mannheim
opera-house on this date.

(January 18) Hasse's opera
"Lucio Popirio" was produced
on this evening at Dresden.

(February 20) Regine Susanna
Bach, daughter of J. S. Bach
(6th generation) was born (died
1809, December 14). She did
not marry.

(February 22) J. S. Bach's
daughter Regine Susanna Bach
was baptized on this day.

1742(cont.)

(March 4) Johann Heinrich Egli, Swiss composer, was born at Seegraben, Zürich (died 1810, December 19 at Zürich).

(March 6) Anton Romberg, a German bassoonist, was born at Westphalia (died 1814, December 14). He concertised in Hamburg and played some concerts with his youngest son, Anton, jr.

(March 23) Hasse's oratorio, "I pelligrini al sepolcro di N.S." (libretto by Pallavicino) was produced at this time in Dresden.

(March 24) Handel's secular choral work "Hymen" (English concert version of the opera "Imeneo") was heard on this date at the Music Hall on Fishamble St. in Dublin.

(April 8) A public rehearsal was heard on this date at the "New Musick Hall in Fishamble Street'. The rehearsal was for the first performance of Handel's "Messiah".

(April 10) Joseph Mondonville's first opera, "Isbe" was performed at the Opéra on this evening. It was a failure.

(April 13) Handel's "Messiah" was first performed on this date at the Musick Hall on Fishamble Street, Dublin. The performance was for the benefit of the Society for relieving prisoners, the Charitable Infirmary and Mercer's Hospital, The text to this work was by Jennens, taken from the Bible and the Prayer Book.

(April 13) S. M. Cibber sang in the first performance of the

(cont.) "Messiah" on this evening at Dublin.

(April 20) "Merope", a version of Pergolesi's "L'Olimpiade", was given at this time in London (see also May 1).

(May 1) Pergolesi's "Olimpiade" was presented in London on this date under the title of "Meraspe, overo L'Olimpiade", a pasticcio with libretto by Rolli. Monticello's performance had a strong effect on the London audience (see also April 20 for conflicting date).

(May 1) Joseph Barnabé Saint-Sevin L"Abbé, on this date became a violinst in the opera orchestra at Paris. He remained there for twenty years and then retired to teach and compose. He innovated the writing out of cadenzas.

(May 2) Gluck's Italian opera "Demetrio" (Libretto by Metastasio) was produced at the Teatro San Samuele on this day in Venice. This work is also called "Cleonice" and "Demofoonte".

(May 6) Arne's "Miss Lucy in Town" was produced on this date at the Drury Lane Theatre in London.

(May 25, 27) J. Oswald announced his "A Second Collection of Curious Scots Tunes" in "The Champion" on these days.

(June 9) Omobono Stradivarius, son of Antonio, was interred in the family vault on this date.

(June 24) G. Scarlatti's opera "Siroe" was produced this evening at the Teatro della

1742(cont.)

Pergola at Florence. The libretto was by Metastasio.

(July 1) Bohuslav Matěj
Cernohorský, Bohemian composer,
died on this date at Graz (born
1684, February 16 at Nymburk,
Bohemia).

(July 12) Evaristo (Felice)
Dall'Abaco, Italian violinist
and composer, died on this day
at München (born 1675, July 12
at Verona).

(July 21) Mrs. Arne and Mrs.
Cibber sang "favourite songs
and duettos" by Arne, Handel
and Hasse for Mrs. Arne's
benefit this evening.

(July 21-28) The American Weekly
Mercury during this week advertised that "A choice Collection
of Hymns with several new translations from the Hymn Book of
the Moravian Brethren" had been
published at Philadelphia.

(July 22) Andrea Adami di
Bolsena, Italian musical scholar,
died at Rome on this date (born
1663, October).

(August 11) William Felton on
this day was ordained a priest
by the Bishop of Hereford.

(August 22) J. J. Rousseau
propounded his new theory on
music writing in a paper he
read on this date before the
Academy of Sciences. He was
introduced by M. de Réaumur.

(August 25) Carlos Seixas,
Portuguese composer, organist
and harpsichordist, died on
this date at Lisbon (born 1704,
June 11 at Coimbra). He was
a close associate of D. Scarlatti.

(August 30) J. S. Bach's
"Peasant Cantata" was performed
on this date of succession of
Carl Heinrich von Dieskau to
some property. The text was
"Mer hahn en neue Oberkeet"
and it was a secular cantata
(#212).

(October 5) Burkat Shudi at
this time moved from Meard's
Street to #33 Great Pulteney
Street, Golden Square, London.
This was announced in the
"Daily Advertiser".

(October 7) Hasse's opera
"Didone abbandonata"(libretto
by Metastasio), was produced on
this date at Hubertusburg near
Dresden.

(October 1) Avondano's opera
"Berenice" was produced at
this time at Macerata, Italy.

(November 2) Arias by Brivio
were included in the pasticcio
"Gianguir" performed on this
evening at the King's Theatre
in London.

(December 2) A new opera house
in Berlin was opened on this
date with Carl Heinrich Graun's
opera "Cleopatra e Cesare"
(see also December 7).

(December 2) Isaiah Warner
reprinted Watts' Hymns at this
time with the 14th edition of
the same book that Benjamin
Franklin reprinted.

Catherine Plunkett gave a
benefit concert on this evening
in Fishamble Street Music Hall.

(December 7) The new opera
house in Berlin was not fully
completed, but on this date it
opened with great ceremony.

1742(cont.)

Graun's opera "Cleopatra e Cesare" was performed (see also December 2).

(December 7) The new opera house in Berlin was opened under Frederick II with Graun's "Rodelinda" on this date. Note conflict with other sources on December 2 and the entry before this one.

(December 12) Brivio's opera "Mandane" was produced this evening at the King's Theatre in London.

(December 16) Bellinzani on this date requested three years' leave, since he was in debt because of his low salary. He had also received an offer elsewhere providing an opportunity to satisfy his creditors.

(December 19) Hasse's opera "Issipile" (libretto by Metastasio), was produced on this date at Naples.

(December 26) Gluck's "Demofoonte" was produced at this time at the Teatro Regio Ducal in Milan (libretto by Metastasio).

(December 30 and 1743, February 10) The Pennsylvania Gazette on these dates advertised that "every evening (was acted) An agreeable Comedy or Tragedy by changeable figures of two feet high. A Sight of the Sea and Ships. A Merry Dialogue between Punch and Joan his wife. With several other pleasing Entertainments".

(Winter) V. L. Ciampi's "Lionora" writeen in collaboration with Logroscino was performed at the Teatro Nuovo during this (cont.) season.

(March) "Mr. Charles" arrived at Dublin during this month.

(May) "Mr. Charles" played concertos on the horn and clarinet and "select pieces" on the hautbois d'amour and "Shalamo" at this time in Dublin.

(June) Arne and his wife went to Dublin this month.

(June) Johann Stamitz gave a concert this month in Frankfort am Main and was advertised as a "famous virtuoso" on violin, viola d'amore, cello and contreviolon, as well as a composer. At this concert Carl Theodor heard him play. The concert was for the coronation of Charles VII.

(Summer) Hasse's opera "L'Agilo d'amore" (libretto by Metastasio) was produced at this time in Naples.

(December) Auletta this month was commissioned to write the first Carnival opera for the Royal Theatre at Turin ("Caio Fabricio").

(December-1743, February) Philadelphians enjoyed a puppet show (Comedy and Tragedy) during this period.

Felice Alessandri, Italian composer was born this year at Rome (died 1798, August 15 at Casinalbo).

Pedro Aranaz, Spanish composer, was born this year at Tudela (died 1821 at Cuença).

Benedikt Anton Aufschnaiter,

German composer, died this year
at Passau (birthdate unknown).

Marc Antoine Desaugiers, French
composer, was born at this time
at Fréjus, Provence (died 1793,
September 10 at Paris).

Henry Eccles, violinist, died
this year at Paris (born c.
1670 at London). This information has been questioned.

André Ernest Modeste Grétry,
Belgian composer and last of the
great masters of the classic
opéra comique, was born this
year in Belgium (died 1813).

Matteo Gofriller, violin maker,
died at this time (born 1670).

Ralph Guest, English organist,
was born this year (died 1830).

Anne Hunter (born Home),
Scottish amateur poet and musician, was born at this time
(died 1821).

Jean Baptiste Aimé Joseph
Janson, Netherlands cellist and
composer, was born this year at
Valenciennes (died 1803,
September 2 at Paris).

Vassily Alexeyevich Pashkevich,
Russian violinist, conductor
and composer, was born at this
time (died 1800).

Robert Rawlings, violinist and
son of Thomas Rawlings, was
born this year at London (died
1814 at London). He was a pupil
of his father and later of
Barsanti.

Augustin Schelle, a learned
Benedictine monk, was born
this year (died 1805).

Robert Wornum, English music
publisher and instrument
maker, was born at this time
in Berkshire (died 1815 at
London).

John Alcock this year left his
position as organist of St.
Andrew's Church, Plymouth,
in order to become organist at
St. Lawrence's Church at
Reading.

Jean Le Rond d'Alembert at
this time acquired fame which
spread rapidly because of the
historic "Alembert principles".

Karl Philipp Emanuel Bach this
year wrote the slow movement
of his first sonata.

Johann Caspar Bachofew succeeded
Johann Kaspar Albertin as
cantor of the minster and as
director of the "Chorherren-
Gesellschaft".

Barsanti settled in Edinboro
prior to this date.

J. A. Benda joined his family
this year on their way from
Bohemia to Prussia to join
the eldest son there.

At this time Royal patronage
was bestowed on Blanchard in
the form of a priory, a pension
and an abbey. He gave them up
however, when he married.

Brivio apparently arrived in
London this year.

DeLange returned to Liège at
this time and became first
violinist at the Collegiate
Church of St. Paul.

During his residence at Dublin,
Dubourg led the orchestra at

the performances produced by Handel during his visit to Ireland this year.

Dubourg was one of the best violinists of the English school at this time. While playing "the Messiah" in Dublin under Handel he modulated several times and when he found the right key, Handel, who was conducting, remarked, "Welcome home, Mr. Dubourg".

The Ranelagh Gardens were opened this year and Michael Festing was appointed director of music.

Caterina Galli, Italian mezzo-soprano, went to London this season.

Gustavus Hasselius was a Swedish spinet manufacturer in Philadelphia as early as this date.

In its first years starting this season, the repertory of the newly built Royal Opera in Berlin consisted almost entirely of operas by Graun and Hasse.

After the dissolution of the Eisenach court chapel this year, Johann C. Hertel was appointed Konzertmeister at the Court of Strelitz.

Karl Hoeckh became Konzertmeister to the court at Zerbst this year. He was recommended by his teacher, F. Benda.

Gottfried August Homilius became organist this year at the "Frauenkirche" in Dresden.

Willem Kennis at this time became chapel master of Saint-Gommaire, Lierre.

Samuel Lee was employed this year by Handel as a copyist.

Thomas Lowe sang in Handel's "Samson" this season.

Galliard's translation of Tosi's "Treatise on Singing" this year carried a footnote which read: "Nicolini had both qualities (acting and singing) more than any that have come hither since. He acted to perfection, and did not sing much inferior. His variations in the airs were excellent; but in his cadences he had a few antiquated tricks".

When R. Pockrich's distillery failed at this time he applied, unsuccessfully, for the position of master of the choristers at Armagh Cathedral.

Manuscripts and the libretto of "Statira" this year showed that Porpora had become maestro of another of the Venetian music-schools for girls, the "Ospedale della Pietà".

J. J. Rousseau probably met La Pouplinière during this season.

Hopkinson stated that a "Le Clerc cataloque (Scarlatti) of this date (1742) mentions a first and second "Livre de Clavecin" but not the third or the "Pièces Choisis".

A volume of Scarlatti's sonatas was copied out for Queen Maria Barbara this year. The range of the sonatas is only four and one-half octaves. Most of the existing sonatas that appeared previous to the "Essercizi" of this year appeared in the volume for the Queen ("Royal Sonatas"). The manuscript, known as Venice XIV, also contained most sonatas that were contemporary with the "Essercizi".

Christian Friedrich Schale was royal chamber virtuoso this year in all probability at Berlin.

Johann Scheibe this year became director of the court opera at Copenhagen, and also conducted the court orchestra there.

Robert Smith became Master of Trinity at this time.

When Ombono Stradivari died this year, Antonio's younger son, Carlo Bergonzi, went to live in Stradivarius' house at the Piazza San Domenico.

Cecilia Young went to Dublin this year and sang in "Comus" and other operas by her husband, Arne.

Girolamo Abos made his début as an operatic composer this year at Naples with "Le due zingare simili".

Andrea Adolfati's opera "L'Artaserse" was produced this season at Rome.

K. P. E. Bach's opus 1, "6 Prussian Sonatas" was issued this year.

Johann Sebastian Bach's "Goldberg Variations", written for the harpsichordist Johann T. Goldberg this year, were included in Clavierübung, Vol. IV.

Alexander Baillie's "A Collection (cont.) of Old Scots Tunes" was published by Francesco Barsanti this year at Edinboro.

Carey's "A Choice Collection of Six Favourite Songs never before publish'd" appeared at this time.

Chiarini's "Amor fa l'uomo cieco" was performed this year with his "Artaserse" at both Genoa and Verona.

Chinzer's last opera "Atalo" was produced at Venice this season.

J. G. Clement composed a Requiem performed this year at the funeral of Emperor Charles VI.

William Corbett published a series of suites for string orchestra this year. One of them, "Alla Veneziana", ended in 2 "Purlana".

Domenico Fischietti made his debut this season as an opera composer with his "Armindo" at the Fiorentini theatre.

The 1st Wesleyan tune-book, "A Collection of Tunes, set to Music, As they are commonly Sung at the Foundry", also known as "Foundery Tunes", was printed by A. Pearson this year. This was the latest date found for her work.

Johann Joseph Fux' "Gradus ad Parnassum", the German edition, was published in Leipzig at this time.

Johann Ernst Galliard this year published a translation of Pier Francesco Tosi's "Opinioni di cantori antichi e moderni, o

sieno Osservazioni sopra il
canto figurato".

Baldassare Galuppi wrote his
opera "Enrico" (libretto by
Vanneschi) at London this year.

Baldassare Galuppi wrote his
opera "Scipione in Cartagine"
at this time in London (libretto by Vannexchi).

Francesco Geminiani's "Guida
armonica" was published this
year.

Johann Valentin Görner's first
set of music composed to
Hagedorn's poems was published
at this time. It was titled
"Collection of New Odes and
Songs".

C. P. Grua's opera "Meride"
was given this season at
Mantua.

C. P. Grua's oratorio "Il
fligliuol prodigo" was sung
this season at Mantua.

Handel's 22 Italian Duets with
Continuo including #17,"Nò di
voi non vuò fidarmi" (another
setting) and #18 "Beato in
ver chi puo" (Horace translation) was still in progress
at this time.

Handel composed his "Forest
Music" for treble and bass
(violin and harpsichord) this
year.

Hasse's "La Clemenza di Tito"
was produced this season at
Moscow at the Coronation of
the Czaritza Elizabeth.

Hasse's pasticcio "Gianguir"
was performed this season at
London.

William Hayes this year composed
"Collins's Ode on the Passions",
vocal and instrumental music
containing: I. The Overture &
Songs in The Masque of "Circe",
II. A Sonata or Trio, & Ballads,
"Airs & Cantatas", III. An
"Ode, being part of an exercise
performed for a Batcheldor's
Degree in Music".

James Hoey published the word-
book to "Messiah" at this time.

Illuminato da Tarino wrote his
"Canto ecclesiastico diviso in
3 libri" with plainchants
this year at Venice.

Jommelli's secular dramatic
works for this year included
"Don Chidulio", intermezzo,
"Eumene", and "Semiramide"
(libretto by Silvani) produced
at Rome, Bologna and Venice
respectively.

Giovanni Battista Lampugnani's
aria was interpolated into the
pasticcio "Meraspe" given at
London and his aria was also
interpolated into "Gianguir"
both this season.

Leo's "Dixit Dominus", for
S.A.T.B., S.A.T.B. and orchestra
in C was published at this time.

Leo this year wrote "L'ambizione
delusa", "L'impresario delle
Isole Canarie", "L'Andromaca"
and air added to Hasse's
"Issipile".

N. Logroscino's "Amore ed
amistade" was produced at this
time.

N. Logroscino's "Lionora" was
produced this season.

Mouret's "Le Mariage de Ragonde
etc" was performed this year at

the Opéra as "Les Amours de Ragonde".

Mouret wrote a book of motets this year for the Académie royale.

John Parry at this time published his book "Ancient British Music".

John Parry was a great collector of Welsh airs and his 1st work which appeared this year was the earliest known collection devoted to Welsh melodies.

Porpora's opera "Statira" was performed this year at the Teatro San Giovanni Crisostomo in Venice.

Rameau's "Castor et Pollux" was revived this year in excerpts.

Rameau's "Hippolyte et Aricie" was revived this year in France. Phaedra's solo "Cruella mère des Amours" was removed from the work.

Bishop La Ravallié this year published 63 songs of the 13th century, King of Navarre and Court of Champagne-Thibaut IV.

Rousseau published his "Le Nouveau Dedale" this year in which "he studies 'the art of flying in air'".

The 14th volume of D. Scarlatti's violin sonatas (61) was published this year.

Jakob von Stählin, German historian and author, wrote the prologue "La Russia afflitta e riconsolata", set to music this year by Domenico Dall'Oglio.

At this time John Stanley, composer and organist, published "Six Cantatas for a Voice & instruments". The words were by Hawkins, the future historian of music.

Pier Francesco Tosi's "Opinioni de'cantori antiche e moderni, o sieno osservazioni sopra il canto figurato" was published this year after his death in London by Galliard as "Observations on the Florid Song, or Sentiments of the Ancient Modern Singers".

Benjamin Franklin again this season reprinted Watt's Hymns (Warrington).

Zellbell composed a string overture at this time.

A primitive form of a piano in which the hammer was knocked by a block at the end of the key was found this year in a square piano in the Musikhistorische Museum Neupert Bamberg. It was made by"Joh. Söchur in Obern Sonthafen Allgau 1742", the oldest existing dated square piano. This proved that Friederici did not invent the square piano.

Rameau in his "Concerts en trio" this year wrote on broken chords.

A new opera house was opened this year at Berlin.

The Teatro dei Rinnovati at Siena was burned down this year.

Dauberval, the French ballet dancer, was born at this time (died 1806).

Fielding this year published
a novel, "Joseph Andrews" in
England.

Edward Young's "Night Thoughts"
was published this year. It
was the most comprehensive
expression of "The Time spirit
on The Theme of life, death &
immortality".

Rivera, Spanish Baroque architect, died this year (born
c.1683).

François Boucher this year
painted "The Bath of Diana".
(oil on canvas, 22 1/2 x 28 3/4")

François Boucher this year
painted "Diana Resting After
The Bath". The picture is at
the Louvre in Paris.

Ignaz von Born, originally a
Jesuit who studied law and
natural science, was born this
year in Karlsburg, Transylvania
(died 1791, July 24 at Vienna).

John Hervey, 1st Earl of Bristol,
died at this time (born 1688).

Lenz "Hofrat" in Altenburg was
initiated into the lodge
"Archimedes zu den drei Reiss-
brettern" at this time.

Charles Town this year had a
population of less than seven
thousand.

Girolamo Abos was assistant to
Feo at the Conservatorio dei
Poveri di Gesù Cristo this
season.

(1746, 1755) Richard Cooper
engraved Gibbons' "Collections
of Scots Tunes" in three books
at the dates given above.

(and 1749) The volumes of
Scarlatti's sonatas that have
since been numbered XIV and
XV were actually the earliest
from these two years respectively. They preceded the
thirteen volumes of the series
proper.

(and 1749) Two unnumbered
volumes of Scarlatti's sonatas
bear these dates. (Venice) See
previous entry.

(to 1748) The "Venetian Ballads
Compos'd by Sig. Hasse And all
the Celebrated Italian Masters",
edited by Adamo Scola, was
published during this period
in 3 volumes.

(to 1752) William Felton was
the vicar of Diddlebury during
this period.

(to 1754) Adolfati wrote about
10 operas for Genoa, Venice and
Modena during this time. They
were not very successful.

(to 1755) Durante taught
at the Conservatorio di Santa
Maria di Loreto for these
thirteen years.

(to 1756) Carl Heinrich Graun
wrote 28 operas for the opera
house in Berlin during these
years.

(to 1759) Michael Broome
engraved music at Birmingham
during this period.

(to 1760) Girolamo Abos taught
at the Conservatorio di Sant'
Onofrio for these eighteen
years.

(to 1774) Benedetta Emilia
Agricola was engaged at the
Berlin Opera throughout these
years.

1742(cont.)

(to 1774) B. E. Moltena was attached to the court of Frederick II of Prussia during this period.

(to 1787) Karl Philipp Emanuel Bach wrote a great number of sonatas throughout these years.

c.1742

Giacomo Insanguine, Italian organist and composer, was born this year at Monopoli, Bari (died 1795, February 1 at Naples).

Christoph Transchel was Bach's pupil and friend at this time.

J. S. Bach's Cantata #122, "Das neugebor'ne Kindelein" was written this year for the Sunday after Christmas Day.

Johann Sebastian Bach's "Clavier-übung", or "Exercises for the Clavier, consisting of an Aria with Several Variations, for a Clavier with two manuals. Published by Balthasar Schmidt at Nürnberg" was issued at this time.

Part II of Johann Sebastian Bach's "Well-tempered Clavier" was completed this year.

The Prussian ambassador to London, C. W. von Borck this year translated into German Charles Coffey's farce "The devil to pay, or the Wives metamorphos'd".

1743

(January 1) Caterina Galli made her singing debut on this date in Galuppi's "Enrico" in London.

(January 12) Maria Barbara Scarlatti, daughter of Domenico, fourth generation of the Scar-

(cont.) latti family, was born on this day (died after 1762). Her mother was Anastasia.

(January 13) The baptismal certificate of Maria Barbara Scarlatti bore this date.

(January 20) Caffarelli appeared on this evening at the first performance of Sarro's "Alessandro nell'Indie" with a live elephant at the San Carlo Theatre in Naples.

(January 24) C. W. von Borck's German translation of Charles Coffey's farce "the Devil to Pay, or the Wives metamorphos'd" was produced at Berlin on this date with the original English music.

(February 1) Giusepph (Ottavio) Pitoni, Italian composer, died on this date at Rome (born 1657, March 18 at Rieti).

(February 3) William Felton on this day was appointed a vicar-choral at Hereford Cathedral.

(February 12) The first performance of Favart's "Don Quichotte chez la duchesse" was produced on this date at Paris. The music was by Boismortier.

(February 18) Handel's "Samson", an oratorio, was produced on this date at Covent Garden in London. The text was by Newburgh Hamilton based on Milton's "Samson Agonistes", "Hymn on the Nativity".

(February 18) Avoglio on this evening sang the famous "Let the bright seraphim" at the first performance of Handel's "Samson".

(February 19) Luigi Boccherini,

Italian cellist and composer,
was born on this date at Lucca
(died 1805, May 28 at Madrid).

(February 22) Porpora's opera
"Temistocle" was performed
this evening at the King's
Theatre in the Haymarket,
London. The text was by Metastasio and not by Zeno. Both
Burney and Loewenberg thought it
to be a revival of "Temistocle"
as it appeared in 1718 but this
was an error.

(Spring) V. L. Ciampi's "Fla-
minia" was produced at the
Teatro Nuovo this season.

(March 23) Handel's "Messiah"
was first performed in England
on this date at Covent Garden
in London.

(March 29) Paris Francesco
Alghisi, Italian composer, died
on this date at Brescia (born
1666, June 2 at Brescia).

(March 31) Favart's "Le Coq
de village" was first performed
on this evening at Paris.

(April 7) Françoise Rose
Gourgaud, actress, was born on
this date at Marseilles (died
1804, October 5 at Paris).

(April 12) Hasse's oratorio
"La caduta di Gerico" (libretto
by Pasquini) was produced on
this date at Dresden.

(May 13) Francesco Stradivarius
was interred in the family
vault on this date. He was the
son of Antonio Stradivarius.

(May 23) Benedikt Friedrich
Zinck, German organist and
composer, was born on this day

(cont.) (died 1801).

(May 26) Antoine Laurent
Baudron, French violinist,
composer and conductor, was
born on this date at Amiens
(died 1834 at Paris).

(May 27) J. S. Bach wrote his
cousin Johann Elias on this
day thanking him for a gift
of wine the latter had sent
him at Leipzig.

(June 3-1743, July 4) Handel
wrote his oratorio "Semele"
during this period. It has
also been referred to as a
serenata. The text is based
on an opera libretto by
Congreve and is considered to
be one of Handel's greatest
works.

(June 26) The victory of
Dettingen on this date was the
one celebrated by Handel's
"Te Deum".

(July 6) Valentin Adamberger,
German tenor, was born on this
date at München (died 1804,
August 24 at Vienna).

(August 16) Matthias Klotz,
violin maker, died on this
day at Mettenwald (born 1653,
June).

(September 9) Gluck's Italian
opera "Il Tigrane" was produced
this evening at Crema. The
libretto was by Goldoni.

(Autumn) E. R. Duni's opera
"Baiazette" was produced this
season at the Teatro della
Pergola in Florence.

(Fall-1744, Whitsuntide)
Rousseau, a foreign diplomat
at the time was given boxes at

1743(cont.)
San Chrysostomo, San Angelo,
San Salvatore and San Samuele.

(September 30) Jeronymo Francisco de Lima, Portuguese
conductor and composer, was
born on this date at Lisbon
(died 1822, February 19 at
Lisbon).

(September 30) Christian
Ehregott Weinlig, German
organist and composer, was born
this day at Dresden (died 1813,
March 14).

(October 4) Henry Carey,
English composer and playwright,
died on this day at London
(born c. 1687, probably at
Yorkshire). He has also been
referred to as an American
composer.

(October 16) Hasse's opera
"Antigone" (libretto by
Metastasio) was produced on
this date at Hubertusburg.

(November 27) Handel's
"Dettingen Te Deum" was first
performed on this evening at
the Chapel Royal, St. James's.
It's text was "The King Shall
Rejoice" and it was written to
celebrate the English military
victory at Dettingen.

(December 7) Johann Heinrich
Viktor Rose, German cellist,
organist and composer, was
born on this date (died 1820,
March 9). He studied several
instruments under his father's
tutelage.

(June-1745, June) Charles
Simon Favart was stage manager
of the Opera-Comique de la
Foire Saint-Germain, at a
salary of 2,000 livres during
this period.

(July) Handel's "Dettingen
Te Deum" was started this month.

(October) Baildon sang in
Handel's "Alexander's Feast"
this month at Ruckholt House,
Essex.

(October) Giuseppe Gazzaniga,
Italian composer, was born
this month at Verona (died
1818, February 1).

(November) "Mr. Charles" this
month was announced to perform
at Salisbury on the clarinet,
horn, hautbois d'amour and
"shalmo. The instruments
had never been heard here before."

(December) Gluck's Italian
opera "Arsace" was produced in
Milan this month. The author
of the libretto is not known.

Lucrezia Aguiari, Italian
soprano, was born on this date
at Ferrara (died 1783, May 18
at Parma).

Johann Bernhard Bach, organist
at Ohrdruf, son of J. Christoph,
grandson of J. Ambrosius, and
member of the 6th generation of
the Bach family died (born 1700,
November 24).

Johann Christian Bach, clavier-
ist, son of Georg Michael,
grandson of Jakob, and member
of the 6th generation of the
Bach family was born this year
(died 1814). He taught music
at Ruhla.

Johann Elias Bach (6th generation) married his first wife
this year. She died two years
later.

Johann Friedrich Bach, schoolmaster, (6th generation) died
this year (born 1706).

1743(cont.)

Karl Ludwig Bachmann, violist, was born this year at Berlin (died 1809, May 26 at Berlin).

Michel de la Barre, famous French flutist, died at this time (born 1675).

Anton Bemetzrieder, Alsatian writer on music, was born this year at Alsace (died at London). Some sources gave his birth as 1748.

Pascal Boyer, French composer and writer on music was born at this time at Tarascon (died after 1793 at Paris).

George Savile Carey, poet, actor, dramatist and possibly a composer, was born this year (died 1807).

Francis Forcer, musician, died at this time (birthdate unknown).

Georg Anton Kreusser, German violinist, conductor and composer, was born this year at Heidingsfeld (died 1810 at Frankfort am Main).

Elias Placht, founder of a family of violin makers who lived mainly at Schönbach, was born at this time (died 1833).

A. G. Schwarz, English bassoonist, was born at this time (died 1804).

Karl Raphael Ungar (originally Unger), Director of the University library at Saaz, was born this year (died 1807). He was a secular priest and imperial councillor.

Antonio Vivaldi, celebrated (cont.) Italian composer of chamber music, died this year (born 1680). He was a violin virtuoso and head of a girl's conservatory, the "Ospedale della Pietà" at San Marco.

J. Elias Bach received 20 thalers this year for writing two sets of church cantatas.

John Beard performed at the Drury Lane Theatre in London until this date.

In the librettos of his early operas, up to this year (mostly performed at Venice) Andrea Bernasconi was still considered a "dilettante".

Raniero Simone Francesco Calzabigi was a financier in Naples at this time.

"Mr. Charles" was back in England by this year.

Catherine Clive was selected this year by Handel to sing the part of Delilah in his oratorio "Samson".

Gioacchino Conti left London for Lisbon at this time.

B. Cooke (ii) this year at age 9 was placed under the tutelage of Pepusch.

Christoph Förster went to Rudolstadt this year as assistant conductor to Johann Graf.

Frederic Adolphus was elected successor to the Swedish throne this year and Johnsen followed him to Stockholm.

"But lo, the angel of the Lord" in Handel's "Messiah" was originally conceived as a

recitative. The "arioso" was
an afterthought interpolated
for the first time in this
year's London performance.

Holzbauer at this time married
Rosalie (last name unknown),
a singer.

Höpken was released as a
prisoner of war from Russia
at this time.

Jommelli was appointed director
of the Conservatorie degli
Incurabili at Venice this year.

Jakob Kleinknecht was a flutist
this year at the Bayreuter
court.

Giovanni Battista Lampugnani
went to London this season to
succeed Galuppi as composer to
the King's Theatre.

Thomas Lowe sang in Handel's
"Susanna" this season.

Thomas Lowe sang in "The
Provoked Wife" in Dublin this
year.

While studying with Predieri
this year, A. Mazzoni became
an associate of the Bologna
Accademia dei Filarmonica.

Metastasio's "Didone abbandonata" of this year was exceedingly tragic for opera of this
period since it ended with
Dido's death.

Johann Molter returned to
Durlach at this time to occupy
his former position of court
conductor and remained there
until his death.

Leopold Mozart this year was
appointed violinist in the

(cont.) Archbishop of Salzburg's
private orchestra.

J. C. Neruda at this time was
appointed choirmaster of the
Premonstratensian Abbey of
Strahov at Prague.

The name of "Pallavicini,
Vincenzo, bresciano, del 1743,"
appeared among those composers
of some pieces of manuscript
music at Bologna's Liceo
Musicale. There were trial
compositions for election to
the Accademia dei Filarmonica
of Bologna.

R. Pockrich played on the
musical glasses this season
at Dublin.

There is no evidence that
Porpora returned to England
this year, but it is not
impossible.

From the time of Maria Barbara's
birth this year and probably
even from that of Domenico's
second marriage, the Scarlatti
family was living in "casas de
administración" in the Calle de
Leganitos.

Vittoria Tesi, the singer,
married a barber and from this
year on appeared as "Tesi-
Tramontini, virtuosa di Camera
della Gran duchessa di Toscana".

Francesco Antonio Baldassare
Uttini, singer and composer,
was a member of the Bologna
Accademia dei Filarmonici at
this time.

German comic opera or Singspiel
began this year with C. F.
Weisse's translation of the
English ballad opera "The Devil
to Pay".

The version of Auletta's "Orazio" given at Venice this season was attributed to Latilla and Pergolesi in the libretto.

Constantin Bellermann's most important work is "Programma in quo Parnassus Musarum voce, fidibus, tibiisque resonans, sive musices divinae artis laudes diversae spelies singulares effectus atque primarii autores succincte enarrautur". It appeared this year at Erfurt.

Bodin de Boismortier's comic opera "Don Quichotte" was produced this season. The libretto was by Favart and the full title was "Don Quichotte chez la duchesse".

Bouvard's "Idylle sur la naissance de Jésus-Christ" appeared at this time.

Boyce composed an anthem for the annual Three Choirs Festival this year, apparently used as part of a "Grand Concert of Musick" in which members of London choirs brought by Maurice Greene participated.

Boyce's serenata "Solomon" was composed at this time.

Briseux published his "L'Art de bâtir des maisons de campagne" this year.

The Prussian ambassador to London at this time was von Brock, who translated Shakespeare's "Julius Caesar" into German. It was performed as "Der Teufel ist los!" this season at Berlin.

Bury made his debut as a composer this year at the Académie Royale de Musique. His work was an opera-ballet, "Les Caractères de la folie".

A collected edition of Carey's principal dramatic works was published at this time.

A third edition of Carey's songs was published this year.

Le Cerf's "comparaison" were republished this year for the last time together with an "Histoire de la musique depuis son origine jusq'à présent", under the name of Bourdelot. Le Cerf's authorship, however, was never questioned.

Louis Nicola Clerambault at this time composed the cantata "Les Francsmaçons".

G. Cocchi produced his first opera "Adelaide" this year at Rome.

Charles Coffey's ballad opera, "The Devil to Pay" appeared in Germany this year as "Der Teufel ist los!".

Francesco Feo's oratorio "Ruth" was published in Rome at this time.

Christoph Förster this year wrote a short Italian opera, called "drama per musica".

Baldassare Galuppi wrote his opera "Sirbace" this year at London. The libretto was by Stampa.

Francesco Geminiani's "Pièces de clavecin" was published this year at London.

Gluck's "Demetrio" with libretto by Metastasio (re-arranged) was performed this season at Reggio.

Carl Heinrich Graun's opera "Artaserse" was produced this season at Berlin.

Maurice Greene published his "Forty Selected Anthems" at this time.

Handel this year wrote his libretto, "Joseph".

Niccolò Jommelli's oratorio "Betulia liberata" was composed at this time.

Jommelli's opera "Demofoonte" was produced this season at Padua.

Jommelli's "Tito Manlio" was produced this season at Turin.

Giovanni Battista Lampugnani's new version of "Rossane" called "Alessandro nell'Indie" was produced this season at the Haymarket Theatre at London, but Lampugnani was not active in the performance.

Leo wrote "Decebalo", "Il fantastico od Il nuovo Don Chisciotte", and "Serenata del felice parto della regina di Napoli" this year.

N. Logroscino's "Ricciardo" was produced this season.

Nicola Logroscino's "La spedizione di Giosué contro di Amalachiti" was performed this season.

Gennaro Manua's opera "Siroe" was produced this season at Venice.

Gennaro Manua's opera "tito Manlio" was produced this year at Rome.

Moreau's "Titon du Tillet, Le Parnasse françois" (the 1743 supplement) appeared at this time.

Metastasio's libretto "Il Vero omaggio" was first set this year by Reutter (see also Hertel).

Jean-Jacques Rousseau published his "Disertation sur la musique moderne" at this time.

Rousseau composed his ballet "Les Muses galantes" this year.

Sammartini produced his second opera "L'Agrippina moglie di Tiberio" this season. In construction of arias and melody it was similar to Gluck's earlier operas.

Terradellas' opera "Merope" was produced this season at both Florence and Rome.

Evrard Titon de Tillet this year issued a supplement to his book "Le Parnasse françois".

Madeleine Guimard, French ballet dancer, was born this year (died 1816).

"A Choice Collection of Hymns" appeared this year at Philadelphia.

In the Pennsylvania Magazine of History, Vol. XVI this year, it was stated: "In the Moravian Church, at the corner of Race and Broad Street, there were two organs in 1743" (Madeira) and from this year . . . "dates the History of the American Pianoforte, for Gustavus

1743(cont.)
Hessclius manufactured Spinets in Philadelphia as early as 1743."

From this year forward St. Peter's Church in Salem, Massachusetts had an unbroken record of organs.

A concert association was founded this year that ultimately became the nucleus for the Gewandhaus Concerts. The first concert was given this season. This was the orchestra of which Mendelssohn became the conductor many years later.

Robert Blair's "The Grave" was published this year. The theme of life, death & immortality was its subject.

The final revision and extension of Pope's "The Dunciad" was at this time.

Nicolas Lancret, French painter, died this year (born 1690).

Hyacinthe Rigaud, French painter, died this year (born 1659).

Thomas Jefferson, 3rd U. S. President, was born at this time (died 1826).

The English defeated the French this year in the Battle of Dettingen. This inspired Handel's "Te Deum".

(to 1744) Jean Marie Leclair "l'aîné" visited the court of Don Philip of Spain at Chambéry during this period.

(to 1744) Rousseau was secretary to the French Embassy at Venice during this year.

(to 1744) Tiepolo painted the ceiling perspectives at the Church of the Scalzi in Venice at this time.

(to 1745) Hogarth painted the "Marriage à la Mode" series during this period. It was a particularly satirical work and is at the National Gallery at London.

(to 1748) John Beard was engaged at Covent Garden for these five years.

(to 1748, March) Elizabeth Hare carried on the business in another shop "Viol and Hautboy" in Birchin Lane during these years. She stayed until March of 1748 when the shop was destroyed by fire.

(to 1754) Isfrid Kayser, German 18th century composer, published his masses, psalms, 3 suites ("Parthiae"), opus 4, for harpsichord at Augsburg during this period.

(to 1761) Meinrad Spiess, German priest and composer, was a member of Mizler's "Society of Musical Sciences" for these eighteen years at the end of which he died.

(to 1778) These were the dates assigned to the Mannheim School, a group of musicians that formed the elector palatine's court orchestra at Mannheim during the reign of the Duke Carl Theodor.

(to 1772) "Vierzehnheiligen", a façade done by Neumann, the German Baroque architect, during these years was 361' wide.

(to 1782) Martin Smith was or-

1743(cont.)

ganist at Gloucester Cathedral for this long term.

c.1743

Richard Meares, jr., English instrument maker, music printer and publisher, died at this time in London (birthdate unknown).

Barsanti's "Concerti grossi . . .(for strings, wind and kettledrums) . . .," opus 3 was issued at this time at Edinboro.

6 concertos for violin by Francesco Geminiani were published this year at London.

Walsh's first collected edition of Handel's "Coronation Anthems for George II" appeared this year. The order was different from previous printings and #2 was omitted.

Handel's 22 Italian Duets with Continuo appeared with #19, "Fronda leggiera e mobile" included.

Handel's "Water Music" was issued this year in an augmented edition for harpsichord.

Jean Marie Leclair "l'aîné" wrote "Six concerto" in a second book this year.

1744

(January 3) Giovanni Battista Lampugnani's opera "Alfonso" was produced on this date at London.

(January 8) Hasse's opera "Ipermestra" (libretto by Metastasio) was produced this season at Vienna.

(January 13) Gluck's Italian opera, La Sofonisba" (libretto by Francesco Silvani) was produced on this date at the Teatro Regio Ducal in Milan. The work was also called "Siface" and was dedicated to a member of Prince Lobkowitz' family.

(January 15) Charles Hubert Gervais, French composer, died on this date at Paris (born 1671, February 19).

(January 19) Johann Friedrich Lampe's"The Queen of Spain, or Farinelli in Madrid" was produced at the Haymarket Theatre in London on this evening.

(January 21) Clegg was declared insane at this time and confined to Bedlam Hospital.

(January 23) Altnikol was awarded four thaler on this date to help him finance his return to his fatherland.

(January 27) Miss Plunkett, who was billed as "a scholar of Mr. Dubourg's lately arrived from Dublin", gave a concert this evening at the Haymarket Theatre in London.

(February 10) The first performance of Handel's "Semele" took place on this date at London. The words were by William Congreve (arranged by Pope) and the production was at Covent Garden.

(February 15) František Václav Mica, Moravian composer and tenor, died on this day (born 1694, September 5 at Třebíč, Moravia).

(February 18) Arne's oratorio

"The Death of Abel" was performed this evening at Smock Alley Theatre in Dublin.

(February 20) Alexandre Guenin, French violinist and composer, was born this year at Maubeuge (died 1819).

(February 27) Miss Plunkett, the violinst, appeared again this evening at the Haymarket Theatre in London.

(March 1) Arne's incidental music for "The Rehearsal" was performed this evening at the Aungier Street Theatre in London.

(March 1) The Royal Decree dealing with D. Scarlatti's Portuguese assets was issued on this date.

(March 2) Handel's oratorio "Joseph and his Brethren" with words by James Miller was premiered on this date at Covent Garden in London.

(March 9) Doles on this date conducted the first performance of his festival cantata in celebration of the anniversary of the founding of the Gewandhaus Concerts.

(March 10) Arne's "Alfred" was produced this evening at Dublin.

(March 13) Anselm Bayly was admitted priest of the Chapel Royal at this time.

(March 13) Veracini's "Sonate accademiche a violino Solo" was licensed for publication in England this year by King George II.

(March 18) Charles Simon Favart's

(cont.) "Acajou" was first performed this evening at Paris.

(Spring) After considerable re-arranging and re-casting, Rameau's less than successful "Dardanus" was revived this season at the Royal Academy of Music in Paris. Three of the acts were rewritten.

(March 31) Joseph Campra, double-bass player, died on this date (baptized 1662, September 10 at Aix).

(April 3) Hasse's oratorio "La deposizione della croce" (words by Pasquini) was produced on this date at Dresden.

(April 12) Casanova on this date returned to his native Venice. He had been on a brief journey in Italy. He made the trip after taking his vows.

(April 16) Johann Friedrich Lampe's "The Kiss Accepted and Returned" was produced on this date at the Haymarket Theatre in London.

(April 23) Gluck appears on this evening at a small theatre in Haymarket where he performed on a glass harmonica.

(April 23) N. Logroscino's "Leandro" was produced on this date.

(April 24) Giovanni Battista Lampugnani's opera "Alceste" was produced on this date at London.

(April 26) Arne's incidental music for "Theodosius, or The Force of Love" was performed this evening at the Smock Alley Theatre in London.

1744(cont.)

(April 30) Gluck's "Rasserna" was performed on this evening.

(May 4) Marianne Martinez (s) was born on this date at Vienna. She was an Austrian composer of Spanish descent and studied under Metastasio, who shared his apartment with her, her sister and her father.

(May 13) Gluck's Italian opera "La finta schiava" (libretto by Silvani) was produced on this date at Venice.

(May 18) Joseph Beer, Bohemian clarinetist, was born at this time at Grünewald, Bohemia (died 1811 at Potsdam).

(May 24) The Pennsylvania Gazette in this issue reported, "among other curiosities Eight Bells ringing truly, both round Ringing and Changes, much in the Imitation of Ringing in England".

(June 8) William Black on this date made the following entry in his journal, "I rose from my Bed and pass'd two Hours in writing' the rest of the time 'till Breakfast I spent with my Fiddle and Flute . . . ."

(June 17) Georg Sigismund Gebel married the daughter of organist Johann Georg Hofmann at this time.

(Summer) Handel obviously appreciated S. M. Cibber's singing. This was shown by his writing to Charles Jennens at this time saying that he had "some hopes" she would sing for him.

(June 29) Andre Campra, French composer of Italian descent,

(cont.) composer of Italian descent, died on this date at Versailles (born 1660, December 4 at Aix-en-Provence). He followed in Lully's footsteps.

(July 12 and August 2) The Pennsylvania Gazette in these issues advertised an Unparallelled (sic) Musical Clock, made by "Master of Machinery David Lockwood".

(July 19-August 17) Handel composed his secular oratorio "Hercules" between these dates. The words were by the Rev. Thomous Broughton and it was announced as a "musical drama" although it was both performed and published as an "oratorio".

(July 20) Clegg was discharged as cured from Bedlam Hospital on this date.

(August 11) Johann Gottlieb Schwencke, German bassoonist and composer, was born at this time in Saxony (died 1823, December 7).

(August 19) Carlo Arrigoni, Italian composer, died on this day at Florence (born 1697, December 5 at Florence).

(August 23, September 5, September 10) Handel's "Belshazzar" was dated on the original autograph with these dates. He started composing the work on the first date given, ended the first part and scored it on the second, and finished it on the third.

(Autumn) G. Scarlatti's opera "Ezio" was given at the Teatro Pubblico in Pisa (libretto by Metastasio).

1744(cont.)

(October 17) Giuseppe Bartolomeo Guarneri, Italian violin maker, died at this time in Cremona (born 1692, August 21).

(October 31) Leonardo Leo, Italian composer, died at Naples at this time (born 1694, August 5). Among his pupils were Jommelli and Piccini.

(November 2) The first subscription concert at Manchester was performed on this date.

(November 21) Gluck's Italian opera "Ipermestra" (libretto by Metastasio) was produced this evening at the Teatro San Giovanni in Venice.

(December 8) Pierre Joseph Candeille, French composer, was born on this date at Estaires' (died 1827, April 24 at Chantilly).

(December 15) Clegg was once admitted to Bedlam Hospital on this date.

(December 26) Gluck's Italian opera "Poro" (libretto by Metastasio) was produced at the Teatro Regio Ducal in Milan this evening.

Hasse's opera "Semiramide riconosciuta" (libretto by Metastasio) was produced on this date at Venice.

(December 29) (Don) Pompeo Canniciari, Italian composer, died at this time at Rome (born 1670 at Rome).

(January) A letter from Altnikol written this month stated that he had been "Choralis" in the Church of

(cont.) St. Maria Magdalena at Breslau for four years and was anxious to return to his native land.

(January) E. R. Duni's opera "Artaserse" was produced this season at the Teatro della Pergola in Florence.

(February) Cardonne's first published composition, an "air tendre" was printed this month in the "Mercure de France".

(July) Casanova's first opportunity to become known as a dancer came this year during a journey to the Near East. Here he became acquainted with an adventurer, Count Bonneval. The latter was known throughout Europe as Achmet Pasha. By this time Casanova had changed from clerical clothing to a uniform.

(December) Handel's "Semele" was produced this month at the King's Theatre, Haymarket in London.

Giovanni Ansani, Italian composer and tenor, was born this year at Rome (died 1826, July 15 at Florence).

Michel de La Barre, French flutist and composer, died this year at Paris according to a major source (born c.1674).

Caspar Bohrer, trumpeter and double-bass player, was born this year at Mannheim (died 1809, November 14 at München).

William Broderip, English organist, was born at this time at Canterbury (died 1770 at Canterbury).

1744(cont.)

Marianne Davies, singer, harp-sichordist, flutist and har-monica player, was born this year, possible at London (death date unknown).

John Abraham Fisher, English violinist and composer, was born this year, either at Dunstable or London (died 1806, May).

Henri Hamal, church musician, author and composer, was born this year at Liège (died 1820, September 17 at Liège).

Johann Gottfried Herder, writer and music critic, was born (died 1803).

Johann Friedrich Lampe (ii), German composer, singer and clavier player, was born at this time in Wolfenbüttel (deathdate unknown).

Zophar Lyon, possibly the father of James, "Yeoman of the Town of Newark" died (birthdate unknown).

Gasparo Pacchierotti, Italian and a famous "evirato" who settled in Padua after his retirement was born this year (died 1824).

Friedrich Ramm, oboist, was born at this time in Mannheim (died 1811).

Domenico Sarro, Italian com-poser, died this year at Naples (born 1679).

Santo Seraphin, violin maker, died at this time (born 1699).

John Simms, English organist, was born this year at Stour-

(cont.) bridge (died 1824).

Richard Woodward, Irish or-ganist and composer, was born at this time in Dublin (died 1777, November 22).

Joseph Zistler, violinist, was born this year (died 1794, March 18).

Altnikol became a pupil of J. S. Bach's this year at the Thomasschule in Leipzig.

Arne and his wife remained in Dublin until this date.

During his absence this year, Astorga's Sicilian estates were sold. The previous year his wife and sister whom he had deserted had applied for permission to sell since they were heavily in debt.

Johann Andreas Bach was organ-ist at Ohrdruf from this date forward.

J. S. Bach's prolific writing slowed down at this juncture.

K. P. E. Bach married Johanna Maria Dannemann at this time. She was the daughter of a wine merchant and they were married at Berlin

Bellinzani mentioned his "advanced age" this year.

Pierre Montan Berton made his début this season as a bass at the Paris Opéra.

Josse Boutmy was appointed first organist to the Royal Chapel at this time.

Bernard de Bury became Royal music-master at this time.

C. Cannabich joined the Mannheim orchestra this year as a "scholar" (presumably an apprentice).

Caporale, Cervetto, and Pasqualini were playing at the concerts at Hickford's Room this season.

Casanova this year came to live with the family of a comediat at Ancona. The household included a mother, 2 daughters and 2 sons. One of the sons was posing as the castrato Bellino, however, "he" was later revealed to be female. The girl later sang under the name of Teresa Lanti.

Chiarini lived at Venice at least up to this time.

Henri de Croes this year became a first violinist in the Royal Chapel at Brussels.

Dauvergne was taken into the Paris Opéra orchestra at this time.

Doles was appointed cantor of Freiberg this year.

William Felton at this time was one of the stewards at the Three Choirs meeting at Hereford.

Jean-Joseph Fiocco resigned this year from court service, only two years before his death.

Louis Fuzelier, librettist of Rameau's "Las Indes Galantes", this year joined La Bruere, librettist of Rameau's "Dardanus" as editor of "Mercure de France".

Martin Gerbert von Harnau was ordained a priest at this time.

C. A. Grenser established himself this year as an independent woodwind-maker in Dresden.

Thomas Griffin at this time arranged to have an organ built in the church at St. Mildred.

Petrus Hallendaal was living in Amsterdam this year and was married there.

J. L. Krebs was appointed organist at Zeitz this year.

Joseph Mondonville succeeded Gervais this season as "Surintendant de la Chapelle du Roi".

Angelo Monticelli sang this year in "Alfonso". He had not previously attempted to sing arias as bravura as these.

Antonio Montagnana sang in Porpora's "Onorio" at the Theatre in Lincoln's Inn Fields this season.

C. Nichelmann, in Berlin, this year was appointed second harpsichordist to the Royal Chapel. He accompanied Frederick the Great, a flutist of quite some ability.

Francois Philedor, at the age of 18 this year, was one of the finest chess players and was able to earn a living at the game.

There was no trace of Catherine Plunkett after this year.

R. Pockrich performed on the musical glasses this season at Dublin.

When the position of maestro
of the Royal Chapel at Naples
was vacated this year on the
death of Leo, Porpora applied
for the job.

Porpora was certainly at Venice
at this time, however, no
longer teaching at the "Ospedale della Pietà".

William Savage this year
became a Gentleman in Ordinary
in the Chapel Royal as a bass.

Pietro Scarlatti applied for
the position of maestro di
cappella this year at Naples.
He was not accepted.

Adamo Scola was a Governor
of the "Decayed Musicians
Fund" at this time.

Burkat Shudi this year made
a single manual harpsichord,
#160.

Johann Stamitz, Bohemian
composer, violinist and conductor, married this year.
He had 4 children, composers
Carl and Anton and 2 daughters,
Franziska and a child who died
in infancy.

In the "avertissement" of his
"Sonate Accademiche" this year,
Veracini stated "If each of
these sonatas comprises 4 or 5
movements, remember that this
has been done for the sake of
the richness and enhancement
of the book, and in order to
give greater diversion to
lovers and dilettanti of music".

S. Weiss at this time became
the highest paid instrumentalist at the Dresden Court.

Cecillia Young returned to
London this year.

E. Young was in the original
cast of Handel's "Semele"
this year at Ruckholt House,
Essex.

Avison's "Twelve Concertos"
were issued this year at
London.

J. S. Bach's cantata #116,
"Du Friedefürst, Herr Jesu
Christ" was written this year
for twenty-fifth Sunday after
Trinity.

The second part of J. S.
Bach's "Das Wohltemperierte
Clavier" was finished at this
time at Leipzig. The 24
preludes and fugues in all
keys was actually a compilation
of some early works and many
later works. They are arranged
in systematic order. The
collection was prominent among
Bach's latest compositions.

K. P. E. Bach this year revised
his Sonata in d minor, written
twelve years earlier.

K. P. E. Bach's opus 2,
"6 "Württemberg Sonatas" were
published at this time.

Wilhelm Friedemann Bach
dedicated six sonatas to Dr.
Georg Ernst Stahl at this time.

Blanchard's "Te Deum Laudamus"
(ms.) was completed this year.

Metastasio's libretto to
"La Danza" was first set this
year by Bonno (see also Gluck
and Hasse).

The third edition of Carey's
"Musical Century" was published

this year by John Simpson at
London.

Chiarini at this time wrote
a Christmas oratorio at Venice.

Chiarini's opera "Meride e
Selinunte" appeared at this
time.

V. L. Ciampi's "Arminio" was
produced this year at the
Teatro Nuovo.

Corselli's "Achille in Sciro"
was completed at this time.

William Felton's first set of
six concertos for organ or
harpsichord, opus 1, was
published this year at London.

Francois Francoeur wrote his
operas "Les Augustales" and
"Le Retour du Roi" at this
time.

Caterina Galli sang in Handel's
"Joseph and his Brethren"
this season.

Baldassare Galuppi wrote his
opera "Ricimero" this year at
Milan (libretto by Silvani).

Gluck's "Demetrio" was presented
this season at Bologna. It
was also know as "Cleonice".

Johann Valentin Görner's
second set of music composed
to Hagedorn's poems was published at this time.

Carl Heinrich Graun's operas
"Alessandro e Poro", "Catone
in Utica" and "La Festa del
Imeneo" were produced this
season at Berlin.

Maurice Greene wrote his
oratorio "The Force of Truth"
at this time.

Metastasio's libretto for
"Antigone" was first set this
year by Hasse (see also Cafaro,
Conforto, Durán, Galuppi, Gluck,
Jommelli, Lampugnani, Paisielo,
Piccinni, Traetta, and
Zingarelli).

Metastasio's libretto for
"Ipermestra" was first set this
year by Hasse (see also Cafaro,
Duni (E.G.), Feo, Fortunati,
Galuppi, Giacomelli, Gluck,
Jommelli, Martin y Soler,
Morlacchi (altered by S. Sca-
tizzi), Naumman, Paisiello,
Piccinni, Sarti).

Hellendaal's opus 1, "6 Sonate
a violino Solo a basso" was
published this year at
Amsterdam.

Holzbauer wrote the ballet music
for Hasse's setting of
"Ipermestra" produced this
season at the Burg Theatre.

Samuel Howard at this time
composed the music for the
pantomime "The Amorous Goddess
or Harlequin Married".

Jommelli's "Alessandro nell'
Indio" and "Ciro riconosciuto"
were both produced this season
at Ferrara.

Giovanni Battista Lampugnani's
"La finta schiava" was produced
this season at Venice.

Leo wrote "La contesa dell'Amore
colla Virtù", "La fedeltà
odiata" and "Vologeso" at this
time.

Leo composed for Royal Chapel

introits, graduals, offertories and communions for the Sundays of Lent this year.

N. Logroscino's "La ciommetella correvata" was produced this season.

The Lully-Marais "Alcide" was revived again this season.

Pescetti's opera "Aristodemo" was performed this season at London.

Porpora's "Le nozze d'Ercole e d'Ebe" was performed this season at the Teatro S. Giovanni Crisostomo this season on the last evening of Carnival.

Rameau's incidental music for the Fair Theatres, "Les Jardin de l'Hymen on la Rose" to a pastorale by Piron written this year has been lost.

Christopher Saur of Germantown this year published "Das Psalter . . . des David".

G. Scarlatti's opera "Pompeo in Armenia" was produced at the Teatro Pubblico in Pisa this season. The libretto was by Vitturi.

Domingo Terradella's "Artaserse" was produced this season at Venice.

The eleventh printing of the Reverend John Tufts' "A Very Plain and Easy Introduction to the Whole Art of Singing Psalm tunes" was completed this year at Boston.

F. M. Veracini's opera "L' errore di Salomone" was completed at this time.

The Italian opera "Rodelinda" of this year may have been composed by Veracini.

Zelbell's opera-ballet "Sueas hogtid" was performed this season.

The Castle Society Concerts were held for about 14 years after this date at the Haberdashers' Hall.

The Conservatorio dei Poveri was in existence until this year.

The Moravian's Collegium Musicum was founded at Bethlehem at this time. They rehearsed choral and instrumental music.

The Josephine Theater was closed this year in order to remodel it into a ballroom.

David Allan, artist known for his vignettes and drawings, was born this year (died 1796).

Alexander Pope, great English satirical poet, died at this time (born 1688).

Dr. Samuel Johnson this year wrote the biography of Richard Savage, a "Scapegrace" poet and friend of his.

Frederick William II, King of Prussia was born this year (died 1797). His reign included the years 1786-1797).

The Count of Saint-Germain made a visit to London at this time.

William Black, Secretary of the Commissioners, was appointed this year by Governor Gooch

1744(cont.)

of Virginia to unite Colonies of Pennsylvania and Maryland to negotiate with Iroquois Indians who were living at Philadelphia.

(to 1745) Theresa Cornelys was in Vienna during this season.

(to 1745) Henry Waylett published Davis' "Solos for a German Flute" during this period.

(to 1745) Elisabeth Duparc participated in Handel's "Belshazzar", "Hercules" and "Joseph" during these seasons.

(to 1745) The "Thesaurus musicus" was published at this time by John Simpson.

(to 1745) At the Thomasschule, a "Chorordnung for 1744-45" listed the distribution of parts in the four choirs.

(to 1745) The "second Silesian war" occured in Europe during this period.

(to 1747) From the date of the Venice production , "Enzio", Pescetti's return to Italy must have taken place during these years.

(to 1749) F. X. Brixi studied music at the monastic college at Kosmonosy for these five years.

(to 1771) Giuseppe Maio succeeded Leo as first master of the Neapolitan Royal Court in 1744 and held the position throughout this period.

(to 1793) Lorenzo Fago was

(cont.) first maestro at the Conservatorio della Pietà dei Turchini during this long term.

1745

(January 5) The first performance of Handel's "Hercules" was on this date at the King's Theatre, Haymarket in London. The words were by Thomas Broughton.

(January 17) Arne's "The Temple of Dullness" was produced on this evening at the Drury Lane Theatre in London.

(January 24) Wincenty Maxylewicz, Polish composer, died on this date at Cracow (born 1685).

(January 25) Johann Friedrich Lampe's "Pyramus and Thisbe" was produced this evening at Covent Garden in London.

(January 31) Gluck's Italian opera "Ippolito" (libretto by Gioseffo Gorino Corio) was produced at this time at the Teatro Regio Ducal in Milan. It was also known as "Fedra".

(February 1) Venturini was listed as a violinist among the court musicians at Stuttgart, and was pensioned as such effective this day.

(February 2) Johann Peter Salomon, German violinist and composer, was baptized in Bonn at this time.

(February 9) Two arias by Brivio were included in the pasticcio "L'inconstanza delusa" performed on this date at the King's Theatre in London. The work has also been referred to as an opera and one source placed the performance at the Little Haymarket Theatre.

(February 11) Arne's "The Picture, or The Cuckold in Conceit" with incidental music only, was performed this evening at the Drury Lane Theatre in London.

(February 18) Nicola Fago ("Il Tarantino"), composer and teacher, died this day at Naples (born 1677, February 26).

(February 22) João de Sousa Carvalho, Portuguese composer, was born at this time at Estremoz (died 1798 probably at Borba).

(February 23) Rameau's comedy-ballet "La Princess de Navarre" was given this evening in the Grande Écurie at Versailles. Voltaire provided the text.

(March 4) Charles Dibdin, English composer, author and entertainer, was born at Southampton and baptized on this date (died 1814, July 25 at London).

(March 6) Willem de Fesch' serenata, "Love and Friendship" was performed at Covent Garden this evening.

(March 13) L. N. Clérambault's "L'Idylle de Saint-Cyr" was performed at this time at the Paris Opéra.

(March 17) François Francoeur's one-act opera "Zélindor, roi des silphes" was produced on this date at Versailles.

(March 19) Nicolas Séjan,

(cont.) French organist and composer, was born this day at Paris (died 1819, March 16).

(March 20) Arne's "Alfred" was produced at this time at the Drury Lane Theatre in London.

(March 20) Bernhard Theodor Breitkopf, printer, was born on this date at Leipzig (died 1820 at St. Petersburg). This publishing house has continued to the present time with various slight changes in ownership.

(March 25) Nicolas Étienne Framery, French author and musician, was born on this day at Rouen (died 1810, November 26).

(March 27) Handel's oratorio "Belshazzar" was produced this evening at the King's Theatre in London. The words were by William Jennens.

(March 29) Rosa Scarlatti, daughter of Domenico and Anastasia and member of the fourth generation of the Scarlatti family, was born on this date (died sometime after 1757).

(March 30) The baptismal certificate for Rosa Scarlatti was dated as above.

(March 31) Rameau's opera "Platéo" was performed this evening at Versailles at a celebration for the wedding of the Dauphin Louis and Maria-Theresa of Spain. The text was by Autreauad Le Valois d'Orville.

(JOHANN GEORG) LEOPOLD MOZART
1756-1791

1745(cont.)

(April 15) Arne's "King Pepin's Campaign" was performed this evening at the Drury Lane Theatre in London.

(April 18) Francesco Venturini, Italian or possibly French violinist and composer, died on this date at Hanover (birthdate unknown).

(April 26) Jean-Baptiste Cupis played this evening at Prince d'Axdore's on the occasion of the Dauphin's marriage.

(April 29) Giovanni Battista Paganini (Niccolò Paganini's paternal grandfather was married on this date to Maria Angela Teresa Gambaro, a native of Montesignano in the province of Genoa. They resided at Vico dei Parmigiani after being married in Genoa.

(May 7) Karl Philipp Stamitz, composer, violinist, violist and son of Johann Stamitz, was born at this time at Mannheim (died 1801, November 9 at Jena).

(June 28) Antoine Forqueray, one of the greatest viol players and a major composer of his time, died on this day at Nantes (born 1671). Another major source placed his birth at 1672).

(July 1) Matthias van den Gheyn became town carillonist of Louvain at this time.

(July 12) Westen Linnert, a member of the Stockholm Royal Orchestra, died on this date (birthdate unknown).

(July 15) Friedrich Wilhelm

(cont.) Heinrich Benda, German composer, was born at this time at Potsdam (died 1814, June 19 at Potsdam).

(August 5) Ranuri Calzabigi, a future collaborator with Gluck, produced his first libretto, "L'impero dell'universo, diviso con Giove" for the marriage of the Dauphin to the Infanta Maria Theresa of Spain. Manna composed the music which with the libretto was completed at Naples.

(August 8) Gerhard Heinrich Romberg, German clarinetist and music director at Münster, was born on this date. He was a brother of Anton Romberg born in 1742. They lived at Bonn.

(August 10) François Francoeur's one-act opera "Zélindor, roi des silphes" was produced at the Paris Opéra this evening.

(August 18) Ludwig Fischer, German bass, was born on this date at Mainz (died 1825, July 10).

(August 20) The last Manchester concert for which any record has survived was performed at this time.

(September 18) This date marked the first public singing of "God Save the King".

(Autumn) V. L. Ciampi's "L'amore ingegnoso" was produced this season at Fiorentini.

(Autumn) Gluck accompanied Prince Lobkovitz to London at this time. He stopped in Paris en route and perhaps met Rameau, who had recently produced a new work, "Les Fêtes de Polymnie".

(Autumn) G. Scarlatti's opera
"L'Olimpiade" was produced
this season at the Teatro
Pubblico in Pisa (libretto by
Metastasio).

(September 21) Henry Waylett
issued the first edition of
"Rule Britannia" sometime
shortly after this date.

(September 28) The news of the
defeat of Sir John Cope's army
at Prestonpans became known
on this day at London.

(October 7) Johann Hasse's
second version of "Arminio"
(libretto by Pasquini) was performed on this date by command
of Frederick the Great when he
entered Dresden after the battle
of Kesselsdorf. It was not
the same work as the same
titled work in 1730.

(October 12) Rameau's opera-
ballet "Les Fêtes de Polymnie"
was produced this evening at
Paris. This was Rameau's
first collaboration with
Cahusac.

(November 22) J. S. Bach's
cantata #116, "Du Friedefürst,
Herr Jesu Christ" was performed
on this day at Leipzig.

(November 23) The following
appeared on the title page of a
libretto by Locatelli this
year. "Diana nelle Selve.
Componimento Drammatico da
reppresentarsi in Musica nelle
Ellettorale Corte il 23
Novembre 1745 per Festiggiare
il Glorioso Nome di Sua Altezza
Serenissima Elettorale Clemente

(cont.) Augusto Arcievesco di
Colonia, Prencipe ed Elettore
di Sacro Romano Imperio. La
Poesia del Sig. Gio Battista
Locatelli."

(November 27) Rameau's opera-
ballet "Le Temple de la Gloire"
(libretto by Voltaire) was
produced on this date at
Versailles in the Grande
Ecurie.

(November 30) Johann August
Bach, lawyer and oldest son of
K. P. E. Bach, grandson of
J. Sebastian and member of the
seventh generation of the Bach
family, was born on this date
(died 1789, April 24).

(December 6) Christoph Förster,
German composer, died at this
time in Rudolstadt (born 1693,
November 30).

(December 12) Charles Simon
Favart on this date married
Marie Duronceray, an actress,
singer and playwright.

(December 23) Jan Zelenka,
Bohemian composer who worked
mostly in Dresden as a court
composer, died at this time
(born 1679, October 16).

(December 24) Matthias van den
Gheyn married Marie Catherine
Lints on this date. They had
seventeen children.

(December 26) D. Perez's opera
"Alessandro nell'Indie" was
produced at this time in Genoa.

(January) Giovanni Lorenzo
Gregori, Italian violinist and
composer, died this year at
Lucca (born 1663).

(January) Johann Peter Salomon,

German violinist, opera impresario and composer, was born
this month at Bonn (died 1815,
November 28).

(January) Durante again became
"primo maestro" at the Conservatorio di Sant'Onofrio
this month.

(February) Marie Justine
Benoîte Favart performed this
month in Charles Simon Favart's
"Les Fêtes publiques" at the
Opéra-Comique.

(May) Rameau by this time had
become a court musician and
was granted a pension and the
title of "Compositeur du
Cabinet du Roi".

(August) Richard Fitzwilliam,
who donated his art and music
collection to the University
of Cambridge, was born this
month (died 1816, February 14).

(September) Burney arranged
"God Save the King" at this
time for Covent Garden.

(December) Casanova arrived back
in Venice this month. He was
poor, having lost all his
possessions at Corfu where
he moved with questionable
companions.

(December) King Friedrich II
of Prussia occupied Dresden
at this time.

Tommaso Albinoni, Italian
violinist and composer, died
this year (born 1674).

Jacques Autreau died this year
at 89 shortly after the performance of Rameau's setting
of his text at court.

Maximus Sozontovich Berezovsky,
Russian composer, was born this
year at Glukhov in the Ukraine
(died 1777, March at St.
Petersburg).

T. Bertin de la Dové, French
composer, died at this time
in Paris (born c.1680 at
Paris).

Adam Horacy Casparini, Polish
organ builder, died this year
at Wroclaw (born 1676 at
Wroclaw).

Ann Catley, English soprano,
was born this year at London
(died 1789, October 14 near
Brentford).

Wilhelm Cramer, violinist, was
born at this time at Mannheim
(died 1799, October 5 at
London).

Dr. George K. Jackson was
born this year (died 1822).

John James, English composer
and organist, noted for his
skill in improvisation, died
at this time (birthdate unknown).
His published compositions included only a few songs and
organ pieces.

Nicolas Jean Mereaux, French
organist and composer, was born
this year at Paris (died 1797
at Paris).

Franz Mitscha, music director
to Count Questenberg in Jaro-
meritz, died on this date
(birthdate unknown).

Jean Baptiste Morin, French
composer, died this year at
Paris (born c.1667 at Orléans).

Louis Henri Paisible, French

violinist and composer, was born this year at Paris. He shot himself and died as a result (died 1783 at St. Petersburg).

John Parke, oboist and composer, was born at this time in London (died 1829, August 2 at London).

Theodoric Pedrini, Italian (probably) musician and priest, died this year in China. While he composed violin sonatas under the name "Nipredi" and taught the sons of the Chinese emperor, he also built instruments (born 1670).

Abbé Pellegrin died this year (born 1663).

Francois André (Danican) lived in Amsterdam at this time.

John Ravenscroft, the English violinist and composer, died this year at London. He was noted for the composition of hornpipes (birthdate unknown).

Paolo Antonio Testore, violin maker, died this year (born 1715).

Francesco Valle, Spanish composer, died at this time (born 1665).

Arne was once more engaged as a composer this year at Drury Lane Theatre. He produced "The Temple of Dullness", a comic opera in two acts.

Gottlieb Friedrich Bach became court painter at the Meiningen court at this time.

Most of Bartolomeo Bernardi's works written for the Danish (cont.) court apparently perished this year in the fire at Copenhagen.

Annibale Pio Fabri, Italian tenor and composer, this year was made president of the Accademia Filarmonica of Bologna. This was the third time he held the position.

Marie Justine Benoîte Favart went to Paris this year with her mother.

William Felton was awarded the Master of Arts degree this year by St. John's College at Cambridge.

Christoph Förster succeeded Johann Graf at this time as conductor of Rudolstadt. This was also the year of his death.

Early upright pianoforte #1631 preserved at the Museum of the Conservatoire Royal de Musique at Brussels was made by Friederici and carried this date.

Johann Ernst Galliard had a benefit concert this season at Lincoln's Inn Fields Theatre.

Giuseppe Giordani, a singer, left Naples this year with his family.

Christoph Willibald Gluck this season was invited to the Haymarket Theatre at London.

J. N. Hamal became an imperial chaplain this year.

Henry Harrington entered Queen's College, Oxford at this time to take orders but instead he developed a craving for music and poetry.

Joseph Haydn's brother, Michael,

this year became a fellow-chorister at the choir school of St. Stephen's in Vienna.

During his second visit to Scotland at this time, Denis Hempson played before Prince Charles at Edinboro.

Arvid Hopken was made a cavalry captain at this time.

Francis Ireland was awarded the Bachelor of Arts degree this year at Dublin.

H. Johnsen became a court organist at this time.

H. Johnsen became organist at St. Clara's, Stockholm this year.

Gennaro Manua succeeded Francesco Feo as maestro de cappella of the St. Annunziata Church this season.

William Mason was awarded the Bachelor of Arts degree at this time from Cambridge.

Franz Meyer von Schauensee lived in Lucerne at this juncture and divided his time between music and his career as a civil servant.

Philippo Nicoloni's troupe of "Enfants Pantomimes" were a great success in Frankfurt and Potsdam this year.

François Philidor, under pressure from his creditors, went to Amsterdam this year. He played chess successfully against Stamma, the author of "Les Stratagèmes du jeu d'échecs".

T. Pinto this year married Sibilla Gronamann, daughter of a German minister.

Porpora was unable to leave Venice at this time and the position of maestro at the Royal Chapel in Naples went to Giuseppe di Maio.

The second opera period began at this time with Rameau's appointment to the court of Louis XV.

Tontines were taken out by Rameau this year for his wife, daughter and second son.

J. H. Roman retired from active musical life in the capitol at this time. He spent his remaining years on his estate at Haraldsmåla.

Rameau this year entered the La Pouplinière establishment.

David Rutherford, Scottish music publisher, at this time worked in London at St. Martin's Court near Leicester Fields "at the sign of the Violin and German Flute".

This was the fourth year of J. Stamitz' position at the Mannheim court. He became concert master and director of chamber music with the highest salary payable to any court musician.

Antonio Tonelli, cellist, organist and composer, left Alassio this year. He returned to Capri and opened a free school for singing for poor children.

Burney this season heard F. M. Veracini conduct the orchestra at Hickford's Rooms.

Voltaire at this time noted Rameau's poverty and gave him all the payment for "La Princesse de Navarre" including his own share.

Noverre appeared this season as a solo dancer in Berlin.

Jan Zach this year became conductor of the Prince Elector's orchestra at Mainz.

Arne's "God bless our noble King" appeared at this time.

Arne's vocal duet "Partoral Dialogue" was written this year.

Avossa wrote a serious opera "Ifigenia in Aulide" this season at Naples.

Wilhelm Friedemann Bach's D major Sonata was published this year at Dresden.

Bertoni's first opera "La vedova accorta" was performed this season at Florence.

Blamont's "Jupiter Vainqueur des Titans" was composed at this time.

Bury and his uncle wrote "Jupiter vainqueur des Titans" and it was performed this season at Versailles.

Cafaro's oratorio "Il figlio prodigo" was written this year.

A motet by Cardonne was sung this season at the French court.

Chilcot produced "Twelve English Songs, the words by

(cont.) Shakespeare and other celebrated poets" at this time.

L. N. Clérambault's "Le Départ du Roi" was performed this season.

Diderot this year wrote a fine survey of the position of the partisans of French (Lully) opera and the proponents of Italian (Rameau) opera.

William Felton published his "Andante with Variations of the third concerto" this year. It was more often known as "Felton's Gavotte".

Willem de Fesch this season wrote his second oratorio, "Joseph". However it was never performed.

Christoph Förster this year wrote the second of two short Italian operas, called "drama per musica".

Baldassare Galuppi wrote his opera "La forza d'amore" this year at Venice (libretto by Panicelli).

Lewis Granom's "Six Sonatas for two German Flutes and a Bass" was published this season.

Carl Heinrich Graun's opera "Adriano in Siria" was produced this season at the Berlin Opera.

Carl Heinrich Graun's opera "Lucio Papirio" was produced this season at the Berlin Opera.

The dramatic pastoral, "Love's Revenge" with music by Maurice Greene, and Handel's "Acis" were performed this season at the Boothall, Gloucester

during the Three Choirs
Festival.

Maurice Greene composed his
"Te Deum" in D major at this
time.

Guillemain published his
Opus XIII, a volume of harpsichord sonatas at this time.
He added a violin accompaniment
"to conform to present-day
taste".

Handel's 22 Italian Duets with
Continuo including #20, "Ahi
nelle sorti umane", appeared
this year in a second edition.

Handel's "Occasional Oratorio"
of this year was composed in
honor of the failure of the
Jacovite uprising.

Handel's song "Stand round
my brave boys" was composed at
this time.

Hasse's pasticcio "Oronte,
re dei Sciti" was heard this
season at Hamburg.

The German march "Hohen fried-
berger" was published at this
time.

Henry Holcombe this year
published as opus 1, solos for
a violin and about the same
time published two collections
of songs, "The Musical Medley
or A Collection of English
Songs and Cantatas set to
Musick" and "The Garland, a
Collection of 11 Songs and
Cantatas".

N. Logroscino's "Don Paduano"
was produced this season.

N. Logroscino's "Li zite" was

(cont.) produced this season.

Gennaro Manua's Opera "Lucio
Papirio" was produced this
year at Rome.

Gennaro Manua's opera "Lucio
Vero" was produced this season
at Naples.

J. J. Rousseau's work "Les
Muses galantes" was performed
this year before le Duc de
Richelieu.

Johann Scheibe this year
published a second edition of
his "Critischer Musikus" at
Leipzig.

Johann Sigismund Scholze (also
known as Sperontes) wrote a
song included in a Masonic
Collection of Songs for
freemasons issued this year.

G. C. Wagenseil wrote "Ariodante"
this year at Venice for production in Italy.

Henry Waylett published C.
Corena's "6 sonatas for 2
German Flutes" at this time.

John Worgan wrote his "Ode on
the Rebellion" at this time.

The Opéra-Comique in Paris was
closed this year because of
its success which created
jealousy on the part of the
large theatres in the area.

The war song "Adieux de la
Tulipe" was popular at this
time with the soldiers of
France.

The Austrian architect Lucas
von Hildebrandt died this year
(born 1668).

Hogarth this year painted
"Portrait of the Artist with
His Dog Trump". It is at the
Tate Gallery in London.

Hogarth finished the engraving
"Marriage à la Mode" at this
time. It is at the Metropolitan
Museum in New York.

British satirist Jonathan
Swift died this year (born 1667).

In the rebellion of this year
John Brown distinguished
himself at the siege of
Carlisle.

Joseph Emanuel Canal, Count
of Malabaila, officer and
humanist, was born this year.
He was partially responsible
for the founding of St. John's
orphanage at Prague (died 1826).

Gerhard von Suneten, father of
Baron Gottfried van Swieten,
returned to Vienna from Leyden
this year. He became Maria
Theresa's favourite physician.

The Pretender this year made
a last effort against the House
of Braunschweig.

The Prussian army laid siege to
Leipzig at this time destroying
the surrounding countryside.

Rebels once again tried this
year to replace the Catholic
Stuart succession, as they had
in 1715. This rebellion also
failed.

(and 1746) Angelo Monticelli
still belonged to the Opera in
London during this period.

(Michelmas and 1747, May)
Altnikol was assistant bass

(cont.) singer at St. Thomas'
and St. Nicholas' churches at
Leipzig at this time. He was
paid "for assistance".

(to 1747) The fife which had
fallen into disuse in military
bands was reintroduced during
this period at Flanders.

(to 1748) John C. Smith
travelled on the European
continent throughout these
three years.

(to 1749) Rameau during this
period composed two ballet-
operas, "Le Temple de la
Gloire" and "Les Fêtes de
l'Hymen et de l'Amour" and two
pastorales héroiques, "Zais"
and "Nais", in which pastoral
divertissements played important parts. In these four
plays the best of his pastoral
music was found.

(and 1750) John Baston's "The
Delightful Pocket Companion
for the German Flute containing
a Choice Collection of . . .
Tunes, curiously adapted to
that Instrument . . ." was
printed in two editions at
London by John Simpson on these
dates, the second and revised
and enlarged edition at the
later date.

(to 1750) Tiepolo painted
"Neptune offering Venice the
Treasures of the Sea" during
these years. The picture is
at the Palazzo Ducale in Venice.

(to 1750) Bernhard C. Weber
wrote "Das wohltemperierte
Clavier" at this time.

(to 1752) Zappis was second
maestro di cappella at Bonn
during this period.

1745(cont.)

(to 1752) The Opéra-Comique de la Foire Saint-Germain was in a state of suppression for these seven years.

(to 1752) The "Essex Inventories" for this period are extant.

(December to 1754) When Zelenka died, Breunich was chosed as his successor as church composer at Dresden and retained the position during this period.

(to 1754) Michael Haydn, having studied the fundamentals of music with the village schoolmaster at Rohrau, became a chorister at St. Stephen's Cathedral in Vienna where he remained for these nine years.

(to 1759) William Felton published four sets of six concertos and one set of eight, plus two sets of eight suites, during this period. The publisher was John Johnson.

(to 1760) Eberlin composed Latin dramas for the pupils of the Benedictine monastery at Salzburg during this decade.

(and 1763, May 14) Having burned in 1745, the Teatro Malvezzi was replaced by a new building designed by Antonio Bibiena. This became the Teatro Comunale which opened on May 14, 1763 with Gluck's "Il trionfo di Clelia" (libretto by Metastasio). Gluck was present at the opening.

(and 1765) Breitkopf passed the printing business on to his only son in 1745 and in 1765 the firm became B. C. Breitkopf

(cont.) & Sohn.

(to 1765) The establishment of the Waylett family of music sellers in London took place at this time.

(to 1770) Tommaso Guarducci appeared successfully at most of the chief Italian theatres throughout these years.

(to 1782) Joseph Seegr was organist at the church of the Knights of the Cross in the Old Town during this period.

c.1745

Gennaro Astaritta, Italian composer, was born this year probably at Naples (deathdate unknown).

Francesco Benucci, Italian bass, was born this year (died 1824, April 5 at Florence).

Nicolas Dezède (Dezèdes, Desaides), French composer, was born at this time (died 1792 at Paris).

Francesco Feo died according to one source (see 1761 for generally accepted date).

Bras Francisco de Lima, composer of oratorios, was born this year (died 1813).

Gaetano Guadagnini, Italian violin maker, was born this year at Piacenza (death date unknown).

Lorenzo Guadagnini, Italian violin maker, died this year at Piacenza (born c.1695).

Joseph Harvis, English composer, was born at this time at Birmingham (died 1814 at

Ivan Evastafievich Khandoskin, Russian violinist and composer, was born (died 1804 at St. Petersburg).

Gaetano Manna, Italian composer, was born this year at Naples (death date unknown).

Navoigille (actually Guillaume Julien), French violinist and composer, was born this year at Givet (died 1841, November at Paris).

Anna Maria Ries, German soprano, was born this year at Bonn (death date unknown). She was the daughter of Johann Ries and was appointed a singer at the Electoral Court at Bonn.

Abiell Whichello, English musician, died at this date in London (birthdate unknown).

Andrea Adolfati was a pupil of Galuppi and church music director of Santa Maria della Salute at Venice until about this year. He then entered the service of the court of Modena.

E. R. Duni was "maestro di cappella" at San Nicola, Bari at this time.

The incorporation of the minuet into symphonies by Stamitz started at this time.

Barsanti's "Nove Overture a Quattro . . .", opus 4, appeared at this time at Edinboro.

Bickham engraved the frontispiece for Simpson's "Delightful (cont.) Pocket Companion" of this year.

Boyce's "Twelve Sonatas for Two Violins, with a Bass for the Violoncello or Harpsichord" was issued this year.

E. R. Duni's only oratorio "Giuseppe riconosciuto" was written at this time.

"Musica Curiosa" was published this year. It contained marches taken from operas.

J. C. Mondonville's "Pièces de Clavecin avec voix ou violin" appeared at this time.

Rousseau's "Recueil de douze chansonnettes italiennes" was engraved this year. It has disappeared.

The Foot Guards reintroduced the fife into the British army at this time.

Piranesi completed the etching "The Prisons" this year.

Joseph Vernet this year painted "The Ponte-Rotto". It is at the Louvre in Paris.

(to 1750) Girolamo Besozzi, oboist, was born during this period at Naples (died 1785 at Paris).

(to 1750) Burk Thumoth's "Twelve English and Twelve Irish Airs" was published this year at London by J. Simpson.

(to 1750) Burk Thumoth's "Twelve Scotch and Twelve Irish Airs" was published this year at London by J. Simpson.

(to 1760) The twelve books of

c.1745(cont.)
James Oswald's "The Caledonian Pocket Companion" were published at this time in London.

1746

(January 7) Theresa Cornelys (La Pompesti) made her first appearance in London this year as "seconda donna" in Gluck's "La caduta dei giganti".

(January 18) Gluck's Italian opera "La caduta de giganti" (libretto by Francesco Vanneschi) was produced on this date at the King's Theatre in London.

(January 21) Gottfried Kirchhoff, German organist and composer, died on this day at Halle (born 1685, September 15 at Mühlbeck near Bitterfeld).

(January 21) Wilhelm Friedemann Bach's new position was at Halle, where the death of Gottfried Kirchhoff, Zachau's talented successor as organist of the Church of Our Lady (Liebfrauen-Kirche or Unserer Lieben Frauen Kirche) had created a vacancy. On his first Sunday (Whit-Sunday) he directed a performance of his own cantata, "Wer mich liebet".

(January 26) Giovanni Battista Lampugnani's opera "Il gran Tamerlano" was produced on this date at Milan.

(January 28) Theresa Cornelys (La Pompesti) appeared this evening in Galuppi's "Il trionfo della continenza".

(January 31) Arne's incidental music for "The Tempest" was performed on this date at the Drury Lane Theatre in London.

(February 13) Giovanni Giuseppe Cambini, Italian violinist and composer, was born on this day at Leghorn (died 1825, December 29 at Bicêtre near Paris).

(February 14) Handel's "Occasional Oratorio" was first performed on this date at Covent Garden in London. The words were probably by Thomas Morell from Milton's Psalms.

(February 19 and 26) Handel's "Occasional Oratorio" had repeat performances on these dates at Covent Garden in London.

(February 27) Giovanni Francesco Fortunati, Italian composer, was born at this time in Parma (died 1821, December 20).

(March 3) Arne's "Harlequin Incendiary, or Columbine Cameron" was performed this evening at the Drury Lane Theatre in London.

(March 3) Jélyotte on this date produced "Zélisca", a comedy-ballet by Sauve de la Nove with music by Jélyotte at the court.

(March 4) Theresa Cornelys (La Pompesti) appeared this evening in Gluck's "Artamene".

(March 13) Arne wrote incidental music for "The She-Gallants" performed on this date at the Drury Lane Theatre in London.

(March 15) Gluck's Italian opera "Artamene" (libretto by Bartolomeo Vitturi) was produced this evening at the King's Theatre in London.

(March 25) Gluck and Handel

on this date appeared together
at a concert at the King's
Theatre.

(March 27) Johann Caspar
Ferdinand Fischer, German com-
poser, died on this dat at
Rastatt (born c.1665).

(March 30) Jean-Joseph Fiocco,
organist and composer, died on
this date at Brussels (born
1606).

(April 9) Hasse's oratorio
"Sant'Elena al Calvario"
(libretto by Metastasio) was
produced this evening at
Dresden.

(April 15) Theresa Cornelys
(La Pompesti) appeared this
evening in Lampugnani's
"Alessandro nell'Indie".

(April 15) Giovanni Battista
Lampugnani's opera "Rossane"
was produced on this date at
London.

(April 16) Altnikol was at this
time recommended by Wilhelm
Friedemann Bach to succeed
him as organist at the Sophien-
Kirche in Dresden. This was
the date of W. F. Bach's
resignation brought on by a
need for greater independence
and a larger income.

(April 16) Wilhelm Friedemann
Bach became organist at Halle
on this date.

(April 23) Gluck had a benefit
concert this evening at the
Little Theatre, Haymarket in
London. He played a concerto
on either 26 glasses or a glass
harmonica (reports conflict
on the instrument).

(May 4) Antonio Pollarolo
(Polaroli), Italian composer,
died on this date at Venice
(born 1680 at Venice).

(May 13) Theresa Cornelys (La
Pompesti) appeared this evening
in Galuppi's "Antigono" at
London. It was the last opera
in which A. Monticelli appeared
on the London stage.

(May 16) Ezekiel Younglove of
Reddistown married Mary Lyon
on this date.

(May 29) Gluck's "Le nozze
d'Ercole ed'Ebe" was performed
this evening at the Castle of
Pillnitz in Germany.

(June 3) James Hook, English
organist and composer, was
born on this date at Norwich
(died 1827 at Boulogne).

(July 2) A. O. Zinck, German
musician, was born at this time
(died 1832, February 15).

(July 7) Ludwig Wenzel Lachnith,
Bohemian horn player and com-
poser, was born this date at
Prague (died 1820, October 3).

(July 9) "Judas Maccabaeus",
an oratorio, was started by
Handel on this date.

(August 1) Marie Jeanne Trial
(née Milon), soprano, was born
on this dat at Paris (died
1818, February 13 at Paris).

(August 9 or 10) Margherita de
L'Épine, Italian or Franco-
Italian soprano, died at this
time in London (birthdate
unknown).

(August 10) Pepusch' wife died
on this date.

1746(cont.)

(August 11) Handel completed his oratorio, "Judas Maccabaeus" today, one month and two days after he started work on the opus.

(August 22) A decree was issued on this date that granted Beethoven's grandfather, Ludovicum van Beethoven, an additional 100 thalers annual salary as court musician.

(September 7) The French ambassador wrote to Paris on this date and reported on the new court as follows: "The only Italians here that deserve attention are two musicians, one a harpsichord player named 'Scarlati', the other a singer named 'Farinello'".

(September 10) A letter from Girolamo Chiti to Padre Martini that bore this date referred to a mass performed at Rome that called Durante "Scolaro di Pittoni".

(September 20) Christian Benjamin Uber, composer, was born on this day at Breslau (died 1812 at Breslau).

(Autumn) La Pompesti was engaged at Vienna this season. Kheven-höller noted in his diary, "The show (Hasse's "Alessandro nelle Indie") was so poor and so confused on account of the absense of one of the characters (the singer Pompesti having been overtaken with labor pains as she entered the theatre)that I was ashamed." The singer delivered her son, Joseph, later to be claimed by Casanova as his son.

(September 26) J. S. Bach visited

(cont.) Naumburg at this time.

(September 28) (Sir) William Jones, English lawyer and orientalist, was born on this date in London (died 1794, April 27 at Calcutta).

(October 4) Domenico Corri, an English singing-master, composer and publisher, was born this day at Rome (died 1825, May 22 at London).

(October 4) Jean Marie Leclair's ("l'aîné") "Scylla et Glaucus" was performed this evening at the Paris Opéra. The opera ends with the "petrification of the heroine and the desolation of the hero". It was a tragic mythological opera.

(October 4) Pergolesi's "La Serva Padrona" was performed on this evening at Paris.

(October 7) William Billings, American composer, was born this day at Boston, Massachusetts (died 1800, September 29 at Boston). He was a strong force in music in the early days of the colonies.

(October 9) Johann Friedrich Lampe's "Kirchen-Music", celebrating the repression of the Stuart Rebellion of this year, was sung in German at the Savoy Chapel on this date and published at Hanover.

(October 10) Fernando VI and Queen Maria Barbara made their state entry into Madrid on this day amid great celebrations with parades, bullfights and fireworks.

(October 13) Clegg was finally discharged from Bedlam Hospital.

1746(cont.)

(October 26) Franz Anton Rössler, Bohemian double bass player, conductor and composer, was born on this date at Niemes (died 1792, June 30)

(November 28) Jacques Loeillet, Flemish musician, died on this day at Versailles (born 1685, July 7).

(December 19) Maria Magdalena Kevench, wife of Johann van Beethoven and mother of the famous composer, was born on this date (died 1787).

(December 19) Venanzio Vauzzini was born in Camerino, Italy at this time. He was a male soprano and composer (died 1810, April 8 at Bath). Rauzzini studied at the Papal Choir in Rome and was a fellow-pupil of Domenico Corri and Clementi.

(June) The latest date of works written for Porpora's pupils was this month at the Ospedaletto and was a "Laudate pueri".

(August) Theresa Cornelys (La Pompesti) was back in Vienna at this time.

(September J. S. Bach's "O holder Tag, erwünschte Zeit" was composed for a wedding this month.

(October) There is a solo cantata in the library of the Naples Conservatorio bearing this date, but it gives no indication of Porpora's position at that time.

Anna Carolina Philippina Bach, daughter of K. P. E. Bach and member of the seventh generation of the Bach family, was born on

(cont.) this date (died 1804).

Johann Egidius Bach, schoolmaster and member of the sixth generation of the Bach family, died this year (born 1709).

Lady Grizel Baillie, author and poetess, died at this time (born 1665).

Gerhard Johan Baltzar of Heidenstam, a Swedish ambassador to the Porte, was born this year (died 1803).

Ernst C. Colson, husband of Anna P. F. Bach, was born at this time (died 1795).

Ernst Ludwig Gerber, German organist and lexicographer, was born this year at Sondershausen (died 1819, June 30).

Ludwig August Lebrun, oboist and composer, was born this year at Mannheim (died 1790, December 16). He was a renowned virtuoso who played in court orchestras at both Mannheim and München.

Johann Frederick Peter, who directed the Moravians' musical life at Bethlehem, was born this year (died 1813). He composed chamber music and was a fine organist.

Joseph Reicha, cellist, composer and conductor, was born at this time in Prague (died 1795 at Bonn).

Karl Stamitz, Bohemian composer and son of Johann Stamitz, was born this year (died 1801).

Jan Stefani, Bohemian violinist and composer, was born at this time in Prague (died 1829,

February 24, at Warsaw).

Ignaz Umlauf, Austrian violinist, conductor, composer and
playwright, was born at this
time in Vienna (died 1796,
June 8 at Vienna).

Augusta Elizabeth Wendling,
singer, was born this year
(died 1794).

Adolfati's setting of Metastasio's serenata "La pace fra
la virto e la bellezza" of this
year has been preserved at the
Biblioteca Estense in Modena.

Johan Joachim Agrell was conductor this season at the city
of Nürnberg.

At the time of the revaval of
Shakespeare's "Tempest" this
year at the Drury Lane Theatre
Arne supplied new music for the
masque and the son "Where the
Bee sucks", a composition
of renowned beauty.

Johann Elias Bach married his
second wife at this time.

Karl Philipp Emmanuel Bach
became Kammermusikus to Frederick the Great of Prussia this
year.

The 1918 Bach-Jahrbuch had a
frontispiece that was a copy
of an oil portrait of Bach by
Haussmann (copied by J. M.
David in 1746). Haussmann was
a court painter at Dresden.

Wilhelm Friedemann Bach left
his position at Dresden this
season for an important position
at Halle.

Doña Barbara de Braganza, a

(cont.) pupil of Domenico
Scarlatti's became Queen of
Spain at this time.

Casanova this year was a
second violinist at San Samuele
until April 15.

S. M. Cibber gave herself up
entirely to the stage after
this year.

Catherine Clive was engaged
by Garrick for Drury Lane
Theatre this season.

At the age of 12 this year,
B. Cooke (ii) acted as deputy
for John Robinson the organist
at Westminster Abbey.

Marianna Cornelys was in
England this season.

This year's date appeared on
a horn made by Friedrich Ehe,
now in the de Wit collection.

Willem de Fesch played first
violin at the first performance
of Handel's "Occasional
Oratorio" this season.

Caterina Galli sang in Handel's
"Judas Maccabeus" this year
with great success.

Gluck left London at this time
to go to Hamburg.

A temporary patron of Gluck's
who took Gluck to Italy this
year as a chamber musician,
Prince Francesco Saverio Melzi,
became involved in a conspiracy
against the Austrian Empress,
Maria Theresa.

Johann Hiller this year graduated from the "Gymnasium" at
Görlitz and went to the Kreuz-
schule at Dresden, where he

studied harpsichord and
thorough-bass under Homilius.

Hermann von Keyserlingk went to
Berlin this year as a Russian
ambassador.

Thomas Lowe sang in Handel's
"Joshua" this season.

Pierre van Maldere became
second violinist this year in
the Royal Chapel at Brussels.

Spazier maintains that F. W.
Marpurg was secretary to General Rothenburg in Paris this
year and while there associated
with Voltaire, Maupertuis
d'Alembert and Rameau.

Angelo Monticelli sang in
Gluck's "Caduta de'giganti"
this season.

Pierre Mortan Berton sang at
Marseilles this year.

Philippo Nicoloni's troupe of
"Enfants Pantomimes" were
enthusiastically received this
season at München.

John Parry visited London at
this time and his playing was
said to have been admired by
Handel.

Pepusch wrote a paper this year
on the "ancient genera". It
was read before the Royal
Society and published in
"Philosophical Transactions"
for 1746. He was then elected
Friend of the Royal Society.

Reutter jr. was appointed
second court conductor at this
time.

J. H. Rolle took the organist's

(cont.) place at St. John's
church, Magdeburg this season.
He became town musician and
worked there with great zeal
and success.

Juan Antonio, the eldest son in
the Scarlatti family, entered
the university of Alcala this
year as a "clerigo de prima
tonsura".

Three pianos made by Gottfried
Silbermann were acquired by
Frederick the Great at this
time.

John Stephens, English composer
and organist, suceeded Edward
Thomson this season as organist
at Salisbury Cathedral.

Antonio Stradivari's son,
Paolo Bartolomeo, his wife
Elena Templari and their four
children, left the house in the
Piazza San Domenico this year.

Antonio Stradivarius leased his
house in the Piazza San Domenico this year to Stradivarius'
pupil, Carlo Bergonzi, who
stayed there until 1758.

Domenico Terradellas, Spanish
composer, was in London at
this time.

The famous Florentine violinist,
Veracini, was shipwrecked this
year while sailing from London
to Leghorn. The two violins
made for him by Marcus Stainer
(christened "St. Peter" and
"St. Paul") were lost in the
wreck.

J. Zach went to Italy this year.

Geronimo Abos' opera,
"L'Artaserse", was produced
this season at Venice.

J. S. Bach wrote Canonic
Variations on "Vom Himmel hoch"
for organ at this time. The
work was published also.

Pirro maintains that J. S.
Bach's Choral Variations were
engraved this year at Nürnberg.

J. S. Bach wrote his motet
"Singet dem Herrn" at this time.

W. F. Bach this year wrote his
first cantata, "Wer mich liebet",
in Dresden.

Blainville published a "Harmonie
théorético-pratique" this year.

Bollioud-Mermet's "La Corruption
du Goût" appeared at this time.

Breunich's "Diana vendicata"
was heard this year at Warsaw.

Cafaro's oratorio "Il trionfo
di Davidde" was composed this
season.

Chiarini's "Il geloso schernito"
was produced this year at
Venice along with Michieli's
serious opera "Zenobia".

V. L. Ciampi's "Arcadia in
Brenta" was produced this season
at Piacenza.

Conforto made his début this
year at the Teatro dei Fiorentini
in Naples during the carnival,
along with a comic opera, "La
finta vedova".

Costanzi's oratorio "San Pietro
Alessandrino" appeared at this
time.

Destouches' opera "Marthésie",
première Reine des Amazones"
was revived at this time.

Baldassare Galuppi wrote his
opera "Antigono" this year at
London (libretto by Metastasio).

Baldassare Galuppi this year
wrote his opera "Il trionfo
della continenza" at London
(libretto by Piovene).

Seven violin concertos in eight
parts by Geminiani were published this season.

Gluck's set of six trio sonatas
were published this year at
London by John Simpson.
He wrote them in Milan during a
period of Sammartini's influence.
The sonatas were all light,
quick, and anti-contrapuntal.

In Venice this year Gluck performed a sinfonia in G major
for strings and two horns as a
"concerto symphony". The piece
was originally the introduction
to "Ipermestra".

Görner's "Collection of New
Odes and Songs" was published
this year.

Carl Heinrich Graun's opera
"Caio Fabricio" was produced
this season at Berlin.

Carl Heinrich Graun's opera
"Demofoonte" was produced this
season at Berlin.

François Lupin Grenet's "Le
Triomphe de l'harmonie" was
performed again this year at
Lyons.

Habermann's "Missae XII" was
published this year at Prague.
The work has not yet been found.

Handel's song "From scourging
rebelion" with words by John
Lockman appeared at this time.

1746(cont.)

Handel's oratorio "Judas Maccabaeus" was composed this year.

Handel wrote the "Occasional Oratorio" this year to honor the Duke of Cumberland for his victory over the Jacobite rebels at Culloden.

Hasse's pasticcios "Annibale in Capua", "Faramondo" and "Ixion" were produced this season, the first at London, the latter two at Braunschweig.

The following works of this year are doubtful and mis-attributed works to Hasse. "Lo starnuto d'Ercole" and "Eurimedonte e Timocleone, ovvero I rivali delusi" were both puppet operas performed at Venice. (Hasse is stated to have been the composer, but more likely his name was merely used as a decoy.)

Jommelli's works of this year included the following produced in the cities indicated: "Sifonisba" (Venice); "Don Trastiello" (Rome), sometimes performed as "La cantata e disfida di Don Trastiello"; "Caio Mario" (Rome); "Antigone" (Lucca); "Tito Manlio" (Naples), second version.

Johann Friedrich Lampe this year set to music Charles Wesley's hymns and called them "Hymns on the Great Festivals".

Giovanni Battista Lampugnani's aria was introduced into the London pasticcio "Annibale in Capua" this season.

The first official Masonic song book or "Frey-mäurer Lieder" by Ludwig Friedrich Lenz appeared at this time in Retenburg.

C. Nichelmann's serenata "Il sogno di Scipinoe" was performed this season at Berlin for the King.

This year's performances of Rameau's "Le Temple de la Gloire" contained a moving entr'acte between the first and second acts.

Schürer's opera "La Galatea" was produced this season at Dresden.

Josiah Street, a musician, issued "A Book containing great variety of Anthems in two, three and four parts" at London in a second edition this year.

G. C. Wagenseil this year set Metastasio's libretto "La Clemenza di Tito" to music.

G. C. Wagenseil published "Demetrio" this year at Florence.

Reverend T. Walter's "Grounds and Rules of Music" in a pamphlet edition this year gave ("some brief and very plain Instructions for Singing by Note.")

We know from Parliamentary reports that the foot guards had fifes at this time.

Robberies at this time had become so frequent and the robbers so daring that the proprietor of Marylebone Gardens was forced to have

1746(cont.)
guards to protect the visitors to and from the town.

Guillaume Coustou, French sculptor, died this year (born 1677).

Francisco de Goya y Lucientes (Goya), Spanish court painter, was born this year (died 1828).

Nicolas de Largillière, French painter, died at this time (born 1656).

William Collins published his "Odes" at this time.

Jemmy Dawson, the Manchester Jacobite, was executed this year.

John Brown was chaplain to the Bishop of Carlisle at this time.

Philip V of Spain died this year and succeeded by Ferdinand VI.

(to 1747) Andrea Bernasconi was chorus master at the Ospedale della Pietà, Venice, where he performed a Latin oratorio, "Adonais" during this season.

(to 1749) A collection of Lieder by Fritsch was published during these years.

(to 1757) François Francoeur and Rebel were inspectors of the Opéra in Paris during these eleven years.

(to 1759) The reign of Ferdinand VI of Spain spanned these years.

(to 1763) Wilhelm Friedemann Bach probably resided with Gotthilf Georgi, an excise

(cont.) official during this period.

(to 1764) Wilhelm Friedemann Bach wrote a large number of cantatas, a Symphony in D Major, the unfinished Eb Major Clavier Concerto, twelve Polonaises, the Eb Clavier Sonata and smaller works during these eighteen years.

(to 1766) Euler during these years was director of the mathematics section of the Berlin Academy of Science.

(to 1770) W. F. Bach lived and worked in Halle all this time.

(and 1770) Bury wrote additions for the revival of Lully's Persée" at these two dates.

(and 1776, 1802) After being restored in 1746 and renovated by Francesco Tadolini in 1776, the Teatro Formagliari was burned to the ground in 1802.

c.1746
Jan David Holland (Johann David) Polish composer of German birth, was born this year at Herzberg near Osterode, Harz (died c.1815 probably at Cracow).

John Mahon, clarinettist and composer, was born at this time (died 1832 at Dublin).

J. S. Bach composed "Einige Kanonische Veränderungen" this year.

J. S. Bach's six Schübler Chorale Preludes were published at this time.

The earliest instruction book in English "The Compleat Tutor for the FRENCH HORN" was

c.1746(cont.)
written by Winch and published
by John Simpson.

(to 1747) Several of M.
Dubourg's compositions were included in John Simpson's
"Delightful Pocket Companion
for the German Flute" during
this year.

(to 1747) Several of M.
Dubourg's compositions were included in Walsh's "Musica
bellicosa, or a Warlike Musick"
this season.

1747
(January 18) Antonio Literes
died this day at Madrid (born
c.1670 near Madrid).

(March 2) The certificate of
matriculation for Juan Antonio
Scarlatti at the University of
Alcala de Henares was issued
on this date.

(Spring) J. S. Bach visited the
Prussian King in Berlin at this
time.

(March 15) Rameau's and
Calhusac's opera-ballet "Les
Fêtes de l'Hymen et de l'Amour"
was performed at Versailles for
the Dauphin's second wedding.

(March 24) Domenico Terradellas'
opera "Bellerofonte" was produced on this date at the King's
Theatre in the Haymarket at
London.

(March 29) Johann Wilhelm
Hässler, German organist,
pianist and composer, was born
on this date at Erfurt (died
1822, March 29 at Moscow).

(Spring) Johann Sebastian Bach,
with his son Wilhelm Friedemann,

(cont.) visited Potsdam at
this time.

(March 31) Johann Abraham
Peter Schulz, German organist,
conductor and composer, was
born this day at Lüneburg
(died 1800, June 10).

(April 1) Handel's "Judas
Maccabaeus" was produced
this evening at Covent Garden
in London. The words were by
Morell.

(April 29) Boyce's "Peleus and
Thetis" was heard on this date
at Swan Tavern, Exchange Alley.

(May 2) Johann Ries at this
time became court trumpeter
at Bonn with a salary of 192
thalers.

(May 7) J. S. Bach arrived for
a visit at the court of King
Frederick II in Prussia on
this day at Potsdam.

(May 11) Spener, who first
recorded Bach's arrival in
Potsdam on this date, noted
his Majesty's command that
Bach be admitted at once.

(May 19) Pierre Jean Burette,
medical man and writer on
musical subjects, died this
day at Paris (born 1665,
November 21 at Paris).

(May 25) Regina Mingotti made
her debut at Dresden in
Scalabrini's "Merope" this
evening.

(May 28) The Pennsylvania
Gazette advertised Benjamin
Franklin's reprinting of Watts'
"Divine and Moral Songs"
(Warrington), and the "Scotch
Psalms" in this issue.

(June 1, June 24, July 4) "Alexander Balus", oratorio (words by Thomas Morell and music by Handel) bore these dates on the autograph: begun June 1, 1747; end of second part, fully scored 24 June do.; end of third part, fully scored, 4 July do.

(June 1) Charles Simon Favart's "Les Nymphes de Diane" was premiered at Brussels on this date.

(June 14) Hasse's opera "La Spartana generosa, ovvero Archidamia" (libretto by Pasquini) was performed this evening at Dresden.

(June 29) Gluck's Italian opera "Le nozze d'Ercole e d'Ebe" was produced at this time at Pillnitz, near Dresden. The librettist was unknown. The work included an allegro from one of Sammartini's symphonies.

(July 6) Coelestin Ferdinand Jungbauer, German priest and composer, who wrote masses and other church music as well as songs with pianoforte, was born on this date at Grattersdorf (died at Grossmehring near Ingolstadt)

July 7) Bach wrote a letter bearing this date to Fredrick the Great, telling him of Bach's dedication of a piece of music to him in his honor. The work, published at this time, was "Das Musikalische Opfer" for flute, violin and continuo, and contained a ricercar for three parts, a canon perpetuus, five canons and a fuga canonica.

(July 11) Domingo Pio Scarlatti, son of Domenico and member of the fourth generation of the Scarlatti family, was born on this date (died sometime after 1815).

(July 12) The baptismal certificate of Domingo Scarlatti bore this date.

(July 18) Porpora's opera "Filandro" was performed at this time in Dresden.

(July 19) Handel began to compose his oratorio "Joshua" on this date.

(August 4) "Il re pastore" by King Frederick II, Quantz, Graun, and Nichelmann was performed this day at Charlottenburg.

(August 5) Pergolesi's "Livietta e Tracollo" had its first performance abroad, as "Il finto pazzo" on this date at Dresden.

(August 12) Handel finished his oratorio "Joshua" on this date just 24 days after he had embarked on the project.

(August 14) Adrien Joseph van Helmont, Netherlands composer, son and pupil of Charles Joseph van Helmont, was born on this date at Brussels (died 1830, December 29 at Brussels).

(August 26) G. Scarlatti's opera "Artaserse" was produced at this time at the Teatro Pubblico in Lucca (libretto by Metastasio).

(September 12) Anna Carolina Philippina Bach, daughter of K. P. Emmanuel, granddaughter

of J. Sebastian and member of
the seventh generation of the
Bach family was christened on
this day.

(Autumn) G. Scarlatti married
Barbara Stabili, a singer, in
Lucca at this time.

(September 23) Esteban Artenga,
Spanish scholar, was born this
day at Tervel (died 1799,
October 30 at Paris).

(September 27) Ezekiel Younglove
presented his child, Dorcas on
this date for baptism in the
Morristown Church.

(October 7) Dickenson, the first
president of Princeton, died
at this time.

(October &) Hasse's opera,
"Leucippo" (libretto by Pasquini)
was produced this evening at
Hubertusburg.

(November 14) Handel's pasticcio
"Lucio Vero" (taken chiefly
from other works by Handel) with
a libretto by Zeno was produced
on this date at the King's
Theatre in London.

(November 21) Leopold Mozart
married Anna Maria Pertl on
this day.

(January) Hasse's intermezzo
"Il bresitone" was premiered
this month at Dresden.

(May) Princeton was opened at
the end of this month at
Elizabethtown.

(June) Forkel stated that Bach's
"Einige Kanonische Veränderungen" was engraved after this

(cont.) date, when Bach joined
Mizler's Society. Spitta
agreed with this assumption.

(June) J. S. Bach at this time
became a member of the
"Society of the Musical
Sciences", founded by Mizler.
Its German title was "Societät
der musikalischen Wissen-
schaften".

(July) The Queen Mother
Elisabeth was ordered to leave
Madrid at this time. She was
the widow of King Philip V
and had been his second wife.

(December) J. S. Bach's
"O angenehme Melodei" was performed this month while he
visited Dresden.

Gabriel da Annunciacao,
Portuguese composer, died this
year at Lisbon (born 1681 at
Ovar).

Ernst Christian Bach, cantor
and member of the seventh
generation of the Bach family,
was born this year (died 1822).

Johann Christoph Georg Bach,
organist and member of the
seventh generation of the Bach
family, was born at this time
(died 1814).

Ernst Friedrich Benda, German
chamber musician, was born this
year (died 1785).

Carlo Bergonzi, Italian violin
maker, died this year at
Cremona (born c.1683 at Cremona).

William Billings, tanner and
psalmodist from Boston, was
born this year (died 1800).

1747(cont.)

Giovanni Bononcini, Italian composer, died at this time according to a major source (born 1670) (see also 1750 and 1755).

Henrique Carlos Correa, Portuguese composer, died after this date (born 1680 at Lisbon).

Louis Cardon, French harpist of Italian descent, was born this year at Paris (died 1805 in Russia).

James Cervetto (called Cervetto the Younger), English violoncellist and composer, was born this year at London (died 1837, February 5 at London).

Gasparo Ghiretti, second cellist of the Royal Orchestra of Parma and composition teacher to Niccolo Paganini in 1795 as well as earlier to Ferdinand Paer, was born this year. He was appointed to the Ducal Orchestra at Parma in 1774 (died 1797).

Dominik Gorączkiewicz, Polish organist, was born at this time at Cracow (died 1803, February 3).

Franz Andreas Holly, Bohemian conductor and composer, was born this year at Lub, Bohemia (died 1783, May 4 at Breslau).

Sophie Kronauer was born on this date (died 1830).

Justin Morgan, American musician, was born at this time (died 1798).

Antonio Puccini, conductor of the Cappella della Signoria in Lucca until 1806 and later

(cont.) maestro di cappella at the Cathedral of San Martino, was born this year (death date unknown).

Raynor Taylor, English composer who wrote a number of ballad operas while in America, was born at this time (died 1825).

François Tourte, violin-bow maker, was born this year at Paris (died 1835, April at Paris).

Francisco Valls, Spanish composer, died (birthdate unknown).

Alembert's discovery of the calculus of partial differences this year was recognized by the Berlin Academy.

Altnikol, after Bach's recommendation, was appointed organist this season at Niederwiesa near Greifenberg.

Amiconi came to Spain at this time to design scenery for Farinelli's opera productions and to paint in the palaces at Buen Retiro and Aranjuez.

Bach accepted themes from Frederick the Great at Potsdam this year while visiting there.

J. S. Bach this year while at Berlin was shown the new Opera House.

The "Musical Offering" of this year was inspired by Bach's visit to the court of Frederick II in Potsdam. K. P. E. Bach served as harpsichordist at the court.

Wilhelm Friedemann Bach and

J. S. Bach visited both Berlin and Potsdam this season.

Battishill became a chorister of St. Paul's Cathedral this year under William Savage.

Bertoni's first oratorio was performed this season at Venice.

Bini found an additional Roman patron in Cardinal Troiano Acquaviva. After the latter's death this year, however, Rome was unkind to him through his enemies and rivals.

Anne-Jeanne Boucon married Mondonville at this time.

Viktorin Ignác Brixi was appointed rector of the local school at Poedbrady this year.

C. Cannabich was appointed ordinary violinist of the Mannheim orchestra this season.

C. Chabran became a member of the Royal Chapel at Turin this year.

V. L. Ciampi was at Palermo at this time.

Annibale Pio Fabri, singer and composer, was named president of the Accademia Filarmonica of Bologna (for the fourth time) this year.

Miss Falkner this year appeared as principal singer at Maryle-bone Gardens. Admission was raised to 2 shillings.

A Venetian opera buffa of this year by Buini and Galuppi, "Il protettore alla moda", may be

(cont.) viewed as a prototype ("Monsò Voraigne") for the mad artist in Gluck's "La Recontre imprévue".

Garrick became manager of the Drury Lane Theatre this season.

Georg Gebel this year became Konzertmeister at Rudolstadt.

Gluck visited his home this year when his father died.

Gluck this season left London and joined the Italian opera company of Pietro Mingotti at Leipzig.

Gaetano Guadagni was singing this season at Parma.

Karl Haudek at this time was appointed court virtuoso at Dresden. It was there that he met Hampel and the two after-ward worked together as teachers and duo-performers.

Among Maria Ippolito's (Marie Hippilyte) Vestris and Violante Béatrix de Dominique Bruscagli's eight children, the four best-known settled in Paris this year.

The Duke of Chandos' organ was sold at this time at auction. The Jordans then repaired it and moved it to Trinity Church, Gosport.

Jakob Kleinknecht was violinist at the Bayreuth Court this year.

Johannes Lohelius this year became a friar at the Premon-stratensian Abbey at Strahov.

The college James Lyon attended moved from Neward this year. This was not the psalmodist.

James Lyon from Ireland moved
to Setauket, Long Island this
year as successor to Rev.
Isaac Brown. He was an Episco-
palian.

Philippo Nicoloni's troupe of
"Enfants Pantomimes" were again
feted in Vienna this year.

J. Oswald this season set up a
music shop on the north side
of St. Martin's Church at the
corner of St. Martin's Lane.

Nicolas Philidor played the
serpent in the King's private
orchestra at this time.

N. Porpora first went to
Dresden this season.

Burkat Shudi made harpsichord
#190 for Hugo Worch this year.
It was a two-manual which has
survived.

Gottfried Silbermann at this
time built the instrument on
which Bach played.

A bassoon by T. Stanesby, jr.
bearing this date has survived.

Domenico Terradellas, the
Spanish composer, returned to
Rome this year from London by
way of Paris.

The singer Vittoria Tesi
went to Vienna this year or
next and opened a school for
vocal instruction.

Maria Antonia Walpurgis was
married to Prince Frederick
Christian this year and con-
tinued her musical studies with
Porpora and later going to
Hasse at Dresden.

Girolamo Abos' opera "Pelopida"
was completed at this time
at Rome.

Maria Teresa Agnesi's pastoral
cantata "Il Ristoro d'Arcadia"
appeared at this time.

Johann Sebastian Bach wrote a
sonata for violin, flute and
clavier, in C minor this year
that was included in the
"Musical Offering".

J. S. Bach composed a set of
five canonic variations on the
Christmas hymn "Vom Himmel
hoch" at this time. Sources
disagree to the exact year.

About four hundred of the
chorales that appeared in
Ephrata, many by Beissel himself, were printed, the majority
of them in the "Turtel Taube",
the Ephrata hymnal of this year.

Boismortier's opera-ballet
"Daphnis et Chloé" appeared
at this time.

Cafaro's oratorio "L'invenzione
della croce" was composed this
year.

Calzabigi wrote "Il sogna
d'Olimpia" this year on the
occasion of Prince Filippo's
of San Carlo's birth.

V. L. Ciampi's "Bertoldo,
Bertoldino e Cacasenno" was
produced this season.

V. L. Ciampi's oratorio
"Betulia liberata" was produced
this season at Venice.

G. Cocchi's "La maestra"
appeared this year at Naples.

Claude Denis at this time

1747(cont.)

wrote "Nouveau Système de musique pratique" while at Paris.

Eberlin's "IX toccate e fughe per l'organo" (Lotter) appeared this year at Augsburg.

William Felton this year published his second set of six keyboard concertos, opus 3 at London.

Antoine Forqueray's "Pièces de viole" were composed at this time at Paris.

Baldassare Galuppi wrote his opera "L'Arminio" this year at Venice (libretto by Salvi).

Baldassare Galuppi wrote his opera "Evergete" this year at Rome (libretto by Silvani).

Baldassare Galuppi this year wrote the opera "Il protettore alla moda" at Venice (libretto by Buini).

Baldassare Galuppi's opera "L'Olimpiade" was produced this year at Milan (libretto by Metastasio).

Georg Gebel's opera "Die Grossmuth" was produced this season at Rudolstadt.

Gluck's "Demetrio" was revived this season at Milan.

Carl Heinrich Graun's opera "Le feste galanti" was produced this season at Berlin.

Habermann's "Litaniae VI" was produced this year at Prague. Dlabac mentioned the work but it has not been found.

Six "Philonela pia" by F. V. Habermann were published this year at Kraslice.

Hasse's intermezzo "Il baron Cospuglio" (known by its libretto only and possibly a title variant) was heard this season at Madrid.

A new version of Hasse's opera "Semiramide riconosciuta" appeared at this time.

Hasse's pasticcio, "Antonino Comodo" was performed this season at Braunschweig.

Holzbauer this year wrote the ballet music for Hasse's "Arminio".

Jommelli's "Didone abbandonata" was produced this season at Rome.

Jommelli's "Componimento drammatico" was composed this year for the wedding of the Dauphin Louis, son of Louis XV and Maria Josepha of Saxony at Rome.

Jommelli's "Eumene" appeared at this time.

Giovanni Battista Lampugnani's opera "Tigrane" was produced this season at Venice.

N. Logroscino's "La costanza" was produced this season.

N. Logroscino's "Il governadore" was produced this season at Naples.

Guiseppe Maio at this time wrote his serenata "Il sogno di Olimpia" as well as the opera seria "Arianna e Teseo".

GIOVANNI BATISTA PERGOLESI
1710-1736

G. Martini's "VI Sonate per organo e cembalo" was published this year at Bologna.

Mizler's "Neu eröffnete musikalische Bibliothek" was published this year. The invention of a clavier equipped with hammers and partly with springs was claimed in the work by Schröter.

Nebra's opera "Antes que celos, y Amor la piedad llama al valor, y Achiles en Troya" appeared at this time.

D. Paradisi's "Fetonte" was produced this season at the King's Theatre in London.

Pescetti's opera "Enzio" was performed this season at Venice.

J. J. Rousseau this year wrote an opera "Les Muses galantes" which was performed at le Theatre de L'Opéra in Paris. One source said the production was at the house of La Pouplinière.

G. Scarlatti's opera "Il giocatore" was produced this year at the Teatro di Via del Cocomero in Florence.

Benjamin Franklin at this time reprinted Watts'"Divine and Moral Songs" (Warrington) and "The Scotch Psalms, in a small neat pocket volume".

Zellbell this year compiled a book of chorales.

The quick arpeggios and closing broken chords that belonged to the new concerto style reoccurred this year in "La Dauphine".

American architecture: Medford, Massachusetts, Royall House (45' x 36').

Samuel Johnson this year issued proposals for a Dictionary of the English Language.

(and 1748) A few more of Auletta's works were performed during these two years.

(to 1748) Caffarelli sang at Florence this season.

(to 1749) J. S. Bach's "Mass in B minor" was probably completed during these years.

(to 1749) J. S. Bach collected and revised his book of Eighteen Chorales during this period.

(and 1749, 1752) Alembert's "Recherches sur la courge que forme une corde tendue mise en vibration" (1747)("Histoire de l'Académie Royale des Sciences", P.214, Berlin, 1749) (do.) Berlin, 1752, pp.355, 415) was published at the indicated dates.

(to 1750) J. S. Bach had his "Sechs Chorale" for organ published during this time by his pupil, Johann Georg Schübler.

(to 1750) Gluck spent these three years with Mingotti's opera company.

(to 1750) Pierre de Jélyotte performed as a cellist in the "petits appartements" of Mme. de Pompadour during this period.

(to 1751) Porpora was the singing teacher of electoral Princess Maria Antonia for

1747(cont.)
these four years.

(and 1752, 1754) Amiconi was
called to Madrid to design
scenery in 1747; and was
succeeded after his death in
1752 by Antonio Jolli and later
by Francisco Bataglioli, who
arrived in 1754.

(to 1755) Abbé Guillaume
Raynal's "Nouvelles litteraires"
appeared during these years.

(to 1764) Wilhelm Friedemann
Bach was organist of the Liebfrauen Kirche, Halle during
this period.

(to 1768) Gregorio Sciroli
wrote more than twenty operas
for Italian theatres during
this twenty-one year period.

(to 1769) Franz Xaver Richter,
a Moravian, came to Mannheim
from his home and was a singer,
violinist and composer in the
ducal band during these years.

(to 1770) Ludwig August Lebrun's
father was oboist in the
Mannheim orchestra at this time.

(to 1886) Catalogus Collegii
Neo-Caesariensis Princetoniae
was one of several volumes
that appeared during this
period.

c.1747
Raynor Taylor, U.S. composer,
was born this year (died 1825).

Giovanni Verocai, Italian
violinist and composer, died
this year at Braunschweig
(born c.1700 at Venice).

Tommaso Antonio Vitali, composer
and son of Giovanni Battista

(cont.) Vitali, died at this
time (born c.1665).

Giovanni Andrea Fioroni settled
in Milan this year.

A "Signor Borosini" this year
collected "One Hundred Cantici
in Italian after the manner
of English Canons and Catches"
(published by J. Simpson).

Bury's "La Prise de Berg-op-
Zoom" was published at this
time.

Jean Marie Leclair "l'aîné"
wrote "Sonatas for 2 violins
without Bass"(second book)
this year.

James Oswald, Scottish composer,
wrote "The Tulip" at this time.

(to 1750) J. S. Bach wrote the
"Eighteen Choral Preludes" for
organ during this period.
Some sources place these as
1747-1749).

1748
(January 1) Giovanni Furno,
Italian teacher and composer,
was born this year at Capua
(died 1827, June 20).

(January 13) Pierre Lagarde's
opera-ballet "Aegle" was performed on this day at
Versailles.

(January 26) Aloys Förster,
German theorist, teacher and
composer, was born at this
time in Niederstein, near
Glatz, Silesia (died 1823,
November 12).

(February 3) Josef Fiala,
Czech oboist and viola da
gamba player, was born on this
date at Lochovice (died 1816).

1748(cont.)

(February 5) Christian Gottlob Neefe, German composer and organist, was born at this time at Chemnitz in Saxony (died 1798). He was an early teacher of Beethoven and a freemason.

(February 9) Hasse's opera "Demofoonte" was produced on this day at Dresden. The libretto was by Metastasio.

(February 13) Arne wrote the incidental music for "The Foundling", performed on this date at Drury Lane Theatre in London.

(February 29) Rameau's ballet "Zaïs" (libretto by Cahusac) was produced on this date in Paris. It has also been referred to as a pastorale héroïque.

(March 5) William Shield, English violinist and composer, was born on this date at Whickham, Durham (died 1829, January 25). He wrote songs as well as operas.

(March 7) William Corbett, English violinist and composer, died on this day at London (birthdate unknown).

(March 9) Handel introduced the mandoline into the "Alexander Balus" production on the above date.

(March 9) Handel's oratorio "Joshua" with words by Morell, was produced on this date at Covent Garden in London.

(March 9) Handel's oratorio "Alexander Balus" (words by Thomas Morell) was produced on this evening at Covent

(cont.) Garden in London.

(March 10) Giovanni Perroni, Italian composer, cellist and husband of Anna, died on this date at Vienna (born 1688 in Italy).

(March 17) Charles King, English singer, organist and composer who composed several services and anthems, died on this day at London (born 1687 at Bury St. Edmunds).

(March 21) Arne wrote the incidental music for "The Provok'd Wife", performed on this evening at Drury Lane in London.

(Spring) E. R. Duni's opera "Ciro riconosciuto" was produced this season at the Teatro del Falcone in Genoa.

(March 22) Power of Attorney was granted to Fernando Ferrera de Silva by Scarlatti on this day in Lisbon.

(March 23) Johann Christoph Gottfried Walther, German composer and musical lexicographer, died on this date at Weimar (born 1684, September 18).

(April 6) David Kellner, German organist, lutenist, carillonist and composer, died this day at Stockholm (born 1670 at Leipzig).

(April 7) Georg Wenzel Ritter, German bassoonist, was born on this date at Mannheim. He played in the Mannheim orchestra (died 1808, June 16 at Berlin).

(April 13) Porpora was made Kapellmeister at Dresden on this date "until further notice".

1748(cont.)
His salary was 1200 thaler per
year.

(April 20) Georg Michael
Telemann, German composer,
was born on this date at Plön,
Holstein (died 1831, March 4
at Riga).

(April 25) Pierre Louis
Ginguene, French historian of
literature and writer on music,
was born on this day at Rennes
(died 1816, November 16).

(May 5) Francesco Azopardi,
Maltese theorist and composer,
was born this day at Rabat,
Malta (died 1809, February 6
at Rabat).

(May 14) Gluck's Italian opera
"Semiramide riconosciuta"
(libretto by Metastasio) was
produced this evening at the
Burg Theatre in Vienna.

(May 15) L. N. Clérambault's
"Le Retour du printemps" was
performed this evening at the
Jesuit College of Louis-le-
Grand.

(June 11) William Leeves,
English cellist and composer,
was born on this date at London
(died 1828, May 28).

(June 17) Catterina Stradivarius,
daughter of Antonio Stradivarius,
died on this date (born 1674,
March 25).

(June 18) Cattarina Stradivari
was interred in the family vault
on this date.

(July 7) Charles Simon Favart's
"Cythère assiégée" was first
performed on this date at
Brussels.

(July 11) "Galatea ed Acide"
by Frederick II, Hasse, Graun,
Quantz and Nichelmann, was
performed on this evening at
Potsdam.

(July 25) Nicolas Couperin,
organist and erstwhile composer, died this day at Paris
(born 1680, December 20 at
Paris).

(August 4 or 7) Maximilian
(Abbé) Stadler, Austrian
organist, clavier player and
composer, was born on this
date at Melk, Lower Austria
(died 1833, November 8 at
Vienna).

(August 11) Joseph Schuster,
German composer, was born this
day at Dresden (died 1812,
July 24).

(August 24) Handel's oratorio
(in 3 parts) "Susanna" was
completed on this date (author
or words unknown, however one
source credits them to Handel
himself).

(August 27) Rameau's "Pygmalion",
an acte de ballet, was produced
on this evening at Paris.

(August 31) Johannes Jäger,
a great cellist of his day, was
born on this day at Schlitz,
Hasse (death date unknown).

(September 14) Johann Paul
Schulthesius, German theorist
and composer, was born on this
date at Fechheim (died 1816,
April 18).

(Autumn) V. L. Ciampi went to
England this season as "maestro"
for a company of Italian
singers who had great success
briefly at London with comic

operas from their Venetian repertory.

(September 26) K. P. E. Bach's third child was christened on this day. He named the child after his father.

(October 27) Thomas Vincent jr,'s "opera secunda" (copy-righted on this date) was "A Sett of Familiar Lessons for the Harpsichord, op. 2, published by John Cox, London, and Six Solos for a Hautboy, German Flute, Violin, or Harpsichord".

(November 1) Christoph Reineck, German composer, was born in Memmingen on this day. He wrote many songs and several operas (died 1797, July 29 at Memmingen).

(November 2) J. S. Bach wrote a letter bearing this date to his cousin, Johann Elias Bach, thanking him for his gift of wine and telling him of his daughter's marriage.

(November 9) Newark College on this day had its first commence-ment.

(November 14) Arne wrote the incidental music for "Much Ado About Nothing", performed this evening at the Drury Lane Theatre in London.

(November 15) Joseph Haydn's voice began to break this year and Reutter assigned the "Salve Regina" to Michael, who sang it so well that the Emperor and Empress gave him 24 gold ducats. Joseph, replaced by his brother, considered castration to help save his voice, but his father

(cont.) came to Vienna and stopped him.

(November 23) Étienne Joseph Floquet, French composer, was born on this date at Aix-en-Provence (died 1785, May 10).

(November 27) Rameau's opera-ballet "Les Surprises de l'Amour" was performed on this date at the Théâtre des Petits Appartements at Versailles. The text was by Bernard.

(December 16) Ferdinand (Philippe Joseph) Staes, Netherlands harpsichordist, organist and composer, was born on this date at Brussels (died 1809, March 23 at Brussels).

(December 27) William Marshall, Scottish violinist and composer, was born on this day at Fochabers, Banffshire (died 1833, May 29 at Dandaleith).

(January) E. R. Duni's opera "ipermestra" was produced this season at the Teatro del Falcone in Genoa.

(January) N. Logroscino's "Giunio Bruto" was produced during this month.

(January) A. Wesstrom was con-ductor of the Royal Orchestra at this time.

(March) Philippo Nicolini's troupe "Enfants Pantomimes" went to Prague from Vienna and remained there until this time.

(September) K. P. E. Bach's younger son, Johann Sebastian, member of the seventh genera-tion of the Bach family, was born (died 1778 at Rome). He became a painter. One source

1748(cont.)
gave his deathdate as 1774.

(September) Gluck joined
Mingotti's company as a conductor this month.

Anton Bemetzrieder, Alsatian
writer on music, was born this
year at Alsace (died 1817 at
London). See also 1743.

Carl Hermann Heinrich Benda,
German musician and composer,
was born this year (died 1836).
Sources disagree as to his
birth year.

Philip Cogan, Irish composer
and organist was born at this
time at Cork (died 1833,
February 3 at Dublin).

Johann Michael Demmler, German
composer, was born this year at
Gross-Altingen near Augsburg
(died 1785 at Augsburg).

Lewis Edson, American musician,
was born this year (died 1820).

Jean Laguerre, Anglo-French
tenor, died at this time in
London (born c.1700).

Simon Leduc ("l'aîné"), violinist, composer and publisher,
was born this year at Paris
(died 1787, January).

Niccolò Mestrino, Italian
violinist and composer, was
born this year at Milan (died
1790, September at Paris). He
was a musician in the service
of Prince Esterhazy and, when
imprisoned for a prank,
practiced judiciously.

Theodor von Schacht, German
composer, was born at this time

(cont.) in Strasbourg (died
1823, June 20).

Emanuel Schikaneder, actor and
theatrical manager, was born
this year (died 1812). He
was closely affiliated with
Mozart.

Robert Wainwright, English
organist and composer, was
born at this time in Stockport
(died 1782).

Karl Friedrich Abel this year
obtained a position under Hasse
in the court orchestra at
Dresden. He remained there
ten years.

Altnikol was appointed organist of St. Wenceslaus,
Naumburg this season.

Two letters written this year
from J. S. Bach to Johann
Elias Bach revealed Bach's
frugality.

Haussmann painted a famous
portrait of J. S. Bach at this
time.

At the 100th anniversary of the
Peace of Westphalia, Doles
wrote a "Singspiel" which
caused a dispute among Bieder-
mann, Mattheson and Bach.

Johann Ernst Bach was associated
with his father this year as
organist at Eisenach.

Pierre Montan Berton went to
Bordeaux at this time and
stayed for five years as conductor and organist.

Richard Bridge this season lived
in Hand Court, Holborn, London.

Burney became organist of a

136

city church this year, St.
Dionis' Backchurch.

Camerloher at this time took
holy orders and became a canon
at St. Veit.

Theresa Cornelys was singing
at Hamburg this season.

At this date Armand-Louis
Couperin became organist at
Saint-Gervais and stayed there
until his death.

Hawkins maintained that
Cuzzoni returned to London this
year and sang in "Mitridate".

The number of lamps at Marylebone Gardens was increased and
Defesch was engaged as first
violinist this season.

In his early "Mémoires" of this
year, Diderot confessed his
ignorance of music.

E. R. Duni went to Parma this
year by way of Genoa.

George England was said to
have been trained by the Younger
Harris and to have lived in
Hand Court, Holborn, London at
this time.

Willem de Fesch conducted the
orchestra this season at
Marlebone Gardens.

Giulia Frast this season
played a leading role in the
pasticcio "Lucio Vero", as well
as in operas by Hasse.

Baldassare Galuppi became
assistant maestro di cappella
at St. Mark's this year.

From this time forward, Baldassare Galuppi supplied Venice
regularly with operas.

Georg Sigismund Gebel became
organist at the Breslau Church
of the Holy Trinity at this
time.

Felice (de') Giardini started
on a concert tour of Germany
and England as a violinist
this season.

Joseph Gibbs this year became
organist at the Church of St.
Mary le Tower in Ipswich.

Giuseppe Giordani, the singer,
travelling with his family
this year, reached Graz.

Gaetano Guadagni went from
Parma to London at this time.

Johann Michael Haydn sang a
"Salve Regina" at the Festival
of St. Leopold this season
and performed well.

Henry Harrington was awarded
his Bachelor of Arts degree
this year and dropped his idea
of the ministry. He began to
study medicine.

M. Heighington was organist
at St. Martin's, Leicester
this season.

Francis Ireland was awarded
the Master of Arts degree this
year at Dublin.

William Jackson, who showed a
strong desire for music at
this time, went to London and
became a pupil of John Travers.

Johann Friedrich Lampe and his
family left London this year
and went to Dublin.

1748(cont.)

Jean Marie Leclair ("l'aîné")
this year was appointed first
violinist in the private orchestra of the Duc de Gramont.

Jan Mareš went to Russia at
this time, having been recommended to a Russian grandee as
an excellent music teacher.

The libretto for G. B. Mele's
"Il vello d'oro conquestato"
(words by Pico della Mirandola)
has been preserved at the
British Museum.

Luis Missón was this year
admitted to the Royal Orchestra
at Madrid as a flutist and
oboist.

Cantor Mittag, Wilhelm
Friedemann Bach's colleague,
was dismissed at this time for
irregularity in attendance.

Until this year Davide Perez
was master of the Real Cappella
Palatina at Palermo.

François Phelidor spent some
time this year at Aachen,
Germany, while working on the
principles of chess.

Teresa Pompesti appeared this
season at London as a member
of the Mingotti opera troupe
and later with the same
company at Copenhagen.

Jean de la Pouplinière, who had
a private orchestra in Bris this
year, added horns, on the advice
of Johann Stamitz.

La Pouplinière and his wife
separated at this time.

The wealthy fermier général,

Riche de La Pouplinière,
brought the horn in its
orchestral form from Germany
this year and added it to his
own private orchestra. It
became known as "le nouveau
cor de chasse allemand".

Jean-François Rameau was involved in a quarrel at the
Opera this season and was
imprisoned in the For l'Eveque.

Joseph Royer became director
and lessee of the Concert
Spirituel at this time.

William Savage this year
became a vicar-choral, almoner
and Master of the Choristers
at St. Paul's Cathedral.

Paolo Scalabrini became conductor to the Danish court
at Copenhagen this season.

In a letter of this year,
Johann Stamitz (attached to
the court at Mannheim) discussed
the possibilities of his
accepting a highly paid position
at the court of Stuttgart.
The Duke of Württtenberg, however,
later appointed Holzbauer, then
Jommelli.

Tommaso Traetta at this time
was teaching singing and
occasionally wrote some
sacred music for several
churches at Naples.

M. C. V. Vestris arrived in
Paris this year.

J. B. Wending appeared in Paris
this season at the Concert
Spirituel.

John Worgan was awarded the
Bachelor of Music degree by
Cambridge this year.

K. P. E. Bach wrote his Concerto
in D minor for clavier this
season.

W. F. Bach's Sonata in E flat
was published at this time.

Blamont's "Cléopâtre" appeared
this year.

Boismortier's opera-ballet
"Daphné" was completed at this
time.

Breunich's cantata "La modera-
zione nella gloria" was heard
this season at Warsaw.

Burney's "Six Sonatas for Two
Violins, with Bass" appeared
this season.

The second book of Carolan's
works was issued at this time.

V. L. Ciampi's "opera seria"
"Adriano in Siria" was produced at the Teatro San Cassiano
during this year's carnival
season.

V. L. Ciampi's opera "Bertoldo,
Bertoldino e Cacasenno" was produced at Venice this year.

Corradin's "Polifemo" was produced at carnival this year at
the court theatre of Buen
Retiro.

Diderot's "Les Bijoux indiscrets"
Assézat edition, IV, appeared
at this time.

Diderot's "Mémoires suf
differents sujets de mathema-
tiques" was published this year
at The Hague.

Diderot's "Principes généraux

(cont.) de l'acoustique, 1745;
Assezat, IX was issued at this
time.

Baldassare Galuppi wrote the
opera "Clotilde" this year at
Venice (libretto by Passarini).

Baldassare Galuppi wrote his
opera "Demetrio" this year at
Vienna (libretto by Metastasio).

Baldassare Galuppi this season
wrote his opera "Vologeso" in
Rome (libretto by Zeno).

Georg Gebel's opera "Der durch
Krieg beschützte Friede" was
produced this season at
Rudolstadt.

Georg Gebel's opera "Die
Jagdlust" was produced this
season at Rudolstadt.

Joseph Gibbs this year published
his "Eight Solos for a Violin
with a Thorough Bass for the
Harpsichord or Bass Violin".

Carl Heinrich Graun's opera
"Cinna" was produced this
season at Berlin.

Carl Heinrich Graun's opera
"Europa galante" was produced
this season at Berlin.

Carl Heinrich Graun's opera
"Ifigenia in Aulide" was produced this year at Berlin.

Maurice Greene wrote his
pastoral "Phoebe" at this time.

C. P. Grua's opera "La clemenza
di Tito" was given this season
at Mantua.

Handel borrowed the overture
from Blow's "Begin the song"

for his oratorio "Susanna",
composed at this time.

"Solomon" by Handel was written
this year according to one
source only.

Hasse's pasticcios "L'ingrati-
tudine punita" and "Galatea ed
Acide" were performed this
season, the former at London,
the latter at Potsdam.

Johann Hemmorlein's "Mass"
was published at this time.

Jommelli's works this year
were performed as follows:
"Ezio" (a new version) at Naples,
"L'amore in maschera" at Naples,
"Merope" at Venice, and "Semira-
mide riconosciuta" at Turin.

Giovanni Battista Lampugnani's
opera "Andromaca" was produced
this season at Turin.

Giovanni Battista Lampugnani's
aria was inserted into the
London pasticcio "L'ingratitu-
dine punita" this season.

Giovanni Battista Lampugnani's
opera "L'Olimpiade" was produced this season at Florence.

N. Logroscino's "La contessa di
Belcolore" was produced this
year.

N. Logroscino's "Li despiette
d'ammore" was produced this year.

A lesser known composer, Luc
Marchand, organist in ordinary
to His Majesty, this year published a volume of "Pièces de
clavecin avec accompagnement de
violon, hautbois, violoncelle

(cont.) ou viole, divisées en
six suites dont les deux
dernières sont pour le clavecin
seul, dédiées à mgr. le Duc de
Luynes, par de France, ...
Oeuvre Ier".

F. Meyer's opus 1, "De semine
bono flos vernans" (40 arias)
appeared this year. Opus 2
through 6 were undated.

Pagin published 6 Sonatas with
bass in Paris this year dedicated to Prince de Grünberghem.

Porpora's "Il verbo incarnato"
or "Il verbo in carne" was performed this season at Dresden.

Robert Smith, mathematician,
published his book "Harmonies,
or the Philosophy of Musical
Sounds" at this time.

G. C. Wagenseil set Metastasio's
libretto "Alessandro nell'
Indie" to music this year.

Woodmason's "Psalm-Tunes"
was issued at this time at
London.

Pizzicato appeared this year
in an aria by Hasse written
for Mingotti.

The position of fife-major in
the Royal Artillery was mentioned at this time.

A fife-major was appointed this
year in the Artillery. He
supervised the fifers.

The Aberdeen Musical Society
was founded at this time.

Oxford college's Holywell
Music Room was opened this
season.

1748(cont.)

In Pennsylvania this year the dancing assembly was founded and an organ was mentioned in St. Joseph's, Willing's Alley, the 1st Roman Catholic Church in the United States.

At Salisbury, the meeting to celebrate St. Cecilia's festival was extended this year to two days.

Ludwig Heinrich Christoph Hölty, lyricist, was born this year (died 1776).

Eoghan Ruadh Ó Súilleabháin, Irish poet, was born at this time (died 1784).

Richardson's novel "Clarissa" was published at this time.

Smollett published his novel "Roderick Random" this season.

James Thomson's poem "The Castle of Indolence" was published this year in England.

Jacques Louis David, neo-classic French painter, was born this year (died 1825).

The English decorator William Kent died this year (born 1685).

Wyatt, the architect, was born this year (died 1813).

Count Albrecht Wolfgang of Schaumburg-Lippe died at this time (birthdate unknown).

Leopold Aloys Hoffmann, a professor of German language at the University of Pest, was born this year (died 1806).

Adam Weisshaupt was born this year at Ingolstadt (died 1830).

(to 1749) Bernacchi was president of the Accademia Filarmonica of Bologna during this period.

(to 1749) Caffarelli sang in Rome this season.

(to 1749) B. Cooke composed two anthems for the Founder's Day at the Charter House both of these years.

(to 1749) Cecillia Young went to Dublin again at this time.

(to 1750) J. S. Bach's "Die Kunst der Fuge" was composed during these years.

(to 1750) Fogliazzi, the famous Milanese dancer, performed in Florence during these years; also under the name "C. Angiolini di Firenze" at Venice.

(to 1750) Georgian architecture: Harrison, Newport, Redwood Library (portico-c. 26'wide).

(to 1750, April) Giuseppe Sarti was organist of the cathedral in Faenza during this period.

(to 1752) N. Pasquali lived in Dublin and wrote his oratorio "Noah" at this time.

(to 1754) Of the 8 one-act pieces Rameau composed between these dates, "Pygmalion" has been considered the best.

(to 1756) A. K. Kunzen's "Lieder zum unschieldigen Zeitvertreib" appeared during this period.

(and 1757) Blanchard was made director of the pages at the Royal Chapel after Campra's

1748(cont.)

death this year, but sold the office in 1757.

(to 1759) John Beard was again at Drury Lane during these years.

(to c.1764) Joseph Barnabé Saint-Sevin L'Abbé, violinist, composed two books of violin sonatas with continuo during this time.

(to 1788) Georg Benda was chapel master at Gotha for these forty years.

(to 1789) Armand Louis Couperin, son of Nicolas Couperin, was the organist of St. Gervais during this period.

(to 1799) William Ayrton was organist of Ripon Cathedral during these years. He died at the end of the time.

c.1748

J. S. Bach's "Canonic Variations on the Christmas hymn Vom Himmel hoch da komm' ich her" was published this year.

Giovanni Battista Bononcini, composer, died this year according to a major source (born 1670).

Louis-Thomas Bourgeois returned to Paris this year.

G. Haydn left the choir-school this year with the help of Spangler, a chorister at St. Michael's, plus a loan of 150 florins from a Viennese man, rented an attic in the old Michaelerhaus. He studied composition and the music of K. P. E. Bach.

Johann Friedrich Lampe's songs were in the collection "Ladies' Amusement" published this year in Dublin.

Joseph Mondonville's "Harpsichord pieces with voice or vn." was composed at this time.

(to 1749) Gainsborough painted "Portrait of Mr and Mrs. Robert Andrews" during this period. The picture is at the National Gallery at London and measures 27" x 47".

1749

(January 2) Arne wrote the incidental music for "Lethe, or Esop in the Shades", performed on this date at the Drury Lane Theatre in London.

(January 2) Boyce's "Lethe, or Esop in the Shades" was revived this evening at the Drury Lane Theatre in London.

(January 7) Hasse was made "Ober-Kapellmeister" at Dresden on this date.

(January 20) Johann Christoph Altnikol, the organist, married J. S. Bach's daughter, Liessgen (Elisabeth Juliane Frederike) on this day.

(February 3) André (Cardinal) Destouches, French composer, died this day at Paris (born 1672, April at Paris).

(February 10) Handel's oratorio in 3 parts "Susanna" was produced this evening at London (author of text unknown). The performance was at Covent Garden.

(February 21) Arne's "The Triumph of Peace" was performed

1749(cont.)
on this date at the Drury Lane
Theatre in London.

(February 22) Johann Nicolaus
Forkel, German writer on the
history and theory of music,
was born on this date at
Meeder, Saxe-Coburg (died
1818, March 20).

(February 23) Gertrude Elizabeth Mara (née Schmeling),
German soprano, was born at
this time in Cassel (died 1833,
January 20 at Reval).

(February 26) Pierre Lagarde's
opera-ballet "Silvie" was performed at this time in
Versailles.

(March 9) Gluck's Italian opera
"La contesa dei numi" (libretto
by Metastasio) was produced
this day at the court in
Copenhagen.

(March 10) Lorenzo da Ponte,
Italian poet and imperial court
poet at Vienna, was born on
this date (died 1838, August
17 at Ceneda, Venetia). He
was born Emanuele Conegliano
and was best known as a
librettist for Mozart. He also
taught at Columbia University.

(March 17) Handel's oratorio
"Solomon" (author of words
unknown) had its first performance on this evening at
Covent Garden in London.

(March 21) The Pennsylvania
Gazette on this date advertised
"John Beals, Musick Master from
London . . .teaches the Violin,
Hautboy, German Flute, Common
flute and Dulcimer by note".

(March 24) Bernard Jumentier,

(cont.) French composer, was
born on this date at Lèves near
Chartres (died 1829, December
17 at Saint-Quentin).

(March 31) Arne's "Henry and
Emma, or The Nut-Brown Maid"
was performed at this time at
Covent Garden in London.

(April 9) Gluck's "La contesa
de'numi" was performed on this
date at Copenhagen with a
second introduction again
borrowed from Sammartini.

(April 14) William Hayes on
this day directed the performance at the opening of the
Radcliffe Library and was
made a Doctor of Music.

(April 21) A rehearsal of
Handel's "Royal Fireworks
Music" took place this day at
Vauxhall Gardens. He used
the contrabassoon in this work.

(April 22) Rameau's pastoral
heroique, "Naïs" (libretto by
Cahusac) was performed on this
date at Paris.

(April 27) Handel's "Royal
Fireworks Music" was performed
in London on this date at the
Green Park, on the occasion of
the Peace of Aix-la-Chapelle.

(April 29) Boyce's elder child,
Elizabeth, was born on this day
(death date unknown).

(May 4) Handel at this time
offered to give a performance
of vocal and instrumental music
at the Foundling Hospital.

(May 6) Johann Friedrich Edelmann, Alsation composer, was
born on this date at Strasbourg
(died 1794, July 17 at Paris).

(May 8) Antonio Scarlatti, son of Domenico and member of the fourth generation of the Scarlatti family, was born at this time (died after 1799).

(May 11) The baptismal certificate for Antonio Scarlatti bore this date.

(May 21) Thomas Kelway, English organist, composer and brother of Joseph Kelway, died at this time at Chichester (birthdate unknown).

(June 8) Johann Gottlob Harrer auditioned on this date for the position in Leipzig that would be vacant if J. S. Bach died.

(June 11) Johann Bernhard Bach, Eisenach organist, son of J. Egidius, grandson of Johann and member of the sixth generation of the Bach family, died on this date at Eisenach (born 1676, November 23 at Erfurt).

(June 12) Anselm Bayly graduated from the Chapel Royal on this date as B. C. L.

(June 15) The Abbé Georg Joseph Vogler, pianist, organist and teacher of Weber and Meyerbeer, was born at this time in Wurzburg (died 1814, June 15).

(Summer) V. L. Ciampi's company of Italian singers visited Brussels at this time.

(June 22) John Smith, in his ms. Journal, showed that on this day, Addison's "Cato" was performed at Philadelphia.

(June 27) William Hayes was admitted as a chorister of Magdalen College, Oxford on this date.

(July 1) Boyce set William Mason's ode to music for the installation of the Duke of Newcastle as Chancellor of the University of Cambridge. It was performed in the Senate House on this evening.

(July 2, 3) Boyce's anthem "O be joyful" with orchestral accompaniments, was performed as a test for the degrees of Bachelor and Doctor of Music which were conferred on him at this time.

(July 8) Louis Auguste Joseph Janson, Netherlands cellist, composer and brother of Jean Baptiste Janson, was born on this day at Valenciennes (died 1815, probably at Paris).

(July 9) King Philip V of Spain died at this time and Fernando was proclaimed King (born 1683). See also 1746 for alternate death date.

(July 17) Philip Hart, English organist and conductor, died on this date at London (birthdate unknown).

(August 5) Marie Justine Benoîte Favart made her debut this evening as an actress with the "Comédiens Italiens".

(August 7) Daniel Gottlieb Treu, German violinist and composer, died on this date at Breslau (born 1695 at Stuttgart).

(September 4) John James Heidegger, a Swiss impresario and librettist in the King's Theater, died at this time at Richmond, Surrey (born 1666, June 13 at Zurich).

(Autumn) Abos' opera "Alessandro

1749(cont.)
nell'Indie" was given this
season at Lucca.

(Autumn) V. L. Ciampi's "Il
negligente" was produced at
San Moisè this season.

(September 23) Joseph Mondonville
on this date produced at the
Opéra "Le Carnaval du Parnasse",
an opera-ballet in three acts.

(October 4) J. S. Bach's grandson and manesake, Johann
Sebastian, was born on this day
according to two sources (see
1748 for consensus opinion).

(October 4) Jean Louis Duport,
French cellist, was born on
this date at Paris (died 1819,
September 7 at Paris).

(October 6) James Vincent,
organist and composer, died
at this time at London (birthdate unknown but at London).

(October 7) Hasse's opera "Il
natale di Giove" (libretto by
Metastasio) was produced on
this date at Hubertusburg.

(October 8) Rosalie Levasseur,
French soprano, was born this
day at Valenciennes (died 1826).

(October 10) Heinrich Christoph
Koch, German violinist and
author, was born on this date at
Rudolstadt (died 1816, March 12
at Rudolstadt).

(October 19) D. Scarlatti
completed his last will and
testament at this time.

(October 26) Louis Nicolas
Clerambault, French composer
and organist, died on this date
at Paris (born 1676, December 19

(cont.) at Paris). He was
essentially a cantata composer.

(November 27) Gottfried
Heinrich Stölzel, German composer, died at this time in
Gotha (born 1690, January 13
in Grunstadlth, Saxony).

(December 2) Boyce's opera
"The Chaplet" was produced
on this date at the Drury
Lane Theatre in London.

(December 5) The first performance of Rameau's and Cahuzac's
tragédie en musique, "Zoroastre",
was given on this date at Paris.
It was their fourth such work
and the most important of
Rameau's later period.

(December 17) Domenico Cimarosa,
Italian opera composer, was
born on this date at Aversa,
Naples (died 1801, January 11
at Venice).

(December 19) Francesco
Antonio Bonporti, Italian
composer, died this day at
Padua (born 1672 at Trento).

(December 23) Johann Lukas
Schubaur, German composer,
was baptized on this day at
Lechfeld, Suabia.

(December 31) Juan Antonio
Scarlatti at this time was
assigned a benefice in the
parish church of Alijar in the
archbishopric of Seville.

(December 31 to 1752, March)
Juan Antonio Scarlatti, son of
Domenico and member of the
fourth generation of the Scarlatti family, died sometime
during this period (born c.1729).

(June) Michael van Beethoven

died this month at Bonn. He was Ludwig's great-grandfather (born 1684 at Malines).

(November) V. L. Ciampi's company of Italian singers fell out with their manager, Signor Croza, at this time and with-drew to a smaller theatre, where Ciampi's "Il negligente" was performed.

(November) J. Haydn was dismissed as a choirboy at the Cathedral of St. Stephen in Vienna due to a change in voice at this time. He succeeded by his brother Michael.

(November) Willem Kennis left Lierre this month to become chapel master at St. Peter's Church at Louvain.

(December) Mary Louise van Beethoven, Ludwig's great-grandmother, died this month at Bonn (birthdate unknown).

(December) Johann Lukas Schuhaus, German composer, was born at this time in Lechfeld, Suabia (died 1815, November 15 at München).

Joseph Agus, French composer, was born this year (died 1798, May). Confusion in this matter leads some to believe this was Henri Agus.

Richard Burnham, English Baptist who composed lyrics to hymns, was born at this time (died 1810).

Charles Nicolas Justin Favart, son of Marie Justine Benoite Favart and Charles Simon Favart; an actor, writer and singer, was born this year at Paris (died 1806, February 2).

Johann Ernst Galliard, German oboist and composer, died at this time in London (born c.1680 or 1687).

Francesco Gobetti, violin maker, died this year (born 1690).

John Percy, English tenor, organist and composer, was born this year (died 1797, January 24 at London).

Johann Ernst Rembt, German organist and composer, was born at this time in Suhl, Thuringia (died 1810, February 26 at Suhl). His birth has also been given as 1750. He was a devoted follower of J. S. Bach.

Jean Pierre Tulou, French bassoon player, was born this year at Paris (died 1799 at Paris).

Pietro Urbani, singer, singing teacher, composer and theorist, was born at this time in Milan (died 1816, December at Dublin).

Polly Young, well-known English singer, was born this year (died 1799, September 20).

Franz Zöhrer, Austrian Member of lodge "Zu den drei Adlern" in Vienna and conductor to Count Palm in Regensburg, was born this year at Zwettl (death date unknown).

Albanese studied at Naples, but left for Paris this year and was engaged for the Royal Chapel there.

John Alcock this year was appointed organist, master of the choristers and lay vicar at Lichfield Cathedral.

d'Argenson, who neither cared for Rameau's music nor him personally, was able this year to forbid that more than two of his operas be given in any one year.

Mrs. Lampe sings in "Acis and Galatea" this season with Mrs. Arne at Dublin.

The version of Auletta's "Orazio" given this year at Brussels was attributed to Auletta on one page of the libretto and to Galuppi on another page.

Johann Ernst Bach this year dedicated a set of "Fables" he had set to music to Prince Ernst August Constantin.

A disease of the eyes left J. S. Bach nearly blind. He underwent an operation this year by Chevalier John Taylor, who was a surgeon and oculist to King George III.

Barsanti's overture and concertos appeared in this year's catalogue of The Aberdeen Musical Society.

J. A. Benda remained as a second violinist in the Berlin royal orchestra up to this time.

Boyce this year became organist of All Hallows Great and Less on Thames Street.

Buffardin was pensioned off this year with 700 thaler per annum.

Burney joined the Royal Society of Musicians this season.

Rameau's librettist for this year's "Zorastre", Cahuzac, complained about the incongruity of having a large chorus on stage, proclaiming a catastrophe and yet standing absolutely still as in the fourth act of this work.

On a trip to Parma this year, Casanova met a girl he referred to only as "Henriette". The girl was a fine musical artist and awaked in Casanova a genuine appreciation since prior to this meeting he was not especially interested in music.

The cantata was cultivated by N. Clérambault who died this year.

Gioacchino Conti was invited by Farinelli to sing at the Madrid with Mingotti this season.

Theresa Cornelys was in Copenhagen this year.

Antonio da Costa fled his native country toward the end of this year in a rather bizarre fashion.

Cotumacci was appointed organist at the Santa Casa dell' Annunziata at this time.

Henri de Croes this year became master of the music in the Royal Chapel at Brussels.

Exaudet, French violinist and composer, was engaged for the Opéra this year at Paris.

Benjamin Franklin at this time was able to accept the low level of music in the colonies as unavoidable.

Giulia Frasi this season sang
in two of Handel's oratorios,
"Solomon" and "Susanna".

D. Paradisi's pupil, Cassandra
Frederick, gave a concert this
year at the Little Haymarket
Theatre in London and played
compositions by Handel and
Scarlatti.

Galuppi's works were performed
at the Mannheim school this
season.

Georg Sigismund Gebel this year
became principal organist at
St. Elizabeth's Church in
Breslau.

Johann Georg Gebel this year
became an organist at the Church
of the Holy Trinity at Breslau.

Francesco Geminiani, the great
violinist, moved from London to
Paris this year.

Gluck gave a concert at Copenhagen this year and played a
concerto on 26 glasses.

Melchior Grimm arrived in Paris
at this time and quickly became
involved in the cultural life
of the city.

Charles Helmont was appointed
Chapel Master at Brussels
Cathedral this year.

A son and three daughters of
Caix D'Hervelois were mentioned
this year as performers on the
viola da gamba at the French
Royal Chamber.

Nicolaas Godfried Heyns this
year became organist at the
church in Cape Town, South
Africa.

Jommelli went to Vienna this
season and produced his
"Achille in Sciro" and "Catone
in Utica". Both librettos
were by Metastasio.

Niccoló Jommelli arrived in
Vienna this year with his
German version of "Merope",
based on a libretto by Zeno.

Jacob Kleinknecht was second
"Konzertmeister" at the
Bayreuth court this season.

A. K. Kunzen was appointed
Konzertmeister to the Duke of
Mecklenburg-Schwerin this year.

Thomas Lowe sang in Handel's
"Solomon" this season.

Pierre von Maldere this year
became first violinist at
the Royal Chapel of Brussels.

F. W. Marpurg edited three
successive papers this year.

William Mason was awarded the
Master of Arts degree this
year from Cambridge.

Mongeot was in Paris at this
time, but never composed any
opera.

Pierre Monsigny went to Paris
at this time and became a
clerk in the "Bureaux des
Comptes du Clergé".

The three organists of the
Royal Chapel in Spain at this
time were Nebra, Sebastian
Albero, and Joaquín Oxinaga.

Palestrina at this juncture was
viewed as a typical figure of
his time, so much so that his
style became the basis for the
study of strict counterpoint

after Fux' death this year.

M. Palotta was reinstated this year as a court composer at Vienna.

The first edition of François Philedor's book "Analyse du jeu des éches" was published this year at London where he had gone at the invitation of the Duke of Cumberland.

Rameau used clarinets in Paris this year in his "Zorastre" following the lead of Johann Stamitz at Mannheim.

Rameau met his librettist, Marmontel this season at La Poupliniére's.

Royer, with Caperan, continued the "Concert Spirituel" this year at Paris.

"The pathos and seriousness of opera suit us less well than dancing" was a quote this year from the pen of Rémond de Saint-Mard.

Giuseppe Santarelli became a singer (alto) in the Sistine Choir this year.

Sarti this season succeeded Johann Scheibe as director of the court opera at Copenhagen.

A volume of Scarlatti's sonatas was copied out for Queen Maria Barbara at this time.

Burkat Shudi made a harpsichord this year for a Mr. Warre; #229, two manual. It has survived.

John Shore at this time married a Mrs. Speed in London.

A jubilee of this year celebrated Cardinal Archbishop Sigismund von Kollonicz' fiftieth year in the priesthood.

Victoria Tesi this season sang the lead in Jommelli's "Didone". She was heard and admired by Metastasio, who claimed she made him feel twenty years younger.

Voltaire, recognizing Rameau's poverty at this time, gave him all the payments from "Le Temple de la Gloire", giving up his own share.

John Worgan became organist this year at St. Andrew Undershaft and St. Mary Axe.

Johann Friedrich Agricola this year published two pamphlets on French and Italian taste under the pseudonym of Flavio Anicio Olibrio.

Aliprandi's setting of the "Stabat Mater" appeared at this time.

Johann Ernst Bach's "Sammlung auserlesner Fabeln mit dazu verfertigten Melodeyen" was composed at this time.

K. P. E. Bach wrote his "Magnificat in d minor" this year at Berlin. The work was for solo voices, chorus and orchestra.

Johann Sebastian Bach's "The Art of the Fugue" ("Die Kunst der Fuge" was written this year according to most sources.

J. S. Bach's "Phöbus und Pan" was revived this season.

W. F. Bach wrote his cantata "Lasset uns ablegen" this year.

At Chemnitz this year a "Kurz-gefasstes musikalisches Lexikon" by One Barnikel was published anonymously.

Boyce this year became a theatre composer by reviving the masque "Peleus and Thetis" and adding songs to Garrick's farce "Lethe" at the Drury Lane Theatre in London and also composing music to the successful entertainment "The Chaplet".

V. L. Ciampi's "Bertoldo, Bertoldino e Cacasenno" was produced this season during the carnival at the Teatro San Moisè.

V. L. Ciampi's "La favola dei tre gobbi" was performed this season at the Teatro San Moisè.

Domenico Fischietti's "L'abbate Collarone" was produced this year at the Teatro della Pace.

Fritsch at this time wrote the music for "Der Frühling, ein Singspiel von Sperontes".

Baldassare Galuppi wrote his opera "Alcimena, principessa dell'isole fortunate" this year at Venice (libretto by Chiari).

Baldassare Galuppi wrote his opera "L'Arcadia in Brenta" this year at Venice (libretto by Goldoni). The opera had its first production at Venice this year as well.

Baldassare Galuppi wrote his opera "Arcifanfano, re de' matti" this year at Venice

(cont.) (libretto by Goldoni).

Baldassare Galuppi wrote his opera "Artaserse" this year at Vienna (libretto by Metastasio).

Baldassare Galuppi wrote his opera "Il conte caramella" this year at Verona (libretto by Goldoni). The opera also had its first production there this season.

Baldassare Galuppi wrote his opera "Il Demofoonte" this year at Madrid (libretto by Metastasio).

Baldassare Galuppi wrote his opera "Olimpia" this year at Naples (libretto by Trabucco).

Baldassare Galuppi's opera "Il Protettore della Moda" was performed frequently this year. Casanova may have heard it with his beloved Henriette.

Baldassare Galuppi wrote his opera "Semiramide riconosciuta" this year at Milan (libretto by Metastasio).

Georg Gebel's opera "Iphis" was produced this season at Rudolstadt.

Georg Gebel's opera "Die siegende Weisheit in Cyro" was produced this year at Rudolstadt.

Georg Gebel's opera "Zeroide" was produced this season at Rudolstadt.

Francesco Geminiani's "Treatise of Good Taste" was published this year at London.

Carl Heinrich Graun's "Angelica e Medoro" was produced this

1749(cont.)
season at Berlin.

Carl Heinrich Graun's opera "Coriolano" was produced this season at Berlin.

Habermann's "Conversio peccatorio", an oratorio known by the preserved libretto only, was published this year.

Handel's Foundling Hospital Anthem "Blessed are they that consider the poor", was composed at this time.

Handel wrote the libretto for "Theodora" at this time.

Hasse's pasticcios "Ercole al Termodonte" and "Tomiri" were both produced this year at Braunschweig.

John Hebden, Eighteenth Century instrumentalist, this year played a piece for five cellos by Abaco at a concert.

Charles Helmont's "divertissement pour la paix" called "Le Retour désiré" was performed this season.

James Hoey this year printed a book of songs with symphonies and thorough-bass by Lampe, who was living in Dublin at the time. Some pieces by Pasquali were included in the volume.

Jommelli's opera "Artaserse" was produced this season at Rome.

Jommelli's operas listed below were performed this year at the locations indicated: "Achille in Sciro" (Vienna); "Arteserse" (Rome); "Catone in Utica"

(cont.) (Vienna); "Demetrio" (Parma); "Ezio" (Vienna), new version.

G. B. Lampugnani's opera "Andromaca" was given this year at Turin.

Giovanni Battista Lampugnani's opera "Artaserse"was produced this season at Milan.

Gaetano Latilla's "La finta giardinera" appeared this season at London as "Don Colascione".

Metastasio's libretto for the canzonetta "La Partenza" was set to music by himself.

F. Meyer's "Festival Mass for Three Choirs" was composed this year at Beromünster.

Davide Perez' "La clemenza di Tito" was performed this season at the Teatro San Carlo in Naples.

Ciampi introduced a version of the song "Tre giorni son che Nina" (generally attributed to Pergolesi) into N. Pesta's "Li tre cicisbei ridicoli" this year at London. Many thought that Ciampi had composed it himself.

The first edition of François Philidor's book "Analyse du jeu des echecs" was issued at this time.

Rameau's "Platée" was performed this year at the Opéra in Paris.

Remond de Saint-Mard's "Réflexions sur l'opéra, Oeuvres, V," was published this year.

Metastasio's libretto to the cantata "L'Augurio di felicità" was first set this year by Reutter.

Pierre-Charles Roy's "Lettres sur l'opéra; in Lettres sur quelques ecrits de ce Temps, II" was issued this year.

G. Scarlatti's opera "Partenope" was produced this year at the Teatro Regio in Turin (libretto by Stampiglia).

The fifteenth volume of D. Scarlatti's violin sonatas was published at this time.

Scarlatti's volume of sonatas of this year was illuminated with gold. The indications, tempo markings and titles were all included in this technique.

Johann Scheibe's libretto "Thusnelda" was published at this time in Copenhagen.

The first Masonic Collection appeared this year. It was by a German musician, Johann Adolf Scheibe.

G. C. Wagenseil this year set Metastasio's libretto "L'Olimpiade" to music.

Geminiani's "Treatise of Good Taste" of this year (privilege, 1739) described acciaccatura, used broken chords, and showed staccato as "one half and once reducing the note".

Scarlatti's sonatas of this year were "flashy and relatively youthful".

The pairwise arrangement first

(cont.) makes its appearance this year at Venice in Volume 15 of D. Scarlatti's sonatas.

In the Queen's volume of Scarlatti sonatas this year, the range included the fifty-six notes from G_1 to d_3.

The Papal Encyclical published this year made specific recommendations for the improvement of sacred music.

The introduction of drama and opera in Philadelphia took place at this time.

Seilhamer stated this year ". . .the Philadelphia performers of 1749 are . . . in part actors who had (had) some experience in England and in part amateurs . . ."

The "Musikausübende Gesellschaft" was founded this year at Berlin.

The College of Philadelphia was founded at this time. Conceivably it could have been 1753.

An organ was built this year in the Church of St. Margaret Pattens.

Hogarth this year painted "Calais Gate" (31" x 37 1/4"). The picture is at the National Gallery in London.

Jean-Baptiste Perroneau this year painted "Portrait of Madame de Sorquainville" (oil on canvas, 39 3/8 x 33 1/2").

Johann Wolfgang von Goethe, the immortal poet and author of "Faust" was born this year (died 1832). Some of the greatest composers used his texts.

Sir John Hawkins this year
joined Samuel Johnson's Ivy
Lane Club, and became one of
its earliest members. This club
lasted seven years.

William Collins' "Ode on the
Superstitions of the Highlands
of Scotland" was written at
this time.

Fielding published his novel
"Tom Jones" in England this year.
The work is still considered to
be a model for the novel.

David Hartley wrote "Observations on Man" this year. The
book gave full treatment to
the chief materialistic psychol-
ogy of the time, "Association".

Johnson's poem "The Vanity of
Human Wishes" was published at
this time.

Jean-Jaques Rousseau this year
proclaimed the philosophical
foundation of the time by
stressing the moral ignorance
of an era only interested in
reason and scientific discovery.

Andrew Law was born this year
at New Haven, Connecticut
(death date unknown).

Lorenz Leopold Haschka, a member
of St. Joseph Masonic lodge,
was born (died 1827).

Arvid Hopkin this year became
lieutenant-colonel at
Stralseend.

(to 1750) J. N. Hamal during
these years returned to Rome
and Naples to perfect his

(cont.) composition. He made
friends with Jommelli and
Durante, who gave him counsel.

(to 1750) Johann Stamitz,
Bohemian conductor, composer
and violinist, paid a visit to
his parental home at this time
while one of his brothers
assumed his duties at Mannheim.

(to 1750) Franz Haydn wrote his
first Mass during this period,
"Missa Brevis in F Major" for
two sopranos, four-part chorus,
two violins, organ and bass.

(to 1750) Friedrich Wilhelm
Marpurg wrote his treatise
"Der critische Musicus an der
Spree" during these years in
Berlin.

(to 1750) Robert Feke, American
painter, this year did his
"Self-Portrait" (50" x 40").

(to 1751) Petrus Hellendaal
studied at the University of
Leyden during this period.

(to 1752) Elizabeth Hare was at
the "Viol and Hautboy" opposite
the Mansion House at Cheapside
during this period. Nothing
is known of his death or the
termination of the business.

(and 1752-1757) Handcrossings
were rare from 1752 to 1757,
compared with Scarlatti's
earlier sonatas of 1749.

(to 1754) Élie Freron's "Lettres
sur quelques ecrits de ce
Temps" was completed during
these years.

(to 1757) Three of Domenico
Scarlatti's children died
during this period.

1749(cont.)
(to 1757) Alexandro Scarlatti, son of Domenico and member of the fourth generation of the Scarlatti family, died sometime in this period (born c.1736).

(to 1757) Mariana Scarlatti, daughter of Domenico and member of the fourth generation of the Scarlatti family, died sometime in this period (born sometime between 1732-1735).

(to 1757) The first published book of Scottish secular instrumental music was published sometime during this time span.

(to 1758) John Beals, music master from London, taught "the Dulcimer by note", among other instruments for these nine years.

(to 1758) Giovanni Guadagnini, violin maker, moved from Piacenza to Milan during these years.

(to 1759) Dr. John Alcock was organist at Lichfield Cathedral for these ten years. He was disappointed that the only music fit for his use, he had either bought or composed.

(to 1762) Ignazio Fiorillo lived in Braunschweig during this period. His son, Federico, was born while he was there.

(to 1771) Philippo Nicolini was in Braunschweig as head of the "Compania dei piccoli Hollandesi" for these twenty-two years.

c.1749
Nicholas Matteis, English violinist of Italian descent, died this year at Shrewsbury (birthdate unknown).

John Simpson, English instrument seller, engraver and publisher, died this year at London (birthdate unknown).

Count Francesco Algarotti was compelled by illness to return to Italy this year.

Domenico Ferrari, violinist, began to tour this year as a concert artist. The tour was generally successful.

B. Galuppi's association with Carlo Goldini at Venice this year was considered a turning point in the history of "opera buffa".

Gregorio Sciroli was teaching at the Conservatory of Palermo this year.

Johann Sebastian Bach this year wrote the secular wedding cantata, "O holder Tag", known also as "O angenehme Melodei".

J. S. Bach's cantata #50, "Nun ist das Heil und die Kraft" was composed at this time for Michaelmas.

Handel's Concerto in D Major for two oboes, bassoon, four horns, two trumpets, drums, strings and continuo was composed at this time.

Handel's "Concerto in F major" for two oboes, bassoon, four horns, strings and continuo was composed this year.

1750
(January 12) Hasse's opera "Attilio Regolo" (libretto by Metastasio) was written in 1740 for Vienna, but not performed at that time. It was performed on this date at Dresden.

154

GEORG PHILIPP TELEMANN
1681-1767

(January 17) Tommaso Albinoni, Italian composer, died on this day at Venice (born 1671, June 8 at Venice).

(January 25) Johann Gottfried Vierling, German organist and composer, was born on this date at Metzels near Meiningen (died 1813, November 22 at Schmal Kalden).

(February 10) Stanislao Mattei, Italian composer and teacher, was born at this time in Bologna (died 1825, May 12 at Bologna).

(February 15) Arne's "Don Saverio" was performed this evening at the Drury Lane Theatre in London.

(February 22) Pietro Filippo Scarlatti, Royal Chapel organist in Spain, died on this day at Naples (born 1679, January 5).

(February 24) Boyce's "The Roman Father" with incidental music was performed on this date at the Drury Lane Theatre in London.

(February 24) Tartini wrote to Algarotti at this time and suggested that Frederick the Great should be asked about the possibility of Bini's entering the service of the Prussian court.

(February 25) Pierre Lagarde's opera-ballet "La Journée galante" was performed on this date at Versailles. It consisted of "Aegle" and two additional acts.

(February 26) The New York Gazette in this issue wrote, "Last week arrived here a company of comedians from Philadelphia".

(March 6) The Pennsylvania Gazette in this issue reprinted "Last week arrived here a company of comedians from Philadelphia".

(March 12) Tartini, on behalf of Bini, wrote to Prince Lobkowitz's secretary on this day concerning the matter of choice of a "maestro di cappella".

(March 15) Boyce's "The Rehearsal, or Bay in Petticoats" with incidental music, was produced this evening at the Drury Lane Theatre in London.

(March 16) Handel's oratorio "Theodora" with words by Morell had its first performance on this date at Covent Garden in London.

(March 27) Pergolesi's "La Serva Padrona" was given this evening at the Haymarket Theatre in London.

(March 28) Hasse's oratorio in operatic style, "La Conversione di Sant Agostino" (The Conversion of St. Augustine), composed at Dresden had a production at this time. The text was by Maria Antonio Walpurgis of Saxony.

(April 2) Michael Arne made his debut this evening at Galli's concert in the Little Theatre, Haymarket in London.

(April 8) A serenade, "L'Asilo

d'Amore", with text by Metastasio, music by Corselli, and decorations by Jolli, was produced on this date.

(April 8) The British Museum has preserved the libretto for Corselli's "L'asilo d'amore" (Buen Retiro).

(April 9) Francois Giroust, French composer, was born on this date at Paris (died 1799, August 28).

(April 12) The opera "Armida Aplacata" was performed on this date in the Coliseo. The libretto was by Migliavacca based on Metastasio; the music was by Mele.

(April 16) Arne's "The Sacrifice of Iphigenia" was performed this evening at New Wells (Saddler's Wells) in London.

(April 20) Caroli succeeded G. A. Perti on this date at the Congregazione dell'Oratorio.

(April 21) The "Gaceta de Madrid" for this date provided an elaborate description of performances of "L'Asilo d'Amore" and "Armida Aplacata".

(May 1) J. A. Benda on this date was appointed "Kapellmeister" at the Thuringian court of Gotha.

(May 1) Handel at this juncture was one of the governors and guardians of the Foundling Hospital. He had donated an organ to the chapel this year and opened the chapel with a concert on the organ.

(May 23) Burney stated that

(cont.) Cuzzoni this year made her third visit to London where she sang a benefit concert.

(May 29) Giuseppe Porsile, Italian composer, died this day at Vienna (born 1680 at Naples).

(June 14) Franz Anton Maichelbeck, German composer, died at this time at Freiburg i/B (born 1702, July 6 at Reichenau near Constance).

(June 25) J. J. Kreigk, German violinist and cellist, was born on this day at Bibra, Merseburg (died 1813 at Meiningen).

(June 28) Handel's "The Choice of Hercules" was begun on this date.

(July 5) Handel's "The Choice of Hercules" was finished on this day.

(July 18) Johann Sebastian Bach, ten days before his death, was suddenly able to see again and worked until the moment of his collapse.

(July 18) Isaac Lyon and John Crane on this day were appointed as guardians of James Lyon.

(July 28) Johann Sebastian Bach on this date dictated the chorale prelude "Before thy Throne, My God, I Stand" to his son-in-law.

(July 28) Johann Sebastian Bach, monumental organist and composer, son of J. Ambrosius, grandson of Christoph and member of the fifth generation of the Bach family died on this day at Leipzig (born 1685,

1750(cont.)
March 21 at Eisenach). His demise took place at the Thomasschule residence at 8:45 p.m. on a Tuesday.

(July 30) Forkel incorrectly gave this as Johann Sebastian Bach's death date (see July 28).

(July 31) Johann Sebastian Bach was buried on this date at the churchyard of the Johannis Kirche in Leipzig. The burial took place early on a Friday morning.

(August 7) Cajetano Mattioli, Bonn musician, was born at this time (death date unknown).

(August 18) Antonio Salieri, Italian opera composer, was born on this date at Legnago (died 1825, May 7). He was a pupil of Gluck and also taught vocal composition to Beethoven (died 1825).

(August 25) André Gretry on this day at Nine years of age was placed in the choir of Saint-Denis.

(September 2) Pehr Frigel, Swedish composer, was born this day at Kalmar (died 1842, November 24).

(September 15) Gluck at this time married Marianna Pergin, daughter of a rich merchant and banker. The marriage brought Gluck a considerable fortune.

(September 17) Michael Woldemar, French violinist and composer, was born on this day at Orléans (died 1815, December 19).

(September 22) Christoph Gottlob Breitkopf, son of the printer, was born this day at Leipzig (died 1800, April 4 at Leipzig).

(September 28) Arne wrote the incidental music for "Romeo and Juliet", performed this evening at Covent Garden in London.

(October 1) Boyce's "Romeo and Juliet" was performed on this date at the Drury Lane Theatre in London.

(October 3) Georg Matthias Monn, Austrian organist and composer, died on this date at Vienna. His symphonies, trio sonatas, quartets and other works were in a transitional style typical of the pre-classical period (born 1717 in Lower Austria).

(October 15) Silvius Weiss, German lutenist and composer, died on this date at Dresden (born 1686, October 12).

(October 18 and 24) Jean-Jacques Rousseau produced "Le Devin du village" before the King at Fontainebleu at this time. Since it pleased the court, it was quickly printed in Paris.

(October 30) Boyce's "The Secular Masque", with music for the revival, was produced on this date at Drury Lane Theatre in London.

(November 11) Apostolo Zeno, writer, librettist and historian, died this year at Venice (born 1668, December 11 at Venice).

1750(cont.)

(November 15) Pantaleon Heben-
streit, German dulcimer player
who had been a dancing master
and violinist, died at Dresden
at this time (born 1669 at
Eisleben).

(November 20) Pascal Joseph
Taskin, instrument maker, was
born on this date at Theux
(died 1829, February 5 at Paris).

(November 30) The Marshal
Maurice de Saxe died at this
time (birthdate unknown).

(December 3) The first performance of "The Beggar's Opera"
in America took place on this
evening.

(December 3) Johann Franz
Xaver Sterkel (Abbé Sterkel),
German priest and amateur
musician, was born this day at
Würzburg (died 1817, October 21
at Würzburg).

(December 17) Elizabeth, Mar-
gräfin of Auspach and English
amateur composer, was born on
this day at London (died 1828,
January 13 at Naples).

(December 25) John Christmas
Beckwith, English organist,
composer and painter, was born
on this date at Norwich (died
1809, June 3 at Norwich).

(December 26) Oswald's pantomime,
"Queen Mab" was produced on this
day at the Drury Lane Theatre
in London by the Society of
the Masque of Alfred.

(January) Louis-Thomas Bourgeois, French singer and composer, died this month at Paris
(born 1676, October 24 at
Fontaine-l'Evêque, Hainault).

(April) Herbain was a captain
in a cavalry regiment when some
minuets of his appeared in the
"Mercure de France".

(May) J. G. Müthel went to
Leipzig this month to study
under J. S. Bach.

(July-August) Handel's last
visit to Halle at this time
coincided with J. S. Bach's
fatal illness. It was the
former's third visit to
Germany.

(September) Johann van Beethoven
this month took part in the
annual school play at the
Gymnasium. It was customary
for the (Musae) Bonnenses to
give this play.

(September) Holzbauer succeeded
Brescianello this month as
court conductor at Stuttgart.

Jean-Baptiste Christophe
Ballard, English printer, died
this year (birthdate unknown).

G. B. Bononcini, Italian composer's death date was given
as this year by one source
(see 1747 and 1755).

Cyprian Cormier, Italian
violinist and composer, was
born this year at Venice (died
1789 at Warsaw).

Giacomo Davide, Italian tenor,
was born this year at Presezzo
near Bergamo (died 1830,
December 31 at Presezzo).

William Gawler, English organist, composer and publisher,
was born this year at London
(died 1809, March 15).

Johann Georg Gebel, German

organist and composer, died this
year at Breslau (born 1685).

Maria Anna Katharina Gilowsky,
who frequently appeared in
Mozart's correspondence as
daughter of the "Antecamera-
Kammerdiener" was born at this
time (died 1802).

Marcin Groblicz, II, Polish
violin maker, died this year
at Warsaw (birthdate unknown).

Maria Barbara's father João V
of Portugal died at this time
after six years of paralysis.

Wenzel Krumpholz, Bohemian
violinist and brother of
Johann, was born this year
probably at Zlonice near Prague
(died 1817, May 2 at Vienna).

Wincenty Lessel, Polish composer of Bohemian origin, was
born this year in Bohemia
(death date unknown).

Johann Gottfried Müthel, J. S.
Bach's pupil, was living in his
house at the time of the latter's
death.

Karl Pachelbel, who had served
as organist in Newport, Rhode
Island, and later until his
death in Charleston, died this
year (born 1690). He was the
son of the famous German organist.

Giovanni Francesco Maria
Paganini, first son of Giovanni
Battista Paganini, was born
this year. He did not survive
his childhood (death date
unknown).

Pelling died this year and left
a large fortune to his nephew,

(cont.) J. Pigott (birthdate
unknown). The latter resigned
the Eaton organist's position
immediately after his inheri-
tance.

F. A. Rössler, Bohemian composer, was born this year
(died 1792). He has also been
referred to as Rosetti.

Johann Sigismund Scholze,
composer and lawyer, died at
this time (born 1705).

Johann Samuel Schroeter,
pianist, was born this year
(died 1788).

John Stafford Smith, English
organist, composer and tenor,
was born this year in Gloucester (died 1836, September
21). He was the composer of
"To Anacreon in Heaven", the
song from which the music to
the "Star Spangled Banner"
was taken.

John Tufts, publisher of a
book on musical notation, died
at this time (born 1689).

Francesco Maria Veracini,
Italian violinist and composer,
died this year near Pisa (born
1690 at Pisa).

Thomas Woodcock, English
violinist, died at this time
(birthdate unknown).

Alcock became organist, master
of the choristers and lay-vicar
of Lichfield Cathedral this
year.

The "Encyclopédie" by Diderot
and d'Alembert described the
minuet "of a noble and elegant
simplicity; the movement is
moderate rather than quick".

1750(cont.)

Bernardo Aliprandi at this time was appointed conductor ("Konzertmeister") of the Munich court orchestra.

The death of his father in 1750 denied Johann Christian Bach the university education his older brothers had received.

Johann Christoph Friedrich Bach became "Kammermusikus" this year to Count von Lippe at Bückeburg.

Johann Ernst Bach married Florentina Malsch this year.

When J. S. Bach died this year, he left cash and bonds worth 360 thalers, silver plate worth 251 thalers, instruments worth 371 thalers, furniture worth 29 thalers, books worth 38 thalers and a share in a mine valued at 60 thalers. The total estate was valued at 1158 thalers, a little less than two years of income.

After J. S. Bach's death, the Passion was treated by composers either in cantata or oratorio form.

K. P. E. Bach at this time applied unsuccessfully for the vacant cantorship at Leipzig formerly held by his father.

Wilhelm Friedemann Bach was in Leipzig this year to wind up family affairs after his father's death.

Wilhelm Friedemann Bach was reprimanded at this time for a prolonged absence from the Liebfrauen-Kirche. He had been in Leipzig working on problems created by his father's death.

The types used by the Ballard family remained in use as late as this year.

The printing business was continued after this year by Jean-Baptiste Christophe Ballard's widow and their son, Christophe Jean François.

Vielle, or hurdy-gurdy music, reached its peak this year in the virtuosity of two brothers, Charles and Henri Baton. The former played the vielle and the latter played the musette.

Bordoni and her husband had great success in Paris this season.

The introduction of separate movable music type this year by Johann Gottlob Immanuel Breitkopf brought about a revolution in the music industry.

John Brown was awarded the degree of Doctor of Divinity this year by Oxford.

Caffarelli sang at Lucca, Turin and Venice this season.

Calzabigi went to Paris this year with his brother and persuaded Metastasio to issue a Paris edition of his (Metastasio's) works, to which Calzabigi wrote a preface.

Casanova this season saw Campra's "Fêtes Venetiennes" at the Paris Opéra. He was highly critical of the stage sets and found Campra's music uninteresting.

Castrucci went to Dublin at this time.

V. L. Ciampi's company of
Italian singers enjoyed minimal
success this season.

A. Dijonnais musician, Balbâtre,
came to Paris this year and
entered the La Poupliniere
circle.

Count Durazzo was called to
Vienna at this time by Count
Kaunitz to serve as Genoese
ambassador there.

Annibale Pio Fabri, composer
and tenor, was named president
of the Accademia Filarmonica
of Bologna this year for the
fifth and final time.

Farinelli this year was awarded
the Cross of Calatrava, one of
the highest orders in Spain.

Farinelli's opera productions
reached their peak this season
with the celebrations for the
wedding of the Infanta Maria
Antonia.

Giulia Frasi this season sang
in Ciampi's "Adriano in Siria"
and Pergolesi's "La Serva
Padrona".

Giulia Frasi sang in "Theodora"
this year.

Johann Gabler built the famous
organ in the abbey of Weingarten at this time.

Gabrielli, the famous singer
nicknamed Cuochetta, came to
Naples this year. Metastasio
heard her there and brought her
to Vienna where she became a
favorite singer of Francis I.

Pierre LaGarde served this year
as assistant conductor at Paris
Opéra.

Giuseppe Giordani, a singer
travelling with his family,
reached Frankfurt am Main at
this time.

Maurice Greene at this time
inherited an estate in Essex
worth 700 pounds per year
from a cousin.

Friedrich von Grimm moved to
Paris this year.

Johann Gronemann became organist at The Hague this season.

Johann Gottlob Harrer became
cantor at the Thomasschule in
Leipzig this year succeeding
J. S. Bach.

Anton Buchholz, a merchant
and Marktrichter from Vienna,
this year loaned F. J. Haydn
150 florins, an enormous sum
to Haydn at the time.

The impresario Hébert this
season engaged a company of
French actors to perform at
court. They quickly began to
perform opéra comique as well.
Ten years later, Durazzo used
some of these works for the
Viennese court with Gluck
conducting.

The other known works of José
Herrando were all subsequent
to this year.

J. S. Kleinknecht followed his
brothers to Bayreuth this year
to complete his studies under
Döbbert and Götzel and also
became a member of the court
chapel.

Johann Friedrich Lampe went to
Edinburgh at this juncture and
died there.

Samuel Lee opened a music shop
this year at the Little Green
and printed music there.

Thomas Lowe sang in Handel's
"Theodora" this season.

Locatelli, director of Italian
opera at the Kotzen Theater,
invited Gluck there and he
performed Gluck's opera "Ezio"
this season.

Empress Maria Theresa and her
consort Francis I were staying
at Köln this year. Locatelli
staged the opera "Zenobia" and
the performance became a major
musical event of the season.

Perti's friend Padre Martini
stated in his "Saggio di Con-
trapunto" (II, 142) that he
communicated on musical subjects with Perti as late as
this date.

J. B. Neruda at this time was
an outstanding member of the
electoral chapel at Dresden.

A. N. Pagin returned to Paris
this year and performed at the
Concert Spirituel with success,
but not of a lasting variety.

U. Panormo went to Paris this
year. Failing to establish
himself as a violin maker there,
he went on to Marseilles.

D. Paradisi gave instruction in
harmony and thorough-bass to
Thomas Linley in England this
year. This was the last time
Paradisi was heard of in
England.

The Venetian Academy was founded
this year and Giambattista
Piazzetta was its first

(cont.) principal.

T. Pinto played often at this
time as a leading violin
soloist at benefit concerts at
the Worcester and Hereford
Festivals, at the Drury Lane
Theatre in London and also
followed Giardini at the King's
Theatre.

Rameau this year was given a
further pension chargeable to
the Opéra at Paris.

Rameau's daughter, Marie-
Louise, went into a convent at
this time and he provided her
with a dowry.

Giovanni Albert Ristori, with
J. H. Hasse, was appointed as
an assistant "Kapellmeister".
He chiefly wrote operas and
church music at this time.

Giuseppe Scolari, composer,
was in Barcelona this year.

Sodi played solos on the
mandoline in Paris this season.

Several new symphonies by
Johann Stamitz were introduced
in Paris this season and
enthusiastically received by
French audiences.

G. C. Wagenseil's position as
organist to the Dowager
Empress Elisabeth Christine
ended this year when she died.

G. C. Wagenseil at this time
had written at least five
operas, wholly or partly by
him, while he was in Vienna.

J. Zach suffered a mental
collapse this year.

F. Zellbell (II) was appointed

conductor of the Swedish court
orchestra this season.

"Opera seria" originated in
reforms by the Italian librettist Zeno, who died this year.
He removed comical characters
from the stories and divided
the action according to musical
contrast between recitative
and aria.

Geronimo Abos' opera "L'Adriano"
was completed this year at Rome.

A cantata by Johann Friedrich
Agricola,"Il Filosofo convinto
in amore", was performed this
season before Frederic the
Great. It made a great impression on the King and he
conferred on Agricola the position of "Hof-componist".

Count Francesco Algarotti's
"Saggio sopra l'opera in
musica" was published this
year. It was a treatise on
"operatic dramaturgy".

Arne's "Ode on Cheerfulness"
appeared at this time.

Louis Aubert's violin sonatas
with a bass were composed this
year.

Six symphonies by Johann
Christian Bach were published
this year.

Johann Sebastian Bach's "The
Art of the Fugue" ("Kunst der
Fuge") was engraved on copper
and published at this time. It
was not received with any great
enthusiasm.

K. P. E. Bach wrote his Concerto
in a minor for clavier this year.

John Barrow's "A New Book of
Psalmody" was issued this year
at London.

"The Beggar's Opera" was performed in Paris this season
as "L'Opéra du gueux".

"The Beggar's Opera" was first
heard this year in New York
City and Philadelphia.

Blamont's "Les Festes de Thétis"
appeared at this time.

Breunich's setting of Metastasio's "Il Parnaso accusato e
difeso" was completed this year.

Burney "Six Songs" and "A
Favourite Cantata" appeared
this year.

Burney provided music for
"Robin Hood" by Mendez and
"Queen Mab" by Henry Woodward.
Some of the music was published
this year.

N. Conforto set Metastasio's
"Antigono" to music this
season for the San Carlo
Theatre at Naples.

J. F. Dandrieu's "Nouveaux
Cantiques spirituels proven-
çaux" appeared this year at
Avignon.

Antonio Ferradini and Logroscino wrote additional music
this year for a revival of
Leonardo Leo's "Amor vuol
sofferenza" under the title of
"La finta Frascatana".

Ignazio Fiorillo published six
harpsichord sonatas this
season at Braunschweig.

François Francoeur wrote his
opera "Ismène" this year.

Baldassare Galuppi's opera "Il mondo alla roversa" (libretto by Goldoni) was produced this season at Venice.

Baldassare Galuppi's opera "Il mondo della luna" (libretto by Goldoni) was produced this season at Venice.

Galdassare Galuppi wrote his "L'oracolo del Vaticano" in Venice or Vicenza this year (the text was by Goldoni).

Baldassare Galuppi wrote his opera "Il paese della Cuccagna" this year at Venice (libretto by Goldoni).

Baldassare Galuppi wrote his opera "La vittoria d'Imeneo" this year at Turin (libretto by Bartoli).

Georg Gebel's opera "Die beständige Liebe" was produced this season at Rudolstadt.

Gluck's Italian opera "Ezio" (libretto by Metastasio) was produced this year at Prague during the carnival season.

Carl Heinrich Graun's opera "Fetonte" was produced this season at Berlin.

Carl Heinrich Graun's opera "Mitridate" was produced this season at Berlin.

C. P. Grua's oratorio "Sant' Elena al Calvario" was sung this year at Mantua.

Handel's stage work "Alceste" with libretto for a play by Tobias Smollett was written this year for a performance at Covent Garden, which did not

(cont.) take place.

Hasse's pasticcios as listed below were produced this season at Vienna: "Andromeda", "Armida placata", "Euridice".

Hasse's works were performed this year at the Mannheim school.

Haydn's first quartet was written this year according to Griesinger.

Francis Ireland published a medical book at Glasgow at this time.

Johnsen's first work, as far as is known, was a pastoral which was sung this year at court on the birthday of the prince.

Jommelli's works listed below were produced this year at Vienna: "Andromeda" (pasticcio, only partly by Jommelli), "Euridice"(pasticcio, only partly by Jommelli) and "L'uccellatrice" (intermezzo).

William Knapp's "New Church Melody" appeared in its first edition this year.

Gaetano Latilla's "Madama Ciana" was given this season at the King's Theatre in London.

Leo wrote airs for "Andromedo" this year.

Giovanni Locatelli's company performed Gluck's "Ezio" this year at Prague.

N. Logroscino's "La finta Frascatana" was produced this season.

James Lyon was influenced more by a collection of tunes issued this year than by earlier works.

Marpurg's "Critische Musicus an der Spree" was published this year at Berlin.

Marpurg's "Die Kunst das Clavier zu spielen" was published this year in Berlin.

"XII English Songs in Score", containing songs of N. Pasquali, was published this year at London.

"Semiramide" by Davide Perez was produced this season at the Teatro della Dame in Rome.

James Ralph's "The Fashionable Lady" was produced this season in New York.

Rameau's "Demonstration du principe de l'harmonie" was published this year. It was Rameau's most readable writing.

Metastasio's libretto to "La Ripettora tenerezza" had its first setting this year by Reutter.

Smollet wrote "Alceste" (from Euripides) this year. Handel wrote incidental music for the work but it was never performed.

Vivaldi's "L'Estro Armonico" was published at this time by Le Clerc, le Cadet in Paris.

"Contributions to the History of the Theater" was published this year at Stuttgart. The work paid tribute to Zanetta's accomplishments.

Zellbell (II) wrote a cantata this year for the succession of Adolf Fredric to the Swedish throne.

Marpurg's "Kunst das Clavier zu spielen" of this year attempted to establish an exact notation for appoggiaturas. The work also stated that the dots in appoggiaturas had to be sustained and that the first of each two slurred notes had to be accented. The tails of small notes were turned to indicate passing appoggiaturas to the left. No mention was made of the double dot.

From this date forward the use of smaller notes for unmeasured ornamental passages of all kinds existed.

By this time the author of "The Academie" could write that "a Taste for Musick, Modern Languages, and other polite Entertainments of the Gentlemen have succeeded to Clubs and Bacchanalian Routs." The Oxford weekly musical meetings had received new impetus from Handel's visit.

The middle class in Austria began to become more interested in music at this time.

The style of music at this time was simple. There were many graceful songs for voice with harpsichord accompaniment.

After this date commercial concerts spread throughout Europe.

The German comic opera ("Singspiel") started to appear at this time.

1750(cont.)

Prior to this date, the Moravian settlement at Bethlehem, Pennsylvania had founded a "collegium musicum". It was probably the first musical society in the colonies deserving of such a name.

A dispute this year between French musicians and dancing-masters was settled in favor of the musicians by decree of the Paris Parliament.

Modal improvisation in the music of Synagogues had assumed monstrous proportions by this time. Consequently an ancient tune could be recognized only by its incipit.

Instrumental music written in the 200 years ending this year could only be properly judged by careful listening.

The question of "regular" versus "natural" singing was largely settled by this time, but other improvements came far more slowly.

The number of performers engaged at the Académie de Musique had risen to 179 by this year.

Playwright Heribert von Dalberg was born this year (died 1806).

Cardinal Albani, Italian cardinal, secretary of state, and librarian to Pope Pius VIII, was born this year (died 1835).

Abbé Jean Terrasson, French professor of Greek at College de France, died this year at Paris (born 1670 at Lyons).

The elegant "perruque" was the (cont.) height of fashion in German poetry at this time.

Early this year, The Recorder, William Allen, afterwards Chief Justice of the Province, reported that people "took it upon themselves to act plays in the city".

Reverend Robert Harding this year took charge of St. Joseph's Church, Willing's Alley.

(and 1751) Agricola's "La ricamatrice divenuta drama" was performed both these seasons at Potsdam.

(to 1751) C. G. Jöcher's "Compendiöses Gelehrten-Lexicon" appeared at this time.

(and 1751) The company of Kean and Murray advertised their weekly performances in the newly fitted "Theater in Nassau Street" in the New York Gazette during both these years.

(to 1752) Andrea Adolfati's operas "L'Arianna", "Adriano in Siria" and "La Gloria ed il Piacere" were produced in Genoa during this period.

(to 1752) Johnson's bi-weekly "Rambler" was published for these two years, containing his own essays.

(to 1752) Joshua Reynolds, the painter, spent this time in Italy.

(to 1753) Johannes Theodosius Cuypers settled at The Hague during these years.

(to 1753) Tiepolo painted the ceiling perspectives at the Residenz, Würzburg during these three years.

(to 1755) Bach's successor at
the Thomasschule, Gottlob
Harrer was cantor for these
five years.

(to 1756) Stefano Storace,
eminent Italian double-bass
player, and father of soprano
Ann Selina Storace, taught music
in Dublin during this period.

(to 1759) Diderot's "Le Neveu
de Rameau" appeared during
these years.

(to 1759) Haydn wrote his first
"Mass in F major" at the beginning of this decade.

(to 1759) R. Pockrich toured
England during these years
when musical glasses were in
vogue.

(to 1760) Italian cello players
Canavasso and Ferrari appeared
in Paris during these seasons.

(to 1760) Carlo Ferdinando
Landolfi, violin maker, lived
at the Via Santa Margherita
in Milan during this decade.

(to 1770) In spite of regula-
tions, most regiments had from
four to six fifers and twice
as many drummers during this
period.

(to 1770) Georg Klotz's violins
were made between these dates.
They had lost their distinctive
Tyrolesian cut without gaining
the true Italian style and were
covered with a thin, brittle
spirit varnish.

(to 1771) Rimbault listed 18

(cont.) instruments made by
the younger John Byfield during
these years.

(to 1780) The pandurina returned to popularity during
these years under the mane
Milanese mandoline and several
pretty specimens have survived.

(to 1850 and 1856 to 1891)
Constantin von Wurzbach's
"Biographisches Lexicon des
Kaiserthums Oesterreich"
has been published throughout
these years.

(to 1850) Britain developed a
portraiture during these years
that was bourgeois without being
provincial, unaffected without
being trivial, and a landscape
art that linked the Dutch
17th century with Impressionism
of the 19th century.

(to 1870) Repeat signs were
found in nearly all the examples of sonata-form written
during these years.

c.1750
Gioacchino Albertini, Italian
conductor and composer, was
born this year at Pesaro
(died c.1812 probably at Rome).

Maddalena Allegranti, Italian
soprano, was born this year at
Florence (died after 1798 in
Ireland).

Francesco Bernardi ("Senesino")
Italian male mezzo-soprano,
died at this time in Siena
(born c.1680).

Giuseppe Calegari, Italian
opera composer, was born this
year (death date unknown).

Giovanni Battista Cerrutti,

Italian violin maker, was born this year at Cremona (died 1817 at Cremona).

Giovanni Chinzer, Italian composer, died at this time (born c.1695).

John Clegg, Irish violinist, died this year at London (born 1714 at Dublin).

Joseph Dale, English music publisher, was born this year (died 1821 at London).

Cecilia Davies, English soprano, was born this year probably at London (died 1836, July 3 at London).

Johann Edeling, German clarinetist and composer, was born this year at Falken near Eisenach (died at Weimar).

Franciscello (first name unknown), Italian cellist, died at this time in Genoa (birthdate unknown).

Joseph Gehot, Walloon violinist and composer, was born this year (death date unknown).

Giovanni Battista Grazioli, Italian composer, was born at this time in Venice (died c.1820).

Franz Xaver Hammer, German violinist, cellist and composer, was born this year at Oettingen (died c.1813 at Schwerin).

Henry Holcombe, English composer, died at this time in London (born c.1693 probably at Salisbury).

James Johnson, Scottish music engraver, was born this year (died 1811, February 26 at Edinboro).

Johann August Just, German pianist and composer, was born at this time at Groningen near Magdeburg (death date unknown).

William Mahon, English clarinetist and violinist, was born this year (died 1816, May 3 at Salisbury).

Alessandro Marcello, Italian philosopher, mathematician and composer, died at this time in Venice (born c.1684 at Venice).

Antonio Leal Moreira, Portuguese composer, was born this year at Lisbon (died 1819, November 21 at Lisbon).

Michele Mortellari ("The elder"), Italian composer, was born this year at Palermo, Sicily (died 1807, March 27 at London).

Giuseppe Maria Orlandini, Italian composer, died at this time in Florence (born 1688, February 4 at Bologna).

José Palomino, Spanish composer, was born this year at Madrid (died 1810, April 9 at Las Palmas).

Giovanni Domenico Perotti, Italian composer and brother of G. Agostino Perotti, was born at this time at Vercelli (died 1824, probably at Vercelli).

Friedrich Wilhelm Pixis, sen., German composer, was born at this time (died at Mannheim).

François Tourte, who perfected
the violin bow, was born this
year (died 1835).

Pierre (Emmanuel) Verheyen,
Flemish composer and tenor,
was born this year at Ghent
(died 1819, January 11 at Ghent).

Andrea Adolfati was conductor
of the music at the Church of
the Annunciation from this date
until his death.

The founders of the Austrian
firm of music publishers,
Cesare, Domenico and Giovanni
Artaria, settled in Vienna
late this year.

Carl Barbandt settled in London
at this time.

Barsanti returned to London
this year.

Andrea Bernasconi was is Vienna
at this time.

Boyce lived in Quality Court,
Chancery Lane at this time.
He stayed there after his
marriage to Hannah.

Paul César Gibert settled in
Paris at this time as a teacher
and composer.

Pierre and Jean Louvet were
eminent hurdy-gurdy makers in
Paris at this time.

Content, order and title of the
"Well-Tempered Clavier" were
imitated at this time by the
organist, Weber, whose cycle
was at one time thought to have
been the model for Bach. It
dated, however, from this year
and was musically poor.

Johann Werner (Neustadt-
Dresden) this year made the
first Inventionshorn, as designed by Hampel.

J. S. Bach composed two
concertos for two claviers and
orchestra, No. 1 in c minor and
No. 2 in C major this year.

J. S. Bach's compositions for
organ this year included
"Prelude and Fugue in Eb major"
("St. Anne"), "Prelude and
Fugue in C major" and "Prelude
and Fugue in e minor ("Wedge").

Barsanti's "Sei Antifone . . .
", opus 5, appeared at this
time in London.

William Bates wrote six
sonatas for two violins (his
earliest work) this year.

An edition of tunes from "The
Beggar's Opera" was published
this year by Walsh.

The German march, "Coburger",
was published at this time.

William Felton's opus 3, "8
Suits of Easy Lessons for the
Harpsichord . . ." was published
this year.

Handel's concertos for organ
and orchestra were composed
at this time.

Handel this year wrote the
following hymns with words by
Charles Wesley: "O Lord divine,
How sweet Thou art", "Rejoice,
The Lord is King" and "Sinners,
obey the gospel word".

Handel composed his Sonata in
C major at this time.

Haydn composed trios #15-20 for
two violins and violoncello

at this time.

Hiller's "Das Orakel (words by Gellert) was composed this year but not performed.

"18 Divertimento's for 2 Guitars or 2 Mandelines (sic), Properly adapted by the best Masters" was published in London at this time by Oswald.

"Sonata a Quattro in d minor" by Alessandro Scarlatti appeared at this time.

John Travers at this time published "The Whole Book of Psalms for one, two, three, four and five voices, with a thorough bass for the harpsichord". Travers was an organist and composer.

Henry Waylett this year published T. Davis' "20 familiar English & Scotch Airs for 2 German flutes".

Bernhard Christian Weber wrote his "Well-Tempered Clavier" this year with a forged date: 1689.

J. Wren this year published "The Harp", "The Spinet", "The Violin", and others from "The Musical Miscellany".

"Yankee Doodle" was composed this year by a fife-major of the Grenadier Guards.

The oboe reed was pictured in Diderot's "Encyclopedie" of this year. Up to this time the upper c^{111}, the original top note of the oboe was played with all note-holes open. The second partial d^{11} was obtained through

(cont.) the same fingering by pinching the reed to make it sound at the octave.

The many concerts in the cities at this time show how quickly stylistic trends of England country found repercussions in the colonies.

"Singing Birds", mechanical devices that imitated bird-songs were introduced during this time.

The classical sonata started as a rather free type comprised of two or three movements.

The influence of the Roman School showed strongly in Poland, and its effect on Polish sacred music continued until this time.

The standard symbol for crescendo and diminuendo started to be used this year.

The left hand e-flat^1 on the oboe was generally discontinued after this date.

Robert Feke, American painter, died at this time (born c.1705).

(to 1760) Boyce wrote eight symphonies during this period.

(to 1772) Abbé Aubert was a serpentist at Notre-Dame, Paris during these years.

(to 1780) Richard Duke flourished during this period.

(to 1784, September 14) Jean Adam was attached to the Saxon court at Dresden from about 1750 until his death as shown above.

(January 12) At this time privileges were granted to Charles Nicholas Le Clerc to publish "Oeuvres de Musique Instrumentale de Scarlatti".

(January 14) Corona Schröter, German composer, soprano and actress, was born on this date at Guben (died 1802, August 23).

(January 20) Hasse's opera "Ciro riconosciuto" (libretto by Metastasio) was produced on this day at Dresden.

(February 4) Blas Laserna, Spanish composer, was born at this time in Corella, Navarre (died 1816, August 8).

(February 8) Franziska Haydn, the composer's sister, married a baker, J. Vieltzwiser, on this date.

(February 12) Johann Florian Deller on this day was appointed a violinist in the court orchestra at Stuttgart. He went there from Vienna and remained for twenty years.

(February 12) Christian Latrobe, English composer and music editor, was born on this date at Fulneck (died 1836, May 6).

(February 14) François Lays, French singer, was born at this time in Old Gascony (died 1831, March 30).

(February 18) Pierre LaGarde's opera-ballet "Aeglé" was performed on this evening at the Paris Opéra.

(February 18) Karl Haack, Ger-

(cont.) man composer and violinist, was born on this day at Potsdam (died 1819, September 28 at Potsdam).

(February 21) Castrucci gave a benefit concert on this date at Fishamble Street in Dublin.

(February 22) Pietro Filippo Scarlatti, member of the third generation of the Scarlatti family, died on this day (born 1679, January 5).

(February 23) Vernon sang in "Alfred" this evening.

(February 25) Wilhelm Friedemann Bach married Dorothea Elisabeth Georgi at this time.

(February 25) Georg Kaspar Schürmann, German conductor, composer and singer, died this day at Wolfenbüttel (born c.1672).

(March 1) Handel's "The Choice of Hercules" was produced on this date at Covent Garden in London. The words were taken by Morell or Smollett from "Polymetis" by Robert Lowth.

(March 3) Jan Křtitel Kuchař, Bohemian organist and composer, was born at this time at Chotec (died 1829, February 18 at Prague).

(March 9) Marie Justine Benoîte Favart sang in Charles Favart's "Les Amants inquiets" this evening at the Comédie-Italienne.

(March 18) Isabella Young first

1751(cont.)
appeared at the New Theatre in Haymarket, London on this date.

(Spring) F. J. Haydn at this time joined a party of pilgrims going to the miraculous shrine of the Virgin at Mariazell.

(Spring) "Demetrio" by Davide Perez was produced at the Teatro San Samuele in Venice on this date.

(March 26) Isabella Young (Lampe) went to Edinboro at this time.

(April 3) Jean Baptiste Lemoune, French conductor and composer, was born on this date in Périgord (died 1796, December 30).

(April 6) Jean Lebrun, French horn player, was born on this date at Lyons (died c.1809).

(April 17) A performance of John Worgan's "Dirge to the Memory of Frederick, Prince of Wales" was held this day.

(April 24) Leveridge on this date sang his last performance at Covent Garden.

(April 29) John Rippon, English church-music editor, was born this day in Tiverton. He was a doctor of divinity and had a meeting-house for many years at Carter Lane, Tooley Street in London (died 1836, December 17 at London).

(April 30) Marianne Davies first appeared on this day at London in Hickford's Rooms. She played a concerto for German flute and a concerto by Handel for the harpsichord, as well as singing several songs.

(May 8) Blamont was decorated on this day with the Order of St. Michael.

(May 20) Domenico Terradellas, Spanish composer, died at this time at Rome (born 1713, February at Barcelona).

(Mah 23) Antonio da Silva Leite, Portuguese composer, was born on this date at Oporto (died 1833, January 10).

(May 29) Salvatore Lanzetti gave a concert at Frankfurt am Main this evening.

N. Conforto's setting of Metastasio's "Festa cinese" was performed at Aranjuez on this date.

(May 31) Salvatore Lanzetti on this day gave a concert at Frankfurt am Main.

(June 2) Antoni Weinert, flutist and composer of Czech origin, was born at this time in Lusdorf (died 1850, June 18 at Warsaw).

(July 8) Kean and Murray managed a company of comedians from Philadelphia who played at New York up to this date.

(July 25) Johann Friedrich Lampe, German-English bassoonist and composer, died on this day at Edinboro (born c.1703).

(July 28) Johann Friedrich Lampe was buried this day in the Canongate Churchyard.

(July 30) Maria Anna (Marianne) Mozart, Austrian child prodigy, teacher and sister of W. A. Mozart, was born at this time in Salzburg (died 1829, October 29 at Salzburg).

1751(cont.)

(August 12) August Christian Andreas Abel, violinist, was born on this date at Braunschweig (died 1834, August 3 at Ludwigslust).

(August 12) Johann Baptist Lasser, Austrian singer and composer, was born on this date at Steinbrücken, Lower Austria (died 1805, October 21).

(August 23) Louis François Beffara, French collector, was born at this time at Nonancourt, Normandy (died 1838, February 2 at Paris).

(September 1) Emanuel Schikaneder, German actor, singer, playwright and theatre manager, was born on this date at Straubing (died 1812, September 21).

(September 4) Maria Magdalena Spangler was born on this day (death date unknown).

(September 10) Bartolomeo Campagnoli, Italian violinist and composer, was born on this date at Cento near Bologna (died 1827, November 7 at Neustrelitz).

(Autumn) E. R. Duni's opera "La semplice curiosa" was produced this evening at Florence in the Teatro del Cocomero.

(September 21) Rameau's acte de ballet "La Guirlande" (Marmontel) was produced this evening at Paris.

(October 21) Lavinia Fenton on this date married Charles, the third Duke of Bolton, at Aix-en-Provence.

(October 30 to 1760, June 10) Maria Scarlatti, daughter of Domenico and member of the fourth generation of the Scarlatti family, died during this period (born 1738, November 9).

(November 3) Antoine Marcel Lemoine, noted music publisher, was born on this date at Paris (died 1817, April).

(November 4) Tommaso Traetta's first opera, "Farnace" was produced at the Teatro San Carlo at Naples this evening.

(November 9) Rameau's pastoral heroique "Acante et Céphise" (Marmontel) was produced on this date at Paris. On this occasion Rameau introduced clarinets into the orchestra of the Paris Opéra.

(November 19) Boyce's "The Shepherd's Lottery" was produced this evening at the Drury Lane Theatre in London.

(November 19) Vernon played the part of Thyrsis in Boyce's "The Shepherd's Lottery" on this evening.

(December 24) Christian Heinrich Schreyer, German composer and clergyman, was born this day at Dresden (died 1823, January 24).

(December 18 to 1761, December 26) The opera "Ipermestra" was written by Pasquale Cofaro during this period.

(December 27) J. Oswald wrote music for a production this evening at the Haymarket Theatre in London called "The Old Woman's Oratory". This

1751(cont.)
work was for the "Society of
the Masque of Alfred".

(February) Giuseppe Matteo
Alberti, Italian violinist and
composer, died this month at
Bologna (born c.1685 at Bologna).

(February) Ignazio Fiorillo
became court conductor at
Braunschweig this month,
succeeding G. C. Schürmann.

(February) Mrs. Wrighton, English singer, was born this
month (died 1796, August 11 in
U. S. A.).

(June) Gervais DeLarue, French
priest and writer on music,
was born this month at Caen
(died 1833 at Caen).

(July) Samuel Lee was one of a
syndicate which assumed a lease
of the Crow Street Music Hall
for six years starting at this
time.

(July) Jean-François Marmontel's
"Examen des réflexions de M.
d'Alembert sur la liberté de la
musique; in Mercure de France"
appeared at this time.

(September to 1762, July 15)
Barbara Scarlatti, daughter of
Domenico and member of the
fourth generation of the Scarlatti family, married Eugenio
Cachurro sometime during this
period.

Johann Georg Bach, organist,
lawyer and member of the seventh
generation of the Bach family
was born this year (died 1797).

Johann Philipp Bach, court organist at Meiningen and member

(cont.) of the seventh generation of the Bach family, was
born at this time (died 1846).

Supply Belcher, an American
musician, was born this year
(died 1836).

Karol Józef Birnbach, Polish
violinist, conductor and composer, was born this year at
Köpernick-on-Nysa (died 1805,
May 29 at Warsaw).

Antonio Bruni (Bartolommeo),
Italian composer and violinist,
was born this year at Cuneo
(died 1821, August 6 at Cuneo).

Joseph Noël Carbonel, a tabor-
pipe player, was born at this
time (died 1804).

Pierre Cardon, singer and
cellist, was born this year at
Paris (death date unknown).

John Crosdill, English cellist,
was born this year at London
(died 1825, October at Eskrick,
Yorkshire).

"La Caramba" (Maria Antonia
Fernández), Spanish singer,
was born at this date at
Motril, Granada (died 1787
at Madrid).

Nicolas Joseph Hüllmandel,
Alsation pianist and composer,
was born this year at Strasbourg (died 1823, December 19
at London).

Haydn's mother, Maria Koller,
died at this time (born 1707
at Rohrau).

Ferdinand Kauer, American
composer, was born this year
(died 1831).

1751(cont.)

Pierre Leduc, French violinist and publisher, was born this year at Paris (died 1816).

A singer, Maddalena Musi (nicknamed Mignatta), died at this time (born 1669).

Salimbeni, the castrato, died this year at Laibach while on a trip from Germany to Italy.

(to 1757) Alexandro Scarlatti, grandson of Domenico, son of Alexandro and member of the fifth generation of the Scarlatti family, was born during this period (died between 1783, April 12 and 1800).

Rosa Scarlatti, daughter of Domenico and member of the fourth generation of the Scarlatti family, died after this date (born 1745, March 29).

Lorenzo Storione, an Italian violin maker, was born this year at Cremona (death date unknown).

Frederick II this year appointed Johann Friedrich Agricola as court composer at Leipzig. The latter then studied composition with J. S. Bach.

Agricola married the soprano Benedetta Molteni this year.

Michael Arne sang this season at Marylebone Gardens.

J. A. Benda married this year.

Burney at this time fell into an alarming state of "premature decay".

Caffarelli sang at Venice again this season.

Carlin, a well-known maker and teacher of the cor-de-chasse at Paris, supplied two of them to the Paris Opéra this year.

C. Chabran went to Paris at this time and met with great success.

From this date until his death Jan Ciecilowicz was the director and conductor of the band at the court of Prince Radziwill at Nieśwież.

N. Conforto went to Madrid this year.

W. Corbett's collection of instruments were sold this year at auction "at the Great Room over against Beaufort Buildings in the Strand, formerly known as "Hoop Tavern". He had died in 1748 on March 7.

John Cox married Ann Simpson probably as early as this time.

Carl Friedrich Fasch, German harpsichordist, accompanied Franz Benda this year and received great praise from the latter.

Frederick II was so enraged by Benedetta Emilia Agricola's marriage this year, that he reduced the couple's joint salary.

Karl Friberth, an excellent tenor, was engaged by the Esterhazy orchestra this season.

Quirino Gasparini at this time was a member of the Accademia Filarmonica at Bologna.

Felice (de') Giardini, violinist, started subscription

concerts this season with
Thomas Vincent, an oboist.

François Joseph Gossec went
to Paris this year with a letter
of introduction to Rameau. He
arrived there from Belgium.

Alexander Jean-Joseph le Riche
de la Poupliniére this year
engaged Gossec as director of
his concerts at Passy. Poupliniére was a wealthy tax farmer
who staged concerts as well as
an amateur musician who maintained a private theater. He
brought Johann Stamitz before
the Paris public.

John Taylor was said to have
operated on Handel this year,
but Streatfield felt it was
Samuel Sharp.

Handel at this time used the
pitches A=423 c.p.s., and
S=2'3.

Dismas Hatǎs, a member of the
Gotha court orchestra from this
date forward, wrote some symphonies and violin solos which
have been preserved at Schwerin.

Anna Hatǎs married Dismas Hatǎs
this year.

Haydn repaid the loan of 150
florins to Anton Buchholz one
year after the original dealing.

Johann Hiller at this time
attended the University of
Leipzig, where in addition to
his legal studies, he devoted
considerable attention to music,
"partly from choice, partly from
necessity". He took part in the
"Grosses Concert" both as a
flutist and singer, and began
to pursue his career as a com-

(cont.) poser and author.

Jommelli this year returned
to Rome where he produced
"Ifigenia in Aulide" and
"Talestri".

Anton Korner of Vienna flourished at this time as a horn
maker and was considered to
have been the most reputed
maker of concert horns of his
time by LaBorde.

The second edition of Georg
Keyssler's "Recent Journeys
Through Germany, Bohemia,
Hungary, Switzerland, Italy
and Lorraine" was published
at this time. George Keyssler
was a tutor to Baron Andreas
Gottlieb von Bernstorf, who
was Prime Minister to the
Elector of Braunschweig-Lune-
berg.

Kirnberger entered the service
of Frederick the Great in
Berlin this year as a violinist.

One of Bach's last pupils at
the Thomasschule at Leipzig,
J. Kittel's first position was
that of organist at Langensalza
this season.

The Jesuit, Jean-Baptiste de
Laborde built an electric
piano at this time.

Samuel Lee this season was
appointed conductor of the City
Music or Corporation Band.

Locatelli's company performed
Gluck's "Ezio" this season
at Leipzig.

J. A. Marersck, a horn player
attached to the court of the
Empress Elizabeth of Russia
this year, conceived the idea

of forming a band exclusively composed of hunting-horns.

Regina Mingotti this season sang with Gizziello in the operas directed by Farinelli in Spain.

According to some sources, Mozart wrote the C major Mass to commemorate the "crowning" of an image of the Virgin Mary at Salzburg this year.

Henry Mountain was one of the Rotunda band at Dublin at this time.

William Neale added "a very elegant additional room to the New Musick Hall at Fishamble Street".

Corselli's neglect of the Royal Chapel due to his time being taken up with Italian opera, led to the creation of the new position of vice-master. Nebra was appointed this year.

N. Porpora at this time was given a pension of 400 thaler a year and apparently left Dresden a year later.

Rameau was still living under La Pouplinière's this year in Paris.

Reutter (jr.) acquired his fourth position this season.

French musicians and actors burned Jean Rousseau in effigy this year in the courtyard of the Royal Academy of Music for writing the following: "From which I conclude that the French have no music, and cannot have any or if they ever have any, it will be so much

(cont.) the worse for them".

Scarlatti's domicile was noted this year.

Burkat Shudi this year made harpsichord #260 for F. Fairley, Newcastle. It was a single manual that has survived.

Ann Simpson, the music publisher and widow of John Simpson, married John Cox this year.

One of Johann Stamitz' symphonies had been played in Paris prior to his visit this year.

Martini il Tedesco was organist of the Jesuit seminary at Neustadt on the Danube at this time.

John Trusler this year became proprietor of Marylebone Gardens; "Master Arne" appeared as a singer, balls and masquerades were given, the doors were opened at 7, the fireworks were discharged at 11 and "a guard was appointed to be in the house and gardens, and to oblige all persons misbehaving to quit the place".

Francesco Antonio Baldassare Uttini, the composer and singer, was "Prince" of the Bologna Accademia dei Filarmonici at this time.

Vernon made his first appearance at Drury Lane Theatre in London this season as a soprano.

Isabella Vincent first appeared at Vauxhall this year as Miss Burchell.

G. Waltz's last appearance at

Covent Garden was this season.

James Worgan this year resigned as organist at Vauxhall Gardens.

E. Young appeared in Handel's "The Choice of Hercules" this season.

G. Abos' opera "Tito Manlio" was produced this season at Naples.

Bertoni's opera "Le pescatrice" was performed this year at Venice.

Béthizy's "Exposition de la Théorie et de la pratique de la musique suivant les principes de M. Rameau" appeared this year.

C. H. Blainville' "L'Esprit de l'art Musical" was issued this year at Geneva.

Blainville's "Essai sur un troisième mode" was completed at this time.

Blanchard's "Berti omnes" of this year was composed in honor of the birth of the Duke of Burgundy.

Burney's "Six Cornet Pieces. Proper for Young Organists . . ." appeared at this time.

Bury's "Titon et l'Aurore" was heard this year at Paris.

Dauvergne's "Concerts de Symphonies", opus 3 and opus 4, were both completed this year.

Thomas Davis this year issued a set of country-dance tunes.

Destouches' opera "Amadis de

(cont.) Grèce" was frequently revived up until this date.

Pierre Estève's "Nouvelle découverte du principe de l'harmonie" was completed this year.

James Evison's "A Compleat Book of Psalmody" was published this year in a second edition.

François Francoeur wrote his opera "Les Génies tutélaires" at this time.

Baldassare Galuppi wrote his opera "Antigona" this year at Rome (libretto by Roccaforte).

Baldassare Galuppi wrote his opera "Dario" this year at Turin (libretto by Baldanza).

Baldassare Galuppi wrote his opera "Lucio Papirio" this year at Reggio (libretto by Zeno).

Georg Gebel's opera "Chelonida" was produced this season at Rudolstadt.

Georg Gebel's opera "Die Gewalt der Musik: was produced this season at Rudolstadt.

Georg Gebel's opera "Oedipus" was produced this season at Rudolstadt.

Geminiani's "Art of Playing the Violin" was engraved and published this year by the Phillips family in London.

"L'eroe Cinese" by Gluck was an opera written for a festival given by the Field-Marshal of Saxe Hildenhausen at Schlosshof this year in honor of Empress Maria Theresa (libretto by Metastasio).

ENGRAVED BY E. HEINEMANN.

BEETHOVEN'S MOTHER, AFTER A PAINTING BY CASPAR BENEDICT BECKENKAMP.

THE RECORD OF BEETHOVEN'S BIRTH.

FACSIMILE FROM THE BIRTH REGISTER AT BONN

1751(cont.)

Carl Heinrich Graun's opera "Armida" was produced this season at Berlin.

Carl Heinrich Graun's opera "Britannico" was produced this season at Berlin.

James Green's "A Book of Psalmody" was issued in its eleventh edition at London.

Handel's choral drama "Jephtha" was composed this year. Handel used material from Habermann's "Philomela Pia" for this work.

Handel's hunting song "The Morning is charming" with words by Charles Legh was composed this year.

Hasse's intermezzo "La donna accorta" appeared this year at Florence. It is known only by its libretto and could be a variation of another title.

Hasse's opera "Ipermestra" appeared this year in a new version.

Haydn's "Asmodeus der krumme Teufel" was produced this season at Vienna.

Haydn this year wrote the music to a singspiel entitled "Der Neue Krumme Teufel".

A. Höpken wrote his first composition this year, a Christmas oratorio in the rococo style, "Försök af en pastorale på wår Herres och Frälsares Jesu Christi nådericka födelse", based on a text by his wife Baroness Helene Hammerhielm.

At this time Jommelli's works were performed at the Mannheim

(cont.) school.

Jommelli's "Artaserse" was presented at Mannheim this year.

Jommelli's opera "Ifigenia" was produced this season at Rome.

The following works by Jommelli were produced this year at the locations indicated: "Cesare in Egitto" (Strasbourg), "Componimento drammatico" (Rome, for the birthday of the King of Portugal), "Ifigenia in Aulide" (Rome), "Ipermestra" (Spoleto), "Talestri" (Rome).

Giovanni Battisti Lampugnani's opera "Alessandro Sotto le tende di Dario" was produced this year at Piacenza.

N. Logroscino's "Amore figlio del piacere" was produced this season.

Giuseppe Maio this year wrote his opere serie "Semiramide".

Mr. Mallet wrote "The Redemption of the Danish Invasion by Alfred the Great" in affiliation with Thompson. Mallet altered and improved it this year.

Gennaro Manna's opera "Didone abbandonata" was produced this season at Venice.

Metastasio's libretto for "Il Re Pastore" had its first setting this year by Bonno. See also Agnesi, Galuppi (M.T.), Giardini, Giordiani (?), Gluck, Hasse, Höpken, Jommelli, Lampugnani, Mozart, Nichelmann, Piccinni, Rush ("Royal Shepherd"), Sarti and Uttini.

Oswald's "Caledonian Pocket Companion" appeared at this time.

Pepusch this year dictated "A Short Account of the Twelve Modes of Composition and their Progression in every Octave" but it was never published.

The eleventh edition of "A Book of Psalm-tunes, with variety of Anthems in four parts" was published this year.

Johann Joachim Quantz's "Versuch einer Anweisung die flute traversière zu spielen" was published at this time.

J. P. Rameau's "Éléments de musique Théorique et pratique suivant les principes de M. Rameau" was completed this year.

Rameau's "In convertendo" was revived this year at the Concerts Spirituels, during Holy Week.

Metastasio's libretto to "La Virtuosa emulazione" (a cantata) was first set this year by Reutter.

Rousseau's "Le Devin du Village" was first played this season.

Rousseau's "Symphonie à cors de chasse" was composed this year.

William Tansur's "The Melody of the Heart, or the Psalmodist's Pocket Companion" appeared this year in its third edition at London.

H. Waylett at this time published "24 Country Country Dances for the year 1751".

Clarinets were available for

(cont.) Acante et Céphise" this year.

The French minuet was at this time defined by Diderot as "noble and elegant . . . moderate rather than quick".

In Virginia an orchestra was formed this year to accompany "The Beggar's Opera".

The Munich Residenz theatre was opened this season. It was a typical "rococo" theatre.

From this date forward the Concert Spirituel in Paris had two regular horn players.

The Teatro dei Rinnovati at Siena was burned down this year for the second time.

Jacob Reinhold Michael, dramatist, was born this year (died 1792).

Richard Brinsley Sheridan, playwright of a number of English comedies of manners, was born this year in Ireland (died 1816). He went to Harrow at an early age and later eloped with a young professional singer. Determined to support her, he began to write plays. He gained immediate success, and at 31 was made a member of Parliament.

Thomas Gray's "Elegy Written in a Country Churchyard" was published this year. It treated the theme of life, death and immortality with great power, bringing universal qualities to the poem.

Smollett published his novel "Peregrine Pickle" this year.

Ralph Earl, American painter,
was born this year (died 1801).

Johan Heinrich Wilhelm Tisch-
bein, German painter, was born
this year (died 1829).

Pietro Longhi at this time
painted "The Rinoceros".

Clemens August paid 468 thalers
this year for painting the in-
terior of the Bonn Comedy House.
This place was past the University Archaeological Museum
portion near the Coblenz Gate.

(to 1752) Bouvard's "Les
Délices de Comus" was published
at this time.

(to 1752) V. L. Ciampi's "12
Sonatas for two vns. + bass",
opus 1 and opus 2, were published by Johnson at London
this year.

(to 1752) Giulia Frasi sang
at Ranelagh this season.

(to 1752) Gaetano Guadagni at
this time sang at Dublin with
great success.

(to 1752) Rameau during these
years produced a tragédée,
"Linus" (the music was lost).

(to 1752) J. B. Wendling
appeared in Paris this season
at the Concert Spirituel.

(to 1753) Herbain was stationed
in Corsica at this time and
three of his Italian operas, an
intermezzo, "Il geloso" and two
serious works, "Il trionfo dei
gigli" and "Lavinia" were performed at Bastia.

(to 1753) Pierre von Maldere was

(cont.) in Dublin these years
and conducted the "Philhar-
monick Concerts" and published
two books of "Sonatas for Two
violins with thorough bass for
the Harpsichord".

(to 1755) Bernard de Bury was
superintendent of the King's
music during this period.

(to 1756) A considerable amount
of V. L. Ciampi's instrumental
music was brought out by
English publishers during these
five years.

(to 1757) Jan Mareš (Maresch)
was an instructor of Prince
Narishkin's hunting band for
these six years.

(to 1759) B. Cole engraved
"The New Universal Magazine"
with illustrated music pages
during this period.

(to 1759) Antonio Ferradini
during these years wrote nine
operas for different Italian
stages.

(to 1764) John Cox was at
Simpson's music shop, Sweeting's
Alley, opposite the east door
of the Royal Exchange, London
for these many years.

(to 1765) D. Diderot and J. R.
d'Alembert's "Encyclopédie ou
dictionnaire raisonné des
sciences, des arts, ..."
was completed during this
period. Some sources claimed
it was completed in 1767.

(to 1767) A. Mazzoni held the
position of chapel master of
the Church of San Giovanni in
Monte at this time.

(December to 1769, September)

1751(cont.)

C. T. Carter remained at St. Werburgh's Church during this period.

(to 1769) Haydn wrote twelve minuets during these years.

(to 1770) J. C. Walther was music director and organist at the Cathedral of Ulm during this period.

(to 1771) F. X. Brixi composed more than 440 works during these two decades.

(to 1771) Alembert was associated with Diderot in the famous "Encyclopédie" at this time.

(to 1772) Ducharger's "Encyclopédie, ou dictionnaire raisonné, des sciences, des arts et des métiers" was written during these years.

(to 1776) In the Encyclopedie edited by Diderot and other eminent men, the spirit of the 18th century became obvious.

(to 1777) The monument of 18th century rationalism was d'Alembert's and Diderot's "Encyclopédia" of this time.

c.1751

Giuseppe Sammartini, Italian oboist and composer, died this year at London (born c.1693).

Karl David Stegmann, German tenor, conductor and composer, was born at this time (died 1826, May 27 at Bonn).

Dressler studied at Halle, Jena and Leipzig this year.

(to 1752) Joseph Haydn this year composed his first Mass

(cont.) (F major). It showed considerable talent. Haydn, in his old age, rediscovered it and inserted extra wind parts.

1752

(January 17) Casanova translated Cahusac and Rameau's "Zoroastre" into Italian and on this date the opera was performed at Dresden with Metastasio and Hasse's "Adriano in Siria". Casanova commented on his work as follows, "I was to adapt the words to the choral music, a difficult task. The music did indeed retain its virtues, but there was no sparkle to the Italian verses!" Count Van Looz, a Pole, urged Casanova to take on the task.

(January 23) Muzio Clementi, Italian pianist and composer, was born on this day at Rome (died 1832, March 10 at Evesham, England).

(January 24) Johannes Theodosius Cuypers on this date was officially enrolled at The Hague as a citizen.

(January 28) Giuseppe Carpani, Italian poet and writer on music, was born at this time at Villalbese, Como (died 1825, January 22 at Vienna).

(February 7) The opera "Zoroastro" was produced at Dresden on this date. It was translated from the French by Casanova and the original music by Rameau was in a new setting by Adam, except for the overture and several choruses.

(February 11) Arne's "Harlequin Sorcerer" was performed this evening at Covent Garden in

London.

(February 15) A review on this date in the "Dresdener gelehrte und politische Anzeiger" read" "The tragedy "Zoroaster", performed during the carnival season at the Royal Theater in Dresden, deserves special attention on account of the excellent production, the fine decorations, the music, and the dancing".

(February 22) Charles Knyvett (I), organist and alto, was born on this date, probably at London (died 1822 at London).

(February 26) Handel's oratorio "Jephta" (libretto by Thomas Morell) was first performed on this date at Covent Garden in London.

(February 29) Pietro Castrucci, Italian conductor, violinist and composer, died on this day at Dublin (born 1679 at Rome).

(March 3) On this date a power of attorney in connection with a transfer to Fernando Scarlatti was consummated. It had to do with a benefice previously assigned to Juan Antonio Scarlatti.

(March 7) Carl Friedrich Cramer, German editor and writer on music, was born on this day at Quedlinburg (died 1807, December 8 at Paris). He headed the "Magazin der Musik".

(March 17) Arne wrote incidental music for "The Oracle", performed on this date at Covent Garden in London.

(Spring) Haydn's opera "Der

(cont.) Krumme Teufel" libretto by J. F. Kurz-Bernadon, based on LeSage's "Le Diable boiteux") was produced this evening at the Kärntner Theatre in Vienna.

(Spring) A letter from Scarlatti to Don Fernando de Silva y Alvarez de Toledo, Duke of Huescar, later twelfth Duke of Alba, was written at this time.

(April 2) Edward Jones, Welsh harper and musical editor, was born on this date at Llanderfer, Merionethshire (died 1824, April 18).

(Arpil 4) Nieda Antonio Zingarelli, Italian composer, was born on this day (died 1837, May 5).

(April 5) Sébastien Érard, instrument maker, was born on this date at Strasbourg (died 1831, August 5 near Passy).

(April 11) Pierre Lagarde's opera-ballet "Les Fêtes de Thalie" was performed this season at Bellevue.

(May 11) G. Scarlatti's opera "L'amor della patria" was produced this season at the Grand Canal in Venice (libretto by Goldoni).

(June 20) Johann Palsa, an excellent cor-alto, known chiefly as a duo-performer with Carl Thurschmidt, was born at Jermeritz, Bohemia (died 1792, January 24 at Berlin).

(July 17) Cardonne's pastoral "Amaryllis" was sung this evening at a concert at Compiègne.

1752(cont.)

(July 20) Johann Christopher
Pepusch, composer of the
"Beggar's Opera" and a student
of ancient music, died at this
time in London (born 1667 at
Berlin).

(July 24) Michael Festing,
English violinist and composer,
died on this day at London
(born c.1680).

(August 1) The revival of
Pergolesi's "La Serva Padrona"
at this time in Paris was by
Bambini's company of Italian
opera singers. This signalled
the start of the invasion of
Italian musical art into France.

(August 15) M. C. V. Vestris
sang at the Concert Spirituel
this evening.

(September 4) Friedrich Ludwig
Benda, the composer, was born
on this date at Gotha (died
1792, March 20 at Königsberg).

(September 10) Johann Friedrich
Christmann, German clergyman,
composer, pianist, flutist and
writer on music theory, was
born on this date at Ludwigsburg (died 1817, May 21 at
Heutingsheim near Ludwigsburg).

(September 25) Solar entered
the monastery of the Escorial
on this date as a novice.

(September 25) Carl Stenborg,
Swedish singer and composer,
was born at this time at
Stockholm (died 1813, August 1
at Djurgarden).

(September 30) Justin Heinrich
Knecht, German composer, was
born on this date at Biberach,
Swabia (died 1817, December 1

(cont.) at Biberach).

(October 6) The German version
of Charles Coffey's farce,
"The Devil to Pay, or the Wives
metamorphos'd" was produced
with new music by J. D. Standfuss in Leipzig this season
as "Der Teufel ist los, oder
Die verwandelten Weiber".
German comic opera may be said
to have started at this time.

(October 18) The first pro-
duction of Rousseau's "le
Devin du Village" was held at
Fontainebleau on this date.
Louis XV and his court were
present. The tile has been
translated as "The Village
Soothsayer".

(October 22) Andreas Kyrillo-
vitch, fourth son of the younger Razumovsky, was born at
this time.

(October 22) Ambrogio Minoia,
Italian composer, was born
this day at Ospitaletto near
Lodi (died 1825, August 3
at Milan).

(November 4) The famous male
soprano, Caffarelli, sang the
role of Sextus on this evening
at the first performance of
Gluck's "La Clemenza di Tito"
at the Teatro San Carlo in
Naples.

(November 4) Gluck's Italian
opera "La Clemenza di Tito"
(libretto by Metastasio) was
produced at the Teatro San
Carlo in Naples on this date.

(November 11) G. Scarlatti's
opera "I portentosi effetti
della madre Natura" was produced this evening at the
Teatro San Samuele in Venice

1752(cont.)
(libretto by Goldini).

(November 18) Blavet's opera
"Le Jaloux corrigé" was produced on this date at Berny.

(November 20) John Shore, English trumpeter and lutenist,
died this day at London (born
c.1662).

(November 25) Johann Friedrich
Reichardt, German composer and
writer on music, was born on
this date at Königsberg (died
1814, June 26). He composed
approximately 700 lieder.

(December 3) Georg Friedrich
Fuchs, German clarinetist and
composer, was born this day at
Mainz (died 1821, October 9).

(December 3) Henri Guillaume
Hamal, harpsichordist, cellist,
singer and composer, died on
this date at Liege (born 1685,
December 3 at Liege).

(December 9) Leopold Koželuch,
Bohemian composer, was born on
this date at Velvary (died 1818,
May 7 at Vienna).

(December 26) Girolamo Nicolo
Laurenti, Italian violinist and
composer, died on this day at
Bologna.

(December 26) Johann Mederitsch,
Bohemian conductor and composer,
was born on this date at Vienna
(died 1835, December 18 at Lwów).

(December 30) Anton Kraft,
cellist and composer, was born
at this time at Rokican near
Pilsen (died 1820, August 28
at Vienna).

(February) M. Grimm this month

(cont.) published a letter on
Destouche' opera "Omphale".
He attacked the work but
eulogized Rameau. He also
described "Platée" as a
"sublime work".

(March) Gluck this month was
commisioned to write a festival
opera for the birthday of
Charles III of Naples. The
libretto chosen was Metastasio's
"La clemenza di Tito".

(Easter) Karl Philipp Emmanuel
at this time commissioned
Marpurg to write a preface to
"Art of Fugue" and the subsequent new edition was published at the Leipzig Fair.

(April) Marie Justine Benoîte
Favart became a "sociétaire"
of the Comédie-Italienne this
month.

(June) G. Scarlatti's opera
"Demetrio" was produced this
season at the Teatro Nuovo
in Padua (libretto by Metastasio).

(July) Rameau at this time was
made an honorary member of the
Societé littéraire of Dijon.

(August) Casanova traveled
from Paris to Dresden this
month. His mother was an
actress there by appointment to
the Royal Court of Saxony. His
journey was made during the
middle of the month.

(August) Gluck and his wife
arrived in Naples this month
to start work on "La clemenza
di Tito".

(September) All of Michael
Festing's books, instruments
and other goods were sold this

month at his house in Warwick
Street, Golden Square, London.
This, of course, was after
Festing's death.

(December) Gluck returned to
Vienna this month from Naples.

(December) M. C. V. Vestris
was in London at this time.
She married violinist Felice
de Giardini while there.

Jacopo Amiconi, an Italian
artist, died (born 1675 at
Venice).

Johann Philipp Bach, organist
and painter, son of Georg
Friedrich and member of the
seventh generation of the Bach
family, was born this year
(died 1846).

Wilhelm Adolf Bach, son of W.
Friedemann, grandson of J.
Sebastian and member of the
seventh generation of the Bach
family, died at this time (born
1752). He obviously died as an
infant.

Jan Jiři Benda, German musician
and composer, died this year
(born 1715).

Franz Benda's daughter, Marie
Karoline, was born at this time
(died 1783).

Francesco Bianchi, Italian
composer and conductor, was born
this year at Cremona (died 1810,
November 27 at London). One
source gave his death date as
1811.

Dmitri Stepanovich Bortniansky,
Rissian composer, was born this
year at Glukhov, Ukraine (died
1825, October 10 at St. Peters-

(cont.) burg.

John Dodd, one of the greatest
English bow makers, was born
at this time at London (died
1839 at Richmond, Surrey).

Girolamo Donnini, Italian
composer, died this year at
Bonn (birthdate unknwon).

Joseph Fodor, violinist and
composer, was born this year
at Venlo (died 1828, October 3).
Louis Fuzelier, playwright
and librettist to Rameau,
died at this time (birthdate
unknown).

Thomas van den Gheyn, Flemish
organist and son of Matthias,
was born this year (death date
unknown).

Anna Friederike Heinel, actress,
known as the inventor of the
pirouette, was born at this
time (died 1808).

José Lidón, Spanish organist
and composer, was born at this
time in Bejar, Salamanca
(died 1827, February 13 at
Madrid).

John Marsh, English composer,
was born this year at Gosport
(died 1828 at Chichester).

Mrs. Elizabeth Porter, who
married Samuel Johnson, died
at this time (birthdate unknown).

Joseph Ritson, who discovered
Wynkyn de Worde's songbook and
several other early musical
manuscripts, was born this
year (died 1803).

Juan Antonio Scarlatti died
prior to this date according
to a major source.

Nikolaus Simrock, German founder of the Simrock music publishing firm, was born this year at Bonn (died 1833).

Anton Cajetan Adlgasser married his teacher's daughter, Eberlin, at this time.

Maria Teresa Agnesi married Pietro Antonio Pinottini this year.

Abbé François Arnaud from Carpentras, a literary and scientific man, arrived in Paris at this time.

Jacques Aubert this season retired from his position as first violinist in the orchestra of the Paris Opéra.

Charles Avison tried to reconcile theory with practice in his "Essay on Musical Expression" written this year.

Following Roseingrave's original publications and their reprints, Charles Avison's transcriptions for string orchestra and twelve sonatas by Dr. John Worgan appeared this year. The manuscript had belonged to Sebastian Albero, organist at the Royal Chapel in Madrid.

J. S. Bach's widow was receiving charitable relief payments by this time.

Johann van Beethoven entered the electoral chapel this year as a chorister. He sang soprano.

Bertoni this year was appointed organist at St. Mark's in Venice.

Guillaume Boutmy was granted an appointment in the Post Office by the Prince of Thurn and Taxis this year.

Charlotte Brent was the daughter of a fencing master and alto who was the original Hamor in Handel's "Jephtha" thi this year. When the production at Ranelagh (1759) of Bonnell Thornton's burlesque "Ode on St. Cecilia's Day" with Burney's music took place, she accompanied Beard in the Saltbox Song "on that instrument".

C. Chabran went to London this season.

B. Cooke (II) was appointed successor to Pepusch as conductor at the Academy of Ancient Music this year.

M. Dubourg succeeded Festing as leader of the King's band this season at London.

Since he was not satisfied with the resources of the palace and gardens, Farinelli offered his rulers a miniature fleet on the the Tagus, with frigates for the royalty, each with its own orchestra. Smaller boats were to be provided for the rest of the court.

Antoine Fel, French singer and composer, retired this year as a singer at the Paris Opéra.

Giulia Frasi sang in "Jephtha" this season.

Mme. Geoffroi-Bodin at this time had been engaged for the Vienna stage at a salary of 5,775 gulden. She was the wife of dancer Bodin, a friend of Casanova's from Turin.

Felice de Giardini this season became the leader of the orchestra at the Italian Opera, succeeding Festing.

Giuseppe Giordani, a singer with his family in tow, reached Amsterdam at this time.

Gluck was commissioned by Locatelli this year to write an opera to Metastasio's "Issipile" for the Prague carnival.

Gluck was invited to become conductor of Prince Hildburghausen's orchestra this season at Vienna.

Johann Valentin Görner was Kapellmeister at the cathedral in Hamburg this year.

A company of comedians from London, backed by William Hallam and managed by Lewis Hallam the elder, came to the colonies this year and played first in Williamsburg, Virginia.

Hallam's London company of comedians arrived in Yorktown this year.

Forkel maintained that Handel visited Germany this year for the third time.

J. Haydn this year made his first attempt at composition with a serenata for three instruments.

Petrus Hellendaal visited London this year to give several concerts and stayed there for eight years.

F. W. Herschel this year at the age of 14, joined the band (cont.) of the Hanoverian regiment of guards.

John Immyns was appointed lutenist at the Chapel Royal this season.

An organ made this year by Jacobus Kirkman has survived. The details are as follows: 2x8' stops only, F-F 5 octaves without bottom F#. Present owner is Benton Fletcher College in London.

Jean Louis Larvette joined the Opéra-Comique this year as an actor and tenor.

Jean François Lépine, senior, built the organ at the Cathedral at Lodève at this time.

Manelli and la Tonelli, both members of Bambini's troupe, performed this year in "La Serva Padrona" and helped to start the conflict called "Guerres des Bouffons".

Two books of sonatas by Padre Martini "were published one in Amsterdam and the other in Bologna in 1752" according to Fayolle. It has been said they were modeled after Corelli's opus III.

Mattheson's "Philologisches Tresespiel" was published this year. He wrote "Rameau: infatuated, pedantic and affected imitator of Lulli".

Giovanni Ambrosio Migliavacca this year produced the opera "Soliman" by Hasse and also wrote the libretto for Gluck's opera "Thetis". He came from Dresden.

Monet this year received per-

mission to reestablish Opéra-
Comique at the Fair of Saint-
Germain.

Davide Perez accepted an invitation to Lisbon at this time
and composed "Demofoonte" there.

P. Pisari was admitted to the
Pope's Chapel this season as
supernumerary and remained as
a member until his death in
1778.

N. Porpora left Dresden at this
time and returned to Vienna.

Quantz, in Berlin this year
described as the ideal musical
style one made up of the best
features of music of all nations:
"a music that is accepted and
recognized as good not by one
country only . . . but by many
peoples . . . must, provided it
is based as well on reason and
sound feeling, be beyond all
dispute the best".

Quantz at this time complained
that although most Italian
composers of the time were
talented, they started writing
operas before they had learned
the regimen of musical composition. Also that they did not
take time to be properly ground-
ed and worked too fast.

An anonymous critic in Soisons
this year issued a prospectus
announcing a "Traité general de
la musique" in which he criticized some of Rameau's theories.
Claude Rameau, the composer's
brother, issued a "Lettre" in
defense of the composer.

Johann Philipp Sack, an organist
at the Cathedral in Berlin,
founded a "Musikausübende

(cont.) Gesellschaft" this year.

Giuseppe Sarti became director
of the theatre in Faenza this
season.

The quality of the series of
Scarlatti's sonatas collected
by the Queen's copyists up to
this year far exceeded that of
his surviving earlier keyboard
works.

The two existing pictures that
are supposedly contemporary
portraits of Scarlatti, the
Lemoine lithograph and a detail
in an engraving after a painting made by Amiconi this year,
are not completely authenti-
cated.

The first two volumes of the
Queen's manuscripts by Scarlatti
(Venice I and II, 1752) con-
sisted of odds and ends.

The systematic copying of
Scarlatti's harpsichord works
began this year and continued
until his death.

There is no evidence to dispel
the astonishing hypothesis that
most of Scarlatti's sonatas
dated from his late years.

Scarlatti's alleged portrait
by Amiconi this year showed
him to be very thin.

Scarlatti was ill and confined
to his house at this time
according to a major source
who quoted a letter from the
Duke of Alba.

Early this year Scarlatti had
been asked to score two hymns
written in honor of two ancestors of the King's major domo.

F. Meyer von Schauensee, when his first music teacher, J. W. Müller, died this year, resigned his various positions and took holy orders. He became Müller's successor as organist and Kapellmeister at the collegiate church. He held the position with great distinction until he died.

Thomas Schwarbrook improved the organ of Worcester Cathedral at this time.

Gregorio Sciroli was in the service of the Prince of Bisignano this year.

John Snetzler at this time built an organ for the Aberdeen Musical Society.

Antonio Soler became a monk of the Order of St. Jerome at Lérida Cathedral this year.

J. C. Standfuss originally set Coffey's ballad opera "The Devil to Pay" at this time.

Carlo Giuseppe Toeschi, an Italian violinist and composer, entered the Mannheim orchestra this season.

William Tuckey, who was vicar-choral at Bristol, was brought from England this year to be clerk of Trinity Parish.

John Worgan at this time was granted licence to print the works of D. Scarlatti.

Girolamo Abos' opera "Erifile" appeared this year at Rome.

Agricola's comic opera "La citella ingannata" was performed this season at the inauguration (cont.) of the new theatre in Antwerp.

Alcock this year edited a collection of psalm tunes by various composers arranged for four voices and titled "The Harmony of Sion".

d'Alembert this year published "Éléments de musique théorique et practique suivant les principes de M. Rameau".

Almeida's "Ippolito", a sere-nata for six voices appeared this year.

Arne's songs in Charles John-son's "Country Lasses" were composed prior to this date.

Louis Aubert's "Simphonies à quatre" for 3 violins and a bass appeared at this time.

Charles Avison's "Essay of Musical Expression" was written this year. In it he criticized any composer who replaced an opportunity for expression with the compositional device of imitation.

Bach's "The Art of the Fugue" was published by Marpurg this year.

Bertoni set Goldoni's libretto "Le pescatrici at this time.

Metastasio's libretto to "L'Eroe cinese" was first set this year by Bonno. See also Cimarosa, Galuppi, Giordani (T), Hasse, Rauzzini (V.) and Sacchini.

Bonno's opera "L'Eroe cinese" was produced this year at Schönbrunn near Vienna.

Metastasio's libretto for "L'Isola disabitata" was first set this year by Bonno. See also Arne (adapted by Murphy), Beck (F.), Benda, Haydn, Holz-bauer, Jommelli, Ouseley, Pérez (D.), Rota, Spontini and Traetta.

Briseux this year issued both his "Traité du Beau essentiel dans les Arts, appliqué particu-lièrement à l'Architecture" and his "Traité des Proportions harmoniques".

Casali's opera "Antigona" was produced this season at Turin.

N. Conforto's opera "Siroe" was produced this season at Madrid.

A volume of clavecin pieces by Armand-Louis Couperin was published this year.

Dauvergne's ballet "Les Amours de Tempé" was produced this season at the Paris Opéra.

Destouches' opera "Omphale" was revived until this year.

William Felton published a third volume of six keyboard concertos, opus 4 at this time in London.

Louis Marc Fouquet's third book of harpsichord pieces was published this year.

Baldassare Galuppi this year wrote his opera "La calamità de'cuori" at Venice (libretto by Goldoni).

Baldassare Galuppi's opera "Didone abbandonata" was pro-

(cont.) duced this season at Madrid.

Baldassare Galuppi this year wrote his opera "Le virtuose ridicole" in Venice (libretto by Goldoni).

Francisco Xavier García this year composed his oratorio "Tobra"

Georg Gebel's opera "medea" was produced this season at Rudolstadt.

Georg Gebel's opera "Tarquinius Superbus" was produced this season at Rudolstadt.

Gluck's Italian opera "Issipile" (libretto by Metastasio) was produced at the Carnival in Prague this year by Locatelli's company.

Johann Valentin Görner's third set of music composed to Hagedorn's poems was published at this time ("Neue Oden und Lieder").

Carl Heinrich Graun's opera "Il giudizio di Paride" was produced in Berlin this season.

Carl Heinrich Graun's opera "Orfeo ed Euridice" was pro-duced in Berlin this season.

Melchior Grimm's "Lettre sur Omphale" appeared this year.

Grimm this year published his satirical pamphlet "Le Petis Prophète de Boehmischbroda" which ushered in the "Guerre des Bouffons".

Handel's "Samson" was performed at Worcester at the Three Choirs

Festival this season.

Höpken this year wrote an
Italian opera-drama with text by
Metastasio, "Il re pastore".

Jommelli's intermezzo "I rivali
delusi" was produced this
season at Rome.

Christian Gottfried Krause
wrote his "Von der musicalischen
Poesie" this year at Berlin.

Jacques Lacombe's "Dictionaire
portatif des beaux-arts" was
published this year at Paris.

N. Logroscino's "Lo finto
perziano" was produced this
season.

N. Logroscino's "Friselda"
was produced this season.

This season a parody of Lulli's
"Acis et Galatée" was conducted
by Gluck.

N. Pasquali's oratorio "Noah"
was produced this season at
Fishamble Street Music Hall in
London.

Pergolesi's works were performed
at the Mannheim school at this
time.

J. J. Quantz's "Versuch einer
Anweisung die Flöte Traversiere
zu spielen", an important
treatise on every phase of flute
playing, was published this
year at Berlin. It was dedicated to Frederick the Great,
Quantz's pupil. In the book
Quantz covered many areas. He
estimated tempi through a relationship to pulse-beats; he
stated that "the notes must not
sound as though glued together";

(cont.) he allowed greater
liberties in regard to "ada-
gios"; he granted the sarabande
the tempo of the gigue--MM80
to the quarternote; as for the
violin he said it might "Increase or diminish the tone
when required"; he spoke of a
"continual play of light and
shade" and even gave rules for
grading the volume of each
successive chord according to
the degree of dissonance; he
described harpsichord technique.
In the chapter on trills he
discouraged very slow and very
fast trills, advised faster
trills on high notes than on
low notes and suggested slow
trills on "sad pieces" and more
rapid on "gay pieces".

Jean-Jacques Rousseau's "Lettres
à M. Grimm au sujet des remarques de la Lettre sur
Omphale, 1752" appeared at this
time.

Rameau published his "Nouvelles
Réflexions sur sa démonstration
du principe de l'harmonie"
this year.

The Academy of Music played
Rousseau's "Devin du Village"
this season.

Rousseau's "Salve Regina", a
motet for soprano and orchestra
was composed for Mlle. Fel,
a cantatrice, at this time,
however in manuscript only.

Giuseppe Sarti's opera "Pompeo
in Armenia" was produced this
season at Faenza.

Christopher Saur published
"Fuenff Schoene Geistliche
Lieder"(Warrington) this year.

The first and second volumes of

D. Scarlatti's violin sonatas were published this season.

G. Scarlatti's opera "Adriano in Siria" was produced this season at the Teatro San Cassiano in Venice (libretto by Metastasio).

G. Scarlatti's opera "L'impostore" was produced this season at Barcelona.

Volumes I-V of Scarlatti's sonatas were issued at this time at Parma.

J. S. Standfuss, a German musician, composed the musical numbers for "Julius Ceasar" which was performed this year.

C. W. Van Borck's German version of Charles Coffey's farce, "The Devil to pay, or the Wives metamorphos'd" was altered this year by Christian Felix Weisse. To his text J. C. Standfuss composed new music. Standfuss thus was the first composer of German "Singspiele". The work was produced at Berlin.

James Turner's tunes were engraved this year at Boston and also bound with Barnard's "New Version of the Psalms".

The year the price of admission to Marylebone Gardens was reduced to 6d., although the expense was supposedly £ 8 per night more than the preceding season.

At this time the Kean and Murray Company presented the "Beggar's Opera" in Maryland. An orchestra was used instead of only a spinet.

The "Company of Comedians from Annapolis" went to Upper Marlborough, Maryland this year to open a new theatre.

The "Guerre des Bouffons" started this year. It was a contest between the partisans of Italian and French music. The great violence was not so much between musicians as between the patrons and audiences.

An Italian company of singers "Les Bouffons" arrived in Paris at this time and produced Italian intermezzi.

Joseph de Laporte this year founded the "Almanach historique et chronologique de tous les spectacles de Paris".

Adolf, Freiherr von Knigge and famous author of "Ueber den Umgang mit Menschen" was born this year (died 1796).

The Genoese Conte Giacomo Durazzo this year was transferred to the Austrian Imperial service as an honorary privy councillor.

Thomas Chatterton, "fraud poet", was born this year (died 1770).

Pierre-Louis d'Aquin de Château-Lyon this year wrote "Lettres sur les hommes célebres dans les sciences, la littérature et l'art sous le règne de Louis XV".

Henry Fielding's "The History of Amelia" was published at this time in London.

Friedrich Maximilian von

1752(cont.)

Klinger, German dramatist, was born this year (died 1831).

Johann Anton Leisewitz, German dramatic poet, was born this year (died 1806).

John Brown, English artist, was born at this time (died 1787).

John Robert Cozens, a landscape painter revered by John Constable who felt he was the greatest genius that ever touched land- scape, was born this year (died 1797).

Stefan Fofanelli, director of the Instituto di Belli Arti in Lucca, was born this year (died 1812). He painted Elise Bonaparte several times.

Sir John Nash, English archi- tect, was born this year (died 1835).

Sir John Soane, the Enlish architect, was born this year (died 1837). One source has his birthdate as 1753.

J. F. de Troy, French painter, died at this time (born 1679).

(and 1753) Blavet wrote several operas for the Count of Cler- mont's private theatre at Berny.

(and 1753) Gaetano Latilla's works were given by the bouffons at the Paris Opéra during these seasons.

(and 1753) The middle period of Scarlatti's sonatas (Venice III and IV) was at this time.

(and 1753) The sonatas of Venice (III and IV) at this time

(cont.) approached the fully mature Scarlatti.

(and 1753) The contemporary issues of new Scarlatti sonatas began at this time with the Parma sonatas (Volume IV) which were not copied into the Queen's set (Venice III) until 1753.

(to 1754) The "Guerre des Bouffons", a name given to the historical quarrel dividing Paris society, as partisans of French and Italian music, during the performances given by the Italian "buffi" (Fr. bouffons) during these seasons.

(to 1754) Le Clerc de la Bruère served as editor of the "Mercure" for these two years.

(to 1754) Rameau's "Pygmalion" was a huge success at this time and held its own against the opera-comique (bouffons).

(to 1755) "Capperan" appeared in the Royal Chapel at Turin for these three years.

(and 1755) In addition to works by resident composers, Corselli and Corradini, Mele, who left in 1752 and Conforto, who had arrived in 1755, Farinelli also produced operas by Galuppi, Hasse, Jommelli and others.

(to 1755) French architecture: E. Nancy, Gate at Stanislas.

(to 1756) Santo Lapis during this period lived in Holland and published pieces for harpsichord and also for flute.

(to 1756) Samuel Lee led the band at Marlborough Green for these four years.

1752(cont.)

(to 1756) It was during the Fall vacation of the Spanish court at the Escorial during these years that Soler befriended Scarlatti.

(to 1757) William Felton was the vicar of Philip Hay during this period.

(to 1757) Scarlatti's thirteen volumes, each containing thirty sonatas (except for volume X which contained thirty-four) were prepared for Queen Maria Barbara during this five year period.

(to 1757) An additional fifteen volumes of Scarlatti's sonatas, largely duplicating the Queen's series, were copied during this period, some at least by the same copyist.

(and 1759, 1762, 1766, 1772, 1779) Alembert's "Elémens de musique, theorique et pratique, suivant les principes de M. Rameau" of this year enjoyed great success and appeared

in five other editions.

(to 1763) Albanèse sang at the Concert Spirituel during these eleven years.

(to 1766) Sir John Hawkins was a member of the Madrigal Society during this period.

(to 1767) François Joseph Giraud, French cellist and composer, during these years played in the Paris Opéra orchestra.

(to 1774) Jan Mares was employed in the imperial Russian orchestra as a horn player during

(cont.) this period.

(to 1789) The most complete German treatise on the method of flute-playing by Johann Joachim Quantz, "Versuch einer Anweisung die Flöte traversiere zu spielen" apperaed in several editions during these years.

c.1752

Isidore Bertheaume, French violinist and composer, was born this year at Paris (died 1802, March 20 at St. Petersburg).

Claude Denis, French theorist, died this year at Paris (born c.1680).

Johann Samuel Schröter, German pianist and composer, was born this year in Warsaw (died 1788, November 2).

Maximilian Ulbrich, Austrian composer, was born this year at Vienna (died 1814, September 14 at Vienna).

D'Alembert maintained this year that the Opéra orchestra played too loud or too soft, but never "à demi jeu".

After returning to Vienna at this time, Gluck was given the title of Kapellmeister by Prince Joseph Friedrich von Sachsen Hildburghausen.

1753

(January 1) An article on this date in "The Daily Advertiser" probably referred to "Scarlatti's 12 Sonatas".

(January 1 to 1757) William Tuckey was choir head at Trinity Parish in New York City

1753(cont.)
during this period.

(January 9) On this date Joseph
Mondonville's opera "Titon et
l'Aurore" was performed at the
Paris Opera. Its success was
due to his having been chosen
as champion of the National
school in the "Guerre des
Bouffons".

(January 9) Luiza Rosa d'Aguiar
Todi, Portuguese mezzo-soprano,
was born on this date at Setubal
(died 1833, October 1 at Lisbon).

(February 5) Hasse's opera,
Solimano" (libretto by Giovanni
A. Migliavacca) was premiered
this day at Dresden.

(February 6) Barnabus Gunn,
English organist and composer,
died on this date at Birmingham
(born c.1680).

(February 7) James Lyon of
Ireland was married on this day.

(February 7) Edward Moore's
"The Gamester", produced on this
dayte, included one song by
Boyce. It took place at Drury
Lane Theatre in London.

(February 7) J. Oswald wrote
one song for Moore's tragedy
"The Gamester", produced on
this date at Drury Lane Theatre
in London.

(February 24) Karl Türrschmidt,
German horn virtuoso, was born
on this date at Wallerstein,
Bavaria (died November 1, 1797
at Berlin).

(February 25) François Lupin-
Grenet, French composer, died
on this day at Lyons (born
c.1700).

(March 1) Rousseau's "Le Devin
du Village" was produced on
this date at the Paris Opera.

(March 9) J. J. Imbault, French
violinist and music publisher,
was born on this date at Paris
(death date unknown).

(May 2) On this day Johann
Friedrich Lampe's wife,
Isabella, sang at a benefit
performance at Covent Garden
in London.

(May 11) Mary Worgan became
organist at St. Dunstan's in
London on this date.

(May 12) G. Scarlatti's opera
"Alessandro nell'Indie" was
produced this day at the Teatro
Pubblico in Reggio (libretto
by Metastasio).

(May 15) Richard Broadway's
oratorio "Solomon's Temple"
was performed at this time at
the Philharmonic Room on
Fishamble Street "for the
benefit of sick and distressed
Free Masons".

(May 19) Jacques Aubert was
buried on this date.

(May 23) Giovanni Viotti,
founder of modern school of
violin playing, was born on
this date at Fontanetto da
Po (died 1824 at London).

(June 13) Nicolas Dalayrac,
French composer, was born on
this day at Muret, Languedoc
(died 1809, November 27 at
Paris).

(July 30) Dauvergne's greatest
success was unquestionably on
this date at the production of

JOHANN VAN BEETHOVEN
(Born c. 1739)

1753(cont.)

"Les Troqueurs", an interlude in one act with words by Jean Joseph Vadé, after La Fontaine (opéra-comique). It was supposedly an adaption of an Italian opera buffo.

(August 4) Charles Simon Favart's "Les Amours de Bastien et Bastienne" was first performed in Paris on this date. The work was performed at the Comédie-Italienne.

(August 4) Gottfired Silbermann, German organ, clavichord and piano maker, died this day at Dresden (born 1683, January 14). He invented the "cembal d'amore".

(August 19) Johan Fredrik Palm, Swedish musician who taught clavier, was born on this date (died 1821, March 15 at Edsberg).

(August 28) Johann Braun, German violinist and composer, was born this day at Cassel (died 1795 at Berlin).

(Septemger 24) Georg Gebel, German organist, harpsichordist and composer, died on this date at Rudolstadt (born 1709, October 25).

(October 3) Scarlatti petitioned Pope Benedict XIII for a plenary indulgence for himself and his wife and family on this date.

(October 4) Dancer Mlle. Heinel was born this day at Bayreuth (died 1808, March 17 at Paris).

(October 4) Hasse's opera "L'eroe cinese" (libretto by Metastasio) was produced on this date at Hubertusburg.

(October 10) André Grétry entered the music school at La Cigogne on this day.

(October 10) Frau Eva Katharina Keverich, Johann van Beethoven's father-in-law's mother, died at this time (born 1664).

(October 14) Franz Anton Dimmler, German composer, was born on this date at Mannheim (died c.1819 at München).

(October 30) Rameau's "Daphnis et Églé", a pastorale héroique (Colli), was heard at this time at Fontainbleau.

(November 3) Friedrich Christoph Gestewitz, German composer, was born on this date at Prieschke, near Meissen (died 1805, August 1).

(November 3) Antoine Marcel Lemoine, guitarist and performer on viola, was born on this day at Paris (died 1817, April).

(November 4) Johann Nikolaus Bach, Jena organist, son of J. Christoph and grandson of Heinrich, died on this date (born 1669, October 10).

(November 13) Dauvergne's "La Coquette trompée" was performed on this date before the court at Fontainbleau. Favart provided the text.

(November 13) Rameau's "Les Sybarites", acte de ballet, was produced this day at Fontainbleau (Marmontel).

(November 16) Nicolas Racot de Grandval, French composer and harpsichordist, died at this time in Paris (born c.1676).

(November 19) The "Beggar's Opera" was performed at New York by a company of comedians on this evening.

(November 19) Stanislas Champein, French composer, was born on this date at Marseilles (died 1830, September 19 at Paris).

(November 25) Otto Carl Erdmann Kospoth, Freiherr was born on this date at Mühltroff, Saxony (died 1817, June 23 at Mühltroff, Saxony). He was a German amateur composer.

(November 30) Johann Schenk, Austrian composer, was born this day at Wiener Neustadt (died 1836, December 29). He wrote Singspiels and was a teacher of Beethoven.

(December 1) Boyce's incidental music to "Boadicia" was heard this evening at the Drury Lane Theatre in London.

(December 13) Robert Bremner gave a concert on this date at the High School in Leith.

(December 17) Cocchi's opera "Gli amanti gelosi" was produced this evening at Covent Garden in London.

(December 27) The Pennsylvania Gazette on this date advertised that Josiah Davenport taught "Writing in all the different hands, arithmetick in a good and easy method and 'psalmody in several necessary and useful parts'".

(December 27) G. Scarlatti's

(cont.) opera "De gustibus non est disputandum" was given this day at the Teatro San Cassiano in Venice (libretto by Goldoni).

(December 28) Johan Wikmanson, Swedish musician and composer, was born on this day at Stockhorm (died 1800, January 16).

(January) The Pennsylvania Gazette in this month mentioned a Robert Coe as the "exponent of Secular Music" whose occupation was drawing Bills, Bonds, Indentures, Leases, etc. and a teacher of the German Flute.

(January) Valentine Snow became Sargeant-Trumpeter to the King this month.

(April) Locatelli this year applied for an extension to his contract with the Prague "Gubenium" and it was granted this month.

(May) Jacques Aubert, French violinist and composer, died at this time at Belleville near Paris (born 1689, September 30).

(August) "Il trionfo della fedelta" by Agricola, Benda, Frederick II, Graun, Hasse and Maria Antonia Walpurgis was performed at this time in Potsdam.

(October and November) Rameau produced three one-act ballets during these two months: "Daphnis et Églé", "Lysis et Delie" and "Les Sybarites".

(November) Jeanne-Thérèse Goermans this month was installed as a favorite at La Pouplinère's establishment at

1753(cont.)
the Rue de Richelieu.

(November) Rousseau's "Lettre sur la Musique Française" appeared this month. The work was involved with the controversy over his musical philosophy.

(December) Joseph Royer this year bought from B. de Bury the position of Maitre de Musique de la Chamber du Roy. This month he was appointed inspector at the Opera, a position he held until his death.

John Beard's wife, Lady Henrietta, died this year.

Karl Franz Benda, German chamber musician, was born this year (died 1817).

Lorenz Hübner, a former Jesuit, was born at this time (died 1807).

Franz Lamotte, violinist and composer of undetermined nationality, was born this year (death date unknown).

Gottlieb August Meissner, writer and Prague University professor, was born at this time (died 1807).

Lucien-Joseph Raoux was born in Paris this year. He was another member of the famed Raoux Family and made concert horns for most of the leading soloists of his time, including Dauprat, Gallay, and Puzzi (death date unknown, but he died at Paris).

Giuseppe Rovelli, Italian cellist, was born this year at Bergamo. He was the son of

(cont.) Giovanni Battista Rovelli (died 1806, November 12 at Parma).

Giovanni Battista Rubinelli, Italian singer, was born at this time at Brescia (died 1829 at Brescia).

Johann David Schiedmayer, instrument builder, was born this year at Erlangen (died 1805, March 20).

Anton Schweitzer, German composer, was born this year (died 1787).

Anton Stadler, Austrian clarinettist and close friend of Mozart, was born this year (died 1812, June 15 at Vienna).

Anton Stamitz, Austrian musician, was born this year according to a major source (died 1820).

Armand Vanderhagen, Belgian clarinettist, was born this year at Antwerp (died 1822, July at Paris).

Gustavus Waltz, German bass, died at London at this time (birthdate unknown).

James Worgan, English organist, died this year at London (born 1715).

Carl Friedrich Zimdar, actor and writer of several "Singspiel" librettos, was born at this time (died 1792).

Dall'Abaco this year left the Bonn court and went to live near his family at Verona and with his wife.

A legal document of this time

listed five children, not
including Ludwig, as the only
surviving children of Henry
Adelard.

Adolfati's opera "La clemenza
di Tito" has been preserved at
the National Library in Vienna.

Maria Teresa Agnesi wrote her
own libretto this year for her
opera "Ciro in Armenia".

Altnikol at this time was a
candidate for the vacant organ
at St. John's Church in Zittau.
W. F. Bach was a competing
candidate.

In the male line Johann
Christoph Bach's descendants
were extinct or expatriated by
this year.

K. P. E. Bach was ready by now
to seek employment at Zittau.

Wilhelm Friedemann Bach applied
for the organist's position
at the Johannis-Kirche at
Zittau, made vacant this year
by the death of G. Krause.

Christlieb Sigmund Binder at
this time was appointed church
organist at Dresden.

During the carnival season of
this year, Bini was still at
Pesaro directing the orchestra
at the Teatro del Sole.

"Dr. William Boyce" was a
bondsman for John Boyce, junior,
when he was elected Beadle
this season.

C. Cannabich studied composition
under Jommelli in Rome up to
this date.

Caffarelli requested permission
to go to France this season.

Caffarelli sang at Modena this
season.

Casanova renewed his acquaintance with Theresa Cornelys
this season at Venice.

Casanova this year wrote, "I
had seen her (Teresa Pompeati-
singer, La Pompeati) in Venice,
and at the time we had taken
each other a little more ser-
iously. She then departed for
Bayreuth, where she became the
mistress of the Margrave. I
had promised to visit her, but
C. C. and my fair nun M.M. left
me with neither the time nor
the desire. Soon afterwood
the Leads engulfed me and I
had other things to think of
besides redeeming a promise."

Gioacchino Conti retired from
the stage and settled in
Arpino, Naples at this time.

The house that Rudolfo Corelli
had attempted to destroy in
1632 was utterly destroyed
under the sinister name of
"Guasto dei Corelli" (The
Devastation of the Corellis).
The site was to remain deserted
until this year, when the Abbe
Marquise Giulio Corelli deeded
it so that the Church del Pio
Suffragio (of the Devout
Supplication) might be built
there.

The contredanse was brought
into French stage music in
Dauvergne's "Les Troqueurs"
of this season.

Diderot along with his friends
d'Alembert, d'Holbach and
Grimm, took part this season in

the famous though trivial "Guerre des Bouffons" which created some stir from this date forward.

Giacomo Durazzo was appointed assistant this year to Count Esterhazy, in charge of theatrical affairs.

Domenico Ferrari this season became a member of the orchestra of the Duke of Württemberg at Stuttgart.

C. A. Grenser was appointed woodwind maker to the court of Saxony at this time.

Sir John Hawkins married Miss Storer this year.

Johann C. Hertel was pensioned at this time. He composed many works for orchestra and chamber music which have remained in manuscript.

Holzbauer this year was summoned to Mannheim and for twenty-five years was in charge of the opera there and conducted the most famous orchestra in existence at the time.

Johann Holzbogen was a pupil of Tartini in Italy at this juncture.

Pierre Iso (Yzo), French composer, took part in the "guerre des bouffons" by publishing (under the name of Yso) one or two answers to Rousseau's "Lettre sur la musique française" this year.

Jommelli this season became court conductor at Stuttgart to the Duke of Würtemberg.

Samuel Lee's salary as Conductor of the Ciry Music or Corporation Band was increased from 40 pounds to 60 pounds a year at this time.

Queen Louisa Ulrika of Sweden founded an "Opéra-Comique" after the Parisian model this season at Stockholm.

J. G. Müthel became organist at the Lutheran Church in Riga this year and stayed there for the rest of his life.

One of Antonio Tonelli's pupils, Rosa Parteggotti, appeared in public this year at six years of age and sang and accompanied herself on the spinet with extraordinary dexterity.

The opera "Il maestro di musica" was erroneously attributed to Pergolesi this year at Paris.

La Pouplinière this season fell into the clutches of an "intrigante", Jeanne-Thérèse Goermans.

The Rameaus spent this summer at Passy for the last time.

The Abbate Vincenzo Rota of Padua published his peom "L'incendio di tempio di S. Antonio" at Padua this year. Every stanza in the preface celebrated the genius of Giuseppe Tartini, violinist, composer and teacher.

According to Jean-Jacques Rousseau, in his "Lettre sur la musique françoise" of this year, Corelli spent his time after his stay at Bologna in France.

Rousseau this year delivered his most devasting blow to the decaying edifice of French Baroque opera in his "Lettre sur la Musique Française". "The ear will no longer tolerate the scholarly nonsense of your gugues and double fugues, inverted cannons and bassi obligati". He further declared "the French cannot have any music".

Anna Scarlatti, daughter of Pietro, was awarded 30 ducats by the city of Naples this year after she had requested sustenance.

With the two sonatas in F sharp major (sonatas 318 and 319) Scarlatti had by this time completed his set of tonalities.

Philipp Schöller of München, one of the first to make the Inventionshorn as designed by Hampel, supplied two of his horns to the electoral court orchestra this year at München.

Solar took his vows at this time.

William Tuckey, after serving in Bristol Cathedral, came to New York this year as clerk of Trinity Church. He soon established himself as organist and a great protagonist of Handel's works.

Francesco Antonio Baldassare Uttini, singer and composer, was at Copenhagen this season.

John Worgen becomes organist at St. Botolph's at Aldgate this year.

Girolamo Abos' last work for the stage, "Medo", was produced this season at Turin.

Alcock this year published a "Morning and Evening Service in E minor".

Pierre-Louis d'Aquin de Chateau-Lyon wrote "Siècle littéraire de Louis XV, ou lettres sur les hommes célèbres" this year at Amsterdam.

François Arnaud wrote "Reflexions sur la musique en general et la musique francaise en particulier" and it was issued this season at Paris.

The first known performance of Astorga's "Stabat Mater" took place at the Oxford Music Room shortly before this year.

A shortened version of Auletta's "Orazio" with additions by other composer, was published in Paris this year under Pergolesi's name, as "Il maestro di musica".

Six arias by Aurisicchio were sung this season in an opera at the Teatro Argentina at Rome.

The second edition of Avison's "An Essay on Musical Expression" appeared this year.

K. P. E. Bach wrote his Concerto in C minor for clavier at this time.

Odes with Melodies, containing songs by Karl Philipp Emanuel Bach, Graun, Quantz and others, was published this season.

The first part of K. P. E. Bach's "Versuch über die wahre Art das Clavier zu spielen" was published this season. Other sources considered less reliable gave the complete work as appearing at this time.

This year Barbella's opera "Elmira generosa", written in collaboration with Logroscino, was produced at Naples.

Bellinzani's opus 6 "Ester", an oratorio, was heard this year at Ancona.

Bertonio set Goldoni's libretto "I bagni d'Albano" at this time.

Rinaldo di Capua's opera "La Zingara" was produced this season at Paris.

Corrette's "Maître de clavecin" appeared at this time.

Diderot's brochure "Arrêt rendu à l'ampithéâtre de l'opéra" was issued this year.

Diderot's brochure "Au Petit Prophète de Boehmischbroda, au Grand Prophète Monet" was issued this year.

Diderot's "Les Trois Chapitres, ou La Vision de la nuit du Mardi-Gras au Mercredi des cendres" appeared at this time.

Durante's oratorio "S. Antonio di Padova" was completed this year.

Errichelli's operas "Il finto Turco" and "La serva astuta" were both completed this season.

Domenico Fischietti's opera "La finta sposa" was produced this season at Palermo.

Baldassare Galuppi and Bertoni wrote their opera "I bagni d'Abano" (libretto by Goldoni) this year at Venice.

Baldassare Galuppi wrote his opera "L'eroe cinese" (libretto by Metastasio) this year at Naples.

Baldassare Galuppi wrote his opera "Sofonisba" (libretto by Roccaforte) this year at Rome.

Georg Gebel's opera "Marcus Antonius" was produced this season at Rudolstadt.

Georg Gebel's opera "Sophonisbe" was produced this season at Rudolstadt.

François Joseph Giraud's "Les Hommes" (libretto by Saint-Fox) was produced this season at the Comédie-Française.

Gluck's aria "Pace, Amor" (text by Metastasio) was performed this year.

Carl Heinrich Graun's opera "Silla" was produced this season at Berlin.

Friedrich von Grimm's "Le Petit Prophete de Boemisch-Broda" was published at this time.

Hasse's pasticcios of this year were "Nerone" (produced at London) and "Il trionfo della fedelta" (produced at Charlottenburg). Hasse also wrote part of the music of an opera with the latter title by his pupil, the Princess Maria Antonia Walpurgis of Saxony, performed at Dresden in 1754. It was a different work.

Holzbauer's Italian opera, Il figlio delle selve", was performed at the summer residence of Schwetzingen this

season.

Arvid Höpken wrote an Italian opera-drama, "Catone in Utica", with text by Metastasio this year.

Six organ fugues of Henrik Johnsen's and 24 odes were both published this year.

Jommelli's secular dramatic work "Attilio Regolo" appeared this year at Rome.

Jommelli's secular dramatic work "Bajazet" appeared this season at Turin.

Jommelli's secular dramatic work "La clemenza di Tito" appeared this year at Stuttgart.

Jommelli's intermezzo "Don Falcone" was produced this season at Bologna.

Jommelli's secular dramatic work "Fetonte" (libretto by Villati) appeared this season at Stuttgart.

Jommelli's cantata "La reggia dei fati" (with G. B. Sammartini) was heard this season at Milan.

William Knapp's "The New Church Melody" appeared this year. It was reissued in 1756 and 1764. The final edition was the fifth.

Giovanni Battista Lampugnani's opera "Vologeso" was produced this season at Barcelona.

Jean Louis Larvette's name appeared this year as a composer of songs in "Le Boulevard" and "Le Plaisir et l'innocence".

Gaetano Latilla's "Madama Ciana"

(cont.) was given this season as "Gli artigiani arrichiti" at the Paris Opéra.

Jean Marie Leclair "l'aîné" wrote "Ouvertures et sonates en trio, 2 violins and continuo" at this time.

N. Logroscino's "Elmira generosa" was produced this season.

N. Logroscino's "Olimpiade" was produced this season.

N. Logroscino's "La pastorella scaltra" was produced this season.

P. van Maldere's "VI Sonatas for violins . . ." was published this year in two volumes at Dublin.

Pergolesi's "Stabat Mater" was performed by the Concerts Spirituel in France this season.

Rousseau's "Le Devin du Village" was performed this season at Brussels.

Jean-Jacques Rousseau this year wrote the witty "Lettre d'un symphoniste de L'Académie Royale de Musique a ses comrades de l'orchestre.

Giuseppe Sarti's opera "Il re pastore" was produced this season at Venice.

The 3rd, 4th, 5th and 6th volumes of D. Scarlatti's violin sonatas were published at this time.

Volumes VI-VIII of Scarlatti's sonatas were published this year at Padua according to a reliable source (see previous

1753(cont. entry for conflict).

Tommaso Traetta's "I pastori felici" was produced at Naples this year at the Teatro San Carlo.

Christopher Saur this year at Germantown published "Die Kleine geistliche Harfe" and "Neu vermehrt und vollstaendiges Gesangbuch"(Warrington).

Watts' "Psalms of David" (16th edition) was reprinted at this time.

Zoppis' "Vologeso" was performed this season at Prague.

In K. P. E. Bach's book "Versuch über die wahre Art das Klavier zu spielen" of this year he discussed many facets of key-board playing. The book dealt essentially with ornamentation and rhythm. Concerning dynamics he stated "For each case met even by the best rule there will be an exception".
  He discussed "broken chords" and gave careful instructions for certain irregularities of rhythm within the bar and ad-vised the speed of the fastest passage work be taken into account to prevent hurrying. The double-dotted note was used very tentatively by him.
  He encouraged harpsichordists to play staccato on occasion as the normal tone of the instru-ment was legato to provide a singing tone.
  He stated, "Probably no one has ever doubted the necessity of embellishments" and dis-cussed the trill, mordent and turn. He maintained that the "ornament takes the beat". He described the ascending turn

(cont.) as "Doppelschlag von Unten" and stated that the "brilliance (of the mordent) is often increased by raising (chromatically) the lower note".

The Royal Artillery at a review in Green Park this year had a drum major, six fifers and ten drummers.

The first regular theatre was erected this season in Man-chester.

This year the bowling-green was added to Marleybone Gardens and the fireworks were on a larger scale than previously.

J. Holdroyd's "Spiritual Man's Companion" appeared this year in its 5th edition.

At this time the "Ordre de Sainte-Cecile Royale" or "Confrerie de St. Cecilia" received the right to use "a chamber" in the city, The Hague, for the purpose of giving concerts. The conductor was Albert Groneman.

Federico Bencovitch, Dalmation painter, died this year (born 1677).

Neumann, a German architect, died at this time (born 1687).

Soane, an architect, was born this year (died 1837).

Oudry, French painter known for chronicling the "Hunts of Louis XV" this year painted "The White Duck", which showed an outstanding handling of color.

The English leader of taste and fashion, Lord Burlington, died at this time (born 1695).

1753(cont.)

(and 1754, 1764) Raphael Courteville for some years had
practically neglected his duties
as organist. He was warned in
1753 and 1754; and in 1764 his
assistant, Richardson, was con-
sulted concerning repairs to
the organ.

(to 1754) Marpurg's "Abhandlung
von der Fuge" with 62 plates
was published at this time at
Berlin.

(and 1755) Andren Bernasconi
was appointed vice chapel master
at the electoral court at
München, under Giovanni Porta,
during this period. He succeeded
Porta in 1755.

(to 1756) During this period
Frederick II wrote the following
librettos in French, later
translated into Italian by
Giampietro Tagliazucchi: "Silla",
"Montezuma", "I fratelli nemici"
and "Merope".

(to 1756) Kellner's published
works during these years included "Manipulus Zeitvertreib
vors Clavier" (Arnstadt), four
pieces, partly suites and partly
sonatas.

(to 1756) During this period
Samuel Lee printed "Lee's
Masque, a collection of Popular
Songs", four in each group,
"price a British sixpence each".

(to 1757) Niccolò Porpora,
famous Italian composer and
singing teacher, lived in
Vienna at this time.

(to 1757) A. M. G. Vestris was
admitted to the ballets in
Paris during these years.

(to 1762) K. P. E. Bach's

(cont.) "Versuch über die
wahre Art das Klavier zu
spielen", in two parts, was
published complete during
this period.

(and 1762, 1763) Robert
Bremner was the author of
the treatise "The Rudiments
of Music" which ran through
three editions at the
years noted above.

(to 1763) Carl Barbandt gave
subscription concerts at the
little theatre in the Haymarket
during this period.

(to 1766, c.1870) Eighteen
manuscripts of Brusa's church
music, mostly hymns and
psalms, dated 1753-1766, were
recovered by Fantoni about
1870.

(to 1769) Niccolò Jommelli
stayed in Stuttgart as court
composer and chapel-master
during these sixteen years.

(to 1776) Pigalle sculpted
"Tomb of the Marechal de
Saxe" during this period
(St. Thomas: Strasbourg) in
marble (15', 11" tall).

(to 1790) During this period
the "Correspondance littéraire,
philosophique et critique"
was circulated (edited by
Friedrich von Grimm).

c.1753

Samuel Baumgarten, English
bassoonist, was born at this
time (died 1784).

Giuseppe Giordani, Italian
composer, was born in Naples
this year (died 1798, January
4).

A. Duni reappeared as the

c.1753

conductor of a traveling opera company in Northern Germany at this time.

Haydn's Quintet ("Cassatio"), a divertimento for two violins, two viola and cello in G major appeared at this time.

(to 1756) Carl Barbandt appeared in public as a virtuoso on both the oboe and the clarinet during these years.

1754

(February 2) Francesco de Paula Grua, Italian composer, was born on this date at Mannheim (died 1833, July 5).

(February 6) Hasse's opera "Artemesia" (libretto by Migliavacca) was performed this day at Dresden.

(February 19) Matteo Babbini, Italian tenor, was born on this date at Bologna (died 1816, September 22 at Bologna).

(February 23) Johann David von Apell, German composer and author, was born on this date at Cassel (died 1832, January 30 at Cassel).

(February 25) Fridolin Weber died on this day at Freiburg, Baden (born 1691, June).

(March 1) The Duke of Württenberg on this date appointed Bini director of the concerts as well as chamber composer at Stuttgart. His salary was to be 400 ducats per annum with furnished apartments as well.

(March 2) Thomas Stanesby, jr., English bassoon maker, died on this day at London (born 1692

(cont.) at London).

(March 4) Dieudonné Pascal Pieltain, violinist and pupil of Giornovichi, was born on this date at Liège (died 1833, December 10 at Liège).

(March 5) Johann Ries was formally appointed court musician at Bonn at this time. He served as a violinist.

(March 6) Josepha Dušek (born Hambacher), Bohemian soprano, was born on this day at Prague (died 1824, January 8 at Prague).

(March 23) Willem de Fesch' operetta"The London 'Prentice"" was produced at Drury Lane this evening in London.

(March 25) Arne's "The Sheep-Shearing, or Florizel and Perdita" was produced this evening at Covent Garden in London.

(March 31) Francesco Geminiani's "La Forêt enchantée" was produced in Paris on this date.

(April 9) Antonin Frantisek Beuzwarzowsky, Bohemian composer, was born on this day at Mlada, Boleslav, Bohemia (died 1823, May 15 at Berlin).

(April 11) The Pennsylvania Gazette in this issue advertised about Robert Coe, "as some Gentlemen are afraid to undertake it (German Flute) by Reason of its taking more wind than they think they can well spare . . . has invented a Mouth Piece, made either of Tin or Silver and does not . . . alter the Tone of the Flute . . . ." Coe's claim was that he had an "easy method".

1754(cont.)

(April 25) The Pennsylvania Gazette on this date advertised "The company of Comedians from London, which opened the New Theatre in Water Street on April 15, 1754".

(May 12) Franz Anton Hoffmeister, German composer and publisher, was born on this date at Rottenburg, Württemberg (died 1812, February 9 at Vienna).

(May 15) Pierre Dutillieu, French composer, was born on this day at Lyons (died 1797 at Vienna).

(May 16) Giovanni Clari, Italian composer, died on this date at Pisa (born 1677, September 27 at Pisa).

(May 29) Arne's "Eliza" was produced this evening at the Haymarket Theatre in London.

(May 29) Innocenz Danzi entered the Mannheim orchestra on this date.

(May 30) In Naples Caffarelli appeared this night for the last time in an opera there.

(June 17) Music played a prominent part in only one performance by Company of Comedians-- "Pantomime Entertainment, called Harlequin Collector, or the Miller Deceived".

(June 18) Vincente Martín y Soler, Spanish composer, was born on this day at Valencia (died 1806, January 30 at St. Petersburg).

(Summer) Maria A. Walpurgis'

(cont.) opera "Il trionfo della fedelta" with libretto by herself and alteration by Metastasio, was produced at Dresden at this time.

(June 27) The last performance at Plumstead's Warehouse by Company of Comedians from London was held on this evening.

(July 9) Power of Attorney was granted by Scarlatti to Nicolás Olivier in Lisbon on this date.

(July 11) Robert Bremner began business in Edinburgh shortly before this date on which he advertised in an Edinburgh newspaper.

(July 11) The Pennsylvania Gazette in this issue advertised David Chamber's publication of "The Youths' entertaining Amusement", or a plain Guide to Psalmody; in two parts, viz. Treble and Bass, By W. Dawson, Writing Master and Accomptant, at the Hand and Pen, in Third Street, Philadelphia".

(July 18) Sixtus Bachmann, Austrian organist and composer, was born this day at Kettershausen (died 1818 at Marchtal).

(August 14) On this date Pergolesi's "La serva Padrona" was again revived, this time in a French version by Baurans. By the end of the following January, it had had 96 performances at the Comédie-Italienne.

(August 15) P. van Maldere conducted the Concert Spirituel in Paris on this evening.

(August 23) King Louis XVI of

France was born on this date. Rameau wrote "La Naissance d'Osiris" in his honor. The King was a member of the House of Bourbon and ruled from 1774 to 1792. He was executed in 1793.

(September 4) Thomas Charles Auguste Dallery, French organ builder, was born on this date at Amiens (died 1835, June 1 at Jovy-en-Josas, Seine-et-Oise).

(September 5) Elizabeth Ann Linley, English soprano, was born this day at Bath (died 1792, June 28 at Bristol).

(September 8) Anton Teyber, Austrian composer, was born on this day at Vienna (died 1822, November 18 at Vienna).

(September 23) Johann Joachim Bellermann, German musical scholar, was born on this date at Erfurt (died 1842, October 25 at Berlin).

(September 24) Gluck's Italian opera "Le cinesi" (libretto by Metastasio) was produced at Schlosshof, near Vienna, on this day on the occasion of Maria Theresa's visit to Gluck's patron, Prince Joseph Friedrich.

(September 25) Luigi Caruso, Italian composer, was born on this day at Naples (died 1822 at Perugia).

(October 12) Rameau's acte de ballet, "La Naissance d'Osiris" (text by Cahusac), was produced on this date at Fontainbleau.

(October 23) Rameau's acte de ballet "Anacreon" (text by Cahusac), was produced on this date at Fontainbleu.

(October 29) Joseph Mondonville's "Daphnis et Alcimadure", a pastoral in the Langue d'Oc, in which he introduced many Provençal airs, was produced before the court at Fontainebleau on this date.

(November ( ) Ciprandi made his first appearance in London on this evening when he sang "Danao" in "Ipermestra" at the King's Theatre.

(November 9) Rosa Curioni made her début this evening at the King's Theatre in London, as "seconda donna" in "Ipermestra" by Hasse and Lampugnani.

(November 24) Anton (Johann Baptista) Stamitz was born on this date at Mannheim. He was a composer, violinist and brother of Karl Stamitz (died probably before 1809 at Paris).

(February) This month in "Les Adieux du goût" by Patu and Portelance the actor who played the part of Plutus imitated La Pouplinière's voice and mannerisms.

(May) Gluck went to the summer residence of Prince Hildburg-hausen at this time.

(August) Peter von Winter, German composer, was born this month at Mannheim (died 1825, October 17).

(September to 1755, June) Caporale played in Dublin during this period.

1754(cont.)

(September) Johann Stamitz went to Paris this month and stayed there for a year.

(October) Johann Christian Hertel, German violist, violinist and composer, died this month at Strelitz, Mecklenburg (born 1699 at Öttingen).

Gotthilf Wilhelm Bach, son of W. Friedemann, grandson of J. Sebastian and member of the seventh generation of the Bach family, was born at this time (died 1756).

Johann Michael Bach, son of Johann Elias, theoretician, composer, lawyer and member of the seventh generation of the Bach family, was born this year (death date unknown).

Wilhelm Hieronymus Bach, son of Johann Christoph and member of the sixth generation of the Bach family, died this year (born 1730).

Ignaz Bolck, a horn player, was born at this time (death date unknown).

Briseux, an associate of Rameau, died this year (born 1680).

Le Clerc de la Bruère, a librettist for Rameau, died in Rome this year of smallpox (born 1717).

Charles, third Duke of Bolton, died this year leaving Lavinia Fenton a widow (birthdate unknown).

The theme of the"follia" remained for a long time in Brittany, since Honore Fleury, born at Quintin this year, re-

(cont.) called dancing them as a boy at an entertainment given by the masters of his college, Saint-Brieuc (death date unknown).

Hans Gram, a Dane born this year, was "liberally educated at Stockholm" (died 1804).

Karl Hanke, German composer, was born this year at Rosswalde near Troppau, Silesia (death date unknown).

Philipp Joseph Hinner, German harpist and composer, was born at this time at Wetzler (death date unknown, but possibly at Paris).

Johann Friedrich Kranz, German composer, was born this year at Weimar (died 1807 at Stuttgart).

Giovanni Felice Mosel, Italian violinist and composer, was born this year at Florence (death date unknown).

Franceso Antonio Maria Paganini, father of Niccolò Paganini, was born this year at Genoa to Giovanni Battista Paganini and Maria Teresa Gambaro.

Matteo Rauzzini, Italian composer and singing teacher, was born in Camerino, Italy at this time. He wrote "Le Finta gemelle", "L'opera nuova" and "Il re pastore". He settled in Dublin as a singing-teacher (died 1791 at Dublin).

Antoine Sallantin, French oboist, was born this year at Paris (death date unknown).

Richard Walond, singer, was born at this time (death date unknown).

Michel Yost, French clarinettist, was born this year (died 1786, July 5).

Gregorio Ballabene this year was made a member of the Accademia dei Filarmonici at Bologna.

Carlo Besozzi at this time joined his father as a member of the Dresden court orchestra.

Britton this year found singing masters in New York.

John Brown at this time was vicar of Great Horkesley, Essex.

G. G. Brunetti was chapel master at the cathedral in Pisa this year.

John Burton gave concerts in Germany this season with great success.

Calzabigi succeeded in having Count Durazzo called to Vienna this year to direct the theatre at Vienna.

During the carnival season this year while he was having his love affair with the Venetian nun, Casanova attended a masked ball in the guise of Pierrot. He danced a minuet and tnen 12 "furlanas".

Most of Černohorský's works were probably destroyed in a fire at his monastery this year.

Diderot and other friends of F. A. Philidor summoned him to Paris this season.

Domenico Ferrari visited Paris this year for the first of two occasions and played with

(cont.) great success.

Caterina Gabrielli made her first operatic appearance at Venice in Galuppi's "Antigona" this season.

The intendant of Viennese theatres, Count Durazzo, commissioned Gluck as Capellmeister this year to compose music for the court.

Gaetano Guadagni sang at Paris and Versailles this season.

Lewis Hallam, an English actor and manager, arrived in New York this year heading a troupe which performed ballad operas.

Johann E. Hartmann at this time became a violinist in the orchestra of the prince-bishop of Breslau.

Ludwig C. Hesse this year became a member of the royal chapel in Berlin.

Johann Hiller entered the household of Count Brühl, the Saxon minister this year, as tutor to his nephew.

Rosalie Holzbauer this year sang the title part in her husband's "Issipile" and either died or retired from the stage shortly after.

Francis Hopkinson's name did not appear in connection with music until this date when he took up the harpsichord.

Francis Hopkinson's illustration of his "Ode on Music" are included in his book of this period.

Jommelli arrived at Stuttgart
this season.

Salvatore Lanzetti remained
in favor in England after his
visit to Germany this year.

Charles Love, the musician in
Lewis Hallam's company, came
to Philadelphia this season.

Mr. and Mrs. Charles Love,
members of the Company of
Comedians from London, performed
a benefit at New York with
the "Beggar's Opera" this year.

William Mason took orders and
became rector of Aston at this
time.

William Mason was appointed
chaplain to Lord Holderness at
this time.

Metastasio this year engaged
Haydn as a teacher for Marianne
de Martinez.

Charles Nichelmann became second
accompanist this year at the
court of Berlin, along with
K. P. E. Bach.

Cuthbert Ogle arrived in Virginia this season from London
and brought musical instruments
and personal belongings that
proved he was above the "itinerant class".

G. Paisiello this season entered
the Conservatorio di Sant'
Onofrio, Naples where he studied
with Durante, Contumacci and
Abos.

François Philidor returned to
Paris this year and began to
compose his "Motets à grand
choeur" at once.

N. Piccinni left the Conservatorio di Sant'Onofrio, Naples
at this time.

La Pouplinière, who kept a
private orchestra in Paris,
was apparently the first to
introduce clarinets into a
Parisian orchestra this year.

Cahusac this year observed
"L'Europe galante" is the
earliest of our lyric works
which was not like a Quinault
opera".

There exist two genealogical
tables for Jean Rameau's wife,
Claudine Demartinecourt, one
for this year.

The author of the "Lettres sur
la musique Françoise en résponse
à celle de J. J. Rousseau"
of this year accused the Italians of his generation of having
forgotten the old simplicity
in order "to shine, to flit
about, and to caper".

For many years it has been said
that "Scarlatti returned to
Naples in 1754".

A four-voice "a cappella" Mass
by Scarlatti was copied into
one of the choir books of the
Royal Chapel at this time.

Probably after this year the
dates of Scarlatti's compositions did not appreciably antedate the copying into the Venice
and Parma manuscripts. This
was in regard to the Royal
sonatas.

The Venetian sonatas (Vol. VIII)
of this year started D. Scarlatti's final great period.

Giuseppe Scarlatti returned to

BENJAMIN FRANKLIN (*His reception at the French Court*)

1754(cont.)
Naples this season.

John C. Smith at this time was appointed first organist at the Foundling Hospital Chapel.

John Snetzler this year introduced the "Dulciana" on the organ he built for St. Margaret's Church at Lynn Regis.

Travenol indicated in his "La Galerie de l'Académie Royale de musique" this year that it was really the French who patterned Italian music for Corelli and acknowledged that Corelli owed his music to Lully, a French composer.

Valesi this year was appointed court singer to the Prince-Bishop of Freising.

Vernon became a tenor this year.

J. B. Wendling was in the court chapel at Mannheim this season.

Garrett Wellesley was awarded the Bachelor of Arts degree this year by Dublin University.

Agricola's "La nobiltà delusa" (libretto by Goldoni) was performed in Berlin this season.

Philippo de Annunciacão published a set of "Acompanhamentos para orgão de Hymnos, Missas . . ." at this time.

Abbe François Arnaud this year wrote a "Lettre sur la musique à Monsieur le Comte de Caylus".

Arne's songs in "The Winter's Tale" were part of "The Sheep-Shearing" of this year.

Avison this year re-published

(cont.) his "An Essay on Musical Expression" with a reply to Hayes' "Remarks on Mr. Avison's Essay on Musical Expression".

J. S. Bach's "canon triplex a 6 voc" was posthumously printed this year in the journal of L. C. Mizler's "Sozietät der musikalischen Wissenschaften".

The earliest catalogue of J. S. Bach's compositions, published this year, enumerated among his unprinted works "Fünf Passionen, worunter eine Zweychörige befindlich ist".

K. P. E. Bach's "Gellers geistliche Oden und Lieder" appeared at this time.

Karl Philipp Emmanuel Bach with Agricola wrote about J. S. Bach in the "Nekrolog" issued at this time.

K. P. E. Bach wrote his trio in G major at this time.

Charles Bâton this year published an "Examen de la lettre de M. Rousseau sur la musique francaise".

Blainville published "L'Esprit de l'art musical" at this time.

Blamont's "Essai sur les goûts anciens et modernes de la musique francaise" was issued this year at Paris.

Burney's "Six Sonatas or Duets for Two Violins or German Flutes" was completed at this time.

Louis de Calhusac's "La danse

ancienne et moderne" was completed this year.

Père Louis-Bertrand Castel's "Lettres d'un Academicien de Bordeaux sur le fond de la musique' in Journal de Trévoux" appeared at this time.

N. de Caux de Cappeval's "Apologie du goût français relativement à l'opéra, poème, avec un discours apologétique et des adieux aux bouffons, en vers" appeared this year.

Chiarini's last known work was an intermezzo which was produced at Cremona this year. It was "La donna dottoressa".

V. L. Ciampi's "6 concertos in six parts for stgs. + bass, Op. 6" was published by Walsh this year.

V. L. Ciampi's "Didone" was produced this season at London.

The six fugues for harpsichord included in Clementi's "Practical Harmony" were taken from the violin sonatas of this year.

W. Dawson's "The Youth's entertaining Amusement, or plain guide to Psalmody" appeared this year at Philadelphia.

"The Divine Musical Miscellany" was issued this year at London.

Errichelli's opera "Issipile" was completed at this time.

Baldassare Galuppi wrote his opera "Il filosofo di campagna" this year at Venice (libretto by Goldoni).

Baldassare Galuppi wrote his

(cont.) opera "Il povero superbo" this year at Venice (libretto by Goldoni).

Baldassare Galuppi wrote his opera "Siroe" this year at Rome (libretto by Metastasio).

Francisco Xavier Garcia wrote an intermezzo, "La finta schiava" at this time.

François Joseph Giraud's ballet "L'Amour fixé" was produced this season at the Comédie-Française.

Gossec published his first symphonies this year.

Carl Heinrich Graun's opera "Semiramide" was produced in Berlin this season.

This year marked the publication of an oratorio by Habermann, "Deodatua e Gozzone", however only the libretto has survived. In the same category was a school play he wrote for the Prague Jesuits, "Artium Clementinarum solemnia".

Handel's "Judas Maccabaeus" was performed at Gloucester this season at the Three Choirs Festival.

Hasse's pasticcio's "Ipermestra" and "Penelope" both appeared at London this season.

J. Michael Haydn wrote a full-length mass this year at Temesvar, Hungary. It was his first full-length mass.

William Hayes' pamphlet "Remarks on Mr. Avison's Essay on Musical Expression" appeared this year.

Holzbauer this year wrote two pantomimic ballets, "Chacun à son Tour" and "L'Allégresse du jour", both stage works.

Holzbauer's Italian opera "L'isola disabitata" was performed this season at the summer residence of Schwetzingen.

Holzbauer's opera "Issipele" was performed at Mannheim this season.

Holzbauer this year wrote an oratorio "La Passione di Gesù Cristo" for Mannheim.

William Knapp's "A Set of New Psalms and Anthems" appeared this year in its 6th edition at London.

Jommelli's secular dramatic work "Lucio Vero" appeared this year at Milan.

An aria by Giovanni Battista Lampugnani's was introduced into the London pasticcio "Ipermestra" this season.

Santo Lapis this year wrote and had published the score of his opera "L'infelice avventurato".

"Platée" was revived this season in opposition to Leo's "I Viaggiatori" and the "Mercure" commented on it with great praise.

N. Logroscino's "Le chiaiese cantarine" was produced this season.

Gennaro Manua's opera "Demofoonte" was produced this season at Turin.

G. Martini wrote the choruses for Varano's tragedy "Giovanni di Giscala" produced this season.

In Lorenz Christoph Mizler's Volume IV of his Journal, he and K. P. E. Bach and Agricola collaborated in the obituary notice, or "Nekrolog", on J. S. Bach.

Pescetti this year wrote an opera with Cocchi, "Tamerlano" and it had its first production at Venice.

N. Piccinni made his debut this year as a composer with the opera "La donne dispettose" at the Teatro Fiorentini in Naples.

Porpora's six Latin duets on the Passion appeared at this time.

Twelve violin sonatas by N. Porpora were completed this year.

Porpora, in his "XII Sonate per Violino e Basso", published in Vienna this year, linked the two books of Padre Martini directly to the style of Opus V.

Rameau wrote "Observations sur notre instinct pour la musique et son principe" this year and in it emphasized the supremacy of harmony over melody.

Rameau's "Castor et Pollux" was revived this season in France.

Rameau this season produced two one-act ballets, "Anacréon" and "La Naissance d'Osiris".

Metastasio's libretto to "Il Tributo di rispetto e d'amore" had its first setting this year by Reutter.

Rochemont's "Réflexions d'un patriote sur l'opéra français et l'opéra italien, Lausanne" appeared this year.

Rousseau's "Le Devin du Village" was published at the end of this year.

Joseph Barnabe Saint-Sevin L'Abbe, a violinist, composed symphonies for three violins and continuo at this time.

Giuseppe Sarti's opera "Vologeso" was produced this season at Copenhagen.

The 7th, 8th and 9th volumes of D. Scarlatti's violins sonatas were published at this time.

Volumes IX-XI of D. Scarlatti's sonatas were published this year at Parma.

John C. Smith composed the opera "The Fairies" at this time.

Giuseppe Tartini's work "Trattato di musica" was published this year at Padua.

John Wynne's "Ten English Songs set to Musick" were published this year.

Some sonatas by D. Scarlatti required a full five-octave range after this date. This was far greater than in the earlier works. The works referred to here were the "Royal Sonatas". In the group there was one sonata (#27) calling

(cont.) for only four octaves and in measure #35 it was obvious it was written for an instrument with no low "B".

Surviving harpsichords by the Kirkman Family are as follows: one made by J. Kirkman, with two manuals owned in 1946 by Messrs. J. G. Morley, 2x8', 1x4'.

The Silbermann organ built this year at Dresden was tuned as follows: A=415 c.p.s., S=2'0.

The organ at York Minster was enlarged this year.

The Paris opera orchestra at this time included 16 violins, 6 violas, 12 cellos and double basses, 6 flutes and oboes, 0 clarinets, 3 bassoons, 2 horns, 7 trumpets, 0 trombones, 7 timpanii and two viole da gamba among the basses.

The theater at Aranjuez was rebuilt at this time.

By this year Boston had built a concert hall where concerts of "Vocal and Instrumental Musick to consist of Select Pieces by the Masters" were performed.

Unfortunately for the Hallam company, Philadelphia at this time still frowned on the theater.

There was a singing school in New York this year.

The park built on the slopes of the Leitha hills, originally owned by Prince Paul Esterházy, was "arranged in the style of the gardens at Versailles".

Clement's "Les cinq années littéraires: 1748-1752" was published this year at The Hague.

Houdar de La Motte's "Réflexions sur la critique; in Oeuvres, III, I" was published this year.

Claude Pierre Patu, attorney and friend of Casanova, wrote a play, "Les Adieux du Goût", this year. It concerned itself with the operatic controversy that was rampant.

Thomas Warton's "Observations on the Faerie Queene of Spencer" was published this year. The "historical method" of criticism was advocated in the work.

Boffrand, the French architect, died this year (born 1667).

Asmus Jacob Carstens, a German painter and engraver, was born (died 1798).

Gibbs, an English architect, died this year (born 1682).

Jean-Baptiste Regnault, a French painter, was born this year (died 1829).

Utamaro, the Japanese painter, was born this year (died 1806).

Wood, the English architect, died this year (born c.1704).

Wood, English architect: Bath, the Circus house (c.35'x49').

Count Stainville at this time was made Ambassador to the Papal Court. He brought his son's valet, Hubert Robert, with him and influenced by

(cont.) Pannini and Piranesi, became a "ruin painter".

Paul I, Czar of Russia, was born this year. He reigned from 1796-1801 (died 1801).

(and 1755, 1765) Three songs by Bury appeared in the "Mercure de France" at these dates.

(to 1755) Caffarelli sang in several of Pérez' operas at Lisbon this season.

(to 1755) Three new operas by N. Conforto appeared at Naples, Reggio and Rome during this period.

(to 1755) Marpurg's "Kritische Beyträge" was published at this time.

(to 1755) The handcrossings of the earlier sonatas became increasingly rare in the earlier volumes of the Queen's collection. Later they completely disappeared in volumes V and VI and VII to X which appeared during this period.

(to 1755) Tiepolo painted the ceiling perspectives at the Pietà in Venice during this year.

(to 1757) Carl Barbandt advertised concerts of clarinets and horns with kettledrums in London during these three years.

(to 1757) Scarlatti's late sonatas (Venice VII to XIII, Parma XV) appeared during this period.

(and 1758, 1759) Two Baildons sang in the Foundling Hospital performances of the "Messiah"

at these dates. One was evi-
dently a chorus leader.

(to 1758) Texts written by Kurz-
Bernardon were contained in
"Teutsche Comedie Arien" pub-
lished during these four years.

(to 1759) Girolamo Abos was
second "maestro" at the
Conservatorio della Pietà dei
Turchini during this time span.

(to 1760, March) Anton Filtz
was leader of the cello section
in the Mannheim orchestra for
these six years.

(to 1760) Marpurg published
"Historisch-critische Beyträge
für Aufnahme der Music" at
this time.

(to 1762, 1778) Marpurg published
the "Historisch-kritische
Beitrage zur Aufnahme der Musik"
in Berlin at these dates.

(to 1764) Edmund Ayrton was
elected organist, auditor and
"rector chori" of the collegiate
church of Southwell, where he
remained during this decade.

(to 1764) Christoph Willibald
Gluck spent this decade in the
service of the imperial opera
at Vienna.

(to 1772) Giuseppe Sarti wrote
24 Italian operas at Copenhagen
during these years.

(to 1778) Friedrich Wilhelm
Marpurg's "Historisch-Kritische
Beyträge zur Aufnahme der Musik"
appeared in five volumes during
these 14 years at Berlin.

(to 1780) Destouches' "Les
Éléments" was revived until

(cont.) 1754 and single acts
until 1780.

(to 1790) Élie Fréron's
"L'Année litteraire" was completed during these years.

(to 1792) Michael Haydn's works
during these years included:
    Church Music; About 360
compositions including 2 Re-
quiems, 24 Masses, 4 German
Masses, 114 Graduals, 64
Offertories, 8 Litanies, 11
Vespers, 5 "Salve Regina",
3 Responses, 3 "Tenebrae",
"Regina coeli", etc.
    Sacred Vocal Works; Many
oratorios, cantatas, several
German songs.
    Secular Vocal Works; Several
operas (including "Andromede
e Porseo", 1776), mythological
operettas, pastoral(Die Hochzeit auf der Alm", 2 collections
of four-part songs, several
songs with pianoforte, 6 canons
in 4 and 5 parts.
    Instrumental Works; 30 sym-
phonies and partitas, serenades,
marches, 12 minuets for full
orchestra, one concerto, sextet,
3 quintets.
    Theoretical Work; "Partutur-
Fundament", edited by M.
Bischofsreiter, finished in
1792.

(to 1808) Giovanni Gualberto
Brunetti was chapel master at
Pisa Cathedral during this
period.

c.1754

Thomas Billington, English
pianist, harpist, singing-
master and composer, was born
this year at Exeter (died 1832
at Tunis).

"Seedo", German musician, died
this year at Potsdam (birthdate

J. Christian Bach at this time
left his family to go to Italy.

(to 1756) Carestini was engaged
at St. Petersburg at this time.

1755

(January 2) Giuseppe Scarlatti's
return to Naples for the production of his "Caio Mario"
at the San Carlo Opera on this
date was probably the source
for erroneous reports of
Domenico's return to Naples.

(January 6) Karl H. Graun's
opera "Montezuma" (libretto by
Frederick II) was presented in
Berlin on this date.

(January 8) J. C. F. Bach on
this date married Lucia Elisabeth Münchausen, a court singer.

(January 14) Giovanni Battista
Lampugnani's opera "Siroe, re
di Persia" was produced in
London at this time.

(January 19) Joseph Mondonville's
"Daphnis et Alcimadure" was
performed on this evening at
the Paris Opéra.

(February 3) Frederick Charles
Reinhold on this date made his
début on stage at the Drury
Lane Theatre in London as
Oberon in J. C. Smith's opera
"The Fairies".

(February 12) Charles Simon
Favart's "Le Caprice amoureux,
ou Ninette à la cour" was
first performed on this date
at Paris.

(February 15 to 1761) Caterina
Gabrielli, Italian soprano, was
(cont.) in Vienna during this
period.

(February 28) Countess Maria
Theresia Ahlefeldt, German-
Danish amateur composer, was
born on this day at Ratisbon
(died 1823, November 4 at
Prague).

(March 2) Antoine Frédéric
Gresnick, Walloon composer,
was baptized on this date at
Liège.

(March 10) Araia's opera
"Cephalus and Procris" was
produced on this date at St.
Petersburg. It was the first
opera to be written in the
Russian language (libretto by
Alexander Sumarokov).

(March 10) Francois Joseph
Herold, a pianist, was born
on this day at Seltz, Alsace
(died 1802, September at
Paris).

(March 10) Philipp Christoph
Kayser, German composer, was
born on this date at Frankfurt
am Main (died 1823, December
24 at Zurich).

(March 12) Arne's "Abel" was
revived on this day, including
the "Hymn of Eve" which became
exceedingly popular. The performance was at Drury Lane
Theatre in London.

(March 14) Pierre-Louis
Couperin, organist and composer, was born this day at
Paris (died 1789, October 10
at Paris).

(March 26) Carl Heinrich
Graun's "Tod Jesu" was first
sung this evening at the
Cathedral of Berlin.

(March 31) A new theatre in Lisbon opened this day with Perez's opera "Alessandro nell' Indie".

(April 5) Hasse's Intermezzo "Il giocatore" was produced on this date at Frankfurt. This work has also been attributed to Orlandini.

(April 5) Vincenc Masek, Czech musician and son of Thomas, was born on this day at Zvikovec (died 1831, November 15 at Prague).

(April 12) Rosa Curioni sang four parts at London up to this date.

(April 14) Hasse's intermezzo "Il Calandro" was produced on this date at Frankfurt. This is not positively by Hasse.

(April 17) Gluck's opera "Le Cinesi" was produced at Vienna on this date.

(April 18) "Il re pastore" by Frederick II, Quantz, Graun and Nichelmann was performed this date at the Haymarket Theatre in London.

(April 25) J. W. Hertel and his friend, the dramatist Johann Friedrich Lowen, wrote and produced a German operetta, "Sieg dir Liebe", on this date at Schwerin.

(April 25) Jacob Kirkman, I became naturalized on this day.

(May 5) Caterina Gabrielli sang "Nice" in "La Danza" on this day.

(May 5) Gluck's Italian opera

(cont.) "La danza" (libretto by Metastasio) was produced at Lavenburg near Vienna on this evening.

(May 9) Arne's "Britannia" was produced this evening at Drury Lane Theatre in London.

(May 12) Giovanni Battista Viotti, Italian violinist and composer, was born on this date at Fontanetto Po Vercelli (died 1824, March 3 at London). Sources disagree on this date.

(May 13) Gluck's pastoral cantata "La danza" was produced this evening at Vienna.

(June 1) Federico Fiorillo, Italian violinist and composer, was born this day at Braunschweig (death date unknown).

(June 6) Alcock was awarded the degree of Bachelor of Music by Oxford University on this day.

(June 18) Louise Rosalie Dugazon, French singer, was born on this date at Berlin (died 1821, September 22 at Paris).

(June 21) Giovanni Porta, Italian composer, died at this time at München (born c.1690 at Venice).

(Spring) G. Scarlatti's opera "La madamigella" was produced at the Teatro dei Fiorentini in Naples (libretto by Palomba).

(June 23) Johann Caspar Bachofen, Swiss singing teacher and composer, died on this date at Zurich (born 1695, December 26 at Zurich).

(June 24) From "Extracts from the Diary of Daniel Fisher 1755," contributed by Mrs. Conway Robinson Howard, Richmond, Virginia, to the Pennsylvania Magazine of History: ". . . I should observe that on St. John the Baptist Day (June 24) there was the Greatest Procession of Free Masons to the church . . ."

(June 27) A pianoforte made at Hamburg was bought by Rev. William Mason, who referred to it in a letter to Gray bearing this date.

(July 5) Cornelius van Beethoven on this day married for the second time, Anna Barbara Marx.

(July 9) Johann Gottlob Harrer, German organist and composer, died on this date at Leipzig (born 1703 at Gorlitz).

(July 28) Charles Simon Favart's "La Bohémienne" was first performed this day at Paris (music by Rinaldo di Capua).

(August 1) Giuseppe Antonio Capuzzi, Italian violinist, was born on this date at Brescia (died 1818, March 18 at Bergamo).

(August 18) Francesco Durante, Italian composer, died at this time at Naples (born 1684, March 31 at Frattaggiore near Naples).

(August 14) Jean-Baptiste Anet, French violinist and composer, died on this date at Lunéville (born c.1661).

(September 22) Christian Kalkbrenner, German composer and father of F. W. M. Kalkbrenner, was born at this time at Minden, (cont.) Westphalia (died 1806, August 10 at Paris).

(September 26) Hermanus Dahmen, horn player, was born on this date at Sneek (died 1830 at Rotterdam).

(September 30) As a composer, Pierre Mortan Berton first appeared on the opera scene when he on this date with Francois Joseph Giraud provided the music for Saint-Foix's opera-ballet "Deucalion et Pyrrha".

(October 7) J. C. F. Bach's daughter, Anna Philippina Friderica, was baptized on this day.

(October &) Hasse's opera "Il re pastore" (libretto by Metastasio) was produced on this evening at Hubertusburg.

(November 1) Caffarelli survived the Lisbon earthquake on this day.

(November 10) Franz Ries, violinist, was born on this date at Bonn. He was a brother of Anna Maria Ries and able to take his father's place in the orchestra at age 11. He studied with J. P. Salomon (died 1846, November at Godesberg).

(November 12) Sabina Hitzelberger, German soprano and accomplished fiortura singer with a range of three octaves, was born on this date at Randersacker (death date unknown).

(November 23) So many singers from the Lisbon opera took refuge in Madrid that Sir Benjamin Keene wrote on Novem-

ber 23: "your musicians come
tumbling in naked upon us
every day".

(November 25) Georg Johann
Pisendel, German violinist
and composer, died at this
time at Dresden (born 1687,
December 26 at Cadolzburg,
Bavaria).

(November 29) Arne's "Eliza"
was produced this evening at
Dublin.

(November 29) Charlotte Brent,
a pupil of Arne, first appeared
in Dublin, singing in Arne's
opera "Eliza" on this evening.

(November 30) Johann Elias Bach,
cantor, son of J. Valentin,
grandson of Georg Christoph
and member of the sixth
generation of the Bach family,
died on this date (born 1705,
February 12).

(December 1) Maurice Greene,
English organist and composer,
died on this date at London
(born 1695).

(December 8) Gluck's Italian
opera "L'innocenza giustificata" (libretto by Giacomo
Durazzo and Metastasio) was
produced this evening at the
Burg Theatre in Vienna. The
performance was in honor of
the birthday of Francis I.

(December 8) Caterina Gabrielli
sang "Elisa" in "L'innocenza
giustificata" this evening.

(December 9) Jean Baptiste
Stuck, French composer of
German descent, died on this
date at Paris (born c.1680
at Florence).

(December 26) G. Scarlatti's
opera "Antigono" was produced
this evening at the Teatro
Regio Ducal in Milan (libretto
by Roccaforte).

(January) Azzolino Bernardino
Della Ciaia, Italian organist,
composer as well as amateur
organ builder, died on this
date at Pisa (born 1671, March
21 at Siena).

(January) G. Scarlatti's opera
"Caio Mario" was produced
this evening at the Teatro
San Carlo in Naples (libretto
by Roccaforte).

(March) A symphony by J.
Stamitz with clarinets and
horn was part of a program
at a Concert Spirituel this
month.

(April) Ciprandi appeared in
several parts in London up
until this month.

(August) Johann Stamitz's
"Mass" was performed at the
Jacobin Church this month.

(September) One Baildon sang
in "Samson" at the Three Choirs
Festival this month at Worcester.

(September) Gregorio Ballabene
at this time applied for an
appointment at Marcerata.

(September) Johann Stamitz,
the Bohemian composer, returned from Bris this month
after a year away.

(November) The Lisbon earthquake occurred and upset the
entire Spanish court. Most of
the records of the musicians
at Joãn V's court were
destroyed.

1755(cont.)

(December) Thomas Busby, English organist and composer, was born on this day at London (Westminster) (died 1838, May 28 at London).

Pasquale Artaria, art dealer and music publisher, was born this year (died 1785).

Anna Philippine Friederike Bach, daughter of J. C. Friedrich and member of the seventh generation of the Bach family, was born (died 1804).

Samuel Friedrich Bach, minister and member of the seventh generation of the Bach family, was born (died 1841).

John Edward Betts, English violin maker, was born this year at Stamford, Lincs (died 1823 at London).

Joseph Bodin de Boismortier, French composer, died this year at Paris (born 1691 at Perpignan).

Giovanni Bononcini died this year probably at Vienna. The portrait in the Bologna Liceo assers he was old and forgotten (born 1670, July 18 at Modena).

William Dance, English pianist and violinist, was born this year at London (died 1840, June 5 at London).

Albert (Christoph) Dies, German author, was born this year at Hanover (died 1822, December 28 at Vienna).

Manuel Doyagüe, Spanish church musician and composer, was born this year at Salamanca (died 1842 at Salamanca).

James Fisin, English composer, was born this year (died 1847, September 8).

François Joseph Garnier, French oboist and flautist, was born this year at Lauris (died 1825).

Baron von Gemmingen, Master of the Masonic Lodge at Mannheim and author, was born (died 1836).

Antoine Frédéric Gresnick, Walloon composer, was born this year at Liège (died 1799, October 16).

Johann Baptist Krumpholz, Bohemian harpist and composer, was born this year at Zlonice near Prague (died 1790, February 19 at Paris).

Pierre Leduc, violinist, publisher and brother of Simon Leduc, was born at this time at Paris (died 1816).

Luigi Marchesi, one of the best of the famous Italian male soprani, was born this year at Milan (died 1829, December 18).

Cuthbert Ogle died this year in Virginia (birthdate unknown).

Joseph Petrides, a brilliant horn player who with his brother Peter (Prague, 1766) were the original first and second horns with the Philharmonic Society, was born this year (death date unknown).

Cozio di Salabue, born this year, collected instruments but started to dispose of them before his death. After his death the remaining ones passed to Marquis Dalle Valle of Casali Monfenato, and from him to Giuseppe Fiorini, who presented them to the city of Cremona (death date unknown).

Jean Pierre Solié, French singer and composer, was born this year at Nîmes (died 1812, August 6).

Adolfati's Genoa opera "Sesostri" appeared this year.

Agricola's "Il tempo d'amore" was completed at this time.

Francesco Algarotti's treatise "Saggio soppa l'opera in musica" was written this year although not published until 1763 according to some sources.

K. P. E. Bach's "Versuch über die wahre Art das Clavier zu spielen" was published this year according to one source.

Wilhelm Friedemann Bach composed a Kyrie in g minor this year.

Wilhelm Friedemann Bach composed a setting of the 100th Psalm, "Dienet dem Herrn mit Freuden" this season.

Johann Caspar Bachofen's "Musicalische Ergezungen" appeared at this time.

Johann Caspar Bachofen's 12 monthly numbers containing sacred airs arranged in concert sytle for two and three voices appeared this year in its fourth edition.

The manuscript of G. G. Brunetti's "Fuga a cappella" for four voices came from this year.

Burney's "Six Sonatas for Two German Flutes" appeared this season.

Calzabigi's essay "Dissertazione su le Poesie Drammatiche del Sig. Abate Pietro Metastasio" was issued at this time.

Campra's "L'Europe galante" was performed up until this year.

V. L. Ciampi's 6 Sonatas for harpsichord were published this year at London by Walsh.

William Crisp's "Divine Harmony" appeared this year at London.

E. R. Duni's opera "L'Olimpiade" was produced at Parma's Teatro Regio Ducal this season during Carnival.

Four volumes of clavecin pieces by Du Phly were published at this time.

Favart's parody "Ninette à la cour", published this season, exerted considerable influence on the development of French comic opera.

William Felton published a fourth volume of six concertos for keyboard, op. 5 this year at London.

A considerable number of songs by Fesch were published in one volume this year.

Giovanni Andrea Fioroni's only opera, "Didone abbandonata", was published this year at Milan.

Domenico Fischietti this year wrote his opera "Lo speziale",

his greatest success (libretto
by Vincenzo Pallavicini).

Baldassare Galuppi wrote his
opera "Attalo" this year at
Padua (libretto by Papis).

Baldassare Galuppi this year
wrote his opera "La diavolessa"
in Venice (libretto by Goldoni).

Baldassare Galuppi wrote his
opera "Le nozze" this year at
Bologna (libretto by Goldoni).

Baldassare Galuppi wrote his
cantata "I presagi" this year
at Venice (words by Gasparo
Gozzi).

Francisco Xavier García wrote
his opera "Pompeo Magno in
Armenia" at this time.

Francisco Xavier Garcia,
Spanish composer, wrote an
intermezzo, "La pupilla", this
year.

Francesco Geminiani's "The
Art of Accompaniment" was
published at this time.

Francesco Geminiani published
his 6 concertos in 7 parts for
violin this year at Paris and
London.

Gluck's ballet "Alessandro"
was produced this season at
Vienna.

Gluck's opera "Les Amours
champestres" was produced this
season at Schönbrunn, near
Vienna.

"Les Amours champêtres" was
performed under Gluck's direction at Schönbrunn this year.

A collection of six cantatas

(cont.) by Nicolas Racot de
Grandval was published this
year posthumously.

Carl Heinrich Graun's opera
"Ezio" was produced in Berlin
this year (libretto by Metastasio).

Hasse's pasticcio "Demofoonte"
was produced this season at
London.

Hasse's opera "Ezio" (libretto
by Metastasio) was produced
this season in a new version
at Naples.

Franz Joseph Haydn wrote his
first string quartet at this
time. It was Opus 1, #0 but
appeared as #1 in Hummel and
Bremner's editions of 1765
and again in the edition of
Opus 1 by Longman and Broderip.
It was again omitted in the
edition by La Chevardiere in
1764 at Paris.

Holzbauer's Italian opera "Don
Chisciotte" was performed at
the summer residence of
Schwetzingen this season.

Höpken this year composed a
comic opera on an Italian
text by an unknown librettist,
"Il bevitore; intermezzi per
musica".

Francis Hopkinson's Memorandum
in manuscript was from this
year.

William Jackson this year published a set of "Twelve Songs"
which were so simple and elegant that they quickly became
popular.

An American tune collection,
"Engraved, Printed and Sold by
Thomas Johnston, Brattlestreet,

1755(cont.)

Boston" appeared this year.

Jommelli's opera "Enea nel Lazio" (libretto by Mattia Verazi) was produced this year at Stuttgart.

Jommelli's opera "Il giardino incantato" was produced this year at Stuttgart.

Jommelli's opera "Pelope" was produced this season at Stuttgart.

Jommelli's "Isacco", an oratorio, was composed at this time.

N. Logroscino's "Rosmonda" was produced this season.

Marpurg published his "Handbuch bey dem Generalbasse" this year.

Marpurg published his "Historical and Critical Essays on Music" at this time.

Nichelmann's treatise on the nature of melody, "Die Melodie nach ihrem Wesen . . ." was completed at this time.

V. Pallavicini's opera buffa "Lo speziale" was performed at the Teatro San Samuele in Venice this season.

A new edition of the "Dramma-turgia" by G. B. Pasquali appeared this year at Venice.

Rameau wrote his "Erreurs sur la musique dans l'Encyclopédie" at this time.

Metastasio's libretto "La Gara" had its first setting this year by Reutter.

Walsh issued an English edition

(cont.) of "Concertini" this year and attributed it to Ricciotti. It had been attributed to Pergolesi before.

The tenth and eleventh volumes of D. Scarlatti's violin sonatas were published this year.

Volume XII of Scarlatti's sonatas were published this season at Parma.

At Venice this year the usual number of thirty sonatas per volume by D. Scarlatti had been extended to thirty-four. This was in order to catch up with the end of Parma's Volume XII and to give Parma's Volume XIII the same contents as Venice' Volume XI .

J. C. Smith's opera "The Fairies" was produced this season at London.

William Tansur's "The Royal Melody Compleat, or New Harmony of Zion" came out this year in its first edition at London.

Évrard Titon de Tillet this year issued a second supplement to his book "Le Parmasse françois".

Tommaso Traetta's opera "L'incredulo" was produced this season at Naples at Teatro San Carlo.

Tommaso Traetta's opera "Le nozze contrastate" was produced this season at Rome.

G. C. Wagenseil's "Le caccia-trice" was produced this year at Saxenburg palace.

G. C. Wagenseil wrote his oratorio "La Redenzione" at this time.

Benedetta Emilia Agricola sang the great soprano aria in Graun's "Tod Jesu" at its first performance on this date.

The compositions of Fernando de Almeida, which were in the library of João IV at Lisbon, were destroyed this year in the earthquake.

Editors of this year's edition of Allacci's "Drammaturgia" attributed the opera "Astianatte" to A. M. Bononcini.

Gabriel da Annunciacão's compositions were destroyed in the Lisbon earthquake this year.

The library of João IV, destroyed in this year's earthquake, contained works by Manuel Leitão de Avilez for eight and twelve voices.

After the Lisbon earthquake at this time Avondano received an important position in the reorganization of the brotherhood of Santa Cecilia, to which the musicians almost all belonged.

Johann Christian Bach went to Milan this year to study with Martini of Bologna.

Thomas Baildon was appointed Gentleman of the Chapel Royal at this time.

William Boyce carried out the duties of Mastor of the Queen's Music this year.

Robert Bremner at this time

(cont.) changed his sign to the "Harp and Hautboy".

Some of Estevao de Brito's works were lost in this year's Lisbon earthquake.

At the Three Choirs Festival this year at Worcester, the solo singers included a Miss Turner, Beard, the famous tenor, and Wass of the Chapel Royal. Abraham Brown led the orchestra.

"Capperan" appeared this season as cellist in the orchestras of both the Paris Opéra and Concert Spirituel.

Caroli was "principe" of the Accademia Filarmonica this season.

At the age of 10 this year, Ann Catley sang in public houses in the neighborhood of Tower Hill.

"Mr. Charles" appeared as a clarinettist this season at Edinburgh.

Charlotte Cibber, who married Charke, often spoke of the way he ill-treated her in a book she published this year.

John Conquest held the position of drum-major general at this time.

When Durante died this year, Cotumacci succeeded him at the Conservatorio di Sant' Onofrio.

Dauvergne was composer to the King and master of his chamber music this season.

The Reverend Samuel Davies,

while leading a Presbyterian
mission in the South this year,
was deeply impressed by the
slaves' response to the hymnals
that were among many religious
books he had received for his
use at Hanover, Virginia.

Diaz' church music, part of the
catalogue of the library of
João IV, was lost in the Lisbon
earthquake this year.

Durante taught at the Conservatorio di Sant'Onofrio until
this year.

Giovanni Ferrandini at this
time left his position as director of electoral chamber music
at the court in Munich.

Maximilien Léopold Philippe
Joseph Gardel made his dancing
debut at the Paris Opéra this
season.

Francesco Geminiani moved from
Paris to London this year.

Giovanni Andrea Giuseppe Giulini
was "Kapellmeister" of Augsburg
Cathedral from this date forward.

Maruice Greene, who was this
year trying to make a collection
of the best English cathedral
music, was forced by his health
to leave the project to his
friend, Boyce, requesting
that he complete it.

On his death this year Maurice
Greene was buried at St. Olave's
Jewry.

Gaetano Guadagni narrowly es-
caped death this year in the
Lisbon earthquake.

Baron Karl Joseph Edler von

(cont.) Fürnberg this year
engaged Franz Joseph Haydn as
the conductor of his orchestra.
While there Haydn wrote his
first twelve string quartets,
opus 1 and 2. The quartet in
Bb Major, now known as Opus 1,
#5, was however not part of
the group.

At Philadelphia Francis
Hopkinson and his teacher-friend
James Bremner sponsored a
series of concerts this season.

Robert Hudson was assistant
organist of St. Mildred on
Bread Street this season.

The musical collector, Joao IV
of Portugal, accumulated a
musical library of which only
the catalogue survived the
earthquake of 1755.

Until this year Pierre de
Jélyotte took part in all the
important productions and
revivals of Lully, Rameau and
other's music.

Zweig adapted for Richard
Strauss Ben Jonson's play
"Epicoene, or The Silent
Women" placing the action in
the London of 1750. It was
known as "Die Schweigsame Frau".

Among the surviving harps made
by the Kirkman family this year
are two: the first with two
manuals, 2x8', 1x4'(lute)
presently owned by O. J. S.
Moore, made by J. Kirkman, and
the second with one manual,
now in the Steinert collection
and also made by J. Kirkland.
The latter one was once
apparently owned by Napoleon
Bonaparte.

Pierre Lagarde was joint con-

ductor at the Paris Opéra this
season.

Locatelli was in debt and even
his short guest engagement at
Dresden this year did not make
it possible for him to meet
his obligations.

Mazzoni was in Lisbon for the
production of his "La clemenza
di Tito" this season.

Frederick Messing played at the
Three Choirs Festivals at
Worcester this year.

Noverre went to London at this
time and became acquainted with
David Garrick and his "dumb
show".

Georg Pasterwitz was ordained
a priest at this time.

Perez visited London this year
and produced "Enzio" with
marked success.

Claude Rameau this year became
organist of St. Lazare's
cathedral at Autan.

The music collection of Richard
Rawlinson this year went to
the Music School of Oxford
University.

Louis Charles Joseph Rey went
to Paris at this time to study
with Berteau and became a
cellist in the theatre orchestra at Montpellier.

Possibly Scarlatti took most of
his Italian church music to
Portugal with him where it
perished in the Lisbon earthquake.

Gerard Smith was organ repairer

(cont.) to Chelsea Hospital at
this time.

John Snetzler opened an organ-
building factory in London
this season.

Christian Gottfeld Tag, the
German composer, became cantor
at Hohenstein, Saxony this
year.

The Prince of Clermont urged
Giuseppe Tartini to visit
Paris and London this year;
however, Tartini did not go.

Giovanni Battista Toeschi
became a violinist in the
Mannheim orchestra this season.

Valesi this year was acclaimed
the greatest singer in Germany
and appeared with great success
both in Amsterdam and Brussels.

Vernon married Miss Poitier,
a singer, at Drury Lane early
this year.

Francis Waylett was involved
in the publishing of Scarlatti's
"Thirty-six Ariettas" this year.

Cecillia Young went to Ireland
again this year with her husband, sister and nieces.

Almérie (an anagram of Lemaire)
was a kind of lute invented
by Jean Lemaire (M. de
Marolles) this year and mentioned in "Memoires", Vol. III,
206.

Marpurg wrote on the "turn
ornament" this year.

Bruton Parish had an organ
at this time.

"T. Ebdon, 1755" was carved

on the oak screen which divided
the choir of Durham Cathedral
from one of the aisles.

The first successful concert
of all hunting-horns was performed this season at Moscow.

Performances of "opéra comique"
began in Vienna at this time.

"Hob in the Well", an opera,
was performed this season at
Charleston and was considered
to be the first ballad opera
performance in the United States.

James Hoey printed the words
to Arne's "Eliza" this year.

Johnson's "Dictionary of the
English Language" was published this year.

Montdorge's "L'Art d'imprimer
les tableaux en trois couleurs"
was issued this year in France.

Christian-Heinrich Schmid's
"Chronologie des deutschen
Theaters" was published this
year at Leipzig.

Gilbert Stuart, American painter,
was born at this time (died
1828).

Elisabeth Vigée-Lebrun, French
painter (portraitist), was
born this year (died 1842).

Greuze this year painted "The
Head of the Family Reading the
Bible to his Children".

Quentin de la Tour this year
painted "Portrait of Madame de
Pompadour". It hangs at the
Louvre in Paris and is pastel
on paper (68 7/8" x 50 3/8").

Immanuel Kant, German philosopher, this year wrote "Allge-
meine Naturgeschichte und
Theorie des Himmels".

Louis XVIII le Désiré, King of
France, was born this year.
He ruled from 1814-1824 and
was the first in the restora-
tion of the House of Bourbon.

(to 1756) During his second
visit to Dublin during this
period, Arne and his wife were
estranged, and he returned to
London by himself, leaving her
behind with her niece, Polly
(or Mary) Young.

(to 1757) Sarah Bates (born
Harrop) was born at this time
at Lancashire. She was an
English soprano (died 1811
at London).

(to 1760) During this period
Haydn's string quartets included Pleyel & Eulenburg
scores:
    No. 1 (Op. 1, #1 in Bb major)
    No. 2 (Op. 1, #2 in Eb major)
    No. 3 (Op. 1, #3 in D major)
    No. 4 (Op. 1, #4 in G major)
    No. 5 (Op. 1, #5 in Bb major)
    No. 6 (Op. 1, #6 in C major)
#5 appeared as a string quartet
in La Cheoardiere's publication
of Opus 1, but is a version of
a symphony for 2 oboes, 2
horns and strings.

(to 1760) Tiepolo painted
"Apollo Pursuing Daphne" at this
time (National Gallery of Art,
Washington).

(to 1761) Gennaro Manna was
maestro di cappella of the
Conservatory of Santa Maria
di Loreto at Naples during
these years.

JOHANN MICHAEL HAYDN
1737-1806

1755(cont.)

(to 1762) Marpurg's theoretical work "Handbuch bey dem General-basse und der Composition" founded on Rameau's system (3 parts) was published during this period at Berlin.

(to 1762) Joseph Mondonville was director of the Concert Spirituel during these years.

(and 1763) Two volumes of tune-books by Tans'ur and Aaron Williams, 1755 and 1763 respectively, were most influential in the stream of American publications.

(to 1779) William Boyce was Master of the King's music during these twenty-four years.

(to 1798) T. Cahusac, senior, was "at the sign of the Two Flutes and Violin opposite St. Clement's Church afterwards 196 Strand" during this entire period.

c.1755

Pedro Albéniz, Spanish composer, was born this year at Biscay (died c.1821).

(November 5) Thomas (Hamly) Bitler, English composer, was born this year at London (died 1823 at Edinboro).

Jacques Foignet, French composer, was born at this time at Lyons (died 1836, May).

Adriana Gabrieli, Italian soprano, was born this year at Ferrara (death date unknown).

Paul Ignaz Kürzinger, German composer and son of Ignaz Franz, was born at Würzburg (died after

(cont.) 1820 probably at Vienna).

František Tuček, conductor, composer and singer, was born this year at Prague (died 1820 at Pest).

Carl Barbandt's 6 sonatas for 2 violins, 2 German flutes or 2 "hoboys", Op. 1 of this year, were dedicated to the Princess of Wales. He referred to himself as "Musician to His Majesty at Hanover".

Tiepolo painted the "Story of Cleopatra" at this time (Palazzo Labia, Venice).

1756

(January 12) Tommaso Giordani's opera "La comediante fatta cantatrice" was produced this evening at Covent Garden in London.

(January 19) Rameau's "Zoro-astre" was revised on this date at Paris with a new second, third and fifth act.

(January 20) Cafaro's opera "La disfatta di Dario" (libretto by Nicola Giuseppe Morbilli), was produced on this date at the Teatro San Carlo in Naples.

(January 21) Michael Arne's "Florizel and Perdita, or The Winter's Tale" was per-formed this evening at Drury Lane in London.

(January 21 and 1757, March 24) Boyce contributed one trio to "Florizel and Perdita, or The Winter's Tale" on this date at Drury Lane in London and again at its revival in 1757, March 24.

(January 22) Vincenzo Righini,

Italian singer, conductor and
composer, was born this year at
Bologna. As a boy he was
chorister at San Petronio,
Bologna. He had a fine voice,
but because of an injury he
became a tenor of dubious
quality and turned to theory
which he studied with Martini
(died 1812, August 19).

(January 27) Wolfgang Amadeus
Mozart, one of the greatest
composers of all time, was born
on this date at Salzburg. He
was a child prodigy and his
father, Leopold, early on
brought him to sing and play
before the court (died 1829,
October 29 at Vienna).

(February 2) "Il re pastore"
by Frederick II, Quantz, Graun
and Nichelmann was performed
on this date at the Great
Room in Soho.

(February 3) Johann Ernst Bach
on this day was appointed
"Kapellmeister" "von Haus aus"
(non-resident) to the ducal
court at Weimar.

(February 9) Gluck's Italian
opera "Antigono" was produced
on this date at the Teatro
Argentina in Rome (libretto by
Metastasio).

(February 9) Gluck's Italian
opera "Il re pastore" (libretto
by Metastasio) was produced at
the Burg Theatre in Vienna
on this day which was Francis
I's birthday.

(February 10) The opera "L'Olimpiade" was produced this season
at London.

(February 12) Metastasio wrote
to Farinelli at this time.

(February 16) Hasse's opera
"L'Olimpiade" (libretto by
Metastasio) was produced on
this date at Dresden.

(March 16) Battishill appeared
as a singer in Handel's "Alexander's Feast" on this evening
at the Little Haymarket
Theatre in London.

(March 16) "Il re pastore" by
Frederick II, Quantz, Graun and
Nichelmann was performed again
on this date at the Great
Room in Soho, London (see also
February 2).

(March 18) Carl Barbandt's
oratorio "The Universal
Prayer" with words by Pope,
was performed on this evening
in the Haymarket Theatre at
London.

(March 19) A petition was
written on this day to Elector
Clemens August for a decree
making Joan van Piethoffen
accessist in the court music.

(March 20) Arne's "The Pin-
cushion" was produced on this
date in Dublin at the Smock
Alley Theatre.

(March 20) Elizabeth Young made
her first appearance in Dublin
on this evening.

(March 23) Georg G. Wagner,
German composer and violinist,
died on this day at Plauen
(born 1698, April 5).

(March 25) Carl Barbandt's
oratorio "Paradise Regained"
(from Milton) was performed
this evening at the Haymarket
Theatre in London.

1756(cont.)

(March 25) a decree was issued
on this day accepting Johann
van Biethofen as court musician
at Bonn. He was 16 years old.

(March 25) Pennsylvania Journal
on this date stated that the
Philadelphia Regiment of 1000
men marched "thro' the Town in
Three Grand Divisions . . . with
Hautboys and Fifes in Ranks
. . .(and) Drums between the
third and fourth Ranks".

(March 27) A report was made on
this day to Elector Clemens
August requesting work for
Joan van Betthoffen in the
court music.

(March 27) Several papers
occurred at this time that re-
lated to the Beethoven family
and showed the entire process
of appointment to membership
in the electoral chapel.

(April 10) Girolamo Abos'
"Tito Manlio" was heard on this
evening at London.

(April 10) Giocomo Antonio
Perti, Italian composer, died
on this date at Bologna (born
1661, June 6 at Bologna).

(April 21) A letter from Venice
bearing this date was included
in Succi's catalogue of Inter-
national Musical Exhibition at
Bologna in 1888. The letter
from V. Pallavicini to Padre
Martini deplored the recent
death of G. A. Perti.

(May 5) Thomas Linley, jr.,
violinist and composer, was
born on this date at Bath
(died 1778, August 5 at
Grimsthorpe).

(May 11) J. Pigott resigned
on this dat as organist at
St. George's Chapel and was
succeeded by Edward Webb.

(May 13) W. Zywry, Bohemian
teacher and composer, was born
on this date (died 1842,
February 21 at Warsaw).

(June 20) Joseph Martin Kraus,
Swedish conductor and composer
of German origin, was born on
this date at Miltenberg near
Mainz (died 1792, December 15
at Stockholm).

(July 25) Edward Miller at
this time was elected organist
of Doncaster on the recommendation of Nares.

(August 10) Daniel Gottlob
Türk, theorist and composer,
was born on this date at
Clausnitz near Chemnitz (died
1813, August 26 at Halle).

(August 14) Olof Åhlström,
Swedish composer, was born on
this date at Vårdinge, Soder-
manland (died 1838, August 11
at Stockholm).

(August 19) On this date at
the Theatre de la Foire, Saint
Laurent in Paris, "Le Diable
a quatre, ou La Double Meta-
morphose" was performed. The
libretto was by J. M. Sedaine
after Charles Coffey's "The
Devil to Pay" and the music
for the opera was supposedly
arranged by F. A. Philidor.

(September 14) Only thirty
copies of J. S. Bach's "The
Art of Fugue" were printed by
Marpurg, and the plates, 60
in all, fell into the hands
of K. P. E. Bach, who on this
date in a highly characteristic

advertisement, offered them for
sale at any reasonable price.

(September 23) N. Conforto's
"Nitteti" (Buen Retiro) appeared
at this time.

(September 28) Herbain's one-
act opera-ballet "Célime, ou
Le Temple de l'indifférence
detriut par l'amour" was produced on this date at the
Académie Royale de Musique.

(October 3) William M'Gibbon,
Scottish violinist and composer,
died on this day (birthdate
unknown).

(November 15) Franz Teyber,
Austrian composer, was born
at Vienna on this day (died
1810, October 22 at Vienna).

(November 21) Cordeiro da Silva
on this date became a member of
the St. Cecilia brotherhood
at Lisbon.

(November 30) Ernst Chladni,
Italian-German acoustician,
was born this day at Witten-
berg (died 1827, April 3 at
Breslau).

(December 8) Francesca Gabrielli, Italian singer, sang
"Tamiri" in Gluck's "Il re
pastore" on this evening. It
was her first role.

(December 18) N. Piccinni's
opera "Zenobia" (libretto by
Metastasio) was produced on
this date at the Teatro San
Carlo in Naples.

(December 26) E. R. Duni's
opera "La buona figliuola"
was produced on this day at
Parma at the Teatro Regio
Ducal.

(December 27) Arne's "Mercury
Harlequin" was produced on
this evening at the Drury Lane
Theatre in London.

(December 30) Paul Wranityky,
Austrian violinist and composer, was born on this date at
Nova Rise (died 1808, September
28).

(January) Johann Friedrich Doles
became Cantor at the Thomasschule in Leipzig this month
succeeding Gottlob Harrer.

(March) Johann van Beethoven
this month wrote a petition
after serving at the chapel
for four years. According to
a report by Gottwald, he
(Beethoven) had only served in
the chapel for "2 years" but
the discrepancy was probably
due to the voice change.

(March) Antonio Bernacchi,
Italian male soprano and sing-
ing-master, died this month at
Bologna (born 1685, June 23 at
Bologna).

(May) J. C. F. Bach was promoted to "Konzertmeister"
this month.

(June) Charles Dibdin was
admitted a chorister to Winchester Cathedral this month.

(December) Quirino Gasparini's
opera "Artaserse" was produced at this time in Milan.

(December) F. Philidor's opera
"Le Retour du printemps"
(libretto by J. Rouhier-
Deschamps) was privately performed this month at Paris.

Guillaume-Alexis (Alexandre),
Belgian conductor and composer,

was born this year at Liege
(died 1840, January 30 at St.
Petersburg).

Joseph Maria Babo, author and
director, was born this year
(death date unknown).

Gotthilf Wilhelm Bach, son of
W. Friedemann, grandson of J.
Sebastian and member of the
seventh generation of the Bach
family, died this year (born
1754).

Johann Christoph Bach, cantor
and member of the sixth generation of the Bach family, died
this year (born 1702).

Johann Günther Bach, teacher
and musician, son of J. Christoph, grandson of J. Christian
and member of the sixth generation of the Bach family, died
this year (born 1703).

A daughter was born to Cornelius
van Beethoven and Anna Barbara
Marx at this time.

Berteau (Berteaud, Berthau),
French violoncellist, was born
this year at Valenciennes
(died 1756 at Paris).

François Bouvard, French composer, died this year at Paris
(born c.1670 at Paris).

Johann Michael Breunich, German
composer, died after this date
at Dresden (birthdate unknown).

Jean Baptiste Bréval, French
violoncellist, was born this
year (died 1825 at Chamoville
near Laon).

Riccardo Broschi, Italian composer, died this year at Madrid

(cont.) (born c.1700 at Andria).

Franziska Danzi, composer and
soprano, was born this year at
Mannheim (died 1791, May 14
at Berlin).

Johann C. Eley, foreign bandmaster in the British Army,
was born this year (died 1832).
He was with the Coldstream
Guards.

Carl August Grenser II, an
instrument maker, was born
(died 1814).

Józef Jawurek, Polish pianist,
conductor and composer of
Bohemian origin, was born this
year at Benešov, Bohemia (died
1840 at Warsaw).

Jan Kleczynski, Polish violinist
and composer, was born this
year (died 1828, August 6
at Vienna).

Franziska Lebrun, soprano and
wife of Ludwig August Lebrun,
was born this year at Mannheim
(died 1791, May 14).

Domenico Montagnana, violin
maker, died at this time
(born 1683).

Erdmann Neumeister, composer
and librettist, died at Hamburg
(born 1671).

Alexander Reinagle, son of
Joseph Reinagle and important
musician in Philadelphia, was
born this year in Portsmouth
(died 1809, September 21 at
Baltimore). He taught George
Washington's adopted daughter
piano.

Ernst Schick, Dutch or German
violinist and composer, was

1756(cont.)
born this year at The Hague
(died 1815, February 10).

Vincente Martin y Soler was
born this year according to
one source.

Johann Stadler, Austrian clarinettist and brother of clarinettist Anton Stadler, was
born this year (died 1804, May
2 at Vienna).

J. C. Standfuss, German composer,
died this year at Hamburg
(birthdate unknown).

Catherine Tofts, English
soprano, died this year at
Venice (birthdate unknown).

Elizabeth Vietz, Schubert's
mother, was born at this time
(died 1812, May 28).

Johann Christoph Vogel, German
composer, was born this year
at Nürnberg (died 1788, June
26 at Paris).

A new organ by Gilfert Ash was
inaugurated at City Hall this
year with a concerto by Hasse
and a song, "The Sword that's
Drawn In Virtue's Cause" by
Handel.

At the outbreak of the Seven
Years' War this year, J. C.
Bach left Berlin for Italy.

The plates for Johann Sebastian
Bach's "Art of Fugue" were sold
this year by his heirs.

K. P. E. Bach, court accompanist
at Berlin at this time, had his
salary raised from 300 to 500
thalers.

Joah Bates obtained a scholar-

(cont.) ship at Eton this year.

Johann van Beethoven this year
received his decretum as
"accessist" on the score of
his singing skill and experience, including violin playing.

Franz Brentano's father married
his first wife at this time.

Franz Buttstett left Erfurt at
this time and became organist
at Weckersheim.

"History of music" by Caffoaux
was advertised at this time
for publication.

Carestin this year left the
stage to retire to his native
country.

At the "Inquisition" in Venice
this year, Casanova was arrested and thrown into the Leads
Prison from which he made
two escapes.

V. L. Ciampi was surely back
at Venice late this season.

N. Conforto settled in Spain
permanently this year.

The poet Cowper this year
commented on the versicles and
responses, saying that "there
was no need for them to be
screamed".

In his "Generalbass in drey
Accorden" of this year, Daube
proved himself a musician of
advanced ideas quite similar
to Rameau.

"Le Retour au village", sometimes quoted as an independent
work, was the title of the
Vienna score of E. R. Duni's
setting of "Le Caprice amoureux"

of this season.

Carl Friedrich Fasch, German
harpsichordist, was appointed
(on the recommendation of
Franz Benda) accompanist to
Frederick the Great in Berlin.
Fasch was twenty years old this
year and worked in this position
as assistant to K. P. E. Bach.

Pietro Grassi Florio, flutist,
was principal flute in the
famous orchestra at Dresden
this season.

Giulia Frasi sang in "Joshua"
this year at Oxford.

Caterina Gabrielli sang "Elisa"
in "Il re pastore" this season.

Gluck conducted "Le Chinois
poli en France" this year at
Luxembourg.

Johann Gronemann, with his
brothers Antoine and Konrad,
assisted at the musical society
at Arnhem at this time.

Hasse engaged A. Monticelli for
the Dresden theatre this season.

On his return to Vienna this
year, Haydn found himself in
demand as a performer and
teacher. Among his pupils was
Countess Thun.

Musgrave Heighington was appointed to a position as organist
at Dundee at this time.

Robert Hudson was appointed
vicar choral of St. Paul's
Cathedral this year.

The opening "Kyrie" of Jommelli's
Requiem in Eb major, written at
Stuttgart this year, was

(cont.) printed as Haydn's in
some editions of the latter's
Mass in the same key.

Gaetano Latilla at this time
returned north to become
chorus master at the Conservatorio della Pietà at Venice.

In Warsaw, Giuseppe da Loglio
(a member of the Imperial
Russian Orchestra) was entrus-
ted with a diplomatic mission
to the Republic of Venice
where he went this year.

Johannes Lohelius became choirmaster of the Premon-Stratensian
Abbey in Strahov this season.

James Lyon this year moved with
the College from Newark to
Princeton in the Fall of the
year.

Kirkpatrick discovered much
valuable information in a
testament drawn up this year
by Queen Maria Barbara. It
is now in the library of the
Royal Palace in Madrid.

William Mason became prebendary
of York Minster at this time.

Frederick Messing played at
Hereford and Lysons this season.

Luis Missón became conductor
of the royal orchestra in
Madrid this year.

L. Mozart this year mentioned
concertos written for "these
little violins" but added that
the instrument was put aside
in his day.

Leopold Mozart's "Violin School"
of this year was translated into
English by E. Knocker in 1948
at Oxford. The original work

was published in Augsburg.

This year at Madrid Nebra drew
up plans for his choir: 4 sopranos (castrati), 4 altos,
4 tenors, 3 basses, 3 organists
(Nebra, Literes, Rabassa).
The orchestra was to include:
2 flutes, 2 hautboys, 2
fagotes, 3 bajones, 2 horns,
2 trumpets, 12 violins, 4 violas,
3 cellos, 3 basses and 18 voices
in an extra choir.

The three organists of the
Madrid chapel this year were
Nebra, Antonio Literes, and
Miguel Rabaxa.

Nichelmann this year was dismissed from the Royal Chapel
at Berlin, but continued living
in Berlin by giving private
lessons.

N. Piccini married his pupil
Vincenza Sibilla at this time.

Claude Rameau married again
this year. The bride was
Jeanne Guyot.

Johann Rose was taken by the
Princess Amalia of Prussia to
Berlin this year to study
cello with Mara and Graul.

Scarlatti's thoughts frequently
carried him back to Naples and
the memories of his youth as
was made obvious in the exquisite little Christmas pastorale that was copied out
this year (sonata #513).

Joseph Tacet, English flutist,
first appeared in London this
season.

Valesi became chamber singer to
the Duke of Bavaria at this time.

Mateo Veraci (or Verazi) was
appointed court poet at the
Palatine Court in Mannheim
this year. At the same time
he was also Italian private
secretary to the Elector.

Vernon again appeared on the
stage this season.

P. Walmsley's publishing and
violin making business was
taken over by Thomas Smith, a
pupil, this year.

Franz von Weber fought against
Frederick the Great at Rosbach
this year a suffered a wound.

Karl Westenholz this year was
a singer in the court chapel
at Schwerin-Mecklenburg.

J. Zach lost his position this
year because he went insane.

Jean Adam published a collection of ballet airs this year.

The fourth edition of John
Arnold's "The Compleat Psalm-
odist" appeared this year at
London.

Brusa's opera "Le statue"
was completed at this time.

Caffiaux wrote a history of
music that was advertised
for publication this year.

No doubt "Mr. Charles" was
identified with the composer of
"Twelve Duettos for two French
Horns or two German Flutes"
appended to "Apollo's Cabinet"
and published this year by
John Sadler at Liverpool.

Chilcot produced two sets of
harpsichord concertos at this
time.

FRANZ JOSEPH HAYDN
1732-1809

1756(cont.)

V. L. Ciampi's 6 concertos for organ or harpsichord, Op. 7, were published this year by Salsh.

C. F. N. Clérambault this year produced revivals of Racine's "Esther" and "Athalie" at Saint Cyr's.

Metastasio's libretto to "Nittete" was first set this year by Conforto. See also Bertoni, Gatti (L.), Hasse, Holzbauer, Jommelli, Piccinni, Poissl (German opera), Traetta.

No trace has been discovered of Henri de Croes' opera that E. van der Straeten said was performed this year.

Destouches' opera "Le Carnaval et la folie" was revived until this year.

A collection of cantatas in Maria Teresa Agnesi's honor by Pier Domenico appeared this season.

E. R. Duni's opera "Le Caprice amoureux, ou Ninette à la cour" was composed at this time.

Favart's "Tircis et Doristée" was performed under Gluck's direction this year.

Domenico Fischietti this year in collaboration with Goldoni wrote the opera "La ritornata di Londra".

Friedrich Gottlob Fleischer's "Oden und Lieder mit Melodien", first part, was published at this time.

Pierre Fournier this year pub-

(cont.) lished "Essai d'un nouveau caractère de fonte pour l'impression de la musique" at Paris.

Barthold Fritz published his "Anweisung, wie man Claviere . . . in allen zwölf Tönen gleich rein stimmen könne . . ." this year at Leipzig.

Baldassare Galuppi wrote his opera "Idomeneo" during this year at Rome. The librettist was unknown.

Baldassare Galuppi wrote his opera "La cantarina" this year at Rome (libretto by Goldoni).

Baldassare Galuppi wrote his opera "Le nozze di Paride" this year at Venice (libretto by Chiari).

Francisco Xavier García wrote his intermezzo "Lo scultore deluso" at this time.

Salomon Gessner's "Idyllen" appeared at this time.

Gluck's opera "Le Chinois poli en France" (libretto by Louis Anseaume) was produced this season at Laxenburg, near Vienna.

Gluck's opera "Le Déguisement pastoral" (libretto by Charles Simon Favart) was produced this year at Schönbrunn near Vienna with Gluck himself conducting.

An aria from Gluck's "Il Rè Pastore" was published at this time in Benoît Andrez' journal, "L'Echo".

1756(cont.)

Goldoni this year wrote a preface for his libretto "Statira".

Carl Heinrich Graun's opera "I fratelli nenici" was produced this season at Berlin.

Carl Heinrich Graun's opera "Merope" was produced this year at Berlin.

Carl Heinrich Graun wrote his famous "Te Deum" at this time.

Joseph Haydn wrote an organ or clavier concerto in C major this year. The orchestration included 2 oboes, 2 horns, 2 violins, viola and bass. Haydn said he wrote it for a student colleague, Therese Keller, whom he fell in love with. She, however, became a nun in 1760.

Haydn's three movement "Salve Regina" in E major was composed at this time for alto, tenor, bass, ripieno, 2 violins, bass and organ. He also wrote two other Salve Reginas, one in G major and one in F major, but the dates of these are unknown.

Holzbauer's "Le nozze d'Arianna" and "I cinesi" (Italian operas) were performed at Mannheim this season.

Hutchinson's "Select Set of Psalms and Hymns" appeared this year.

G. Insanguine wrote his opera "Lo funnaco revotato" at this time.

Jommelli's operas "L'isola disabitata" and "Endimione" (later titled Il trionfo d'amore") were both produced

(cont.) this season at Genoa.

"Sentiments d'un harmonophile sur différents ouvrages de musique", a periodical published this year in Paris, was edited by M. A. Laugier.

Jean Louis Larvette wrote "Les Arnans trompés", a full-length "comédies mêlées d'ariettes" this year.

N. Logroscino's "I disturbi" was produced this season.

N. Logroscino's "Le finte magie" was produced this season.

P. van Maldere's opéra-comique "Le Deguisement pastoral" of this year is preserved at the National Library at Vienna.

F. W. Marpurg's "Kunst das Clavier zu spielen" was issued this year in a French edition.

Marpurg's "6 Sonaten für das Cembalo" was published this year at Nürnberg.

Leopold Mozart's great violin method, "Versuch einer gründlichen Violinschule" was published this year at Augsburg.

Rameau's "Les Fêtes d'Hébé" was revived this year in France.

Jean-François Rameau this year produced a book of harpsichord pieces published by Veuve Boivin.

Rameau this year wrote a "Suite des erreurs . . ."

Metastasio's libretto to "Il Sogno" was first set at this time by Reutter.

Alexander and Patrick Russell
this year published their book
"The Natural History of Aleppo"
containing a description of
music.

Giuseppe Sarti's "Ciro riconosciuto" was published at this
time in Copenhagen.

Giuseppe Sarti's opera "Gram
og Signe" was produced this
year at Copenhagen.

Volumes XIII-XIV of D. Scarlatti's sonatas appeared this
year at Parma.

The twelfth volume of D. Scarlatti's violin sonatas was
published this year probably
in the Venetian edition.

Giuseppe Scolari's opera "La
cascina" was produced in Venice
this season.

John C. Smith composed the opera
"The Tempest" at this time.

William Tansur's "The Royal
Melody Compleat" was issued
this year in its first edition.

William Tansur's "A New Musical
Grammer and Dictionary" appeared
this year in its third edition
at London.

William Tansur's "A Compleat
Melody . . ." was issued this
year in its third edition in
London.

Tommaso Traetta's opera "La
fante furba" was produced this
season at the Teatro San Carlo
in Naples.

Vento made his first appearance
as an opera composer in Rome

(cont.) this year with the
intermezzo "Le deluse accor-
tezze".

In Marpurg's "Principes" of
this year he wrote on undotted
slides, the "springer" ornament,
the ascending trill (tremble-
ment coulé en montant), the
ordinary trill and also accented
turns, standard and inverted,
tied turn.

In his violin method Leopold
Mozart used the double dot
which he may have found in the
music of Raison. He said that
one must sustain dots in
appoggiatura and accent first
of each two slurred notes. He
also said "the mordent must
be used only when it is desired
to give special emphases to a
note" and to "take the prolonged mordent from below and
invariably from the semi-tone".
He further explained the mordent. He also used the term
"passing appoggiatura". The
"ribattuta" (ornament) was
mentioned and trills for sad
slow pieces and for fast lively
pieces were discussed. The
author further said the accel-
lerating trill is used mostly
in cadenzas and recommended
increasing volume in proportion
to speed. He mentioned "ti-
rates" (passing notes) and
called the vibrato, "tremolo".

Surviving harpsichords made by
the Kirkman family this year
included one made by J. Kirkman
with two manuals owned by G. C.
Bushby, described as follows:
2x8', 1x4' (lute) F-F, 5
octaves without bottom F#.

The choir of the Royal Chapel
at Madrid this year included
four sopranos (castrati), four

altos, four tenors, and three basses.

The Mannheim orchestra at this time consisted of 20 violins, 4 violas, 4 cellos, 4 basses, 2 flutes, 2 oboes, 2 bassoons, 4 horns, 1 trumpet and 2 tympani.

There were a number of short-lived musical magazines, the earliest being published this year.

Breitkopf this year printed an opera in full score and in three volumes entitled "Il trionfo della fedeltà, dramma per musica di E.T.P.A."

After this year (Venice XI and Parma XIII) the contents of the corresponding volumes of each set of Scarlatti sonatas were identical except that Parma XV included the last twelve sonatas that were never in the Venice manuscripts.

The building at Lincoln's Inn Fields was converted into a barrack this year and later served as a warehouse.

The "Apollo's Cabinet" was published in Liverpool this year.

Burke published his "Inquiry into the Origin of our Ideas of the Beautiful and Sublime" at this time in England.

Henry Raeburn, Scottish portraitist, was born this year (died 1823).

Thomas Rowlandson, the English painter, was born this year. He commented on social satire (like Hogarth) and brought

(cont.) Rococo delicacy to his landscapes (died 1827).

John Trumbull, American painter, was born this year (died 1843).

Jean Baptiste Champagny, Napoleon's foreign minister from 1807-1811, was born this year (died 1836).

William Godwin, English philosopher, was born at this time (death date unknown).

Count de Lacépède, scientist and man of letters, was born at this time (died 1825).

This year marked the birth of Friedrich Franz Joseph Spaur, a canon at Salzburg, a position he held also at Brixen and Passau, and that of Domdechant at Salzburg (died 1841).

(to 1757) Handcrossings occurred in the latest Scarlatti sonatas of the Queen's series published during these years.

(and 1758) Geronimo Abos' opera "Creso" was produced both these seasons at London.

(to 1758) Francis Waylett published Joseph Bryan's "The Muse's Choice, a favorite collection of Songs" at this time.

(to 1759) Felice (de') Giardini was manager of the Opera in London during this period.

(to 1763) The period of the Seven Years' War included these years.

(to 1763) During the Seven

1756(cont.)

Years' War Breitkopf organized "a warehouse of German, English, French and Italian music, both manuscript and printed, and started a special trade in music, with the publication of systematic descriptive catalogues referring to the stock and embracing the whole field of musical literature".

(to 1764) As a consequence of the Seven Years' War the operahouse in Berlin was closed during this period.

(to 1765) Gasparo Angiolini was ballet-master in Vienna during these nine years.

(to 1767) G. F. Brusa wrote seven operas for Venice, Pesaro and Forli during this period. They were: "Semiramide riconosciuta", "Angelica", "Le statue", "Adriano in Siria", "La cascina", "La ritornata di Londra" and "L'Olimpiade" (with Guglielmi and Pampani). Because of the large time-gap between this series of operas and a previous one, some sources believe that there were two composers (father and son) by the same name.

(to 1772) James Read engraved music during these years.

(to 1774) Giuseppe Sarti wrote nine Danish operas at Copenhagen during these years.

(to 1778) Pierre Montan Berton was conductor at the Paris Opéra at this time.

(to 1780) J. L. Krebs was organist at Altenburg for these twenty-four years.

(to 1789) Doles was director of the two principal churches at Leipzig during this period. He was Leipzig's cantor.

(to 1799, November 11) When his master, James Nares resigned in 1756, John Camidge was appointed organist of York Minster where he stayed until 1799, November 11.

c.1756

Brigitta Giorgi Banti, Italian soprano, was born at this time at Monticelli (died 1806, February 18 at Bologna).

Giuseppe Bertini, Italian composer and theorist, was born this year at Palermo (died after 1847).

Andrea Caporale, Italian violoncellist and composer, died this year at London (birthdate unknown).

August Friedrich Kollmann I, German organist, theorist and composer, was born this year at Engelbostel, Hanover.

Antoinette Cécile Saint-Huberty (actually Clavel), French soprano, was born this year (died 1812, July 22).

Capron made his debut at about sixteen this year in the orchestra of the Paris Opéra-Comique.

1757

(January 11) Louis Bertrand Castel, French theorist and writer on musical subjects, died this day at Paris (born 1688, November 11 at Montpellier).

(January 20) Cafaro's opera

1757(cont.)

"L'incendio di Troia" was produced on this date at the Teatro San Carlo in Naples.

(January 20) "The first public Concerts on record . . . took place in 1757". They were advertised in the Pennsylvania Gazette in this issue.

(January 20, 27 and February 3, 10) These issues of the Pennsylvania Gazette discussed Francis Hopkinson's playing harpsichord at a College Hall concert.

(January 20, 27 and February 3, 10) The Pennsylvania Gazette on these dates gave detailed accounts of "The Redemption of the Danish Invasion by Alfred the Great".

(January 21) J. Oswald wrote one song for Smolett's farce "The Reprisal, or The Tars of Old England" produced on this date at Drury Lane Theatre in London.

(January 25) The Pennsylvania Gazette advertised "On Tuesday next, the 25th instant, at the Assembly Room, in Lodge Alley will be performed a Concert of Music, under . . .Mr. John Palma . . ." George Washington purchased tickets for the concert.

(February 1) Francis Hopkinson wrote "To Miss Lawrence, on the same" (a poem) in Philadelphia this day.

(February 3) Caporale's performance in Dublin on this date was mentioned in Faulkner's Journal (#3107) on this day.

(February 12) Christian Latrobe,

(cont.) English musical editor and amateur composer, was born on this date at Fulneck, Leeds (died 1836, May 6).

(February 15) Friederica Sophia Bach, daughter of Wilhelm Friedemann, granddaughter of J. Sebastian and member of the seventh generation of the Bach family, was christened on this day.

(February 17) Antonio Calegari, Italian composer, was born on this date at Padua (died 1828, July 28 at Padua).

(February 25) Paolo Benedetto Bellinzani, Italian composer, died on this date at Recanati (birthdate unknown but at Mantua).

(March 4) George Thomson, a promoter of good music, "reviver of ancient Scottish melody" and secretary to the Board of Trustees for the Encouragement of Arts and Manufactures in Scotland, was born on this date at Limekilns, Dunfermline (died 1851, February 18 at Leith).

(March 8) N. Conforto's opera "Antigono" was produced on this date at the King's Theatre in London.

(March 11) Handel wrote his last composition, an oratorio, The Triumph of Time and Truth", at this time and it was first produced at Covent Garden in London on this date. The words were based on "The Italian of Panfili" adapted by Morell.

(March 20) Johann Paul Kuntzen, German organist, singer and composer, died on this date

1757(cont.)

at Lübeck (born 1696, August 30 at Leisnig, Saxony).

(March 24) The Pennsylvania Journal on this date made no mention of the musician who arranged the entertainment for a second "Concert of Music" in Philadelphia.

(March 25) Hasse's oratorio "I pellegrini" was performed on this day at London.

(March 25) The Second Concert of Music in the Assembly Room in Lodge Alley at Philadelphia was held on this evening.

(March 27) Johann Stamitz, leader and founder of the Mannheim School, died on this date at Mannheim (born 1717, June 17 or 19).

(March 27) Richard John Samuel Stevens, an Englishman and the first composer who "succeeded in adapting the sonata-form to the glee", was born on this day at London (died 1837, September 23 at London).

(April 6) Alessandro Rolla, Italian violinist, violist, conductor and composer, was born on this day in Pavia. He first studied piano, but changed to violin and studied with Renzi and Conti. His compositions had considerable success and he was the teacher of Paganini (died 1829, July 23 at Warsaw).

(April 12) Boyce's "Ode in Commemoration of Shakespeare" was performed this day at the Drury Lane Theatre in London.

(April 27) The Pennsylvania

(cont.) Journal on this day stated that Josiah Davenport kept a "Singing School, (for the Summer Season Evenings) . . . where any Person may be instructed in Psalmody, that is capable to learn that agreeable Art . . ."

(April 30) Felice (de') Giardini's opera "Rosmira" was given in London on this date.

(May 8) P. van Maldere played before the Empress Maria Theresa in Vienna this evening.

(May 14) Bartolommeo Cordans, Italian composer, died on this date at Udine (born c.1700 at Venice).

(June 1) Ignaz Pleyel, pupil and rival of Haydn, was born on this date at Ruppertsthal, lower Austria. Pleyel also became a leading piano maker (died 1831, November 4 at Paris).

(June 4) Correr, the Venetian Ambassador, had his farewell audience before leaving Vienna on this day. It is not certain whether Porpora left with him.

(June 13) Christian Ludwig Dieter, German composer, was born on this date at Ludwigsburg (died 1822 at Stuttgart).

(June 18) Sometime after this date a "Te Deum" of N. Porpora's was performed in Vienna during the battle of Kolin. This indicated that Porpora stayed in Vienna and did not leave on June 4 with Correr.

(Summer) Anseaume's "Le Peintre amoureaux de son

modèle" with music by E. R.
Duni, was produced at the Foire
Saint-Laurant this evening.

(June 25) W. Walond I was admitted on this date to the
privileges of the University of
Oxford and was described as
"organorum pulsator".

(July 5) W. Walond I was granted
his degree this day at Christ
College, Oxford.

(July 7) Giuseppe Andreol,
Italian double-bass player and
harpist, was born this date at
Milan (died 1832, December 20
at Milan).

(July 23) Domenico Scarlatti,
harpsichordist and composer,
died on this day at Madrid or
Naples (born 1685, October 26).
Sources disagree on where he
died, but the judgement here
is Madrid. He received the last
rites of the Church. He was
the son of Alessandro and in
his own right the leading keyboard composer and virtuoso of
his time.

(July 23) The death certificate
and will of Domenico Scarlatti
bore this date.

(July 26) E. R. Duni's opera
"Le Peintre amoureux de son
modèle" was produced on this
evening at the Paris, Théâtre
de la Foire Saint-Laurent.

(July 29) A private rehearsal
of a Mass composed by Johann
Christian Bach took place on
this date at Milan under
Martini's supervision. Johann
Christian referred to here was
J. Sebastian's son.

(August 19) J. P. Rameau on
this date wrote a letter to
Arnand asking help in drafting
the prospectus for his "Code".

(August 23) A public performance
of a Mass by J. Christian Bach
(son of J. Sebastian) took
place on this date at the
Church of San Fedele.

(September 2) The Pennsylvania
Gazette advertisement offering
a Reward for run-away Charles
Love was dated "Williamsburg,
Sept. 2, 1757".

(September 18, 19, 20, 22, 30,
October 30) An accounting of
the portion of Scarlatti's
estate allotted to Domingo
Scarlatti, and of the Royal
Pension accorded Scarlatti's
widow and children appeared
on these dates according to
a major source.

(September 18, 19, 20, 22, 30,
October 30) An accounting of
the portion of Scarlatti's
estate alloted to Maria Scarlatti, and of the Royal Pension
accorded Scarlatti's widow
and children appeared on these
dates according to a major
source.

(September 21) Johann Joseph
Kenn, a notable "cor-basse",
was born on this date in
Germany (death date unknown).

(Autumn) From this date forward
Signora Mattei, impresario at
the King's Theatre in London,
employed a musician of the
Neapolitan school, Gioacchino
Cocchi, as composer to London's
Italian opera.

(Autumn) No new opera by G.

Emanuele Kant.

1724-1804

Cocchi was produced in Italy
after this date when he went
to London.

(Autumn) Traetta's opera "Didone
abbandonata" (libretto by Metastasio) was produced at this
time at the Teatro San Moisè
in Venice.

(October 6) The Pennsylvania
Gazette on this date advertised
"Run away from the Subscriber,
at Stratford . . . on Sunday
the 28th of August, Charles Love
. . .", offering a Reward;
written up by Philipp Ludwell
Lee.

(October 11) Zacharias Hildebrand, German organ builder,
died on this date at Münster-
berg, Silesia (born c.1690).

(October 13) Nicolo Pasquali,
Italian composer and violinist
who emigrated to Edinboro, died
this year (birthdate unknown).

(November 2) Charlotte (Caroline
Wilhelmine) Bachmann, (born
Stöwe), singer, pianist and
composer, was born at this time
in Berlin (died 1817, August 19
at Berlin).

(November 4) Piccinni's opera,
"Nitteti" (libretto by Metastasio), was performed on this
day at the Teatro San Carlo at
Naples.

(November 6) Louis Abel Beffroy
de Reigny, French playwright
and composer, was born on this
date at Laon (died 1811,
December 17 at Paris).

(November 8) G. Cocchi made his
London debut this evening with
the pasticcio "Demetrio, re di

(cont.) Siria" at the King's
Theatre.

(November 20) G. Scarlatti's
opera "L'isola disabitata"
was produced on this date at
the Teatro San Samuele in
Venice (libretto by Goldoni).

(December 2) Arne wrote incidental music for "Isabella, or
The Fatal Marriage", performed
on this date at Drury Lane
Theatre in London.

(December 11) Charles Wesley,
English musician, was born on
this date at Bristol (died
1834, May 23).

(December 15) Sophie Arnould
made her debut as a singer on
this evening.

(December 25) Raick was recalled
by the Bishop of Antwerp and
became canon and vicar-choral
at the cathedral at this time.

(January) "The Redemption of
the Danish Invasion by Alfred
the Great" was produced this
month at College Hall at
Philadelphia (an "Oratorial
Exercise"). Francis Hopkinson
supposedly wrote additional
music for the masque. There
were several performances.

(April) Castel's "Éloge historique du Père Castel" appeared
in "Journal de Trevoux" this
month.

(May) Rameau's "Les Surprises
de l'Amour" was given at the
Opéra this month. The prologue
and the addition of a third act
were omitted.

(September) B. Cooke II, became
master of the choristers of

Westminster Abbey at this time.

(September) The list of D. Scarlatti's surviving heirs appeared this month in the accountings prepared for Maria and Domingo.

(September) To honor "la buena memoria de Dn. Domingo Scarlatti" at this time, their Catholic Majesties assigned a pension of three hundred ducats annually to each of his five youngest children.

(September) A portion of Domenico Scarlatti's estate, including two paintings of views of Rome, this month was given to his daughter, Maria.

(December) Antonio Besozzi appeared this month with his son Carlo at the Concert Spirituel in Paris.

(December) Fortunato Cheller, Italian composer of German descent, died this month at Cassel (born 1690, June at Milan).

Francesco Aglietti, a physician who treated Paganini, was born this year (died 1836).

Emanuele d'Astorga, Italian amateur composer, died this year at Madrid (born 1680, March 20 at Augusta, Sicily).

Friederica Sophia Bach, daughter of W. Friedemann, granddaughter of J. Sebastian and a member of the seventh generation of the Bach family, was born (died 1801).

Jan Jiří Benda, a linen-weaver at Staré Benátky, Bohemia, and

(cont.) a talented amateur performer on several instruments, died this year (born 1685).

Anton Boeck, a horn player and brother of Ignaz, was born this year (death date unknown).

Henry Condell, English composer, was born at this time (died 1824, June 24 at London).

John Danby, English organist and composer, was born this year at Dondon (died 1798, May 16 at London).

Jacob Eckhard of Charleston, South Carolina and one of the early American musicians, was born this year (died 1833).

Michel Forqueray, French organist, died this year at Paris (born 1681, February 15).

The wife of Bernard Gates died at this time (birthdate unknown).

Gerhard Hoffmann, composer who also made improvements of the flute and oboe, died at this time (born 1690 at Rastenberg, Thuringia).

Edward Hopkins, French horn player from England, was born this year (died 1790).

Józef Kozłowski, Polish composer, was born at this time in Warsaw (died 1831, February 27 at St. Petersburg).

Lacoste, French composer, died sometime after this date (birthdate unknown).

Christian Ignatius Latrobe, who edited the selection of sacred music which appeared in

London, was born this year
(died 1836).

Abbé Domenico Quilici, a well-
known Italian clergyman and
musician, was born this year
(death date unknown).

Lazare Rameau, Claude Rameau's
son, was born this year (died
1794).

Daniel Read, American musician,
was born this year (died 1836).

William Reeve, English actor,
organist and composer, was
born this year in London. He
was a pupil of Richardson,
the organist of St. James',
Westmenster (died 1815, June 22
at London).

Franz Wenzel, brother of
"Katherl", was born this year
(died 1816).

Avison this year joined John
Garth in editing Marcello's
Psalms, adapted to English
words.

Johann Christian Bach rebelled
against the Picardian third
even as late as this date.

Johann Nicolaus Bach's youngest
daughter married Johann Heinrich
Möller, a Jena organist this
year.

Bertoni this year became choirmaster at the Ospedale San
Lazzaro dei Mendicanti.

Gerber says Bini was still at
Stuttgart this year.

Boccherini was sent to Rome this
year and rapidly made himself
famous both as a composer and

(cont.) player.

Jean-Baptiste Joseph Boutmy
was appointed organist of the
Church of Saint Baafs at this
time.

William Boyce was officially
sworn in as Master of the
Queen's music this year.

Calzabigi established a lottery
this year at Paris with Madame
de Pompadour and Casanova.
She was the "protector".
Calzabigi's brother, Antonio
Maria, was said to be involved
with them.

C. Cannabich succeeded J.
Stamitz this year as leader
of the Mannheim orchestra
after the latter's death.

During the carnival season,
V. L. Ciampi had three different
operas produced at three
different theatres in Venice.

William Cramer entered the
Mannheim orchestra this season.

Rosa Curioni was heard at
Venice this year.

Johann Florian Deller took
lessons in composition from
Jommelli this year.

A. Duni gave private lessons
this year in Russia.

Nearly all the works E. R.
Duni wrote in Paris from this
year forward were published,
translated and imitated.

Fogliazzi, the famous Milanese
dancer, after many tours was
engaged this year as successor
to Hilverding at Vienna.

Giulia Frasi sang in Handel's
"The Triumph of Time and Truth"
this season.

Pascual Fuentes was maestro de
capilla at the cathedral of
Valencia at this time.

Gluck this year began to use the
title of "Cavaliere", indicating
that he had recently received
the Order of the Golden Spur
from the Pope.

Handel this year reset an oratorio by Cardinal Panfili
titles "Il Trionfo del Tempo e
del Desinganno" into the oratorio "The Triumph of Time and
Truth".

This year Michael Haydn, having
had no real instruction in
composition, taught himself
from Fux's "Gradus ad Parnassum"
which he copied in its entirety.

Michael Haydn was Kapellmeister
to the Bishop Count Firmian
this year at Grosswarden.

William Hayes conducted the
Gloucester Festival this season.

Johann W. Hertel, after studying
with his father, entered the
orchestra at Schwerin and this
year became conductor there.

John Holden, Scottish writer
and composer who settled in
Glasgow as a potter, became a
burgess there this year.

Francis Hopkinson graduated
from the College of Philadelphia
this year. He was the first
matriculated student there.

A. K. Kunzen succeeded his
father this year as organist

(cont.) at the Marien-Kirche
at Lübeck.

Durey de Noinville's "Histoire
de Théâtre de l'Académie
Royale de Musique" stated that
Lacoste was still alive this
year.

Jean François Lepine, jr.
built the organ at Pezenas
this year.

Written this year: James Lyon
"can not have entered college
later than fall . . ."

Padre Martini, in his dedication to Maria Barbara of the
first volume of his "Storia
della Musica" this year,
praised her as having learned
from the "Cavaliere" D. Domenico
Scarlatti the most intimate
knowledge of music and its
profoundest artifices".

William Mason was appointed
chaplain to the King this year.

Luis Misson, who was regarded
as the inventor of the Tonadilla, produced his first
stage piece of that "genre"
this season.

Leopold Mozart this year was
appointed court composer to
the Archbishop of Salzburg.

Johann Gottlieb Naumann went
to Hamburg this year, then to
Padua with his teacher,
Wesstrom. His teacher studied
with Tartini but did not allow
Naumann to share in the work.

Nebra completed arrangements
for the choir this year.

Gaspari Pacchierotti this year
was admitted to the choir of

St. Mark's at Venice where
Bertoni was his master, according to G. Pacchierotti's son
but not according to Fétis.

John Palma may have given
Hopkinson lessons on the
harpsichord at this time.

A tablet was placed this year
in memory of Pepusch in the
chapel of Charter House in
England where he was buried.

T. Pinto replaced Giardini
this year at the King's Theatre
in London.

N. Porpora was still drawing
his pension from Dresden this
year.

S. Porter was elected organist
of Canterbury Cathedral this
season.

Jean-François Rameau was married
this year at St. Severin;
however, his uncle and cousins
were not present.

Giuseppe Scarlatti settled in
Vienna this year.

Luigi Tomasini at this time
became a member of Prince Paul
Anton Esterházy's household
at Eisenstadt serving as a
violinist and composer.

M. C. V. Vestris appeared in
the Paris Concert Spirituel
as an Italian singer, under the
name of Vertris-Giardini until
this year.

Garrett Wellesley was awarded
the degree of Master of Arts
this year by the University of
Dublin.

Garrett Wellesley this year
founded the Academy of Music,
an amateur society in which
for the first time, ladies
were permitted to sing in the
chorus.

A. Wesstrom visited Dresden
this year and met J. G.
Naumann.

I. Young sang "Counsel" in the
first performance of "The
Triumph of Time and Truth"
this season.

J. Friedrich Agricola wrote
his treatise "Anleitung zur
Singkunst" this year at Berlin.

Agricola's theoretical works
included a translation of
Tosi's "Opinioni de'cantori
antichi e moderni" in 1723
and his "Anleitung zur Singkunst" of this year.

D'Alembert wrote his "Encyclopédie" at this time.

Fritz Barthold's "Anweisung
wie man Claviere, Clavecins
und Orgeln nach einer mecha-
nischen Art . . . stimmen
Könne" was issued this year
at Leipzig.

Charles Bâton published a
"Mémoire sur la vielle en
D la re" in this year's
"Mercure de France".

Six harpsichord sonatas by
J. A. Benda were published
this year at Berlin.

Bremner published his "Collection of Scots Reels" at this
time.

F. X. Brixi composed "La

1757(cont.)

Bataille beym Dorfe Planyan" this year for harpsichord.

Bury's "La Parque vaincue" appeared this year at Versailles.

There is evidence that T. Cahusac published "Country Dances" this year.

Castel's "Explanation of the Ocular Harpsichord" was issued this year at London.

G. Cocchi's "Semiramide ricono-sciuta" was given this season at Venice.

Francis Waylett published N. Conforto's "The Favorite Songs in Antigono" this year.

This year marked the reprint of the 17th edition of Watts' "Psalms of David" and the publication of "Der Psalter David" by B. Franklin and Armbruster (Warrington). Also Josiah Davenport operated a singing school.

Errichelli's opera "Solimano" was completed at this time.

William Felton published eight suites, opus 6, this year at London.

Antonio Ferradini wrote his opera "Il festino" at Parma this year (libretto by Goldoni).

Domenico Fischietti, in collabo-ration with Goldoni, wrote the opera "Il mercato di Malmantile" at this time.

Friedrich Gottlob Fleischer's "Oden und Lieder mit Melodien", second part, was published this year.

Barthold Fritz's "Anweisung wie man Claviere . . . in allen zwölf Tönen gleich rein stimmen könne . . ." was published for the second time this year at Leipzig.

Baldassare Galuppi wrote his opera "Ezio" in Milan this year (libretto by Metastasio).

Baldassare Galuppi this year wrote his opera "Sesostri" in Venice (libretto by Zeno and Pariati).

Florian Gassmann's opera "Merope" was produced in Venice this season (libretto by Zeno).

Pietro Guglielmi's opera "Lo solachianello 'mbroglione" was produced at the Teatro dei Fiorentini at Naples during this year.

Handel finished "Jephtha" this year.

Handel's "Messiah" was first given in the Boothall at Gloucester at the Three Choirs Festival of this year.

Hasse's pasticcio "La Petite Maison" was heard at Paris this year. It was a parody of Rameau's second "Anacreon", and one air by Hasse was printed in the libretto.

Francis Waylett's publisher's imprint appeared this year on "The Favourite Songs in Il re pastore" by Hasse.

Before this year, Haydn wrote a "nonet" for 2 oboes, 2 horns, 2 violins, viola, cello and double bass

1757(cont.)

A famous Spanish violinist, José Herrando, was said to have been Corelli's pupil. He published a method this year.

Holzbauer's Italian opera "La clemenza di Tito" was performed this season at Mannheim.

Holzbauer wrote an oratorio, "Isacco", for Mannheim this year.

Holzbauer's Italian opera "Nitteti" was performed at Turin this season.

The American Magazine (Philadelphia) published Hopkinson's "Ode 1757" in its October number with an editorial remark.

Jommelli's opera "Creso" and "Temistocle" were produced this season at Rome and Naples respectively.

Musician and theoretician Johann Philip Kirnberger wrote a manual this year showing how compositions could be written mechanically with neither inspiration or musical knowledge, "Der allzeit fertige Polonaisen und Menuetten Komponist". It was published in Poland as a satirical paper.

Jean Louis Larvette wrote "La Fausse Aventurière" at this time.

P. van Maldere's "Six Quatuors pour 2 violons, alto and basse" was issued this year at Brussels.

An English edition of B. Marcello's "Estro poetico-armonico . . ." was published this year at London, edited by Avison and Garth.

Marpurg's "Raccolta" was published at this time.

Marpurg this year issued his "Systematiche (sic) Einleitung in die musikalische Setzkunst" at Leipzig. He did not mention d'Alembert on the title page.

The first volume of G. Martini's "Storia della musica" was published at Bologna this year.

A Mazzoni's opera "Il re pastore" was produced this season.

A. Mazzoni this year composed a setting of Goldoni's opera "Il viaggiator ridicolo" while at Parma.

According to Dretzschmar, D. Perez's most important opera was one to an unknown libretto, "Solimano", produced at Lisbon during this year's carnival.

Phaedra's solo, "Druelle mère des Amours", was put back in Rameau's opera "Hippolyte et Aricie" this year.

Rameau's "Hippolyte et Aricie" was revived a second time this season.

Rameau this year wrote his "Réponse de M. Rameau à M. M. les Editeurs de l'Encyclopédie sur leur dernier avertissement" at this time (see next entry).

Rameau this year wrote a "Réponse" to Diderot's "disparagement" of his statements about Rousseau's "Lettre sur la musique française".

Rameau composed "Les Surprises de l'Amour" at this time.

Rameau's and Marmontel's "Les Sybarites" was included in a revival of "Les Surprises de l"Amour" this season.

Antonio Rodríquez de Hita this year was choirmaster at Palencia in Old Castile. He published a pamphlet of 36 pages for his pupils.

Rousseau's "Ecce sedes hic Tonantis", a motet in six parts for soprano and orchestra, was completed this year in manuscript.

The Queen's series of Scarlattis manuscripts ended with Venice Vol. XIII, copied out this year.

Volume XV of Scarlatti's sonatas in the Parma edition came out this year.

G. Scarlatti's opera "Il mercato di Malmantile" was given at the Burg Theatre in Vienna this season (libretto by Goldoni).

John Stanley produced his "Jephtha" this season.

J. G. Sulzer wrote his treatise "Pensées sur l'origine et les différents emplois des sciences et des beaux-arts" this year at Berlin.

Pier Francesco Tosi's "Opinioni de 'cantori antichi e moderni, o sieno osservazioni sopra il canto figurato" was published in Berlin this year by Agricola as "Anleitung zur Singkunst".

Tommaso Traetta's "Ezio" (libretto by Metastasio) was produced this season at Rome.

Tommaso Traetta's opera "Nitteti" (libretto by Metastasio) was produced this season at Reggio.

There was a singing school in Pennsylvania at this time.

Count de Fontanes, writer and friend of Chateaubriand, was born this year (did 1821).

Joseph Franz von Ratschky, a poet, was born this year (died 1810).

Thomas Gray was offered the position of Poet Laureate of England this year but refused it.

William Collins, English poet, published his "Oriental Ecologues" at this time.

Thomas Gray's "Pindaric Odes" were published at this time.

English mystical poet and artist, William Blake, was born this year. Blake had a fantastic imagination, exercised in his obscure "prophetic books" and his "Songs of Innocence and Experience". He spent a simple and isolated life (died 1827).

Antonio Canova, Italian sculptor, was born this year (died 1822).

McIntire, Irish architect, was born this year (died 1811).

Giandomenico Tiepolo painted "Peasants Resting" this year

while at the Villa Valmarana in Vicenza.

Charles X, King of France, was born this year (died 1836). He ruled from 1824-1830 and was a member of the House of Bourbon.

Baron Heinrich Friedrich Karl von Stein, a Prussian statesman, was born this year (died 1831).

This year marked the victory of British forces under Clive at Plassey, opening an era of British rule in India.

Prague was beseiged at this time.

(to 1758) J. W. Hertel's "Sammlung musikalischer Schriften", translated from Italian and French authors and annotated, was published in Leipzig at this time.

(to 1758) John Greenwood painted "Sea Captains Carousing in Surinam" during this period (37 3/4" x 75 1/4").

(to 1758) P. van Maldere during this period traveled to Austria and Bohemia with Duke Charles of Lorraine under whose protection he was.

(to c.1759) Bremner published his "Thirty Scots Songs" during this period.

(to 1759) Noverre at this time retired to Lyons to devise a new system of dramatic dance.

(to 1760) The sonata in c minor of J. Christian Bach was published during these year (son of J. Sebastian).

(and 1760) J. W. Hertel set to

(cont.) music Löwen's "Oden und Lieder", published in Leipzig in 1757 and Rostock in 1760.

(to 1766) François Francoeur was a director of the Paris Opéra with Rebel during these nine years.

(to 1767) Thomas Phinn engraved music at Edinboro during this decade.

(to 1768) At the College of Philadelphia music played an important part at this time, more than in following years.

(to 1769) William Felton was the vicar of St. Agnes during this period, a position which terminated with his death.

(to 1774) At least 12 concerts were advertised in Philadelphia newspapers during this time.

(to 1778) In the "Liceo musicale" at Bologna, a series of letters from J. Christian Bach (son of J. Sebastian) to Padre Marini written during these years have been preserved.

(to 1781) J. Brown's "A Dissertation on the Rise, Union and Power . . . of Poetry and Music" appeared during these years.

c.1757

Peter Dahmen, composer of chamber music, was born at this time at Deventer according to one source (died 1835 at Sneek).

N. Pasquali wrote "The Art of Fingering the Harpsichord" this year at Edinboro.

(January 4) Mary Linley, English singer, was born this day at Bath (died 1787, July 27 in Clifton, Bristol).

(January 10) Calori appeared on this date at London in Cocchi's "Zenobia".

(January 21) N. Piccinni's opera "Alessandro nell'Indie", which included a fine overture, was produced on this date at the Teatro Argentina in Rome. It was the first setting of this libretto.

(January 27) B. Cooke, II became lay vicar at Westminster Abbey on this day.

(January 31) Calori sang this evening in the pasticcio "Solimano".

(February 1) Arne's "The Prophetess, or The History of Dioclesian" was produced on this date at Covent Garden in London.

(February 4) Pierre Gabriel Gardel, French ballet dancer, was born on this date at Nancy (died 1840, October 18).

(February 5) Bernhard Christian Weber, German organist and composer, died this day at Tennstedt near Erfurt (died 1712, December 1).

(February 13) E. R. Duni's opera "Le Docteur Sangrado" was produced on this date at Paris in the Théâtre de la Foire Saint-Germain.

(February 14) Dauvergne's opera "Enée et Lavinie" was performed on this date at the Opéra in Paris.

(February 21) Boyce's "Agis", music for the procession in Act II and the final chorus, was heard on this date at Drury Lane Theatre in London.

(March 3) Charlotte Brent sang on this date in a concert performance of "Eliza", given at the Drury Lane Theatre in London.

(March 4) E. R. Duni's opera "La Fille mal gardée, ou Le Pédant amoureux" was produced on this date at the "Comédie-Italienne" in Paris.

(March 4) Charles Simon Favart's "La Fille mal gardée, ou Le Pédant amoureux" was first performed on this evening at Paris (music by Duni).

(March 9) Carl Barbandt's oratorio "On the Divine Veracity" (libretto by Elizabeth Rowe) was performed this evening at the Haymarket in London.

(March 13) E. R. Duni's opera "L'Embarras du choix" was performed on this date at the Théâtre de la Foire Saint-Germain in Paris.

(March 14) Calori sang in Cocchi's "Issipile" this evening.

(March 15) Joseph Karl Ambrož (Ambrosch), Bohemian tenor and singing teacher, was born on this day at Netolice (died 1822, September 11 at Berlin).

(March 22) Richard Leveridge, English bass, died this day at London (born c.1670).

(March 28) Matteo Palotta,

1758(cont.)
Italian composer, died on this
date at Vienna (born 1680 at
Palermo).

(March 31) Johann Balthasar
König, German musical editor,
died on this date at Frankfurt
am Main (born 1691, January at
Walthershausen near Gotha).

(April 1) Constantin Bellermann,
German lutenist and composer,
died on this date at Münden
(born 1696 at Erfurt).

(April 23) Matthieu Frédéric
Blasius, French composer and
conductor, was born on this
date at Lauterburg, Alsace
(died 1829 at Versailles).

(April 27) Ján Francisci, Slovak
composer, died on this date at
Banská Bystrica, Slovakia (born
1691, June 14).

(May 9) Joseph Mondonville's
opéra "Les Fêtes de Paplios"
was performed on this evening
at the Paris Opéra.

(May 30) N. Conforto's "La
forza del genio, osia Il pastor
guerriero" was performed at
Aranjuez on this date.

(June 7) Rameau on this day
wrote a letter to Arnaud
asking his advice for the composition of one of his works.

(June 18) Francois Dagincour(t)
(d'Agincour), French composer,
died on this day at Paris
(born 1684 at Rouen).

(Summer) Metastasio received
a disturbing letter from Farinelli at this time stating that
the Queen was in critically bad
health and that the King was

(cont.) behaving strangely.

(June 29) Georg Johann Abraham
Berwald, musician and conductor, was born on this date
(died 1825, January 27 at St.
Petersburg).

(July 17) Bohumil Jan Dlabač,
Bohemian musicographer, was
born on this date at Cerhenice
(died 1820, January 4 at
Prague).

(August 8) The opera-ballet
"Les Festes d'Euterpe" was
performed on this date at the
Opéra in Paris (music by
Dauvergne).

(August 27) After months of
great pain, Queen Maria Barbara
of Spain died on this date.
Nebra's music for the funeral
included a requiem for eight
voices, flute and strings,
published in a modern edition
by Eslava.

(August 31) Henriette Adélaide
Villard de Beaumesnil, French
singer and composer, was born
on this date at Paris (died
1813 at Paris).

(September ( ) E. R. Duni's
opera "Nina et Lindor, ou Les
Caprices du coeur" was pro-
duced on this date at the
Théâtre de la Foire Saint-
Laurent in Paris.

(September 9) Jean Louis
Larvette's wife, Madame
Larvette, made her début this
evening at the Opéra-Comique.

(October 3) Gluck's opera
"L'Isle de Merlin, ou Le Monde
renversé" (libretto by
Anseaume) was produced at
Schönbrunn near Vienna on this

date. Gluck conducted and had twenty-two new songs for the work originally by LeSage and d'Orneval.

(October 5) Thomas Greatorex, English organist, conductor, teacher and composer, was born on this day at North Wingfield, near Chesterfield (died 1831, July 18).

(October 7) Hasse's opera, "Il sogno di Scipione" (libretto by Metastasio), was performed on this date at Warsaw.

(October 7) Paul Winneberger, German violoncellist, organist and composer, was born on this date (died 1821, February 8).

(October 31) Anton Joseph Liber's son, Wolfgang, was born on this date (died 1758, October 31).

(November 5) P. van Maldere's opera-comique "Les Amours champetres" was performed on this date in the Imperial theatre at Schönbrunn near Vienna.

(November 11) One aria by Aurisicchio was introduced into the pasticcio "Attalo" performed at London on this evening.

(November 11) Calori sang in Cocchi's "Attalo" on this day.

(November 23) A masque,"The Sultan", was added to Arne's "The Prophetess, or The History of Dioclesian" on this date.

(December 2) Dodsley's tragedy, "Cleone", was produced at Covent Garden on this date. J. Oswald wrote one song for the work.

(December 3) (Jean) Louis (Johann Ludwig) Adam, Alsatian pianist, teacher and composer, was born on this date at Mütterscholtz, Alsace (died 1841, April 8 at Paris).

(December 3) T. Dupuis was elected a member of the Royal Society of Musicians at this time.

(December 3) Joseph Gelinek, Bohemian pianist and composer, was born on this date at Selč (died 1825, April 13).

(December 5) Johann Friedrich Fasch, German conductor and composer, died on this day at Zerbst (born 1688, April 15).

(December 6) Rameau's opera, "Castor et Pollux", was produced this evening at Parma (in French).

(December 11) Karl Friedrich Zelter, director of the Berlin Singakademie and friend of Goethe, was born on this day (died 1832, May 15).

(December 20) Othon Joseph Vandenbroeck, horn player and composer, was born on this date at Ypres (died 1832 at Passy).

(Winter) N. Piccinni's opera, "La scaltra letterata" (libretto by Palomba), was produced at this time at the Teatro Nuovo at Naples.

(December 27) Traetta's opera "Buovo d'Antona" was produced on this date at the Teatro San Moisè in Venice (libretto by Goldoni).

(December 29) Paolo Scalabrini's opera "Den belønede

THE KING'S THEATRE IN THE HAYMARKET, London

1758(cont.)
kjaerlighed, eller De troe
elskende", was produced at the
National Theatre in Copenhagen
on this evening.

(January) Hasse's opera,
"Nitteti" (libretto by Metastasio), was produced this month
at Venice.

(January) N. Porpora was again
at Naples this month.

(January) Antonio Sacchini became "maestro straordinario di
canto" this month without pay
at Ste. Maria di Loreto Conservatory.

(Lent) Lord Mount Edgcumbe found
B. Mengozzi singing in an oratorio at Naples with Signora
Benini at this time. He later
married her.

(June) John Travers, organist
and composer, died at this time
in London (born c.1703).

(October-1759, January) Casanova
visited the Netherlands during
this period, allegedly on a
diplomatic mission. He claimed
he met with several adventures
in finance, love and mystery.
Gugitz (in his book, "Giacomo
Casanovas Lebensroman") examined
this carefully and rejected most
of it as Casanova's imagination.

(October-December) Pierre Claude
Fouquet was one of four or-
ganists of the Royal Chapel at
Paris during these months.

Charles Bâton ("le jeune"),
French virtuoso on the hurdy-
gurdy ("vielle"), died this
year at Paris (birthdate unknown).

George Bickham, jr., English

(cont.) engraver, died this year
at London (birthdate unknown).

Jacques de Bournonville, French
composer, died this year (born
c.1676 at Amiens).

John Calah, English organist
and composer, was born at this
time (died 1798, August 5 at
Peterboro).

Matthew Camidge, English organist and composer, was born
this year at York (died 1844,
October 23 at York).

Martin Friedrich Cannabich,
German oboist, flautist and
composer, died afther this date
at Mannheim (birthdate unknown).

Louis-Armand Chardiny, French
baritone and composer, was born
this year at Fecamp, Normandy
(died 1793, October 1 at Paris).

Carl Gustaf Düben, director of
the court orchestra, died this
year at Stockholm (born 1700,
at Stockholm).

The list of Johann Ernst Bach's
compositions given by Eitner
included a "Trauer-Ode" on the
death of his patron, Duke Ernst
August II Constantin this year.

Jakob Friedrich Gauss, composer,
was born this year (died 1791).

Carmine Giordani, Italian composer, died this year at Naples
(born c.1685).

Johann Friedrich Grenser,
oboist and son of C. A. Grenser,
was born at this time (died 1794).

Prince Karl Lichnowsky, Austrian
noble and one of Beethoven's
patrons, was born this year

(died 1814, April).

Nicolas Lupot, greatest name
among French violin makers,
was born this year (died 1824).

Bernardo Mengozzi, Italian tenor
and composer, was born this year
at Florence (died 1800, March
at Paris).

Louis François Pique, French
violin maker, was born this
year at Roret near Mirecourt
(died 1822 at Charenton-Saint-
Maurice).

Allan Ramsay, writer and musician, died this year (born 1685).

John Sale, II, English singer,
conductor and composer, was
born this year at London (died
1827, November 11).

Benedikt Schack, German tenor
and composer, was born at this
time at Mirovice (died 1826,
December 11).

Timothy Swan, American musician,
was born this year (died 1842).

Alessandro Toeschi, violinist
and composer, died after this
year at Mannheim (birthdate
unknown).

(and 1763, March 26) A collection of John Christopher Pepusch was bequeathed partly to
John Travers, who died this year.
The rest was sold in 1766, July
and partly bequeathed to
Ephraim Kelner and sold on March
26, 1763.

Richard Wainwright, organist
and composer, was born this
year at Stockport, England
(died 1825, August 20).

Josepha Weber, bravura singer,
was born at this time (died
1819, December 29).

Leopold August Abel was conductor of the court bands of
the Prince of Schwarzburg-
Sonderhausen at this time.

Adlung at this time used the
name "viola da spalla" as a
plain alternative for violoncello.

Michael del Agatha along with
the famous choreographer,
Sauveterre, founded the Opera
and Comedy Ballet at Stuttgart
this year.

Johann Lorenz Albrecht this
year became a teacher at the
grammar school as well as cantor and musical director at
the principal church at
Görmar.

Wilhelm Friedemann Bach applied
for a position at Frankfurt
this year.

Battishill became a member of
the Madrigal Society this year.

John Beals at this time advertised that he "plays on the
Violin at the Assembly Balls,
and teaches the Violin and
other Instruments".

John Beals still lived at
Philadelphia this year.

Carlo Bergonzi (a pupil of
Antonio Stradivarius) gave up
his lease to Stradivarius'
house at this time. The lease
started in 1746.

Boyce was appointed one of the
three organists of the Chapel
Royal this season.

1758(cont.)

Per Brandt this year succeeded
Roman as conductor of the
Royal Orchestra at Stockholm.

John Brown was vicar of St.
Nicholas, Newcastle this season.

Casanova went to Vienna from
Prague at this time. He brought
with him a letter of recommenda-
tion from Dresden librettist
Giovanni Ambrosio Migliavacca,
addressed to the librettist
Pietro Metastasio, imperial
Austrian poet laureate.

With Douglass as manager, the
London Company of Comedians
returned to New York this season.

Johann Gottfried Eckardt lived
in Paris from this date forward.

Charles Simon Favart succeeded
Jean Monnet this year as director of the Opéra Comique.

Marie Fel, French soprano, this
year was forced by health to
retire. She was given a pension
of 1500 livres by the Paris
Opéra.

Carlo Ferrari played the cello
in the Concert Spirituel at
Paris this season.

Filippo Finazzi, Italian male
soprano and composer, somehow
broke both his legs this year.

Karl Franz held his first
position this year under the
Archbishop of Olomouc.

Giulia Frasi appeared and sang
this season in G. Cocchi's
"Issipile".

Gluck conducted "La Fausse
Esclave" this season (the year

(cont.) before "La Fausse
"Aventuriere" at the St. Germain
theatre in France) with all
new vocal numbers.

Giovanni Guadagnini lived and
worked for a few months in
Cremona this year.

Johann Ulrick Haffner started
a music business this year
at Nürnberg and composed
six flute sonatas.

Catherine Hamilton (Barlow)
married the Hon. William
Hamilton this year.

Haydn worked this year on
"Der neue krumme Teufel",
music for a comedy, "Der
krumme Teufel".

At this time A Herbing was
assistant organist and vicar
of Magdeburg Cathedral and
one of the most gifted
revivers of German song.

Johann Hiller this year
accompanied a pupil to Leipzig
in the capacity of tutor. A
few years later he resigned
his position and lived indepen-
dently in Leipzig. There he
was actively working to promote
the revival of public concerts
given up during the Seven
Years' War.

Dr. Robert Hudson was appointed
a Gentleman of the Chapel
Royal this season.

Johann Christoph Kleen, Danish
18th century composer, had
by this date trained enough
Danish singers to produce
a whole season of Danish opera.

Samuel Lee was appointed musical director of Crow Street

1758(cont.)
Theatre this season.

Adrien Lépine this year established himself in Paris.

James Lyon at this time tried to improve and spread the art of psalmody throughout the American Colonies.

V. Manfredini, along with his brother Giuseppe (a castrato singer) went to Russia this year where he succeeded Raupach as court composer.

Gertrude Maria this season went with her father to Vienna to give some violin concerts.

Appended to Queen Maria Barbara's testament after her death this year was an inventory that listed a description of the keyboard instruments in her collection.

Angelo Morigi at this time was appointed 1st violin of the Prince of Parma's orchestra.

Rameau made further investments this year for his eldest son and younger daughter.

Johann Peter Salomon was engaged this year as a violinist in the orchestra of the Elector Clement August.

Jean Georges Siéber went to Paris this year.

At age 10 this year Maximilian Stadler, Austrian organist, clavecinist and composer, became a chorister at the Lilenfeld monastery where he studied music.

Johann Andreas Stein, pianoforte

(cont.) maker and musician, was in Paris this year and stayed there for several years.

Euler this year expounded on Tartini's "Trattato di musica" at the Berlin Academy of Science.

Giusto Ferdinando Tenducci, male soprano and composer, went to London this season.

Traetta was appointed opera composer at the Bourbon court in Parma this year.

The first burletta performed in the Marylebone Gardens was given this year. It was an adaption by Trusler, jr. and the older Storace of Pergolesi's "La serva padrona".

Pierre Vachen, the violinist and composer, played a concerto of his own at the Concert Spirituel this season.

A. M. G. Vestris danced at Stuttgart this year.

Thomas Vincent, jr. was a member of the King's band this year.

Franz von Weber this year became steward to the Prince-Bishop and court councillor at Steuerwald.

Georg Weimar this year became court cantor and chamber musician at Zerbst.

G. Wellesley succeeded his father at this time as Baron Mornington.

A. Wesstrom studied violin this year with Tartini at Padua.

I. Young sang in the "Messiah" at the Foundling Hospital this season.

J. Adlung's "Anleitung . . ." was published this year at Berlin, "et seg."

D'Alembert's "De la liberté de la musique" was published this year. It was a criticism of both French and Italian operas and a plea for the rejuvenation rather than the destruction of the former by some transfusions from the latter.

J. C. Bach wrote his "Te Deum" (T 210/2) this year.

Johann Ernst Bach's contributions on the preface to Jakob Adlung's "Anleitung zu der musikalischen Gelahrtheit" appeared this year.

W. F. Bach wrote his cantata "O Himmel, schone" (F 90) at this time.

Thomas Baildon contributed seven songs to "Clio and Euterpe", a collection published at this time.

Francisco Barbiere this year provided a valuable historical introduction to the "Crónica de la opera italiana en Madrid desde 1758", by L. Carmena y Millán.

Franz Beck's "Sei overture a piu stromenti", opus 1, was published this year.

T. Cahusac published "Twenty-four Country Dances for 1758" at this time.

V. L. Ciampi's opera "Arsinoe" (cont.) was performed this year at London.

V. L. Ciampi's opera "Arsinoe" was produced at the Teatro Regio in Turin this season.

G. Cocchi's "Zenobia" and "Issipile" appeared early this year.

Domenico Fischietti, in collaboration with Goldoni, wrote the opera "Il signore dottore" this year and it was produced at Venice.

William Flackton's (Flacton's) "Six Sonatas for two Violins and a Violencello or Harpsichord", opus #1, was published this year.

Ignaz Fränzl, Johann Toeschi and Christian Cannabich wrote the music for a pantomime to be performed at the Mannheim court this season.

Baldassare Galuppi this year wrote his opera "Ipermestra" at Milan (libretto by Metastasio).

Baldassare Galuppi this year wrote his opera "Il re pastore" at Milan (libretto by Metastasio).

Florian Gassmann's opera "Issipile" was given this season at Venice (libretto by Metastasio).

Twelve violin sonatas by Francesco Geminiani were published this year at London.

Paul César Gibert composed his opera "La Sibylle" at this time.

Gluck's opera "La Fausse Esclave" (libretto by Anseaume and Marcaville) was produced this season at Vienna.

André Grétry composed six small symphonies this year at Liège.

A new version of Hasse's opera "Demofoonte" appeared at this time.

Hasse's pasticcio, "Solimano", was produced this year at London.

A. Herbing composed his "Musicalische Belustigungen" this year.

Jommelli's opera "L'asilo d'amore" was heard this season at Stuttgart.

Jommelli's opera "Ezio" was produced in a new version at Stuttgart this season.

Giovanni Battista Lampugnani's operas "Il re pastore" and "Le cantatrici" were both produced this year at Milan.

Jean Louis Larvette, with Duni, wrote "Le Docteur Sangrado" this year. It was one of the "comédies mélées d'ariettes".

P. van Maldere's "VI Sonatas for 2 violins . . ." was published this year by Walsh in Catherine Street, Strand.

Marpurg's "Anleitung zur Singe-composition" was published at this time in Berlin.

Martinelli's "Lettre familiare e critiche" appeared this year.

F. Philidor's opera "Les

(cont.) Pèlerins de la Mecque" (libretto by Alain René Le Sage and d'Orneval) was produced at the Théâtre de la Foire Saint-Laurent this year at Paris. The original production was in 1726 with music arranged by Jean C. Giller. Philidor wrote new airs for this revival.

This year there was an unidentified private stage performance of a comic opera, "Le Procureur dupe", in which there was a burlesque edict, a caricature of the royal decree which had dismissed the Bouffons. Rameau was the composer according to the manuscript.

Giuseppe Scolari's opera "La conversazione" was produced this season at Venice.

"Ifigenia in Tauride" by Tommaso Traetta was produced in Parma this year.

Tommaso Traetta set Metastasio's "L'Olimpiade" this year and it was produced at Verona.

W. Walond I this year published his setting of Pope's "Ode on St. Cecelia's Day".

Zoppis' "Didone abbandonata" was performed in St. Petersburg this season.

Among the surviving harpsichords made by the Kirkman family were two made this year by J. Kirkman. One had 1 manual and 2x8', 1x4', 2 pedals. Its most recent owner was Miss Perugina Adler of New York. The other had 2 manuals (no further description) and was

1758(cont.)
last owned at Havering-at-Bower.

There were twenty-seven American editions of the Bay Psalm Book and at least twenty in England before the final printing of this year.

"Psalms, Hymns and Spiritual Songs . . ." (American tune collection) was published at Boston this year.

Carl Gottlob Cramer, author, was born this year (death date unknown).

August Julius Lafontaine, the most popular German novelist of the first part of the 19th century, was born this year (died 1831).

John Hoppner, English portraitist, was born this year (died 1810).

Pierre-Paul Prud'hon, French painter, was born this year (died 1823).

Wenzel Tobias Epstein, a man of Jewish descent known for his chess-playing and coin collecting, was granted the title "von Ankersberg" this year.

Prince Ernst August Constantin died (birthdate unknown).

(to 1759) Arne visited Dublin during this year.

(and 1759) Antonio Besozzi and his son, Carlo, played at the Stuttgart court orchestra under Jommelli during these two years.

(to 1759) G. Cocchi's "Attalo" and "Ciro riconosciuto" were both completed during this time.

(to 1759) Santo Lapis was in London at this time and had a book of cello solos, and a book of songs and duets published.

(to 1759) Fétis, in his "Biographie universelle des musiciens", mentioned Mondonville's oratorio as having been written at this time. Casanova said "A motet composed by Mondonville was being given (in the Tuileries). The text was by Abbé Voisenon, to whom I (Casanova) had supplied the theme".

(to 1759) In Germany at this time Mannheim led the way in clarinettists with Quallenberg, a Bohemian, Hampel and Tausch the elder as regular players.

(to 1760) Martini il Tedesco studied at Freiburg and played the organ at the Franciscan monastery there during these two years.

(and 1760 to 1762, 1763) It seems likely that the "Signor Arigoni" mentioned in concert advertisements at Dublin this year and between 1760 and 1762, and as conductor of an Italian intermezzo company at Edinburgh in 1763, was identical with Carlo Arrigoni, in which case he died much later than assumed by many earlier biographers.

(and 1760) J. Christian Bach (son of J. S.) composed a Magnificat for double chorus in C major and a Te Deum for double chorus in D this year. In 1760 he did another setting of the former canticle in C.

(and 1760) Hellendaal's opus 3

"Six Grand Concertos" was
published in 1758 in London and
a second edition was issued by
Johnson in 1760.

(to 1760, April) N. Porpora held
the position of "primo maestro
straordinario" at the Conservatorio di Santa Maria di Loreto
during this period.

(to 1760) Thomas Wright, sr.
was organist at Stockton Chruch
for these two years.

(to 1760) Samuel Johnson's
essays were published at this
time in the "Rambler" and the
"Idler" in England.

(to 1761) Franz Joseph Haydn
served as musical director and
chamber composer for Count
Ferdinand Maximilian Morzin
during this period.

(to 1761) Gluck produced six
new French operas during these
years.

(to 1766) "L'Écho, ou Journal
de musique française et
italienne" was published at
this time at Liege.

(to 1768) John Alcock, II was
organist of St. Mary Magdalen's,
Newark-on-Trent during this
period.

(to 1769) Charles John Frederick
Lampe was organist in the London
church of All Hallows at Barking
for these eleven years.

(to 1769) The following works
by V. Manfredini were performed
at St. Petersburg at this time:
"Semiramide", "L'Olimpiade" and
"Carlo Magno".

(to 1769) The reign of Pope
Clement XIII included these
years. He was born in Venice.

(and 1783) Adlung's "Anleitung
zur musikalischen Gelährtheit"
with a preface by Johann Ernst
Bach, was issued in 1758 at
Erfurt. A 2nd edition was
issued by J. A. Hiller in 1783
at Leipzig.

c.1758

Gottlieb Hayne, a fine organist,
died this year (born 1684).

Catherine Wild, wife of Burkat
Shudi, died this year (born
1704).

Karl Friedrich Baumgarten
settled in London at this time.

Hipkins stated in his "History
of the Piano" that the invention
of the square piano was attributed in Germany to C. E.
Friederici of Gera about this
year.

Handel's Overture in Bb major
for oboes, strings and continuo
was written at this time.

Kürzinger published his opus 1,
eight symphonies titled "David
et Apollo, iste profanus
Parnassi, is sacer coeli
uterque rex et jubilaris
archiphonaesis chori" this
year at Augsburg.

(to 1783) The Castle Society
Concerts were moved to the
King's Arms, Cornhill this
year, where they continued at
least until 1783.

1759

(January 1) F. X. Brixi was
choirmaster at St. Vitus Cathedral from this date forward.

1759(cont.)
He succeeded J. F. Novak.

(January 4) Maria Rosa Coccia,
Italian composer, was born on
this date at Rome (died 1833,
November at Rome).

(January 16) Calori sang in
Cocchi's "Ciro riconosciuto"
at this time.

(January 18) "Der lustige
Schuster" (from Charles Coffey's
"The Merry Cobbler") with music
by J. C. Standfuss, was produced
on this date as a sequel to
"Der Teufel ist los, oder Die
verwandelten Weiber" at Lübeck.

(January 19) Johann Jeremias
Du Grain, German composer (?)
of French origin, was buried
on this date at Danzig (birthdate unknown).

(January 29) Kleen this year
wrote "En musikalisk Prologus"
and several ballets and was
conductor and musical director
of the Danish"Sangspel" during
its early seasons.

(January 31) G. Cocchi's "Il
tempio della gloria" was produced on this day at the King's
Theatre.

(January 31) François Devienne,
French composer and flute and
bassoon virtuoso, was born on
this date at Joinville, Haute-
Marne (died 1803, September 5
at Charenton).

(February 7) G. F. Maio's first
opera, "Ricimero, re dei Goti"
was produced on this day at
Rome.

(February 7) Pierre Monsigny's
first opera, "Les Aveux indis-
cret", was produced this evening

(cont.) at the Théâtre de la
Foire Saint-Germaine at Paris.
The libretto was by La
Ribodière, taken from Lafon-
taine and the work was an
instant success.

(February 15) Arne wrote the
incidental music for "Cymbe-
line", performed on this date
at Covent Garden in London.

(February 27) Johann Karl
Friedrich Rellstab was born
on this day at Berlin. When
his father died, he was forced
to take up his printing
business. He later added a
music branch (died 1813,
August 19 at Berlin).

(March 2) Johann Christian
Friedrich Haeffner (Haffner),
Swedish organist, conductor
and composer of German origin,
was born on this date at
Oberschönau, Henneberg (died
1833, May 28 at Uppsala).

(March 5) Metastasio at this
time appealed to Farinelli to
help obtain a small pension
from the King of Spain for
N. Porpora.

(March 9) F. Philidor's opera
"Blaise le savetier" (libretto
by Sedaine, after Lafontaine)
was produced on this date at
the Teatre de la Foire, St.
Germain at Paris.

(March 17) A letter signed
"Marcellinus" appeared in the
"Newcastle Journal" on this
day stating that Avison had
refused the organist's
position at York Minster, and
also other appointments.

(March 28) Ignazio Maria Conti,
Italian composer, died on this
date at Vienna (born 1699 at

1759(cont.)
Florence).

(April 6) Jean Lebrun, French
horn player, was born on this
day at Lyons (died c.2809).

(April 3) Dom Bédos was elected
a member of the Academie des
Sciences of Bordeaux on this
date.

(April 5) Karl Friedrich Abel
gave his first concert on this
date at the "freat room in Dean
Street, Soho" at London. He
gave concerts in London with J.
Christian Bach (son of J. S.
Bach).

(April 21) Calori appeared in
Perez' "Farnace" on this date
at London.

(April 14) George Frideric
Handel (Händel), great English
(naturalized) composer of German birth, died at London on
this date (born 1685, February
23 at Halle). Handel is regarded by all as one of the
great masters of all times and
was a superb organist and
violinist as well.

(May 3) Benjamin Franklin on
this date attended a performance
of the "Messiah" at Foundling
Chapel, London, thirteen days
after the composer's death.

(May 3) Giulia Frasi sang in
the "Messiah" at the Foundling
Hospital this evening.

(May 9) Tommaso Traetta's
"Ippolito ed Aricia" (libretto
by Carlo Innocenzio Frugoni)
was produced on this date at
Parma. The text was a translation by Frugoni of Rameau's
work.

(May 15) Maria Theresia
Paradies, Austrian pianist,
singer and composer, was born
this day at Vienna (died 1824,
February 1 at Vienna).

(May 16) Jakob Scheller,
Bohemian violinist, was born
on this date at Schettal
(died 1803). He has been
described as a strange mixture
of genius and charlatanism and
did many musical "tricks".

(May 22) Gervais-François
Couperin, organist and composer,
was born on this day at Paris
(died 1826, March 11 at Paris).

(May 24) J. C. F. Bach's first
and only son, Wilhelm Friedrich
Ernst, was baptized on this day
at Bückeburg (died 1845,
December 25 at Berlin).
Another source gave 1759, May
27 as the birthdate, which
would negate this date of
baptism.

(May 26) A dirge and funeral
for Handel were performed in
the chapel of the Foundling
Hospital on this date. John
Christopher Smith directed it.

(May 27) Wilhelm Friedrich
Ernst Bach, later cembalist to
Queen Louisa of Prussia, was
born on this date according
to a conflicting source.

(June 19) Laurent François
Boutmy, harpsichord player,
organist and composer, was born
on this date at Brussels
(died 1838, November 3 at
Brussels).

(July 2) G. Cocchi's double
cantata, "La vera lode" and
"Il marito coronato", were
written for the installation

1759(cont.)

of John Fane, Seventh Earl of
Westmorland, as Chancellor of
Oxford University on this date.

(July 6) The University of
Oxford awarded the degree of
Doctor of Music to Arne on this
date.

(July 25) Johann Christoph
Altnikol was buried on this date.

(August 2) Heinrich Keverich,
Johann van Beethoven's father-
in-law, died on this day at
Molzberg (born 1701).

(August 7) Rameau wrote Beccari
on this day asking for criticism of his "Nouvelles reflexions . . .".

(August 8) Karl Heinrich
Graun, German tenor and composer,
died on this date at Berlin
(born 1704, May 7).

(August 10) Fernando, King of
Spain, died on this day.

(August 12) The Prussian army
was annihilated near Kunersdorf
at this time.

(September 6) Guillaume André
Villoteau, French writer on
music, was born on this date
at Bellême, Orne (died 1839,
April 27 at Tours).

(September 16) The Russian
opera-ballet, "Virtue's Refuge"
(with Raupach), ballet music by
Josef Starzer, was produced in
St. Petersburg on this date.

(September 17) F. Philidor's
opera "L'Huitre et les plai-
deurs ou Le Tribunal de la
chicane" (libretto by Sedaine)
was produced on this date at

(cont.) the Théâtre de la
Foire, St.-Laurent.

(Autumn) G. Scarlatti's opera,
"La serva scaltra", was produced at the Teatro San Moisè
in Venice at this time (author
of libretto unknown).

(September 24) E. R. Duni's
opera, "La Veuve indécise"
was produced at Paris on this
date in the Théâtre de la
Foire, Saint-Laurent.

(September 26) James Lyon,
a member of the class of '59
at Princeton, was awarded his
first degree in music at
commencement.

(September 27) The commencement of the previous day was
communicated to the "New York
Mercury".

(October 1) The "New York
Mercury" printed an account of
the commencement where James
Lyon had received his first
degree on September 26. Lyon
had set music to an ode for
the occasion.

(October 3) Gluck's opera,
"L'Arbre enchante ou Le
Tuteur dupe" (libretto by
Moline), was produced on this
evening. The story was taken
from Bocaccio.

(November 4) Hasse's opera,
"Achille in Sciro"(libretto
by Metastasio), was produced
at Naples on this date.

(November 4) "Ciro riconosciuto", an opera by N.
Piccinni (libretto by Metastasio), was heard at this time
at the Teatro San Carlo in
Naples.

1759(cont.)

(November 27) Franz Krommer,
Austrian violinist and composer
of Moravian origin, was born on
this date at Kamenice near
Třebíč (died 1831, January 8
at Vienna).

(November 29) The Pennsylvania
Gazette in this issue advertised, "Violin is taught in the
best and neatest taste according
to the new Italian Method by
the Subscriber, an Italian born
. . . Francis Alberti".

(December 1) Hawkesworth's
version of Southerne's tragedy
"Oroonoko", with songs by John
Stanley, was performed at the
Drury Lane Theatre in London on
this evening.

(December 4) Johann Sigmund
Gruber, German lawyer and
musicographer, was born on this
date at Nürnberg (died 1805,
December 3).

(December 5) The Pennsylvania
Journal in this issue stated
that "Vocal Music was taught in
the School House behind the
Revd Dr. Jenny's near the
Church . . ."

(December 6) The Pennsylvania
Journal in this issue advertised "teaching of Vocal Music
in School House" (Singing-School).

(December 9) The marriage certificate of Fernando Scarlatti
bore this date.

(December 27) Francis Hopkinson
may have played harpsichord in a
performance at a theatre on
Society Hill, as stated in the
Pennsylvania Gazette in this
issue.

(December 27) The Pennsylvania
Gazette in this issue advertised that business men began
to consider music a commercial
factor.

(December 31) Michael Arne's
"Harlequin's Invasion, or A
Xmas Gambol" was performed
on this date at the Drury Lane
Theatre in London.

(December 31) Boyce's
"Harlequin's Invasion, or A
Christmas Gambol" was heard
on this date at the Drury
Lane Theatre in London.

(February) Casanova this month
returned to Paris from the
Netherlands where he had
conducted financial transactions profitable to the French
government. He earned money
and furthered his reputation
by this move.

(March) André Gretry left
Liège this month and went to
Rome on foot. He was later
admitted to the Collège de
Liège at Rome.

(March) N. Porpora this month
was in Vienna in dire need
owing to the misfortunes of
Saxony in the Seven Year's War.

(July) Johann Christoph
Altnikol, German organist and
composer, died this month
at Naumburg (born 1719,
December at Berna, Silesia).

(July) Iso's "Fragments
héroiques" was produced this
month.

(August) The Ode in this issue
of New American Magazine filled
two pages and bore the signa-

MOZART AT THE AUSTRIAN COURT

ture of "Nassovian" under date of "E. Jersey . . ."

(September) James Lyon's ode, which he set to music, was performed at Commencement (Nassau Hall) in the College of New Jersey, or Princeton.

(September) The New American Magazine (Woodbridge, N. J.) in this issue contained an "original ode" entitled "Louisburg Taken".

(September) Josef Starzer's Russian prologue, "The New Laurels" (with Raupach), was produced in St. Petersburg either this month or in 1764.

(November) Charles Dibdin remained in the choir at Winchester Cathedral until this time.

Johann Christoph Altnikol, a pupil of J. S. Bach, died this year (birthdate unknown).

Wilhelm Friedrich Ernst Bach, son of J. C. F. Bach and member of the seventh generation of the Bach family, was born at this time (died 1845).

A second daughter was born this year to Cornelius van Beethoven and Anna Barbara Marx.

Herman Christian Benda, German violinist, was born this year (died 1805).

Johann Friedrich Braun, German oboist, was born this year (died 1824).

Othon Joseph van den Broeck, Flemish horn player and composer, was born this year at Ypres (died 1832, October 18 at Passy near Paris).

Jan Ciecilowicz, Polish conductor, died this year at Nieświez (birthdate unknown).

Joseph Čzerwenka (Cervenka), Bohemian oboist, was born this year at Benadek, Bohemia (died 1835, at Vienna).

Salomea Deszner (Teschner), Polish actress and singer, was born at this time at Bialystok (died 1809 at Grodno).

Charles Duquesnoy, Netherlands tenor and composer, was born this year at Beuzet in the province of Namur (died 1822, May 9 at Brussels).

François Joseph Garnier, oboist who wrote a "Méthode", was born this year (died 1825).

Simon Gaveaux, French musician and brother of Pierre, was born at this time at Béziers (death date unknown).

Giuseppe Gherardeschi, Italian composer, was born this year at Pistoia (died 1815).

Gluck's niece, Marianne Hedler, was born at this time (death date unknown).

Alexander M'Glashan, Scottish violinist, was born this year (died 1797).

Richard Pockrich, Irish amateur musician, died this year at London in a fire at the Royal Exchange (born c.1690 at Derrylusk, County Monaghan, Ireland).

Friedrich Rellstab, who wrote critiques and articles on music, was born this year (died 1813).

Catalan composer and organist,
Felipe Rodriquez, was born this
year (death date unknown).

Luis Serra, Spanish oratorio
composer, died this year (death
date unknown).

Franz Stanislaus Spindler,
German composer and singer, was
born this year at Steingaden,
Bavaria (died 1819, September
8 at Strasbourg).

Ignaz Walter, Austro-Bohemian
tenor and composer, was born
this year at Radovice, Bohemia
(died 1822, April at Ratisbon).

Agricola this year succeeded
to the directorship of the Royal
Chapel of Frederick the Great
of Prussia on the death of
Graun.

John Beard this year married
Charlotte, daughter of John
Rich, proprietor of Covent
Garden Theatre.

Berezovsky sang the part of
"Poro" in Araia's "Alessandro
nell'Indie" this season. He
was only a boy of fourteen at
the time.

Jean-Baptiste Joseph Boutmy
visited Paris this year.

Pascal Boyer succeeded Gauzargues
as chapel master at Nîmes Cathedral at this time and stayed
there for six years.

Robert Bremner this year moved
his music business to another
shop in the High Street.

Buroni this year procured
lessons for Muzio Clementi in
thorough-bass from an organist,

(cont.) Cordicelli.

Cafaro became "secondo
maestro" at the Conservatorio
della Pietà de'Turchini at
Naples this year. He had
attended the Conservatory as
a student.

When Prince von Hildburghausen
dismissed his orchestra this
year, he procured a place for
Ditters in the empress' Opera.

A Company, headed by Mr.
Douglass, arrived at New York
in the Autumn (1758) and, after
performing there, it moved
to Philadelphia in the Spring
of this year.

Durazzo approached one of the
directors of the Parisian
Opéra-Comique this year with
the intention of creating a
purified, elevated type of
comic opera.

Paul Anton Esterházy at this
time had a detailed catalogue
of manuscript scores he had
collected in Italy and Germany
made by the violinist Champee.

At this point Charles III
became the ruler of Spain
and Farinelli was ordered
to leave the kingdom.

William Forster, English
maker of spinning-wheels and
violins, went to London as a
cattle-drover this year.

Karl Friebert was engaged as
a singer by Prince Esterházy
this season.

Caterina Gabrielli sang the
leading role in Gluck's
"Ippolito ed Aricia" this
season.

1759(cont.)

Francesco Geminiani moved from London to Ireland this year.

"Le Diable à quatre" was conducted by Gluck this year.

Friedrich Graf went to Hamburg this season as a flute virtuoso.

Karl Heinrich Graun, who died this year, was in Frederick the Great's service for a long period.

J.-N. Hamal became a canon of the Church of St. Giles at this time.

Sir John Hawkins came into a legacy this year and bought a house at Twickenham. Here he had Horace Walpole, Garrick, Kitty Clive, poet Paul Whitehead and other interesting people as neighbors.

F. J. Haydn left Vienna this year.

F. J. Haydn this year took charge of music at the court of Count Ferdinand Maximilian Morzin in Lukaveč, near Pilseň. The Count had a small private orchestra at Lucaveč near Plzeň. Karl Joseph von Fürnberg recommended Haydn.

Karl Hoeckh became Kapellmeister at the court at Zerbst this season.

Arvid Höpken became a Colonel in the Queen's life-guards in Pomerania this year.

Francis Hopkinson became Secretary of the "Library Company" at this time.

Francis Hopkinson's undated

(cont.) collection of "Songs" was started this year.

W. C. Hulett taught violin and dancing in New York at this time.

Pierre de Jélyotte asked to retire at this time but when offered the sum of 48,000 livres, he remained.

James Lyon had perhaps mastered the rudiments of music prior to this date.

James Lyon moved to Philadelphia either early in 1760 or shortly after graduation this year. In the latter case he may have been the founder of one of the Singing Schools.

Joseph Mahoon's name this year appeared in Rider's "Court Register" as a harpsichord maker to the King.

Pierre Alexandre Monsigny made his debut this year, probably at Paris.

Eberlin contributed five pieces to Leopold Mozart's collection for the "Hornwerk" at Hohen-Salzburg, "Der Morgen und der Abend", published by Lotter this year.

François André Philidor made his debut this year, probably at Paris.

Joseph Raoux, a member of the Raoux family famous for making excellent French horns, had his name appear in "Le Tableau de Paris" this year as a professor of the horn. His birth and death dates are unknown but he died at Paris.

Rameau this year submitted to the "Accademia delle Scienze dell'Instituto di Bologna" a manuscript entitled "Nouvelle réflexions sur le principe sonore".

At an auction of N. Seelhof at The Hague this year, two harpsichords by "P. E. Johannes Couchet, Antverpiae" were mentioned, one dated 1662.

Josef Starzer this season followed the choreographer Franz Hilferding to the Russian court in St. Petersburg where he remained for ten years.

Neil Stewart, Scottish music publisher, was at the sign of the "Violin and German Flute" in the Exchange at Edinboro this year.

Carlo Giuseppe Toeschi this season became conductor of the Mannheim orchestra.

At the end of this year composer Tommaso Traetta accepted the appointment of maestro di cappella and teacher of singing to the princesses, offered by Don Felipe, Infante of Spain and Duke of Parma.

Christian Felix Weisse visited Paris at this time.

Garrett Wellesley this year married the Honorable Anne Hill Trevor.

John Worgan this year wrote an anthem for a Thanksgiving for victories.

Edward Young this year showed in his "Conjectures on Original Composition" that men of genius (cont.) created not by the intellect but with the aid of divine inspiration.

John Arnold's "The Leicestershire Harmony" was issued in its first edition this year at London.

Johann Caspar Bachofen's "Passion" (by Brockes) appeared at this time.

Battishill's earliest contribution to the stage was a song he wrote for the Rev. James Townley's farce, "High Life below Stairs", produced this season at the Drury Lane Theatre in London.

A collection of Benoît Blaise's songs appeared this year in three books.

Bremner's "Collection of Scot's Reels" was issued at this time.

Bremner published his "Curious Collection of Scot's Tunes" this year.

Giuseppe Brunetti wrote an opera, "Didone abbandonata", this year for Siena.

Two airs by one Brunetti contained in the London pasticcio, "Vologeso", may be either by Giuseppe Brunetti or by Giovanni Gualberto Brunetti.

Burney this year set to music for Ranelagh, Bonnell Thornton's humerous "Ode on St. Cecilia's Day", announced as being adapted to "Ancient British Music".

Burney's "Six Sonatas for Two Violins and a Bass" were completed this year.

Errichelli's opera "Siroe" appeared this season.

Bartolommeo Felici's oratorio, "La notte prodigiosa", was published in Bologna at this time.

William Felton published his last volume of eight keyboard concertos, op. 7 this year at London.

One of Fedele Fenaroli's two operas, "I due Sediarii", was produced this season at Naples.

Ignazio Fiorillo this year wrote a "comische opera pantomima" called "Die Begebenheiten des Arlequins in dem Harz Gebürge".

François Francoeur's opera "Pirame et Thisbé" was revived for the second time this season at Paris.

Baldassare Galuppi wrote his opera "Melite riconosciuta" this year at Rome (libretto by Roccaforte).

Baldassare Galuppi wrote his opera "La ritornata di Londra" this year at Rome (libretto by Goldoni).

Florian Gassmann's opera "Li uccellatori" was given this season at Venice (libretto by Goldoni).

A volume of musical settings of texts by Gellert was published this year.

Paul César Gibert composed his opera, "Le Carnaval d'été", this year.

Gluck set Charles Simon Favart's "Cythère assiégée" to music and it was produced this season at Schwetzingen near Mannheim. Gluck conducted this performance and also one at Vienna. He contributed 26 new vocal selections to the work.

Gluck's opera, "Le Diable à quatre" (libretto by Jean Michel Sedaine), was produced at Laxenburg this season.

Gossec published his first string quartets at this time.

André Grétry wrote a "Messe solennelle" for four voices this year.

Handel's "Messiah" was first given in the cathedral at Hereford this year. This marked the beginning of oratorio performances in the cathedral. Clack, the organist at Hereford, conducted.

Haydn's first symphony was written this year. It had 3 movements and was scored for 2 oboes, 2 horns and strings in D major. Haydn was at Lukavec at the time, employed by Count von Morzin.

A. Herbing's "Musicalische Versuche an Febeln und Er-zählungen" was published this year by Gellert.

Holzbauer's Italian opera "Alessandro nell'Indie" was performed this season at Milan.

Holzbauer's Italian opera Ippolito ed Aricia" was performed this season at Mannheim.

Francis Hopkinson's manuscript collection of this year con-

tained the 23rd Psalm on page
179.

Francis Hopkinson's "Earliest
composition of his 'extant'
and on record, a pastoral song,
cannot be dated earlier".

The two earliest recorded
compositions of Hopkinson and
Lyon were written this year,
one with great probability,
the other with certainty.

Francis Hopkinson's "Book of
Songs" was dated "Philadelphia,
Domini 1759". Page 63 of the
collection was definitely
written this year.

Francis Hopkinson wrote his
first song, "My Days Have Been
So Wondrous Free", at this time.
It was the first known secular
composition by a native American.

Jommelli's opera "Nitteti"
was produced this season at
Stuttgart.

Giovanni Battista Lampugnani's
opera "Il conte Chicchera" was
produced this season at Milan.

Jean Louis Larvette at this time
wrote two of the comédies
"Mêlées d'ariettes", "Cendrillon"
and "L'Yvrogne corrigé".

Coffey's "The Merry Cobler"
was heard this year at Lubeck.

James Lyon this year set an
"Ode on Peace" to music for
commencement exercises.

P. van Maldere's "Six Symphonies
pour 2 violons altos, basse,
2 hautb. et 2 cors" was released
this year at Brussels.

Marpurg's "Kritische Einleitung
in die Geschichte der . . .
Musik" was published this
year at Berlin.

For the Academy of Ancient
Music Cooke this year added
choruses and accompaniments
to Pergolesi's "Stabat Mater".

An oratorio, "Le Passage de la
mer Rouge", by Luis Persius'
father appeared this year.

N. Piccinni's opera "Siroe"
(libretto by Metastasio) was
produced this season at Naples.

"Platée" had its last performance in the 18th century
this year.

"Demetrio", an opera by
Giuseppe Ponzo, was produced
this year at Genoa during the
carnival season.

Porpora's Latin oratorio,
"Israel ab Aegyptiis liberatus",
was performed this season at
the Ospedale degli Incurabile
in Venice.

Publications of the "Vollstaen-
diger Marburger Gesangbuch"
by Christopher Saur, Germantown, and the "Liturgische
Gesaenge der Bruder Gemeinen"
by H. Miller, were issued this
year at Philadelphia (Warrington).

The second edition of Robert
Smith's "Harmonies, or The
Philosophy of Musical Sounds"
was published this year.

The "singspiel" with music by
J. C. Standfuss, "Der stolze
Bauer Jochen Tröbs", was given
this season at Hamburg.

1759(cont.)

Tommaso Traetta's "Demofoonte" (libretto by Metastasio) was produced this season at Pesaro.

At this year's carnival at Parma Tommaso Traetta's "Solimano" was produced.

Henry Waylett published "Minuets for the year 1759".

On Robert Smith's organ at the Chapel of Trinity College, Cambridge, the pitch had been lowered to that of Roman pitch-pipes made about 1720; A=395 c.p.s. S=1'l.

Two horns were added this year to the permanent personnel of the Opéra orchestra at Paris.

According to Rockstro this year's London orchestra of Handel was comprised of 12 violins (1st and 2nd), 3 violas, 3 cellos, 2 double basses, 0 flutes, 4 oboes, 0 clarinets, 4 bassoons, 2 horns, 2 trumpets, 0 trombones, 1 timpani.

The Teatro Nuovo was founded this year in competition with that of the Obizzi at Padua.

This year marked the appearance of the Orpheus Club of the College, and the witnessing of the third attempt at opera in Philadelphia.

This year marked the birth of Robert Burns, poet and hero of Scotland. He had very little schooling and until his late twenties was a farm laborer who wrote poetry in his free time. After his first poetic successes he went to Edinboro and joined the literary society of the Scottish capitol. Later he be-

(cont.) came a farmer and held a job as an exciseman as well. This life discouraged him, however, and he died unhappy at only 37 years of age (died 1796).

Friedrich Schiller, German poet and dramatist, was born this year (died 1805).

Francesco Gianni, Roman poet and extemporizer, was born this year. His revolutionary sympathies made him "persona non grata" in his native city. He came to Genoa in 1795 and in 1800 went to Paris, where Napoleon gave him a title and an annual salary of 6,000 francs (died 1822).

The treatise "Briefe die neueste Litteratur betreffend" was published this year and was a great success in Germany.

Everyone at this time was sure that "Brave Wolfe" was in-spired by the capture of Quebec.

President Davies this year composed his "Odes of 1759" (correctly 1760), one on Science and the other on Peace.

Samuel Johnson's philosophical romance, "Rasselas", appeared this year in England.

Thomas Gainsborough, the Eng-lish painter, moved to Bath at this time.

G. F. Bach this year painted a triple portrait of the Duchess Philippina Elisabeth Caesar of Saxe-Meiningen, her daughter and a lady-in-waiting.

Wolfe ascended the "Heights of

1759(cont.)
Abraham" and captured Quebec
this year, thus ending French
rule in Canada.

(and 1760) Frederick the Great
beseiged the Saxon capital
both these years.

(to 1760) Francis Hopkinson's
collection of songs in his book
began and ended during these
two years.

(to 1760) Samuel Webbe at this
time published "Mr. B.'s yearly
subscription of new music, to
be deliver'd monthly".

(to 1761) Araia returned to
Italy from Russia during this
period.

(to 1762) K. P. E. Bach wrote
a treatise on harpsichord
playing during these years
at Berlin.

(to 1763) "Kritische Briefe
über die Tonkunst", edited by
F. W. Marpurg, was published
during this period at Berlin.

(to 1765) Martin Gerbert von
Hornau, musical historian,
travelled through Germany,
France and Italy during these
years, establishing relations
with various learned societies.

(to 1767) Sterne wrote his
great novel, "Tristam Shandy",
during this period.

(to 1771) Giovanni Guadagnini
made his violins at Parma at
this time.

(to 1789) Robert Bremner had
moved to a shop higher up the
High Street "at the back of the
Cross Well" or "opposite Cross

(cont.) Well" during these
years, where he remained
until 1789.

(to 1788) The reign of Charles
III of Spain encompassed these
years.

(to 1790) Hiller cultivated
the lied ("Lieder mit Melodien
an meinen Kanarienvogel",
"Letztes Opfer in einigen
Lieder Melodien") for this
long period of years.

c.1759
Andrew Ashe, Irish flutist,
was born this year at
Lisburn (died 1838 at Dublin).

Johann Conrad Schlick, German
cellist and composer, was born
at this time in Münster (died
1825).

Richard Vincent, jr. married
Isabella Burchell this year.

(to 1760) During this period
Haydn composed a "Divertimento
a sei" for 2 violins, 2 horns,
English horn and bassoon, and
a Symphony in D major. The
form of the latter is quite
similar to that of the Bb
major Symphony (Op. 1, #5)
though the treatment is more
mature.

(to 1767) Isabella Vincent
sang as Mrs. Vincent during
these years.

1760
(January 1) Hyper-religious
people vigorously opposed
Douglass and his company and
a bill was passed forbidding
the erection of play-houses or
the acting of plays in Pennsylvania after this date.

(January 10) J. Zumsteeg, German conductor and composer, was born on this date at Baden (died 1802, January 27).

(January 13) Jacques-Georges Cousineau, French harp maker and harpist, was born on this day at Paris (died 1824 at Paris).

(January 15) Calori sang in Cocchi's "Clemenza de Tito" this evening at London.

(January 17) G. Scarlatti's opera "La clemenza di Tito" was produced on this date at the Teatro San Benedetto in Venice (libretto by Metastasio).

(January 18) William Shrubsole, English organist, was born on this date at Canterbury (died 1806, January 18).

(January 20) N. Logroscino's "Il natale d'Achille" was produced on this evening.

(January 24) Arne wrote incidental music for "The Desert Island" performed on this date at Drury Lane Theatre in London.

(January 24) Lavinia Fenton, English singer and actress, died this day in Greenwich (born 1708).

(January 25) Louis Alexandre Clicquot, French organ builder, died on this date at Paris (birthdate unknown).

(January 21) Fernando Scarlatti, member of the fourth generation of the Scarlatti family, married Maria Lorena de Robles at this time.

(February 3) Lavinia Fenton was buried in Greenwich Church on this date.

(February 6) "La Cecchina, ossia La buona figliuola", an opera by N. Piccinni (libretto by Carlo Goldoni based on Samuel Richardson's "Pamela") was produced on this date at the Teatro delle Dame at Rome.

(February 6) Maria A. Walpurgis' opera "Talestri, regina delle Amazoni" (libretto by herself) was given this evening at the castle of Nymphenburg near Munich.

(February 7) P. A. Monsigny's opera "Le Maître en droit" (Pierre René Lemonnier) was produced at Paris at the Théâtre de la Foire Saint-Germaine on this date.

(February 11) Nicolo Jommelli's opera "Alessandro nelle Indie" was first performed on this date in celebration of Duke Charles Eugene's birthday. The performance was at Stuttgart.

(February 12) Jan Ladislav Dussek, Bohemian pianist and composer, was born on this day at Cáslav, Bohemia (died 1812, March 20 at Saint-Germain-en-Laye).

(February 12) Rameau's "Les Paladins", a comedie lyrique, was produced on this date at Paris (the text was by Mounticourt).

(February 14) François Colin de Blamont, French composer, died on this date at Versailles (born 1690, November 22 at Versailles).

(February 14) "Il re pastore"
by Frederick II, Quantz, Graun
and Nichelmann, was given this
evening at the Great Room in
Soho, London.

(February 15) Jean François
Lesueur, French composer, was
born on this date at Drucat-
Plessiel near Abbeville (died
1837, October 6).

(February 18) Ignacio Antonio
de Almeida, Portuguese ecclesiastic and composer, was born
this day at Guimarães (died
1825, October 25 at Pedro de
Penedono).

(February 19) Katharina Cava-
lieri, Austrian soprano, was
born on this day at Währing
near Vienna (died 1801, June
30 at Vienna).

(February 27) Anna Magdalena
Wülken, youngest daughter of
Johann Caspar Wülken (court
trumpeter at Weissenfels),
court singer at Cöthen and
second wife of J. S. Bach,
died (born 1701). She died
an almswoman.

(March 5 to April 2) Casanova
was in Stuttgart during this
period.

(March 5) Tartini on this date
wrote a letter to Signora
Maddalena Lombardini and gave her
a recommendation for the "car-
riage of the left hand". There
were also instructions on bowing
and fingering in the letter and
he said, "trills of different
speeds must be practiced. The
same shake will not serve with
equal propriety for a slow movement as for a quick one". One
source called the addressee

(cont.) "Maddalena Sirmen" but
it is assumed here that this
is an error and that the
recipient mentioned above is
the correct one.

(March 6) F. A. Philidor's
"Le Quiproquo, ou Le Volage
fixe" (libretto by Mouston
after Lafontaine) was produced on this date at the
Comédie-Italienne at Paris.

(March 12) John Stanley's
"Zimri" was performed at
Covent Garden in London on
this date.

(March 13) Calori sang in
Jommelli's "L'isola disabitata"
this evening at London.

(March 14) Anton Filtz, German
cellist and composer, was
buried on this date at Mannheim.

(March 20) During the month
preceding this date, Rameau's
"Les Paladins" was performed.
It was a failure and was
criticized by all.

(March 27) Marie Jean Augustin
Vestris, natural son of
Gaetano Vestris and a ballet
dancer, was born on this date
at Paris (died 1842, December
5 at Paris).

(April 9) Louis Alexandre
Frichot, a French instrument
inventor, was born on this
date at Versailles (died 1825,
April 9).

(April 12) Ernst Theophil
(Gottlieb) Baron, German
lutenist and composer, died
on this date at Berlin (born
1696, February 17 at Breslau).

(April 12) Franz Bühler

(Biehler), German organist and composer, was born at this time at Schneidheim (died 1824, February 4 at Augsburg).

(April 23) Cervetto the Younger appeared this evening at a concert given at the Little Theatre in the Haymarket at London.

(April 24) The Pennsylvania Journal in this issue stated "Besides the Youth that are to receive their Bachelors Degree as usual, the Class that obtained their first Degree of the Institution in May, 1757, being now of standing for their Master's Degree, will receive the same".

(May 1) On this day Francis Hopkinson's "Anthem from the 114th Psalm" was sung and played (at least for the 1st time) in College Hall (commencement). An ode by Lyons was sung at the same exercises.

(May 8) James Lyons' proposals for printing by subscription, "Urania" were dated on this date (Philadelphia) and appeared in the Pennsylvania Journal on May 15.

(May 8) Pennsylvania Journal and Gazette: "Conditions" for "Proposals for Printing by Subscription" was dated (Philadelphia) as above.

(May 10) Christoph Graupner, German composer, died on this date at Darmstadt (born 1683, January 13).

(May 15) The "Pennsylvania Gazette" on this date mentioned F. Hopkinson's playing of the organ at Commencement.

(May 15) The Pennsylvania Journal's proposals for printing "Lyon's psalm-tune collection'Urania'" by subscription first appeared in this issue.

(May 17) Baron Johann Friedrich Hugo von Dalberg, German amateur composer, was born on this day at Herrnsheim near Worms (died 1812, July 26 at Herrnsheim).

(May 22) The "Pennsylvania Journal" and "Pennsylvania Gazette's" "Proposals for Printing by Subscription A Choice Collection of Psalms Tunes and Anthems . . ." with a prefix by James Lyon appeared in this issue.

(May 22) Traetta's opera "Buovo d'Antona" was first performed abroad on this date at Barcelona.

(May 28) Paul de Villesavoye, French composer, died on this day at Strasbourg (born 1683 at Paris).

(May 30) Porpora's opera "Il trionfo di Camilla" (second version) was performed this evening at the Teatro San Carlo in Naples.

(May 31) Calori sang in Cocchi's "Erginda" this evening at London.

(June 2) Carvalho left Lisbon on this date.

(June 10) A receipt by Margarita Rossetti Gentili for a loan from Fernando Scarlatti carried this date.

(Spring) Cecilia Grassi sang the role of "Sabina" in Galuppi's "Adriano in Siria" at the Tea-

1760(cont.)
tro di San Salvatore in Venice
at this time.

(June 25-December 28) Douglass
erected a wooden theatre on
"Society Hill" and gave a series
of performances during this
period.

(June 30) Teresa Albuzzi-
Todeschini, Italian contralto,
on this date died at Prague
(born 1723, December 26 at
Milan).

(July 10) Durán's "Antigono",
a setting of Metastasio's
libretto, was performed at
Barcelona on this date.

(July 13) The new King, Charles
III, on this date made his
triumphal entry into Madrid.

(July 24) In the "Pennsylvania
Journal" of this date, James
Lyons advertised that "with less
than 200 subscriptions, the said
Tunes would be printed".

(August 1) The "Pennsylvania
Journal" and "Gazette" mentioned
conditions ". . . if that
Number of Subscribers (400)
cannot be found, . . . the
money shall be returned . . ."
by August 1st.

(August 1) Tommaso Scarlatti,
a tenor and a member of the
second generation of the Scarlatti family, died (born between
1669-1672). He was Alessandro's
younger brother.

(August 12) Nikolaus Ephraim
Bach, organist, son of Jakob,
grandson of Wendel and a member
of the fifth generation of the
Bach family (died (born 1690).
He was organist to the Abbess

(cont.) Elizabeth of
Gandersheim.

(August 12) Annibale Pio
Fabri, Italian tenor and com-
poser, died on this day at
Lisbon (born 1697).

(August 14) F. A. Philidor's
opera "Le Soldat magicien"
(libretto by Anseaume) was
performed on this date at the
Téâtro de la Foire Saint-
Laurent in Paris.

(August 14) In the "Pennsylvania Gazette" this issue
James Lyons advertised that
with less than 200 subscriptions, the said Tunes would
be printed.

(August 19) Angelo Tarchi,
composer, was born on this day
at Naples (died 1814, August
19 at Paris).

(August 24) The company under
Mr. Douglass performed the
"Beggar's Opera" on this
evening.

(September 2) The bill opposing
Mr. Douglass and his Company
was set aside on this day by
the King in Council.

(September 8) Samuel Harrison,
English tenor, was born on
this date at Belper, Derbyshire (died 1812, June 25 at
London).

(September 14) Johann Brandl,
German violinist, pianist,
conductor and composer, was
born on this date at Rohr near
Ratisbon (died 1837, May 25
at Karlsruhe).

(September 14) (Maria) Luigi
(Carlo Zenobio Salvatore)

FARINELLI (CARLO BROSCHI),
1705-1782

1760(cont.)

Cherubini, Italian composer, was born on this day at Florence (died 1842, March 15 at Paris). On the house on the Via Fiesole there is a placque commemorating the event.

(September 15) Cherubini was baptised on this date at the Basilica of Saint John the Baptist in Florence.

(Autumn) "Il re pastore", an opera by N. Piccini (libretto by Metastasio) was performed on this date at the Teatro della Pergole in Florence.

(Autumn) G. Scarlatti's opera "Issipile" was produced on this date at the Burg Theatre in Vienna (libretto by Metastasio).

(September 23) Isabella Vincent sang in "The Beggar's Opera" at Drury Lane Theatre in London this evening.

(September 25) At Princeton's Nassau Hall, the anniversary Commencement of the College of New Jersey was held on this date.

(October 2) The "Pennsylvania Journal" in this issue printed an account of the September 25th anniversary commencement of the College of New Jersey.

(October 5) Campioni's dramatic cantata "Venere placata" was produced on this date for the wedding of the Archduke Joseph and Isabella of Bourbon at Leghorn.

(October 8) Caterina Gabrielli sang in a production of "Tetide" this evening.

(October 8) Gluck's Italian opera "Tetide" (libretto by Gianambrosio Migliavacca) was produced on this date at the court in Vienna.

(October 23) This issue of the "Pennsylvania Journal" advertised, "Notice is hereby given that the Singing-School, lately Kept in the Rooms over Mr. William's School in Second street, will again be opened on . . . the 3rd of November next . . ."

(November 5) Petrus Hellendaal was appointed organist at St. Margaret's Chruch at King Lynn on this date. He succeeded Burney.

(November 6) Pierre Gaviniès' comic opera "Le Prétendu" was given this evening at the Comédie-Italienne in Paris.

(November 9) Henri Philippe Gérard, Belfian singer, violinist, pianist, teacher and composer, was born on this day at Liège (died 1848, September 11).

(November 17) The masque "The Tears and Triumphs of Parnassus" with songs by John Stanley was performed on this date at the Drury Lane Theatre in London.

(November 22) Calori sang in Galuppi's "Il mondo alla luna" this evening at London.

(November 26) F. J. Haydn married Maria Anna Aloysia Apollonia Keller, Therese's older sister on this date. She was far less attractive than Therese and she and Haydn had a very poor marriage.

(November 28) Arne's "Thomas and Sally" was produced this evening at Covent Garden Theatre in London. It was also called the "Sailor's Return" and the libretto was by Isaac Bickerstaffe.

(December 2) Joseph Graetz, German pianist, theorist and composer, was born on this date in Bavaria (died 1826, July 17).

(December 11) Johanna Helena Averdank, singer and pupil of Johann van Beethoven, was born at this time at Bonn (died 1789, August 13).

(December 27) The last performance for the benefit of the Pennsylvania Hospital was given by the Company under Douglass on this date.

(December 27) In this issue of the Pennsylvania "Gazette" was advertised, ". . . raising of a Fund for purchasing an Organ to the College Hall . . . and instructing the Charity Children in Psalmody" by benefit concert at Pennsylvania Hospital".

(December 29) E. R. Duni's opera "L'Isle des foux" was produced at the Comédie-Italienne in Paris on this evening.

(December 30) Boyce's "The Conscious Lovers" included one song written for the revival at Drury Lane Theatre in London on this date.

(March) Anton Filtz, German cellist and composer, died this month at Mannheim (born c.1730).

(March or May) Josef Starzer's ballet "La Victoire de Flore sur Borée" was produced in St. Petersburg during this month.

(April) Gluck's opera "L'Ivrogne corrigé" (libretto by Anseaume) was produced at the Burg Theatre this month at Vienna. Gluck conducted the work, which was taken from Lafontaine's fable "The Drunkard in Hell".

(April) Tommaso Traetta's opera "I Tintaridi" (libretto by Frugoni) was produced this month at Parma.

(May) François Joseph Gossec's "Messe des morts" was first performed this month.

(May) James Lyons lived in Philadelphia this month after his graduation.

(July) Francis Ireland at this time was appointed lecturer in chemistry at Trinity College, Dublin.

(August) Henry Needler, English violinist, died this month at London (born 1685 at London).

(September to 1761, September) On the resignation of Abos at the end of September 1760, N. Porpora became maestro of the Conservatorio di Sant' Onofrio at Naples again and remained there a year.

(October) Girolamo Abos, Maltese composer of Spanish descent, died this month at Naples (born 1715, November 16 at Valetta).

(October) The first setting of

Metastasio's libretto to "Alcide al bivio" was by Hasse and was performed on this date at Vienna (see also Paisiello and Righini).

(December) An Italian opera "Siroe" (libretto by Metastasio with Raupach) with Josef Starzer's ballet music, was produced in St. Petersburg this month.

Teresa Bocciardo, Italian mother of Niccolò Paganini, was born this year at Genoa (death date unknown).

Prospero Castrucci, director of the Castle Society Concerts and a violinist, died at this time, probably in London (birthdate unknown but probably at Rome).

Lucius Chapin, singing master, was born this year at Springfield, Massachusetts (died 1842).

César Francois Nicolas Clérambault, French organist and composer, died this year at Paris (born c.1700 at Paris).

Louis Hippolyte Cornette, an organist of the Cathedral of Amiens, was born this year (died 1832).

Johann Georg Distler, Austrian violinist and composer, was born this year at Vienna (died 1798 at Vienna).

Franz Gleissner, German composer, was born this year at Neustadt-on-Waldnab, Bavaria (died after 1815).

Johann Bernhard Hummel, German pianist and composer, an ex-

(cont.) cellent performer who composed pianoforte sonatas. songs, etc. and wrote a book on "Modulation", was born this year at Berlin (birthdate unknown but at Berlin).

Franz (Joseph) Otter, German violinist and composer, was born this year (or 1764) in Bavaria (died 1836, September 1).

Anna Perroni, Italian singer of French parentage, died after this year (born c.1690 at Modena).

The youngest of Claude Rameau's children was born this year and was 44 years younger than his eldest brother.

Claude Joseph Rouget de l'Isle, who wrote "Le Marseillaise", was born this year (died 1836).

Bernard Václav Stiastný, Czech violoncellist, was born this year at Prague (died 1835 at Prague).

John Weaver, English dancing-master, died this year (born 1673 at Shrewsbury).

Aloysia Weber, singer, was born this year in Zell, Baden. She was Mozart's first love (died 1839).

Many of Vincenzo Albrici's works were probably destroyed during the bombardment of Dresden this year.

Alcock resigned appointments of both organist and master of the choristers of Lichfield this year and retained only that of lay-vicar.

Arne was able to use clarinets
for "Thomas and Sally" by this
date.

Apparently as a consequence of
a difference with Garrick,
Arne transferred his services
this year to Covent Garden
Theatre.

William Ayrton was the son of a
barber-surgeon of Ripon who was
magistrate of the borough and
this year became Mayor.

J. Christian Bach (son of J. S.)
became organist at Milan Cathedral this year.

J. Christian Bach (son of J. S.)
was employed at Reggio and
Parma this year to hear singers
engaged for the opera at Turin.

Claude Balbastre, who studied
under Rameau this year, was the
organist at a number of churches
in Paris.

When Baretti visited Mafra this
year, he found his Majesty's
bell-ringer playing Handel and
the "most difficult lessons of
Scarlatti" on a sort of xylo-
phone he had invented himself.

Joah Bates went to Cambridge
this year and became fellow and
tutor at King's College.

Johann van Beethoven this year
appeared in the court calendar
as an accessist (Bonn).

Pierre Montan Berton was master
of the King's music at this time.

Guillaume Boutmy maintained
the keyboard instruments at the
Brussels Court this year.

Jean-Baptiste Joseph Boutmy
this year appeared as organist
in the accounts of the Church
of Sint Jan.

Burney returned to London at
this time.

Caroli was "principe" of the
Accademia Filarmonica this
year.

Casanova took a trip this year
to Florence. He was expelled
from the city because of an
obscure financial matter.

Chabanon entered the Academy
of Inscriptions at this time.

F. H. Clicquot succeeded his
father this year.

Theresa Cornelys returned
to England at this juncture.

Maurice Whitaker was manager
for John Cox this year.

Farinelli left Spain at this
time, but only on order of
King Charles III.

Geminiani held Avison in very
high esteem and this year paid
him a visit at Newcastle.

Cecilia Grassi sang in two
oratorios this year: Jommelli's
"Passione" and "Gioa", by J.
Christian Bach (son of J. S.).

Grétry studied in Rome this
season.

Johann Gronemann this year
left his position as organist
at The Hague.

In the siege of Dresden during
the Seven Years' War, Johann
Hasse lost his collected manu-

scripts.

F. J. Haydn this year fell in love with a student of his, a daughter of Johann Peter Keller, Therese Keller. She did not return his feelings and entered a convent.

In his compositions written before this year, Haydn followed the model of the "preclassical" school.

William Hayes conducted the Gloucester Festival this season.

Francis Hopkinson was awarded the degree of Master of Arts this year by the College of Philadelphia.

M. Kamiénsk, after being educated in Vienna, went to Poland this year and settled at Warsaw.

F. K. Kratzer became a member (bass) of the Cracow Cathedral choir this season.

Joseph Johann Felix von Kurz ("Bernardon") left Vienna this year. He was a librettist.

No other collections of Lyon's were advertised during 1760 except his "Urania".

James Lyon's "Urania" (The Warrington II copy) contained the ink memorandum, "Mary Thane's the Gift Book of Capt. Wright now Majr. Wright.176(?)"

Perhaps James Lyon's "Ode on Peace" of this year was identical to the "Ode on Peace" of the previous year.

James Lyon this year worked out "plainest and most necessary

(cont.) Rules of Psalmody" as used by psalmodists then.

James Lyon could not have left Philadelphia until late this year.

J. B. Malchair this year was appointed leader of the Oxford Music Room orchestra.

Giambattista Mancini, having become a famous teacher of singing, settled this year at Vienna as a singing teacher to the Imperial Princess.

F. Meyer von Schauensee founded the public musical college of Lucerne this year.

Johann Naumann met Hasse this year.

The English "burletta" was actually created by Kane O'Hara of Dublin, who, this year decided to produce a species that would rival the Italian "burletta".

Carlo d'Ordonez was born in Spain according to Hanslick and in this year, he became registrar and later a secretary of the Landgericht.

M. Overend was organist at Isleworth this season.

Anna Perroni was listed in records at Vienna at this time.

After this year Rameau's harpsichord music, like his operas, started to vanish into obscurity.

Rameau returned this year to comédie lyrique at the age of 76 with a libretto by Monticourt, in comparison with whom,

Colle, said, "the late Cahusac was a Quinault".

Collé maintained this year that "Platée" contained the most striking and strongest music Rameau had ever written.

Rameau at this time wrote a personal letter to d'Alembert "sur ses opinions en musique ensériés dans les articles "Fondamental' et 'Gamme" de l'Encyclopedie". The letter started, "It is clear enough that you have chosen the articles . . . to declare open war on me".

Rameau this year said "F is foreign to C". His use of the subdominant (he invented the term) was a new thing. "In his harmonic system the dominant . . . . is part of the natural resonance of the tonic, whilst the subdominant, belonging to the lower harmonics, is 'refused' by the tonic and therefore brings with it a feeling of strangeness" is a quote from Girdlestone.

Rameau this year reiterated "Talents are not acquired but they develop as by degrees the ear is educated, and to that end one should listen often to music of all tastes".

Rameau this year declared that "true music is the language of the heart".

Ramm made his first concert tour this year which took him to Frankfurt am Main and The Hague.

Countess Schaffgotsch, Austrian composer, took Jan Vaňhal to Vienna when she returned

(cont.) this year where he studied under Dittersdorf.

The soprano, Anna Maria Scheffstas, was engaged by the Esterházy orchestra this season.

Johann Schobert entered the service of the Prince de Conti this year in Paris.

A fire destroyed all the manuscripts of Heinrich Schütz this year at Dresden.

Nicolas Séjan was employed at the Paris Church of Saint-Andre-des-Arts this season.

Shudi this year became bailiff and Royal Councillor at Metz.

Burkat Shudi this year made a harpsichord for H. J. Dale; #407, 2-manual. It still survives today.

Maddalena Sirmen at this time returned to Venice from Padua.

John Stanley, organist and composer, joined J. C. Smith this year in producing oratorio performances formerly conducted by Handel. He composed "Zimri" for these.

This year the Elector Clement Augustus at Bonn made Joseph Touchemoulin conductor of his orchestra, in preference to Beethoven's grandfather.

"Mrs. Vernon" sang this year at Drury Lane at London in T. A. Arne's "Thomas and Sally".

G. Wellesley was created Viscount Wellesley and Earl of Mornington at this time.

John Worgan this year became organist at St. John's chapel, Bedford Row.

Zumpe started the manufacture of square pianofortes this year.

"Réponse de M. D'Alembert a M. Rameau" appeared this year.

Giorgio Antoniotto's "L'arte armonica", a treatise on the composition of music in 3 books, translated by Johnson, appeared at this time.

C. Ashworth's "A Collection of Tunes" was issued this year in its first edition at London.

K. P. E. Bach dedicated his "Sonaten mit veränderten Reprisen" of this year to Princess Amalia.

Boccherini's first six trios dated from this year.

Robert Bremner's "The Harpsichord or Spinnet Miscellany" was published this year at London by Brown and Stratton.

F. X. Brixi composed a "Sinfonia" this season.

V. L. Ciampi's opera "Gianguir" was produced this year at Venice in the Teatro San Benedetto.

B. Cole printed "Orpheus Britannicus, or the Gentleman and Lady's Musical Museum" at this time.

Giuseppe Colla's earliest recorded works were additional airs for Jommelli's "Caio Fabricio" this season at Mannheim.

Johann Florian Deller this year

(cont.) wrote the ballet music for his master's opera "Alessandro nell'Indie".

Friedrich Gottlob Fleischer's "Kantaten zum Scherz und Vergnügnen" was published at this time.

François Francoeur this year wrote his opera "Le Prince de Noisy".

Baldassare Galuppi wrote his opera "L'amante di tutte" (libretto by Antonio Galuppi) for this year's production at Venice.

Baldassare Galuppi wrote his opera "La clemenza di Tito" (libretto by Metastasio) this year at Turin.

Baldassare Galuppi wrote his opera "Solimano" in Padua this year (libretto by Migliavacca).

Florian Gassmann's opera "Filosofia ed amore" was produced this season at Venice (libretto by Goldoni).

Francesco Geminiani's "The Art of Playing the Guitar" was published at this time.

Paul César Gibert wrote his opera "La Fortune au village" this year.

Goldini's "Buona Figliuola" appeared this year at Rome.

Karl Heinrich Graun's oratorio-Passion "Der Tod Jesu" was published this year.

Hasse's opera "Artaserse" (libretto by Metastasio) was produced this year in a new version at Venice.

Haydn this year wrote a piano (harpsichord) concerto in C major. It was scored for 2 violins, 2 horns or trumpets, drums (ad. lib.) and bass. Breitkopf in 1763 listed it for clarinets, oboes, 2 violins, viola and bass.

Haydn this year wrote his divertimento for 2 oboes, 2 horns, and 2 bassoons in F major.

Haydn this year wrote his octet for 2 horns, 2 English horns, 2 violins and 2 bassoons.

Prior to this year Haydn wrote his quartets Op. 1, Nos. 1-4, Op. 1, No. 6, Op. 2, Nos. 1-6, and the "No. 0".

Haydn's Sonatas for piano listed below were written prior to this year:
    #1, C major
    #2, Bb major
    #7, C major
    #8, G major
    #9, F major (published 1766)
Several of them were originally written as divertimenti (Nos. 1 7, 8, 9) and No. 2 was originally a partita.

Haydn wrote his 2nd Symphony in C major this year and it was published by Venier in 1764 at Paris. It was scored for 2 horns and strings.

Haydn's Trio #2 for two violins and violoncello was written after this year.

Ernst Heinsius' (Dutch or German 18th century organist and composer) following compositions appeared this year at Amsterdam: 6 Violin Concertos, 6 Symphonies, opus 2.

Hiller's "Musikalischer Zeitvertrieb" was published this year, the first of his "collecting works" in which he saved many of his contemporaries' works from oblivion.

Holzbauer wrote an oratorio "La Betulia liberata" this year for Mannheim.

In Francis Hopkinson's "Collection of Songs" of this year, there was an anthem dated "F. H. 1760" on page 180.

Jewett ("Ballads and Songs of Derbyshire") gives an illustration of "Singing Sam" this year using the drone.

Jommelli's opera "Caio Fabricio" was produced this year at Mannheim.

J. Philipp Kirnberger wrote his treatise "Konstruktion der gleichschwebenden Temperatur" at this time in Berlin.

Giovanni Battista Lampugnani's opera "Amor contadino" was produced this year in Venice. His opera "Giulia" was produced this same year.

N. Logroscino's "La furba burlata" was produced this season.

Nicola Logroscino's "Stabat Mater" in Eb was performed this year.

The first collection of Gaelic airs, made by the Rev. Patrick MacDonald and his brother this year, was published.

Reverend M. Madan's "A Collection of Psalms and Hymns" was published this year at London.

J. Mainwaring this year published his "Memoirs of the Life of Handel" at London.

P. van Maldere's opera "Les Précautions inutiles" appeared this year.

P. van Maldere's "VI Sinfonie a più Stromenti", dedicated to the Duc d'Antin, was issued this year at Paris.

Marpurg this year published his "Critische Briefe über die Tonkunst".

Joseph Mondonville published an amusing "jeu d'esprit" at this time.

C. Nichelmann's collection of clavier pieces and odes, "Musikalisches Allerlei" appeared at this time.

Noverre's book on dramatic ballet, "Lettre sur la danse et sur les ballets", appeared this year. In the work he paid tribute to Rameau, by this time an aged musician.

"The Art of Fingering the Harpsichord" by N. Pasquali was published this year at Edinboro.

"The Real Story of John Carteret Pilkington", an anonymous book containing information on the life of Richard Pockrich, was published this year at London.

Rameau's "Code de musique pratique ou méthodes pour apprendre la musique, même à des avengles, etc" of this year, was published at Paris by the Imprimerie Royale. Rameau added "Nouvelles Reflexions sur le principe sonore" as a post-(cont.) script.

Rameau's "Dardanus" was revived this year with Sophie Arnould.

"Nouvelle Héloise" by Jean-Jacques Rousseau appeared at this time.

Rameau's 2nd comédie lyrique "Les Paladins" was produced this year on the stage of the Opéra in Paris.

John C. Smith composed the opera "The Enchanter" at this time.

John C. Smith's "Paradise Lost" was produced this season at Covent Garden in London.

William Tans'ur this year published his "The Psalm Singer's Jewel".

William Tans'ur's "The Royal Melody Compleat, or New Harmony of Zion" appeared this year in its second edition at London.

Évrard Titon du Tillet this year issued a 3rd supplement to his book, "Le Parnasse François".

Traetta composed an opera this year to Frugoni's Italian translation of Rameau's "Castor et Pollux", changing the name to "I Tindaridi" and added choral and ballet trappings "alla francese" for the production at Parma.

Tommaso Traetta's opera "Enea nel Lazio" (libretto by Mattia Verazi) was produced this season at Turin.

Tommaso Traetta's opera "Le

feste d'Imeneo" was produced
this season at Parma.

Tommaso Traetta's opera "Stor-
dilano" was performed this
season at Parma.

Four books, each containing
"VI divertimenti da cembalo",
were published by G. C. Wagenseil
in Vienna this year and dedicated to the Archduchesses Mariana,
Marie Christina, Elizabeth
and Amalia, his pupils.

Reverend T. Walter's "Grounds
and Rules of Music" appeared
in its fifth edition this year
at Boston.

Zoppio's "Galatea" was produced
in St. Petersburg this season.

A surviving harpsichord made by
J. Kirkman this year had 1
manual + stops 2x8', 1x4', and
no pedals. It was restored
by A. Dolmetsch in 1897 and was
recently owned by Messrs.
Hubbard and Dowd in Boston,
Mass.

Prior to this year concerts
were the private concern of
members of the Court Chapel
at Stockholm.

Before this year Philadelphia
was not most important of the
four Musical Centres (Boston,
Charleston, New York and
Philadelphia).

Music in the colonies progressed rapidly after this date.

After this year journals
emerged in England, France,
Italy and Russia.

Philadelphia's population this

year was 23,750.

Sir John Hawkins at this time
published his annotated
edition of Walton & Colton's
"Compleat Angler". This
edition has been reprinted
at least 9 times. The latest
edition was in 1893.

Claude Henri, Count of Saint-
simon, French philosopher,
was born this year (died 1825).

Gianantonio Guardi, painter
and brother of Francesco, died
this year (born 1699).

Hokusai, Japanese painter, was
born this year (died 1849).

After this year Francesco
Guardi's "vedute"scenes were
totally different from Canaletto's art. "His equable,
careful, peaceful style &
preoccupation with regular
form structure were replaced
by evocations of fairyland"
("Arcade of the Doges' Palace",
"The Isola San Giorgio",
"The Piazzetta", "Gondola
on the Lagoon").

Alexander Baron of Proney,
writer and later general
inspector of the Lutheran
Church in Hungary, was born
at this time (died 1839).

The Count of Saint-Germain
made a trip to London at
this time.

Prince Hildburghausen was
defeated at the battle of
Rossbach this year. This
brought on the dissolution
of his orchestra.

(to 1761, Winter) Clemens
August made a long-desired

1760(cont.)
visit to his family in
München at this time.

(to 1761) During this year
Goldsmith wrote a book of
witty criticism of manners,
"The Citizen of the World".

(to 1762) Johann Christian Bach
(son of J. S.) was organist at
Milan Cathedral for these two
years.

(and 1762) Franz Beck's "Six
Symphonies à 4 parties et cor
de chasse" were published,
opus 2 in 1760 and another set,
opus 3 in 1762.

(to 1762) V. L. Ciampi was
l'maestro" of the Venetian
Ospedale degli Incurabili
during this period and composed
several Latin oratorios for
his female pupils.

(to 1762) Teresa Lanti was
"prima donna" at Florence
during this time.

(to 1762) Franz Beck wrote the
music for Favart's "Soliman
Second" performed during these
seasons at Bordeaux.

(to 1763) Joseph MacDonald's
"A Compleat Theory of the
Scots Highland Bagpipe" was
compiled between 1760 and 1763.

(to 1763) James Macpherson's
"Ossian" was published at this
time. It was a collection of
poems purported to be "genuine
remains of ancient Scottish
poetry".

(to 1763) S. F. Maio wrote six
more operas for various Italian
towns during this period.

(to 1765) Richard Alderman
engraved music during these
five years.

(to 1765) During this period
Haydn composed the following:
C major Sonatina #10, G major
Sonatina #11 (published in
1767).

(to 1765) "12 Airs for one or
two guittars composed by
John Parry, harper to His
Majesty" was published during
this period.

(to 1765) "A collection of
Welsh, English and Scotch
Airs . . . also Four New Lessons
for the Harp or Harpsichord"
by John Parry was published
during these years.

(to 1768) Kedleston by architect Robert Adam was completed
during this period.
    South front, 125'wide
    Total width, 360'

(to 1768) Noverre's stay at
Stuttgart embraced these years.

(to 1768) Maddalena Sirmen
toured Italy as a violinist for
these eight years.

(to 1769) Haydn's "12 Minuets"
for clavier were composed at
this time.

(to 1769) Haydn wrote 40
symphonies during this period.

(to 1769) During these years
Haydn's writing was in a
transition period with new and
old elements combining.

(to 1769) Jefferson won the
friendship of Governor Francis
Fauquier during this period.
The latter indulged his own love

for music with weekly concerts
in the governor's palace.

(to 1769) Along with other
musicians probably less talented,
Tuckey offered concerts and
balls at New York by subscriptions during the 1760's.

(and 1770) Giorgio Antoniotto
was apparently in London during
this decade.

(to 1770) Salvatore Galeotti,
Italian violinist and composer,
at this time lived in London
where he wrote violin concertos
and sonatas.

(to 1770) The clarinet became
an integral part of the instrumentation of Army bands during
this period.

(to 1770) During this decade
Leonzi Honauer, a German composer published a large number
of his compositions for chamber
music, especially harpsichord
sonatas with and without violin
accompaniment. Some of his
works appeared in London at this
time along with Schobert's.

(to 1770) Only between these
years did the piano begin to
truly compete with the harpsichord for sovereignity.

(to 1777) Theresa Cornelys
began to give musical entertain-
ments at Carlisle House, Soho
Square, during this period.
She attracted the attention of
London society.

(to 1778, 1788) Boyce was the
collector and editor of the
three volume work "Cathedral
Music, being a collection in
score of the most valuable and

(cont.) useful compositions
for that service by the several
English masters of the last two
hundred years". The first
volume was published in 1760
and the second edition was
issued in 1788 by John Ashley.

(to 1778) François Francoeur
was Superintendant de la
Musique du Roi for these
eighteen years.

(to 1778) Maurice Whitaker
established his music shop at
"The Violin" in London at
this time.

(to 1780) William Bates was
well known as a dramatic
composer for these twenty
years.

(to 1780) Haydn's 35 sonatas
for the pianoforte were composed during this period.

(to 1785) Stefano Galeotti,
Italian cellist and composer,
published books of sonatas,
minuets and a divertimento
during these years.

(to 1787) Breitkopf and Härtel
at this time issued about 25
thematic catalogues of musical
works "not made public through
printing and now procurable
in correct manuscript copies".

(to 1788) Haydn's Symphonies
Nos. 2-92 were written for
Prince Esterházy's orchestra
during this long period.

(to 1790) This was the Classical
age of English painting.

(to 1791) Jeremiah Clarke, II
published three volumes of
songs and one volume of
"Sonatas for Harpsichord or

1760(cont.)

Piano Forte" with additional string parts, between these years.

(to 1800) Beuchner reported singing schools operative for 160 years and divided their era into four equal parts. The second, being this one, continued to improve congregational singing while enriching the musical part of the service with longer musical pieces, by adding a trained choir to sing the anthem.

(to c.1810) Ferdinand Gagliano, Italian violin maker, worked at Naples during these fifty years.

(to 1820) George II, House of Hanover, ruled England and Great Britain during these years.

(to 1837) This span of years represented the period of the wide tide of Romanticism in English literature.

c.1760

Harriet Abrams, soprano and composer, was born this year (death date unknown).

Andrea Adolfati, Italian composer, died this year at Genoa (born 1711 at Venice).

George Astor, founder of an Anglo-American firm of musical instrument makers, was born this year at Waldorf near Heidelberg (death date unknown).

Antonio Brunetti, II, Italian composer, was born this year at Florence (deathdate after 1814).

Louis de Caix d'Hervelois, (cont.) French violinist and composer, died at this time in Paris (born c.1670 at Paris).

Johan Arnold Dahmen, violoncellist, was born this year at The Hague (died 1794 at London).

William Dixon, English composer, writer, teacher and music engraver, was born this year at London (died 1825 at London).

Francesco Gardi, Italian composer, was born this year at Venice (died after 1809).

Friedrich Haack, German composer and violinist, was born at this time at Potsdam (death date unknown but probably at Stettin).

Magdalena Jasińsha, Polish singer, was born this year at Podlasie (died c.1800 at Warsaw).

Count Moritz Lichnowsky, Austrian noble, brother of Prince Carl and music patron, was born this year (death date unknown).

Jean-Baptiste Rey, II, French cellist and composer, was born this year at Torascon (died 1827 at Paris).

Abraham Adams lived at Shoreham, Kent this year.

Theodore Aylward this year became organist of Oxford Chapel, London.

At about the age of 15 at this time, Ann Catley was apprenticed by her father to William Bates to receive regular in-

1760(cont.)
struction in the art of singing.

Davaux went to Paris this season.

Delusse this year made simple second-order levers for the primary holes of his flutes.

Giovanni Ferrandini, who was living and working in München, returned to Italy this year and settled at Padua.

Baltimore and Annapolis had concerts on Musical Glasses at this time. These probably were the improved Harmonica on which Benjamin Franklin experimented in Paris this year, thereby establishing a European reputation for himself equal to that associated with his invention of the lightening rod.

In London this year, Franklin heard a performance on a set of musical glasses filled with water.

Benjamin Franklin was credited with the invention of the "armonica" this year.

The "amorshorn" or "amorschall" was a kind of horn invented about this time by Köbla, a Russian musician.

J. Ernst Bach's two sonatas in F and G were published at this time in Nürnberg.

Battishill wrote a song for Edward Moore's "Gamester" this year.

Burney's "Six Concertos in Seven Parts" (4 violins, viola, cello and continuo) appeared at this time.

Burney's "Six Concertos in Eight Parts" appeared this year.

Campioni's chamber music was published in London this year.

"Six Duets for Two Violins, intended to Improve and Entertain Practitioners, by Messrs. Clagget" appeared this year at Edinboro.

"La Grande Encyclopédie" was published this year (author unknown).

Handel's "A Second Set of Six Concertos for the harpsichord or organ" (the first two concertos with instrumental parts) were published this year.

Prior to this year Haydn wrote his Concerto for Clavier in C major (2 horns, 2 violins and bass). The work has been lost.

Haydn's Concerto for Clavier in F major was written at this time (2 violins, viola and bass).

Haydn's divertimenti listed below were composed at this time: Six Scherzandi (flute, 2 oboes, 2 horns, 2 violins and bass), No 1 in F major, No. 2 in C major, No. 3 in D major, No. 4 in G major, No. 5 in E major, No. 6 in A major (published later by Artaria in a version of 2 violins and bass).

Haydn's quartet, opus 1, No. 5 was written after this year.

Haydn's quartet opus 3 was written after this year.

GIOVANNI PAISIELLO
1740-1816

Haydn's Symphony #3 in G major was composed at this time (2 oboes, 2 horns and strings).

Haydn's Symphony #4 in D major was written this year (2 oboes, 2 horns and strings).

Haydn's Symphony #5 in A major was written this year (2 oboes, 2 horns and strings).

Haydn's Symphony #11 in Eb major was written at this time (2 oboes, 2 horns and strings).

Works by Lidarti for the "viola pomposa" existed at this time.

Leopold Mozart wrote 6 divertimenti at this time.

"Thirty Favourite Marches which are now in Vogue" was published this year containing operatic marches.

Francis Waylett this year published Christopher Dixon's "Two English Cantatas and four Songs".

We know about drum and fife music from Walsh's "Warlike Music" of this date.

After this year "the organization of all that had been thrown on the surface by the activity of the earlier symphonists" existed.

Up to this date "The figured bass or thoroughbass, realized on some organ, harpsichord, or lute, was an indispensable feature of all music, whether it was instrumental or vocal, solo, chamber, or symphonic music".

The hornpipe at this time underwent a radical change, being changed into common time from triple-time.

Hogarth this year painted "The Painter's Servants" (National Gallery, London).

Hogarth at this time painted "The Shrimp Girl" (National Gallery, London).

(to 1763) Haydn Symphony #10 in D major was composed during these years (2 oboes, 2 horns and strings).

(to 1763) Haydn's Symphony #17 in F major was composed during this period (2 horns, ad. lib. and strings). Breitkopf & Härtel dated this work 1764.

(to 1763) Haydn's Symphony #16 in Bb major was composed at this time (2 oboes and strings).

(to 1763) Haydn's Symphony #19 in D major was composed during this period (2 oboes, 2 horns and strings).

(to 1764) Haydn's Symphony #18 in G major was composed during this period (2 oboes, 2 horns and strings).

(to 1764) Haydn's Symphony #20 in C major was composed at this time (2 oboes, 2 horns, 2 trumpets, drums and strings).

(to 1764) Haydn's Symphony #25 in C major was composed during this period (2 flutes, 2 horns and strings). Breitkopf and Härtel dated this work as 1765).

(to 1765) Haydn's Symphony #27 in G major was composed at this time (2 oboes and strings).

c.1760(cont)

(to 1765) Haydn's Symphony #32 in C major was composed at this time (2 oboes, 2 horns, 2 trumpets, drums and strings).

(to c.1790) Giuseppe Gagliano, Italian violin maker, worked at Naples during this period.

(to 1790) On English oboes of this period (a type peculiar to that country) the split g' hole was discontinued and the f#' hole enlarged, in order to simplify the fingering of that note.

1761

(January 3) Willem de Fesch, Dutch organist, violinist, cellist and composer, died on this day at London (born 1687).

(January 3) "La vicenda della sorte", an opera by N. Piccinni (libretto by G. Petrosellini based on Goldoni's "I portentosi effetti"), was produced on this date at the Teatro Valle in Rome.

(January 3) Traetta's "Armida" (text by Durazzo with versification by Migliavacca) was performed on this date.

(January 6) Calori sang in Galuppi's "Il filosofo di campagna" this evening at London.

(January 10) Arne wrote incidental music for "The Way to Keep Him", performed on this date at the Drury Lane Theatre in London.

(January 12) Nicola Sala's opera "Zenobia" was performed this evening at Naples.

(January 15) Carvalho on this day entered the Naples Conservatorio di Sant' Onofrio.

(January 21) Carl Barbandt's oratorio "David and Jonathan" was performed on this date in the Haymarket at London.

(January 22) Georg Nikolaus von Nissen, Danish statesman and musical biographer, was born on this date at Hoderslev (died 1826, March 24 at Salzburg).

(January 31) Michael Arne's "Edgar and Emmeline" was performed this evening at Drury Lane in London.

(February 2) Rosalie Levasseur at this time went to Paris where her parents married.

(February 4) Monsigny's opera "Le Cadi dupé" was produced on this date at Paris in the Theatre de la Foire, Saint-Germaine (libretto by P. R. Lemonnier).

(February 5) Clemens August on this day arrived at the palace of the Elector of Trèves at Ehrenbreitstein.

(February 6) Clemens August died on this date at Ehrenbreitstein (born 1700, August 17 at Brussels).

(February 7) Calori sang in Cocchi's "Tito Manlio" this evening at London.

(February 18) F. A. Philidor's opera "Le Jardinier et son seigneur" (libretto by Sedaine after Lafontaine) was produced this evening at the Théâtre de la Foire, St. Germaine.

1761(cont.)

(February 18 or 19) Josef Starzer's ballet "Le Judgement de Paris" was produced on this date at St. Petersburg.

(February 20) Johann Christoph Ludsig Abeiller, German pianist, organist and composer, was born at this time in Bayreuth (died 1838, March 2 at Stuttgart).

(February 22) Benjamin Blake, English violinist and violist, was born on this day at London (died 1827 at London).

(February 22) Erik Tulindberg, Finnish composer, was born on this date at Vähäkyrö (died 1814, September 1 at Abo).

(February 27) T. A. Arne's oratorio "Judith" was performed this evening at the Drury Lane Theatre in London.

(March 14) Calori sang in Perez' "Didone abbandonata" this evening at London.

(March 28 and December 8) Gray, a poet of Peterhouse, at this time spoke with great enthusiasm about DeLaval's glasses in a letter to James Brown, Master of Pembroke, and on December 8 he once more referred to a charming set of glasses that sing like nightingales".

(April 6) Maximilian Friedrich was elevated to the electorship in Bonn on this day.

(April 7) William Hayes was awarded his Bachelor of Arts degree by Magdalen College, Oxford on this date.

(April 9) Charles Simon Favart's

(cont.) "Soliman Second, ou Les Trois Sultanes" was first performed on this date at the Comédie-Italienne in Paris (Music by Gilbert).

(April 20) Johann Gottlieb Karl Spazier, German composer and musical editor, was born on this date at Berlin (died 1805, January 19 at Leipzig).

(April 28) Bertoni's opera "Le pescatrici" was performed this evening at the King's Theatre in London.

(April 28) Calori sang in Bertoni's "Le pescatrici" on this date at London.

(April 29) Florian Gassmann's opera "Catone in Utica" was produced on this date at Venice (libretto by Metastasio).

(May 1) Franz Joseph Haydn became second Kapellmeister for Prince Paul Anton Ester- házy on this date at his estate in Eisenstadt. Five years later he became first Kapell- meister. Werner was first conductor and Haydn was 29 years of age.

(May 15) Antonio Sacchini, became second "maestro" at Ste. Maria di Loreta on this day.

(May 22) The Academy of Dijon on this day elected Rameau a member.

(May 23) James Lyon may have witnessed a performance of one of his anthems at commencement on this date. An ode by Hopkinson was on the same pro- gram.

1761(cont.)

(May 28) The Pennsylvania
Gazette in this issue reported
on the commencement at College
in Philadelphia "on Saturday
last".

(June 3 and September 19) G.
Cocchi's double cantata "Le
speranze della terra" and "Le
promesse del cielo" was produced on both these occasions
at London.

(June 10) Piccinni's opera "La
buona figliuola maritata"
(libretto by Goldoni, a sequel
to Richardson's "Pamela") was
produced on this evening at
Venice.

(June 13) Anton Wranitzky,
Austrian violinist and composer,
was born on this date at Nova
Riše (died 1820, August 6).

(July 12) Meinrad Spiess, German
priest and composer, died at
this time at Yrsee, Bavarian
Swabia (born 1683, August 24
at Honsolgen, Swabia).

(July 16) A decree was issued on
this day appointing Beethoven's
grandfather, Ludwig van Beethoven, Kapellmeister at Bonn.

(July 20) Joseph Lefebvre,
French composer, was born on
this date (died after 1822).

(July 24) Dom Bédos wrote an
account of his survey of the
organ at Saint-Martin de Tours,
built by Nicolas le Fevre on
this date in the "Mercure de
France".

(August 16) Eustigney Ipatovich
Fomin, Russian conductor and
composer, was born on this day
at St. Petersburg (died 1800,
April).

(August 22) The "grande bande"
continued to exist until this
date when King Louis XV
dissolved it by decree.

(August 22) F. A. Philidor's
opera "Le Maréchal Ferrant"
(libretto by Antoine François
Quétant) was produced on this
date at the Theatre de la
Foire, St. Laurent in Paris.

(September 1 and 3) W. A.
Mozart on this date took part
in a comedy, "Sigismundus
Hungariae Rex", set to music
by Eberlin, the court organist.

(September 13) F. A. Philidor
on this date wrote additional
music for the revival of the
opera, "L'Huitre et les plai-
deurs Le Tribunal de la
chicane".

(September 14) Pavel Lambert
Mašek, Czeck musician and brother of Vincenc, was born on
this date at Zvíkovec (died
1826, November 22 at Vienna).

(September 14) Monsigny's
opera "On ne s'avise jamais
de tout" (libretto by Sedaine
after a story by Lafontaine)
was performed on this date at
the Théâtre de la Foire, St.
Germaine at Paris.

(September 21) Petrus Hellendaal resigned his appointment
in Norfolk on this date.

(Autumn) Oscar Sonneck indicated that the date of Franklin's invention (the "armonica") which was also popularly
known as the "glassy-chord"
cannot have been later than
this Fall.

(September 22) E. R. Duni's

opera "Mazet" was produced on this evening at the Comédie-Italienne in Paris.

(September 24) Friedrich Ludwig Aemilius Kunzen, clavier player, editor and composer and son of Adolph Karl, was born at Lübeck (died 1817, January 28 at Copenhagen).

(September 28) Audinot was the original author and part-composer of one of the earliest French "opéras-comiques", "Le Tonnelier", which was first produced at the Théâtre de la Foire Saint-Laurent in Paris on this evening.

(October 7) Hasse's opera "Zenobia" (libretto by Metastasio) was produced this evening at Warsaw.

(October 17) Gluck's ballet "Don Juan" (scenery by Angiolini, choreography by Angiolini) was produced on this date at Vienna.

(October 17) A performance of Noverre's pantomimes in Angiolini's "Le Festin de pierne" was held at this time in Stuttgart.

(October 20) Wilhelm Friedemann Bach on this date petitioned his superiors at Halle for a raise in salary. It was not granted.

(October 23) Nicolas Gilles Forqueray, organist, died on this day at Paris (born 1703, February 15).

(October 25) Gioacchino Conti, Italian male soprano, died on this date at Rome (born 1714, February 28).

(November 2) Miss Ann Ford was the author of the first and only method for the glasses which was published on this date with the title "By Miss Ford, Instructions for playing on the Musical Glasses, so that any person who has the least knowledge of music, or a good ear, may be able to perform in a few days if not in a few hours".

(November 10) Domenico Fischietti's opera "Il mercato di Malmantile" was performed in London on this date.

(December 13) Johann Andreas Streicher, German music teacher and pianoforte maker, was born on this date at Stuttgart (died 1833, May 25 at Vienna).

(December 19) Giuseppe Scolari's opera "La cascina" was produced on this date at Dublin.

(December 26) Cafaro's opera "Ipermestra" was heard at this time.

(December 30) F. A. Philidor's opera "Le Triomphe du temps" (libretto by Legrand) was produced on this date at Versailles.

(February) Gottfried Heinrich Bach, son of J. S. Bach and Anna Magdalena, died at this time (born 1724, February 26). He was an imbecile. Spitta had his death as 1763.

(May) "Demofoonte", an opera by N. Piccinni (libretto by Metastasio) was heard this month at Reggio.

(August) Pierre Gaveaux, French tenor and composer, was born this month at Béziers

1761(cont.)
(died 1825, February 5).

(August) Josef Starzer's ballet "Prométhée et Pandore" was produced this evening at Oranienbaum.

(September) J. C. Bach's setting of John Lockman's "Ode on the Auspicious Arrival and Nuptials of Queen Charlotte" appeared this month.

(November) The first meeting of the "Catch Club" was held at this time.

(November) Sir John Andrew Stevenson, Irish composer, was born this month at Dublin (died 1833, September 14 at Kells, County Meath).

(December) The Italian "burletta" season began this month at the Smock Alley Theatre in Dublin.

(December) Gluck's opera "Le Cadi dupe" (libretto by Pierre René Le Monnier) was produced this month at the Burg Theatre in Vienna. Gluck conducted the work which was taken from a tale from the Arabian Nights.

Johann Caspar Altenburg, German trumpeter, died this year (born 1688).

Dr. Sira Borda, born this year, gave Paganini the diagnosis of veneral disease (syphilis) around 1822-1823. Borda was one of the most renowned Italian physicians of his day (died 1824).

Burney's wife died this year (birthdate unknown).

Giovanni Battista Cimadoro, Italian composer, was born this

(cont.) year at Venice (died 1805, February 27 at Bath).

Giacomo Costa, Italian who taught composition to Niccolò Paganini, Giovanni Sena, Francesco Gnecco, and Camillo Sivari, was born on this date at Genoa. He was Genoa's leading violinist and a capable teacher (death date unknown).

Francesco Feo, Italian composer, died this year at Naples (born 1691).

Jacob Haibel, Austrian composer and singer, was born at Graz (died 1826, March 24 at Djakova, Yugoslavia).

John Hindle, English composer, was born this year at London (died 1796 at London).

Johann Schmidt, husband of Friederica Sophia Bach, was born this year (death date unknown).

Johann Karl Stamitz, "German composer of unusual talent, now underestimated", died this year (born 1717).

Johann Triemer, German violoncellist and composer, died this year at Amsterdam (born c.1700 at Weimar).

(or 1765) Vittorio Trento, Italian composer, was born this year at Venice (died 1833 at Lisbon).

Abingdon this year was awarded the degree of Master of Arts at Magdalen College, Oxford.

Alcock was awarded the degree of Doctor of Music this year by Oxford.

Mrs. Mary Andrews left a will
this year stating that she had
left £100 towards the purchasing of an organ for Christ
Church.

Michael Arne appeared this year
as a dramatic composer with a
piece he had written.

Franz Asplmayr seems to have
spent his whole life in Vienna,
where he appeared at this time
in the court "état" as a ballet
composer of the German theatre
with a salary of 400 Florins.

J. S. Bach was referred to in
the "History of the Travels and
Adventures of the Chevalier
by John Taylor" published this
year.

Battishill this year became a
member of the Royal Society of
Musicians.

When Rich died this year, John
Beard became, in right of his
wife, proprietor and manager of
Covent Garden Theatre.

Franz Beck's career in France
was almost unknown until this
year when he settled at Bordeaux.

Bertheaume appeared as soloist
this year at the Concert Spirituel in Paris.

Blanchard this year was appointed "maître de musique" and held
the position until his death.

John Broadwood married Barbara
Shudi at this time.

The firm of John Broadwood &
Sons (piano makers) originated
when John Broadwood came from
the north of England and joined
Shudi.

Ramieri Calzabigi, the librettist who opposed Metastasio so
strongly and inspired Gluck,
came to Vienna at this time.

When Calzabigi went to Vienna
this year, he established
personal contact with Metastasio and appointed himself
Chamber Councillor to the
Couts of the Netherlands.

Capron appeared as a soloist
at the Concert Spirituel this
season.

Casanova went to Augsburg
this summer and participated
in the peace negotiations as a
plenipotentiary of the Portuguese Government. He did little
to honor the Government he was
representing.

After a visit to the Teatro
via Pergola in Florence this
year, Casanova stated, "I
took a box next to the orchestra, to eye the artists rather
than to hear the music of
which I was never an enthusiastic admirer". Still in other
passages he professed to be
a great music lover.

Late this year Casanova returned to Paris to complete his
hoax with the Marquise d'Urfé.
He convinced her in a great
farce that he could turn her
into a man.

This year Casanova visited his
mother, Zanetta, in Prague
where she had fled with the
Dresden Court after the siege
of Frederic the Great.

F. H. Clicquot this year
worked on the organs at Versailles Cathedral.

This fall the dancer Maria Corticelli appeared in ballet at the opera in Prague, "La Clemenza di Tito", presumably composed by Jommelli or Giuseppe Scarlatti.

Ditters started with Gluck this year on a professional tour in Italy, where his playing was well received.

M. Dubourg was appointed Master of Her Majesty's Band of Musick this year at £200 a year.

J. P. Duport played this season with great success in Paris at the Concert Spirituel.

Farinelli left the Spanish court this year and permanently settled in Bologna.

Domenico Fischietti joined the company of the impresario Bustelli this season and conducted performances at Prague.

Philip Vickers Fithian composed many "tunes" after this year.

Caterina Gabrielli sang in Gluck's "Armida" this season at Vienna.

Angiolini (Fogliazzi) danced the part of Don Juan in Gluck's "Don Juan" this season. Mme. Geoffroi-Bodin danced the part of Donna Elvira. Angiolini created the parts in this ballet as he also had created the ballets for Gluck's "Orfeo".

Haydn became Kapellmeister at Eisenstadt this year and promoted Luigi Tomasini to 1st violin the same year.

Johann Haessler this year was (cont.) appointed organist of the Barfüsserkirche at Erfurt.

Haydn's works were known to the Moravians even at this time.

Francis Hopkinson's "Patriotic Ode" was sung with organ at the College of New Jersey commencement this year.

Francis Hopkinson was acquainted with Lyon by this time.

Francis Hopkinson studied law at this time under the Honorable Benjamin Chew and was later admitted to the bar.

When Queen Charlotte arrived in England this year, Kelway was appointed her instructor.

Jakob Kleinknecht was Kapellmeister at the Bayreuth Court this season.

James Lyon's copy of "Urania" is in the possession of the New York Public Library and has on the first page, "Hetty Chambers . . .1761", signifying it was delivered to her.

Mozart, when only 5½ years old this year, gave his first public performance in the "Aula" of the University.

Johann Naumann went to Naples this year with a student named Pitscher, to study dramatic music for six months. He then went to Naples to study counterpoint with Padre Martini.

Thomas Norris appeared this season at the Worcester Festival.

James Oswald this year was appointed chamber composer to King George III.

Giuseppe Scolari, the composer, visited Spain and Portugal at this time.

Burkat Shudi this year made a 1-manual harpsichord, #423, which has survived.

Burkat Shudi this year made a 1-manual harpsichord, #427, which has survived.

Burkat Shudi this year made a harpsichord, #428, which has survived.

Tommaso Traetta went to Vienna at this time to witness the performance of his "Armida", written especially for the Austrian capital.

Pierre Vachon, violinist and composer, was appointed leader of the Prince de Conti's band this year.

A. M. G. Vestris was engaged at Stuttgart this season.

E. T. Warren this year became a member of the Noblemans and Gentlemans "Catch Club".

Joseph F. Weigl entered Prince Esterházy's orchestra at Eisenstadt this year as first cellist.

Ernst Wilhem Wolf was leader of the orchestra at Weimar at this time.

John Worgan this year was appointed composer at Vauxhall Gardens.

C. G. Alexandre's "Georget et Georgette" was produced this year. It was the earliest "Shakespearean" opera and two

(cont.) scenes were adapted from "The Tempest".

T. A. Arne's "Thomas and Sally" was published this year by the composer himself, in a folio with an engraved date coinciding with this one. Other sources give J. and S. Phillips as the publisher.

J. Christian (son of J. S.) Bach's "Artaserse" was produced this year at the Teatro Reggio in Turin. It was a three-act opera.

J. Christian (son of J. S.) Bach's opera "Catone in Utica" was produced this season at the Teatro de San Carlo in Naples.

J. Christian (son of J. S.) Bach's "Catone in Utica" was produced this year at Florence.

J. C. Bach's two first symphonies, overtures to "Artaserse" and " atone in Utica", were written at this time.

Joseph Barnabé Saint-Sevin L'Abbé, violinist, this year composed five collections of airs arranged for one and two violins, with variations, etc., and a pedagogical work, "Les Principes du violon".

Boroni's first opera, Metastasio's "Demofoonte", was performed this season at Treviso.

Burney's "Six Sonatas or Lessons for the Harpsichord" were issued this year.

V. L. Ciampi's "Amore in caricatura" was produced at the Teatro Sant' Angelo in

Venice during this year's carnival season.

Raphael Courteville published a pamphlet, "Arguments Respecting Insolvency" at this time.

Ducharger's "Réflexions sur divers ouvrages de M. Rameau" was published this year at Rennes.

Friedrich Gottlob Fleischer's "Sammlung von Menuetten une Polonoisen" was published at this time.

The Italian edition of Johann Joseph Fux's "Gradus ad Parnassum" was published this year at Carpi.

Baldassare Galuppi wrote his opera "Il caffè di campagna" (libretto by Chiari) this year at Venice.

Baldassare Galuppi's opera "Il filosofo di campagna" was produced this season at London's Haymarket Theatre.

Baldassare Galuppi wrote his opera "Li tre amanti ridicoli" (libretto by Chiari) this year at Venice.

Florian Gassmann's opera "Ezio" was produced this season at Florence (libretto by Metastasio).

Carlo Goldoni's "Commedie" was published in Venice at this time.

Gossec's opera "Le Périgourdin" was privately performed this season at Prince de Conti's (librettist unknown).

Johann Mattheson's "G. F.

(cont.) Händel's Lebensbeschreibung" was published this year at Hamburg.

Prior to this date Haydn's Divertimento in C major was written (2 clarinets, 2 bassoons, 2 horns).

The six "Russian" Quartets, op. 33, by Haydn were completed this year.

Haydn wrote his 3rd Symphony this year.

Haydn wrote six symphonies this year.

Some of the most notable of Haydn's Symphonies, Nos. 6, 7 and 8, known as "Le Matin", "Le Midi", and "Le Soir", were composed this year. "Le Matin" was for flute, 2 oboes, bassoon, 2 horns, violin and cello concertante and strings. "Le Midi" was for 2 flutes, 2 oboes, bassoon, 2 horns, 1st and 2nd violin concertante, cello concertante and strings. "Le Soir (et La Tempesta)" was for flute, 2 oboes, bassoon, 2 horns, 1st and 2nd solo violins, solo cello, solo bassoon and strings. Haydn started work also this year on Symphonies #7 and #8.

Hellendaal's opus 4, "6 Solos for a Violin with a Thorough Bass for the Harpsichord" was completed this year at London.

Karl Hoeckh's 7 "Parthien" (suites) were published this year. He also composed 10 symphonies, violin concertos, solos, "Capricietti" for violin (together with Benda), but these were all in manuscript.

1761(cont.)

Jommelli's opera "L'Olimpiade" was produced this season at Stuttgart.

William Knapp's "New Church Melody" appeared at this time in its 4th edition.

James Lyon's "Urania", the first collection of hymns and psalm tunes done by a native American, appeared this year.

James Lyon's "Two Celebrated Verses" (in "Urania") were published this year by Stern-hold and Hopkins.

M. Overend this year composed an "Epithalamium" for the marriage of King George III.

N. Piccinni wrote 6 operas this year, 3 serious and 3 comic.

The last complete performance of Rameau's "Les Indes Galante" took place this season.

Richardson's "Pamela" was set by Piccinni at this time.

Jean-Jacques Rousseau's "Les Muses galantes" was performed at this time before "M. le Prince de Conti".

Rousseau's "La Nouvelle Heloise" was completed this year.

Gregorio Sciroli's opera "Merope" was produced this season at Milan.

John Stanley this year set to music Robert Lloyd's dramatic pastoral "Arcadia, or the Sheperd's Wedding". It was written in honor of the marriage

(cont.) of King George III and Queen Charlotte.

G. C. Wagenseil's "The divertimenti per cembalo" was published this year at Vienna.

E. W. Wolf wrote one or more sonatas for two performers at this time when he was musical director at Weimar.

The great vogue of vocal chamber music in England at this time was obvious in the Noblemen and Gentlemen's "Catch Club", where a selected Royal membership and aristocracy were complemented by noted professionals.

The only persons allowed to play symphonies at the King of France's apartments at this time were the musicians of his chamber and chapel.

Three of the harpsichords made this year by J. Kirkman fit the following description: #9, 2 manuals and stops, 2x8', 1x4', lute; #10, 2 manuals and stops 2x8', 1x4', lute; #11, 1 manual and stops 2x8', 1x4'. They have all survived and #9 is currently owned by J. G. Morley, #10 by Mrs. A. F. Hill and #11 by the Hochschule für Musik in Berlin.

By this time the Light Dragoons were already using "horns like post boys" for certain calls.

The theatre of the Paris Opéra was burned down this year.

The Noblemen and Gentlemen's "Catch Club" was formed at this time.

August Friedrich Kotzebue,

German dramatist, was born this year (died 1819).

Friedrich V. Matthisson, German poet, was born this year (died 1831).

Louis-Léopold Boilly, French painter, was born this year (died 1845).

Greuze this year painted "The Village Bride", 36" x 46½" (Louvre).

Giesecke was born this year at Augsburg. He studied law and mineralogy (died 1833).

Sir John Hawkins became a Middlesex magistrate at this time.

(to 1762) J. Christian Bach (son of J. S.) succeeded G. Cocchi at the King's Theatre this season.

(to 1762) Geminiani was M. Dubourg's guest at Dublin this year.

(to 1762) Hiller wrote his collection "Raccolta delle megliore sinfonie . . . accomo- date al clavicembalo" at this time. There were 24 numbers in 4 parts.

(to 1762) Mozart during this period wrote "El, Kl", a Minuet and Trio in G major while at Salzburg.

(to 1763) Johann Naumann during these years produced his first opera at the Teatro San Samuele in Venice.

(to 1763) Domingo Scarlatti worked in the Secretaria de la

(cont.) Nueva España during this period.

(to c.1764) Friedrich Graf gave subscription concerts in Hamburg at this time.

(to 1766) Martini il Tedesco during this period was in the household of King Stanislas, who was then living at Lunéville.

(to 1766) Gregorius Werner during these years wrote six- teen masses, five "Salve Reginas" and nine other sacred works.

(and 1767, January 14) John Broadwood was employed by Shudi as a harpsichord maker this year according to the "Gazateer" and "Daily Advertiser" issued on January 14, 1767.

(to 1769) Joseph Weigl was a member of the Vienna court or- chestra during these seasons as a violoncellist.

(to 1772) Cimarosa attended the Conservatorio Santa Maria di Loreto at Naples for these eleven years.

(to 1780) Many of Karl Fried- rich Abel's works were published by Bremner of London and Hummel of Berlin during this nini- teen year period.

(to 1780) Alembert's "Recherches sur les vibrations des cordes sonores avec un supplément sur les cordes vibrantes" ("Opuscules mathématiques", Paris, 1761-1780) appeared at this time.

(to 1784, 1794) The electors under whom three Beethovens served as musicians were Max

EMPRESS CATHERINE (THE GREAT) OF RUSSIA
1729-1796

1761(cont.)
Friedrich, who held the See from
1761 to 1784; and Max Franz who
ruled until the French armies
occupied the Rhine country in
1794.

(to 1786) Alcock was the organist of Sutton Coldfield Church
for these twenty-five years.

(and 1786 to 1788) Grose
("Military Antiquities", 1786-
1788) stated that in 1761 there
were some troops of light dragoons who used horns like post-
boys.

(to 1794) Warren was secretary
of the "Catch Club" for these
many years.

(to 1810) The "Fuguing tune" was
popular throughout this time.

c.1871
Theodosia Abrams, contralto, was
born this year (died after 1864).

Ernst Haüsler, German cellist,
singer and composer who developed a falsetto voice to such
an extent that he appeared as
a soprano, was born this year
at Stuttgart (died 1837, February 20 at Augsburg). He also
composed cantatas, songs and
some chamber works. Sources
disagree on his date of birth
and it has also been given as
1760 and 1766.

Jacques Hotteterre, son of
Marin, died at this time (death
date unknown but died at Paris).

Joséf Todeusz Benedykt Pekalski,
Polish ecclesiatic, conductor
and musical theorist, died this
year (birthdate unknown).

Bernard Viguerie, French com-

(cont.) poser, teacher and
music publisher, was born this
year at Carcassonne (died 1819,
March at Paris).

Joshua Reynolds this year
painted "Portrait of Countess
Spencer and Her Daughter"
(Earl Spencer Althorp Collection at Northants).

(to 1765) Haydn's Symphony
#72 in D major was written
during this period (flute
obbligato, 2 oboes, 4 horns,
solo violin and strings).
There is some disagreement over
this date as another source
simply refers to the work as
having been composed prior to
1781.

1762
(January 1) Casanova on this
date wrote to dancer Maria
Corticelli in Prague saying he
would meet her and her mother
at Metz.

(January 1) Marchese di Villa-
rosa, Italian musical lexicographer and author, was born
on this date at Naples (died
1847, January 30 at Naples).

(January 20) J. Christian (son
of J. S.) Bach's opera "Alessandro nell' Indie" was produced
on this day at Naples.

(January 22) Kane O'Hara's
light musical "Midas" opened
on this date at the Crow
Street Theatre in London.

(February 2) "Artaxerxes", an
opera by T. A. Arne, was produced this evening in London
at the Covent Garden Theatre.
The work used recitative
rather than spoken dialogue
and the text was by Metastasio.

1762(cont.)

(February 2) Charlotte Brent reached the peak of her career on this date in Arne's "Artaxerxes" supposedly written for her.

(February 2) Girolamo Crescentini, Italian male mezzo-soprano, was born on this date at Urbania near Urbino (died 1846, August 24 at Naples).

(February 3) "Artaserse", an opera by N. Piccinni (libretto by Metastasio), was produced this evening at the Teatro Argentina in Rome.

(February 3) The "Comédiens du Roi" joined the Opéra-Comique at this time in Paris.

(February 9) Andrew Shirrefs, Scottish musician and poet, was born on this date at Aberdeen (died c.1801 or c.1807).

(February 15) Charles Simon Favart's "Annette et Lubin" was first performed this evening at Paris (music by Gibert).

(February 26) Arne's "Beauty and Virtue" was produced at Drury Lane Theatre in London on this date.

(March 4) Mozart's Allegro in Bb major was composed on this date at Salzburg.

(March 16) Gaetano Latilla on this date was appointed second maestro at St. Mark's.

(March 18) Prince Paul Anton Esterhazy died on this date (born 1710). He was known best as F. J. Haydn's patron, but was also a violinist and cellist. He was succeeded by his brother

(cont.) Nikolaus, also greatly interested in art and science.

(March 24) Marcos Antonio Portugal (Portogallo) (da Fonseca), Portuguese conductor and composer, was born on this date at Lisbon (died 1830, February 7 at Rio de Janeiro). Another source gave his birthplace as Italy.

(March 24) "Prometeo assoluto" by G. C. Wagenseil was given at the Burg Theatre in Vienna this evening.

(March 24) Ferdinand Waldstein was born on this date in Duchov, Bohemia. He was a musical amateur, but is best known today by the dedication of the "Waldstein" sonata (died 1823, August 29).

(March 30) Vincenzo Legrenzio Ciampi, Italian composer, died on this day at Venice (born 1719 at Piacenza).

(April 2) V. L. Ciampi's death was reported in this issue of the "Nuova Gazzetta Veneta"

(April 7) Pietro Guarneri, Italian violin maker, died on this date at Venice (born 1695, April 14).

(April 13) Karl Friedrich Horn, German organist, theorist, composer and father of Charles Edward Horn, was born on this date at Nordhausen, Saxony (died 1830, August 5 at Windsor).

(April 26) Pierre (Jean) Garat, French tenor-baritone, was born on this date at Bordeaux (died 1823, March 1).

(April 27) Andreas Romberg, son

1762(cont.)

of Gerhard Heinrich Romberg, a
violinist, was born on this
date at Vechta near Münster
(died 1821, November 10 at
Gotha).

(April 27) Hasse's opera, "Il
trionfo di Clelia" (libretto
by Metastasio) was produced
on this evening at Vienna.
(See also Gluck, Jommelli,
Portugal and Vaňhal for other
settings of the same libretto.)

(May 11) Mozart's Minuet in F
major was composed on this date
at Salzburg.

(May 16) Ernst Christian Hesse,
German violinist and composer
who composed 2 operas, church
music, sonatas and solos for
viola da gamba, died on this
date at Darmstadt (born 1676,
April 14 at Grossgottern,
Thuringia).

(May 17) Prince Nikolaus made
his solemn entry into Eisenstadt on this day.

(May 19) E. R. Duni's opera
"La Plaideuse, ou Le Procès"
was produced on this date at
the Paris Comédie-Italienne.

(May 19) Charles Simon Favart's
"La Plaideuse, ou Le Procès" was
premiered on this evening at
Paris (Music by Duni).

(May 29) The name of the earliest
known maker of the armonica was
given in this issue of Jackson's
"Oxford Journal" as Charles
James of Purpool Lane, near
Gray's Inn, who stated that he
manufactured these solely for
Franklin from the very beginning.

(June 3) In the "Pennsylvania

(cont.) Journal" on this date,
the n.b. at the end of the
advertisement indicated that
Lyon's "Urania" had not been
published before.

(June 8) Pietro Maria Crispi
on this date joined the Accademia di Santa Cecilia at Rome.

(June 12) "La bella verita",
an opera by N. Piccinni (libretto by Goldoni) was performed on this date at Bologna.

(June 16) Karl Christian Agthe,
German organist and composer,
was born at Hettstädt on this
date (died 1797, November 27
at Ballenstedt).

(June 19) Johann Ernst Eberlin,
German organist and composer,
died on this day at Salzburg
(born 1702, March 27 at Jet-
tingen near Günzburg in
Bavaria).

(Summer) Ann Catley made her
first appearance in public
this evening at Vauxhall
Gardens.

(Summer) Signora Mattei, the
impresaria at the King's Theatre, London, engaged J. Christian Bach (son of J. S.), who
arrived in England this summer.

(June 23) E. R. Duni's opera
"La Nouvelle Italie" was pro-
duced this evening at the
Paris Comédie-Italienne.

(July 1) B. Cooke, II was
appointed organist of Westminster Abbey on this date.

(July 1) F. J. Haydn at this
time had expanded the Esterhazy
orchestra to 5 violins, 1
cello, 1 double bass, 1 flute,

2 oboes, 2 bassoons, 2 horns,
2 "sopranos", 2 "tenors", 1
"contralto", 1 "bass", a choir
of servants of the Prince.

(July 1) LeBon, a painter, was
given permanent employment at
the estate of Prince Nicholas on
this date on the condition that
his wife and daughter sing in
the choir which Haydn directed.

(July 4) Marco Santucci, Italian
composer, was born at this time
at Camaiore, Tuscany (died 1843,
November 29).

(July 5) Jacob Adlung, German
theologian, scholar and musician,
died on this day at Bindersleben
(born 1699, January 14 at Bindersleben near Erfurt).

(July 5) Mozart's "Minuet in F
major" was composed on this date
at Salzburg.

(July 6) Wilhelm Friedemann
Bach was invited at this time to
succeed Christoph Graupner,
"Kapellmeister" at the Darmstadt dourt.

(July 8) F. Philidor's "Sancho
Pança dans son isle" (Antoine
Alexandre Henri Poinsinet, after
Cervantes) was performed this
evening at the Comédie-Italienne
in Paris.

(July 13) Karl von Doblhof-Dier,
Austrian amateur composer, was
born at Vienna on this date
(died 1836 at Vienna).

(July 15) The testament of Margarita Rossetti Gentili bore
this date.

(July 20) Christoph Nichelmann
German harpsichordist and com-

(cont.) poser, died on this date
(born 1717, August 13 at
Treuenbrietzen, Brandenburg).

(August 28) Wilhelm Friedemann
Bach at this time accepted the
position of "Kapellmeister"
at the Darmstadt court.

(September 17) Francesco Geminiani, Italian violinist and
composer, died on this date
at Dublin (born 1687, probably
December 4). His date of birth
has also been given as 1679 or
1680. His eminence in the
field is great and his
teachers were Corelli and A.
Scarlatti.

(Autumn) Florian Gassmann's
opera "Un pazzo ne fa cento"
was produced on this date
in Venice (author of libretto
unknown).

(September 29) William Bradford
of Philadelphia this year
printed "The Military Glory of
Great Britain. An Entertainment, Given by the late candi-
dates for Bachelor's Degree, At
the close of the Anniversary
Commencement, Held in Nassau-
Hall, New Jersey".

(September 29) James Lyon was
awarded his second degree on
this date at Princeton.

(September 30) The "Pennsylvania
Gazette" on this date printed
an account of Princeton's
commencement.

(October 5) Gluck's Italian
opera "Orfeo ed Euridice"
(libretto by Ranieri Calzabigi)
was premiered on this date at
the Burg Theatre in Vienna. The
public response was highly
favorable and the performance

1762(cont.)
was on the name day of Francis I.

(October 6) J. P. Rameau on this
date wrote a letter to A. M.
Beguillet, in which he discussed
ancient music and tonal intervals. "Why does man prefer
certain intervals to others
after certain sounds?"

(October 6) Andrew Steuart on
this date published the "Pro-
priety Necessity and Use of
Evangelical Psalms in Christian
Worship". "Delivered at a
Meeting of the Presbytery at
Hanover, in Virginia . . ."

(October 8) Ann Catley appeared
at Covent Garden Theatre this
evening as the Pastoral Nymph
in Dalton's adaption of Milton's
"Comus".

(October 11) The "New York
Mercury" in this issue described the commencement exercises at Princeton.

(October 12) Antonio Sacchini at
this time obtained a leave from
the maestro of the Conservatory
at Loreto to go to Venice for
the production of an opera.

(October 15) Samuel Holyoke,
American composer who helped to
compile a collection of psalms
in America, was born on this
date at Boxford, Mass. (died
1820, February 7 at Concord,
N. H.).

(October 21) Jean François
Lépine, sr., the organ builder,
died on this day at Toulouse
(birth date unknown).

(October 21) The "Pennsylvania
Gazette" in this issue described
the commencement at Princeton

(cont.) more fully.

(October 21) Josef Starzer's
ballet "Le Pauvre Yourka"
was produced on this date in
Moscow.

(November 22) Monsigny's opera
"Le Roi et le fermier" (libretto by Sedaine) was produced on this date at the
Comédie-Italienne at Paris.
It was one of his greatest
successes.

(November 23) Vernon composed
songs for "The Witches, or
Harlequin Cherokee" performed
this evening at the Drury
Lane Theatre in London.

(November 24 or 28) John Pigott,
English organist and son of F.
Pigott, died on one of these
dates at Windsor (birthdate
unknown).

(November 26) Evrard Titon du
Tillet, French author, died on
this date at Paris (born 1677,
January 16 at Paris).

(November 27) A reply to a petition from Johann Beethoven at
Bonn was given on this date by
Elector Max Friedrich granting
him special consideration at
court concerning salary.

(December 5) Alexandre Jean
Joseph Le Riche de La Poupe-
linière, French statesman,
patron and musical amateur,
died on this day at Paris (born
1693, July 26).

(December 5) Josef Starzer's
ballet "Le Seigneur de village
moqué" was produced this
season at Moscow.

(December 8) T. A. Arne's "Love

1762(cont.)
in a Village" was produced in London on this date (libretto by Isaac Bickerstaffe).

(December 12) Nicola Sala's opera "Demetrio" was produced in Naples this evening.

(December 16) Franz Tausch, German clarinettist, was born on this date at Heidelberg (died 1817, February 9 at Berlin).

(Winter) N. Piccinni's opera "Il cavaliere per amore" (libretto by Petrosellini) was produced at this time at the Teatro Nuovo in Naples.

(December 22) Vernon composed songs for Shakespeare's "Two Gentlemen of Verona", performed on this date at Drury Lane Theatre in London.

(December 23) The "Pennsylvania Gazette" in this issue complimented Fyring as an organ builder to be the "best Hand at that ingenious Business on the Continent".

(December 25) Michael Kelly, Irish tenor, actor and composer, was born on this date at Dublin (died 1826, October 9 at Margate.

(December 25) An enthusiast signing "C.W.P." heard the organ at St. Paul's on Christmas Day this year and commented, "Thy Name, o Fyring thy deserving Name, Shall shine conspicuous in the roll of fame".

(December 29) E. R. Duni's opera "Le Milicien" was performed this day at Versailles.

(December 30) The enthusiast, "C.W.P." wrote a poem about St.

(cont.) Paul's organ player, Fyring, and it appeared in this issue of the "Pennsylvania Gazette"

(January, February) Benoît Blaise's little pastoral, "Annette et Lubin", was first heard privately at a wedding in January and produced at the Comedie-Italienne a month later. It became a huge success.

(January) Leopold Mozart took Wolfgang and Anna Maria on their first concert tour to Vienna, Linz and München this month.

(January) Mozart's "Minuet in F major" was composed this month at Salzburg.

(February) F. Philidor's opera "Le Triomphe du temps" (libretto by Marc-Antoine Legrand) was performed this month at the Comedie-Francaise in Paris.

(March) It was obvious that d'Alembert did not fully agree with Rameau from his "Lettre à M. Rameau, pour prouver que le corps sonore ne nous donne et ne peut nous donner par lui-même aucune idée des proportions", which Fétis considered "good and sane criticism". The letter appeared in this issue of the "Mercure de France".

(March) The defenders of French music this month wrote in "Mercure de France" that, "It is not our national music but often to the way of playing it that one should attribute the ridicule which foreigners who know it badly or fellow-countrymen who decry it disingenuously wish to shower on it unreflectingly".

1762(cont.)

(June) Felix Baciocchi, a member of an old Genoese family, married Elise Bonaparte (sister of Napoleon) this month. They ruled Piombino and Lucca (died 1841).

(June) James Lyon's "Urania" appeared on the book market for non-subscribers this month.

(July) Johann Valentin Görner, German composer, died this month at Hamburg (born 1702, February 26). He was music director at Hamburg.

(November) Petrus Hellendaal this season became organist of Pembroke College, Cambridge.

(November) Piccinni's opera "Antigono" (libretto by Metastasio) was performed this month at the Teatro San Carlo in Naples.

(November) Tommaso Traetta's "Sofonisba" (libretto by Verazi) was produced at Mannheim this month.

Christine Louise Bach, daughter of J. C. F. Bach and a member of the seventh generation of the Bach family, was born this year (died 1852).

Adelheid Marie Eichner, pianist and singer, was born this year at Mannheim (died 1787, April 5 at Potsdam).

Cäcilia Fischer, Theodor's oldest daughter, was born this year (died 1845).

Joseph Haudek, horn player and son of Karl Haudek who succeeded his father in the Dresden orchestra, was born at this time (died 1832, October 10 at Dres-

(cont.) den.

Felix Janiewicz, Polish violinist, was born this year at Wilno (died 1848, May 21 at Edinboro).

James Leach, English tenor and composer, was born this year at Wardle near Rochdale (died 1798, February 8).

Cellist Giuseppe da Loglio died at this time in Venice (birthdate unknown).

Jacob Augustus Otto, German violin maker, was born at this time in Gotha (died 1830, June at Jena).

Silvestro Palma, Italian composer, was born this year at Palermo (died 1834, August 8 at Naples).

William Thomas Parke, violist, oboist, composer, and brother of John, was born this year at London (died 1847, August 26 at London).

James Ralph, American composer, died at this time (birthdate unknown).

Catherine Rameau, Jean-Philippe's sister, died this year (birthdate unknown).

Joseph Reinagle, brother of Alexander Reinagle, was born this year. He studied horn and trumpet with his father and cello with his brother-in-law, Johann Schetky (died 1825, November 12 at Oxford).

Alexander Reinagle's young brother, Hugh, was born this year and became an eminent violoncellist (death date unknown).

Barbara Scarlatti, daughter of
Domenico and a member of the
fourth generation of the Scarlatti family, died this year
(born 1743, January 12).

Johann Heinrich Schröter, German violinist and composer, was
born at this time in Warsaw
(death date unknown).

Jan Wanski, Polish violinist
and composer, was born this year
in Western Poland (death date
unknown).

Georg Wolf, German composer,
was born this year at Schwartz-
burg (died 1814).

D'Alembert this year answered
Rameau's attack cleverly and
neatly in the "Elements de
musique" and probably destroyed
French music up to the time of
Gounod.

Aliprandi's son, Bernardo
Aliprandi, joined his father
this year as a cellist in the
Munich court orchestra.

Anna Lucia de Amicis was at
first successful only in "opera
buffa" which she sang in London
this year, appearing in "La
pupilla", a pasticcio by John
Christian Bach (son of J.S.).

Araia returned to Italy this
year after the death of Peter
III.

T. A. Arne was able to use
clarinets this year for his
"Artaxerxes".

Theodore Aylward at this time
became organist of St. Lawrence,
Jewry.

J. Christian Bach (son of J. S.)
moved to London this year and
became official composer to
the King's Theatre in London.
He remained in London for the
rest of his life.

When J. Christian (son of J. S.)
Bach arrived in London in the
Fall of the year, Karl Friedrich Abel joined him. They
lived together and jointly
conducted Mrs. Cornelys'
subscription concerts.

Joseph Baildon this season was
appointed organist at the London
churches of St. Luke, Old
Street, and All Saints, Fulham.

Johann van Beethoven was
promised a salary of 100
thalers this year, but received
it two years later.

Franz Beck was in Marseilles
at this time.

Franz Beck this year became
conductor at the Grand Théâtre
in Bordeaux.

Hugh Bond was appointed lay-
vicar of Exeter Cathedral this
year and was also organist
at the church of St. Mary
Arches in that city.

Pasquale Bondini sang "buffo"
parts in opera from this date
forward.

Bremner this year purchased
the famous "Fitzwilliam Virginal Book". He bought it at
the sale of Pepusch' library
for ten guineas and presented
it to Lord Fitzwilliam

(or early 1763) Robert Bremner
actually opened a music-school
at this time although it was

not advertised in the "Pennsylvania Gazette" or "Journal".

Robert Bremner at this time
moved to London and opened a
shop with the "Harp and Hautboy"
sign, in the Strand, opposite
the Somerset House. He still
retained the Edinboro shop
under a manager.

Broadway had become organist of
St. Ann's, Dublin by this time.

Gaetano Brunetti spent the
greater part of his life in
Madrid, from this year on at
least. His name was mentioned
this year in connection with a
comedy, "El Faetón", for which
he wrote incidental music.

Calzabigi, a devoted admirer of
Metastasio, this year wrote
the Italian libretto of "Orfeo"
for Gluck.

Dancourt arrived in Vienna
this year. He was the "Berlin
harlequin", a comedian who had
been involved in the successful
production in Brussels of
Gluck's "La Recontre imprévue".

Dauvergne this season became
one of the directors of the
Concert Spirituel.

Charles Dibdin made his début
this season at the summer
theatre at Richmond.

Durazzo this year earned
"lasting merit" for his patronage of Gluck's "Orfeo".

Fedele Fenaroli, Italian composer, succeeded Sacchini this
year as a teacher at the Santa
Maria Conservatory.

Hipkins stated that Fétis began

(cont.) his musical studies
on a Zumpe square pianoforte
bearing this date.

Ignazio Fiorillo left Braunschweig this year to transfer
his services to the court of
Hesse-Cassel.

Johann Nikolaus Forkel was
appointed a chorister at
Lüneburg this year when he
was thirteen years old.

By this time the "glassy-
chord", invented by Franklin
of Philadelphia was delighting
British audiences.

Philipp Fyring erected an organ
this year at St. Paul's
(Pennsylvania).

Baldassare Galuppi this season
was appointed director of the
Conservatorio degli Incurabili.

Baldassare Galuppi became
maestro di cappella at St.
Mark's this season.

This year Vienna was the first
city to witness the birth of
Gluck's "musical drama".

Thomas Griffin was appointed
professor of music this year
at Gresham College in London.

Gaetano Guadagni sang in
Gluck's "Orfeo" this season.

J. N. Hamal this year ended his
studies of the humanities at
the Jesuit College, Liège, and
was sent to Rome to the
Darchais Foundation.

F. J. Haydn's new patron this
year after Prince Esterházy
died, was Prince Nicholas the
Magnificent.

1762(cont.)

Archbishop Sigismund of Salzburg this year appointed Michael Haydn as musical director and concert master and the latter took up residence at Salzburg.

Eva Ursula Hemmerlein, daughter of Johann N. Hemmerlein and an excellent singer at the Bamberg court, this year married her cousin, Anton.

Johann Gottfried Hildebrand, the principal workman under Silbermann of Dresden, built the organ at St. Michael's, Hamburg this year. It cost £ 4000.

Hill & Sons was founded by Joseph Hill. He carried on business at "The Violin" in Holborn this year and later at the sign of the "Harp & Flute" in the Haymarket.

Hipkins stated that Fétis began his musical studies on a Zumpe square pianoforte which bore this date.

J. Holzbogen was appointed court Konzertmeister at München after his return from Italy this year.

Francis Ireland was awarded the degree of M. D. this year at Dublin.

Giuseppe Francesco Lolli succeeded Eberlin this season as Kapellmeister to the court at Salzburg.

Martini's report on Rameau's "Nouvelle reflexions sur le principe sonore" was finally ready this year. Martini said the style was modern and far from the excellent old Italian school , and that his system

(cont.) could be of value in the secular and theatrical styles but harmful to the polyphonic and church ones.

Under Monet's skilful management the Opera-Comique at Paris had progressed rapidly this year. It joined the Comedie-Italienne and took possession of the room in the Rue Mauconseil.

Mozart was a virtuoso on the clavier by this time.

Thomas Norris appeared this year at the Hereford Festival.

Thomas Norris appeared this season at Drury Lane Theatre in London in "The Spring", a pasticcio.

Piron, Crébillon "fils", Gentil Bernard and others this year founded a new society which became a "cafe" of the Palais-Royal and lasted twenty years.

Samuel Foote, an English humorist, introduced the name Rousoumoffsky (Razumovsky) to European society this year in a farce.

The great influence on Alexander Reinagle's life came from J. Christian Bach (son of J. S.), the "London" Bach, who had come from Italy to England this year.

Joseph Reinagle this season was appointed trumpeter to the King through the influence of the Earl of Kelly.

Antonio Rosales began to write for the stage this year. Besides about 70 "tonadillas", 12 "sainetes" and other smaller pieces, he wrote the music for a successful "zarzuela" to a

libretto by Ramón de la Cruza
called "El tío y la tía".

Barbara Scarlatti married
Eugenio Cachurro prior to this
year.

Johann Schwanenberg this season
became court Kapellmeister
at Braunschweig.

Carlo Tessarini, violinist and
composer, appeared this season
as a soloist at Amsterdam.

At Dublin this season Vernon
created the part of "Apollo" in
Kane O'Hara's "English burletta",
"Midas".

The publishers Breitkopf and
Härtel put many of Vivaldi's
works up for sale at this time.

Peter Welker this year established his music publishing
and sales business at London.

Two songs were reset this year
by T. A. Arne for a revival
of R. Fabian's ballad opera
"Trick for Trick". The songs
were completed prior to this
date.

J. Christian (son of J. S.)
Bach's Latin "Te Deum" was composed this year.

K. P. E. Bach's "Oden mit
Melodien" was published this
season.

K. P. E. Bach's "Symphony in
F major" was written at this
time.

The second part of K. P. E.
Bach's "Versuch über die wahre
Art das Clavier zu spielen"
was published this year.

Franz Beck's Op. 3 Symphonies
were published at this time.

Blaise's opera "Annette et
Lubin" was produced this
season at Paris.

Metastasio's libretto to
"L'Ateneide" was first set
this year by Bonno.

Breitkopf's "Catalogo dei soli,
duetti, trii e concerti per
il violino" was issued at
this time.

Bury's "Hylas at Zélie" (a new
act for a revival of his first
opera) was performed this year
at Paris.

Carey's "The Contrivances"
was performed this season in
America.

V. L. Ciampi's "Antigona"
was produced this season at
the Teatro San Samuele in
Venice.

Colla's opera "Adriano in
Siria" was produced this year
at Milan.

Crispi at this time wrote
several cantatas and oratorios
for various colleges and
churches in Rome.

Crispi's "Isacco" was completed at this time.

W. Dunlap this year printed
"An Exercise containing a
Dialogue and Ode on the
Accession of His present
gracious Majesty, George III,
Performed at the public com-
mencement in the College of
Philadelphia, May 18th,. . ."

Durán's "Temistocles" of this

year was an arrangement of Metastasio's play in Spanish written in less than a month.

Favart published an air this season.

Baldassare Galuppi wrote his opera "Il marchese villano" this year at Venice (libretto by Chiari).

Baldassare Galuppi wrote his opera "Il Muzio Scevola" this year at Padua (libretto by Lafranchi Rossi).

Baldassare Galuppi wrote his opera "L'orfano onorata" this year at Rome (author of libretto unknown).

Baldassare Galuppi wrote his opera "Il puntiglio amoroso" this year at Venice (libretto by Carlo or Gasparo Gozzi).

Baldassare Galuppi wrote his opera "L'uomo Femmina" this year at Venice (author of libretto unknown).

Baldassare Galuppi wrote the opera "Viriate" this year at Venice (libretto by Metastasio).

Ventura Galván, Spanish composer, wrote the music for the comedy "Riesgo, esclavitud y disfraz, ventura, acaso y deidad" at this time.

Ventura Gálvan, Spanish composer, wrote his first "tonadilla" this year.

Martin Gerbert von Hornau at this time published his prospectus for a volume of historical data of church music, in Marpurg's "Critische Briefe".

Hafner wrote his "Megära" this year.

Handel's "Semele" was revived by Smith and Stanley this season.

Henri Hardouin this year wrote a "Méthode nouvelle pour apprendre le plainchant".

The earliest baryton trios were written by Haydn this year.

Haydn composed his "Vivan gl' illustri sposi" for chorus this year.

Haydn wrote the Italian comedies "La Marchesa Nepola", "La Vedova", "Il Dottore", and "Il Sganarello" all at this time.

Haydn this year wrote a concerto for French horn, his first. It was in D major and in the score, Haydn mixed up the staves for oboe and violin. He then added the comment "written while asleep".

Haydn this year wrote the Italian "Acide" (festa teatrale).

Haydn's opera "Il dottore", a comedia, which has been lost, was produced this season at Eisenstadt.

Haydn's opera "La Marchesa Respoli", a comedia, was produced this season at Eisenstadt. Only fragments of the score have survived.

Haydn's opera "Il Sganarello", a comedia, was produced this season at Eisenstadt. The work has been lost since that time.

Haydn's opera "La vedova", a comedia, was produced this season at Eisenstadt. The work has been lost.

Haydn's overture to "Alcide" was composed this year. The work, in D major, was scored for 2 oboes, 2 horns and strings.

William Hayes this year published "Remarks on Mr. Avison's Essay on Musical Expression".

Joseph Hill issued some volumes of music this year that contained sets of lessons for harpsichord by different composers, from "The Harp & Flute" in the Haymarket.

Hiller's instrumental music "Loisir musical" was published this year and included 2 clavier sonatas and some "pièces de galanterie".

Jommelli's opera "L'amante deluso" was produced this season at Prague (possibly an earlier work under a new title).

Jean Louis Larvette's work "Le Guy de Chesne" was performed this season at the Comédie-Italienne in Paris.

Lyon's "Urania: Or a Choice Collection of Psalm Tunes, Anthems, and Hymns from the most approved authors with some entirely new . . . .etc. (Philadelphia 1762)(was) among the first collections to include "fuguing tunes".

Janes Lyon's psalm-tune collection "Urania" was published this year.

P. van Maldere's opera "La (cont.) Bagarre" exists at least in libretto and some extracts at the National Bibliothek in Paris.

P. van Maldere's opera "Les Soeurs rivales" appeared this year.

Marpurg, a German composer, published his "Klavierstücke" this year at Berlin. In this volume was a transcription of Couperin's "Le Rèveil Matin"; pieces by other clavecinists (Clérambault); and some of his own.

General Monckton's March for the 17th Regiment on Foot was written this year and used clarinets.

Mozart composed his first Minuets this year.

"The Real Story of John Carteret Pilkington", an anonymous book containing information on the life of Richard Pockrich appeared this year at Dublin.

Rameau's "Élements de musique théorique et pratique suivant les principes de M. Rameau" appeared this year in its second edition preceded by a "Discours preliminaire".

Jean-Jacques Rousseau's "Emile" was completed at this time.

Breitkopf at this time published a catalogue in which only two symphonies of the four listed under Sammartini's name were attributed to him, the others to Martinelli and Pergolesi.

Giuseppe Sarti's six sonatas

for clavier were published this year at London.

Alois Schmittbauer's serenata "L'isola disabitata" was performed this season at Rastatt.

Robert Smith's "Postscript upon the Changeable Harpsichord" was published this season.

Padre Antonio Soler's "Llave de modulación y antiguedades de la música" was published this year at Madrid.

Stevenson's "Music before the Classic Era" was published this year.

Neil Stewart's "Collection of . . . Reels" was issued at this time.

Tommaso Traetta's opera "Alessandro nell' Indie" (libretto by Metastasio) was performed this season at Reggio.

Tommaso Traetta's "La Francese a Malghera" was produced at Parma this season.

Tommaso Traetta's "Zenobia" was produced this season at Rome.

According to Mattheson, pitch at this time was: A=408 c.p.s. S-1'7.

Surviving harpsichords made by J. Kirkman include three made this year. One is a 1 manual owned by a Mrs. Ramsay; another a 2 manual owned by Benton Fletcher College in London; and the third is a 2 manual, 2x8', 1x4' lute owned by Colonial Williamsburg, Virginia.

The band of the Royal Regiment (cont.) of Artillery was formed this year.

The King of France this year granted the Swiss Guards a band of 4 oboes, 4 clarinets, 4 horns and 4 bassoons.

The Marylebone Gardens were opened this season in the morning, gratis and an organ performance was given from 5 to 8.

The "Musical Society of Edinburgh" moved to St. Cecilia's Hall at this time.

The Opéra-Comique merged with the Comédie-Italienne at this time.

Up until this year the théâtre de la foire and the Italian theater were opposed.

An organ was built this year in the church of St. Michael Bassishaw.

Charles Town (Charleston) musical amateurs were able to form a St. Cecilia Society this year, the first musical society in America.

Johann Gottlob Fichte, German philosopher, was born this year (died 1814).

Vulpius, author of "Rinaldo Rinaldi" and a mason, was born this year (died 1827).

Bishop Richard Hurd's "Letters on Chivalry & Romance" were published at this time advocating "The Gothic Chivalry" and "The spirit of romance".

Samuel Johnson, recognized for his literary distinction, this

THE NEWLY DISCOVERED PORTRAIT OF MOZART
(Owned by Mr. H.E. Krehbiel in 1901)

year was awarded a pension of
300 pounds a year for the
remainder of his life.

James MacPherson this year published a book, "Fingal", which
he claimed was a faithful translation of a poem by a third
century Irish bard, Ossian. It
depicted a society of very noble
primitive men and was a great
success in Europe. Later this
MacPherson was proved to be
a fraud, and "Fingal" was his
own invention.

Pietro Longhi, Venetian genre
painter, died this year (born
1702).

Vignon, French architect, was
born this year (died 1829).

This year marked the beginning
of the reign of Catherine II
(the Great) over Russia.

Empress Elizabeth of Russia
died this year (birthdate
unknown).

King George IV of England, House
of Hanover, was born (died 1830).

Nicholas Esterházy, "the Magnificent", succeeded to the title
of Prince this year.

Maximilian Friedrich this year
was elevated to the ecclesiastical principality of Münster.

Count Anton Willibald Wolfegg
was Canon at Salzburg from this
date forward.

(and 1763) Giuseppe Brunetti
wrote additional music for
Traetta's opera "Enea nel Lazio"
produced both these years at
Braunschweig.

(to 1763) Drury Lane Theatre
was materially altered and
enlarged during this year.

(to 1764) K. P. E. Bach wrote
his clavier Sonatinas during
these years.

(to 1764) Charles Clagget
was said to have been the leader
of the orchestra at the theatre
in Smock Alley, Dublin during
this period.

(to 1764) Mozart's "Sonata in
C major" was composed during
this period at Salzburg,
Brussels and Paris.

(to 1767) The first 48 of
Haydn's baritone trios were
written during these years.
They are as follows:

#1	A major	3/4	Adagio
#2	A major	2/4	Allegretto
#3	A major	2/4	Allegretto
#4	A major	C	Moderato
#5	A major	2/4	Moderato
#6	A major	C	Piu tosto Adagio
#7	A major	2/4	Moderato
#8	A major	2/4	Andante
#9	A major	3/4	Cantabile
#10	A major	C	Moderato
#11	D major	C	Adagio
#12	A major	2/4	Adagio
#13	A major	C	Moderato
#14	D majro	C	Adagio
#15	A major	3/4	Adagio
#16	A major	3/4	Moderato
#17	D major	2/4	Adagio
#18	A major	3/4	Adagio
#19	A major	2/4	Moderato
#20	D major	3/4	Adagio
#21	A major	C	Moderato
#22	D major	2/4	Adagio moderato
#23	A major	3/4	Adagio
#24	D major	C	Moderato (dated 1766)
#25	A major	3/4	Adagio
#26	G major	3/8	Adagio

#27	D major	3/4	Adagio
#28	D major	3/4	Adagio
#29	A major	2/4	Andante
#30	G major	2/4	Moderato
#31	D major	3/4	Cantabile
#32	G major	C	Moderato
#33	A major	3/4	Adagio
#34	D major	C	Moderato
#35	A major	6/8	Adagio
#36	D major	3/4	Adagio
#37	G major	3/4	Andante
#38	A major	2/4	Andante
#39	D major	3/4	Adagio
#40	D major	2/4	Moderato
#41	D major	2/4	Moderato

(dated 1767)

#42	D major	3/4	Adagio
#43	D major	C	Moderato
#44	D major	6/8	Allegro
#45	D major	2/4	Adagio
#46	A major	C	Moderato
#47	G major	3/4	Adagio
#48	D major	2/4	Moderato

(to 1768) Gabriel, French archi-techt: Versailles, Petit Trianon (78'6" wide x 37' high).

(to 1769) John Conquest during this period was drum-major of the Royal household at £100 a year.

(to 1769) Haydn's Concerto for violin No. 1 in C major was written during this period for violino concertante, 2 violins, viola and bass, "Fatto per il Luigi Tomasini".

(to 1770) Thomas Baker engraved music during these eight years.

(to 1770) Lambert Kraus' compo-sitions during this period in-cluded sacred and secular "Sing-spiele", 12 symphonies, 16 masses and other church music.

(to 1770) Karl Stamitz was a violinist in the Mannheim orch-estra during these years.

(to 1770) Gabriel, French arch-itect: Paris, Ministry of Marine (75' high).

(to 1771) Dauvergne, Joliveau and Caperan continued the Concert Spirituel during these years.

(to 1771) Alois Schmittbauer was conductor at the court of the Margrave of Baden at Rastatt for these nine years.

(to 1787) Breitkopf issued catalogues of printed music, both theoretical and practical, in 6 parts, of manuscript music, in 4 parts, and a third, a thematic catalogue of manu-script music only, in 5 parts with 16 supplements during these years.

(to 1796) The reign of Cather-ine II, Empress of Russia, spanned these years.

(to 1800) Michael Haydn was director and concertmaster to the archbishop of Salzburg for this long period.

(to 1878) During this period a spiritual and political rennaiscence was taking place in Bulgaria, during which an interest in folklore awoke.

c.1762

John Johnson, II, English music publisher, died this year (birthdate unknown).

Girolamo (Hieronymo) Stabilini, Italian violinist, was born this year at Rome (died 1815, July 13 at Edinboro).

Marianne Davies at this time achieved considerable reputa-tion for her skill on the "armonica", recently much im-

c.1762(cont.)
proved by Franklin.

J. J. Kriegk played the violin
at the court of Meiningen this
year.

Haydn's Symphony #9 in C major
was composed this year (2 flutes,
2 oboes, bassoon, 2 horns and
strings).

"The Catch Club, or Merry
Companions: . . ." was published
this year by Walsh, jr.

Hoban, an architect, was born
this year (died 1831).

(to 1769) François Joseph
Gossec was "intendant" of the
music of the Prince de Condé
during this period.

1763
(January 1) E. R. Duni's opera
"Le Milicien" was produced on
this date at the Comédie-
Italienne in Paris.

(January 4) Stephen Storace,
English composer of Italian
descent and brother of soprano
Ann Selina Storace, was born
on this day at London (died
1796, March 19 at London).

(January 6) This date marked the
publication of the first edition
of Aaron Williams' "The Universal Psalmodist" which title
read "By A. Williams. Teacher
of Psalmody in London . . .
printed for Joseph Johnson,
at Mead's Head . . ."

(January 6) A. Williams' "New
Universal Psalmodist" included
a preface, "To all Lovers of
Psalmody:, dated London.

(January 6) Constanze Weber,

(cont.) later to be Mozart's
wife, was born on this dat at
Zell, Baden (lower Austria).
She was a talented singer and
had some pianistic ability
(died 1842, March 6).

(January 8) Giuseppe Scolari's
opera "La cascina" was given
this season at London under
the direction of J. Christian
(son of J. S.) Bach.

(January 9) Karl Gottlieb
Umbreit, organist and composer,
was born on this date at
Rehstadt near Gotha (died 1829,
April 28 at Rehstadt).

(January 11) Thomas Griffin was
appointed professor of music
at Gresham College at this
time.

(January 11) Haydn's festa
teatrale "Acide", an opera
seria (libretto by Migliavacca) was performed on this
date at Eisenstadt. The score
is extant.

(January 27) Gottfried Christoph Härtel, music printer,
was born at this time in Schnee-
berg (died 1827, July 25 at
Cotta near Leipzig).

(January 29) G. Niccolini,
Italian composer of opera
and church music, was born on
this date (died 1842, December
18).

(January 30) Maria Magdalena
Keverich (later to be Johann
van Beethoven's wife) married
Johann Laym, valet of the
Elector of Trèves on this date.

(February 5) Charles (Benjamin)
Incledon, English tenor, was
born on this day at St.

1763(cont.)
Keverne, Cornwall (died 1826,
February 18 at London).

(February 11) J. F. Deller's
most famous ballet was "Orfeo
ed Euridice", first performed
on this date with Jommelli's
"Didone abbandonata".

(February 12) Gottfried Heinrich Bach, son of J. Sebastian
and member of the sixth generation of the Bach family, died
on this day (baptized, 1724,
February 27).

(February 17) Christoph Schaff-
rath, German harpsichordist and
composer, died on this date at
Berlin (born 1709).

(February 19) J. Christian
(son of J. S.) Bach's first
opera in England, "Orione,
ossia Diana vendicata", was
produced on this day at the
King's Theatre in London.

(February 19) Adalbert Gyrowetz,
Bohemian composer, was born on
this date at Budějovice (died
1850, March 19).

(February 22) Kane O'Hara's
"Midas", a renowned work of the
2nd period of English ballad
opera, was produced this evening
in London at Covent Garden.

(February 28) F. A. Philidor's
opera "Le Bûcheron, ou Les
Trois Souhaits" (libretto by
Guichard and Castet, after
Perrault) was performed on this
date at the Comédie-Italienne
in Paris.

(March 6) Jean (Xavier) Lefèvre,
Swiss clarinettist and composer,
was born on this date at Lausanne (died 1829, November 9).

(March 19) Joseph (von)
Friebert at this time was
appointed court conductor to
the Prince Bishop of Passau.

(March 20) Max (Joseph) Hellmann, Austrian composer and
instrumentalist, died this
year at Vienna (born 1702).

(Spring) Antonio Sacchini's
opera "Alessandro nell' Indie"
was produced at this time in
Venice.

(April 2) Giacomo Gotifredo
Ferrari, Italian composer, was
born on this day at Rovereto,
South Tyrol (died 1842,
December).

(April 7) Domenico Dragonetti,
Italian double-bass player and
composer, was born on this
date at Venice (died 1846,
April 16 at London).

(April 20) Anna Maria Crouch
(born Phillips), English
soprano, was born at this time
at London (died 1805, October
2 at Brighton).

(April 28, May 5, June 2, June
16) The "Pennsylvania Gazette"
in these issues carried advertisements about "The Lawfulness, Excellency and Advantage
of Instrumental Musick"

(May 5) The "Pennsylvania
Gazette" in this issue advertised William Dunlap as publishing and selling a collection of Psalm Tunes, Hymns
and Anthems.

(May 7) Charles John Frederick
Lampe at this time married a
singer, a Miss Smith.

(May 7-June 11) J. Christian

1763(cont.)

(son of J. S.) Bₐch's "Zanaida" was performed during this period at the King's Theatre in London.

(May 14) The first performance of Gluck's "Il trionfo di Clelia" (libretto by Metastasio) took place on this date at the inauguration of the Teatro Comunale in Bologna. Cecilia Grassi sang Larissa.

(May 15) Franz Danzi, composer, was born on this day at Mannheim (died 1826, April 13 at Carlsruhe).

(May 18) Philip Hayes was awarded the degree of Bachelor of Music at Oxford on this day. He received the greater share of his musical education from his father.

(May 28) Nathaniel Gow, Scottish musician, was born on this date at Inver, near Dunkeld (died 1831, January 19).

(May 28) The Reverend Richard Peters on this date wrote to Rev. William Smith, D.D., First Provost of the College of Philadelphia, about Hopkinson.

(June 2) The Pennsylvania Gazette in this issue advertised "For one Groat may be had a cudgel to drive the Devil out of every Christian Place of Worship. . ."

(June 9) Leopold Mozart, with Anna Maria and Wolfgang, left Salzburg on this date for Paris by way of München, Augsburg, Schwetzingen, Mainz, Frankfurt, Coblenz, Aachen and Brussels, where they concertized at various courts.

(June 14) Johann Simon Mayr, an Italian composer of Gₑrman origin, was born on this day at Mendorf, Bₐvaria (died 1845, December 2 at Bergamo).

(June 16) William Dunlap at this time issued a second edition of a pamphlet, "The Lawfulness, Excellency and Advantage of Instrumental Musick".

(June 16) The "Pennsylvania Gazette" in this issue carried an advertisement for the second edition of "The Lawfulness, Excellency and Advantage of Instrumental Musick" by William Dunlap.

(June 20) James Heseltine, English organist and composer, died on this date at Durham (born 1692 at London).

(Summer) Mozart's Allegro in C major was composed at this time in Salzburg.

(June 22) Étienne Méhul, French composer, was born on this date at Givet near Mézières (died 1817, October 18 at Paris).

(June 29) Johann Sebastian Demar, German organist and composer, was born on this dat at Gauaschach, Bavaria (died c.1832 at Orleans).

(July 2) Peter Ritter, German cellist, conductor and composer, was born on this date at Mannheim. He was a composition pupil of Vogler's (died 1846, August 1 at Mannheim).

(July 4) Charles Simon Favart's "Les Fetes de la Paix" was first performed on this date at Paris. The music was by Philidor and the work was an intermezzo

written on the conclusion of
peace with England. The performance was at the Comedie-
Italienne in Paris.

(July 5) G. Paisiello left
school on this date after nine
years of study.

(July 11) "Livietta e Tracollo"
was performed this evening at
Edinboro as "Tracolla".

(July 11) Leopold Mozart, in a
letter from Württemberg on this
day, described his anti-mili-
tarism.

(July 11) Schubert's father,
Franz Theodor Schubert, was
born at Neudorf near Altstadt
in Moravia (died 1830).

(July 15) Carl Heinrich Graun's
"Te Deum" was first performed
at this time at the end of the
Seven Years' War.

(July 21) E. R. Duni's opera
"Les Deux Chasseurs et la
laitiere" was produced on this
date at the Comédie-Italienne
in Paris.

(August 14) Giovanni Battista
Somis, Italian violinist and
composer, died at this time in
Turin (born 1686, December 25).
He was a pupil of Corelli.

(August 23) DeLange's "Le
Riche malheureux" was performed
on this day at Liege.

(August 24) Maria A. Walpurgis'
opera "Talestri regina delle
Amazoni" was performed on this
evening at Dresden.

(August 29) DaPonte, one of
Mozart's librettists, was of

(cont.) Jewish descent. His
mother was Chella Pincherele,
his father Geremia Conegliano
Corduangerber. The entire
family was baptized on this
date by Bishop Lorenzo da
Ponte, whose name they assumed.

(August 30) Mozart, at six
years old, on this date proved
his "perfect pitch" at a
concert at Frankfurt-am-Main,
Germany.

(September 18) Thomas Wright,
English organist, composer and
inventor, was born in Stockton
on Tees on this day (died
1829, November 24).

(September 26) On this day a
letter was written by Leopold
Mozart mentioning the Kerpen
family of which Franz Jugo
Kerpen was probably a member.

(September 29) Hiller's "Cantate bey der Wiedereröffnung
(sic) des Grossen Concerto"
(text by Clodius) was performed
on this evening at Leipzig.

(October 7) Josef Starzer's
ballet "Pygmalion, ou La
Statue animée" was produced
on this date at St. Petersburg.

(November 2) The organ in St.
Peter's Church was "built"
by Philipp Feyring (Fyring)
this year.

(November 18) Leopold Mozart
and his family arrived in
Paris on this day.

(November 22) E. R. Duni's opera
"Les Rendezvous" was produced
this evening at the Comédie-
Italienne in Paris.

(November 23) Michael Arne contributed three numbers to "A Midsummer Night's Dream", produced at the Drury Lane Theatre on this date.

(November 23) Battishill wrote two songs for "A Midsummer Night's Dream" (Garrick's operatic version), produced on this date at the Drury Lane Theatre in London.

(November 28) Matthäus Fischer, German composer and brother of Anton Fischer, was baptized on this day in Ried, Swabia.

(December 1) Robert Bremner's name did not appear in the Philadelphia papers prior to this date.

(December 1) The "Pennsylvania Gazette" in this issue stated that James Bremner opened his Music School and the paper provided information as to where, and what times for lessons.

(December 2) Johann Chrysostom Neruda, Czech violinist, died on this day at Prague (born 1705, December 1 at Rosice).

(December 5) Josef Starzer's ballet "Apollon et Dauphné" was produced at St. Petersburg on this evening.

(December 13) Felice (de') Giardini's opera "Siroe" was produced on this date at London.

(December 15) The declaration of inventory of the estate of Margarita Rossetti Gentili appeared on this date.

(December 23) John Davy, English composer, was born on this date at Upton Helions near Exeter

(cont.) (died 1824, February 12 at London).

(December 23) The pantomime "Rites of Hecate, or Harlequin from the Moon" was produced on this evening at Drury Lane Theatre in London (music by Battishill and John Potter).

(January) An English doctor, James Grainger, this month mentioned the banjo in his didactic poem "The Sugar Cane", written at Basseterre, British West Indies.

(February) N. Piccinni's opera "Le contadine bizzare" (libretto by Petrosellini) was performed this month at the Teatro Capranica in Rome.

(April) William Dunlap this month printed "The Lawfulness, Excellency and Advantage of Instrumental Musick in the Public Worship of God, Urg'd and Enforc'd from Scripture and the Examples of the far greater Part of Christians in all Ages. Address'd to all (particularly the Presbyterians and Baptists) who have hitherto been taught to look upon the Use of Instrumental Musick in the Worship of God as Unlawful. By a Presbyterian" at Philadelphia.

(April) Abbé Galiani this month wrote a criticism of the French Opéra, complaining that the orchestra and singers were too loud.

(May) Robert Bremner ". . .can hardly have been organist at St. Peters . . . especially not in May" because the editor of Psalm-tune Collection stated that "no organ existed in St.

Peter's".

(May) Robert Bremner, if he was editor of Dunlap's psalm-tune collection, must have been in Philadelphia earlier than this month.

(June) Santo Lapis was in Edinburgh this month where he was harpsichordist for a visiting Italian intermezzo company.

(June) The entire Mozart family, father, mother, Wolfgang, and his talented elder sister, Mariane ("Nannerl") embarked this month on a tour that included lengthy stays in Paris and London.

(June) Antonio Sacchini's opera "L'Olimpiade" was performed this month at Padua.

(August) Mozart as a boy of seven this month rebuked Esser at Mainz for adding too many notes and said he ought to play music as it was written.

(September or October) Maria Linley, English singer, was born at this time in Bath (died 1784, September 5 at Bath).

(September) John Watts, English bookseller and printer, died this month at London (born 1678).

(October) Santo Lapis went to York this month with an Italian intermezzo company.

(November) Cecilia Davies appeared this month at the Theatre Royal in Dublin.

(November) Matthäus Fischer, German composer and brother of Anton Fischer, was born this

(cont.) month at Ried, Swabia (died 1840).

(December) A singer, Madame Lentner, after 4½ years of service in the court at Bonn, this month gave up her appointment. Johann van Beethoven (Ludwig's father) requested a raise in salary from her salary now not used.

? Alday (l'aine), a member of a French family of musicians, was born this year. He was a mandoline player and violinist (death date unknown but probably at Lyons).

Johann Andrers Amon, German conductor and composer, was born this year at Bamberg (died 1825, March 29 at Wallerstein, Bavaria).

John Jacob Astor, founder of the Anglo-American firm of musical instrument makers, was born this year at Waldorf (died 1848 at New York).

Blaze's father, a lawyer and musician, was born this year (died 1833).

Michel Joseph Gébauer, French violinist, oboist and composer, was born this year at La Fère, Aisne (died 1812). He was also a French army bandmaster.

Maria Scarlatti died soon after her father, and left her share in her mother's estate to her grandmother and guardian, Margarita Rossetti Gentili, who herself died this year at the age of eight-three at the house of her step-grandchild, Barbara Scarlatti.

Johann Gottlieb Janitsch,

German lawyer and composer,
died this year at Berlin (born
1708, June 19 at Schweidnitz,
Silesia).

Francesco Giuseppe Pollini,
Italian pianist and composer,
was born at this time at
Ljubljana (died 1846, September
17 at Milan).

John Relfe, English composer,
was born this year in Greenwich.
He studied under his father,
Lupton Relfe (died c.1837 at
London).

Alembert's article on music
"Fondamental" provoked "Observations sur les principes de
l'harmonie, occasionnees par. .
. l'article "Fondamental" de
M. d'Alembert" was issued this
year at Geneva by J. A. Serre,
who had been criticized.

Giuseppe Aprile sang in all the
principal theatres of Italy and
Germany from this date forward.

Arne's "The Birth of Hercules"
was rehearsed at Covent Garden
this year.

J. Christian Bach (son of J. S.)
scored for clarinets in D and
Bb in his opera "Orione" this
season.

Joseph Baildon obtained one of
this year's first prizes given
by the "Catch Club" for a catch.

Battishill this year married
Miss Davies, a singing actress.

Baudron entered the orchestra
of the Comedie-Française at
this time.

Karl Friedrich Baumgarten became leader of the orchestra

(cont.) this season at the
Haymarket Theatre in London.

František Benda wrote an
autobiography this year.

George Berg this year won the
first prize medal awarded
by the "Catch Club" for his
glee "On softest beds at
leisure laid".

Jean-Baptiste Joseph Boutmy
visited The Hague at this time.

James Bremner arrived in Philadelphia this year.

It's not certain whether James
Bremner was engaged as organist
for St. Peter's this season.

As late as this year Casanova
danced the minuet in London.

Ann Catley appeared at Marylebone Gardens this season.

Domenico Corri studied under
Porpora at Naples from this
date forward.

John Crosdill was said to
have been at Westminster
School, but no trace of his
name in the school registers,
which, however, only started
this year.

Charles Dibdin was engaged
at Birmingham this season.

Dressler was employed at the
court of Gotha at this time.

Karl Vilhelm Düben was appointed envoy to the Russian court
this year.

Ebdon this year was appointed
organist at Dorham Cathedral.
He held the position until his
death.

Prince Nicholas Esterházy's
son married the Countess Erdödy
at this time.

Until this year Marie Fel,
French soprano, sang at the
"Musique du Roi".

Benjamin Franklin perfected his
glass harmonica invention this
year.

Frederick the Great at this time
set the size of Prussian army
bands at 2 oboes, 2 clarinets,
2 horns and 2 bassoons, a
combination accepted by several
composers of the Classical
period for wind octet music.

Caterina Gabrielli left northern
Italy at this time to continue
her career in the south.

Gluck, along with Dittersdorf
and the singer, Chiara Marini,
visited Venice and Bologna this
year.

William Hayes conducted the
Gloucester Festival this season.

William Hayes became a competi-
tor for the prizes offered by
the "Catch Club" this year and
won 3 prizes for his canona
"Alleluja" and "Miserere nobis"
and his glee "Melting airs soft
joys inspire".

J. Hiller took charge of the
"Liebhaberkonzerte" this year
at Leipzig. He took steps to
improve the choir right away.

Francis Hopkinson was awarded
the Master of Arts degree this
year from the College of New
Jersey, "gratiae causa".

Francis Hopkinson wrote a

(cont.) third ode, perhaps
for commencement of this year.

Hülpliers at this time con-
sulted bishops and consistories
to collect information about
the history of Swedish organ-
building.

Henrik Johnsen became musical
director of the French court
theatre this season.

C. Kühnau went to Berlin this
year to take lessons in harmony and composition from
Kirnberger.

Kürzinger this year in his
"Getreuer Unterricht" said
that "Lituus" can mean either
a "trompette" or a "Waldhorn".

Ignaz Franz Xaver Kürzinger,
after being a trumpeter in a
cavalry regiment and chapel
master at Mergentheim, became a violinist this year in
the orchestra of the prince-
bishop of Würzburg and later
music director at the Julius
Hospital.

Jean Louis Larvette at this
time married Mlle. Villette,
a favorite singer and actress.

Georg Simon Löhlein this season
went to Leipzig as a violinist
and pianist.

Marylebone Gardens this year
passed into the hands of
Thomas Lowe, the popular tenor.
The admission was raised to 1s
and Miss Catley was among the
singers engaged.

It was doubtful whether James
Lyon took part in the musical
controversy that took place at
Philadelphia this year.

1763(cont.)

James Lyon at this time published a pamphlet, "the Lawfulness, Excellency, and Advantage of Instrumental Musick
in the Public Worship of God".

After gaining a reputation in
Italy, S. Manzuoli went to
Madrid this year where he was
engaged at a high salary by
Farinelli.

William Mason became canon
residentiary and precentor of
York Minster at this time.

A. Mazzoni played second cembalo
in Gluck's opera "Il trionfo
di Clelia" this season at
the inauguration of the new Teatro Publico at Bologna.

Frederick Messing, a leading
English horn player, had his
name in Mortimer's "London
Directory" this year as that
of a "Performer on the French
horn and Violin".

Regina Mingotti sang in
"Cleonice", "Siroe", "Enea e
Lavinia", "Leucippo" and "Sene-
crita" this season probably
at London.

Other makers of the armonica
besides Franklin mentioned in
Mortimer's London Directory of
this year, were John Harris
and William Phipps.

Mortimer's rare London Directory
of this year provided a list of
twenty-eight wind instrumetal-
ists who actually taught, and of
these six were bassoonists.

Leopold Mozart this season received the position of vice-
kapellmeister in the Archbishop
of Salzburg's orchestra.

Mozart at this time gave a
concert in Frankfurt, and
Goethe remembered it years
later.

G. Muffat retired on a pension
this year.

Johann Heinrich Müller came to
the Vienna Hoftheater this
season.

J. Myslivécek went to Venice
this year to study music with
Pescetti.

Johann Naumann returned to
Dresden at this time and was
appointed court composer of
sacred music.

M. Overend this year published
"12 Sonatas for two Violins
& Violoncello".

Vassily A. Pashkevich entered
service of Catherine II this
year as violinist in the court
orchestra and later became a
conductor and court composer.

As long ago as this year, John
Peace found "the unwillingness
and inability of the higher
ranks of the Church in England
to take an active part in the
cathedral service" was the
subject of published comments.

Breitkopf's catalog of this
year listed a flute concerto
by Pergolesi.

Lyon was the editor of a
psalm-tune collection of this
year dedicated to Reverend
Peters.

Emmanuele Conegliano's name
was changed to Lorenzo da Ponte
when the family embraced
Christianity this year.

Porpora owed 60 ducats for rent at this time.

Rameau this year asked Pellegrin for a text for an opera. A story from this period stated that Pellegrin consented on condition of a sizeable payment if the opera failed.

Pietro Pompeo Sales was in the service of the Bishop of Augsburg at this time.

C. G. Schröter of Nordhausen took credit for the invention of a clavier equipped with hammers and partly with springs (Triebfedern) in Mizler's "New eröffnete musikalische Bibliothek". He repeated his claim in Marpurg's "Kritische Briefe" of this year.

Jean Georges Siéber was a horn player in the orchestra of the Comédie-Française at this time.

Cordeiro da Silva held the position of organist at the Royal Chapel at Ajuda this year as well as that of court composer to King Joseph.

William Smith stopped his music publishing business this year.

Oscar G. T. Sonneck maintains that there was no organ in Christ Church at this time, consequently, no organist.

Carl Stenborg, Swedish singer and composer, entered a government office job this year.

John Stephens, English organist and composer, was awarded the degree of Doctor of Music this year by Cambridge University.

Marpurg selected Pietro Francesco Valentini's "con le sue Resolutioni in più di Duemila Modi" as the theme of his "Critical Letters on Music" this year.

At the age of eight this year Viotti already played the violin.

The annual publishing of catches and glees in oblong folders was started this year by E. T. Warren.

Samuel Webbe first appeared as a composer this year.

Mrs. Weichsell was a clarinet player at King's Theatre, Haymarket, London this season.

Clarinets appeared this year for the first tiem at the Three Choirs Festival. Weichsell, an oboist, was one of the players.

Georg Weimar was cantor at Erfurt at the Kaufmannskirche this year.

Williamson, in "Bibliography of Maine" and Sabin, in "Bibliotheca Americana" both mentioned an edition of Urania as 1763, but it "is probably a misprint".

Jean Le Rond D'Alembert's "De la liberté de la musique, 1758, in Mélanges de litterature, d'histoire et de philosophie (2nd ed.), IV; 1763" appeared this year.

Algarotti's "Saggio sopra l'opera, in musica" was published at this time.

Aufossi's first opera "La serva spiritosa" appeared this

MARIA ANNA THEKLE
(Mozart's Cousin)

season at Rome.

T. A. Arne's opera "Love in a Village" this season had its first performance in England.

Avossa's comic opera "La pupilla" was performed this season at Naples.

J. Christian (son of J. S.) Bach's six Concertos op. 1 were published this year at London.

J. Christian (son of J. S.) published six Trios, op. 2 at this time.

J. C. Friedemann Bach wrote his Sonata in Eb this year.

J. C. F. Bach this year wrote a Trio for flute, violin and bass.

According to Spitta only Johann Sebastian Bach's Inventions were published at Leipzig this year.

William Bates wrote single songs for the revival of Galliard's "Rape of Proserpine" this season at Covent Garden in London.

Giovanni Battista Bianchi may have been the same composer who wrote a cantata for the Archiepiscopal Seminary this year at Siena.

Borono's opera "L'Amore in musica" appeared this year at Venice.

Brijon wrote his "Réflexions sur la Musique" at this time.

John Brown's "Dissertation on the Rise, Union & Power, the (cont.) Progressions, Separations, & Corruptions of Poetry & Music" bore this date.

G. G. Brunetti's opera "Arminio" appeared this season at Lucca.

Cooke composed an Ode this year for Christmas Day.

Pietro Maria Crispi this year wrote a cantata, "La Morte de Abele".

Highly detailed descriptions and illustrations of all the French bagpipes were provided in Diderot and d'Alembert's Encyclopedie this year at Paris.

Doni's description of the "Lyra Barberina" was published at Florence this year.

Domenico Fischietti this year wrote an oratorio "La morte d'Abele" and a comic opera "La donna di governo" (libretto by Goldoni).

Baldassare Galuppi wrote his opera "Arianna e Teseo" this year at Padua (libretto by Pariata).

Baldassare Galuppi wrote his opera "Il re alla caccia" in Venice this year (libretto by Goldoni).

Filippo Gherardeschi's first opera, "L'amore artigiano" (libretto by Goldoni) was given this season at Lucca.

Paul César Gibert wrote his opera "Apelle et Campaspe" at this time.

Gluck's "Ezio" of 1750 was revived this season at Vienna.

"Social Harmony, consisting of
a collection of songs and
catches. By Thomas Hale of
Darnhall, Cheshire" appeared
this year. It included Masonic
references.

The earliest edition of Handel's
"Messiah" was published this
year by Walsh.

Hasse's opera "Siroe, re di
Persia" appeared this season
in a new version.

Haydn's sonata for piano #5
in A major was published prior
to this year.

Haydn wrote his Symphony #11
at this time.

Haydn's Symphony #12 in E major
was written this year for 2
oboes, 2 horns and strings.

Haydn's Symphony #13 in D major
for flute, 2 oboes, 4 horns,
drumgs and strings was composed this year. The drums
were added to the manuscript
in another handwriting.

Haydn wrote his Symphony #40
this year.

Numbers 15-20 of Haydn's 21
Trios for two violins and violoncello appeared in a Breitkopf
and Härtel catalogue of this
year.

Haydn's string trio for 2
violins and bass in E major #1
was published prior to this
date by Bailleux. The Breitkopf
catalogue #1 of 1767 listed it
as well.

Haydn's string trios for 2
violins and bass #1 in B major

(cont.) was composed prior to
this year. It has been lost
according to H's catalogue #5.

Haydn's string trios for 2
violins and bass were composed prior to this year.
H's catalog #7 listed them as
follows:
    A major #1 Simrock
    A major #2
    A major #3
    A major #4 La Chevardiere,
        Bremner, Preston
    A major #5 Lost, only left
        "Kleines Quartbuch"
    A major #6 Lost, only left
        "Kleines Quartbuch"

Haydn's string trio for 2
violins and bass #1 in D major
in H's catalog #15 was written
prior to this year. It also
appeared in Breitkopf's catalog of 1766 as published by
La Chevadière of Paris and also
by Longman.

Haydn's string trios for 2
violins and bass were written
prior to this year. They were
listed in H's catalog #16 as
follows:
    C major #1
    C major #2
    C major #3
    C major #4
    C major #5
    C major #6
    C major #7
    C major #8
    C major #9 Most likely not a
        string trio but a diverti-
        mento for clavier accompa-
        niment
    C major #10 Egerton, B.M.,
        Forster

Haydn's string trios for 2
violins and bass were composed
prior to this year. They were
listed as follows in H's

catalogue #17:
    Eb major #5 Breitkopf's
        Cat., 1766, published by
        La Chevardiere, Artaria,
        Mollo, Bremner, Preston
    Eb major #6
    Eb major #7
    Eb major #8
    Eb major #9
    Eb major #10
    Eb major #11 Brussels:
        Leopold Hoffmann
    Eb major #12
    Eb major #13

Haydn's string trios for 2
violins and bass were composed
prior to this year. They were
listed as follows in H's
catalogue #18:
    Bb major #3 Breitkopf's
        Cat. 1766, La Chevardiere
        Longman
    Bb major #4 Simrock
    Bb major #5
    Bb major #6 Lost. Only
        listed in "Kleines Quart-
        buch"
    Bb major #7

Haydn's string trios for 2
violins and bass were composed
prior to this year. They were
listed as follows in H's
catalogue #19:
    E major #3 Breitkopf's
        Cat. 1766. Published by
        La Chevardiere; also
        Longman
    E major #4 Lost
    E major #5
    E major #6

Haydn's string trios for 2
violins and bass were composed
prior to this year. They were
listed as follows in H's
catalogue #20:
    G major #1 Breitkopf's
        Cat. 1766. Published by
        La Chevardiere, Artaria,

        Bremner, Preston, Mollo
    G major #2 La Chevardiere,
        Preston, Bremner
    G major #3 Simrock
    G major #4 Simrock
    G major #5 Lost. Only
        listed "Kleines Quartbuch"
    G major #6 Lost. Only
        listed Fuch's Cat.
    G major #7 Egerton, B.M.,
        Forster

Hayes published his first set
of catches at this time.

Herbain's comic opera "Les
Deux Talents" was produced
at the Comedie-Italienne in
Paris this season.

These compositions for two
flutes by V. A. Holmes were
published this year by Jonathan Fentum: "Twenty-four
Duetts, op. 1", "Twenty-Four
Familiar Airs, op. 3", "Six
Sonatas, op. 4".

Francis Hopkinson's "Collection
of Psalm Tunes with a few
Anthems and Hymns" was issued
at this time in Philadelphia.

Jommelli's opera "La pastorella
illustre" was performed this
season at Stuttgart.

I. F. X. Kürzinger this year
published his "Getreuer Unterricht zum Singen mit Mamieren
und die Violine zu spielen" at
Augsburg.

Giovanni Battista Lampugnani's
opera "Enea in Italia" was produced this season at Palermo.

Jean Louis Larvette wrote
"Le Guy de Chesne, ou La Feste
des Druides" at this time.

N. Logroscino's "L'innamorato balordo" was produced this season.

N. Logroscino's "La viaggia-trice di bell' umore" was produced this season.

Marpurg's "Anleitung zur Musik" was published at this time

G. Martini's "Duetti da camera" was published this year at Bologna.

Pierre Monsigny's opera of this year, "Le Nouveau Monde" (libretto by Charles Simon Favart based on a play by Simon Joseph de Pellegrin), was never produced.

Mozart's Andante in Bb major for piano was composed this year at Salzburg.

G. Paisiello wrote a comic intermezzo this year.

J. & S. Phillips published Warren's "Collection of Catches and Glees" at this time.

N. Piccinni's opera "La donne vendicate" (libretto by Petro-sellini) was produced this year during carnival at the Teatro Valle at Rome.

N. Porpora's "Ouverture royale" appeared at this time.

Antonio Sacchini's "Semiramide" was produced this year at the Argentina Theater in Rome.

G. Scarlatti's opera "Pelopida" was produced this season at the Teatro Regio in Turin (libretto by Roccaforte).

Tommaso Traetta went to Vienna

(cont.) this season to hear a performance of his "Ifigenia in Tauride", written especially for the Austrian capital.

Vento's "La finta semplice" was produced this year at Rome.

"A Collection of Catches, Canons, and Glees, for three, four, five, six, and nine voices, never before published. Selected by Thomas Warren, London for the editor" was published this year at London.

Warren's "Collection of Catches & Glees" was engraved this year by Phillips.

Aaron Williams' "The Universal Psalmodist" appeared this year in its first edition at London.

The surviving harpsichords made this year by J. Kirkman included #15, 1 manual, 2x8' only, currently owned by C. F. Colt; #16, 2 manuals, 2x8', 1x4', current owner, Kenneth Skeading; #17, 2 manuals, 2x8', 1x4', current owner, Stockholm Musik-historiska Museet; #18, 2 manuals, no data on stops, current owner, Miss E. Wilkinson.

It is doubtful whether Christ Church possessed an organ at this time.

A subscription of £500 was raised this year towards the purchase of an organ for Christ Church, Philadelphia.

"The Vestry agreed to the erecting of an organ in Saint Peter's Church" at this time.

A rare booklet was published this year at Philadelphia, "A Collection of Psalm Tunes with a few Anthems and Hymns . . . for the Use of the United Churches of Christ Church and St. Peter's Church in Philadelphia".

The "Catch Club" offered its first prizes this season.

Leipzig's Gewandhaus concerts were resumed this season after an interruption by the Seven Years' War.

The Paris theatre of the Palais Royal, built by Lemercier and 90 years old, was destroyed by fire. This was the Paris Opéra.

Jean Paul (Johann Paul Friedrich Richter), a writer, was born this year (died 1825).

Samuel Johnson at this time founded his Literary Club of which Reynolds, Burke, Goldsmith and Sir John Hawkins were members.

Boswell this year published his "An Account of Corsica, the Journal of a Tour of that Island, and Memoirs of Pascal Paoli".

"A Dissertation on the Union and Power, the Progressions, Separations, and Corruptions of Poetry and Music" by John Brown was issued at this time.

Bulfinch, an architect, was born this year (died 1763).

Kiyomasu, Japanese painter, died this year (born 1679).

George Morland, genre painter of rustic subjects, was born this year (died 1804).

Francesco Guardi this year

(cont.) painted "The Doge Embarking on the Bucentaur" (oil on canvas, 26 3/8" x 39 3/8"). The picture hangs at the Louvre.

Tiepolo painted the ceiling perspectives at the Throne Room, Escorial, Würzburg at this time.

Sir John Hawkins this year was elected chairman of the "Quarter Sessions". He held this position for over 15 years.

Ignaz Joseph was co-adjutor of his uncle Leopold Joseph this year in Brixen.

The Austro-Prussian peace was signed at this time.

The French wars ended this year.

The Jacobite Plot occurred at this juncture.

The "Peace of Paris" marked the triumph of England over France. England became the undisputed "mistress of the seas".

(and 1764, 1768, 1769, 1772) John Brown's "A Dissertation on the Union and Poser, the Progressions, Separations, and Corruptions of Poetry and Music" was reissued the next year as "The History of the Rise and Progress of Poetry" and translated into French (Paris, 1768), German (Leipzig, 1769) and Italian (Florence, 1772), but it did not include music.

(to 1764) Felice (de') Giardini was the manager of the Opera in London during this season.

(to 1764) Haydn composed the "Esterhazy Cantata" this year

1763(cont.)
for Prince Nicholas' name day.
The text was in German and the
work was scored for solo voices,
chorus, flute, oboe, bassoon,
clarinet and strings.

(to 1764) Haydn's string quartets listed below were composed
at this time:
    #13 Op. 3, #1 E major
    #14 Op. 3, #2 C major
      "Fantasia con variazione"
    #15 Op. 3, #3 G major
      "Bagpipe Minuet"
    #16 Op. 3, #4 Bb major
    #17 Op. 3, #5 F major 2nd
      movement "Serenade"
    #18 Op. 3, #6 A major

(to 1764) James Hook at this
time left Norwich for London
where he became organist at
White Conduit House, one of the
famous "tea-houses".

(to 1764) Mozart's Sonata in D
major for violin and piano was
composed this year at Paris.

(to 1764) Franz Adam Veichtner,
German violinist and composer,
was engaged by the Russian Count
Kaiserling at Königsberg for
this season.

(to 1764) Franz Adam Veichtner,
German violinist and composer,
composed several violin concertos this year at Königsberg,
and was later mentioned by
Reichardt in his autobiography.

(and as early as 1766) Franz
Benda left a very detailed and
highly coloured account of his
youthful adventures in a long
autobiographical sketch written
this year, which was used by
Hiller as early as 1766.

(to 1766) Cambini studied the

(cont.) violin with Pohl and
theory under Martini at Bologna
during this period.

(and 1767) Prefixed to John
Brown's "Dissertation" of this
date was the libretto of an
oratorio or "sacred ode", "The
Cure of Saul", which the author
adapted to music by Purcell,
Benedetto Marcello, and Handel.
It was performed this season
after Brown's death, reset by
Arnold and later performed in
1767. It was also revived on
other occasions.

(to 1767) Mrs. Vincent was a
leading singer at Marylebone
Gardens for these four years.

(to 1769) W. Pichl was violinist
with Bishop Patachich's orchestra at Nagyvárad (Hungary)
during this period. The orchestra was then directed by
Dittersdorf with whom Pichl
formed a close friendship.

(to 1770) Cervetto the Younger
toured as a soloist on the
continent for these seven
seasons.

(to 1770) Antonio Sacchini
composed operas during these
years at the Argentina Theater
in Rome.

(to 1776) Karl Franz held a
position under Prince Nicholas
Esterházy at Eisenstadt during
this long period.

(to 1776) Giacomo Rust lived
chiefly in Venice at this time
where a great number of his
operas were performed.

(November 18 to 1774, April 10)
Wolfgang and Anna Maria Mozart
performed concerts in Paris and

at the court in Versailles on these dates.

(to 1777) Crispi wrote a half a dozen comic operas and inter- mezzi during these years.

(to 1794) "Vocal Harmony: A collection of Glees, Madrigals, . . ., including the prize glees from 1763-1794" was edited by William Horsley at this time.

(to 1795) F. W. Marpurg was director of the government lottery at Berlin during this period.

c.1763

Eliza Abrams, singer was born this year (death date unknown).

Pierre Aubert, French violon- cellist, was born at this time in Amiens (died c.1830 at Paris).

Joseph Exaudet, French violinist and composer, died this year at Paris (born c.1710 at Rouen).

Pietro Carlo Guglielmi, Italian composer, was born at this time probably at Naples (died 1817, February 28).

Robert Bremner's "the Harpsichord or Spinnet Miscellany" appeared this year at London, dated by Robert Eitner.

Ann Catley this year became a pupil of Macklin, the actor.

Simon Leduc appeared this year as soloist in several violin concertos at the Concert Spirituel in Paris.

Johann Samuel Schröter went with his father and sister to

(cont.) Leipzig this year.

Walter Clagget's Op. 2, "Six Solos and Six Scots Airs with Variations for the Violin, or Violoncello with a Thorough Bass for the Harpsichord, London, Printed for the Author" appeared this year.

Haydn's Symphony #14 in A major for 2 oboes, 2 horns and strings was composed at this time.

Haydn's Symphony #15 in D major for 2 oboes, 2 horns and strings was composed at this time.

"Six Solos for the Violin", published this year at London, was probably credited to Thomas Mazzinghi.

(to 1765) Haydn's Symphony #33 in C major for 2 oboes, 2 horns and strings was composed during this period.

1764

(January 1) N. Piccinni's opera "Gli stravaganti" (librettist unknown) was produced on this date at the Teatro Valle in Rome.

(January 2) F. Philidor's opera "Le Sorcier" (libretto by Poin- sinet) was produced this evening at the Comédie-Italienne in Paris.

(January 3) "Il Filosofo di campagna", an opera by Galuppi, was performed on this date at the Electoral Theatre in Bonn.

(January 7) Gluck's opera "La Recontre imprévue" (libretto by L. H. Dancourt) was produced this evening at the Burg Theatre in Vienna.

1764(cont.)

(January 8) In Bonn a grand
assembly was held at the palace
including a fine dinner in the
grand gallery and a masked ball.

(January 12) Pasquale Cafaro
wrote a cantata for King Ferdinand IV's birthday at this time.

(January 12) The "Pennsylvania
Gazette" in this issue printed
an advertisement, "On Thursday,
the 19th instant, at the Assembly Room in Lodge Alley, will be
performed a Concert of Musick,
to be continued every other
Thursday, till the 24th of May
. . ."

(January 13) Franz Lauska,
Moravian pianist and composer,
was born on this date at Brno
(died 1825, April 18).

(January 15) William Hayes was
awarded the degree of Master
of Arts by Magdalen College,
Oxford on this date.

(January 19) T. A. Arne's "The
Arcadian Nuptials" was produced
this evening at Covent Garden
in London.

(January 20) Michael Arne's
"Hymen" was produced on this
date at Drury Lane Theatre in
London.

(January 20) Richard Cooper,
Scottish music engraver, died
on this day (birthdate unknown).

(January 20) Vento's opera
"Leucippo" was performed this
evening at the King's Theatre
in London.

(January 25) Felix Joseph
Lipowsky, German musical lexicographer and composer, was born

(cont.) on this day in Wiesen-
steig (died 1844, March 21 at
München).

(February 13) George Berg's
opera "Antigono" was performed
this evening at the Great Room,
Spring Gardens, St. James'.

(February 16) The "Pennsylvania
Journal" in this issue advertised a concert at Assembly Room
under the direction of James
Bremner.

(February 17) Josef Starzer's
ballet "Acis et Galatée" was
produced on this date at St.
Petersburg.

(February 21) James Bremner
directed a Concert which took
place on this date at the
Assembly Room.

(February 22) Alexander Campbell,
Scottish organist, was born on
this date at Tombea, Loch
Lubnaig (died 1824, May 15 at
Eninboro).

(February 29) T. A. Arne produced his second oratorio
"Judith" this evening at the
Chapel of the Lock Hospital
in Grosvenor Place, Pimlico. It
was a benefit for charity.

(February 29) The first of the
concerts at Spring Gardens took
place on this date and J. Christian Bach (son of J. S.) collaborated with Carl Friedrich Abel.
Bach's serenata "Galatea" was
performed.

(March 1) Joseph Legros made his
debut at the Paris Opéra this
evening.

(March 8) Monsigny's opera "Rose
et Colas" (libretto by Sedaine

1764(cont.)

after Lafontaine) was performed
on this date at the Comédie-
Italienne in Paris. It was one
of his most successful operas.

(Spring) Santo Lapis went to
Dublin at this time with an
Italian intermezzo company.

(March 23) "La buona Figliuola"
an opera with music by Piccini,
was performed at the Bonn court
for the second time on this date.

(March 25) Boyce's younger child,
William, who later was well
known as a double-bass player in
London orchestras, was born on
this date (death date unknown).

(March 30) Pietro Locatelli,
Italian violinist and composer,
died on this date at Amsterdam
(born 1695, September 3). He
studied with Corelli.

(April 3) Reverend Dorr at this
time published the vestry-
minutes of both St. Peter's and
Christ Church.

(April 3) The coronation of the
Archduke Joseph as King of the
Romans took place on this day.

(April 3) John Worgan's oratorio
"Hannah" was produced on this
evening.

(April 3) Gluck's "Orfeo" was
performed on this date at the
coronation of Joseph II as King
of the Romans. Goethe, 15 years
old at the time, was in the
audience. The event took place
at Frankfurt-am-Main

(April 15) John Immyns, English
lawyer and amateur musician,
died on this date at London
(birthdate unknown).

(April 17) Johann Mattheson,
German organist, harpsichordist,
singer and composer, died on
this date at Hamburg (born 1781,
September 28 at Hamburg).

(April 18) The "Pennsylvania
Gazette" on this date reported:
". . . Thirty Pounds was raised
for the Benefit of the Charity
Schools belonging to the said
College".

(April 24) Johann van Beethoven
this year was granted a salary
of 100 thalers per annum, based
on his violin-playing skill.
This had been promised to him
two years earlier.

(April 24) Elector Maximilian
Friedrich on this date issued
two decrees. On was to grant
Joannes van Beethoven (Ludwig's
father) a raise; the other
appointed Anna Maria Ries
(Johann's daughter) a court
singer.

(April 24) Hasse's opera "Egeria"
(libretto by Metastasio) was
performed at Vienna on this date.

(April 27) T. A. Arne's opera
"L'Olimpiade" was produced
this evening at the King's
Theatre in London. It was performed in the original language.

(April 27) Elector Maximilian
Friedrich on this day wrote the
Electoral Exchequer at the Bonn
court concerning the two new
salaries to be taken out of
Lenther's salary (since she had
resigned), one for Anna Maria
Ries and the other for Johann
van Beethoven.

(May 3) Count Francesco Algarotti,
Italian scholar, died at Pisa
this year (born 1712, December
11 at Venice).

(May 5) Felice (de') Giardini's opera "Enea e Lavinia" was produced on this day at London.

(May 12) Wilhelm Friedemann Bach resigned his position at Halle at this time.

(May 13) On the Elector's birthday today, "Le Nozze" (music by Galuppi) and two ballets were performed at the Bonn court.

(May 20) "Il Filosofo di Campagna", an opera by Galuppi, was performed at the Bonn court on this date.

(May 21) C. Dibdin wrote "The Shipherd's Artifice", a pastoral which was performed on this date for his benefit. The performance was held at Covent Garden in London.

(May 22 and June 29) The "Pennsylvania Magazine of History", Volume VI, page 124, referred to William Kelby's memorandum in both these issues.

(June 5) Wolfgang and Anna Maria Mozart gave their first concert at the Great Room in Spring Gardens on this date.

(June 5) Musical items in great number and varieties were available in Philadelphia at this time as proved by an advertisement in the "Pennsylvania Gazette" issued on this date.

(Summer) Domenico Dall'Oglio, Italian violinist and composer, died at this time at Narva (born c.1700 at Padua).

(Summer) Elector Max Friedrich went away to Brühl at this time but visited Bonn twice a week

(cont.) when operas were performed.

(June 29) Wolfgang Mozart played the harpsichord and organ at a concert at Ranelagh this evening for the benefit of a useful public charity

(July 1) Georg Christoph Grosheim, German composer and writer, was born on this date at Cassel (died 1841, November 18).

(July 4) Antoine Trial made his debut at the Theatre-Italienne at Paris on this date in Philidor's "Le Sorcier".

(July 5) János de Izsépfalva et Kevelháza Lavotta, Hungarian violinist and composer, was born on this date at Puszafödémes (died 1820, August 11).

(July 6) William Hayes was admitted as a clerk of Magdalen College at this time.

(July 10) Anselm Bayly graduated from the Chapel Royal "D. C. L." at this time.

(August 8) A decree was issued this year at Bonn threatening to take away both the position and salary of Johann Peter Salomon if he was "not returned" by the beginning of September.

(August 11) Philipp Salomon and his daughter (Johann Peter Saloman's father and sister) were appointed court musician at Bonn on this date.

(August 18) Rosine Therese Petronelle ("Rosa") Cannabich, a clavier player, was baptized on this date at Mannheim (death date unknown).

1764(cont.)

(August 23) Jean-Philippe Rameau on this day was attacked by a "putrid fever accompanied by scurvy".

(September 11) Valentino Fioravanti, Italian composer, was born at this time in Rome (died 1837, June 16).

(September 11 or 12 or 22) Jean Philippe Rameau, "France's foremost composer of the 18th century", died on one of these three dates (probably September 12) at Paris of a fever diagnosed as "scurvy" (born 1683, September 25).

(September 13) Richard Edgcumbe, Earl of Mount-Edgcumbe, English musical amateur and composer, was born on this date (died 1839, September 26 at Richmond, Surrey).

(September 21) La Pastorella al Soglio" (composer probably Latilla) was performed on this date at the Bonn court, along with two ballets.

(Autumn) At this time W. Mozart composed four violin sonatas, one in G major, one in A major, one in C major and one in Bb major. All were composed in London.

(Autumn) Rameau worked at a full-scale "tragédie lyrique", "Abaris on Les Boréades", to be performed at the Opéra at this time, but his death in September terminated the rehearsals.

(September 27) A first memorial service for Rameau was celebrated on this day at the church of the Oratorians in the Rue St. Honoré at Paris.

(October 11) A 2nd memorial service for Rameau was held on this day at the Carmelite Fathers near the Luxembourg.

(October 12) John Ross, English organist and composer of Scottish extraction, was born on this date at Newcastle-on-Tyne (died 1837, July 28 at Aberdeen).

(October 15) Martin Gerbert von Hornau was appointed a prince-abbot at this time.

(October 19) Charles Henri Plantade, French instrumentalist and composer, was born at this time at Pontoise (died 1839, December 18 at Paris).

(October 21) János Bihar, Hungarian violinist, bandleader and composer of gypsy stock, was baptized on this date at Nagyabowy, Hungary (now Velky Abon, Czechoslovakia) (died 1827, Aptil 26 at Pest).

(October 22) Jean Marie Leclair, l'aîné, French composer, died on this date at Paris (born 1697, May 10).

(October 23) Jean Marie Leclair. l'aîné was found dead today after being assassinated late the night before.

(October 25) Wolfgang and Anna Maria Mozart on this date were invited to play at court in London.

(November 1) The "Pennsylvania Journal" in this issue advertised the second season of Concerts at the Assembly Room in Lodge Alley.

(November 2) Battishill wrote

1764(cont.)

the English opera "Almena" in collaboration with Michael Arne and it was performed at the Drury Lane Theatre in London this evening.

(November 23) Cocchi's opera "Gli amanti gelosi" was produced on this date at the Smock Alley Theatre in Dublin.

(November 24) J. Christian (son of J. S.) Bach's pasticcio "Ezio" was performed on this date.

(November 24) Ciprandi appeared as "Massimo" in the pasticcio "Ezio" this evening at London.

(December 9) Jeanne Charlotte Saint-Aubin (born Schroeder), soprano, was born at this time (died 1850, September 11).

(December 10) Louis Sébastien Lebrun, French tenor and composer, was born on this date at Paris (died 1829, June 27).

(December 12) T. A. Arne's "The Guardian Outwitted" was produced this evening at Covent Garden in London.

(December 16) A third memorial service for Rameau was held at the Oratoire on this date.

(December 16) "La Calamità di cuori" by Galuppi, along with two balets, was performed at the Bonn Court on this date. This was the first performance by the Mingotti company under Rizzi and Romanini.

(December 20) Joseph Kohault's comic opera "Le Serrurier" was produced this evening at the Comédie-Italienne in Paris.

(December 22) Baron Ludislav von Amadé, Hungarian poet and composer, died on this date at Feldbar (born 1703, March 12 at Kassa).

(December 25) Dauvergne became surintendant at the Paris Opéra on this date.

(December 25) Monsigny's opera "Le Bouquet de Thalie" (libretto by Charles Collé) was produced on this date at Bagnolet, Théâtre du Duc d'Orléans.

(December 27) In this issue of the "Pennsylvania Gazette" a concert on "the famous Armonica, or Musical Glasses, so much admired for their great Sweetness and Delicacy of its Tone" was advertised. Stephen Forrage was to be the performer.

(December 31) Stephen Forrage advertised "A Concert of Music" on this date.

(January) W. Mozart, while at Paris this month, composed E8, K8, a violin sonata in Bb major.

(February) This month "The subscriptions still proved insufficient 'for completing the design'" of St. Peter's church organ.

(April) This month marked the first performance abroad of Gluck's "Orfeo ed Euridice". It was held either at Frankfurt am Main or at Parma on August 24, 1769.

(April) Leopold Mozart and family visited London this year on a concert tour.

(April) W. A. Mozart, when in

1764(cont.)

London this year, became friends with J. Christian(son of J. S.) Bach. Mozart was 8 years old at the time.

(October) An anonymous essay "Essai d'Eloge historique de feu M. Rameau" appeared this month in "Mercure de France"

(October) Florian Gassmann's opera "L'Olimpiade" was produced at this time in Vienna (libretto by Metastasio).

(October) The opening of Marylebone Gardens for tea-drinking was prohibited. This month a morning performance, under the name of a rehearsal, was given and a collection was made in aid of the suffers by destructive fires at Montreal, Canada and Homton, Devonshire.

(November to 1765, April) Ciprandi sang in London during this period.

(November) "La donna vana", an opera by N. Piccinni (libretto by Palomba) was performed this month at the Teatro dei Fiorentini in Naples.

Paul Alday (le jeune), French violinist, was born this year (died 1835 at Dublin).

Count Francesco Algarotti, author of the "Sagio sopra l'opera", died at this time (birthdate unknown).

Cornelius van Beethoven died according to a major source (born 1708).

In his "Lexicon der Tonkünstler" Gerber was four years wrong (cont.) in assigning Cherubini's birth to this year.

Celeste Coltellini, Italian mezzo-soprano, was born this year at Leghorn (died 1829 at Capodimonte near Naples).

Pierre-François Dallery, French organ builder, was born this year at Paris (died 1833 at Paris).

Vincenzo Federici, Italian composer, was born this year at Pesaro (died 1826, September 26).

William Forster, English violin maker, was born this year at 1764 (died 1824).

Giovanni Antonio Giai, Italian composer, died this year at Turin (born c.1700).

Johann Heinrich Grenser, German woodwind maker, was born this year at Dresden (died 1813).

C. F. Henrici (pseudonym,Picander), a Leipzig poet who provided many of Bach's cantata texts, died (born 1700).

Jeremiah Ingalls, one of the earliest compilers to write down and publish folk hymns, was born this year (died 1828).

Angelo Maria Monticelli, Italian male soprano, died this year at Dresden (born c.1710 at Milan).

Wilhelm Hieronymous Pachelbel, German organist, composer and son of Johann Pachelbel, died at this time at Nürnberg (born 1685 at Erfurt).

Jan Stiastny, Czech violoncellist, composer and brother of violoncellist, Bernard Vaclav Stiastny, was born this year at Prague (death date unknown).

Regina Strinasacchi, Italian violinist and guitar player, was born this year at Ostiglia near Mantua (died c.1823 at Gotha).

When Rev. Dr. Fifield Allen died this year, Bayly was appointed to succeed him as sub-dean of the Chapel Royal.

Annibali left Saxony this year and returned to Italy.

Lucrezia Aguiari made her début at Florence this season.

Edmund Ayrton was appointed a Gentleman of the Chapel Royal this year at London. He also held the position of lutenist.

Wilhelm Friedemann Bach this season played the organ and conducted the musical performances at the Liebfrauen Church in Halle.

Fétis maintained that Carl Barbandt was organist at the chapel of the Bavarian ambassador at this time.

Barthélemon played the violin in the orchestra of the Comédie-Italienne in Paris this season.

Joah Bates was awarded the degree of Bachelor of Arts this year.

Karl Friedrich Baumgarten was orchestra leader at Dublin this season.

Johann van Beethoven's father

(cont.) drew up a petition this year stating that his son had been serving in the chapel for 12 years.

Jean-Baptiste Joseph Boutmy resigned his positions at Ghent this year and returned to The Hague to enter the service of the Portuguese ambassador.

J. Bremner and Hopkinson worked together this season in presenting Philadelphia's first subscription concerts.

Robert Bremner purchased some of the plates this year at the sale of the stock-in-trade of Simpson's music shop.

John Broderip was succeeded as organist of Canterbury Cathedral this year by R. Parry.

Burney took two of his daughters to Paris at this time for their education, and began his acquaintance with continental libraries and musical organizations which he extended a few years later.

Burney at this time was elected a Fellow of the Royal Society of Arts.

The last performance of Campra's "Tancrède" took place this year.

C. Cannabich went to Paris this year.

Gianbattista Casanova this year became director of the Dresden Art Academy.

Mathon de La Cour founded the "Journal de musique historique,

Mozart.

théorique et pratique sur la musique ancienne et moderne" this year.

Owing to the state of Mrs. Cox's health, John Cox gave up his music business at this time.

Giuseppe Dall' Oglio lived in Berlin, Warsaw and Venice after this year.

Cecilia Davies appeared this season at the Theatre Royal in Dublin.

Ditters went to Frankfurt am Main with Gluck and Guadagni this year for the election and coronation of the Archduke Joseph as King of the Romans.

From this date until his death, Dretzel was organist at St. Sebald.

Florian Gassmann was called to Vienna this season to succeed Gluck as ballet composer and director of the "opera buffa" company at the Burg Theatre.

Both Durazzo and Gluck left their jobs in Vienna this year, Durazzo to go to Venice as ambassador. He was succeeded by Count Wenzel Sporck, Gluck by Florian Gassmann.

Gluck used bass drum, cymbals and triangle this year.

Gluck, in his "La Rencontre imprévue", used bass drum and cymbals, a true innovation.

Singspiel received a great stimulus this year at Leipzig through J. Adam Hiller, who was influenced by translations of the English ballad operas

(cont.) by Charles Coffey who had come to Germany with these fashionable novelties.

Francis Hopkinson at this time was engaged to translate the "Psalms of David" from Dutch into English.

Francis Hopkinson and Mr. Young were given acknowledgements at this time for teaching and instructing children in psalmody.

Jommelli's opera "Il re pastore" was performed this season at Ludwigsburg.

William Jones was presented to the vicarage of Betheroden, Kent at this time. He later became Rector of Pluckley.

Pierre Lagarde this year became music teacher of the royal children at Paris.

Ludwig August Lebrun entered the Mannheim orchestra this year as an oboist.

Corelli's pupil Locatelli, who died this year, turned the modern concerto into a highly personal vehicle of great virtuosity.

Opera in the style of Lully had been the leader in tragic opera in Paris for 90 years up to this time.

James Lyon was ordained as a Presbyterian minister this year by the Synod of New Brunswick.

J. W. Mangold went to Darmstadt this season and became an instrumentalist in the orchestra. Five of his sons, Georg,

August Daniel, Ludwig, Paul and Carl Friedrich, were musicians at Darmstadt.

Giovanni Manzuoli went to London at this time and by his performance "the serious opera acquired a degree of favour to which it had seldom mounted since its first establishment in this country".

Lord Mornington this year was appointed to the newly created Chair of Music at Dublin University.

As late as this year a German visitor unwilling to praise anything French in the person of Leopold Mozart, commented on the quality of the singing at the Chapel Royal at Versailles.

Mozart as a child may have heard clarinets for the first time when he visited London this season.

Mozart began to write symphonies this year at age 8.

At age 7 this year Mozart came to London with his father. A castrato singer, Tenducci, gave Mozart "his first great impressions in the realm of song".

Rameau's "Nais" was revived this season. A lively loure (a type of bagpipe or a dance) was added.

The "grande clarinette" was mentioned this year by V. Roeser.

Christian Friedrich Schale was organist at the Berlin Cathedral this year.

Johann Paul Schulthesius entered the college at Feldheim this

(cont.) year to study theology.

Anton Stamitz became a violinist in the Mannheim orchestra this year at age ten.

Henry Thorowgood was in business in London this year at the sign of the "Violin & Guitar". He was a music publisher, printer and musical instrument maker.

Antoine Trial, a tenor, went to Paris this season.

Vernon sang in Arne's "Fairy Tale" this season.

"Mrs. Vernon" sang in the London performances of "Midas" this season as "Miss Poitier".

Vernon succeeded Lowe as the tenor at Vauxhall Gardens this year.

The University of Dublin conferred the degree of Mus. D. on G. Wellesley this year and elected him professor of that faculty.

Yale University has a copy of "Second Edition Corrected London, 1764" with same preface as first edition (of "Universal Psalmodist") by Aaron Williams.

R. Woodward this year was awarded the gold medal of the "Glee & Catch Club".

William Yates appeared this season in a concert he himself produced.

Michael Arne's "Almena" was published this year. It included a song with mandolin accompaniement.

1764(cont.)

J. Christian (son of J. S.)
Bach's opera "Catone in Utica"
was produced for the second time
this year at Naples.

K. P. E. Bach's "Zwölf geistliche Oden und Lieder" appeared
at this time.

Béthizy's "Théorie et pratique
de la musique suivant les
nouvelles decouvertes, 1764"
(A 2nd ed. of his "Exposition
de la Théorie . . .") appeared
at this time.

Calzabigi's "Orfeo" was published this year at Paris.

Michel-Paul-Gui de Chabanon's
"Éloge de M. Rameau" appeared
this year.

At age twelve this year, Clementi had an oratorio, "Il
martirio de' gloriosi Santi
Girolamo e Celso", performed
at Rome.

B. Cooke at this time composed
an anthem with orchestral accompaniment for the funeral of
William,Duke of Cumberland.

Fischietti's opera "Vologeso"
was produced this year at
Prague.

Josiah Flagg's "Collection of
the best Psalm Tunes, in two,
three or four parts . . . Engraved by Paul Revere" appeared
this year at Boston printed on
paper made in British America.

Josiah Flagg this year attri-
buted "Morning Hymn" to James
Lyon (not to be confused with
Tansur's "Morning Hymn").

Baldassare Galuppi wrote his
opera "Caio Mario" this year at
(cont.) Venice (libretto by
Roccaforte).

Baldassare Galuppi's opera
"Didone abbandonata" was produced this year at Venice.

Baldassare Galuppi wrote his
opera "La donna di governo"
this season at Venice (libretto
by Goldoni).

Baldassare Galuppi wrote his
opera "Sofonisba" this year
at Turin (libretto by Verazi).

François Joseph Giraud's
"Acanthe et Cydipe" was per-
formed this season at the
Théâtre Nicolet.

Gluck's version of "Le Sage"
and d'Orneval's "Les Pelerins
de la Meque" called "La Recontre imprevue" by Gluck,
were performed this season
at Vienna.

One of Haydn's choral works
with orchestra, "Al tuo
arrivo felice" for chorus
appeared this year. Larsen
felt this was identical with
a choral composition in the
Göttweig collection and perhaps
with the MS cantata "Destatevi
o miei fidi".

Haydn wrote a piano (harpsichord) concerto in C major
this year.

Haydn's "Offertorium St.
Joannis de Deo: Accurrite
hunc mortalis" in G major,
scored for recitative and duet,
2 violins, viola, 2 horns, 2
oboes, bass and organ, was
taken from the cantata dedicated to Prince Esterházy in 1763.

Haydn wrote his Symphony #16
at this time.

1764(cont.)

Haydn's Symphony #21 in A major
was written this year, scored
for 2 oboes, 2 horns and strings.

Haydn's Symphony #22 in Eb major
("The Philosopher") was composed
at this time for 2 English
horns, 2 horns and strings.

Haydn's Symphony #23 in G major
was composed this year for 2
oboes, 2 horns and strings.

Haydn's Symphony #24 in D major
was composed this year for solo
flute, 2 oboes, 2 horns and
strings.

Haydn's "Te Deum" in C major
scored for 4 solo voices, 4-
part chorus, 2 violins, 2 trumpets ad. lib., organ, double
bass and drums appeared at this
time.

Herbain's comic opera, "Nanette
et Lucas, ou La Paysanne
curiuse", was produced this
season at the Comédie-Italienne
in Paris.

Jommelli's "Demofoonte" appeared
this season.

Charles John Frederick Lampe
had his "Six English Songs"
published this year.

Pierre Leclair published his
opus 1, six violin duets, at
this time.

Samuel Long wrote his "Where'er
you tread" this year.

Music of G. F. Maio's appeared
this season in a pasticcio,
"Ezio", produced at the King's
Theatre in London.

P. van Maldere's "An Overture

(cont.) set for the Harpsichord,
organ or Piano-Foret" was published this year at London.

P. van Maldere's "Sei Sinfonie
a più Stromenti" was published
this year by Vernier at Paris
and Longman at London.

P. van Maldere's "Symphonie"
was published this year in
"Symphonies periodiques" at
Paris.

Marpurg's "Kritische Briefe"
was published this year at
Berlin.

Franz Meyer's opus 7, "Par
nobile fratrum" appeared
this year.

Mozart this year wrote a
violin sonata in Bb major
while in London.

Mozart this year composed a
violin sonata in F major
while in Paris and London.

Mozart early this year composed
a violin sonata in G major
while in Paris.

Mozart's Symphony #1 in Eb major
appeared at this time. It was
scored for 2 oboes, 2 horns
and strings while he was in
London.

Mozart composed his first two
symphonies this year and started
to experiment in composition
for his own amusement.

"Il ciralone" and "I Francesi
brillanti", comic operas by
G. Paisiello, were composed
at this time.

Three songs from Pescetti's
opera "Enzio" were introduced

into the London pasticcio performance this year.

F. A. Philidor's "Tom Jones" appeared this year according to a major source.

Rameau's "Abaris ou les Boréades tragédie en musique" (written this year) was never performed. The libretto was probably by Cahusac.

The last complete revival of Rameau's "Les Fêtes d'Hébé" was this season.

Valentine Roeser's "Essai d'instruction à l'usage de ceux qui composent pour la clarinette et le cor" was published this year at Paris.

George Rush' 3 act opera "The Royal Shepherd" (libretto by R. Rolt from Metastasio's "Il re pastore") received its production at Drury Lane Theatre in London this season.

Antonio Sacchini's opera, "Lucio Vero", was performed this season at Naples.

Staromieyski, a Polish composer, wrote "Missa ex C" this year.

Tommaso Traetta"s "Antigono" (libretto by Metastasio) was produced this season at Padua.

Tommaso Traetta's "La buona figliuola maritata" (libretto by Goldoni) was produced this season at Parma.

S. Webbe published his first book of Glees at this time.

Aaron Williams' "The Universal Psalmodist" (2nd edition,

(cont.) corrected) was issued this year at London.

One of the surviving harpsichords made by J. Kirkman carried this year's date. It had 1 manual, stops 2x8', 1x4' and is currently owned by J. G. Morley. It was referred to as #19.

In Philadelphia this year, a series of concerts was offered for public subscription.

Goethe this year described Prince Nicholas as "not tall but well built, vivacious and distinguished, and at the same time without haughtiness and coldness".

Goldsmith's book of poetry, "The Traveler", was issued this year.

Horace Walpole this year published his "The Castle of Otranto", a whimsical, half-cynical horror tale.

Johann Joachim Winckelmann's "History of the Art of Antiquity" appeared at this time.

William Hogarth, English painter, satirist and reformer, died this year (born 1697).

The Royal Palace at Madrid was not ready for occupancy until this year.

(to 1765) Except for a journey to Italy this year, Adlgasser spent his entire life in Salzburg.

(and 1765) Charlotte Brent sang with Tenducci in works by Handel these two seasons at Ranelagh.

1764(cont.)

(to 1765) Mozart's 43 Pieces (mostly for piano) were completed at this time in London.

(to 1766) Pierre Lagarde wrote two collections of vocal music: "Les Soirees de L'Isle Adam" during these years.

(to 1766) Cafaro's cantatas for the birthdays of Ferdinand IV were written each of these years for January 12.

(to 1766) American architecture: New York, St. Paul's Chapel (140' long, 66' wide, 42' high).

(to 1767) Klopstock journeyed to Denmark at this time to gain inspiration from Northern mythology.

(to 1768) Charles Clagget was leader at Crow Street Theatre Royal in Dublin during these four seasons.

(to 1768) F. H. Clicquot and his workmen built the organ at the church of Saint-Gervais during this period.

(to 1768) Hermann Friedrich Raupach met Mozart at this time and they improvised piano duets together..

(to 1768) Johann Baptist Savio, composer, was musical director of the theatrical company run by Joseph von Brunian during these years.

(to 1768) A periodical published in Paris at this time was called "Journal de musique française et italienne".

(to 1769) Boccherini was in the (cont.) town band of Lucca during this period.

(to 1769) Boccherini's two oratorios, "Giuseppe riconosciuto" and "Gioas", were given at Lucca during these years.

(to 1769) Six operas by Filippo Gherarceschi were performed in Pisa and Venice during this period.

(to 1769) Röllig was music director of Ackermann's theatrical troupe in Hamburg for these five seasons.

(to c.1771) Johann Christian Fischer was in the court orchestra at Dresden at this time.

(to 1774) Lord Mornington, father of the Duke of Wellington, was professor of music at the University of Dublin during this decade.

(to 1774) Garrett Wellesley was a professor at the University of Dublin during this period.

(and 1780) Daines Barrington was mentioned as the author of a biography of Mozart during his visit to London in 1764, at eight years of age, in the "Philosophical Transactions" for 1780 (Vol. XI).

(to 1789) Cordeiro da Silva wrote the music for twelve dramatic works performed at Lisbon during this period.

(to 1790) French architecture: Paris, Pantheon by Soufflot (360' x 262' x 265'high).

1764(cont.)

(to c.1798) "Catches, Canons, and Glees. Composed by Samuel Webbe." was issued at intervals during this long period.

c.1764

Francois Cupis (de Camargo), Netherlands violinist and composer, died this year at Paris (born 1719, March 10 at Brussels).

Heinrich Lenz, Polish or German pianist and composer, was born this year (died 1839, August 21).

Hugh Reinagle, brother of Alexander Reinagle, was born this year at Edinboro. He was a pupil of Schetky and a proficient cellist (died 1785, Mauch 19 at Lisbon).

Battishill this year was appointed organist of the united parishes of St. Clement, East-cheap and St. Martin, Ongar.

Van den Bosch was organist at Antwerp Cathedral this season.

Welcher's "Collection of Catches" was published this year at London.

1765

(January 1) J. Christian (son of J. S.) Bach's pasticcio "Berenice" was performed on this date.

(January 5) The opera, "The Maid of the Mill" was first performed on this date at Philadlephia.

(January 6) "Le Aventure di Rodolfo", possibly by Piccinni, and a pantomime, "L'Arlequino

(cont.) fortunato per la Maggia", were given at the Bonn court on this date. After the performance there was a grand supper and masquerade ball.

(January 10) N. Piccinni's opera "Il barone di Torreforte" (librettist unknown) was produced at this time at the Teatro Capranica in Rome.

(January 12) Johann Melchior Molter, German composer, died this year at Durlach (birth-date unknown).

(January 15) Karlmann Kolb, German organist and composer, died on this date at München (born 1703 at Kostlarn, Bavaria).

(January 19) Johan Joachim Ayrell, Swedish composer, died on this date at Nürnberg (born 1701, February at Löth, Sweden).

(January 20) N. Logroscino's "Il tempo dell' onore" was produced on this date.

(January 23) J. Christian (son of J. S.) Bach and Karl Friedrich Abel jointly conducted the first of Mrs. Cornelys' subscription concerts on this date at Carlisle House, Soho Square, London.

(January 24) E. R. Duni's opera "L'École de la jeunesse ou le Barnevelt françois" was produced at this time at the Comédie-Italienne in Paris.

(January 24) Gluck's Italian opera "Il Parmaso confuso" was produced at Schönbrunn, near Vienna this evening (libretto by Metastasio). It was actually a little festival

1765(cont.)

play performed by the four young Archduchesses.

(January 25) Florian Gassmann's opera "Il trionfo d'amore" was given on this date at Schönbrunn (libretto by Metastasio).

(January 25) J. Christian (son of J. S.) Bach's opera "Adriano in Siria" was produced on this date at London).

(January 30) Gluck's Italian opera "Il Telemacco, ossia L'isola di Circe" (libretto by Carlo Sigismondo Capece) was produced at this time in the Burg Theatre at Vienna.

(January 31) Samuel Arnold's pasticcio, "The Maid of the Mill", was performed on this date at Covent Garden in London.

(January 31) Gluck's ballet "Semiramide" (scenery by Calzabigi, choreography by Angiolini) was produced on this date at Vienna.

(February 4) Georg Gruber became Kapellmeister at Nürnberg on this date.

(February 8) Joseph von Eybler, Austrian conductor and composer, was born on this day at Schwechat near Vienna (died 1846, July 24 at Vienna).

(February 11) G. Scarlatti's opera "Gli stravaganti" was produced on this date at the Burg Theatre, Vienna.

(February 13) The oratorio "Ruth" by Felice (de') Giardini and Charles Avison, was performed this evening at the Lock Hospital chapel in London.

(February 18) T. A. Arne's "Artaxerxes" was performed on this date at Dublin.

(February 18) Giusto Ferdinando Tenducci, a male soprano, appeared in Dublin this evening at the Smock Alley Theatre in Arne's "Artaxerxes".

(February 21) Wolfgang and Anna Maria Mozart gave a concert at the Little Theatre, Haymarket on this date, in which "all the overtures were of the little boy's own composition".

(February 23) Charles-Louis-Joseph André, Belgian composer, was born on this day at Ath (died 1839, April 8 at Mechlin).

(February 25) (See also February 27) In Paris at the Comédie-Italienne on this evening an opera by F. A. Philidor, "Tom Jones", was produced (libretto by Poinsinet and Davesne after H. Fielding).

(February 27) "Tom Jones", the opera by F. A. Philidor (libretto by Antoine Alexandre Henri Poinsinet and Davesne after H. Fielding) was produced this evening in Paris at the Comédie-Italienne.

(March 7) Felice (de') Giardini's opera "Il re pastore" was produced on this day at London.

(March 11) William Yates' masque "The choice of Apollo" was performed this evening at Haymarket Theatre in London.

(March 16) Gossec's opera "Le Tonnelier" (libretto by Antoine François Quéfant) was produced at the Comédie-Italienne in Paris on this date.

MARIA ANNA MOZART
(Mozart's Sister)

1765(cont.)

(April 1) At Marylebone Gardens on this date George Berg produced an ode calle "The Invitation".

(April 4 and 18) The "Pennsylvania Gazette" in these issues advertised J. Bremner's Benefit Concert that he arranged and conducted in the College Hall. It was a benefit for the "Boys and Girls Charity School".

(April 10) The "Pennsylvania Gazette" in this issue advertised a concert of "Solemn Musick" in the Hall of College of Philadelphia, for the Benefit of the Charity School.

(May 1) Hiller's "Cantate auf die Ankunft der hohen Landesherrschaft" (text by Clodius) was produced on this date at Leipzig.

(May 5) August Friedrich Graun, German organist and composer, died on this date at Merseburg (born 1699).

(May 13) Wolfgang and Anna Maria Mozart gave their last concert in Hickford's Great Room on Brewer St. on this date and played a piece of Mozart's for 4 hands on the same harpsichord (Mozart also composed all the overtures they played).

(May 18) Charles Simon Favart's "Les Amours de Gonesse" was first performed on this date at Paris (music by Laborde).

(May 28) Jean Baptiste Cartier, French violinist and composer, was born on this day at Avignon (died 1841, at Paris).

(June 6) F. Zellbell, Swedish musician, died on this date

(cont.)(birthdate unknown).

(Summer or Autumn) Mozart arranged "3 Sonatas" by J. Christian (son of J. S.) Bach as Concertos in D major, G major and Eb major at this time at London or The Hague.

(June 27) Gossec's opera "Le Faux Lord" (libretto by Parmentier) was produced this evening at the Comédie-Italienne in Paris.

(July 1) Elector Max Friedrich on this date gave a document to Johann Peter Salomon certifying that he had served faithfully and diligently and was deserving of a recommendation.

(July 2) Aegidius Christoph Möller, German string player and Hof musikus to the Duke of Braunschweig, was born on this date at Görsbach near Nordhausen (died 1841, August 4 at Braunschweig).

(July 16) T. Dupuis married Martha Skelton of Fulham on this day.

(August 6) Hasse's opera "Romolo ed Ersilia" (libretto by Metastasio) was produced this evening at Innsbruck.

(August 11) J. A. Benda's "Xindo riconosciuto" (an Italian opera) was produced on this date at Gotha.

(August 14) Charles Simon Favart's "Isabelle et Gertrude, ou Les Sylphes supposes" was first performed in Paris this evening (music by Blaise).

(August 18) Emperor Francis I died on this day (birthdate unknown).

1765(cont.)

(August 21) Printing privileges were granted to Charles Nicholas Le Clerc on this date for "Musique de Scarlatti".

(August 25) Maret pronounced his eulogy of Rameau before the Academy of Dijon on this day.

(September 7) Prince Oginski Michal Kleofas, writer and composer, was born on this date near Warsaw (died 1833, October 18 at Florence). His works, though simple, were full of deep human feeling and and move toward Chopin.

(September 11) Leopold, Wolfgang and Anna Maria Mozart arrived at The Hague on this date to play before the Dutch court.

(September 12) Mathias Haydn, died at this time (born 1699, January 31 at Hainburg).

(October 16) Frédéric Duvernoy, French horn player, was born on this day at Montbeliard (died 1838, July 19 at Paris).

(October 22) Daniel Steibelt, German pianist and composer, was born this day at Berlin (died 1823, October 2 at St. Petersburg).

(October 26) E. R. Duni's opera "La Fée Urgèle, ou Ce qui plait aux dames" was produced on this date at Fontainebleau.

(October 26) Charles Simon Favart's "La Fée Urgèle, ou Ce qui plaît aux dames" was first performed at this time in Paris (music by Duni; later in the year also set by Grétry).

(October 26) Jan Jakub Ryba, Czech composer and writer on music, was born on this date at Přeštice (died 1815, April 8 at Rožmitál).

(November 12) Thomas Norris on this day submitted 2 anthems for his exercise in graduation from Oxford, "The Lord is King" and "I will always give thanks". They were performed at the Music School.

(November 19) The National Theatre was opened in Warsaw on this occasion.

(November 20) Friedrich (Heinrich) Himmel, German composer, was born on this date at Treuenbrietzen, Brandenburg (died 1814, June 8 at Berlin).

(November 23) Thomas Attwood, English organist and composer, was born on this date at London (died 1838, March 24 at Chelsea, London).

(November 28) Johann Laym, Maria Magdalena Keverich's first husband, died on this date. She married Johann van Beethoven 2 years later.

(December 4) E. R. Duni's opera "La Fée Urgèle, ou Ce qui plaît aux dames" was produced on this date at the Comédie-Italienne in Paris.

(December 6) Arne's "The Summer's Tale" was produced this evening at Covent Garden in London.

(December 6) Samuel Arnold's "The Summer's Tale" was performed at this time at Covent Garden in London.

(December 13) Francis Hopkinson on this date wrote to Benjamin Franklin, "I have finished the translation of the Psalms of David . . ."

(December 15) Thomas Norris was chosen organist of St. John's College on this date.

(December 16) Conrad Friedrich Hurlebusch, German organist and composer, died on this day at Amsterdam (born 1699 at Braunschweig).

(Winter) The "Subscription Concerts" did not continue through the Winter at the Assembly Room in Lodge Alley.

(December 25) Joseph Mazzinghi, English organist, pianist and composer and son of Thomas, was born on this day at London (died 1844, January 15 at Downside near Bath).

(December 25) Antonio Tonelli, violoncellist, organist and composer, died on this date at Capri (born 1686, August 19 at Capri).

(March) Joachim Gigault, French organist, died this month at Paris (born 1676, May 17).

(April) George Berg produced an ode, "The Invitation", this month at Marylebone Gardens in London.

(April) J. Westhoff, German violinist and composer, died in Weimar this month (born 1656).

(July) John Abraham Fisher made his first public appearance as a violinist at the King's Theatre in London during this time.

(July) Mozart's Sonata in C major for four hands was composed this month at London.

(July) Mozart's a capella sacred madrigal (chorus), "God is our Refuge (46th Psalm) was composed this month at London.

(August) Benjamin West wrote to Hopkinson this month from London.

(October to 1766, June) J. A. Benda went (with F. W. Rust of Dessau) on an Italian journey to Venice, Bologna, Florence and Rome during this period.

(October) Mozart's solo aria with orchestra, E23, K23, "Conservati fedele" (text by Metastasio) for soprano and strings, was composed for the Princess of Orange this month at The Hague.

(November to 1766, May) Ciprandi sang in London during this period.

(August) Ozias Thurston Linley, organist and clergyman, was born this month at Bath (died 1831, March 6 at London).

(November) Thomas Norris was awarded the degree of Bachelor of Music this month by Oxford.

(December) Mozart's Symphony #5 in Bb major for 2 oboes, 2 horns and strings was composed this month at The Hague.

Christope Jean François Ballard, of the family of printers died this year (birthdate unknown).

Franz Brentano, Bettina's half-brother, was born this

year (died 1844).

(or 1768) Elizabeth Billington, English soprano and composer, was born this year at London (died 1818, August 25 near Venice).

George William Chard, English organist and composer, was born at this time at Winchester (died 1849, May 23 at Winchester).

Niccolò Conforto, Italian composer, died this year at Madrid (born 1727 at Naples).

Natlae Corri, music publisher, was born this year at Rome (died 1822 at Edinboro).

Louis Antoine Dornel, French organist and composer, died this year at Paris (born c.1685).

František Benedikt Dussek, son of Johann Joseph Dussek, was born this year (died after 1816).

Vincenzo Fabrizi, Italian composer, was born this year (death date unknown).

Gilbert Heathcote, English ecclesiastic and composer, was born this year at London (died 1829, October 19 at London).

Oliver Holden, who helped compile a collection of psalms in America, was born this year (died 1844).

Joseph William Holder, English composer, was born this year at London (died 1832).

Feliks Lipiński, Polish violinist, was born this year (died

Nicola Logroscino, Italian composer of comic operas, died at this time (born 1698). He was nicknamed the "God of Opera Comique".

Anna Barbara Marx, wife of Cornelius van Beethoven, died this year (birthdate unknown).

Antonín Stamitz, organist and teacher and father of Johann Stamitz, died this year (birthdate unknown).

Johann Caspar Vogler, German organist, died this year at Weimar (birthdate unknown).

Charles Weichsell, English violinist and composer, was born at London at this time (death date unknown).

Karl Friedrich Abel confined himself to the viola da gamba from this date forward.

François Arnaud was Abbot of Grandchamp and a member of the French Academy. He won distinction as a writer on music.

In England this season excellent performances were given under the leadership of Johann Christian (son of J. S.) Bach and Karl Friedrich Abel.

An opera of J. Christian (son of J. S.) Bach was given at the King's Theatre in London this season.

J. Ernst Bach was appointed "Kastenverwalter" in Eisenach this year.

Karl Ludwig Bachmann was appointed viola player in the

Royal Chapel this year and ex-
celled as a soloist.

Barthelémon went to London at
this time and was engaged as
conductor of the Opera orchestra.

One of Dom Bédos' surveys was
that of the new organ at Saint-
Lazare, constructed by Pierre
Dallery at this time.

Berezovsky went to Italy this
year to complete his studies
at Bologna under Padre Martini.

Knee-pedals for increasing and
decreasing the sound and for
operating a sordine were mentioned in Berger's (of Grenoble)
description of a harpsichord this
year.

Gaetano Besozzi held an appointment at the court of Naples until
this year.

Gaetano Besozzi, through the
efforts of the French ambassador,
Durfort, was induced to go to
Paris this year, a trip he made
with his father.

Pascal Boyer went to Paris
this season.

Charlotte Brent sang at the
Hereford Festival this year.

Juan Bautista Bruguera y
Morreras won the prize offered
by the "Catch Club" in London
this year for the most remarkable canon, for artifice and
melody.

Cervetto the Younger played
with his father this season at
a concert given by Parry the
harpist.

F. H. Clicquot took Pierre
Dallery into partnership this
year.

G. Cocchi once more conducted
this season at the King's
Theatre in London.

N. Conforto continued to provide the Spanish court with
Italian serenatas and operas
up to this date.

Mme. Cornelys (a singer and
friend of Casanova's) arranged
subscription concerts this
year at which, among others,
Johann Christian Bach (son
of J. S.) conducted.

When Crabanon wrote his "Eloge"
at this time, only a few played
it.

M. Dubourg left Ireland this
year.

Giacomo Durazzo became the
Austrian ambassador to Venice
at this time.

Jan Ladislav Dussek began to
study pianoforte this year at
age 5.

Carlo Ferrari entered the
service of the Duke of Parma
at this time.

Domenico Fischietti succeeded
Hasse as court conductor at
Dresden this season.

Alessandro Maria Antonio
Fridzeri (Frizeri) left Vicenza
at this time and began to
travel in Europe.

Catherine II sent for "Il
Buranello" (Galuppi) this year.
He went to St. Petersburg for
the second time.

1765(cont.)

Ernst Ludwig Gerber entered the University of Leipzig at this time.

Dancing (in Gluck's opera) had become less abstract and more dramatic by this time, but this was not reflected in his ballet numbers other than the 2nd act of "Orfeo".

Gluck and Metastasio this year were commisioned to write an "azione teatrale" for the name day of Emperor Francis (December 8), but since the Emperor died in August, it was never performed.

This year was the advertised date of the performance of a masque by George Graham, "Telemachus" for which Philip Hayes wrote the music. The performance was postponed and never announced again.

Gaetano Guadagni sang in Gluck's "Telemacco" this season in Italy.

Anna Hataš had a great success this season in her brother's Italian opera "Xindo riconosciuta". According to contemporary reviewers, she was a coloratura soprano of rare ability.

Haydn, with the help of Eissler, started work this year on a thematic catalogue of his works.

Haydn's works prior to this year were not reliably listed in Eissler's 1805 catalogue.

William Hayes contributed this year to the "Gentleman's Magazine" in a paper titled "Rules necessary to be observed by all (cont.) Cathedral Singers in This Kingdom".

William Hayes resigned at this time as clerk of Magdalen College when he obtained a minor canonry at Worcestor Cathedral.

Petrus Hellendaal played the violin this year at Lynn, at a concert given by his successor, Harris.

Francis Hopkinson ordered a Kirkman harpsichord at this time.

Francis Hopkinson this year accepted and completed the task as psalmodist for the Dutch Reformed Congregation of New York City, translating their metrical psalter into English.

James won the Catch Club medal this year with his "Parting Catch" and shortly thereafter wrote music for a Richmond pantomime, "The Sacrifice of Iphigenia".

Pierre de Jélyotte retired at this time.

When Arnold and Bickerstaffe selected the music for "The Maid of the Mill" this season they chose as an overture one of Kellie's which remained popular for a long time.

Kozeluch went to Prague this year for his education, taking lessons in composition from his uncle, Jan Kozeluh and in piano from F. X. Dušek.

Dancer François Jacques Lefebvre this year returned with his family to his native Paris.

James Lyon was sent to Nova Scotia by the Presbytery at this time because a minister was needed.

Leopold Mozart and his young son, Wolfgang, went to visit Johann Christian (son of J. S.) Bach this year. The latter was known as the "London Bach".

Leopold Mozart, Wolfgang and Anna Maria stayed at The Hague for some time this year. Here Wolfgang wrote Variations of the Dutch National song, "Wilhelmus van Nassouwe".

Thomas Norris at this time was appointed organist of Christ Church Cathedral, Oxford.

B. Ottani became a member of the Accademia Filarmonica of Bologna this year.

Bishop Thomas Percy at this time published his collection of old English and Scottish ballads under the title "The Reliques of Ancient English Poetry" and this started an interest in folk songs.

Mongeot published Rameau's letter in the "Mercure" this year whild music master to the children of the Princess de Gueménée at Versailles.

The letter Rameau wrote to La Matte asking him for a libretto for an opera he wanted to write was published in the "Mercure" this year after both had died.

Venamzio Rauzzini made his debut in a soprano part at the Teatro della Valle this season. After that, he sang with great success in many important opera

"The Garb of Old Gaul", written at this time, went to the tune of the "Highland March" of General Reid.

Friedrich Wilhelm Rust this year studied violin with G. Benda, Tartini and Pugnani in Italy.

Johann Peter Salomon made a concert tour to Frankfurt and Berlin this year.

Corona Schröter sang in a Leipzig Grosses Konzert this season. She was fourteen years old at the time.

Joseph Schuster went to Italy this year to study composition.

Friedrich Schwindel toured Europe this season, winning praise both as an instrumentalist and as a composer.

Burkat Shudi this year made a harpsichord for Frederick the Great, #496, 2 manuals, which has survived.

Burkat Shudi this year made a harpsichord, #499, 2-manuals, which has survived.

Scarlatti's chief Spanish disciple, Padre Antonio Soler, this year made a reference to "Scarlatti's thirteen volumes for harpsichord".

Ignazio Somis at this time painted a portrait of his two brothers Lorenzo and Giovanni.

The composer Tommaso Traetta left Parma at this time and settled at Venice as principal of the Conservatorio dell' Ospedaletto.

Brown and Stratton wrote under Williams' "New Universal Psalmodist"; the 3rd edition published in London.

R. Woodward was appointed organist at Christ Church Cathedral this year.

Agricola's "Achille in Sciro" appeared at this time.

Arne's "The Birth of Hercules" libretto was published this year.

Astaritta's first recorded opera was "L'orfana insidiata", written in collaboration with Piccinni at this time in Naples.

Avordano's "Il mondo della luna", a comic opera, appeared this season.

J. Christian (son of J. S.) Bach's "6 Italian Canzonette" were completed at this time.

J. Christian (son of J. S.) Bach published his six symphonies op. 3 this year.

J. Christian (son of J. S.) Bach published his six trios, op. 4 this year.

Karl Philipp Emmanuel Bach collected Johann Sebastian's four-part chorals and they were published this year by Birnstiel at Berlin and Leipzig, Part I at this time.

K. P. E. Bach's Concerto in C for solo clavier was published this season.

W. F. Bach announced his completion of 12 Polonaises at this time.

William Bates' serious opera "Pharnaces" was produced this season at Drury Lane Theatre in London.

Battishill wrote one song for a revival this season of Edmund Moore's "The Foundling" at the Drury Lane Theatre in London.

Battishill's "Twelve Hymns" was published this year. It was a valuable contribution to the general hymnal collections.

Pierre Montan Berton's opera "Erosine" appeared at this time.

Pierre Montan Berton's opera "Silviè" appeared this season.

A third edition of Bickham's "The Musical Entertainer" appeared this year.

Benoît Blaise's "Isabelle et Gertrude, ou Les Sylphes supposés" was completed at this time.

Blanchard's "Bonum est confiteri" was completed this year in manuscript only.

Boccherini's opera "La confederazione" was produced this season at Lucca.

"Brady and Tate's Psalms", an American tune collection, was issued at Boston this year.

Burney's "Sonata for Two Violins and a Bass" was brought out at this time.

Bury's "Zénis et Almasie" (written with Laborde) was performed this year at Fon-

CONSTANZA VON WEBER MOZART
(Mozart's Wife)

tainebleau.

Cardonne this year published
some collections of airs and
a book of sonatas for harpsichord with violin, opus 3.

Corette's "Laudate Dominum de
Coelis" was performed this
season.

Diderot's "Encyclopédie" was
issued again this year.

Giacomo Falconi of Venice published his "Manifesto d'una
nuova impresa di stampara la
musica . . ." at this time.

A "Traité historique et critique
sur l'origine et les progrès
des caractères de fonte pour
l'impression de la musique"
was published this year in
Paris by Pierre Simon Fournier.

Baldassare Galuppi wrote his
opera "L'arrivo d'Enea nel
Lazio" in Florence this year
(libretto by Alamanni).

Baldassare Galuppi wrote his
opera "La partenza ed il ritorno
dei marinari" this year at
Venice (librettist unknown).

Baldassare Galuppi wrote his
opera "La virtù liberata" this
year at St. Petersburg (text by
Lazzaroni).

Martin Gerbert von Hornau's
"Iter alemannicum, accedit
accedit italicum et gallicum",
containing accounts of the
author's travels, was published
this year.

Charles Hubert Gervais' opera
"Hypermnestre" was revived this
season at the Paris Académie

(cont.) Royale de Musique,
49 years after its first
production.

Gluck wrote his Italian opera
"La corona" this year, however
it was not performed until 1937.

Gluck's opera "Isabelle et
Gertrude" (libretto by Favart)
was produced in Paris this
season. Actually it was a
group of Gluck's arias fitted
to a French text inserted in
an opera by Blaise.

André Grétry wrote a 5-part
"Antifona" at this time.

Grétry's opera "La vendemmia-
trice" was given this season
at the Teatro Alibert in Rome
(librettist unknown).

Pietro Guglielmi's opera "Il
ratto della sposa" was given
this year at Venice.

Hasse's pasticcios listed below
were all performed this season
at London:
    "Berenice"
    "La clemenza di Tito"
    "Leucippo"
    "The Maid of the Mill"
    "The Summer's Tale"

Haydn's "Capriccio" in G major
for piano was completed this
year.

Haydn's Concerto for Clavier
in D major was composed prior
to this year. It was scored
for cembalo, concertante, 2
violins, viola and bass.

Haydn's Concerto for cello #1
in C major was composed prior
to this year for cello, 2
violins, viola, bass and 2
horns.

Prior to this year Haydn wrote
a Concerto for flute in D major.

Prior to this year Haydn wrote
his Concerto for horn in D major
which was lost. It was first
announced by Breitkopf in 1781.
There is also another possible
horn concerto in D major.

Haydn's Divertimento in C major
was written prior to this year
scored for flute, oboe, 2 violins, cello and bass (cassation).

Haydn's Divertimento in G major
(Cassation) was composed prior
to this year for flute, oboe,
2 violins, cello and bass.

Haydn's Divertimento (minuet,
trio and finale) was composed
prior to this date for string
quartet and two horns.

Haydn's Divertimento (sextet)
in F major was composed prior
to this date for string quartet
and two horns.

Haydn's Divertimentos (sextets)
in C major, D major and G major
(Feld Partitas) were composed
prior to this date.

Haydn's piano sonatas #12, #13,
#14, in A major, E major and
D major, were written before
this date and published in 1767.

Haydn's piano sonatas #3, #4
in C major and D major, referred
to as divertimenti, were written
prior to this year.

Haydn's "Eight lost Sonatas" as
listed below were written about
this time. They are not to be
confused with #3 and #4 in the
entry above this one:
  #3 a minor

#4 A major
#5 E major
#6 Bb major
#7 e minor
#9 C major
#10 A major
#16 D major

Haydn's Symphony #26 in d minor
was composed this year. It
was nicknamed "Lamentatione
oder Weihnachts-symphonie".

Haydn's Symphony #28 in A major
was composed this year and
scored for 2 oboes, 2 horns
and strings.

Haydn's Symphony #29 in E
major for 2 oboes, 2 horns
and strings was composed this
year.

Haydn's Symphony #30 in C major
("Alleluja") was composed this
year for flute, 2 oboes, 2
horns and strings.

Haydn wrote his Symphony #31
in D major ("Hornsignal","Auf
dem Austand") this year for
flute, 2 oboes, 4 horns, solo
violin, solo cello and string
quartet.

Haydn's first "Te Deum" (in C
major) was written before this
year.

Jommelli's opera "Imeneo in
Atene" was produced this season
at Ludwigsburg.

N. Logroscino's "La gelosia"
was produced this season.

G. S. Löhlein's "Piano Tutor",
part I, was published this year.

A. Lucchesi wrote his opera
"L'Isola della Fortuna" and it
was produced this season.

"La clemenza di Tito", performed
at the King's Theatre in London
this year, contained a pasticcio
by G. F. Maio.

Giovanni Maio's opera "Monte-
zuma" (libretto by V. A. Cigna-
Santi) was produced this year at
Venice.

P. von Maldere's "VI Sonatas
for 2 violins . . .",dedicated
to Mgr. de Montmorency, was
published in its second edition
this year at Paris.

The carefully documented "Éloge"
by Dr. Maret was read before the
Academy of Dijon and published
this year.

Metastasio's libretto "La
Corona" had its first setting
this year by Gluck.

Metastasio's libretto "Il
Parnaso confuso" had its first
setting this year by Gluck.

Metastasio's libretto "Romolo
ed Ersilia" had its first setting
this year by Hasse.

Metastasio's libretto "Il
Trionfo d'Amore" had its first
setting this year by Caldara
and Gassmann.

Mozart's solo aria with orchestra, "Va, dal furor portata"
(text by Metastasio), was written
this year at London for the
tenor, Ciprandi. It was scored
for tenor, 2 oboes, 2 bassoons,
2 horns and strings.

Mozart composed his first
Symphony this year.

W. A. Mozart wrote his Symphony
in D major at London this year.

(cont.) It was for 2 oboes, 2
horns and strings.

Paisiello's comic opera,
L'amore in ballo", was composed this year.

Paisiello's comic opera, "I
bagni d'Abano" was composed
this season.

Paisiello's opera seria
"Demetrio" was composed at
this time.

Paisiello's comic opera,
"Madama l'amorista, o Gli
stravaganti" was composed
this year

Paisiello's comic opera, "Il
negligente", was completed
this year.

Paisiello's opera "Le nozze
di Bacco ed Arianna" was composed this year (mascherata
coreografica).

Paisiello's comic opera, "Le
virtuose ridicole", was composed this season.

G. Paolucci's treatise "Arte
practica di contrappunto
dimostrata con esampi de varii
autori e con osservazioni"
was published this year at
Venice by Giacomo Falconi.

Percy published his "Reliques"
at this time.

"Histoire amoureuse de Pierre
le Long . . ." containing
seven romances by F. A.
Philidor appeared this year at
London.

When Piccinni's "La buona
figliuola" was translated
into Spanish and performed in

Madrid this year, Esteve adapted the music and wrote some additional numbers for the work.

Porpora's cantata in praise of St. Januarius was performed this season at Naples in the Cathedral.

Rameau's "Castor et Pollux" was revived again this season in France with a few changes by Pierre Berton.

Antonio Sacchini's operas "La contadina in corte" and "Il finto pazzo per amore" were both produced at Rome this year.

Antonio Sacchini this year wrote the opera "L'isola d'amore" while at Rome.

G. Scarlatti's opera "Bajazet" was produced this season at the Teatro Filarmonico in Verona (libretto by Piovene).

An edition of "The Beggar's Opera" was reissued this year by J. & R. Tonson.

Tommaso Traetta's opera "Semiramide" was produced this season at Venice.

Jean Claude Trial composed "Renaud d'Ast" this year with Vachin.

Jean Claude Trial composed the opera "Sylvie" this year with Berton.

Vento's opera "Demofoonte" was produced this season at London.

Aaron Williams' "Universal Psalmodist" was issued this year in its third edition.

A harpsichord made by J. Kirkman this year has survived. It was #20, 1 manual, stop 2x8', only currently owned by Colonial Williamsburg, Virginia.

"The committee for building an organ for Christ Church, reported that the same was now ready to be put up . . ." this year at Philadelphia.

"At Bethlehem, music was cultivated with much skill and knowledge of Sacred and Secular literature, as no where else in the Colonies" up to this date.

A collegium similar to the Collegium Musicum was set up this year at Lititz.

After this year opera buffa absorbed all attention, even over the opéra comique.

A new series of concerts began this year at London.

"Reliques of Ancient English Poetry" by Thomas Percy, a clergyman and scholar, was published this year. It was a collection of authentic old romances and ballads which he had written down in the 17th century when he found them in manuscript form at a friend's house. This collection familiarized 18th century readers with medieval poetry.

Horace Walpole, novelist and amateur medievalist, published one of the first "Gothic" novels, "The Castle of Otranto", this year.

Theodore Bienaimé, a well-known architect of the period, was born (died 1826).

1765(cont.)

Georgian architecture: Charleston, Brewton House (portico,
c.28' w.).

When he returned to Paris from
Rome this year, Fragonard composed a diploma work directly
inspired by the opera "Callirboé".
It was astonishingly lyrical and
was his only large picture. It
hangs in the Louvre.

Georgian architecture: New
York, Jumel House (portico,
c.33' w.).

King William IV of England
(House of Hanover) was born
(died 1837). He reigned from
1830-1837.

The philosopher Thomas Abbt
took up residence in the court
at Bückeburg at this time.

"Histore de l'Académie Royale
des Sciences de Paris" was
written this year by Berger of
Grenoble.

The Bergakademie ("mining
Academy") was founded this year
at Freiberg.

(to 1766) Felice (dei) Giardini
was the manager of the Opera in
London during this season.

(to 1768) Bortniansky studied
with Galuppi, a court composer,
during these years at St.
Petersburg.

(to 1768) Baldassare Galuppi
was chapelmaster at the court
of St. Petersburg (Catherine II)
during this period.

(to 1768) Johann Naumann during
this period while in Italy,

(cont.) set two librettos by
Metastasio, "Achille in Sciro"
(produced at Palermo, September
5, 1767) and "Alessandro nell'
Indie" (for Venice).

(to 1768) Joseph Schuster produced several of his operas
in Italy, where he was studying
composition during these years.

(and 1769) Johann Sebastian
Bach's "Vierstimmige Choral-
gesänge" were published at
both these dates.

(to 1770) Henri Hamal studied
under his uncle, J. N. Hamal
at the above dates in Italy.

(and 1770) B. Ottani's oratorios were performed at
Bologna during these years.

(to 1771) Andrea Lucchesi was
maestro di cappella at Venice
during this period.

(to 1774) At Hickford's Room
(II) several good concerts
were given during these years,
some directed by J. Christian
(son of J. S.) Bach and Abel.
Also Hayes carried on a Monday
evening subscription series
for several years.

(to 1775) Sarah Phillips continued the music engraving
business after this year when
her husband, John, died. She
moved the shop to Bedford
Court shortly after his death.

(to 1776) Haydn during these
years increased the number of
his symphonies to about 60 and
added opus 9, 17 and 20 to his
quartets.

(to 1777) Work continued inter-
mittently during these years on

a thematic catalogue of Haydn's works. It has provided a valuable source of information.

(to 1785) Henry Mountain was leader of the Dublin City Music for these twenty years.

(to 1793) Composer Gennaro Astaritta was active during this period.

(to 1802) Samuel Arnold produced nearly a hundred operas, musical afterpieces and pantomimes during these years.

(to 1804) Bernardini wrote more than 35 operas for Rome and other Italian towns during these thirty-nine years.

(to 1808) John Caulfield, the elder, the younger Joseph Caulfield, and Henry Caulfield all engraved music during this period.

(to 1810) Friedrich Benda was chamber musician (violinist) in the Royal Orchestra at Berlin during these years.

c.1765

José Maria Aldana, Mexican composer, was born this year (died 1810, February 7).

Jean-Baptiste Bédard, French violinist, conductor and composer, was born this year at Rennes (died c.1815 at Paris).

Wojciech (Adalbert) Dankowski (real name Danek) was born this year (death date unknown).

Charles Dignum, English tenor and composer of Irish descent, was born this year at London (died 1827, March 29 at London).

Anton Eberl, composer, was born this year (died 1807).

John Gunn, Scottish cellist and writer, was born this year at Edinboro (died c.1824).

Jean (John) Jousse, French music teacher, was born this year at Orleans (died 1837, January at London).

Gustavo Lazzarini, Italian tenor, was born at this time at Padua or Verona (death date unknown).

John Phillips, Welsh music engraver, died at this time (birthdate unknown).

Carlo Teodoro Toeschi, violinist and composer, was born this year at Mannheim (died after 1835 at München).

Nicolas Winnen of Paris, who invented the "Bassonore", was born this year (died c.1834).

Campioni moved to Florence this year and was appointed "maestro di cappella" of the cathedral there.

Campioni lived at Leghorn until this year.

A. Duni lived at Riga as a teacher at this time.

Jonathan Fentum, music publisher, at this time located his business at the corner of Salisbury Street in London.

Several sets of Asplmayr's serenatas, quartets and trios were published this year.

Barsanti's "Six Sonatas for

c.1765(cont.)

Two Violins and a Bass . . .",
Op. 6, were published this year
at London.

"Collection of Airs & Marches"
by R. Bremner was published
this year containing operatic
marches.

Hook's choral work "Ode on the
opening of the New Exhibition
Rooms" appeared this year.

Haydn's Concerto for clavier in
G major for 2 violins, 2 violas
and bass was composed at this
time.

Haydn's Concerto for clavier
in F major for 2 violins,
violetta, bass and 2 horns (ad.
lib.) was composed this year.

Haydn's Concerto for clavier
and violin in F major for clavier, violino principale, 2
violins, viola and bass was composed at this time.

Haydn's Symphony #34 in d minor
and D major for 2 oboes, 2 horns
and strings was composed this
year.

The Moravians in America
founded a Collegium musicum
this year at Lititz.

Fragonard painted "The Bathers"
this year (25 1/4" x 31 1/2").
The picture hangs in the Louvre
in Paris.

(to 1770) John Singleton Copley
during these years painted
"Portrait of Paul Revere"
(37 7/8" x 28 1/2").

(to 1785) During this period
there was a performance of
Gluck's mimed drama "Semiramide".

(to 1830) Many travelling
virtuosos and enthusiastic
amateurs played the armonica
all over Europe during these
years.

1766

(January 9) N. Piccinni's opera
"La pescatrice, ovvero L'erede
riconosciuta" (librettist un-
inown) was produced at the
Teatro Capranica at Rome on
this date.

(January 12) Pasquale Cafaro
wrote a cantata for King
Ferdinand IV's birthday at
this time.

(January 12) Jean François
(Johannes Francicus) Cuypers,
violin maker, was born on this
day at The Hague (died 1828,
July 16 at The Hague).

(January 15) Marie Jeanne Trial,
soprano, made her debut at the
Theatre-Italien on this date
singing under the name of Mme.
Mandeville.

(January 15) John Walsh II,
English music seller, instrument maker and publisher, died
on this date at London (birthdate unknown).

(January 30) Susanna Maria
Cibber, English singer and
tragic actress, died on this
dat at London (born 1714,
February 15 London. Her maiden
name was Arne.

(February 13) Luis Missón,
Spanish woodwind player, conductor and composer, died on
this date at Madrid (birthdate unknown but probably at
Barcelona). He invented the
"tonadilla".

1766(cont.)

(February 19) Kohault's opera "La Bergère des Alpes" (libretto by Marmontel) was produced this evening at the Comedie-Italienne in Paris.

(February 24) Samuel Wesley, English organist and composer, was born on this date at Bristol (died 1837, October 11).

August Bernhard Valentin Herbing, German cleric and organist, died at this time at Magdeburg (born 1735, March 9 at Halberstadt).

(March 3) Joseph Sonnleithner, Austrian amateur musician, was born on this date at Vienna (died 1835, December 25).

(March 3) Gregor Werner, German conductor and composer, died on this date in Eisenstadt (born 1695).

(March 4) Robert Lindley, English cellist and composer, was born on this date at Kotherham (died 1855, June 13 at London).

(March 5) G. Werner died on this day and Haydn became sole Kapellmeister. His compositions were already known far outside Austria: at Leipzig, Paris, Amsterdam and London. His symphonies, cassations, trios and quartets were available in print.

(March 17) Leoné performed this evening on the mandoline at Hickford's Rooms in London.

(Spring) Florian Gassmann's opera "Achille in Sciro" was produced on this date at Venice (libretto by Metastasio).

(March 28) Joseph Weigl II, conductor and composer, was born on this date at Kismarton, Eisenstadt (died 1846, February 3).

(April 15) Monsigny's opera "Aline, reine de Golconde" (libretto by Sedaine after Boufflers) was produced on this date at the Paris Opéra.

(April 18) Bernhard A. Weber, German pianist, conductor and composer, was born on this date at Mannheim (died 1821, March 23).

(April 25) Arne wrote incidental music for "Miss in her Teens" at this time performed at the Drury Lane Theatre in London.

(April 30) John Worgan's oratorio "Manasseh" was produced at this time.

(May 9) Johann Daniel Silbermann, German organ builder, died on this date at Leipzig (born 1717, March 31).

(May 24) Barthélemon's opera, "Pelopida" was performed at the King's Theatre in London this evening.

(May 25) Florian Gassmann's opera "Il viaggiator ridicolo" was produced on this date at Vienna (libretto by Goldoni).

(May 28) J. A. Hiller's singspiel "Die verwandelten Weiber oder Der Teufel ist los" (libretto by C. F. Weisse based on Coffey's "The Devil to Pay" and on Sedaine's "Le Diable a quatre") was produced this evening at Leipzig. It was Hiller's revised version

of an earlier setting by J. C.
Standfuss in 1752.

(June 16) Antonio Scarlatti
applied to become a cadet in
the Infanteria de Soria at this
time.

(June &) Gossec's opera "Les
Pêcheurs" (libretto by Adrien
Nicolas Piédefer, Marquis de
La Salle d'Offemont) was pro-
duced this evening at the
Comédie-Italienne in Paris.

(June 12) Mozart's "Kyrie" in
F major for four voices and
strings was finished on this
date at Paris.

(June 13) Anton Eberl, Austrian
pianist and composer, was born
on this day at Vienna (died
1807, March 11 at Vienna).

(Summer) Hiller's Singspiel
"Der lustige Schuster" (libretto
by Weisse, based on Coffey's
"The Merry Cobbler") was produced at this time at Leipzig.
Hiller added an overture and
7 numbers to an earlier setting
by J. C. Standfuss in 1759.

(July 1) "Menalcas" by Joseph
Harris was performed at the
Oxford Music Room in London on
this date.

(July 2) Francis Hopkinson on
this date wrote to his mother
from London Derry (sic).

(July 3) Jacques Marie (Beau-
varlet) Charpentier, French
organist and composer, was born
on this date at Lyons (died
1834, September 7 at Paris).

(July 12) Francis Hopkinson
wrote his mother on this day

(cont.) from Dublin.

(July 16) Male soprano, Giusto
Ferdinando Tenducci, eloped
on this day with a pupil,
Dorothy Maunsell.

(July 17) Barthold Fritz,
German mechanic and instrument
maker, died on this date at
Braunschweig (born 1697).

(July 18) Friedrich Fleisch-
mann, German composer, was born
at this time at Markleidenfeld
near Würzburg (died 1798,
November 30).

(July 24) E. R. Duni's opera
"La Clochette" was produced
on this date in Paris at the
Comédie-Italienne.

(July 24) František Petr
Němeček, Czech writer on music,
was born on this date at
Sadska near Poděbrady (died
1849, March 19 at Vienna).

(August 1) Ignaz Anton Ladurner,
Austrian composer, was born at
this time in Aldein, Tyrol
(died 1839, March 4).

(August 4) Francis Hopkinson
wrote his mother on this date
from London and reported that
he had been received by Benjamin West, famous artist
(and a friend of his family).

(August 22) Joseph Denis
Doche, French composer, was
born on this date at Paris
(died 1825, July 20 at Soissons).

(August 28) Richard Vincent, jr.,
English composer, died on this
date at London (birthdate unknown but at London).

(August 30) C. Dibdin's "The

1766(cont.)
Sailor's Reception" was performed at this time in Richmond.

(September 5) Luigi Bassi,
Italian bass-baritone, was born
on this day at Pesaro (died
1825, September 13 at Dresden).

(September 19) The "Connecticut
Gazette" in this issue printed
"Proposals for Printing by
Subscription a Book . . . 'New
Universal Psalmodist'. . ."
It was dated at New Haven.

(September 23) John Brown,
English divine, poet and writer
on music, died on this day at
Newcastle-on-Tyne (born 1715,
November 5 at Rothbury, North-
umberland).

(September 23) Francis Hopkin-
son, in a letter forwarded home
from London on this date said
"From . . . London I went to
Glocester, where I had the
Pleasure of hearing the
Messiah . . ."

(September 22) Prince Maximilian
of Bavaria on this date conferred the title of Baron on
Dall' Abaco.

(October 2) In this day's issues
of the Massachusetts "Gazette"
and Boston "News Letter",
Josiah Flagg inserted an advertisement, "A Collection of all
Tansur's and a Number of other
Anthems", published and to be
sold.

(October 9) Dionys Weber, Bohemian composer and teacher,
was born on this date at
Velichov, Bohemia (died 1842,
December 25 at Prague).

(October 25) Karl Gottlieb

(cont.) Hering, German music
teacher and composer, was born
on this date at Schandau, Saxony
(died 1853, January 4 at Zittau).

(October 25) Barthélemon contributed one song to "The Country
Girl" performed on this evening
at the Drury Lane Theatre in
London.

(October 28) Thaddäus Gerl,
German bass and composer, was
born on this date at Straubing
(died 1844, April 13).

(October 29) J. A. Benda's
Italian intermezzo "Il buon
marito" was performed on this
date at Gotha.

(November 1) Cecilia Grassi
sang this evening in "Trake-
barne, Gran Mogol" at London.
Her performance was considered
mediocre.

(November 4) N. Piccinni's
opera "Il gran Cid" (libretto
by G. Pizzi) was performed on
this date at the Teatro San
Carlo at Naples.

(November 5) Michael Arne on
this day married Elizabeth
Wright, a vocalist of some
reputation.

(November 8) Josef Starzer's
ballet "Le Chevalier boiteux"
(composer doubtful) was produced this evening at St.
Petersburg.

(November 15) The Connecticut
"Gazette" in this issue printed:
"Proposals for Printing by
Subscription a Book entitled
the New Universal Psalmodist,
or Beautiful Harmony of Zion
. . ."

1766(cont.)

(November 18) Samuel Arnold's "Harlequin Doctor Faustus" was performed this evening at Covent Garden in London.

(November 20) John (Wall) Callcott, English organist and composer, was born at this time at London (Kensington) (died 1821, May 15 at Bristol).

(November 21) Rousseau's "Le Devin du village" was first produced at London's Drury Lane Theatre on this date (adapted by Burney as "The Cunning Man").

(November 25) Hiller's Singspiel "Lisuart und Dariolette oder Die Frage und die Antwort" (libretto by Daniel Schiebeler, based on Favart's "La Fée Urgele") was performed this evening at Leipzig.

(December 20) Cecilia Grassi sang in "Ezio" this evening at London.

(December 21) Mozart's solo aria with orchestra, K. 36, "Or che il dover" (recitative), "Tali e catanti sono" (aria), for tenor, 2 oboes, 2 bassoons, 2 horns, 2 trumpets, drums and strings was composed at this time in Salzburg.

(December 29) Franz Lamotte at this time gave a violin concert at the Burg Theatre in Vienna.

(January) Cafaro's opera "Arianna e Teseo" was performed this month at the Teatro San Carlo in Naples.

(January) The Mozart family went to Amsterdam this month where 2 public concerts were given by Wolfgang and Anna Maria.

(January) Mozart's piano work, variations on "Laat ons juichen" (an air by C. E. Graf) in G major (K.24) was composed this month at The Hague.

(February) Mozart's Piano Concerto in F major for three pianos (K.242), scored for 2 oboes, 2 horns and strings, was composed this month at Salzburg for the Countess Antonia Lodron and her daughters.

(February) Mozart's violin sonatas listed below were written this month at The Hague:

K.26   Sonata in Eb major
K.27   Sonata in G major
K.28   Sonata in C major
K.29   Sonata in D major
K.30   Sonata in F major
K.31   Sonata in Bb major

(February) Mozart's piano work, "Variations on 'Wilhelmus van Nassouwe'" (K.25) was composed this month at Amsterdam.

(February) Nicola (Antonio) Porpora, Italian opera composer, died this month at Naples (born 1686, August 19 at Naples). Naples musicians donated to pay for his funeral.

(March) Mozart's orchestral work "Galimathias musicum" (K.32) for piano, 2 oboes, 2 horns, bassoon and strings was composed this month at The Hague.

(April) Piscetti was succeeded this month in his position at St. Mark's in Venice by Domenico Bettoni.

(June) Antonio Salieri went to Vienna this month with

Gassmann.

(Autumn) Tommaso Traetta's "Le
serve rivali" (libretto by
Pietro Chiari) was produced at
this time at the Teatro San
Moise in Venice.

(October) Hook this month gave
a benefit concert "for the
widow Hook".

(November) Thomas Chilcot,
English organist and composer,
died this month at Bath (birthdate unknown).

(November) Rodolphe Kreutzer,
French violinist and composer,
was born this month at Versailles
(died 1831, June 6 at Geneva).
His parents were German.

(November) Charlotte Brent
became Thomas Pinto's second
wife this month. He was a
violinist.

(November) The American premiére
of T. A. Arne's opera "Thomas
and Sally, or the Sailor's Return" took place this month at
Philadelphia (libretto by Issac
Bickerstaffe).

(November) After a successful
concert tour through Switzerland, the Mozart family returned
to Salzburg this month.

(December) Grétry's opera
"Isabelle et Gertrude, ou Les
Sylphes supposés" was given at
this time in Geneva (libretto
by Favart).

Francesco Besozzi, oboist, was
born this year at Dresden (died
1816 at Dresden).

Girolamo Crescentini, Italian

(cont.) male singer who had a
beautiful mezzo-soprano voice
and supposedly a "perfect
method of vocalization", was
born this year (died 1846).
He was the last of the great
castrati.

Stepan Anikievich Degtiarev,
Russian composer, was born this
year (died 1813, May 5 near
Kursk).

Johann Friedrich Eck, German
violinist, was born this year
at Mannheim (died c.1809 at
Bamberg).

Johannes Adolf Ibach, founder
of Ibach and Sons, was born
at Barmen this year (death
date unknown). The firm
manufactured pianofortes.

Johann Nopomuk Kalcher, German
organist and composer, was
born at this time in Freising,
Bavaria (died 1826 at München).

Jean Dominique Larrey, Napoleon's
chief surgeon, was born this
year (died 1842).

Robert Mackintosh, Scottish
violinist, was born this year
(died 1807).

This year marked the birth of
Count Jean Baptiste Milhaud who
in 1800 was raised to the rank
of brigadier general on
Napoleon's staff (died 1833).

Giovanni Battista Pescetti,
Italian composer, died at this
time at Venice (born c.1704
at Vienna).

Ludovico Piccinni, son of N.
Piccinni who taught him music,
was born this year (died 1827,
July 31 at Paris).

DR. ARNE.

1710-1778

Ann Selina Storace, English
soprano of Italian descent, was
born this year at London (died
1817, August 24 at London).

Franz Xaver Süssmayr, Austrian
conductor and composer who
finished the Mozart Requiem,
was born this year at Schwanen-
stadt, Upper Austria (died 1803,
September 16 at Vienna).

Bernhard Anselm Weber, an imitator of Gluck who traveled as a
virtuoso on glass harmonica,
was born this year (died 1821).

Leopold August Abel was conductor of the court bands of the
Margrave of Schwedt at this time.

D'Alembert described the courante
this year as "une sarabande
forte lente".

Pedro Aranaz became "maestro
de capilla" at the cathedral
of El Pilar at Suragossa.

Joseph Baildon at this time
was awarded a prize for his
glee "When gay Bacchus fills
my breast".

Barthélemon married Mary Young
this year.

Beaumesnil made her debut at
the Paris Opera this season in
"Sylvie", music by Berton and
Trial.

An English gentleman, Peter
Beckford, M.P., induced Clementi's
father to give his consent this
year to the young musician's
going to England.

Bédos, in "L'Art du facteur
d'orgues" this year, spoke of
"the combinations of silences,

(cont.) held and touched
notes to form the articulation
of the music".

Charlotte Brent sang at the
Gloucester Festival this
season.

Britton found singing masters
this year at Maryland.

C. Cannabich went to Paris
at this time.

Cherubini began to learn music
this year at six years of age.

Georges Cousineau at this
time appeared as a music publisher in Paris.

A. Duni was back at Schwerin
this year applying for a
position in the ducal orchestra
there.

The castle of Esterháza, Prince
Nicholas' estate, was built
after his return from France
this year.

Joseph Fodor, violinist and
composer, was studying under
F. Benda this year at Berlin.

Johann Nicolaus Forkel was
appointed chorister at "Chor-
präfect" in Schwerin this
season by the Grand Duke.

Baldassare Galuppi was invited
to St. Petersburg this year by
the Empress Catherine II.

André Grétry left Rome at this
time and settled as a teacher
in Geneva.

Tommaso Guarducci left Italy
this year for England.

Johann S. Hartmann entered the
royal band at Copenhagen this

royal band at Copenhagen this year.

The author of a short article on Haydn this year called the master's music "charming, ingratiating, engaging, naturally humorous and enticing".

The official gazette "Wiener Diarium" spoke of Haydn this year as "our national favorite" and drew a parallel between him and Gellert, at that time a great compliment.

Haydn's "Mouvement de Walze" of this year was a sonata and supposedly was the first known instance of a waltz for pianoforte.

By this time Haydn had composed about 30 symphonies and cassations; a few divertimenti in 5 parts; 6 string trios; a concerto for the horn (1762); 12 minuets for orchestra; concertos, trios, sonatas, and variations for clavier. In vocal music he had finished a "Salve Regina for soprano and contralto, 2 violins and organ; a "Te Deum" (1764); 2 Italian operettas (1762); a pastoral, "Alcide e Galatea"; and a grand cantata.

William Hayes was appointed a minor canon of St. Paul's Cathedral in London this year.

Ludwig C. Hesse joined the Royal Chapel of the Prince of Prussia (later King Frederick William II).

Johann Hiller at this time became connected with the Leipzig Theatre, when he provided new music for Weisse's German version of Coffey's ballad opera, "The Devil to Pay".

James Hook directed his overture "The Sacrifice of Iphigenia" at Norwich this season.

Francis Hopkinson visited England this year. The terminal point of his trip was Hartlebury Castle. He was the guest of a relative, the Bishop of Worcester, and called on John Penn during his trip.

Johann Hummel was established in Amsterdam by this time.

Jean B. Janson made his debut this season as a cellist at the "Concert Spirituel".

A Viennese memoir of Khevenhüller's diary reported this year that Mme. Geoffroi "had herself left the theater in disgust shortly before the departure of Conte Durazzo". She was a dancer and wife of the dancer, Bodin (a friend of Casanova's who came from Turin).

J. S. Kleinknecht toured Germany this year successfully.

François-Joseph Krafft was mentioned this year as being at Brussels as a teacher of harpsichord, organ and composition.

Rosalie Levasseur appeared this season in a fragment of Campra's "L'Europe galante".

John Marsh was finally given musical instruction this year but only in violin.

Carlo d'Ordoniz was admitted as a member of the Imperial Court chapel in Vienna this year.

F. A. Philidor composed a "Requiem" performed this year at the anniversary of Rameau's death.

T. Pinto married singer Charlotte Brent this year after his first wife died.

Lazare Rameau played the organ in Autun Cathedral this season.

William Randall and John Abell took over the extensive business on Catherine Street this year when John Walsh, jr. died.

Friedrich Wilhelm Rust at this time returned to Dessau from Italy and became the life and soul of music there.

John Sale became a lay-clerk of St. George's Chapel in Windsor this year.

Antonio Salieri, Court Music Director and a former pupil and protégé of Gluck, became a resident of Vienna at this time.

Scarlatti's wife Anastasia was still living at this time.

Corona Schröter became acquainted with Goethe this year.

Burkat Shudi this year made two harpsichords for Frederick the Great' 2-manual, #511 and #512, both of which have survived.

Burkat Shudi this year made a harpsichord, #529, which has survived.

A Shudi harpsichord of this date was equipped with the "Venetian swell".

Maximilian Stadler, Austrian organist, clavier player and composer, this year joined the Benedictines at Melk and after taking priest's orders, worked

(cont.) as a parish priest and professor.

John Stephens, the English organist and composer, conducted the Gloucester Festival this season.

Thomas Straight and Thomas Skillern were established this year on Russell St., Covent Garden in London. The firm was Straight & Skillern, an English firm of music engravers and publishers at London.

A. M. G. Vestris married Françoise Rose Gourgaud this year at Stuttgart.

At the age of eleven this year, Viotti received instruction from an itinerant lute player named "Giovannini".

Viotti went to Turin for his studies this year and stayed at the house of the Prince of Cisterna.

Samuel Webbe this year received the "Catch Club" award for "O that I had Wings".

After Werner's death this year F. J. Haydn became Kapellmeister.

T. Wright became organist in Stockton Church this year.

Zumpe's piano was built (the earliest dated square piano in existence) with damper stops this year.

Leopold August Abel composed a "Sinfonia a 8 voci" this year.

Maria Teresa Agnesi's "L'insubria consolata" appeared at this time.

Another section of "Ré Pastore" was published this year in Andrez' journal, "L'Echo".

T. A. Arne's 2nd oratorio "Judith" was completed at this time.

Avossa's comic opera "La pupilla" enjoyed the distinction of a sequel with music by Marescalchi at the performance this year at Lisbon.

J. Christian (son of J. S.) Bach's opera "Catone in Utica" was given this year at the Braunschweig Court.

J. Christian (son of J. S.) Bach's 6 Italian Canzonette were completed by this time.

K. P. E. Bach's "Phillis und Tirsis" was published this year.

K. P. E. Bach's "Der wirt und die Gäste" (Gleim's "Singode") appeared this year.

Franz Beck's "Six Symphonies a plusieurs instruments", opus 4, was written this year.

Bertoni's "Tancredi" was produced this season at Turin.

Capel Bond's "Six Concertos in 7 Parts" appeared at this time.

Boroni's opera "La notte critica" was produced this season at Venice.

G. G. Brunetti's opera "Il trionfo dell' Arno" was performed this year at Pisa.

Burney this year prepared an English version of Rousseau's highly successful pastoral (cont.) dating from thirteen years earlier, "Le Devin du village", under the title of "The Cunning Man". He prepared the work for Garrick.

Cambini this season produced an opera at Naples without success.

Coffey's opera "Die verwandelten Weiber" was given this year at Leipzig. It was a new version, with music by Johann Adam Hiller.

Crispi's "La caduta de Gerico" appeared at this time.

Esteve this year adapted the music and wrote some additional numbers for Giuseppe Scarlatti's Goldoni opera "I portentosi effetti della Madre Natura".

The "Observations sur le traite historique et critique de M. Fournier . . ." was published at this time.

Baldassare Galuppi wrote his opera "La cameriera spirituosa" this year at Milan (libretto by Goldoni).

Baldassare Galuppi this year wrote his "La pace fra la virtù e la bellezza" at St. Petersburg (text by Metastasio).

Tommaso Giordani's opera "L'eroe cinese" was performed this season at Dublin.

Haydn this year composed a mass, "Missa solemnis in Honorem B.V.M." in Eb major, scored for SATB solo, four-part chorus, 2 cors anglais, 2 horns, 2 trumpets, drums, strings and organ obbligato.

It was probably written for the Bergkirche at Eisenstadt.

Breitkopf and Härtel this year announced the Haydn double concerto for violin and piano (or harpsichord) in F major in their catalogue.

Haydn wrote the opera "La canterina" (The songstress) at this time.

Haydn wrote the "Great Organ Mass" (Novello No. 12) this year. Geiringer referred to a solo organ Mass on this date which is presumably the same.

Haydn, prior to this year, composed his piano sonata in G major (#6) which was published this year.

Haydn this year composed a piano sonata in Eb major (called #45 and in another version opus 54, #2). The work was published in 1789.

"Le Diable à Quatre", music by Johann Adam Hiller, was performed this evening at the new Leipzig theatre.

J. A. Hiller's "Wöchentliche Nachrichten und Anmerkungen, die Musik betreffend" appeared at this time.

John Holden at this time published a "Collection of Church Music, consisting of New Setts of the Common Psalm Tunes, with some other Pieces; adapted to the several Metres in the Version authorized by the general assembly . . . principally designed for the use of The University of Glasgow".

Holzbauer wrote an oratorio "Il Giudizio di Salomone" for Mannheim this year.

Jommelli's opera "La Critica" appeared at this time.

Jommelli's opera "Vologeso" was produced this season at Ludwigsburg.

Jommelli's opera "Il matrimonio per concorso" was produced this season at Ludwigsburg.

Jean Marie Leclair's ("l'aine") Trio for 2 violins and bass was published this year posthumously.

A. Lucchesi's "Il marito geloso" was produced this season.

P. van Maldere's "Six Symphonies", dedicated to Prince Charles of Lorraine, was published this year at Brussels.

P. van Maldere's opera, "Le Medecin de l'amour" (libretto written at the Brussels Conservatory) appeared this year.

P. van Maldere's opera, "Le Soldat par amour" (librettist unknown) appeared this season.

Dr. Hughes Maret's "Eloge historiques de M. Rameau" was issued this year at Dijon.

Monsigny's opera "Baucis et Philémon" (libretto by Sedaine, after Lafontaine) was produced this year at Baguolit Théâtre du Duc d'Orléans.

Mozart at this time wrote his first oratorio, "Die Schuldigkeit des ersten Gebotes".

Paisiello's comic opera, "La finte contesse", was produced this year at Rome. The work was later called "Il marchese Tulipano".

Paisiello's comic opera, "Le nozze disturbate", was completed at this time.

Paisiello's comic opera, "La vedova di belgenio" appeared this year.

The first performance of Philidor's "Tom Jones" abroad was this season at Geneva (libretto by Antoine Alexandre Henri Poinsinet).

Piccinni's opera "La pescatrice" was produced this season at Rome.

Sacchini's opera "Colonie" appeared this year.

G. Scarlatti's opera "Armida" was produced this year at the Burg Theatre in Vienna (libretto by Cottellini).

Giuseppe Sarti's opera "Ipermestra" was produced this season at Rome.

Giuseppe Scarlatti's setting of Goldoni's "I Portentosi Effetti della Madre Natura" was transformed into a zarzuela and performed at Madrid this season.

Johann Schobert's opera "Le Garde-chasse et le braconnier" was produced this year at the Comédie-Italienne in Paris.

Jean Baptiste Antoine Suard this year published his "Exposé de la contestation entre Hume et Rousseau" at Paris.

Jean Claude Trial composed his "Ésope à Cythère" this year.

John Trydell at this time issued by subscription a work on the art of music, "Two Essays on the Theory and Practice of Music, Dublin, printed for the Editor . . . 1766, 8 vo.". He was an Irish clergyman and writer on music.

Vento's "Sofonisba" was produced this season at London.

The collection, "La lire Maçonne, ou Recueil de Chansons des Francs Maçons" by the Brothers de Vignoles and du Bois, was published at The Hague this year.

John Wainwright at this time published a collection of anthems, chants, and psalm tunes.

J. C. Walther published three sonatas for clavier this year.

Samuel Webbe wrote "Antiphonae" at this time.

Bedos this year set pitch at A=377 c.p.s., S=0!3.

Surviving harpsichords made by J. Kirkman included 2 of this year: #21 with 2-manuals currently owned by Mostell Priory, and #22, 2-manuals currently owned by Capt. R. Berkeley.

The Christmas Eve concerto remained in the repertoire of the "Concerts Spirituels" until this time.

Dragoon guards and dragoons this year were furnished with

1766(cont.)
trumpets instead of side drums.

The "Anacreontic Society", an aristocratic society, was founded in London this year by several noblemen and some wealthy musical amateurs.

Johann Christoph Gottsched, German poet and critic, died this year (born 1700).

Nikolai Mikhailovich Karamzin, Russian novelist who wrote the novel "Poor Lisa" and "History of Russia", was born this year (died 1826).

Goldsmith's novel "The Vicar of Wakefield" was published at this time in England.

Latrobe, the architect, was born this year (died 1820).

Jean-Marc Nattier, French painter, died this year (born 1685).

The philosopher Thomas Abbt died at this time (birthdate unknown).

Edmund Burke was elected to the English Parliament this year.

Frederick V, King of Denmark, died this year (birthdate unknown).

(and 1767) Gasparo Angiolini was ballet-master at Milan in 1766 and possibly 1767.

(to 1767) Cecilia Grassi was engaged as "prima donna seria" in London this season.

(to 1767) Francis Hopkinson at this time purchased a number of

(cont.) works from Robert Bremner while in England.

(and 1767) At Newcastle a concert was given this season including Handel's "Water Music" and Coronation Anthem (1766), "Messiah" (1767).

(to 1768) Brusa was choirmaster at the Conservatorio degli Incurabili during these years in place of Galuppi, who had left for Russia.

(to 1768) In the books of words for 4 Latin pieces of church music printed at this time, the composer's name was given as Johannes Franciscus Brusa.

(to 1769) Anastasia Maxarti Ximenes, second wife of Domenico Scarlatti, died sometime during this period (birthdate unknown).

(to 1769) Johann Adam Hiller's "Wöchentliche Nachrichten und Anmerkungen die Musik betref-fend" was published during these years at Leipzig.

(to 1770) The "Wöchentliche Nachrichten und Anmerkungen die Musik betreffend" (4 vols., 1766-1770) was the earliest German musical periodical in which news and reviews were the main feature. There were also articles on aesthetics and general controversial subjects. J. A. Hiller was the editor.

(to 1771) Pasquale Fago was maestro di cappella at the Tesoro di San Gennaro during this period.

(to 1771) G. Mara attended Hiller's music school at Leipzig studying voice during these five years.

1766(cont.)

Corona Schröter sang in the Leipzig Grosses Konzerts during these seasons.

(to 1773) In Philadelphia opera showed definite progress during these years.

(to 1775) Rosalie Levasseur took secondary parts under the name of Mademoiselle Rosalie at this time.

(to 1777) Thomas Skillern, the elder, and Thomas Straight were partners during this period.

(to 1778, 1935) "L'Art du facteur d'orgues", a book by Bedos de Celles Dom Francois, appeared in Paris at this time and was published in a new edition in 1935.

(to 1778) "De Poësi Fennica", written in Latin by Henrik Gabriel Porthan, was published during these years.

(to 1779) Wincenty Lessel during these years played as a violist in the court orchestra at Dresden.

(to 1784) Mrs. Weichsell appeared as a ballad singer at Vauxhall for this twelve year period.

(to 1788) Thomas Norris appeared this season at the Gloucester Festival as a tenor and continued to sing at meetings of the Three Choirs until 1788.

(to 1790) Alcock was organist of St. Editha's at Tamworth during this period.

(to 1790) During this period at Esterhaza, Prince Nicolaus' new palace near Süttör, Haydn com-

(cont.) posed nearly all his operas, most of his arias and songs, the music for the puppet theatre and the greater part of his orchestral and chamber works.

(to 1790) The principal and best paid musicians during Haydn's Esterhazy period were: women singers--Weigl, Cellini, Maria and Matilda Bolognia, Raimondi, Nencini, Benvenuti, Rippamonti, Valdesturla and Tavecchia; men singers--Friberth, Bianchi, Gherardi, Jermoli, Moratti, Morelli, Totti (2), Peschi; violinists--Tomasini, Rosett, Rippamonti, Mestrino, Mraw; cellists--Weigl, Rüffel, Marteau, Kraft; flute--Hirsch; clarinets--Griesbacher (2); oboes--Columbazzo (2), Poschwa, Czerwenka; bassoons--Schiringer, Peczival; horns--Steinmüller, Franz, Stamiz, Oliva, Pauer, Lendway.

(to 1792) The libretto of Burney's "The Cunning Man" was published at least 6 times during these years.

(to 1822) Baudron was conductor of the Comédie-Française during this period.

c.1766

John Addison, English double-bass player and composer, was born this year at London (died 1844, January 30 at London).

Jean Marie Raoul, the French government official and cellist, was born at this time in Paris. He wrote sonatas, studies and solos for cello. He also wrote a "tutor" for the cello (died 1837 in Paris).

Hook this year married "Miss

c.1766(cont.)
Madden" often referred to as
"The Heiress".

Theodor von Schacht, German
composer, was a student of
Jommelli this year at Stuttgart.

Joshua Shudi at this time set up
his own harpsichord-making
business on Silver Street,
Golden Square, London.

Zumpe began making square
pianos this year at London with
the G-f''' compass (omitting the
lowest G#)--nearly 5 octaves--
but soon adopted the 5 octaves,
F-f''' in which John Broadwood,
who reconstructed the square
piano, followed his leadership.

Gluck's ballet "L'orfano della
China" (scenario from Voltaire;
choreography by Angiolini) was
produced this year at Vienna.

Haydn composed Six String
Quartets, opus 9 this year.

Haydn's trio #16 in Eb major
was probably written this year
for violin, cello and piano.

1767
(January 2) Michael Arne wrote
the misic for Garrick's dramatic Romance "Cymon", which
was successful and his best
work. It was produced on this
date at the Drury Lane Theatre
in London.

(January 11) In the diary kept
by Prince Khevenhüller-Metsch
this date's entry read: "In
the evening there was the 1st
appearance at the Burgtheater
of the famous dancer Vestris, a
native Italian who had once
lived here with his parents &
brothers & sisters in Sellier's

(cont.) time, dancing on the
very same stage as a boy.
Later he had become 1st dancer
at the Paris Opera, where he had
acquired a great reputation in
his art. He had accepted an
engagement at Stuttgart for
this carnival. But, the Duke
of Württemburg, because of his
well-known peccadilloes, had
agreed with his subjects to
undertake great reforms in his
household himself retiring
to Venice for a while. Thus,
M. Vestris, to keep from
remaining idle, sought an
opportunity to display his
artistry here or in Warsaw."

(January 12) Christ Church's
(Philadelphia) organ was
finished on this date "and
examined by the governors,
Mr. Bremner, the Organist . . ."

(January 29) Mysliveček's 1st
operatic success, "Bellerfonte",
was produced on this date at
the Teatro San Carlo at Naples.

(February 2) Franz Volkert,
German organist, conductor and
composer, was born on this day
at Friedland near Bunzlau
(died 1845, March 22).

(February 3) Francesco Basili
(Basily), Italian composer,
was born on this date at
Loreto (died 1850, March 25 at
Rome).

(February 11) A. Lucchesi's
"Cantata" was performed this
evening.

(February 14) J. Christian (son
of J. S.) Bach's opera
"Carattaco" was produced on this
date at London.

(February 21) C. Dibdin's "Love

425

in the City" was performed
on this date at Covent Garden
in London. He only composed
part of the music.

(March 12 and April 2) Mozart's
sacred cantata "Die Schuldigkeit des ersten Gebotes" (K.35)
was performed by the students
in the University Hall at
Salzburg on both these occasions.
The text was by Jacobus A.
Wimmer and the work was composed
for the Archiepiscopal Court.

(March 13) Heinrich Domnich,
German horn player, was born
on this date at Würzburg
(death date unknown).

(March 19) The opera "Love in a
Village" had its first performance at Philadelphia on
this day.

(March 21) Mozart's sacred work
(K.34) "Offertorium in Festo
Sti Benedicti" (4 voices, 2
trumpets, drums, strings and
organ) was composed at this
time at Seeon Monastery in
Bavaria.

(March 26) Count Lamberg wrote
to Casanova from Augsburg on
this date about the "Pythagorean
Table". He asked whether or not
a similar square of musical
notes could not be contrived
which, "used in various ways,
would represent a minuet, a
gavotte, a sarabande, a fandango,
etc."

(April 4) Cecilia Grassi sang
in Vento's "La conquista di
messico" this evening in London.

(April 4-5) James Grassineau,
English musical lexicographer,
died this night at Bedford (born
c.1715).

(April 6) Michael Arne's
"Linco's Travels" was produced
on this date at Drury Lane
Theatre in London.

(April 6) Vernon composed
songs for Garrick's interlude
"Linco's Travels" produced
on this date at Drury Lane
Theatre in London.

(April 20) Mr. Douglass' performance of "The Disappointment" was announced for this
day.

(April 21) Samuel Arnold's
"Rosamond" was performed
this evening at Covent Garden
in London.

(April 22) Mr. Douglass on
this date announced his with-
drawal from the performance
of "The Disappointment"
because it contained "local
color" that might be offensive.

(April 24) Hiller's singspiel,
"Lottchen am Hofe" (libretto
by Weisse, based on Favart's
"Le Caprice amoureux, ou
Ninette à la cour") was per-
formed on this date at Leipzig.

(April 25) J. A. Benda's Italian
intermezzo "Il nuovo maestro
di cappella" was produced this
evening at Gotha.

(April 26) Florian Gassmann's
opera "L'amore artigiano"
was produced on this date at
Vienna (libretto by Goldoni).

(May 2) Arnoldus Dahmen,
flutist and flute teacher, was
born on this date at Harlingen
(died 1829, December 17 at
Amsterdam).

(May 12) John Wainwright was
appointed organist and singing-

1767(cont.)
man at the Collegiate Church in Manchester at this time.

(May 13) Many festivities were listed in this issue of the "Bonnischer Anzeiger" which celebrated the Archbishop's birthday.

(May 13) Francisco Xavier García's intermezzo, "La finta schiava" was performed this evening at Bonn.

(May 13) Mozart's K.38, "Apollo et Hyacinthus seu Hyacinthi Metamorphosis", a Latin comedy, Intermezzo to "Clementia Croesi" (words by Rufinus Widl) was performed this evening at Salzburg.

(May 23) John Beard retired from the public as "Hawthorne" in "Love in a Village" on this date.

(June 4) At Philadelphia at this time a musical, "The Chaplet", an afterpiece to the comedy "The Country Lasses", was performed for the first time.

(June 5) Monsigny's opera "L'Isle sonnante" (libretto by Collé) was performed on this date at Bagnolet, Theatre du Duc d'Orléans.

(June 20) Gossec's opera "Toinen et Toinette" (libretto by Jean Auguste Julien) was produced at the Comédie-Italienne in Paris this evening.

(June 22) Jean Nicolas Mereaux, organist, pianist, composer and son of Nicolas Jean, was born on this date at Paris (died 1838, February at Paris).

(June 25) The death of his god-father, Telemann, on this date,

(cont.) conveniently opened the door to K. P. E. Bach for escape from Potsdam.

(June 25) Georg Philipp Telemann, a major German composer, died on this date at Hamburg (born 1681, March 14 at Magdeburg).

(June 29) J. W. Hertel wrote incidental music for Lowen's comedy "Das Rätsel" (published at Hamburg on this date, score preserved at Brussels). He also wrote incidental music this year for Cronegk's tragedy "Olint and Sophronia" and Weisse's "Richard III".

(July 3) Matthew Cubourg, English violinist, died on this day at London (born 1703 at London).

(July 18) C. Dibdin's "The Village Wedding, or The Faith-ful Country Maid" was performed this evening at Richmond.

(August 9) Per (Brant) Brandt, Swedish musician, died on this date (born 1713 at Stockholm).

(August 10) Cecilia Davies made her first appearance this evening at London.

(August 23) The governors of the Conservatorio di Sant' Onofrio at Naples decided on this date that Cotumucci taught in "too old-fashioned a way" and divided his stipend of 4 ducats a month between him and his ex-pupil Insanguine.

(August 24) Franz Beck wrote the one-act "bouquet", "La Belle Jardinière", produced on this date at Bordeaux.

(August 24-31) The Pennsylvania

1767(cont.)

"Chronicle" in these issues
advertised John Gualdo's music
store on Walnut Street in
Philadelphia.

(August 28) Johann Schobert,
German harpsichordist and com-
poser, died on this day at
Paris (born c.1720).

(August 30) Christian Friedrich
Gottlieb Schwencke, German
harpsichordist, composer, mathematician and musical editor, was
born on this date at Wachen-
hausen, Harz (died 1822, October
27).

(September 8) Karl August van
Lichtenstein, German theatre
manager and composer, was born
in Lahm, Franconia on this date
(died 1845, September 16 at
Berlin).

(September 9) Hasse's opera
"Partenope" (the 1st setting
of Metastasio's libretto) was
produced on this date at Vienna.
The libretto was also set by
Handel and Martin y Soler.

(September 10) In the diary of
Prince Khevenhüller on this date
was stated that the ballet
"L'Apotheose d'Hercule" had been
performed in Vienna "de la
composition du fameux Sr.
Noverri de Hongard . . . while
yesterday M. Vestris, by special
permission of the King, returned
from Paris for the present
season".

(September 17) Henri Montan
Berton, French composer, was
born on this date at Paris
(died 1844, April 22 at Paris).

(Autumn) Felice Alessandri
went to London at this time.

(Autumn) Felice Alessandri's
wife, the singer Guadagni, made
her debut this evening at the
King's Theatre in London in
Piccinni's opera "La schiava".

(Autumn) Pietro Guglielmi and
Felice Alessandri were engaged
as composers to the King's
Theatre in London at this time.

(Autumn) André Grétry went to
Paris at this time.

(Autumn or December) Mozart's
Symphony K.43 in F major for
2 oboes (or flutes), 2 horns
and strings was composed at
Olomouc and Vienna at this time.

(Autumn) Mozart's Symphony
K.76 in F major for 2 oboes,
2 bassoons, 2 horns and strings
was composed at this time in
Vienna.

(September 24) The Pennsylvania
"Gazette" in this issue stated
that operas were "accompanied
by a Band of Music".

(September 24-November 23)
Philadelphia enjoyed opera
performances during this period.

(September 26) Wenzel Müller,
Austrian conductor and composer,
was born on this date at Trnava,
Moravia (died 1835, August 3 at
Baden near Vienna).

(September 28) Gossec's opera
"Le Double Déguisement" (libretto by Houbron) was produced
at the Comédie-Italienne in
Paris this evening.

(October 2) Isabella Vincent on
this date married Captain John
Mills, one of the survivors
of the Black Hole of Calcutta.

1767(cont.)

(October 3) Hiller's "Nachspiel",
"Die Muse" (text by Schiebeler)
was produced on this date at
Leipzig.

(October 5) Florian Gassmann's
opera "Amore e Psiche" was given
this evening at Vienna (libretto
by Coltellini). It was an
imitation of Gluck's "Orfeo".

(October 21) Francesco Ruggi,
Italian composer, was born on
this date at Naples (died 1845,
January 23 at Naples). He was
a pupil of Fenaroli at the
Conservatoria Santa Maria Loreto
in Naples.

(October 23) Barthélemon's
"Orpheus" was performed this
evening at the Drury Lane
Theatre in London.

(October 27) The pasticcio
"Tigrane" was produced this
evening at London.

(November 3) K. P. E. Bach on
this date was chosen successor
to Telemann as music director of
Hamburg's Johanneum Kirche.

(November 9) The publication of
"The Psalms of David" (a rare
publication) on this date
contained an advertisement "To
the Reader" and was dated by
order of the Consistory,
Joannes Ritzema.

(November 12) Bernhard Romberg,
son of Anton Romberg (born 1742)
and a cellist and composer, was
born on this day in Drinklage
(died 1841, August 13 at Hamburg).

(November 15) A document from
San Lorenzo on this date re-
vealed the difficulties which
Nebra and Sabatini had with

(cont.) mules and drivers in
transporting their instruments.

(November 19) The Pennsylvania
"Gazette" in this issue stated,
"On Tuesday last was held the
public Commencement . . . An
elegant "Dialogue", written
in Verse by Thomas Coombe,
B.A." with allusions to Hopkinson as "worthy Son of the
College".

(July 6) Philadelphia enjoyed
operatic music during theatrical
seasons 1766 and 1767 up to
this date.

(November 22) Carvalho joined
the Brotherhood of Santa
Cecilia at Lisbon on this date.

(November 24) F. Philidor's
opera "Ernelinde,princesse de
Norvége" (libretto by Poinsinet
after Matteo Noris) was produced at the Académie Royale on
this date at Paris.

(November 26) "Lycidas" was repeated at Gyde's Room, Bath,
on this date under the direction
of the composer, William Jackson.

(November 26) The Pennsylvania
"Journal" in this issue advertised a new edition of "Urania".

(December 1) Haydn's Symphony
#35 in Bb major for 2 oboes,
2 horns and strings was composed
at this time. It was dated
"before 1770" by Breitkopf and
Härtel and placed as #40 by
Mandyczewski. Later the autograph score was discovered
bearing the date 1763.

(December 8) The pasticcio
"Siface" was produced this
evening at London.

1767(cont.)

(December 13) August (Eberhardt)
Müller, German keyboard player,
flutist and composer, was born
on this date at Northeim,
Hanover (died 1817, December 3
at Weimar).

(December 14) Thomas Linley,
Sr.'s "The Royal Merchant" was
produced on this date at Covent
Garden (book by Hull).

(December 26) Antonia Bernasconi
made her debut this evening
at Vienna in the title role of
Gluck's "Alceste".

(December 26) Gluck's Italian
opera "Alceste" was produced
on this date at the Burg
Theatre in Vienna (libretto by
Calzabigi).

(January) Quirino Gasparini's
opera "Mitridate, re di Ponto"
was given this month at Turin.

(January-August) John Johnson,
English 18th century music
publisher, during this period
first published "at the Apollo
in the Strand opposite the
New Exchange Coffee Rooms".

(February) Gluck's Italian opera
"Il prologo" was produced this
month at the Teatro della
Pergola in Florence (libretto
by Lorenzo Ottavio del Rosso).

(March) Tommaso Giordani's
oratorio "Isaac" was sung at
the Fishamble Street Music Hall
in London.

(May) W. Clagget's comic opera
"The Power of Sympathy, or The
Innocent Lovers" was performed
this month at Dublin.

(June) Mozart's K.39, Piano

(cont.) Concerto in Bb major
(arrangement of sonata movements by Raupach and Shobert)
for 2 oboes, 2 horns and strings
was composed this month at
Salzburg.

(April) Mozart's Piano Concerto
in F major (K.37) written for
2 oboes, 2 horns and strings
was composed this month at
Salzburg (arrangement of sonata
movements by Raupach at Hanover).

(August) John Gualdo, a wine
Merchant from Italy, opened
a Store of Music this month
at London.

(July) Mozart's Piano Concerto
(K.41) in G major (arrangement
of sonata movements by Honauer
and Raupach) was written this
month at Salzburg for 2 flutes,
2 horns and strings.

(July) Mozart's Piano Concerto
(K.40) in D major (arrangement
of sonata movements by Honauer,
Eckart and K. P. E. Bach)
for 2 oboes, 2 horns, 2 trumpets and strings, was composed
this month at Salzburg.

(October) On the way to Spain
and Portugal from Vienna this
month, Casanova stopped over
in Paris.

(November) "Lycidas", music by
William Jackson, was produced
at Covent Garden at London this
month but never repeated.

(December) Mozart's song (K.53)
"An die Freude" (text by J.
P. Uz) was composed this month
at Olomouc.

Luigi Asioli, Italian tenor
and composer, was born this
year at Correggio (died 1815,

A CARICATURE OF DR. ARNE BY F. BARTOLOZZI

1767(cont.)
November 17 at London).

Amélie Julie Candeille, French
actress, singer and composer,
was born at this time in Paris
(died 1834, February 4 at Paris).

Nicolas Gando, Swiss publisher,
died this year at Paris (birthdate unknown).

Gottlieb Graupner, an American
oboist from Hanover, was born
this year (died 1836).

Johann Ulrich Haffner, German
lutenist and composer, died
this year (birthdate unknown).

John Mackintosh, basson player,
was born this year (died 1844).

Niccolo Porpora, one of the
greatest singing teachers, died
at this time (born 1687).

Luc' Antonio Predieri, Italian
composer, died this year at
Bologna (born 1688, September
13 at Bologna).

Ferdinando Rutini, Italian com-
poser, was born this year at
Modena (died 1827, November at
Terracina).

Giuseppe Sarti's mother died
at this time (birthdate unknown).

Joseph Ignaz Schnabel, German
organist, violinist, composer
and singing teacher, was born
this year at Naumburg am Queis
(died 1831, June 16).

Franz Tunder, German composer,
died this year (birthdate unknown).

Sophie Weber, wife of Haibel,
was born at this time (died
1846).

Edmund Ayrton was installed at
this time as vicar-choral of
St. Paul's Cathedral.

Johann Christian (son of J. S.)
Bach married Cecilia Grassi
this year.

W. Friedemann Bach this year
dedicated his Clavier Concerto
in e minor to Maria Antonia,
Electress of Saxony.

Garrick this season engaged
Barthélemon to compose the music
for the burletta of "Orpheus",
introduced in his farce "A
Peep behind the Curtain" at the
Drury Lane Theatre in London.

Joah Bates was awarded the degree
of Master of Arts this year.

Battishill this year was
appointed organist of Christ
Church, Newgate Street.

Johann van Beethoven married
Maria Magdalena, the daughter
of Keverich, the chief cook at
the court of Ehrenbreitstein.

Ludwig van Beethoven, Sr. at
this time moved from the Fischer
house in the Rheingasse to the
house next north of the
"Gudenauer Hof".

In the rear of the Clasen house,
north, at Bonn, a lodging was
leased to the newly weds Johann
and Maria van Beethoven (Ludwig's
parents) this year.

James Bremner's ". . . name
appears not in the Vestry minutes
of Christ Church and St. Peter's
until 1767 . . ."

James Bremner was organist at
Christ Church this season.

Robert Bremner's name did not appear until this year in the Vestry minutes of Christ Church as published by Rev. Dorr.

Charlotte Brent sang at the Worcester Festival this season.

Burney was appointed an "Extra Musician" in the King's Band at this time.

Burney's second marriage (to a Lynn widow, Mrs. Allen, a book-lover like himself) took place this year.

Franz Buttstett moved to Rotenburg this year.

F. H. Clicquot and his workmen built the organ at the church of Saint-Médard at this time.

Collard's firm of London piano makers was in direct succession, through Muzio Clementi, to Longman & Broderip, the music publishers, located at 26 Cheapside, as the Parish books of St. Vedast showed as early as this year.

Caroli was "principe" of the Accademia Filarmonica this season.

Caroli succeeded Perti this year in his position at San Petronio Cathedral.

Casanova went to Vienna at this time and made a brief stopover in Prague. He arrived in Vienna late in the year.

Dimmler at this time was a pupil of Vogler and of the horn player Joseph Ziwini, and joined his teacher as a horn player in the famous Mannheim orchestra.

Dressler was "Kapellmeister"

(cont.) to Prince Fürstenberg at Wetzlar this year.

French writer, Duclos, on his way home from Italy to Paris this year, stopped off in Bologna to visit Farinelli.

At the age of twelve this year, Louise Rosalie Dugazo made her début as a ballet dancer at the Comedie-Italienne in Paris.

Elizabeth, Margravine of Anspach, married William Craven at this time.

Giovanni Francesco Fortunati, the composer, studied with Padre Martini at Bologna this year.

Gluck had not yet learnt by this time to enter imaginatively into his characters and their situations . . . . :Alceste" was an example of tragic music, rather than a tragedy.

Andre Gretry visited Voltaire this year and asked for a libretto for an opera-comique but Voltaire declined.

After the original performance, Handel revised and rewrote his "Messiah" and it was finally published this year.

"Menalcas", by Joseph Harris, was probably the one-act pastorale the anonymous libretto of which appeared at Salisbury at this time.

Adlgasser and Michael Haydn collaborated with the ten-year-old Mozart this year, each writing one act of "Die Schuldigkeit des ersten Gebotes".

Philip Hayes was appointed a Gentleman of the Chapel Royal this year.

F. W. Herschel at this time was appointed organist of the Octagon Chapel at Bath.

Hildeburn and Warrington correctly named the new edition of "Urania" this year.

When the first Dutch Reformed Church was organized in New York, by French and Dutch settlers this year, the French Psalter with Dutch words and original Bourgeois tunes (known as the Datheen Psalter) was used until this year. Francis Hopkinson was engaged to provide English words for it.

Jean B. Janson went to Italy this season for a concert tour.

Klopstock began work this year on "Hermanns-Schlact", "a tragedy with bardic songs".

Simon Leduc at this time published his own works and the German and Italian compositions of Haydn, J. Christian (son of J. S.) Bach, Nardini and others.

Adrien Lépine restored the great organ of Nantes Cathedral at this time.

Jeronymo Francisco de Lima was elected to the Brotherhood of St. Cecilia this year.

Locatelli filed bankruptcy this year at Moscow. Imperial favor then granted him the historic "Krasny Kabak" or "red travern" at the Katherinenhof, where he staged elaborate banquets for the aristorcracy.

As late as this year, a document in Prague referred to Locatelli as "having fled to Russia".

Lodovico Madonis, a violinist, left his position as concert master at St. Petersburg this season.

Nicolas Mereaux at this time was organist at the Paris church of Saint-Sauveur and also the "Petits Augustins" and the royal chapel.

Jean de Mondonville at this time was "Ordinaire de la Musique du Roi" and composed a set of sonatas.

Mozart used a movement from one of Eckardt's sonatas in the third (K.40) of the four composite keyboard concertos of this year.

Palissot this year wrote, "He (Rameau) was accused of having given us too learned a music, too difficult, too recondite; today for a little he would be accused of a plainness almost equal to that of Lulli".

The New York Historical Society owns "The Psalms of David, with the Ten Commandements, Creed, Lord's Prayer, etc. In Metre . . . Translated from the Dutch. For the Use of the Reformed Protestant Dutch Church of the City of New York, Printed by James Parker, at the New Printing office in Beaver Street MDCCLXVII".

Robert Rawlings this season became violinist in the King's orchestra and the Queen's private orchestra as well.

Antonio Rodríquez de Hita this year made the acquaintance of the Spanish dramatist, Don Ramón de la Cruz and together they produced a series of remarkable

works in the style of the national lyric theatre of Spain.

Rousseau's "Dictionnaire de
musique" was published this year.
In it, Rousseau refuted
Grassineau's claim that de Muris
invented musical notes.

Antonio Sacchini's "Care luci"
was introduced by Guarducci
this year into the pasticcio
"Tigrane".

John Sale this season became a
chorister at St. George's Chapel
in Windsor, and at Eton College.

Ferdinand Staes, the Netherlands
harpsichordist, organist and
composer, this year became a
theatre accompanist.

Tans'ur in his "Elements of
Musick" of this year, described
the "Bell Harp".

The Prince de Conti this year
obtained joint directorship
with Berton of the Opéra in
Paris for Jean Claude Trial,
the composer.

"Urania" copies, "Yale University
I" and "Warrington I", belonged
to the Philadelphia edition of
this year.

Adlgasser's opera "Nitteti"
was performed this season at
Salzburg.

Agricola wrote the incidental
music for a performance of
Voltaire's "Semiramis" held
this year at Hamburg.

Felice Alessandri's first opera
was produced this season at
Venice.

John Arnold's "The Leicester-

(cont.) shire Harmony" appeared
this year at London.

Samuel Arnold's first oratorio
was "The Cure of Saul", completed at this time.

"Six Sonates a violin et basse"
opus 1, by J. Oliver y Astorga
appeared this year.

An opera by J. Christian (son
of J. S.) Bach was given at
the King's Theatre in London.

Wilhelm Friedemann Bach's
Clavier Concerto in e minor
was completed this year.

Andrew Barton's "The Disappointment, or, the Force of Credulity"
was the first comic ballad
opera produced by a native
American and had its publida-
tion this year at Philadelphia.

William Bates wrote new music
for "Flora, or Hob in the
Well", an old ballad opera,
produced this year at the Drury
Lane Theatre in London.

Pierre Montan Berton's opera
"Théonis" appeared at this time.

C. H. Blainville's "Histoire
générale critique et philolo-
gique de la musique" was published this year.

"Thalia, a collection of six
songs by Dr. Boyce . . ."
was completed at this time.

Pascal Boyer's "Lettre à M.
Diderot sur le projet de
l'unité de clef dans la musique
et la réforme des mesures
proposées par M. l'Abbé de La
Cassagne" appeared at this time.

Burney's "The Cunning Man" was
produced this season at Dublin.

1767(cont.)

Dittersdorf's opera "Amore in musica" was completed this year.

Dressler's "Fragmente einiger Gedanken des musikalischen Zuschauers . . ." appeared at this time.

Domenico Fischietti's opera "Il signore dottore" was performed this season at London's Haymarket Theatre.

The German edition of Martin Gerbert von Hornau's "Iter alemannicum, accedit italicum et gallicum" was published this year at Ulm.

Pietro Guglielmi's opera "La sposa fedele" was given this season at Venice.

Haydn's Divertimento in Eb major was composed this year for horn, violin and cello. The auto- graph was formerly in the possession of Edward Speyer in England.

Haydn's Divertimento in Eb major for 2 violins and 2 cellos was composed at this time.

Haydn's Divertimento in C major ("Mann und Weib") for flute, oboe, 2 violins, cello and bass was written this year. It is #11 in Haydn's catalogue.

Haydn's Divertimento (#20) in F major for 2 oboes, 2 horns, 2 violins, viola, cello and double bass was composed this year according to a major source; however, Geiringer placed it as prior to 1757.

Haydn's opera buffa "La cantari- na" (intermezzo) was produced at carnival at Esterhazy this year. The score is extant.

Haydn's sonatas for piano of this year included #15 in C major (divertimento originally for 2 violins, flute, oboe, cello and bass). In 1780 it appeared as a sonata for violin and piano and in 1785 in West- phal's catalogue as "Mann und Weib".

Haydn's piano sonata #19 in D major (other version of opus 53, #2) was completed this year and published in 1789.

Josef Haydn's sonata in E major was written at this time.

Haydn wrote his Symphony #33 prior to this date.

Haydn's string trios for 2 violins and bass were written prior to this date:
Bb major #1 Haydn's catalogue #8
   Breitkopf's catalogue
Bb major #2
B minor # 1 Haydn's catalogue #3
   (Breitkopf 1767, La Chevadiere)
   Bremner and Preston
B minor #2   Haydn's catalogue #14
   lost
F major #1   Haydn's catalogue #2
   (Breitkopf catalogue 1767)
   published by Bailleux, Artaria
Eb major #1 Haydn's catalogue #4
   Breitkopf catalogue 1767
   published by La Chevadiere,
   Bremner, Artaria, Preston
Eb major #2 Lost
Eb major #3 Lost
F major #2   Haydn's catalogue #10
   (Breitkopf catalogue, 1767)
   published by Bailleux
F major #3   La Chevardiere,
   Longman
F major #4   Lost, listed in
   "Kleines Quartbuch"
F major #5   Lost, listed in
   "Kleines Quartbuch"
F major #6
Eb major #4 published by Bailleux
   Simrock

E major #2   Haydn's catalogue #12
    Breitkopf catalogue, 1767
    published by Bailleux

J. A. Hiller this year published
a German translation of Blainville's "L'Esprit de l'art
musical".

This year marked the publication
date of "The Myrtle", a collection of songs in 3 books, of a
service and some chants and many
hymn-tunes by Robert Hudson.

William Jackson this year composed the music for "Lycidas",
altered from Milton's poem,
for the occasion of the death
of Edward, Duke of York.

Jommelli's opera "Il cacciatore
deluso" and "La critica" were
both produced this season, the
former at Tübingen and the latter
at Stuttgart.

Andrew Law's first book, "A
Select Number of Plain Tunes",
was published at this time when
he was eighteen years old.

Jean Marie Leclaire's "L'aîné"
sonatas for violin and bass were
published this year, posthumously.

A. Lucchesi's "Le donne sempre
donne" was produced this season.

In connection with James Lyon's
"Urania", the Warrington II
copy belonged to the 1767
edition in all probability.

Di Majo's opera, "Ifigenia in
Tauride", was completed this
year.

Joseph Mondonville's opera,
"Thesee", was unsuccessfully
performed at this time.

Mozart's choral work with
orchestra (for Holy Week), a
passion cantata (K.42) "Grab-
musik" (words by a local poet)
was composed this year at
Salzburg.

Mozart's opera "Apollo et
Hyacinthus" was produced this
year at Salzburg.

Mozart composed his first
oratorio at this time.

Early this year Mozart wrote
the three sonatas listed
below for organ and strings:
    Eb major (K.67)
    Bb major (K.68)
    D major (K.69)
All three were completed at
Salzburg.

J. Müthel's 2 Concertos, C minor
and D minor for clavier and
strings were published this
year at Riga.

Naumann's opera "Achille in
Sciro" was produced this
season at Palermo.

De Noinville's "Histoire de
l'opéra en France" appeared at
this time.

Paisiello's comic opera "L'idolo
cinese" appeared at this time.

Paisiello's comic opera "Il
furbo malaccorto" was completed at this time.

Paisiello's comic opera "Le
mbroglie de le bajasse" ("La
serva fatta padrona") was completed at this time.

Paisiello's opera seria "Lucio
Papirio dittatore" was composed this year.

Among manuscript "sinfonie"

given in the Breitkopf list of this year (Supplement ii, p.30) was one "di Pallavicini. Accommodata per il cembalo solo".

Charles Palissot's "Rameau; in Le Necrologe des hommes celebres de France, par une societe de gens de lettres, I," appeared this year.

At the Lisbon Carnival this year N. Piccinni's opera "La notte critica" (libretto by Goldoni) enjoyed a production.

Purcell's "King Arthur" was published this year. It included a couple of common-time hornpipes.

The libretto by Andrew Barton for James Ralph's opera "The Disappointment; or, The Force of Credulity" was published in New York this year. Sonneck referred to it as the first American opera.

Rameau's "Hippolyte et Aricie" was revived a third time this year after the composer's death.

William Randall and John Abell at this time issued in large folio the first complete edition of Handel's "Messiah".

Jean-Jacques Rousseau this year published a "Dictionary of Music", the first of its kind in the French language.

The opera "Olympiade" by Sacchini was compoeted at this time.

The "bard of the Messias" this year wrote a paraphrase of Schubert's "Stabat Mater".

Giuseppe Tartini's "De' principi dell' armonia musicale" was published this year at Padua.

Giuseppe Tartini's "Riposta di G. T. alla critica del di lui trattato di musica di Monsieur Serre di Ginevra" was published in Venice this year.

Giuseppe Tartini's 2nd edition of "Trattato di musica" was published at this time at Paris.

Tommaso Traetta's "Siroe" (libretto by Metastasio) was produced this season at München.

Jean Claude Trial with Berton composed "Théonis" this year.

A serenata, "La tutela contrastata fra Giunane, Marte, e Mercurio, col giudizio di Giove" was written this year.

Vento's "Conquista del messico" was given this season at London.

Vento's "La conquista del vello d'oro" was produced this year at London. This may be an incorrect name for the opera in the previous entry.

Samuel Webbe this year wrote the catch "The Man and the Woman".

R. Woodward's "Songs, Canons, and Catches" was published at this time.

Two harpsichords made this year by J. Kirkman have survived; #23, 2 manuarls, currently owned by Mssrs. Rushworth and Dreaper at Liverpool; and #24 2 manuals, stops 2x8', 1x4' lute, currently owned by W. Barrow. Esq., Llandudno.

1767(cont.)

The Teatro della Sala was rebuilt and lasted up to this year
when it was demolished as a
"dangerous structure".

Gotthold Ephraim Lessing's
"Minna von Barnhelm" was
written this year.

Anne-Louise Girodet-Trioson,
French painter, was born (died
1824).

Hadfield, the architect, was
born this year (died 1826).

Ben Marshal, English painter
of sporting animals, was born
this year (died 1835).

English architecture: Adam,
London, Kenwood Library (60'x
22'x24' high).

Karl Wilhelm von Humboldt,
humanist, was born this year
(died 1835).

August Wilhelm Schlegel, the
greatest critic and translator
of German romanticism was born
at this time (died 1845).

The Jesuits were expelled from
Spain this year.

(to 1769) Haydn wrote his
baryton trios #49-#72 during
this period. A list with details appears below:

49	G major	3/4	Adagio
50	D major	2/4	Andante
51	A major	6/8	Adagio
52	D minor	C	Adagio
53	G major	C	Moderato
54	D major	C	Moderato
55	G major	C	Moderato
56	D major	3/4	Adagio
57	A major	3/4	Adagio
58	D major	C	Moderato
59	G major	3/4	Adagio

(cont.)

60	A major	2/4	Adagio
61	D major	C	Allegro
62	G major	C	Allegro
63	D major	3/4	Adagio
64	D major	C	Allegro
65	G major	C	Adagio
66	A major	3/4	Adagio
67	G major	2/4	Allegretto
68	A major	3/4	Adagio
69	D major	2/4	Adagio
70	G major	3/8	Presto
71	A major	C	Moderato
72	G major	2/4	Andante

(to 1768) Haydn's Symphony #58 in
F major for 2 oboes, 2 horns and
strings was written during
these years.

(to 1768) Haydn's Symphony #59
in A major ("Feuersymphonie")
was composed at this time for
2 oboes, 2 horns and strings.

(to 1769, late) Concert life at
Philadelphia was at a low ebb
at this time.

(and 1770) With Trial, Pierre
Montan Berton at this time took
over the management of the
Paris Opéra from Rébel and
Francoeur and remained director
in 1770 until the Opéra was
taken over by the Paris
municipality.

(to 1770) Francis Hopkinson,
his harpsichord and John
Penn's "fiddle" joined in
"small concerts at this time.

(to 1770) The State Library
in Berlin owns a large number
of manuscript arrangements
by L. C. Hesse from operas for
1 and 2 viole da gamba during
this period.

(to 1771) Improvements in
opera were more perceptible

than in Concert Music at this
time in Philadelphia.

(to 1773, 1805, 1785) One of
D'Alembert's outstanding contributions to the literature
of music was the "Traité sur la
liberté de la musique" in his
"Mélanges de littérature et de
philosophie" (Amsterdam 1767-
73) and reprinted in his
"Oeuvres" (Paris, 1805). It may
also be studied in "Della
libertà della musica" in the
"Opere" (1785, Vol. VII)
by Metastasio.

(and 1773) There were further
editions of Lyon's "Urania",
all "Dedicated to the Clergy
of every Denomination in
America" and issued in Philadelphia at these two dates.

(or 1773) A fourth edition
of Lyon's "Urania" was issued
in the newspapers "based (with
revisions) either upon the
Philadelphia edition of 1767,
the New York . . . of 1773 or
directly upon the first
Philadelphia edition of the
collection".

(to 1782) G. Pasterwitz was
Kapellmeister to the abbey
during this fifteen year period.

(to 1780) Sonatas for organ and
orchestra by Wolfgang Amadeus
Mozart appeared during this
period.

(to 1809) Count Durazzo's older
brother served as Doge of Genoa
during these years.

c.1767
Benjamin Flight, English organ
builder, was born this year at

(cont.) London (died 1847).

Henry Fougt, English printer
and publisher, started business
in London (St. Martin's Lane)
this year under the name of
the "Lyre and Owl".

Franz Lamotte was heard this
year in Leipzig while on tour
in Europe. Gerber was impressed
by Lamotte's technique on
violin.

The publishing house, Longman
& Broderip, was founded at this
time.

William Selby was organist
this season at St. Sepulchre's,
London.

Haydn wrote a Divertimento
(#6) this year in C major.
Haydn's catalogue listed it as
#11. It appeared in the 1780's
as a sonata and as a quartet
for flute, violin, viola,
and cello (#3).

Haydn's trio for piano, violin
and cello #25 in F major was
composed at this time.

Theodore Hook this year completed his opus 1, "A Collection
of New English Songs".

Hook's "Five Lessons in an
Easy Familiar Style" appeared
this year.

(to 1768) Haydn's Symphony #26
in D minor, "Lamentatione"
(sometimes called "Weihnachts-
Symphonie") for 2 oboes, 2 hornss
and strings was written during
this period. An ecclesiastical
melody for Passion Week was
included in the "adagio".

1768

(January 1) Casanova visited the two librettists, Metastasio and Calzabigi, on this day. He had met them in Berlin.

(January 4) Monsigny's opera "L'Isle sonnante" (libretto by Colle) was produced on this date at the Comédie-Italienne in Paris.

(January 5) Florian Gassmann's opera "La notte critica" was given this evening at Vienna (libretto by Goldoni).

(January 13) Pierre (Gabriel) Buffardin, French fluties, died on this date at Paris (born c.1690 at Marseilles).

(January 16) Pietro Guglielmi's opera "Ifigenia in Aulide" was produced on this date at London (libretto by Bottarelli).

(January 16) Mozart's Symphony in D major (K.45) for 2 oboes, 2 horns, 2 trumpets, drums and strings was completed this year at Vienna.

(January 18) Voltaire at this time wrote that some of the music intended for "Samson" ended up in Rameau's next opera, "Castor et Pollux".

(January 27) Duni's opera "Les Moissonneurs" was produced on this evening at the Comédie-Italienne in Paris.

(January 27) Charles Simon Favart's "Les Moissonneurs" was first performed on this date at Paris (music by Duni).

(February 2) A "Motet à voix seule de M. le chevalier Gluck, celebre et Savant musicien de (cont.) S. M. Imperiale" was sung on this day at the Concert Spirituel in Paris.

(February 15) Sebastian Ludwig Friedl (Friedel), German string player, was born on this date at Neuburg (died c.1857).

(February 25) C. Dibdin's "Lionel and Clarissa" was produced on this date at London in the Covent Garden Theatre (libretto by Isaac Bickerstaffe). According to a major source Dibdin only wrote two-thirds of the music.

(March 3) Barthélemon's "Oithona" was performed on this date at the Haymarket Theatre in London.

(March 10) Pietro Guglielmi's opera "Sesostri" was produced this evening at London (libretto by Bottarelli).

(March 23) The Vienna "Diarium" on this date reported: "Angelus Pompeati, dancer at the German Theater, wounded himself mortally in a fit of madness. An inquest was held by the court at the old Haar-markt. The deceased was 51 years old.

(March 26) Pietro Guglielmi's opera "Il ratto della sposa" was produced on this date at London.

(April 13) George Walond at this time became a chorister at Magdalen College.

(April 26) Pascual Fuentes, Spanish composer, died on this date at Valencia (birthdate unknown).

1768(cont.)

(April 26) Several papers were written at this time by Kapell-meister Ludovicus van Beethoven relating his position and duties and showing that his life at Bonn court was not always simple.

(April 26) Tommaso Traetta's "L'isola disabitata" was pro-duced at Bologna in the Teatro Comunale on this day.

(May 15) Pierre Philippe Saint-Sevin L'Abbé, cellist in the Paris Opéra orchestra, died on this day (birthdate unknown).

(May 16) At the Bonn court theatre on this date a musical poem in German, written for the birthday of His Highness, and an Italian intermezzo entitled "La Nobilita delusa" were both performed.

(May 18) Hiller's Singspiel "Die Liebe auf dem Lande" (libretto by Weisse, based on Favart's "Anette et Lubin" and on Auseaume's "La Clochette") was performed on this date at Leipzig.

(May 23) F. Philidor's opera "Thémistocle" (libretto by Etienne Morel de Chefdeville) was produced on this date at the Academie Royale de Musique in Paris.

(May 24) Pietro Guglielmi's opera "I viaggiatori ridicoli tornati in Italia" was produced on this evening at London.

(May 25) Siegfried Coesus von Aemingus, German scholar, died on this date (born 1710, December 3 at Mölln, Mecklen-burgh).

(May 25) Felice (de') Giardini's oratorio "Ruth" was sung on this date at the Lock Hospital chapel in London.

(June 2) Johann Christian Fischer made his first concert appearance on this date as an oboist in London, at the Thatched House. J. Christian (son of J. S.) Bach played the piano.

(June 4) Kohault's comic opera "Sophie, ou Le Mariage Cache" (libretto from the "Clandestine Marriage" by Garrick and Coleman) was produced on this evening.

(June 14) The Commission of Domingo Scarlatti in the Infanteria de Soria bore this date.

(Summer) Mozart's song (K.52) "Daphne, deine Rosenwangen" was completed at this time in Vienna.

(July 6) Joseph Harris' "Te Deum and Jubliate" was performed on this date at the Oxford Music Room, and again on July 3, 1770.

(July) On this date at the Comedie-Italienne in Paris, F. A. Philidor's opera "Le Jardinier de Sion" (libretto by Roger Timothee Regnard de Pleinchesne after Fontenelle) was produced.

(July 11) José de Nebra, Spanish composer, died on this day at Madrid (born c.1688).

(July 11) Antonio Rodríquez di Hita produced "Briseida" this evening at the Teatro del Principe in Madrid. It was an attempt to write an Italian opera with Spanish words and Spanish music.

(July 28) Arne's "The Temple of Dullness" was revived on this date as "Capochio and Dorinna" at the Marylebone Gardens in London.

(August 17) On this day Michael Haydn married Maria Magdalena Lipp, daughter of the cathedral organist and a singer at the archbishop's court. She sang the leading soprano parts in several of Mozart's juvenile operas.

(August 20) Gretry's opera "Le Huron" was premiered this evening at the Comédie-Italienne in Paris (libretto by Marmontel). The work was simultaniously published by Beraux.

(August 24) Barthélemon's "The Judgment of Paris" was performed on this date at the Haymarket Theatre in London.

(September 1) Bernhard Wessely, German composer, was born on this date at Berlin (died 1826, July 11).

(September 1) Mozart's violin sonata (K.46d) in C major was composed at this time in Vienna.

(September 1) Mozart's violin sonata (K.46e) in F major was composed at this time in Vienna.

(September 12) Benjamin Carr, American composer, was born on this date at London (died 1831, May 24 at Philadelphia).

(September 21) Louis Emmanuel

(cont.) Jadin, pianist, conductor, teacher and composer, was born on this date at Versailles (died 1853, April 11 at Paris).

(Autumn) Mozart's sacred music (K.47) "Veni sancte spiritus" (for 4 voices, 2 oboes, 2 horns, 2 trumpets, drums, strings and organ) was composed at this time at Vienna.

(September 25) Hiller's "Prolog zur Eröffnung des Weimarer Schloss Theaters" (text by Musaeus) was completed at this time.

(October 3) Charles Dibdin's opera "The Padlock" (I. Bickerstaffe on Cervantes' "El Celoso extremeño") was performed on this date at the Drury Lante Theatre in London.

(October 4) In Spain Gaetano Brunetti wrote an opera, "Jason, o La conquista del vellocino" which was given this evening at Madrid.

(October 8) Pierre Simon Fournier, French engraver and "type-founder", died on this date at Paris (born 1712, September 15).

(October 10) Samuel Arnold's "The Royal Garland" was performed this evening at Covent Garden in London.

(October 21-1769, January 6) Philadelphia enjoyed operatic music in this theatrical season.

(October 24) Hiller, cantor of St. Thomas' in Leipzig, published a favorable review of Gluck's "Alceste" in this issue

JEAN HONORE FRAGONARD
1732-1806

1768(cont.)
of the "Wöchentliche Nachrichten".

(October 26) E. R. Duni's
opera "Les Sabots" was produced
on this date at Paris in the
Comédie-Italienne.

(October 28) Michel Blavet,
French flutist and composer,
died on this day at Paris
(born 1700, March 13 at Besançon).

(November 3) Pierre van Maldere,
violinist, composer and brother
of Guillaume, died on this dat
at Brussels (born 1729, October
16 at Brussels).

(November 6) Dibdin's opera
"The Padlock" was first performed at Philadelphia on this
date.

(December 6) Johann Baptist
Henneberg, Austrian composer
and musician, was born on this
date at Vienna (died 1822,
November 26 at Vienna).

(December 13) Mozart's Symphony
in D major (K.48) for 2 oboes,
2 horns, 2 trumpets, drums
and strings was composed at
this time in Vienna.

(December 14) Dibdin's opera
"Lionel and Clarissa" was first
performed on this date at
Philadelphia.

(December 21) C. Dibdin's
"Damon and Phillida" was pro-
duced this evening at the
Drury Lane Theatre in London.

(December 22) Barthélemon on
this date produced a pastoral
opera called "Le Fleuve
Scamandre" at the Comédie-
Italienne in Paris.

(January) John Wainwright,
English organist and composer,
died this month at Stockport
(birthdate unknown).

(c.January) Gretry's opera
"Les Mariages Samnites" was
given this month at Paris
(libretto by Légier).

(February) N. Piccinni's opera
"L'Olimpiade" in its first
setting (libretto by Metastasio)
was performed on this date at
the Teatro Argentina in Rome.

(March) Angelus Pompeat,
dancer, died this month (born
1717).

(March) K. P. Emanuel Bach
started his position as music
director in Hamburg at this
time. He was director to the
five principal churches in
Hamburg.

(September) William Knapp,
English musician, died this
month at Poole (born 1698).

(September or October) "Bastien
und Bastienne", operetta in
one act by Mozart (K.5), was
produced at this time in
Vienna at Anton Mesmer's garden
theatre. The libretto was by
F. W. Weiskern after Favart's
"Les Amours de Bastien et
Bastienne".

(November) Hasse's opera
"Piramo e Tisbe" (libretto by
Marco Coltellini) was performed
this month at Vienna.

(November) Mozart's "Missa
brevis" in G major (K.49)
for 4 voices, strings and organ
was composed this month at
Vienna.

1768(cont.)

Tobias Friedrich Bach, cantor
and member of the sixth generation of the Bach family died
this year (born 1695).

Johann Georg Heinrich Backofen,
German harpist, clarinet and
basset-horn player, was born
this year at Durlach (died 1839
at Darmstadt).

George Baker, English organist
and composer, was born at this
time at Exeter (died 1847,
February 19).

Carles Baguer, Spanish (Catalan)
organist and composer, was born
this year at Barcelona (died
1808 at Barcelona).

Giovanni Francesco Brusa,
Italian composer, died this year
at Venice (born c.1700 at
Venice).

Francisco Cabo, Spanish organist
and composer, was born at this
time at Nájara, Valencia (died
1832, November 21 at Nájara).

(or 1769) Leonhard von Call,
German guitar player and com-
poser, was born this year in
South Germany (died 1815,
February 19 at Vienna).

Princess Caroline of Braun-
schweig-Wolfenbüttel, who married
the Prince of Wales in 1795
and in 1813 left England and
settled on the Continent, was
born this year. She returned to
England in 1820 when her
husband succeeded to the throne
and died a month after his
coronation (died 1821).

Robert Cooke, English organist
and composer, was born this
year at London (Westminster)

(cont.) (died 1814, August
13 at London).

Margarete Danzi (born Merchand),
soprano, was born at this time
at Frankfurt am Main (died
1800, June 11 at München).

(late, or 1769, early) Charles
Dibdin (Isaac Mungo), playwright, was born at this time
at London (died 1833, January
13 at London).

Antonio Duni, Italian composer,
died after this year (born
c.1700 at Matera, Basilicata).

Carlo Innocenzio Maria Frugoni,
librettist, died this year
(born 1692).

Friedrich Adam Hiller, German
composer, singer and violinist,
was born this year at Leipzig
(died 1812, November 23 at
Königsberg).

Jose Pons, Spanish composer
whom Eslava characterized as
a typical composer of the
Catalan school, was born this
year at Gernoa, Catalonia
(died 1818 at Valencia).

Neopolitan composer Nicola
Porpora died at this time
(born 1686).

Franz (Anton) Schubert, double-
bass player and composer, was
born this year at Dresden
(died 1824).

Paolo Spagnoletti, Italian
violinist, was born this year
at Cremona (died 1834, September 23 at London).

Johann Michael Vogl was born
at this time in Steir, Upper
Austria. He was an Austrian

baritone (died 1840, November 19 at Vienna).

The "Lieblich Gedact" stop on the organ was mentioned this year by Jakob Adlung in his "Musica mechanica organoedi".

Pedro Aranaz became "maestro de capilla" at Zamora at this time.

Astaritta left Naples and Sicily after this year.

Theodore Aylward became organist of St. Michael's, Cornhill at this time.

Karl Philip Emanuel Bach this year terminated his service to the court of Frederick the Great in Berlin.

J. Christian (son of J. S.) Bach played the "hammer" piano this season for the first time in public.

Rameau's "Dardanus" was revived after his death, with additions to the libretto by Joliveau, and to the score by Berton.

Luigi Boccherini this year arrived at the court of Charles III.

Boccherini appeared this season as a cello soloist at the Concert Spirituel in Paris.

Boccherini joined Filippo Manfredi this year as a pupil of Tartini and they toured through Lombardy, Piedmont and the south of France and to Paris which they reached at this time.

Capel Bond this season conducted the first Birmingham Musical

(cont.) Festival.

Boyce resigned this year as organist of St. Michael's, Cornhill.

Cafaro became supernumerary "maestro di cappella" at the royal chapel this year with a salary of 20 ducats a month.

When Casanova tried his luck in this year in Spain, he was fascinated by the Spanish national dance, the "Fandango".

Important modifications and repairs were made to the organ at St. Gervais this year by the organ builder F. H. Clicquot.

John Crosdill became a member of the Royal Society of Musicians at this time.

Marianne Davies began to tour Europe this year with her sister, They went to Paris and Vienna.

C. Dibdin transferred his services from Covent Garden to Drury Lane this season.

Jean Louis Duport made his début this season at the Concert Spirituel.

Dyne's glee "Fill the bowl" was awarded a prize this year from the "Catch Club".

Alessandro Maria Antonio Fridzeri, during his travels in Europe this year, visited Frankfurt.

Karl Friebert at this time married Maria Magdalena Spangler, a singer.

Richard Gaudry, an English

singer and composer, sang this season at the Salisbury theatre.

A fire this year at the monastery of St. Blasien destroyed the nearly complete first volume of Martin Gerbert von Hornau's history of church music.

François Giroust won the two first prizes in an Orléans competition for composition held this year.

Gluck bought this year himself a fine house in the Rennweg in the Landstrasse district of Vienna.

Johan E. Hartmann this year rose to the status of leader and acting conductor of the royal orchestra in Copenhagen.

The Eszterházy ensemble this season performed Haydn's opera "Lo speziale" at the home of a Viennese nobleman, Freiherr von Sumerau.

F. J. Haydn this year engaged Maria Magdalena Spangler as a singer for Prince Eszterházy.

Franz Holly succeeded Johann Baptist Savio this season as musical director at Brunian's theatre at Prague.

Francis Hopkinson married Ann Borden of Bordentown at this time.

H. Koch was appointed to the ducal orchestra at Rudolstadt this year as a violinist.

F. Kratzer at this time was appointed master of the chorus of the boy sopranos as well as cantor of the cathedral school at Cracow.

F. L. A Kunzen and his equally talented sister appeared this year, he as a juvenile produgy in London playing a concerto for two claviers.

Pierre Lahoussaye went to London this year where he became conductor at the King's Theatre.

Honoré François Marie Langlé went to Paris this season by way of Genoa.

Samuel Lee at this time moved his music shop to #2 Dame Street, where he published a miscellaneous batch of music.

Thomas Lowe retired this year from the management of Marylebone Gardens, having met with heavy losses.

John Marsh was at this time "articled" to a solicitor and continued as a lawyer.

F. Meyer von Schauensee created the Helvetic Society of the Concordat this year. They pursued cultural and patriotic aims.

Mozart himself conducted the premiére of his "Bastien et Bastienne" this season.

Mozart and his father visited Vienna at this time.

John Parke was engaged as principal oboist at the Opera this season.

Pietro Pompeo Sales this year became Kapellmeister and court councillor to the Elector of Coblenz.

Domingo Scarlatti became a

cadet in the Infanteria de Soria this year.

Johann Schulz this year taught, and accompanied the Polish Princess Sopieha through France, Italy and Austria.

Joseph Tacet, flutist, J. Christian (son of J. S.) Bach, pianist, and J. C. Fischer, oboist, gave a concert at the Thatched House this year where Bach played a pianoforte for the first time.

Pascal Taskin's clavecin "en peau de buffle" was made at this time (and said to be superior to the pianoforte).

According to Trouflaut, Paschal Taskin this year used a foot-pedal (un tirant) for harpsichord by means of which the "jeu des buffles" or the "jeu des plumes" could be brought on imperceptibly.

Soprano Giusto Ferdinando Tenducci left Ireland this year to go to Edinboro.

A romantic account of the elopement of Tenducci and his pupil Dorothy Maunsell was published by his wife at this time; "A True and Genuine Narrative of Mr. and Mrs. Tenducci".

Luiza Rosa d'Aguiar Todi, a mezzo-soprano, appeared on the Lisbon stage this season in comedy.

Francesco Antonio Baldassare Uttini, singer and composer, visited London this year.

Robert Wainwright this year

(cont.) succeeded his father as organist at Collegiate Church, Manchester.

A harpsichord by Weber from this date is known. It was fitted with the "Venetian Swell".

K. Westenholz was appointed Kapellmeister at Schwerin-Mecklenburg this year.

E. Wolf was court Kapellmeister at Weimar this season.

Count Anton Willibald Wolfegg heard Mozart this year at the home of Prince Galitzin in Vienna.

R. Woodward was awarded the degree of Bachelor of Music this year by Trinity College at Dublin.

H. O. Zinck was a singer at Hamburg this season.

J. Adlung's "Musica mechanica organoedi" was published this year in two volumes at Berlin.

Adlung's "Musikalisches Siebengestirn" was issued this year at Berlin.

Agricola's "Amore e Psiche" appeared at this time.

Alessandri's opera "La moglie fedele" was produced this season.

"Twelve Italian songs and duets for voice and harpsichord, with an accompaniment for a guitar" opus 2 by Oliver y Astorga was completed this year.

J. Christian (son of J. S.) Bach's opera "Catone in Utica"

1768(cont.)

was given this season at the court of Braunschweig.

Boccherini's 6 quartets were published this year at Paris.

Cafaro's opera "Creso" was produced this year at the Teatro Regio in Turin during carnival season.

Capron's "Premier Livre de sonates à violon seul et basse" opus 1, was completed at this time.

"Briseida" by Don Ramón de la Cruz and Don Antonio Rodriguez de Hita appeared this year.

A. Duni was probably still living this year since Gerber records a "Litania della Beata Virgine" as having been published at "Norby" (Norimbergi= Nürnberg).

Esteve's "Los jardineros de Aranjuez" appeared at this time.

Friedrich Gottlob Fleischer's "Sammlung von Menuetten und Polonoisen", 2nd edition, was published this year with four sonatas added to the collection.

Joseph von Fribert this season wrote these operas for the court of Passau: "Angelica", "Dafne", "Galatea", "Il natal di Giove", "Zenobia".

Galuppi's opera "Ifigenia in Tauride" was produced this season at St. Petersburg (libretto by Coltellini).

John Garth's 6 harpsichord sonatas, opus 2 were published this year.

Florian Gassmann's cantata "Amore e Venere" was performed this season at Innsbruck.

Florian Gassmann's additional music for Anfossi's "Lo sposo di tre, e marito a nessuno" was performed this season at Vienna.

Luigi Maria Baldassare Gatti wrote his opera "Alessandro nell' Indie" this year at Mantua.

Giuseppe Gazzaniga, Italian composer, had his first opera "Il barone di Trocchia" produced this year at the Teatro Nuovo.

Gluck's and Calzabigi's famous preface was published this year. It proposed to correct the abuses "which have disfigured Italian Opera".

"L'innocenza giusts ficata", a departure from Metastasian music drama in that actual dramatic action (introducing an active dramactic chorus in its final scene) suited to the plot was used, was revised by Gluck, who re-titled it "La Vestale".

Haydn prior to this year composed "Arietta con variazioni" in A major for piano.

Haydn wrote the cantata "Applausus" this year. It was a "Fest Kantate" with a Latin text possibly written by Prior P. Urban Schaukögel, scored for solo voices, chorus, 2 trumptes, strings and drums.

This year or earlier Haydn wrote his Concerto for violin in G major for Violino Concer-

1768(cont.)

tante, 2 violins, viola and
bass. This work was listed
by Pohl but its authenticity
is questionable.

Haydn's Divertimento (cassation)
in F major for 2 horns, violin
viola and bass was published
prior to this year by La Chevardiere in Paris among the string
quartets, opus 2 (listed as
Cassation in Breitkopf's Catalogue for 1768).

Haydn's "3 Divertimenti" as
listed below were composed
this year:
1. A major
2. G major
3. C major

Haydn's "Offertorium: Motet "O
Jesu, te invocamus" in C major
scored for chorus, 2 violins,
viola, bass, 2 trumpets, and
drums, was completed this year.
Three others were listed but
with date unknown:
Offertorium; "Non nobis Domini" in d minor
Offertorium; "Animae Deo
gratae" in C major
Offertorium; "Jus aeternum
altende nobis" in G major

Haydn's opera buffa "Lo speziale"
(libretto by Carlo Goldoni) was
produced at this time at
Esterhaz. The score has survived. It is generally known as
"Der Apotheker".

Haydn's String Quartets as
follows were written this year:
#19 Op. 9, #1 C major
#20 Op. 9, #2 Eb major
#21 Op. 9, #3 G major
#22 Op. 9, #4 D minor
#23 Op. 9, #5 Bb major
#24 Op. 9, #6 A major

Haydn wrote his Symphony #49
in F minor this year. It is
nicknamed "La Passione" and
scored for 2 oboes, 2 horns
and strings. Mandyeczewski
had placed it as prior to
1775 but the autograph score
places it this year.

John Heck (Johann Caspar),
German 18th century theorist,
this year published "A Complete
System of Harmony, or A
Regular & Easy Method to attain
a Fundamental Knowledge &
Practice of Thoroughbass".

F. W. Herschel at this time
published a Symphony for
orchestra and 2 military
concertos for wind instruments.
He also wrote some occasional
songs for the stage.

Holzbauer's Italian opera
"Adriano in Siria" was performed this season at Mannheim.

Jakób Ibkowski wrote his
"Litaniae de B.M.V. ex D"
(in 7 parts) this year. He
also wrote undated works:
"Missa ex D" (in 5 parts) and
"Missa ex G" (in 8 parts).

John Johnson published
Charles Dibdin's "Lionel
and Clarissa" this year.

John Johnson published Charles
Dibdin's "The Padlock" at this
time.

Jommelli's opera "Fetonte"
was produced at Stuttgart
this season.

Jommelli's serenatas "L'unione
coronata" and "La schiava
liberata" were produced this
season, the former at Stuttgart,
the latter at Ludwigsburg.

J. H. Knecht's singspiel "Kain und Abel" was produced at the Biberach school this year when he was only 12 years of age.

Mozart's opera buffa "La Finta Semplice" ("The Pretended Simpleton" was composed this year at Vienna.

Mozart's Symphony in Bb major K.214(?) for 2 oboes, 2 horns and strings was composed early this year at Vienna.

Mozart's Symphony in G major, K. 221(?) for 2 oboes, 2 horns and strings was composed early this year at Vienna.

C. G. Neefe wrote sonatinas for piano and other pieces included in Hiller's "Wöchentliche Nachrichten" this year.

B. Ottani's most successful opera, "L'amore senza malizia" was completed this year at Venice.

Paisiello's cantata "L'Ebone" was completed at this time.

Paisiello's "Festa teatrale" ("Pelèo") was completed this year.

Paisiello's comic opera "La finta maga per vendetta" was composed this year.

Paisiello's comic opera "La luna abitata" was composed this year.

Paisiello's opera seria "Olimpia" ("Alceste in Ebuda") was composed at this time.

Paisiello's comic opera, "L'osteria di Marechiaro", appeared this year.

Niccolò Piccini's opera "I Napolitani in America" was performed this season at Naples.

Rousseau's "Dictionnaire de Musique" was published this year. It mentioned barcaroles sung in Venice to the poetry of Tasso.

Rousseau's "Quam dilecta Tabernacula", a motet for two voices and bass, written for Madame de Nadaillac, abbesse de Gomerfontaine, was published at this time.

Giuseppe Sarti's opera "La calzolaia di Strasburgo" was produced this season at Modena.

Giuseppe Sarti's opera "La giardiniera brillante" was produced this year at Rome.

Gregorio Sciroli's opera "Le nozze in campagna" was produced this season at Venice.

Straight & Skillern, English firm of music engravers and publishers, issued a set of Country Dances this year.

Giusto Ferdinando Tenducci published "6 sonatas for harpsichord" this year in Dublin.

Tommaso Traetta's "Amore in trappola" was produced this season at Venice.

Tommaso Traetta's oratorio "Salomone" was produced this year.

Tommaso Traetta's "Il tributo campestre" was performed this season.

Henry Foust this year published

1768(cont.)

Francesco Antonio Baldassare Uttini's "Six Sonatas for 2 violins and a bass, one sonata for the violoncello and another for the harpsichord, Op. 1" at London.

Vento's cantata "La musica e la poesia" was given this season at Almack's.

Voltaire wrote the libretto for Gretry's "Le Baron d'Otrante" this year.

Voltaire this year wrote the libretto for "Les Deux Tonneaux" by Gretry.

Samuel Webbe wrote both "From everlasting", a canon, and "A generous friendship", a glee, at this time.

Three harpsichords made by J. Kirkman this year have survived. They are the following: #25, 1-manual; #26, 2-manuals, stops 2x8', 1x4' lute, current owner, M. Salaman; #27, 1-manual, current owner, Gerald Forty, Birmingham.

The French overture at this time was usually an announcement of action to come.

The Birmingham Musical Festival began this year when performances were given at St. Philip's Church and in the theatre on King Street to raise funds for the General Hospital.

Simes said this year "The one (in the band) most capable is to be appointed Master of the Band, under whose care and inspection the others are to be."

The position of Music Master existed at this time.

Zacharias Werner, dramatist, was born this year (died 1823).

Thomas Gray received an appointment this year as professor of history and modern languages at Cambridge, but never delivered a lecture

Laurence Sterne published his novel "Sentimental Journey Through France and Italy" this year. It was a humorous 'though sentimental work.

Antonio Canaletto, or Bernardo Bellotto, Italian painter, died this year (born 1697).

John Crome (known as Old Crome), English painter and founder of the Norwich Society of Artists, was born this year (died 1821).

George Dance, English architect, died this year (born 1700).

Jean-Honoré Fragonard painted "The Swing", one of a pair. They were purchased for the Kress Collection in 1955 for about $350,000 and are now on exhibit at the National Gallery in Washinton, D.C. according to Edith Eisler, a contemporary artist.

Grundmann did an oil painting of Haydn in court uniform this year.

Marie-Guilhelmine Benoist, French painter, was born at this time (died 1826).

Spanish architecture: San Antonio, San Jose

1768(cont.)
Friedrich Schleiermacher, a
German Protestant philosopher,
was born (died 1834).

Robert Smith, English mathematician, died at this time in
Cambridge (born 1689).

(to 1769) Samuel Arnold offered
Hook the position of organist
and composer at Marylebone
Gardens at this time.

(to 1769) Barthélemon visited
Paris several times this
season.

(to 1769) Boccherini and
Manfredi started for Madrid at
this time.

(to 1769) A German publication,
"Wöchentliche Nachrichten und
Anmerkungen die Musik betreffend"
edited by J. A. Hiller, continued
after this year as "Musikalische
Nachrichten und Anmerkungen auf
das Jahr 1770".

(to 1770) Alessandro Felici's
seven operas were performed
during this period at Florence,
Venice and Rome.

(to 1772, August) John Johnson
published during these years at
11 York St., Covent Garden,
London.

(to 1773) Franz von Weber lived
at Hildesheim during these
years to become a practical
musician.

(to 1779) Luigi Maria Baldassare
Gatti was singer and vice
maestro at the Cappella Santa
Barbara at Mantua for these
eleven years.

(to 1780) Lidarti may have lived
in London during this period.

(to 1782) Mozart wrote nine
small and eight great Masses
during these years.

(to 1785) Agostino Accorimboni
wrote eleven comic operas
during these years.

(to 1791) Mozart's "Cadenzas
for his Concertos", K.624,
were composed during these
years at Salzburg and Vienna.

(to 1793) G. B. Borghi during
this period wrote operas for
all the principal theatres of
Italy.

c.1768
J. Adrien, who was to be
choirmaster at the Theatre
Feydeau, was born this year
(died c.1824).

François (Xavier) Desargus,
French harpist and composer,
was born this year at Amiens
(death date unknown but at
Paris).

Jaques Hotteterre "le Romain",
a famous French flutist,
died this year at Paris (birthdate unknown).

Sarah Mountain (born Wilkinson),
English soprano, was born this
year (died 1841, July 3 at
London).

Sebastiano Nasulini, Italian
composer known to have produced
about 30 operas, was born this
year in Piacenza (died 1806 or
before at Venice or Naples).

J. Christian (son of J. S.)
Bach published 5 sonatas for
clavier this year.

Haydn's piano sonata #46 in
Ab major (alternate version
opus 54, #3) was completed

c.1768(cont.)
this year, published in 1789.

Haydn this year year wrote his
String Quartet in F major,
op. 3, #5.

(to 1787) Simon Leduc, composer,
during this period published
two books of sonatas, two
books of duos for violins
without bass, six trios for 2
violins and bass, three violin
concertos and two "Symphonies
concertantes".

1769
(January 1) Pascal Boyer wrote
half a dozen airs for Cailhava's
"comédie-ballet" "Les Étrennes
de l'amour", produced on this
date at the Comédie-Française
in Paris.

(January 2) Maria Anna (Nannette)
Stein, pianist and daughter of
pianoforte maker Johann Andreas
Stein, was born on this date
(died 1833, January 16 at
Vienna).

(January 5) Gretry's opera
"Lucile" was given this evening
at the Comédie-Italienne in
Paris (libretto by Marmontel).

(January 5) Grétry wrote a
small aria for Louise Rosalie
Dugazon in his "Lucile" performed on this date. She performed a small part in the work.

(January 9) James Oswald, English music published, died on
this day at Knebworth (birthdate unknown).

(January 12) Cafaro's opera
"L'Olimpiade" was performed
on this date at the Teatro
San Carlo in Naples.

(January 12) Cecilia Grassi

(cont.) sang in Cafaro's cantata "Ercole ed Acheloo" at the
Teatro San Carlo in Naples this
evening.

(January 14) T. A. Arne's
"Tom Jones"was produced on
this date at Covent Garden
in London.

(January 14) Samuel Arnold's
libretto, "Tom Jones", was
performed this evening at
Covent Garden in London.

(January 14) Mozart's "Missa
Brevis" in d minor (K.65) for
strings and organ was composed
at this time in Salzburg.

(January 17) Ole Andreas
Lindeman, Norwegian musician,
was born on this date at
Surnadel (died 1857, February
26 at Tronditjem).

(January 20) Cafaro's "Ercole
ed Acheloo" was performed
this evening at Naples.

(January 24) F. A. Philidor's
opera "Ernelinde" was revived
as "Sandomir, prince de
Dannemarck" on this date.

(January 26) Domenico
Fischietti's opera "Il mercato
di Malmantile" was revived
for six performances in London
at this time.

(January 26) Mozart's 7 minuets
(K.65a) for string orchestra
without violas was composed
at this time at Salzburg.

(February 12) Johann Friedrich
Rochlitz, German critic and
musical editor, was born at
this time at Leipzig (died 1842,
December 16 at Leipzig). His
vioce procured him admission to
the Thomasschule at the age of

1769(cont.)
thirteen, under the cantorship
of Doles. He spent 6 hears
there.

(February 13-20) John Gualdo
appeared as a musician and
placed an advertisement in this
issue of the Pennsylvania
"Chronicle".

(February 28) Mozart's aria with
orchestra, K.70, Recitative "A
Berenice", Aria "Sol nascente",
was composed at this time at
Salzburg for soprano, 2 oboes,
22 horns and strings, It may
have been written for Maria M.
Haydn.

(March 6) Monsigny's opera "Le
Déserteur" (libretto by Sedaine)
was produced on this date at
the Comédie-Italienne in Paris.

(March 7) Joseph Aloys Ladurner,
Austrian composer and brother
of Isnaz Laduner, was born in
Algund on this date (died after
1835).

(Spring) Mozart's Serenade in
G major for orchestra (K.63)
was composed at this time at
Salzburg for 2 oboes, 2 horns
and strings.

(March 25) Salvatore Vigano,
Italian dancer and composer,
was born on this day at Naples
(died 1821, August 10 at Milan).
Among his ballets were "Il Noce
di Benevento" with music by
Süssmayer, and the "Men of
Prometheus" with music by
Beethoven.

(April 2) Johann and Maria van
Beethoven's first son, Ludwig
Maria, was baptized on this
date. He lived only six days.

(April 7) Joseph-François
Krafft returned to Ghent
and was appointed chapel-master
at his old church, Saint-Bavon
at this time.

(April 11) Johann Georg Lickl,
Austrian composer, was born on
this date at Korneuburg, Lower
Austria (died 1843, May 12 at
Pécs).

(April 11) Giovanni Agostino
Perotti, Italian composer, was
born on this date at Vercelli
(died 1855, June 28 at Venice).

(April 23) T. A. Arne's
"Shakespeare's Garland" was
produced on this day at
Stratford-on-Avon. David
Garrick wrote the ode.

(April 23) Barthélemon's music
for "Shakespeare's Garland"
was performed at Stratford-on-
Avon on this day. See previous
entry for more on this festival.

(April 23) James Sanderson,
English composer, was baptized
in Washington, Durham on this
day.

(April 24) Catherine Clive
retired to Twickenham at this
time.

(May 1) Mozart's opera buffa
"La finta semplice" was produced
on this date at Salzburg although
composed at Vienna. The libretto
was arranged by Cottellini
from Goldoni.

(May 1) Elizabeth Wright, vocalist and wife of Michael Arne,
died on this date (birthdate
unknown).

(May 2) Cardonne's "tragedie
lyrique" "Omphale" was produced

PRINCE NIKOLAS JOSEPH ESTERHAZY
1714-1790

1769(cont.)

on this date at the Opéra in Paris.

(May 2) Hiller's "Allegorisches Ballett am Tage der Erb Huldigung des . . .Churfürsten" was produced this evening at Leipzig.

(May 4) Charles Hague, English violinist and composer, was born on this date at Todcaster (died 1821, June 18 at Cambridge).

(May 7) Giuseppe Farinelli, an Italian composer, was born on this day at Este (died 1836, December 12). He was strongly influenced by Cimarosa.

(May 12) C. Dibdin's opera "The Ephesian Matron" was produced on this day at Ranelagh House in London.

(May 17) "Il Riso d'Apolline" with music by Petz, was given at the Bonn court on the occasion of the Elector's birthday on this date.

(May 29) Charles Dibdin's opera "The Padlock" was given on this date by an American Company in New York.

(May 30) Benedikt Hacker, German violinist and composer, was born at this time in Deggendorf, Bavaria (died 1829 at Salzburg).

(May 30) N. Piccinni's opera "Demetrio" (libretto by Metastasio) was given on this date at the Teatro San Carlo in Naples.

(June 13) Quirino Gasparini and Giuseppe Sordella's "Azione musicale" was given this evening

(cont.) at Turin.

(Summer) Thomas Busby sang at Vauxhall at this time at a weekly salary of ten guineas.

(June 21) C. Dibdin's opera "The Captive" was performed on this date at the Haymarket Theatre in London.

(Summer) Mozart's Cassation in Bb major, K.99 was composed at this time in Salzburg for 2 oboes, 2 horns and strings.

(Summer) Mozart's "March for a Cassation", K.62, in D major for 4 instruments, presumably strings, was composed at this time at Salzburg.

(Summer) Mozart's Serenade in D major, K.100, for 2 flutes, 2 oboes, 2 horns, 2 trumpets and strings was composed at this time in Salzburg.

(June 22) On this date Capron married Anne Soisson, a cousin of Piron, the writer.

(June 24) Alexis Nikolayevich titov, musical dilettante and composer of several operas, was born on this date at St. Petersburg (died 1827, November 20 at St. Petersburg.

(June 27) Metastasio and Hasse wrote an ode performed on this date and sung by Cecilia Davies, accompanied by Marianne on the armonica.

(June 29) Ksawery Józef Elsner, Polish composer, conductor, teacher and writer, was born on this day at Silesia (died 1854, April 18 at Warsaw).

1769(cont.)

(July 4) Luis de Persuis, French violinist and composer, was born on this day at Metz (died 1819, December 20 at Paris).

(July 24) Francisco Scarlatti, grandson of Domenico, son of Fernando and member of the fifth generation of the Scarlatti family was born on this date at #8 Calle de Leganitos (died 1852).

(July 26) The baptismal certificate of Francisco Scarlatti bore this date.

(July 30) Giuseppe Scolari, Italian composer, died at this time in Venice (born 1720).

(August 13) Nicola Sala's opera "Merope" was produced this evening at Naples.

(August 15) J. C. F. Bach's cantata "Der Tod Jesu" was completed on this date (text by C. W. Rambler).

(August 24) Gluck's Italian operas "Le feste d'Apollo", "Il prologo", "Bauci e Filemone", "Aristeo" and "Orfeo" were produced at this time at the court at Parma (libretto by Carlo Innocenzia Frugoni). Gluck was present in Parma for a visit, especially since this was the first performance of "Orfeo" in Italy.

(August 30) Bonifacio Asioli, Italian theorist and composer, was born on this date at Correggio (died 1832, May 18 at Correggio).

(September 2) Charles Simon Favart's "L'Amant déguisé, ou Le Jardinier supposé" was first performed this evening at Paris (music by Philidor).

(September 2) F. A. Philidor's opera "L'Amant deguisé, ou Le Jardinier suppose (libretto by Favart and Claude Henri Fusée de Voisenon) was performed on this date at the Comédie-Italienne at Paris.

(September 8) Marie-Martin Marcel Marin (Viconte), French harpist, violinist and composer of Venetian descent, was born on this date at St. Jean de Luz, Bayonne (death date unknown).

(September 19) James Bartleman, English bass, was born at this time in London (died 1821, April 15 at London).

(September 20) Gretry's opera "Le Tableau parlant" was produced on this date at the Comédie-Italienne in Paris (libretto by Louis Anseaume).

(September 21) John Gualdo in this issue of the Pennsylvania "Journal" advertised that he taught instruments.

(Autumn) Jommelli at this time summoned his close friend Verazi to Ludwigsburg from Schwetzingen. Mateo Verazi was the court poet at Mannheim.

(Autumn) Christian F. D. Schubart became organist at Ludwigsburg at this time.

(September 30) Johann Adolf Hasse on this date wrote a letter to Abbe Giovanni Maria Ortes praising the 12 year old W. A. Mozart and sending a letter of recommendation for him.

1769(cont.)

(October 9) Marian Königsporger, German organist and composer, died on this date at Pröfening near Ratisbon (born 1708, December 4 at Roding, Bavaria).

(October 14) C. Dibdin's opera "The Jubilee" was performed at Drury Lane Theatre in London this evening.

(October 25) Charles Simon Favart's "La Rosière de Salenci" was first performed on this date at Paris (music by Philidor, Monsigny and Van Swieten).

(October 25) Monsigny's opera "La Rosière de Salenci" (libretto by Favart) was produced on this date at Fountainbleau. According to Grimm the music was actually by Philidor, Monsigny, Van Swieten, Blaise and Dun, all collaborating on the work.

(November 8-1770, May 24) Philadelphia enjoyed operatic music during this theatrical season.

(November 9) John Gualdo's first concert was announced by him in the Pennsylvania "Journal" in this issue.

(November 16) A program of John Gualdo's work appeared at this time.

(November 23) C. Dibdin's new setting of the masque in Dryden's "Amphitryon" was performed on this evening at the Drury Lane Theatre in London.

(November 30) The Pennsylvania "Gazette" announced the first concert by subscription in this issue.

(November 30) The Pennsylvania "Gazette" in this issue stated that "The Orchestra, on Opera Nights, will be assisted by some musical Persons . . ."

(December 9) William Felton, English clergyman, organist, harpsichordist and composer, died on this day at Hereford (born 1715).

(December 14) Monsigny's opera "La Rosière de Salency" (libretto by Favart) was produced this evening at the Comédie-Italienne in Paris.

(December 14) F. A. Philidor's opera "La Rosiere de Salenci" (libretto by Favart) was produced on this date at the Comedie-Italienne in Paris. However, note the previous entry for the possibility of an error in this information.

(December 18) William Neale, son of John Neale and from a family of Irish impresarios, printers and publishers of engraved music and musical-instrument makers, died on this day (birthdate unknown).

(December 18) Burkat Shudi, harpsichord maker, at this time received a patent for his "Venetian swell mechanism" under the name of a "harpsichord pedal". The mechanism was on occasion used on some Kirkman instruments.

(January) James Oswald, Scottish dancing-master, violinist, organist and composer, died this month (birthdate unknown).

(April) C. Dibdin's "Shakespeare's Garland" was performed this month at Stratford-on-Avon.

(May) Thomas Carter, Irish composer, was born this month at Dublin (died 1800, November 8 at London).

(September or October) Mozart's "Offertorium pro omni tempore", K.117, for 4 voices, 2 flutes, 2 horns, 2 trumpets, drums and organ was composed at this time in Salzburg.

(October) Mozart's Mass in C major (Dominicus), K.66, for 4 voices, 2 trumpets, drums, strings and organ with 2 oboes, 2 horns, and 2 more trumpets added later was composed this month at Salzburg.

(December) Wolfgang and Leopold Mozart left Salzburg this month for Italy, traveling through Innsbruck where Wolfgang gave a private concert for Count Künigl.

George Bickham, an engraver during Queen Anne's reign, died this year (birthdate unknown).

Maria Theresa Bland (Romanzi), English singer born of Italian Jewish parents named Romanzi, was born this year in Italy (died 1838, January 15 at London).

Benjamin Carr, publisher, was born at this time (died 1831).

Wilhelm Dahmen, jr., horn player, was born this year at Harlingen (death date unknown but in Spain).

Johann Elssler, son of Prince Eszterhazy's music copyist and a godson of Haydn, was born at this time (death date unknown).

Václav Farník, Czech clarinetist, was born this year (died 1838).

John Fawcett, comedian, was born at this time (death date unknown).

August Hermann Francke died this year in Halle (birthdate unknown).

Johanna Rosine Frankenberger, wife of Johann Philipp Bach, was born at this time (died 1817).

Christian Fürchtegott Gellert, German composer, died this year (born 1715).

Francesco Gnecco, Italian composer, was born this year at Genoa (died 1810). He taught N. Paganini at about 1792 and also composed at least 26 operas and many other works.

Jean Jacques Grasset, French violinist and pupil of Berthaume, was born at Paris this year (died 1839).

Thomas Haigh, English violinist, pianist and composer, was born this year at London (died 1808, April at London).

Mrs. Catherine Comerford Hellyer, actress and singer, was born at this time (died 1821).

(Chevalier) d'Herbain, French amateur composer, died this year at Paris (born c.1730 at Paris).

Johann Hermann Mankell, founder of the Swedish branch of the Mangold family, was born this year at Darmstadt (death date unknown but at Karlskrona).

Dominique Della Maria, opera composer, was born this year (death date unknown).

Joseph Muntzberger, Netherlands cellist and composer, was born this year at Brussels (died 1844, January at Paris).

Marquis Gian Carlo di Nigro, a Genoese aristocrat of Gnecco's time who was an enthusiastic patron of the arts and helped Niccolò Paganini in a material way, was born this year (died 1857).

Paravicini (born Gandini), an Italian violinist, was born this year at Turin (died in the 19th century).

Louis Luc Loiseau de Persuis, opera composer, was born this year (death date unknown).

Nicolas Philidor, brother of Francois and later oboist in Grande Ecurie as well as violist in the King's private orchestra, died this year (born 1699, November 3 at Versailles).

Domenico Pino, who was a Field Marshal, friend of Niccolo Paganini and a General under Napoleon, was born this year (died 1826, March).

Louis Riegel, pianist and teacher, was born this year at Paris (died 1811, February 25 at LeHavre.

James Sanderson, English composer, was born this year at Washington, Durham (died c.1841).

John Adams mentions a patriotic dinner of the Sons of Liberty this year celebrating the Stamp Act Riots. Everyone stood and sang "The Liberty Song, or In Freedom We're Born" written by John Dickinson of Delaware.

John Antes at this time was sent as a missionary to Egypt.

Pedro Aranaz became "maestro de capilla" at Cuenca this year where he remained for the rest of his life.

Samuel Arnold took a lease on Marylebone Gardens this year. It was then a fashionable resort which he made more attractive by composing and producing several burlettas performed by the principal singers of the time.

The Empress' privilege was granted this year to Carlo Artaria, the son of Cesare, and to his cousins, Francesco, Ignazio and Pasquale, all to establish an art business in Vienna.

The "Catch Club" this season awarded Theodore Aylward the prize medal for his serious glee "A cruel fate".

Anselm Bayly edited a collection of the words of anthems at this time. He contributed an interesting preface on cathedral music.

Johann van Beethoven this year received a salary increase of 25 florins.

Boyce at this time relinquished his position at All Hallows, Thames Street.

Boyce retained his position as

organist at the chapel royal
after this year when his deafness increased and compelled
him to go into semi-retirement
at Kensington.

John Broadwood married his
employer's daughter, Barbara
(Shudi) at this time.

B. T. Breitkopf this season
composed music to Goethe's
"Jugendlieder".

Burney was awarded both the
Bachelor of Music and the
Doctor of Music degrees this
year at Oxford.

Cherubini began to compose this
year at the age of nine.

An oratorio made up of various
pieces from Cherubini's operas,
with a new tenor aria and two
choruses, was performed this
season for the benefit of the
Jesuits at their church in
Florence. The problem is that
the Jesuits as such did not
exist at this time.

Georges Cousineau was a member
of the guild of instrument
makers at this time.

John Crosdill appeared this
season at Gloucester as principal cellist at the meeting of
the Three Choirs.

C. Dibdin this year composed
some of the music for the
Shakespeare Jubilee at
Stratford-on-Avon.

Douglass' "American Company"
had a good long season in
Philadelphia this year.

Karl Vilhelm Düben held high
office in the Treasury at this

J. P. Duport was attached to
the Prince de Conti's orchestra
until this year.

J. P. Duport travelled to
England at this time.

Jan Ladislav Dussek began to
study the organ this year
at age 9.

Charles Simon Favare retired
this year on a pension of 800
livres, from the Opéra-Comique
in Paris.

William Felton was made chaplain to the Princess Dowager of
Wales and elected custos of
the vicars-choral this year.
This was also the year of his
death.

Johann Nikolaus Forkel at this
time entered the University of
Göttingen to study law.

P. J. Frick, a virtuoso on the
armonica, introduced pads as
early as this year.

Gluck and his wife at this time
adopted their niece, Marianne
Hedler. She traveled with them
and sang at various musical
events.

Gluck became composer at the
court of Parma this season.

Gluck informed Prince Kaunitz
this year that, due to an un-
successful investment in the
Burgtheater, he had wasted much
of his fortune.

Baron Gottfried van Swieten
visited England this year and
became an ardent admirer of
Handel.

Prince Nicolaus' entire musical establishment visited Vienna at this time and under Haydn's direction gave a performance of his opera "Lo speziale".

Petrus Hellendaal won the "Catch Club" medal this season.

Johann Gottfried Herder, German writer, visited Hamburg this year.

Samuel Howard was awarded the Doctor of Music degree this year by Cambridge University.

Nicola Jommelli at this time returned to Naples from Germany and was received coldly by his countrymen, who had found his new style of composition too German for their taste.

Jakob Kleinknecht was Kapellmeister at the Ansbach court from this date forward.

William Leeves, cellist and composer, entered the first regiment of Foots-Guards at this time.

V. Manfredini was displaced at court this season by Galuppi and retired to Italy, first to Bologna where he met Mozart, and later to Venice.

Mozart this year was made concert master to the Archbishop of Salzburg and went to Italy with his father.

Christian Gottlob Neefe went to Leipzig this year to study. While there he befriended J. A. Hiller at St. Thomas' Church.

Ottani went to Dresden this year for performances of two (cont.) new operas of his that had not previously been heard in Italy, "L'amore industrioso" and "Le virtuose ridicole".

Gasparo Pacchierotti returned to Venice at this time and took the place of Guarducci, primo musico at the Teatro San Benedetto, at the time the chief theatre in that city.

The organ built by Parker for the Foundling Chapel this year had 4 quarter notes: Db, D#, Ab, A#. These were not furnished with extra keys but were controlled by a substituting mechanism.

Mme. Rameau moved to Andrésy at this time where her son-in-law, Francois de Gaultier, had an estate.

John Randall composed the music for Gray's "Ode" for the Installation of the Duke of Grafton as Chancellor of the University this year. He also composed some church music.

Reutter, jr. was appointed first court conductor this season.

Franz Xavier Richter left for Strassburg this year from Mannheim.

Elector Maximilian Friedrich at this time issued a decree granting raises to Philipp Salomon, his two daughters, and Beethoven's father, all of whom were Bonn court musicians.

Antonio Sacchini this season became director of the school of music at the Ospedaletto at Venice. He held office little more than a year.

Bernardus Shudi made a 2-manual

harpsichord this year that has
survived.

Josef Starzer, Austrian violinist and composer, returned to
Austria from St. Petersburg
this year and played an important
part in Viennese musical life.

The English firm of music engravers and publishers, Straight
& Skillern, took over the business of James Oswald at this
time and moved to #17 St.
Martin's Lane in London.

Giusto Ferdinando Tenducci,
a soprano, returned to London
from Edinboro this year.

G. J. Vogler was in Wurzberg
at this time where he invented
a system of fingering and
tried to learn the violin and
other instruments without a
teacher.

J. F. Weigl was in the orchestra
of the Imperial Opera of Vienna
this season.

Alessandri's "Il re alla caccia"
was produced this year.

T. A. Arne's opera "Artaxerxes"
was performed at Edinboro this
season.

"Six sonatas for two German
flutes or 2 violins and a bass"
by Oliver y Astorga appeared
at this time.

J. Christian (son of J. S.)
Bach produced Piccinni's
"L'Olimpiade" this year with
additions of his own.

A set of six Divertimenti by
J. Christian Bach were published
at this time.

J. C. F. Bach, with Bock of
Hamburg, published six quartets
for flute, violin, viola and
bass this year.

Kirnberger was responsible for
editing the 1769 volume of
J. S. Bach's Chorales.

K. P. E. Bach at this time
wrote his cantata "Die
Israeliten in der Wüste".

Karl Philipp Emmanuel Bach
arranged for Bach's four-part
Chorales to be published by
Birnstiel this year at Berlin
and Leipzig. This was Part II
of the set.

Capel Bond this year composed
"6 Anthems in Score, one of
which is for Christmas Day".

Bernhard Theodor Breitkopf
at this time composed some
music to Goethe's "Jugendlieder".

John Broderip this season published a volume of "Psalms,
Hymns and Spiritual Songs",
dedicated to Lord Francis
Seymour, Dean of Wells.

Bury's "Palmire" was issued
this year at Versailles.

Cafaro's "La guistizia placata"
was performed this season at
Naples.

Carvalho's opera "L'amore industrioso" was produced this
season at London.

Colla's opera "Lucida e Mopso"
appeared this year at Parma.

"The Laborers of Murcia" by
Don Ramón de la Cruz and Don
Antonio Rodriguez de Hita was

completed at this time.

Dard's "Nouveaux Principes de musique . . ." appeared at this time.

E. R. Duni's collaboration in "La Rosière de Salency" (libretto by Favart) performed this year was dubious.

Esteve's "Los zagales del Genil" appeared this year at Granada.

Alessandro Felici's "L'Amore soldato" was published this year at Venice.

Domenico Fischietti's opera "Lo speziale" was performed at London's Haymarket Theatre this season.

Johann Christian Frischmuth's "Das Mondenreich", as well as some violin and pianoforte music, was published at this time.

Baldassare Galuppi wrote his opera "Il villano geloso" this year at Venice (libretto by Bertati).

Gassmann's operetta "L'Amore Artigiano" was produced this year at Vienna. Monsigny's "Deserteur" was produced in Paris also.

Florian Gassmann's opera "L'opera seria" was produced this season at Vienna (libretto by Calzabigi).

Filippo Gherardeschi's opera "La notte critica" (libretto by Goldoni) was produced this season.

The score of Gluck's opera "Alceste" was published at

(cont.) this time in Vienna.

A second edition of James Grassineau's "A Musical Dictionary . . . of Terms and Characters . . . ." was published by Robson this year.

Hasse's pasticcio, "Tom Jones", was produced this season at London.

Haydn wrote his quartets, opus 9 this year.

Hiller's lied "Lieder für Kinder" (words by his librettist and friend C. F. Weisse) appeared at this time.

Hook's "Love & Innocence" was produced this season at Marylebone Gardens in London.

John Johnson this year published "Shakespear's Garland" by Charles Dibdin.

Klopstock's "Hermanns-Schlacht" was issued this year and dedicated to Joseph II.

Koželuh's opera "Allesandro nell' Indie" (libretto by Metastasio) was produced this season at Prague.

Giovanni Battista Lampugnani's opera "L'Illustre villanella" was produced this season at Turin.

F. Meyer's opera-buffa, "Hans Hältenstock", appeared this year in manuscript.

Joseph Mondonville's opera "Psyché" was performed this year, but was a failure.

Mozart's "Te Deum" in C major (K.141) was composed at the end

of this year at Salzburg for
4 voices, strings and organ.

Mozart's "2 Minuets" for orchestra, K.61g, for 2 flutes and
strings was composed at Salzburg
this year during carnival season.

Mozart's "6 Minuets" for orchestra, K.61h, was composed this
year during carnival season
at Salzburt for 2 flutes, 2
oboes, 2 horns, 2 trumpets and
strings.

Mozart's "Minuet in D major",
K.64, for 2 horns and strings
was composed early this year
at Salzburg.

Mozart's "19 Minuets" for orchestra, K.103, was written this
year during carnival season at
Salzburg for 2 oboes, 2 horns
and strings.

Mozart's "6 Minuets" for orchestra, K.104, was written this
year at Salzburg during carnival
season for piccolo, 2 oboes, 2
horns, 2 trumpets and strings.

Mozart's "6 Minuets" for orchestra, K.105, was composed this
year during carnival season at
Salzburg for flute, 2 oboes,
2 horns and strings.

Johann Naumann produced his
"Metastasian" opera "La
clemenza di Tito" this season
at Dresden.

Paisiello's comic opera "L'Arabo
cortese" appeared at this time.

Paisiello's opera "Don Chisciotte
della Mancia" (after Cervantes)
was completed at this time.

A. Palamino wrote the zarzuela

(cont.) "La mesonerilla" (libretto by Rámon de la Cruz)
this year.

José Palamino this year wrote a
successful "tonadilla", "El
canapé".

Sacchini's "L'isola d'amore"
was given this season at
Vienna (music by Florian Gassmann).

Giuseppe Sarti's opera "L'Asile
de l'amour" was produced in
Copenhagen this year.

Maddalena Sirmen's "Six
Quartettes à deux violons, alto
et basse" were published this
year at Paris.

Baron Gottfried van Swieten this
year committed himself to compose
several of the songs in Favart's
"Rosière de Salency" for its
production at Paris.

Vento's "La zingara" was performed in Vienna this year (music by Florian Gassmann).

At the age of fourteen this year
Viotti wrote his first violin
concerto (in A minor). It was
published as #3.

Two harpsichords made this year
by J. Kirkman have survived and
are listed as follows: #28 with
2 manuals, currently owned by
the Steinert Collection, and
#29, 1-manual, 2x8' only
currently owned by Noel Dilkes,
esq.

The earliest anthems by American
composers were published this
year. By the end of the century
approximately 120 anthems by
twenty-one composers were available.

NAPOLEON BONAPARTE I
1769-1821

1769(cont.)

The first church hymn-book for general use was published this year.

A periodical entitled "Der Musikalische Dilettante" appeared at this time.

The court chapel was transferred this year from Bayreuth to Ansbach.

At Stockholm this year the importance of concerts was emphasized by the creation of a special institution, "Cavalier Concerts", based on the Viennese pattern.

The Bishop of Grosswardein at Pressburg received a rebuke from the Empress at this time because of the laxity of his life. She also dismissed his entire orchestra.

One of the greatest German literary figures, Gotthold Ephradim Lessing, this year wrote "How the ancients pictured death".

Sir Thomas Lawrence, English portraitist and acknowledged successor to Reynolds, was born this year (died 1830).

James Ward, a romantic landscapist and animal painter, was born at this time (died 1859).

The English Royal Academy was founded this year by Joshua Reynolds. His 14 Presidential "Discourses" not only provided the theoretical background for the period, but also were the best written material of their kind in the Enlish language.

Hubert Roberts this year painted (cont.) "Garden of a Roman Palace".

Napoleon Bonaparte, later Emperor of France, was born this year (died 1821).

George III this year granted Lord Aston a pension of 300 pounds per annum under the title of Lord Aston of Forfar.

(to 1770) K. P. E. Bach's "Passion Cantata" was written at this time.

(to 1770) J. F. Deller acted as conductor at Stuttgart this year.

(and 1770) Philipp and Peter Dornaus were born at Coblenz on these dates. They were horn prodigies who became distinguished horn virtuosi in their later lives.

(to 1770) Marie Fel, French soprano, retired this season at a Concert Spirituel.

(to 1770) Haydn wrote his baryton trios #73-96 at this time. They are listed below:

#73	G major	2/4	Andante
#74	D major	3/4	Andante
#75	A major	C	Moderato
#76	C major	2/4	Moderato
#77	G major	6/8	Adagio
#78	D major	2/4	Moderato
#79	D major	2/4	Moderato
(dated 1769)			
#80	G major	C	Moderato
(dated 1769)			
#81	D major	2/4	Adagio
#82	C major	3/4	Adagio
#83	F major	3/4	Adagio
#84	G major	2/4	Adagio
(c.1769)			
#85	D major	C	Adagio
#86	A major	3/4	Moderato
#87	A major	C	Adagio

1769(cont.)

#88	A major	3/4	Adagio
#89	G major	2/4	Moderato
#90	C major	C	Moderato
#91	D major	2/4	Moderato
#92	G major	3/4	Allegro
#93	C major	C	Allegro
#94	A major	2/4	Allegretto
#95	D major	2/4	Allegro
#96	b minor	3/4	Largo

(to 1770) Giuseppe Sarti wrote 3 French operas in Copenhagen during these years.

(to 1770) Jakob von Stählin was the author of the earliest source on the history of music in Russia. His treatise "Nachrichten von der Musik in Russland", published with 2 others (on theatre and ballet) this year in the collection "J. J. Haigold's Beylagen zum neuveränderton Russland" (2 volumes, Riga and Leipzig).

(to 1770) The orchestra in Philadelphia was an established institution during this season.

(to 1771) W. Pichl was conductor of Count Louis Hartwig's orchestra at this time.

(to 1772) Joseph Blaschek was a violinist in the orchestra of Count Esterhazy during these years.

(to 1774) The Papal reign of Clement XIV embraced these years. He was born at Rimini.

(to 1774) Andreas Lidl played the baryton in the orchestra of Prince Nicolaus during this period.

(and 1777, 1786, c.1795) "The Essex Harmony: Being an entire new collection of the most

(cont.) celebrated Songs and Catches, Canzonets, Canons, and Glees. By John Arnold" A later work (c.1795) under this title was published by Bland & Weller.

(to 1780) Audinot founded the Théâtre de l'Ambigu-Comique, Boulevard du Temple at this time. He wrote numerous plays, pantomimes and operettas for the theatre until 1780.

(to 1780) A. M. G. Vestris left the Opéra for the Comedie-Italienne, also at Paris, where he stayed during this period.

(to 1794, August 25) Leopold August Abel was violinist and composer at the chapel of the Duke of Schwerin at Ludwigs-lust during this period.

(to 1795) Franz Adam Veichtner, German violinist and composer, during these years was court conductor to the Duke of Courland at Mitau (Yelyava).

(to 1798) V. Manfredini's opera "Armida" was performed at Bologna during these seasons.

(to 1798) V. Manfredini's opera "Arteserse" was performed at Venice during this period.

c.1769

Charles Henri de Blainville, French violoncellist, teacher of music and composer, died this year at Paris (born c.1711 near Tours).

Domenico Fischietti's opera "Les metamorphoses de l'amour, ou Le Tuteur dupe" was given at Count Brühl's theatre at Pfördten, near Dresden this year.

Etienne Joseph Floquet moved
to Paris this year where his
setting of "La Gloire du
Seigneur" (text by Rousseau)
was first performed at a
Concert Spirituel.

(or 1770) Haydn's overture #1
in C major for 2 oboes, 2 horns,
drums and strings (listed in
Breitkopf's Catalogue for 1782)
was completed at this time.

Haydn's string duo (no number)
for violin solo with accompaniment for viola was written at
this time.

Haydn's string duo #1 in F
major was written this year.
The last movement, "Tempo de
Menuetto", had a theme in
which the first 4 bars are
almost the same as in the
first Minuet in the early
Cassation in F major and in the
Minuet of Haydn's London Symphony in C major #97.

Haydn's string duos, #2 in A
major and #3 in Bb major were
composed this year.

Haydn's string duos, #5 in Eb
major and #6 in C major were
composed this season.

Haydn's string duo #4 in D major
was composed this year. In 1775
it was published in an arrangement for violin and bass by
Bailleux, and issued in 1782 by
W. Campbell, London; and later
by Napier and by Hamilton.

(to 1772) Haydn's "Missa St.
Caecilae" in C major, scored
for solo SATB was written during
this period. It was Haydn's
longest Mass and was quite
possibly composed for the festival at Vienna.

(January 8) N. Piccini's opera
"Didone abbandonata" (libretto
by Metastasio) was produced on
this date at the Teatro Argentina at Rome.

(January 13) Cecilia Grassi
sang "Fulvia" in Guglielmi's
"Ezio" this evening at London.

(January 13) Pietro Guglielmi's
opera "Ezio" was produced on
this date at London.

(January 18) Anton Schweitzer's
one-act "Elysium" was produced
this evening at Hanover.

(January 22) F. A. Philidor's
opera "La Nouvelle École des
Femmes" (libretto by Alexandre
Guillaume Mouslier de Moissy)
was produced on this date at
the Comédie-Italienne at Paris.

(January 26) A revival of
Rameau's "Zoroastre" for the
opening of the newly built
Opera house at Paris was performed on this date.

(January 29) J. A. Hiller's
singspiel, "Die Jagd" (libretto
by Weisse from Sedaine's "Le
Roi Fermier") was performed this
evening at Weimar. The source
gave Colli's "La Partie de
chasse de Henri IV" as an additional basis for the libretto.

(February 1) Pietro Guglielmi's
opera "L'Olimpiade" was produced this evening in London
(libretto by Metastasio).

(February 2) Luigi Belloli, a
French Horn player and one of
the earliest to adopt the "cor-
nixte" type, was born on this
day at Castelfranco (died 1817,
November 17 at Milan).

1770(cont.)

(February 2) Guiseppe Naldi,
Italian baritone, pianist and
cellist, was born on this day
at Bologna (died 1820,
December 15 at Paris).

(February 10) Ferdinando
Carulli, Italian guitarist and
composer, was born at this time
at Naples (died 1841 at Paris).

(February 18) Johann Christian
Heinrich Rinck, German organist
and composer, was born on this
date at Elgersburg, Saxe-
Gotha. He was a pupil of
Kittel (one of Bach's best
pupils) and his talent developed
at an early stage (died 1846,
August 7 at Darmstadt).

(February 19) Grétry's opera
"Silvain" was given this evening
at the Comédie-Italienne in
Paris (libretto by Marmontel).

(February 26) François Hanot,
Flemish violinist, dancing
master and composer, died on
this date at Tournai (born
1698 at Dunkirk).

(February 26) Antonin Reicha,
French composer and teacher of
Bohemian birth, was born on this
date at Prague. He was adopted
by his uncle, Joseph Reicha,
concertmaster at Bonn. He
studied violin, pianoforte, and
flute in Bavaria (died 1836,
May 28 at Paris).

(February 26) Giuseppe Tartini,
great violinist, teacher and
composer from Padua, died on
this date (born 1692, April 8
at Pirano, Istria). He was
the most celebrated of all
Italian virtuosi and established
a school at Padua where he
spent most of his life.

(March 9) Mr. Hallam on this date
conducted the orchestra when
"Comus" was performed for the
first time at Philadelphia by
the old American Company.
(See Pennsylvania "Journal",
March 8)

(March 15) William Gardiner,
English stocking manufacturer
as well as writer and editor
of music, was born on this date
at Leicester (died 1853,
November 16).

(March 15) Mozart's string
quartet in G major, K.80, was
completed on this date at Lodi.

(Spring) Johann van Beethoven
was offered the job of tenor
soloist at the cathedral in
Liège, but he refused the offer.

(March 22) J. Christian (son of
J. S.) Bach's only oratorio,
"Gioas, Re de Giuda", was
published and performed on this
date at the King's Theatre in
London.

(March 23) Jan August Vitásek,
Bohemian composer, was born on
this date at Horín near Mělnik
(died 1839, December 7 at Prague).

(March 25) Carl Friedrich
Ebers, German musician and
composer, was born at this time
in Cassel (died 1836 at Berlin).
One source gave his birthplace
at Mecklenburg.

(March 30) Wolfgang and his
father, Leopold Mozart, arrived
in Florence on this date where
Wolfgang played at court,
accompanying Nardini, the great
violinist.

(March 31) Pietro Guglielmi's
opera "La costanza di Rosinella"

1770(cont.)

(April 1) Ignaz Leutgeb, Austrian French horn player, visited Paris at this time and appeared as a soloist at the Concert Spirituel.

(April 7) J. C. Bach produced Gluck's "Orfeo" with additions of his own on this day at London. It was the first production in England (in Italian) and also perportedly included music by Pietro Guglielmi.

(April 8) Marie Élisabeth Anne Miller, a French dancer, was born on this date in Auxonne, Côte d'or (died 1823, May 18).

(April 10) Esprit Joseph Antoine Blanchard, French composer, died at this time in Versailles (born 1696, February 29 at Pernes, Comtat Venaissin, now called Vaucluse).

(April 13 or 14) Mozart's "Country Dance" in Bb major, K.123, for 2 oboes, 2 horns and strings was composed at this time at Rome.

(April 19) Georg Abraham Schneider, German horn player, oboist, conductor and composer, was born at this time in Darmstadt (died 1839, January 19). He was also an army bandmaster.

(April 25) Mozart Symphony in D major, K.81, was composed at this time at Rome for 2 oboes, 2 horns and strings.

(April 25) Mozart Symphony in D major, K.95, was composed this year at Rome for 2 flutes (or oboes), 2 trumpets and strings.

(May 7) Arne's "The Ladies' Frolick" was produced this evening at the Drury Lane Theatre in London.

(May 10) Charles Avison, English organist, composer and writer on music, died at this time at Newcastle-on-Tyne (born 1709 at Newcastle-on-Tyne).

(May 19) Pietro Guglielmi's "Il disertore" was produced this evening at London (libretto by Badini).

(May 24) Ferdinand Fränzl, German violinist and composer, was born on this date at Schwetzingen (died 1833, November 19).

(May 28) C. Dibdin's "The Maid the Mistress" was performed at Ranelagh on this date.

(May 28) Wolfgang Mozart gave a concert this evening at Naples. It was brilliantly attended and a great financial success.

(June 4) James Hewitt, American (English-born) violinist and composer, was born on this day at Dartmoor, England (died 1827, August 1 at Boston, Massachusetts). He started a dynasty of musicians who spearheaded American music.

(June 7) Arne's "Miss Lucy in Town" was revived on this date as "The Country Mad Cap" at the Drury Lane Theatre in London.

(June 14) Burney on this date heard Gaetano Besozzi at the Concert Spirituel and enjoyed his excellent playing.

1770(cont.)

(June 16) Samuel Arnold's "The Servant Mistress" was performed this evening at the Marylebone Gardens in London.

(June 19 and 22) J. Holzbogen gave concerts at this time at Frankfurt am Main with Leutget, the horn virtuoso.

(June 25) Leopold and Wolfgang Mozart went back to Rome on this day and the Pope decorated Wolfgang with the "Order of the Golden Spur".

(July 4) Barthélemon's "The Magic Girdle" was performed this evening at the Marylebone Gardens in London.

(July 5) G. Scarlatti's opera "L'amor geloso" was produced on this date at the Schönbrunn Palace near Vienna (librettist unknown).

(July 13) Burney visited Alessandro Besozzi and his brother Paolo Girolamo on this day when the two old virtuosi played duets for oboe and bassoon especially for him.

(July 14) Richard Walond matriculated at Christ Church at Oxford at this time.

(July 17) Giovanni Andrea Fioroni was visited on this date in Milan by Burney. Later that year the Mozarts, father and son, also visited Fioroni.

(July 20) C. Dibdin's "The Recruiting Serjeant" was produced at Ranelagh this evening.

(July 20) Wolfgang and Leopold Mozart arrived in Bologna at

(cont.) this time where Wolfgang had the rare distinction of being admitted as "compositore" to the Academia Filarmonica, even though he was not yet 20 years of age.

(July 21) Christian Gottfried Krause, German lawyer, composer and author whom Riemann called "the soul of the Berlin Lieder School", died on this day at Berlin (born 1719 at Winzig, Silesia).

(July 25) C. Dibdin's "Cupid's Frolick" was performed on this date at Sadler's Wells in London.

(July 30) Friedrich Ludwig Aemilius Abel, violinist, was born on this day at Ludwigslust.

(July 30) Ignaz Sonnleithner, Austrian amateur musician, was born at this time in Vienna (died 1831, November 27).

(August 6) Goffredo Cappa, Italian violin maker, died on this date at Saluzzo (born c.1647).

(August 13) Cafaro's cantata written for the Queen's birthday was performed on this date.

(August 13) Cafaro's opera "Antigono" was produced at this time at the Teatro San Carlo in Naples.

(August 21) Barthélemon's "The Noble Pedlar, or The Fortune Hunter" was performed on this date at Marylebone Gardens in London.

(August 28) Samuel Arnold's "The Mad Man" was performed on

NAPOLEON I IN EXILE AT ST. HELENA-July 24, 1820
(From a sketch made by an English officer)

this evening at Marylebone Gardens in London.

(August 28) C. Dibdin's "The Mad Man" was produced on this day at Marylebone Gardens in London (see previous entry as well).

(September 3) Florian Gassmann's opera "La contessina" was given at this time in Moravia (libretto by Calzabigi).

(September 11) Burney, the British music historian, wrote from Florence on this day that he had met the famous impromptu actress, Signorina Maddalena Morelli, that evening. (She was usually called "La Corilla").

(September 16) Haydn's opera buffa "Le pescatrici" (libretto by Goldoni) was produced at Esterház on this evening. The score is extant.

(September 23) Burney visited Pietro Maria Crispi at this time to hear the weekly "accademia" at the latter's house.

(September 28) Fabián García Pacheco's "En casa de nadie no se meta nadie, o El buen marido" was completed by this date.

(October 1) Ann Catley appeared this evening at Covent Garden in London as "Rosetta" in "Love in a Village".

(October 1) Louis Gabriel Guillemain, French violinist and composer, died on this date at Paris (born 1705, November 15).

(October 1-8) The Pennsylvania "Chronicle" during this week advertised a concert directed by Mr. Gualdo.

(October 9) Mozart's sacred "Antiphon", "Quaerite primum regnum Dei" for 4 voices a cappella was composed at this time at Bologna.

(October 20) E. R. Duni's opera "Thémire" was produced this evening at Fontainebleau in Paris.

(October 20) Grétry's opera "Les Deux Avares" was given on this date at Fontainebleau in Paris (libretto by de Falbaire).

(October 31) Domenico Scarlatti on this day visited the Conservatorio of St. Onofrio.

(November 3) Gluck's Italian opera "Paride ed Elena" (libretto by Calzabigi) was produced on this date at the Burg Theatre in Vienna. This was their last collaboration and the opera which had 5 acts was published simultaneously with its première.

(November 4) The record of Burney's French and Italian tour bore this date.

(November 4) Burney on this day visited, as he stated, "Don Carlo Cotumacci, master to the Conservatorio of St. Onofrio, whom I heard play on the harpsichord . . ."

(November 8) The Pennsylvania "Journal" in this issue advertised a concert "two days after Christmas".

1770(cont.)

(November 10) Kohault's opera "La Closière, ou Le Vin nouveau" was produced this evening at Fontainbleau in Paris.

(November 13) Charles Simon Favart's "L'Amitié à l'épreuve" was first performed on this date at Paris (music by Grétry).

(November 13) Grétry's opera "L'Amitié à l'épreuve" was given on this date at Fontaine-bleau (libretto by Favart and Fusée). See previous entry as well.

(November 16) Pietro Maria Crispi was visited by Burney on this evening when six new quartets of Crispi's were performed.

(November 22) Samuel Arnold's "The Portrait" was performed this evening at Covent Garden in London.

(November 26) E. R. Duni's opera "Thémire" was produced on this date at Paris in the Comédie-Italienne.

(November 27) John George Henry Jay, English violinist and composer, was born on this date at Essex (died 1849, September 17 at London).

(November 29) Peter Hänsel, German violinist and composer, was born on this day at Leipa, Silesia (died 1831, September 18 at Vienna).

(December 1) Angélique Dorothée Lucie Grétry, French composer, was born at this time in Paris (died 1790, March).

(December 6) Grétry's opera

(cont.) "Les Deux Avares" was given this evening at the Comédie-Italienne in Paris (libretto by de Falbaire).

(December 10) T. A. Arne's "Love and Resolution" was produced on this date at the Haymarket Theatre in London.

(December 10) Francis Hopkinson at this time succeeded Bremner as organist of Christ Church and in the vestry minutes under this date it so stated.

(December 10) Gotlieb (Theophil) Muffat, German organist, composer of Scottish extraction and son of Georg, died on this date at Vienna (born 1690, April at Pasau). He was baptized on April 25. He was an important contemporary of Bach and Handel.

(December 11) Dr. Johann Thomas Held, noted physician and professor, was born on this date (death date unknown).

(December 13) T. A. Arne's "King Arthur, or The British Worthy" was produced this evening at Drury Lane Theatre in London.

(December 13) John Clarke (later known as Clarke-Whitfeld), English organist and composer, was born on this date at Gloucester (died 1836, February 22 at Holmer near Hereford).

(December 15-16) Ludwig van Beethoven, German composer of Flemish descent and probably the most renowned composer of all time, was born on this night at Bonn, Germany (died 1827, March 26 at Vienna).

(December 17) Ludwig van

1770(cont.)

Beethoven was baptized on this day.

(December 23) Hiller's "Die Schatten", a "nachspiel" (libretto by Johann Benjamin Michaelis), was produced at this time in Leipzig.

(December 26) Samuel Arnold's "Mother Shipton" was performed this evening at Covent Garden in London.

(December 26) Antonia Bernasconi this evening created the part of "Aspasia" in Mozart's opera "Mitridate, rè de Ponto" at Milan.

(December 26) Mozart's opera seria, "Mitridate, rè di Ponto" (libretto by V. A. Cigna Santi after Racine) was premiered this evening at the Teatro Regio Ducal in Milan.

(January) Luigi Maria Baldassare Gatti met the Mozarts this month at Mantua.

(January) William Tuckey performed Handel's "Messiah" this month at New York City.

(February) Mozart's solo aria with orchestra, K.143, Recitative "Ergo interest"; Aria, "Quaere superna" for soprano, strings and organ was composed this month at Milan.

(February or March) Mozart's solo aria with orchestra, K.88, "Fra cento affanni" (text by Metastasio) for 2 oboes, 2 horns, 2 trumpets and strings was composed at this time in Milan.

(February or March) Mozart's solo aria with orchestra, K.79,

(cont.) Recitative, "O temerario Arbace"; Aria, "Per quel paterno amplesso" (text by Metastasio) for soprano, 2 oboes, 2 bassoons, 2 horns and strings was composed at this time in Milan.

(February or March) Mozart's solo aria with orchestra, K.78, "Per pietà, bell' idol mio" (text by Metastasio) for soprano, 2 oboes, 2 horns and strings was composed at this time at Milan.

(March) J. J. Imbault was heard this month as soloist at the third of the concerts organized by Gaveniès for the benefit of the drawing-school of Bahelior.

(March) Mozart's solo aria with orchestra, K.77, Recitative, "Misero me"; Aria, "Misero pargoletto" (text by Metastasio) for soprano, 2 oboes, 2 bassoons, 2 horns and strings was composed this month at Milan.

(April) Pasquale (Pasqualino) Bini, Italian violinist and composer, died this month at Pesaro (born 1716, June 21 at Pesaro).

(April) Mozart's solo aria with orchestra, K.82, "Se ardire e speranza" (text by Metastasio) for soprano, 2 flutes, 2 horns and strings was composed this month at Rome.

(April or May) Mozart's solo aria with orchestra, K.83, "Se tutti i mali miei" (text by Metastasio) for soprano, 2 oboes, 2 trumpets and strings (2 horns added later) was composed at this time at Rome.

(April) Mozart's piano solo, K.94, Minuet in D major, was

1770(cont.)

composed this month at Bologna
or Rome.

(April) Mozart's Symphony in
D major, K.79, for 2 oboes,
2 horns, drums and strings
was composed this month at Rome.

(May) Coignet's "Pygmalion"
first appeared privately at
Lyons this month.

(May) Leutgeb's performance on
French horn was praised this
month in "Mercure".

(May) The Mozarts, father and
son, went to Naples at this
time.

(May) Mozart's "Kyrie"in G major,
K.89, for 5 sopranos, a cappella
was composed this month at Rome.

(June) Burney at this time
began to travel to acquire
information for his history of
music.

(July and August) Mozart's
"5 Riddle Canons", K.89a, for
several voices, a cappella
(Latin texts from the vignettes
in Martini's "Storia della
musica"), was composed at
this time at Bologna and Rome.

(July or August) Mozart's
"Miserere" in A minor for alto,
tenor, bass and organ was
composed at this time at
Bologna.

(July) Mozart's Symphony in D
major, K.84, for 2 oboes, 2
horns and strings was composed
this month at Milan and Bologna.

(July) Anton Schweitzer's
"Elysium" was given this month
at Hamburg.

(August) W. F. Bach left Halle
at this time and began a life
of wandering.

(August) Wilhelm Friedmann Bach's
wife's property at Halle was
announced for sale this month.

(August) E. R. Duni's opera
"Thémire" was produced this
month privately at Passy.

(August) Mozart's Minuet in
Eb major, K.122, for 2 oboes,
2 horns and strings was composed
this month at Bologna.

(September or October) Mozart's
sacred "Antiphon", "Cibavit
eos" for 4 voices and organ,
K.44, was composed at this time
at Bologna.

(October) After completing the
E minor Fantasy this month,
Wilhelm Friedemann Bach moved
his household to Braunschweig.

(November) Giovanni Francesco
Maio (Majo), Italian composer,
died this month at Naples (born
1732, March 24).

(December) James Bremner this
month was listed as "the late
organist" in Vestry minutes of
St. Peter's.

(December) W. Clagget wrote
new accompaniments for a production of Garrick's "Cymon"
this month at Dublin.

(December) Giovanni Battista
Lampugnani played second cembalo
to Mozart's first in Mozart's
"Mitridate" during this month.

(December) Mozart's Symphony in
G major, K.74, for 2 oboes, 2
horns and strings was composed
this month in Milan.

1770(cont.)

(December) Valentine Snow, English trumpeter, died this month at London (birthdate unknown).

Georges Jacques Aelsters, Belgian carillonist and composer, was born this year at Ghent (died 1849, April at Ghent).

Johann Aiblinger, pupil of Simon Mayr, was born this year at Bergamo (died 1867).

Francesco Araia, Italian composer, died before this date, probably at Bologna (born c.1700 at Naples).

Thomas (Ludford) Bellamy, English bass, was born at this time at Westminster, London (died 1843, January 3 at London).

William Broderip, English organist, died this year at Canterbury (born 1744, at Canterbury).

Maria Anna Cuppi Camargo, greatest ballerina in Paris at this time, died (born 1710). She introduced the "entrechat à quatre".

Francesca Cuzzoni, Italian soprano, died at this time at Bologna (born c.1700 at Parma).

Jean Baptiste Édouard Du Puy, Swiss violinist, singer and composer, was born this year at Corcelles, Neuchatel (died 1822, April 3 at Stockholm) Some sources gave his death date as 1771.

August Fryderyk Duranowski, Polish violinist and composer, was born at this time at Warsaw (died 1834 at Strasbourg).

John Jeremiah Goss, English alto, was born this year at Salisbury (died 1817, April 25).

Joseph Gugel, a horn player of outstanding ability, was born at this time in Stuttgart (death date unknown).

The Michael Haydn's only child, a daughter, was born at this time but only lived about a year.

Marianne Kirchgessner, German armonica player, was born this year at Waghäusel near Rastatt, Baden (died 1809, December 9 at Schaffhausen).

Jean Frédéric Auguste Lemière de Corvey, French composer, was born this year at Rennes (died 1832, April 19).

Aloys Mooser, Swiss organ builder and piano maker whose greatest instruments were at Fribourg and in the New Temple at Berne, was born this year (died 1829, December 19 at Fribourg).

Antonio Pasini, a pupil of Muzzi who first held the post of professor of miniature painting in the Academy of Fine Arts in Parma, Italy and in 1822 was made master of "composition and anatomy", was born this year (died 1845).

Reginald Spofforth, English composer, was born at this time in Southwell, Nottingham (died 1827, September 28 at London).

Sergius Nikolayevich Titov, Russian composer of operas who supposedly supplied incidental music to Pleshcheyev's play "The Forced Marriage" was born this year at St. Petersburg

1770(cont.)
(death date unknown).

Johann Georg Vollweiler, German
music teacher, was born this
year (died 1847, November 17).

William Walond, I, English
organist and composer, died
at this time in Oxford (born
1725).

Friedrich Witt, Würzberg Hof-
kapellmeister, was born this
year (died 1837).

John Worgan, II, English
composer, was born at this
time in London (death date
unknown).

Maddalena Allegranti made her
début this season at Venice.

Three authorized copies of
Gregorio Allegri's "Miserere"
for nine voices in two choirs
were produced prior to this
year, one for Emperor Leopold I,
one for the King of Portugal,
and a third for Padre Martini.

Alessandri returned to Italy
at this time.

Giovanni Ansani sang in Copenhagen this season.

Burney heard Giuseppe Aprile
at Naples this year and said
that he had a weak and uneven
voice, but "was perfectly in
tune, had an excellent shake
and great taste and expression".

T. A. Arne presented a garbled
version of Purcell's "King
Arthur" this season.

J. C. F. Bach's secular songs
were included this year in
K. P. E. Bach's "Musikalisches

Vielerley" published at Hamburg.

Karl Ludwig Bachmann, with
E. F. Benda, at this time
founded the "Liebhaber-
Konzerte", which flourished
under the latter's directorship.

Barthélemon this season became
director at Marylebone Gardens
in London, for which he produced
a number of "burlettas".

Barthélemon, as leader at
Marylebone Gardens, had Mrs.
Barthélemon, Bannister and
Reinhold as singers this
season.

The loss of Johann and Maria
van Beethoven's first son
was made up for by the birth
of a new son, Ludwig, at this
time.

"Saint Ciprien et Sainte
Justine Martirs", a French
oratorio, was revived in Italian
and given this season at the
Bonn court (composer unknown).
Beethoven's grandfather, the
Kapellmeister, sang the part
of "Eusebio Sacerdote Christiano
occulto".

William Billings' compositions
were among the earliest by an
American and were mostly
hymn-tunes, primitive in
character. The first was contained in "The New England
Psalm Singer or American
Chorister", published this
year at Boston.

The "Necrologue des hommes
celebres de la France" of this
year included a striking account
of Blavet's extraordinary flute
virtuosity.

Ignaz von Born at this time

became an advisor to the "Münz,-
und Bergmeisteramt" at Prague.

J. G. I. Breitkopf founded a
playing card business and
factory at this time.

John Broadwood this year became
Shudi's partner in the piano
manufacturing business.

Brown and Stratton at this time
wrote under Williams' "Universal
Psalmodist": "London . . . 4th
edition".

John Byfield this year was
"Organ Maker" to the royal
household at London.

Calori was singing at Dresden
this season with great success.

Cambini went to Paris this year
and while there was introduced
to Gossec.

Burney visited Campioni at
this time and told him of the
popularity of his chamber music
in England.

Ann Catley returned to England
this season.

Burney heard Celestino in
Rome this season and considered
him to be the best Roman violinist of the period.

Chrismann's name first appeared
in connection with a monster
organ located at the monastery
of St. Florian near Linz. It
was begun this year, but left
unfinished because of a
quarrel with the provost.

Burney this season found
Ciprandi singing at Milan.

Both g# and f# keys were found
on a 5-key instrument by Collier
of London, dated this year
and in the Keighley Museum.
The instrument was a type of
clarinet.

Ditters of Dittersdorf was made
"Knight of the Golden Spur"
this year.

Burney met G. Dreyer at Florence
this year.

Eichner was a member of the
court orchestra at Zweibrücken
until this season.

Burney, the British music historian, visited Farinelli at
Bologna this year. In describing
this trip Burney offered considerable information on the
character of instruments being
used at the Spanish court.

Alessandro Maria Antonio
Fridzeri at this time returned
from his European travels,
which included Paris.

Giovanni Mane Giornovichi made
his concert debut as a violinist
this year at Paris.

François Joseph Gossec founded
the "Concert des Amateurs"
at this time.

Cecilia Grassi sang "Aristea"
in Guglielmi's "Olimpiade" this
season.

Gaetano Guadagni sang under
J. Christian (son of J. S.)
Bach this season.

A concert of Italian music was
given this year at Philadelphia
in connection with a ball. The
concert was under the direction
of Gualdo.

1770(cont.)

T. Harris became Sargeant-Trumpeter to the Royal Household at this time.

In England this year Thomas Haxby obtained a patent for a "new single harpsichord containing all the stops of a double one, which by use of one pedal only, produces every increase, diminution & variation of tone" (of a double harpsichord).

Breitkopf and Härtel's 1770 catalogue listed six quartets, opus 5, for flute, violin, viola, and cello by Haydn.

Haydn at this time was seized by the "Storm and Stress", emotional movement, more commonly known as "Sturm und Drang".

Johann W. Hertel resigned his position as conductor of the orchestra at Schweren this year and was appointed court councillor and secretary to Princess Ulrike of Mecklenburg.

J. A. Hiller this year described Rameau as "An art difficult, frigid, strained".

Five piano sonatinas and other pieces by C. G. Neefe appeared this year in Hiller's "Wöchentliche Nachrichten".

Burney visited the opera composer Jommelli this season at Naples.

Jommelli at this time had fallen out of favor. He wrote to Verazi from Aversa this year and requested that his friend settle his affairs. Verazi, whom Jommelli owed money, satisfied his debt from the composer's

(cont.) effects. Verazi at the time was court poet at Mannheim.

P. C. Kauper, after studying with Georg A. Sorge at Lobenstein this year, returned to Frankfurt am Main and it was at this time his friendship with Goethe began.

Thomas King, now the proprietor of Sadler's Wells, this season engaged Dibdin to write and compose some small musical pieces to be produced there.

Gaetano Latilla met Burney in Venice this year.

Pierre Leduc made his debut this season as a violinist at the Concert Spirituel.

Jean Baptiste Lemoyne went to Berlin at this time.

Cristiano Giuseppe Lidarti, Italian cellist and composer, lived in Pisa at this time. His birth and death dates are unknown but he was probably born at Pisa.

Elizabeth Ann Linley this season sang oratorios in London and at the Worcester Festival. She was well-received and respected by the public.

Luigi Marescalchi lived in Venice at this time. He was listed by Gerber and Fétis, as a student of P. Martini and he kept a music shop in Venice and in Naples. The Library of Congress in the U.S.A. has a series of operatic texts he wrote.

From this date forward Stanislao Mattei acted as Padre Martini's deputy.

Leopold Mozart, at Naples this
year, commented on C. Hamilton's
"unusual feeling" (as a performer
she played the spinet, harpsichord and pianoforte). She
also mentioned her "Schudi
harpsichord".

Mozart this year submitted to
the examinations at the
Accademia dei Filarmonici.

Mozart this season took down
the notes to Allegri's
"Miserere" while the choir was
performing the work.

Mozart heard the singer Lucrezia
Aguiari this season at Parma.
She could sing C'''.

Mozart at this time studied
counterpoint under Padre Martini
at Bologna.

Mysliweček, while listening
with Mozart to symphonies by
Sammartini this year at Milan,
remarked, "I have found the
father of Haydn's style!"

B. Ottani's oratorios were
performed at Bologna this year
as they had been in 1765.

William T. Parke began his
study of music this year with
his brother John.

Johann Frederick Peter arrived
in Bethlehem, Pa. at this time
with scores by Haydn, Stamitz,
J. Christian (son of J. S.)
Bach, Abel, and Graun. All
were contemporaries.

F. W. Pixis, sr. was a pupil
of Vogler this year at Mannheim.

Rousseau at this time met
Coignet at Lyons.

Antonio Salieri wrote the first
of his more than forty operas
this year.

Reputedly a student of Saunier,
a Lorraine violin and guitar
maker who settled in Paris
this year, Pizue became one of
the best string instrument
makers of the time.

Burney visited a brother of
Domenico Scarlatti's (unidenti-
fied) "whom we found out at
Rome, but in great indigence".

Burkat Shudi and John Broadwood
this year made a harpsichord
for Dr. David Hartley; #625,
2-manual. The instrument has
survived.

Shudi, a piano maker, increased
the compass of his harpsichords
downward to "C".

Anton Stamitz, composer and
violinist, accompanied his
brother to Strasbourg this
year.

Karl Stamitz, composer, violinist and violist, was taken to
Strasbourg this year by his
teacher, Franz Xaver Richter.
Anton accompanied them (see
previous entry).

The numberous solo concertos of
Tartini who died this year,
already showed the "style ga-
lant" which brought an end to
the music of the Baroque
Period.

G. Tartini's "A letter . . .to
Maddalena Lombardini" was
written at Venice at this time
and translated by Burney at
London in 1771.

Girolamo Tiraboschi, the eminent

Italian writer on music, held the position of librarian at Modena this year.

Tuckey this season conducted the first American performance of parts of Handel's "Messiah" in New York. Sixteen numbers were performed with orchestra.

Burney, the British music historian, met Antonio Vandini at Padua this year. He called Vandini one of the greatest cellists in the world and added, "The Italians applied the word 'parlare' to his playing, meaning that it was as expressive as the human voice".

Johann and Gerhard Vogler were established as music sellers and publishers this year at Glasshouse Street, near Burlington Gardens in London.

Aaron Williams' "Universal Psalmodist", fourth edition, was issued this year.

Aaron Williams' fifth edition of "New Universal Psalmodist" was issued at this time.

Mr. Warrington at this time incorrectly states in his "Short Titles" that A. Williams' "New Universal Psalmodist" had 5 editions in one year.

J. Wikmanson this year was sent to study mathematics and instrument making at Copenhagen.

Mrs. Wrighton made her debut this season in "The Recruiting Officer".

Zanetti was maestro di cappella at Perugia Cathedral at this time.

Young Zelter saw Graun's "Phaeton" this season.

J. C. F. Bach's "Musikalisches Vierlerley" was published this year.

The first 3 of J. Ernst Bach's sonatas for clavier and violin were published at this time.

Johann Michael Bach this year published as his "Op. I" six "Concerts aisés pour le clavier" at Berlin.

K. P. E. Bach wrote his cantata "Selma" at this time.

K. P. E. Bach's "12 little pieces for two flutes (or violins) and clavier" were printed at this time.

K. P. E. Bach's "Solfeggio" in C minor was published this season.

A sonata by K. P. E. Bach was published this year.

W. F. Bach wrote his first "Fantasia in E minor" at this time in Halle.

A military march by William Beckford, scored for 2 oboes, 2 clarinets, 2 horns and bassoon was performed this year, but probably with 2 players assigned to the bassoon part.

Bertin's opera "Ajax", his most successful work in this area, reappeared in the repertory until this year. It was parodied at the Opera-Comique in Paris.

William Billings' first book was "The New England Psalm-Singer; or, American Chorister", published at this time in Boston.

Blamont's "Les Festes grecques et romaines" was revived up until this season.

Boyce this year published a selection of twelve overtures from his Royal New Year and birthday odes. They were for use at Vauxhall and at the theatres.

Pasquale Cafaro's cantata for the transfer of the blood of St. Gennaro was composed at this time.

"Captatio benevolentiae" was a book that attempted "to spread the art of psalmody" throughout the Colonies up until this time.

Thomas Chatterton wrote his two burlettas, "The Revenge" and "The Woman of Spirit" this year for Marylebone Gardens and Arnold is said to have set them to music.

Clementi composed his Sonata in C major, opus 2, #1 at this time.

Rousseau's "Pygmalion" with music by Coignet was completed this year.

Domenico Corri this year produced a comic opera at the small Teatro della Pace in Rome. It was called "La Raminga Fedele".

Carl Ditters von Dittersdorf at this time published his "Simphonie sur le genre de cinq nations" (Germany, Italy, England, France and Turkey) this year at Paris.

Carl Ditters von Dittersdorf's "Trois Simphonies a 4 parties, opus 61 . . ." was published

Dittersdorf's opera "Il viaggiatore americano" appeared at this time.

Pasquale Fago's opera "La caffetiera di garbo" was produced at the Teatro Nuovo this year during carnival season.

"The Compleat Tutor for the German Flute" was published in London this year by the Fentum family of music publishers (Jonathan Fentum).

John Abraham Fisher at this time wrote the opera "The Court of Alexander" for the Covent Garden Theatre and other locations.

William Flackton's (Flacton) "Six Solos, three for a Violoncello and three for a Tenor", opus 2 was published this year.

Étienne Joseph Floquet's two Requiem Masses, in memory of the Comte de Clermont, were performed this season at Paris.

Giovanni Francesco Fortunati's opera "I cacciatori e la vendilatte" was written at this time.

Baldassare Galuppi wrote his opera "Amor lunatico" this year at Venice (libretto by Chiari).

Florian Gassmann's opera "Il villano geloso" was produced this season at Vienna (libretto by Bertati).

Tommaso Giordani's opera "Il padre e il figlio rivali" was performed at the King's Theatre in London this season.

John Hawkins' "An Account of the Institution and Progress of the Academy of Ancient Music" was issued this year at London.

Sir John Hawkins published a number of pamphlets on antiquarian and legal subjects at this time.

Haydn's "Missa Sunt bona mixta malis" in D minor, published this year, has been lost.

Haydn's "Salve Regina" (in 3 movements) in G minor scored for 4 solo voices, organ and a few instruments was completed at this time.

Haydn's Concerto for violin, #2 in D major for Violino concertante, 2 violins, viola and bass was composed prior to this year.

Haydn's violin concerti in C and Bb major were written prior to this date. The authenticity of the latter has been questioned.

Haydn's Concerto for violin, #3 in A major for Violino concertante, 2 violins, viola, bass and 2 horns was composed prior to this year. The parts were at the Benedictus Priory at Melk.

Haydn wrote his "Little Organ Solo Mass" at this time.

Haydn wrote his Piano Sonata in C minor this year.

Haydn wrote his Symphony #39 in G minor before this year.

John Heck this year published "The Art of Fingering".

Hellendaal's opus 5, "Eight Solos for the Violoncello with a Thorough Bass" was issued at this time in Cambridge.

John Holden published an "Essay towards a Rational System of Music" this year at Glasgow.

F. A. Holly's singspiel, a new setting of "Der lustige Schuster" was published this year at Prague.

John Hoyle this year published his dictionary of musical terms titled "Dictionarium musica (sic), being a complete Dictionary or Treasury of Music".

Jommelli's opera "Armida abbandonata" was produced in Naples at the San Carlo Theatre this season and was a failure because the Italians did not like the Germanic influences in his style.

Koželuh composed his oratorio, "Gioas, re di Guida" at this time.

The singspiel "Die Liebe unter den Handwerksleuten, ein lustiges Singspiel" was performed this season at Dresden.

P. van Maldere's orchestral work, "A Second Set of Six Favorite Overtures in 8 Parts" was published this year at London by Longman, Luckey and Broderip.

G. Manna composed his oratorio "Assuero" this year.

The 2nd volume of G. Martini's work "Storia della musica" was published this season at Bologna.

1770(cont.)

Mozart's solo aria with orchestra K.71, "Ah piu tremar non voglio" (text by Metastasio) for tenor, 2 oboes, 2 horns and strings was composed this year at Salzburg or Italy.

A sonata for mandore and violin was printed this year at Vienna, "Der musikalische Dilettante".

According to Fétis, this year Ottani produced a successful opera "Il maestro" in München but it cannot be verified.

"Musikalische Nachrichten und Anmerkungen auf das Jahr 1770" was published this year at Leipzig.

André Noël Pagin's 6 Sonatas were published with harpsichord accompaniment this season at London.

Paisiello's comic opera, "Le trame per amore", appeared at this time.

Paisiello's comic opera, "La Zelmera, o sia La marina del Granatello", was completed this year.

D. Paradisi printed his 12 "Sonate di gravicembalo" dedicated to Princess Augusta in its 2nd edition at Amsterdam this year. The publisher was Johnson.

N. Piccinni's opera "Catone in Utica" (libretto by Metastasio) was performed this season at the Teatro San Carlo in Naples.

Rousseau's "Dictionnaire de musique" had appeared in three English editions by this time.

Rousseau's cantata "La naissance de Venus" was published this year. Some sources question the authenticity of the work.

Antonio Sacchini this year wrote three operas, "Scipione in Cartagine", "L'eroe cinese" and "Calliroe", the first two at Munchen, the last at Stuttgart.

Antonio Salieri's opera "L'amor innocente" was produced this season at Vienna.

Antonio Salieri's opera "Don chisciotte alle nozze di Gamace" was produced at Vienna this year.

Antonio Salieri's opera "Le donne letterate" was produced this season at Vienna.

Johann Peter Salomon at this time wrote his opera "Les Recruteurs".

Friedrich Schwindel produced two of his operas, "L'Astronome, ou L"Houreux Moment" and "La Soirée des boulevards" this season at The Hague.

Six trios by Gregorio Sciroli were published this year at Paris.

Giuseppe Tartini published his "Lettera del defonto Sig. G. T. alla Signora Maddalena Lombardini" this year at Venice.

Jean Claude Trial composed his "La Fête de Flore" this year.

Six sonatas for violin and bass by Pierre Vachen, the violinist and composer, were published this year at London.

1770(cont.)

Francesco Antonio Vallotti, the organist and composer, composed a "Requiem" for Tartini's funeral at this time.

Samuel Webbe this year composed a canon, "Alzate o porte".

Aaron Williams' "New Universal Psalmodist" was issued at this time.

Two harpsichords made this year by J. Kirkman have survived. Their description follows: #29a, 1-manual, 2x8' stops, current owner, Rushworth and Dreaper of Liverpool; # 30, 1-manual, stops 2x8' only, current owner unknown.

Arnhem shared the fame of its organs at this time with Holland, especially that at the "Groote Kerk" or cathedral, which was guilt by Silesian builders early this year and destroyed by bombs in 1945 during the second world war.

French operas, between "Cadmus" and this year, "followed their way with a greater simplicity than Italian; the expression was more direct, the music remained closer to the words and there were few display pieces to obscure their meaning".

For many years piano sonatas retained the character of divertimenti until this year. The "mood and style inherited from Wagenseil disappeared from the piano works of Haydn and Mozart, although even after this time they occasionally returned to it for specific reasons".

Sonata form reached the end of its development at about this (cont.) date.

The "Symphonie Concertante", a symphonic work employing two or more solo instruments in addition to the regular orchestra, appeared at this time.

The custom of writing very emotional music emerged powerfully this year.

From this date forward it might be said that everything of consequence in Germany up to the end of the 19th century was "Romantic".

Relations between the court music and the Opera (under Sarti) at this time in Copenhagen became stronger.

The Gentlemen's Concerts were established this year at Manchester and continued in unbroken succession until 1920.

The existing records of the Hibernian "Catch Club" dated from this year when lay members were first admitted.

This year marked the death by suicide of Thomas Chatterton. Another "fraud poet", "he wrote his poems on old parchment in archaic handwriting, and claimed he had found the work of a 15th Century monk, Thomas Rowley, in an oaken chest".

Goldsmith's didactic poem "The Deserted Village" was published this year in England.

François Boucher, French painter, died this year (born 1703).

François-Pascal, Baron Gérard, French painter, died this year

1770(cont.)
(born 1837).

Haronobu, Japanese painter, died at this time (born 1725).

Giambattista Tiepolo, Venetian painter of many large scale works, died this year (born 1696).

Pietro Antonio Lorenzoni, the painter, made a portrait of Anna Maria this year.

Frederick William III, King of Prussia, was born this year (died 1840). His reign embraced the years 1797-1840.

Gautier Dagoty le fils this year wrote "Galerie française ou portraits des hommes et des femmes célèbres qui ont paru en France, Paris, 1770".

La Dixmerie this year wrote "Les deux âges du goût et du génie français, 1770".

The population of Bonn at this time was approximately 9,560.

Churches at Bonn at this time were in an area of Bonn that eventually became an open space.

(and 1771, 1772) Glees by Alcock's won the "Catch Club" prizes in these years.

(to 1771) Casanova was again in Italy during this year.

(to 1771) The periodical "Journal de musique historique, théorique et pratique" was published at Paris during these years.

Jean François Lépine, jr. re-

(cont.) constructed the organ at the church of Saint-Just de Narbonne at this time.

(to 1771) The Pantheon, a building on Oxford Street at London, was erected at this time from designs by James Wyatt. The building was to be used for masquerades, concerts, balls etc. and as a Winter "Ranelagh".

(to 1772) Burney, the British music historian, heard the 5 Baglioni sisters (singers) in Florence during this period (Vincenza, Clementina, Giovanna, Costanza and Rosa).

(to 1772) Michael Kelly was taught the pianoforte by Morland during these two years.

(to 1773) John Broadwood became Shudi's partner, and the arrangement lasted until the death of the senior in 1773.

(to 1773) A periodical "Der musikalische Dillettante: eine Wochenschrift" was published during these years at Vienna and edited by J. F. Daube.

(to 1773) Mozart's Symphonies K.81, 95, 112, 132, 162, and 182, written during this period, all showed Sammartini's influence.

(to 1773) Mozart travelled to Italy during these years.

(to 1773) Marylebone Gardens, in which T. Pinto and Arnold had invested failed, and Pinto fled to Scotland, playing at the Edinboro concerts and also at Aberdeen concerts.

1770(cont.)

(to 1773) Johann Paul Schulthesius studied at the University
of Erlangen at this time.

(to 1775, May 20) Giuseppe
Sarti directed the Danish
court theatre during these
five years.

(to 1775) Zanetti published his
string quintets and sonatas
during this time.

(to 1776) Felice (de') Giardini
was leader of the Three Choirs
Festival during these seasons.

(to 1776) During this period
German Singspiel companies performed Gluck's "La Recontre
imprevue" all over Germany in
translation as "Die Pilger von
Mekka".

(to 1778) Nicolas Étienne
Framery edited the "Journal de
musique historique, théorique
et pratique sur la musique
ancienne et moderne" for these
eight years.

((to 1779) Friedrich von
Hardenberg, arch-romantic poet,
was born during this period
(died 1801).

(to 1779) Astaritta was active
during this period in northern
Italy, chiefly at Turin and
Venice.

(to 1779) Antonia Bernasconi
sang in various Italian towns,
Naples most of all, during
these years.

(to 1779) Burney was organist
of Oxford Chapel, now the
Church of St. Peter and St.
Thomas, on Vere Street during
these years and possibly the
next decade as well.

(to 1779) Haydn's pleasure in
using unexpected ideas mani-
fested itself during these
years.

(to 1779) Haydn wrote about 30
symphonies during this period.

(to 1779) The order of the
"Illuminati" was founded during
these years.

(to 1779) Conrad Poll's name
appeared in the court calen-
dars at this time as one of the
eight electoral footmen.

(to 1779) Chapels in Virginia
and North Carolina were "full
of white and black" at this
time.

(to 1779) By this time experience (enriched by practice in
allied forms such as the sonata,
quartet, and possibly, the concerto) "had elaborated the
simple binary forms of the
dance into something like the
classical sonata form".

(to 1780) Lambert was an eminent
hurdy-gurdy maker at Nancy
during this decade.

(to 1780) Various editions of
many of Johann Schobert's
sonatas and concertos were
published in London during
this period.

(to 1781) John Antes composed
three trios for two violins
and violoncello during these
eleven years.

(to 1782) John Byfield, jr.
was "Organ Maker" to the royal
household for this span of
time.

(to 1783) Carvalho's harpsichord sonatas appeared at

1770(cont.)
this time.

(to 1783) François Krafft was
composer to the royal chapel
during this period.

(to 1790) Dauvergne was manager
of the Paris Opéra three times
during this twenty years.

(to 1797) A. Hülphers wrote 6
volumes on Swedish scenery and
topography during this long
period.

(and 1802, 1809, 1811, 1813,
1814 and 1817) The Music Festivals at Norwich at these dates
all generally consisted of 2 or
more miscellaneous concerts
held either at St. Andrew's
Hall or the theatre, and of
oratorios, and selections of
sacred music performed at the
church of St. Peter Mancroft.

(to 1802) A series of "tutors"
(books) for playing the flute
appeared during this period.

(to 1820) The Clarinette d'amour
was made in great quantities in
Flanders, Germany, Switzerland
and Italy during these fifty
years.

(to 1840) All the famous piano
virtuosi of this era were
heard by Tamaschek at some
time during this period.

(to 1855) Belgium could boast
of the fine bassoon makers,
Tuerlinckx of Mechlin, for this
long period.

c.1770
Ferdinand Adrien, who was "chef
de chant" at the Opera, was
born this year (died c.1830).

Joseph Alexander, German violoncellist, was born this year at
Duisburg (died 1822).

Charles Ashley, violinist, was
born at this time at London
(died, August 21 at London).

Michel Angelo Bergonzi, Italian
violin maker, died this year
at Cremona (born 1722 at Cremona).

Maria Dickons (born Poole),
English soprano, was born this
year at London (died 1833, May 4
at London).

Auguste Frédéric Durand, Franco-
Polish violinist and leader of
the Brussels Opera who toured
Germany and Italy as a soloist
with brilliant technical effects,
was born this year in Warsaw. He
later changed his name to
Duranowski.

J. Bernhard Flies (Fliess),
German amateur composer, was born
at this time in Berlin (death
date unknown).

Gustaf Fredrici, Swedish composer, was born this year at
Stockholm (died 1801).

Guillaume Triébert, wind-
instrument maker, was born this
year at Horndorf, Hesse (died
1848 at Paris).

Samuel Webbe II, English organist, pianist and composer,was
born this year at London (died
1843, November 25).

Charlotte Brent continued to
sing at Covent Garden until this
time when she went on tour
with her husband.

It was not until about this year

that instruments of such perfection as Cristofori's were
made again.

Edelmann went to Paris at this
time.

John Abraham Fisher married
a daughter of Powell this
year.

Henry Fougt this year sold his
printing business to R.
Falkener.

The Goldoni-inspired Venetian
opera buffa underwent a
stylistic reorientation at
this time.

Bartholomew Johnson appeared in
London this year as a soloist.

The English guitar became
very popular at this time
which threatened to ruin the
harpsichord makers. Kirkman
bought a few guitars and gave
them to street singers and
milliner girls, which so
shamed the ladies of the
"beau monde", that they
returned to the harpsichord.

According to Fétis, François
Krafft was chapel-master of
the Church of Notre-Dame du
Sablon as well as teacher of
the harpsichord at this time.

The "Venetian Swell" Harpsichord
was the name given this year
by the London firm of Shudi
& Broadwood to a "crescendo"
or tone-modifying device for
the harpsichord, oddly enough
because of its resemblance to
a Venetian blind.

George Smart began his music
publishing business in London
this year.

Two concertos by J. Christian
(son of J. S.) Bach, in Eb and
A were published this year at
Riga.

J. Christian (son of J. S.)
Bach's six concertos op. 7
were published this year.

William Bates this year wrote
18 duettinos for two guitars,
two horns or two clarinets.

Burney's "Two Sonatas for the
Harpsichord or Forte-Piano
with Accompaniments for a
Violin and Violoncello"
appeared at this time.

Johann Joseph Fux's "Gradus
ad Parnassum" was published
in London this year as "Practical Rules for Learning
Composition".

Paul César Gibert published his
"Mélange musical" this year.

Haydn's Concerto for clavier in
G major was composed at this
time.

Haydn's "Missa brevis St.
Johannis de Deo" ("Kleine Orgel
Messe") scored for SATB solo,
four-part chorus, 2 violins and
organ was probably composed
this year for the Brothers of
Charity at Eisenstadt. It
is numbered Novello #8.

Haydn's overture #10 in G major
appeared at this time. It was
scored for flute, 2 oboes, 2
horns and strings (listed in
Breitkopf's catalogue for 1782).
Pohl did not list the flute but
Breitkopf did.

Haydn's piano sonata #18 in Bb
major was composed this year
(other version, opus 53, #3).

The work was published in 1789.

Haydn's Symphony #41 in C major was completed this year for flute (traverse), 2 oboes, 2 trumpets, drums and strings.

J. W. Hertel's last dramatic work was a setting of Metastasio's "Zl vero omaggio" performed this year at the court of Schwerin.

Hook's Concerto, opus 5 ("Lovely Nancy") was composed this year.

Hook's "Two Favorite Concertos" in D major and F major were performed at Vauxhall Gardens this season.

Samuel Jarvis at this time composed "6 Lessons for the harpsichord or pianoforte", opus 2, an ode, songs and a cantata.

Haydn wrote his trio #84 for baryton, viola and cello this year.

Haydn this year wrote his trio #95 for baryton, viola and cello.

Haydn this year wrote his trio #96 for baryton, viola, and cello.

Monsigny's opera, "Pagamin et Monègue" (libretto by Sedaine) was composed this year but never performed. The score is extant.

The composer Thomas Thackray at this time issued "A Collection of Forty-four Airs, properly adapted for one, or two guittars".

The sixth edition of Aaron

(cont.) Williams' "New Universal Psalmodist" appeared at this time.

The basset-horn was invented at Passau this year.

At this time the hand horn came into usage.

At this time fashion dictated the adoption of the name "oboe" for the instrument. This was obviously an Italianate form.

The pianoforte now began to supercede its forerunners and a repertoire of music for the instrument rapidly took form.

At about this time compositions in three or more movements, such as quartets, symphonies, etc., more ofte than not used the sonata form in the first movements and occasionaly in the final movement.

The impact of the "Sturm und Drang" period in German literature arrived at this time.

Gainsborough painted "The Blue Boy" this year (San Marino Collection, Huntington Art Gallery).

(to 1775) Bremner had a branch establishment at 108 New Bond Street during these years.

(to 1775) Adrien Helmont was conductor at the Amsterdam Schouwburg, and a comic opera called "Het nagt-gevegd, of De leevende doode" (The undated libretto of which is in the British Musium) was probably produced there during this period.

(to 1775) Ignazio Raimondi went to Amsterdam during these years

c.1770(cont.)
where he directed concerts and
wrote his symphony.

(to 1786) Samuel Babb was
established in London at
132 Oxford Street during this
period.